EARTH 2
WORLD'S END

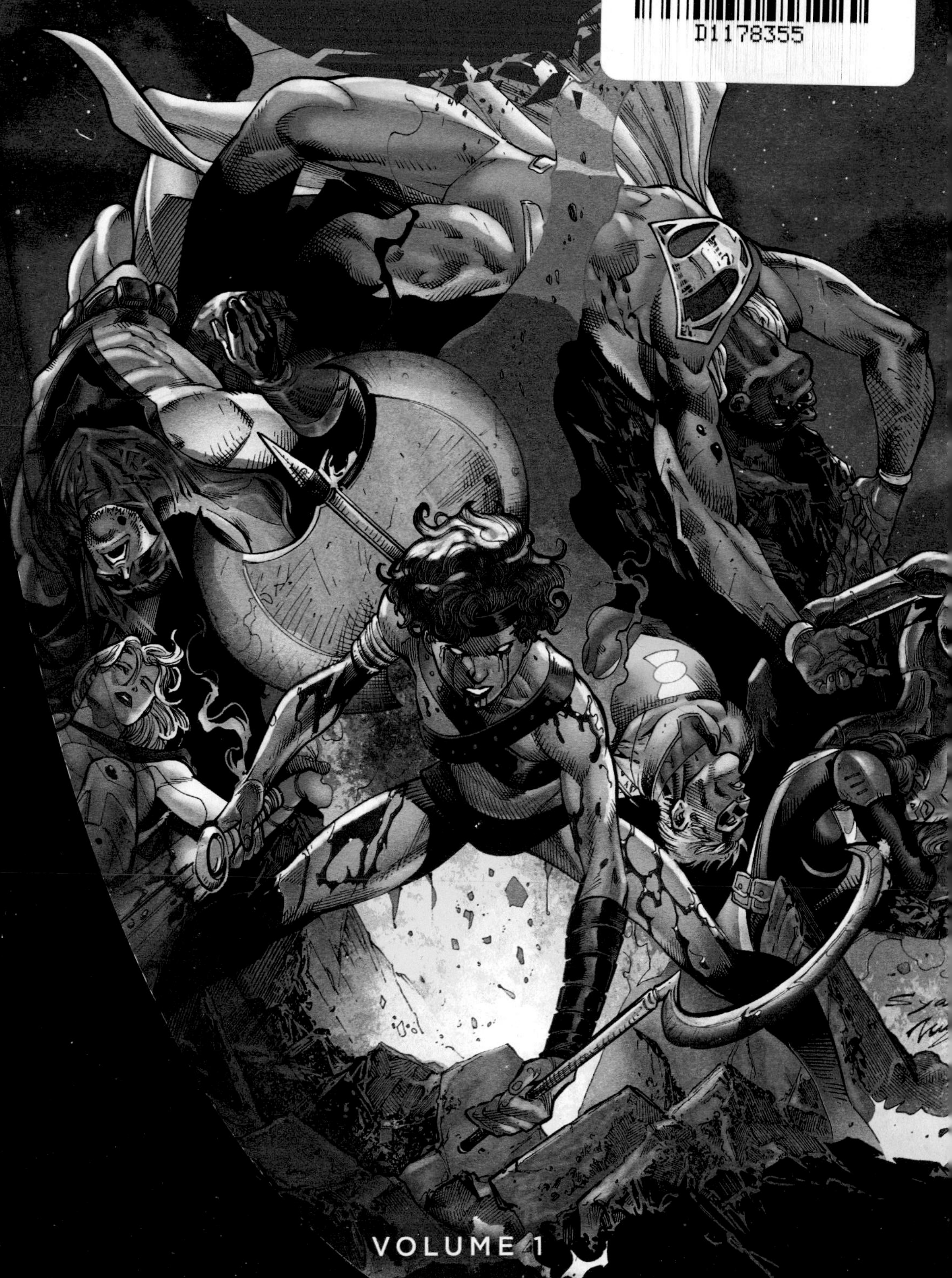

VOLUME 1

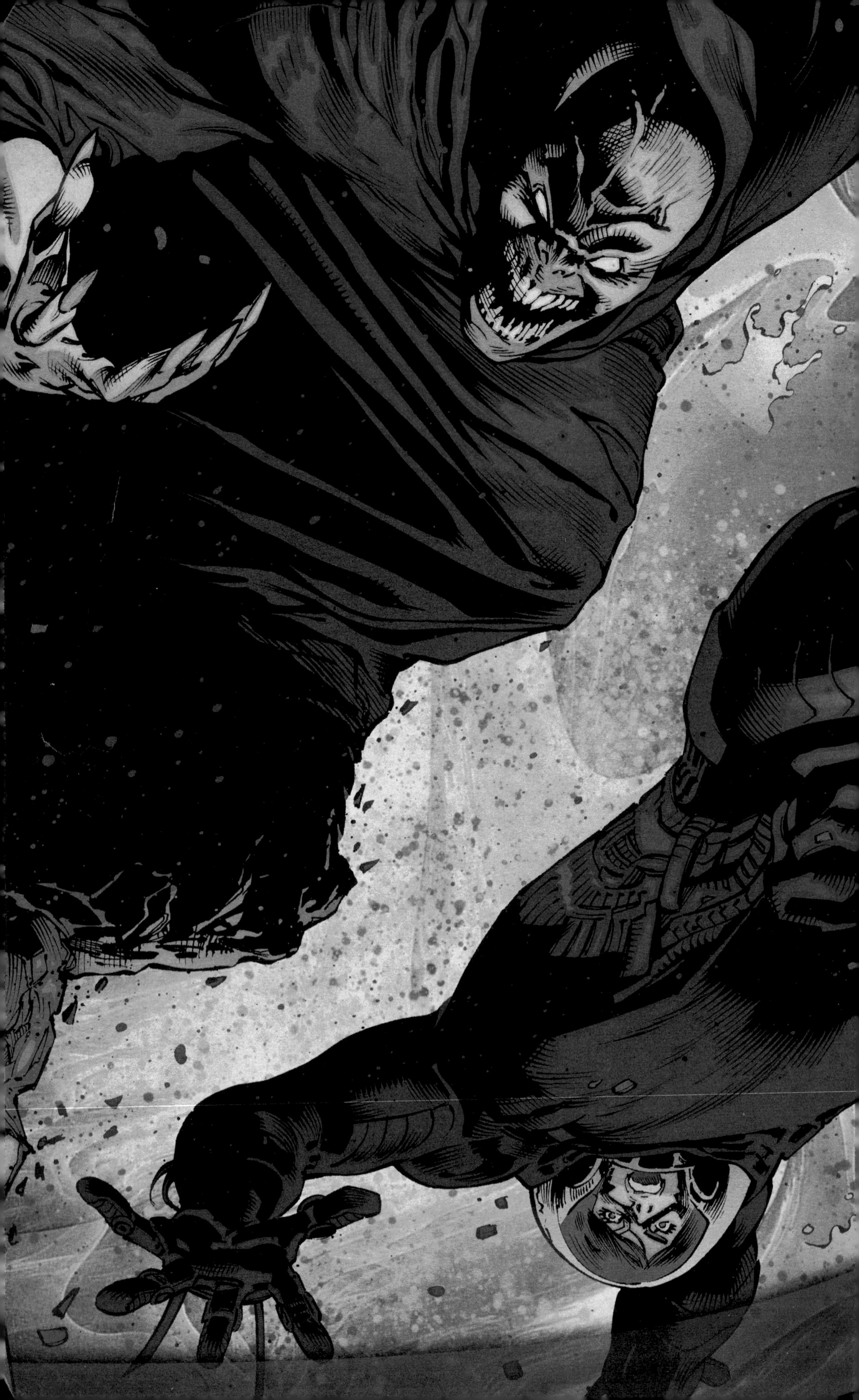

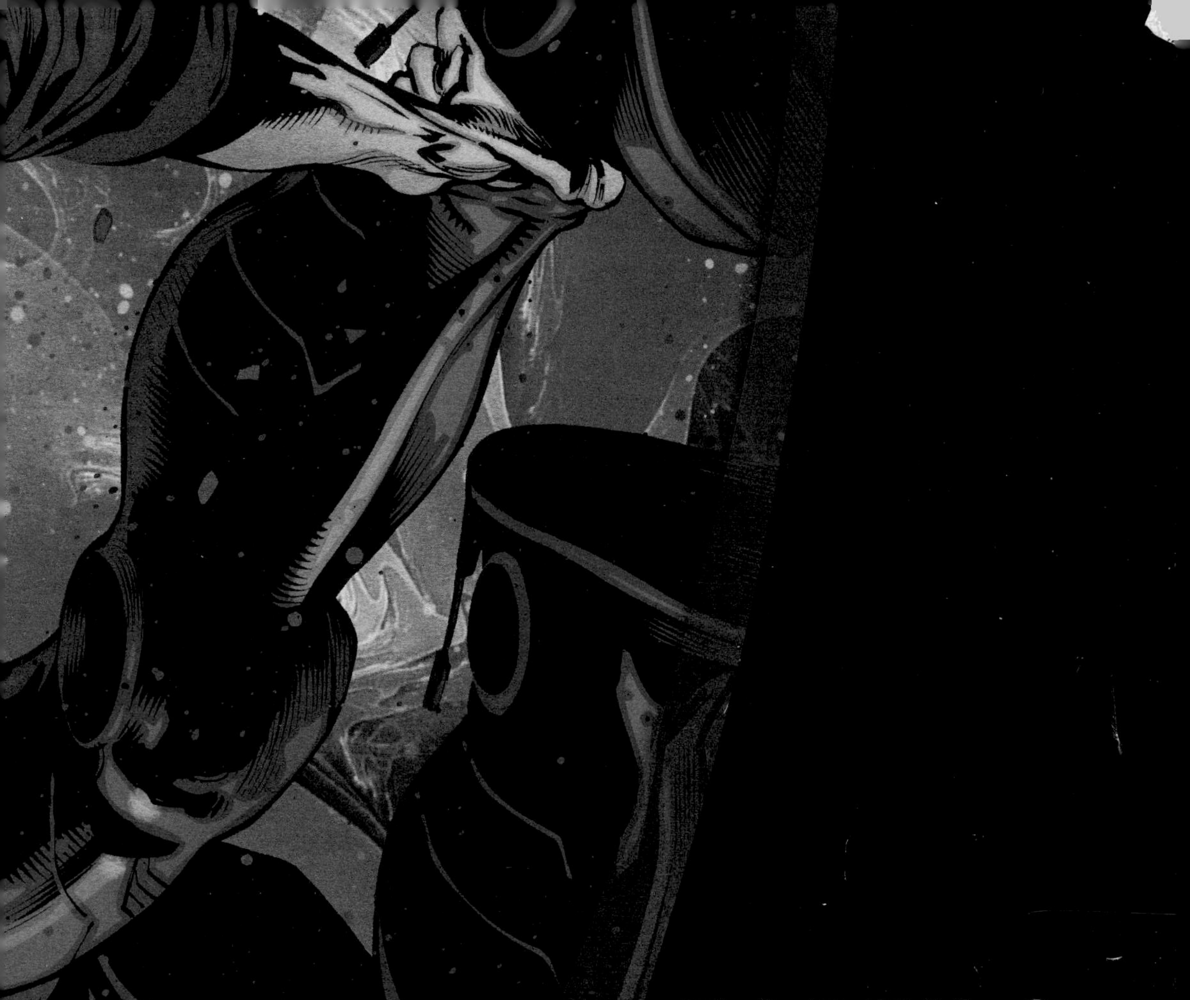

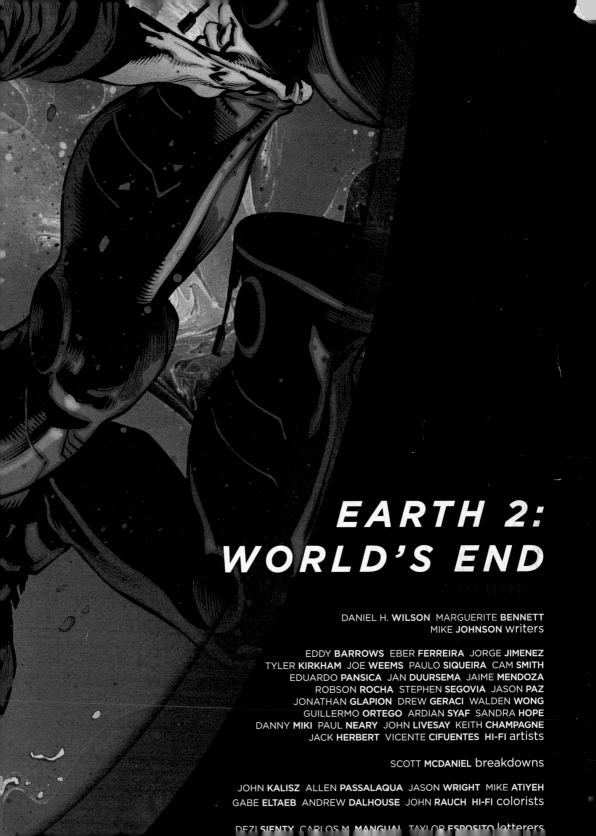

EARTH 2: WORLD'S END

VOLUME 1

DANIEL H. **WILSON** MARGUERITE **BENNETT**
MIKE **JOHNSON** writers

EDDY **BARROWS** EBER **FERREIRA** JORGE **JIMENEZ**
TYLER **KIRKHAM** JOE **WEEMS** PAULO **SIQUEIRA** CAM **SMITH**
EDUARDO **PANSICA** JAN **DUURSEMA** JAIME **MENDOZA**
ROBSON **ROCHA** STEPHEN **SEGOVIA** JASON **PAZ**
JONATHAN **GLAPION** DREW **GERACI** WALDEN **WONG**
GUILLERMO **ORTEGO** ARDIAN **SYAF** SANDRA **HOPE**
DANNY **MIKI** PAUL **NEARY** JOHN **LIVESAY** KEITH **CHAMPAGNE**
JACK **HERBERT** VICENTE **CIFUENTES** **HI-FI** artists

SCOTT **MCDANIEL** breakdowns

JOHN **KALISZ** ALLEN **PASSALAQUA** JASON **WRIGHT** MIKE **ATIYEH**
GABE **ELTAEB** ANDREW **DALHOUSE** JOHN **RAUCH** **HI-FI** colorists

DEZI **SIENTY** CARLOS M. **MANGUAL** TAYLOR **ESPOSITO** letterers

MIKE COTTON Editor – Original Series RICKEY PURDIN Associate Editor – Original Series
LIZ ERICKSON Editor ROBBIN BROSTERMAN Design Director – Books

BOB HARRAS Senior VP – Editor-in-Chief, DC Comics

DIANE NELSON President DAN DIDIO and JIM LEE Co-Publishers GEOFF JOHNS Chief Creative Officer
AMIT DESAI Senior VP – Marketing & Franchise Management AMY GENKINS Senior VP – Business & Legal Affairs
NAIRI GARDINER Senior VP – Finance JEFF BOISON VP – Publishing Planning
MARK CHIARELLO VP – Art Direction & Design JOHN CUNNINGHAM VP – Marketing
TERRI CUNNINGHAM VP – Editorial Administration LARRY GANEM VP – Talent Relations & Services
ALISON GILL Senior VP – Manufacturing & Operations HANK KANALZ Senior VP – Vertigo & Integrated Publishing
JAY KOGAN VP – Business & Legal Affairs, Publishing JACK MAHAN VP – Business Affairs, Talent
NICK NAPOLITANO VP – Manufacturing Administration SUE POHJA VP – Book Sales
FRED RUIZ VP – Manufacturing Operations COURTNEY SIMMONS Senior VP – Publicity Bob Wayne Senior VP – Sales

EARTH 2: WORLD'S END VOLUME 1

DC Comics, 4000 Warner Blvd., Burbank, CA 91522
A Warner Bros. Entertainment Company.
Printed by RR Donnelley, Salem, VA, USA. 4/10/15. First Printing.
ISBN: 978-1-4012-5603-6

Library of Congress Cataloging-in-Publication Data

Wilson, Daniel H. (Daniel Howard), 1978-
Earth 2, world's end volume 1 / Daniel H. Wilson, Marguerite Bennett ; illustrated by Eddy Barrows.
pages cm. -- (The New 52!)
ISBN 978-1-4012-5603-6 (paperback)
1. Graphic novels. I. Bennett, Marguerite, author. II. Barrows, Eddy, illustrator. III. Title.
PN6728.E25W55 2015
741.5'973—dc23
2015006066

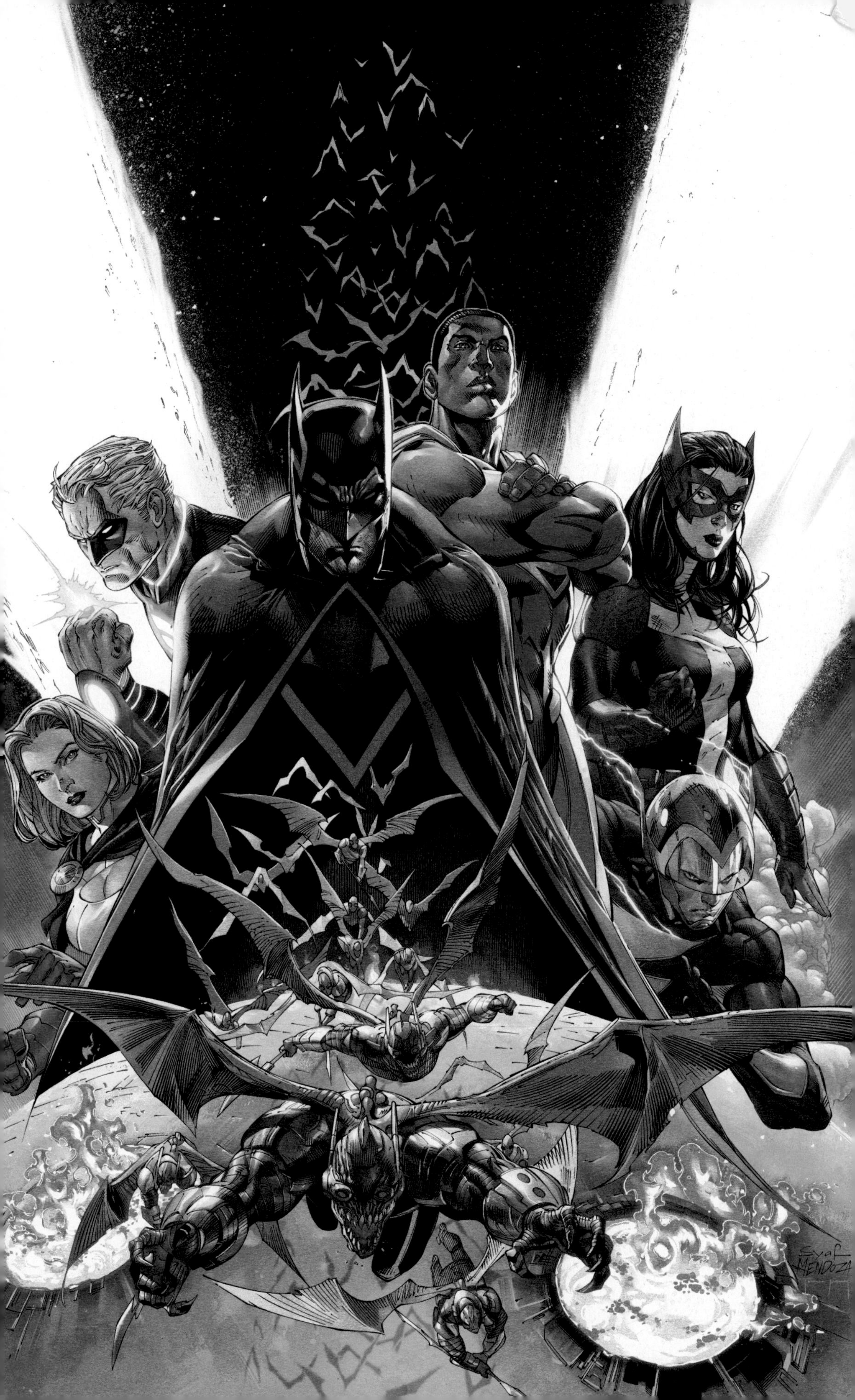
Syaf
MENDOZA

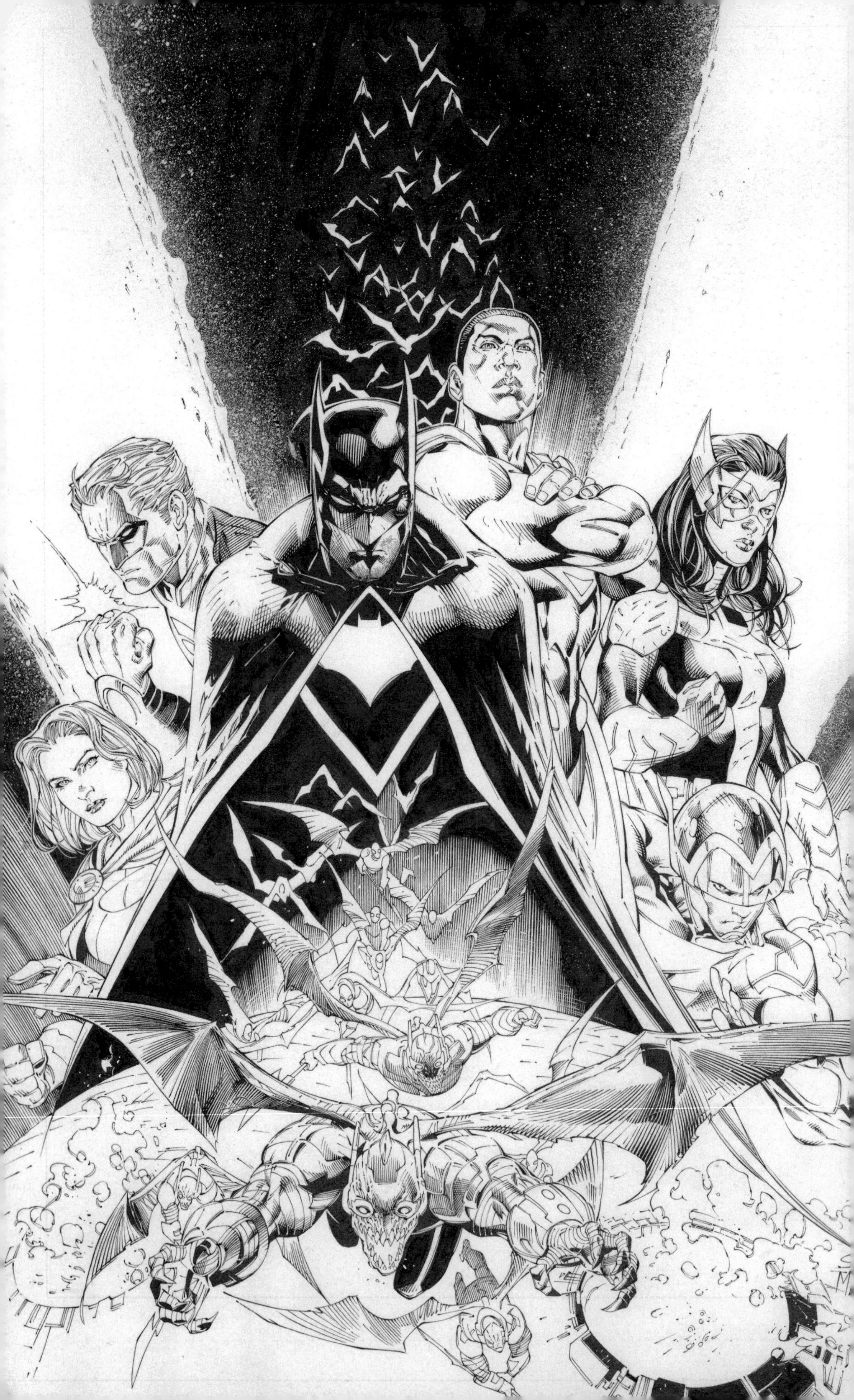

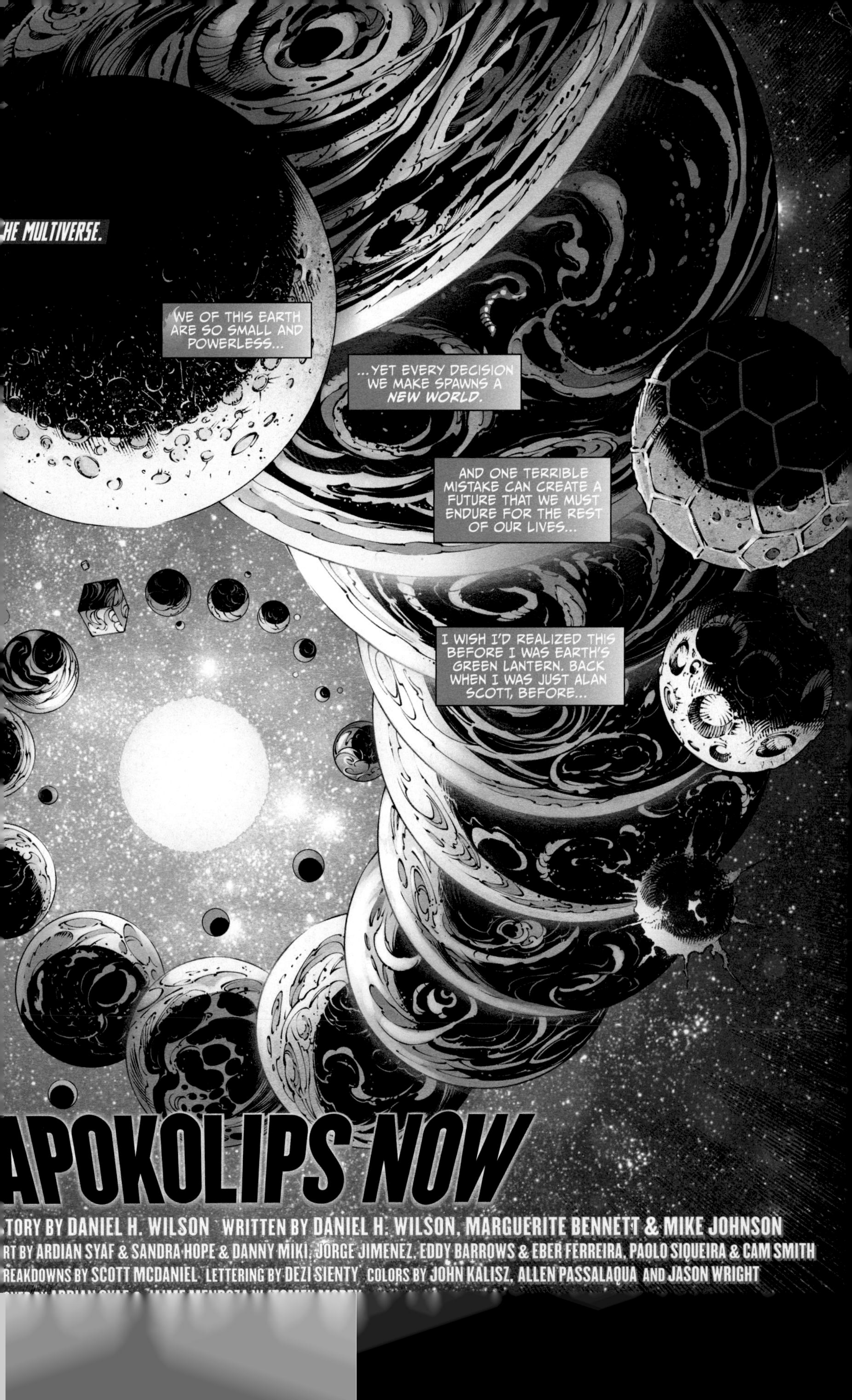
HE MULTIVERSE.
WE OF THIS EARTH ARE SO SMALL AND POWERLESS...
...YET EVERY DECISION WE MAKE SPAWNS A *NEW WORLD.*
AND ONE TERRIBLE MISTAKE CAN CREATE A FUTURE THAT WE MUST ENDURE FOR THE REST OF OUR LIVES...
I WISH I'D REALIZED THIS BEFORE I WAS EARTH'S GREEN LANTERN. BACK WHEN I WAS JUST ALAN SCOTT, BEFORE...
APOKOLIPS NOW
TORY BY DANIEL H. WILSON WRITTEN BY DANIEL H. WILSON, MARGUERITE BENNETT & MIKE JOHNSON
RT BY ARDIAN SYAF & SANDRA HOPE & DANNY MIKI, JORGE JIMENEZ, EDDY BARROWS & EBER FERREIRA, PAOLO SIQUEIRA & CAM SMITH
REAKDOWNS BY SCOTT MCDANIEL LETTERING BY DEZI SIENTY COLORS BY JOHN KALISZ, ALLEN PASSALAQUA AND JASON WRIGHT

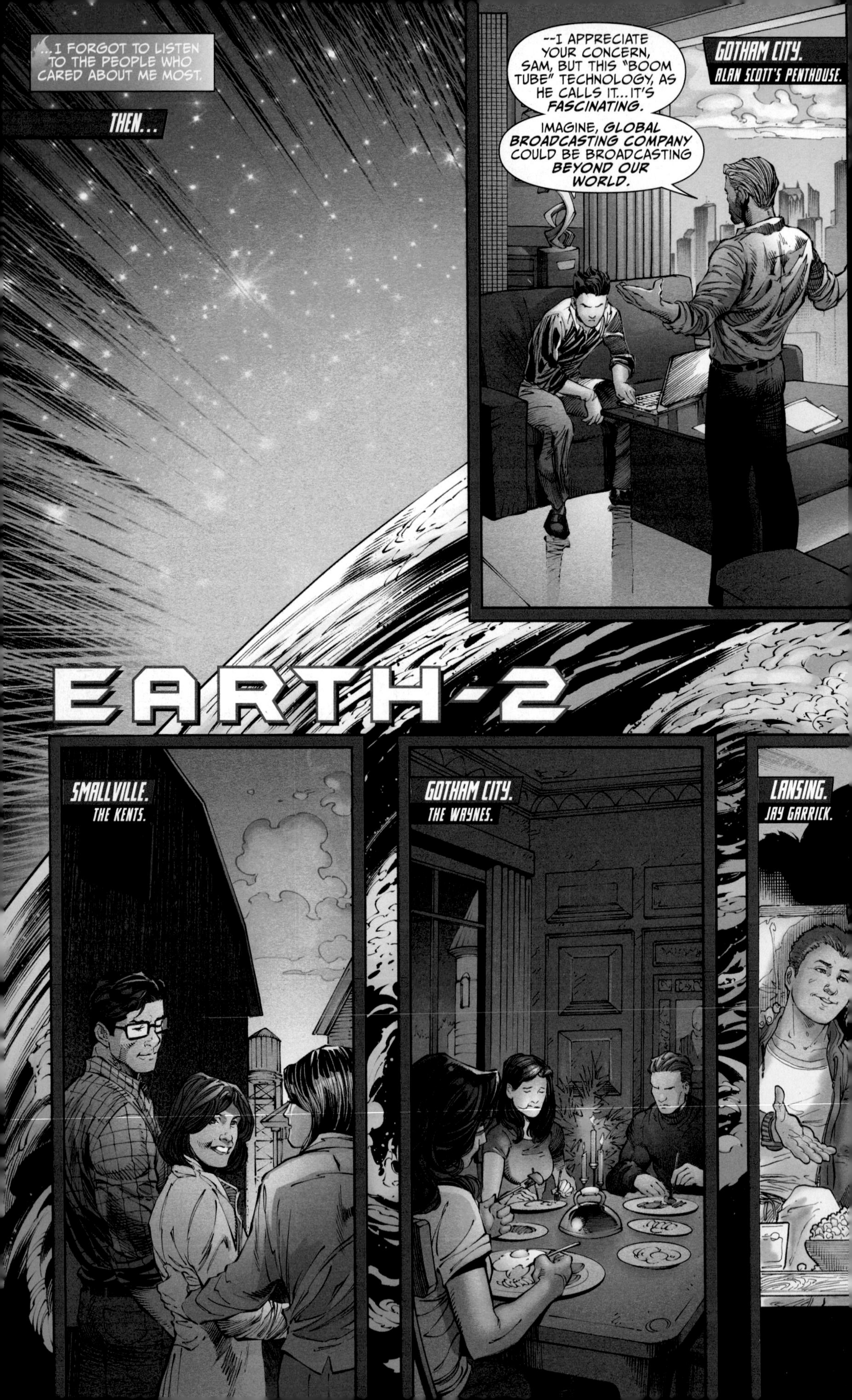
...I FORGOT TO LISTEN TO THE PEOPLE WHO CARED ABOUT ME MOST.
THEN...
GOTHAM CITY.
ALAN SCOTT'S PENTHOUSE.
--I APPRECIATE YOUR CONCERN, SAM, BUT THIS "BOOM TUBE" TECHNOLOGY, AS HE CALLS IT...IT'S FASCINATING.
IMAGINE, GLOBAL BROADCASTING COMPANY COULD BE BROADCASTING BEYOND OUR WORLD.
EARTH-2
SMALLVILLE.
THE KENTS.
GOTHAM CITY.
THE WAYNES.
LANSING.
JAY GARRICK.

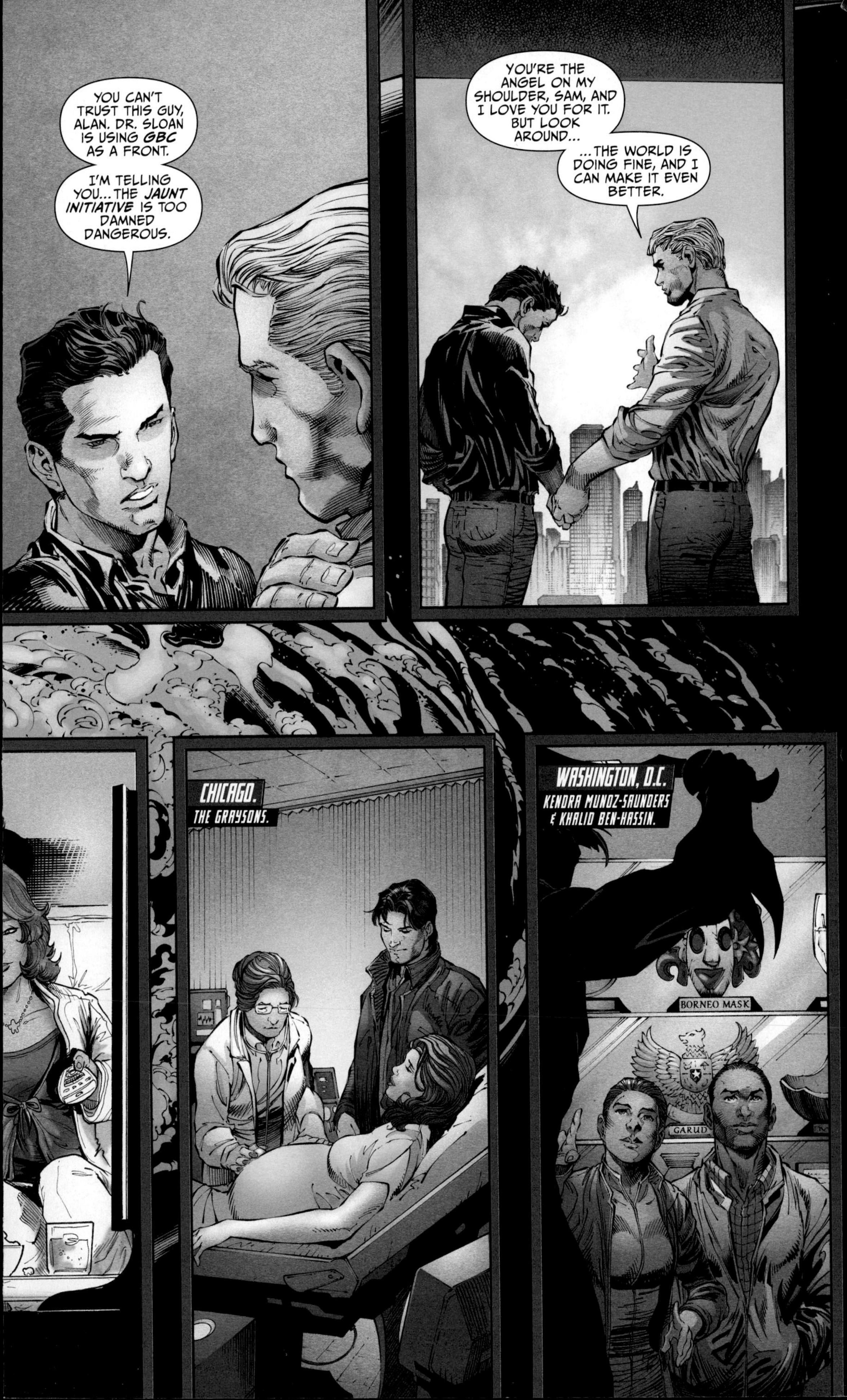
YOU CAN'T TRUST THIS GUY, ALAN. DR. SLOAN IS USING GBC AS A FRONT.
I'M TELLING YOU... THE JAUNT INITIATIVE IS TOO DAMNED DANGEROUS.
YOU'RE THE ANGEL ON MY SHOULDER, SAM, AND I LOVE YOU FOR IT. BUT LOOK AROUND...
...THE WORLD IS DOING FINE, AND I CAN MAKE IT EVEN BETTER.
CHICAGO.
THE GRAYSONS.
WASHINGTON, D.C.
KENDRA MUNOZ-SAUNDERS & KHALID BEN-HASSIN.
BORNEO MASK
GARUD

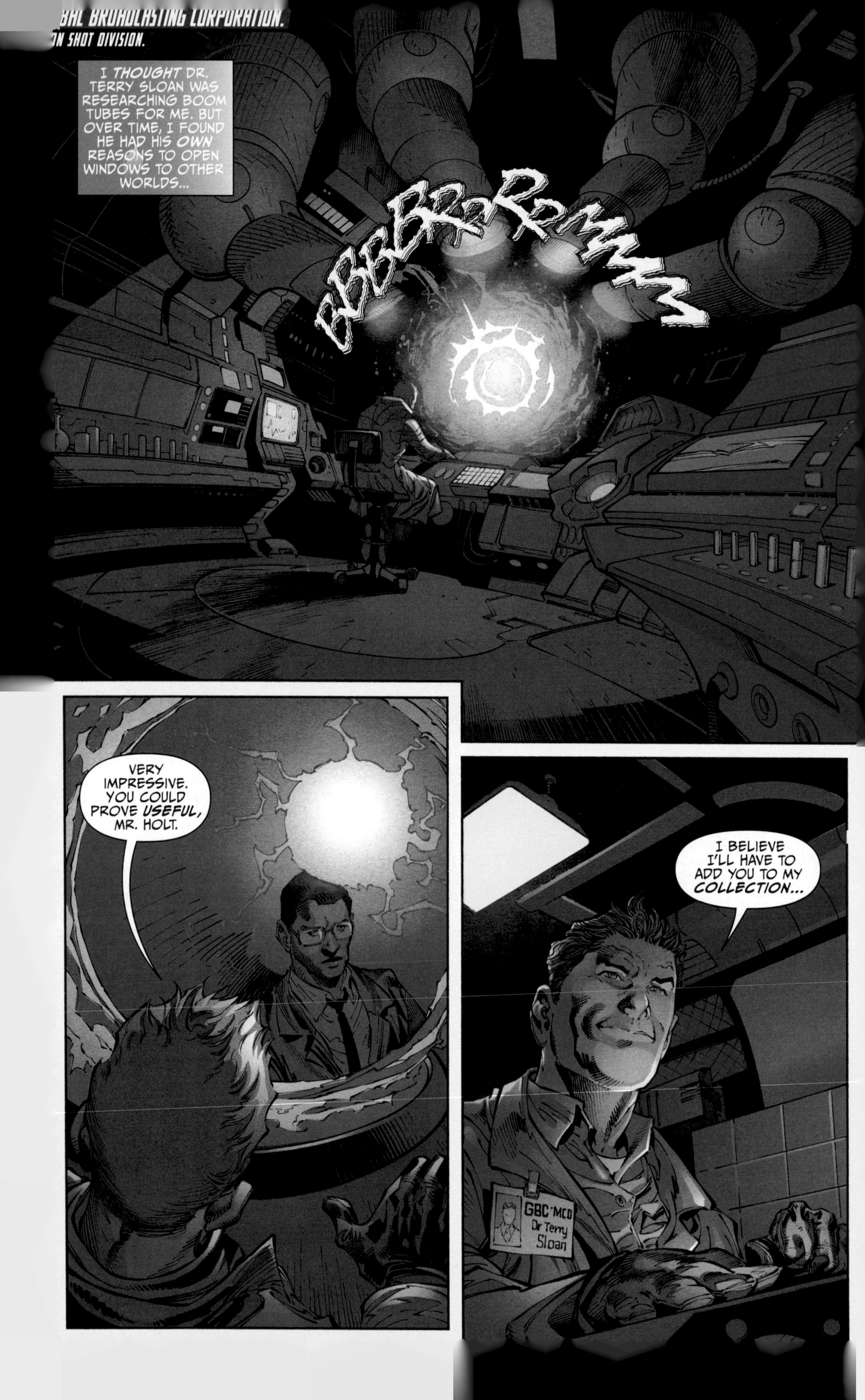
BAL BROADCASTING CORPORATION.
ON SHOT DIVISION.
I THOUGHT DR. TERRY SLOAN WAS RESEARCHING BOOM TUBES FOR ME. BUT OVER TIME, I FOUND HE HAD HIS OWN REASONS TO OPEN WINDOWS TO OTHER WORLDS...
VERY IMPRESSIVE. YOU COULD PROVE USEFUL, MR. HOLT.
I BELIEVE I'LL HAVE TO ADD YOU TO MY COLLECTION...
GBC
Dr Terry Sloan

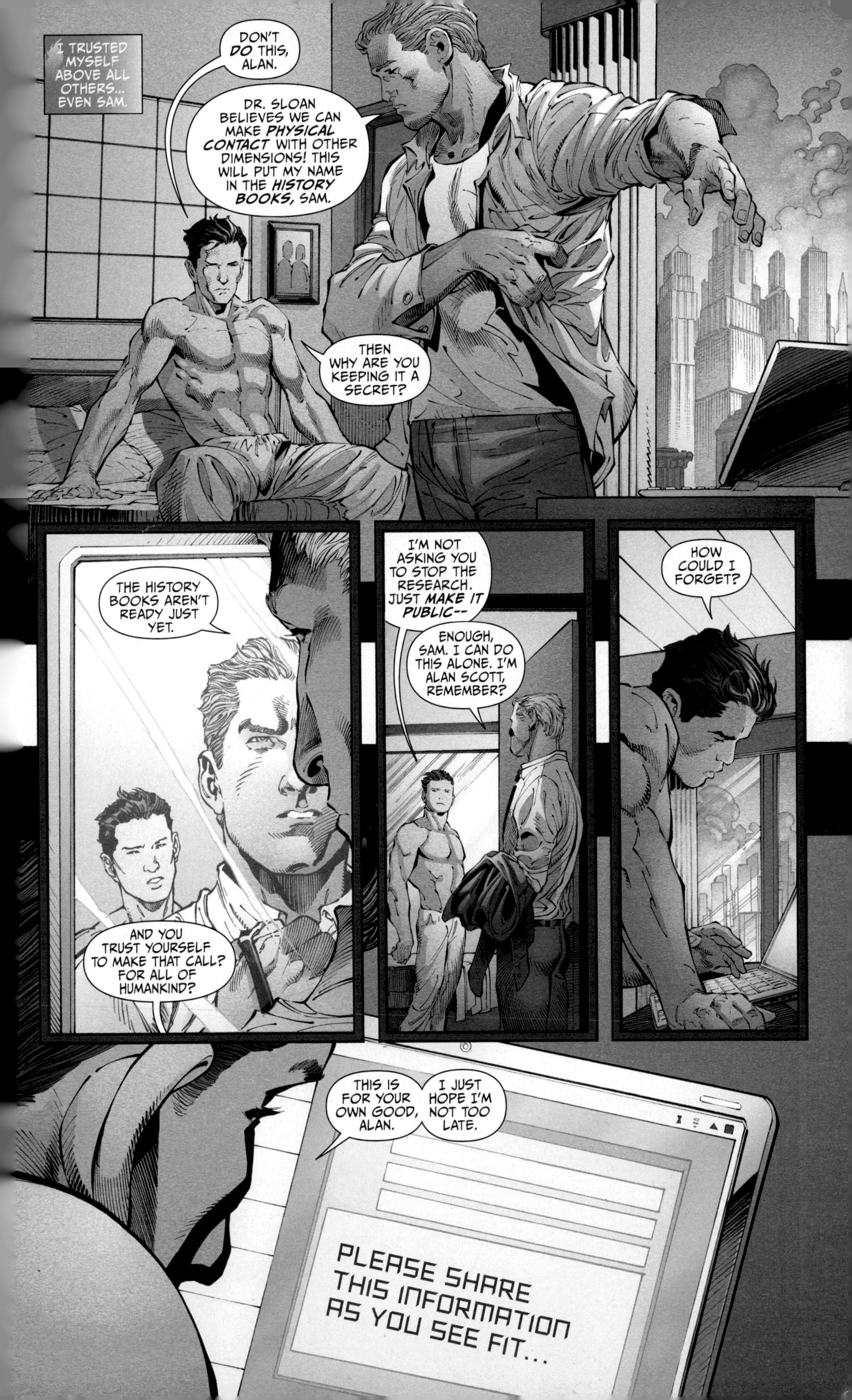
I TRUSTED MYSELF ABOVE ALL OTHERS... EVEN SAM.
DON'T DO THIS, ALAN.
DR. SLOAN BELIEVES WE CAN MAKE PHYSICAL CONTACT WITH OTHER DIMENSIONS! THIS WILL PUT MY NAME IN THE HISTORY BOOKS, SAM.
THEN WHY ARE YOU KEEPING IT A SECRET?
THE HISTORY BOOKS AREN'T READY JUST YET.
AND YOU TRUST YOURSELF TO MAKE THAT CALL? FOR ALL OF HUMANKIND?
I'M NOT ASKING YOU TO STOP THE RESEARCH. JUST MAKE IT PUBLIC--
ENOUGH, SAM. I CAN DO THIS ALONE. I'M ALAN SCOTT, REMEMBER?
HOW COULD I FORGET?
THIS IS FOR YOUR OWN GOOD, ALAN.
I JUST HOPE I'M NOT TOO LATE.
PLEASE SHARE THIS INFORMATION AS YOU SEE FIT...

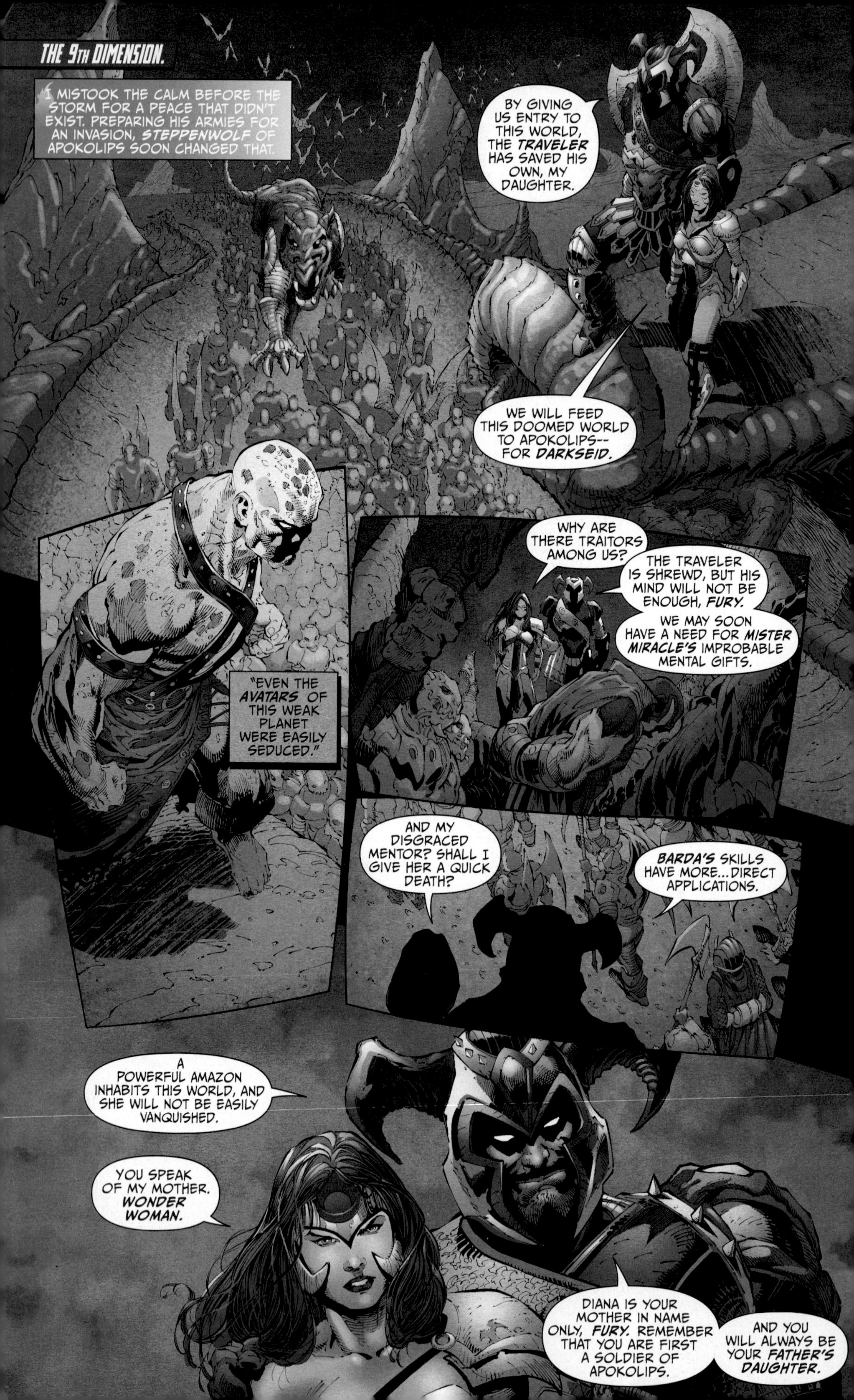
THE 9TH DIMENSION.
I MISTOOK THE CALM BEFORE THE STORM FOR A PEACE THAT DIDN'T EXIST. PREPARING HIS ARMIES FOR AN INVASION, STEPPENWOLF OF APOKOLIPS SOON CHANGED THAT.
BY GIVING US ENTRY TO THIS WORLD, THE TRAVELER HAS SAVED HIS OWN, MY DAUGHTER.
WE WILL FEED THIS DOOMED WORLD TO APOKOLIPS--FOR DARKSEID.
"EVEN THE AVATARS OF THIS WEAK PLANET WERE EASILY SEDUCED."
WHY ARE THERE TRAITORS AMONG US?
THE TRAVELER IS SHREWD, BUT HIS MIND WILL NOT BE ENOUGH, FURY.
WE MAY SOON HAVE A NEED FOR MISTER MIRACLE'S IMPROBABLE MENTAL GIFTS.
AND MY DISGRACED MENTOR? SHALL I GIVE HER A QUICK DEATH?
BARDA'S SKILLS HAVE MORE...DIRECT APPLICATIONS.
A POWERFUL AMAZON INHABITS THIS WORLD, AND SHE WILL NOT BE EASILY VANQUISHED.
YOU SPEAK OF MY MOTHER. WONDER WOMAN.
DIANA IS YOUR MOTHER IN NAME ONLY, FURY. REMEMBER THAT YOU ARE FIRST A SOLDIER OF APOKOLIPS.
AND YOU WILL ALWAYS BE YOUR FATHER'S DAUGHTER.

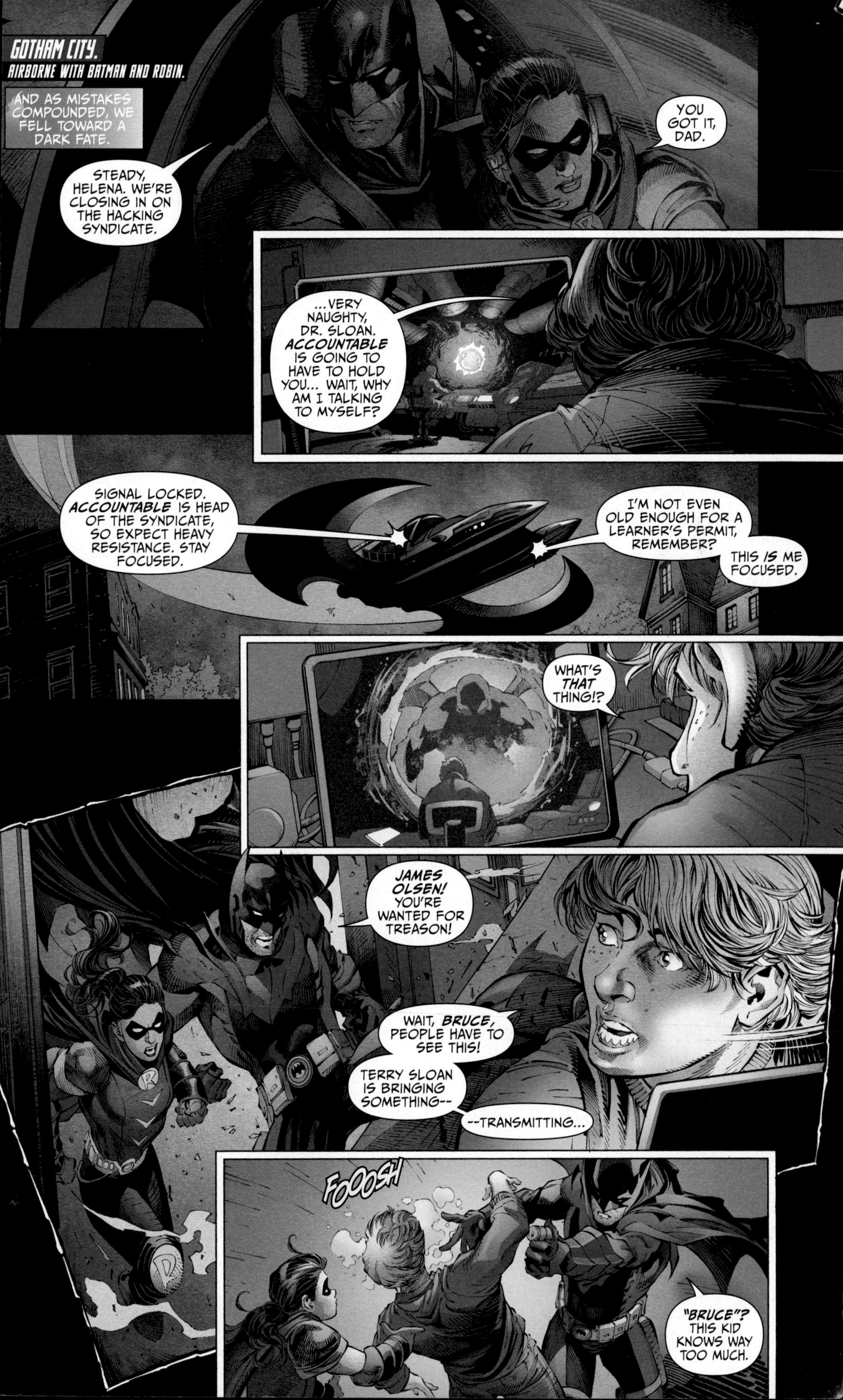
GOTHAM CITY.
AIRBORNE WITH BATMAN AND ROBIN.
AND AS MISTAKES COMPOUNDED, WE FELL TOWARD A DARK FATE.
STEADY, HELENA. WE'RE CLOSING IN ON THE HACKING SYNDICATE.
YOU GOT IT, DAD.
...VERY NAUGHTY, DR. SLOAN. ACCOUNTABLE IS GOING TO HAVE TO HOLD YOU... WAIT, WHY AM I TALKING TO MYSELF?
SIGNAL LOCKED. ACCOUNTABLE IS HEAD OF THE SYNDICATE, SO EXPECT HEAVY RESISTANCE. STAY FOCUSED.
I'M NOT EVEN OLD ENOUGH FOR A LEARNER'S PERMIT, REMEMBER?
THIS IS ME FOCUSED.
WHAT'S THAT THING!?
JAMES OLSEN! YOU'RE WANTED FOR TREASON!
WAIT, BRUCE, PEOPLE HAVE TO SEE THIS!
TERRY SLOAN IS BRINGING SOMETHING--
--TRANSMITTING...
FOOOSH
"BRUCE"? THIS KID KNOWS WAY TOO MUCH.

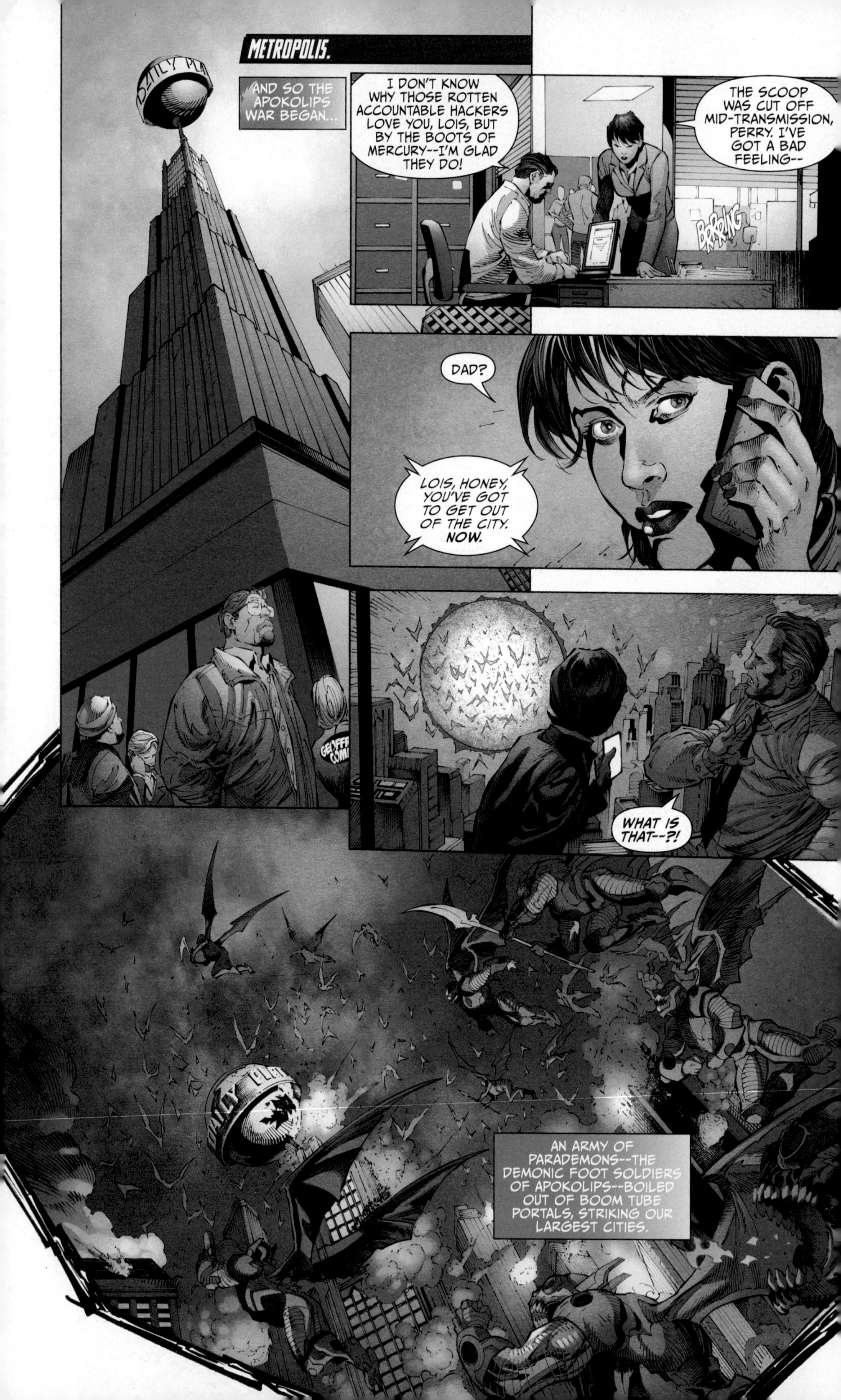
METROPOLIS.
AND SO THE APOKOLIPS WAR BEGAN...
I DON'T KNOW WHY THOSE ROTTEN ACCOUNTABLE HACKERS LOVE YOU, LOIS, BUT BY THE BOOTS OF MERCURY--I'M GLAD THEY DO!
THE SCOOP WAS CUT OFF MID-TRANSMISSION, PERRY. I'VE GOT A BAD FEELING--
BRRRING
DAD?
LOIS, HONEY, YOU'VE GOT TO GET OUT OF THE CITY. NOW.
WHAT IS THAT--?!
AN ARMY OF PARADEMONS--THE DEMONIC FOOT SOLDIERS OF APOKOLIPS--BOILED OUT OF BOOM TUBE PORTALS, STRIKING OUR LARGEST CITIES.

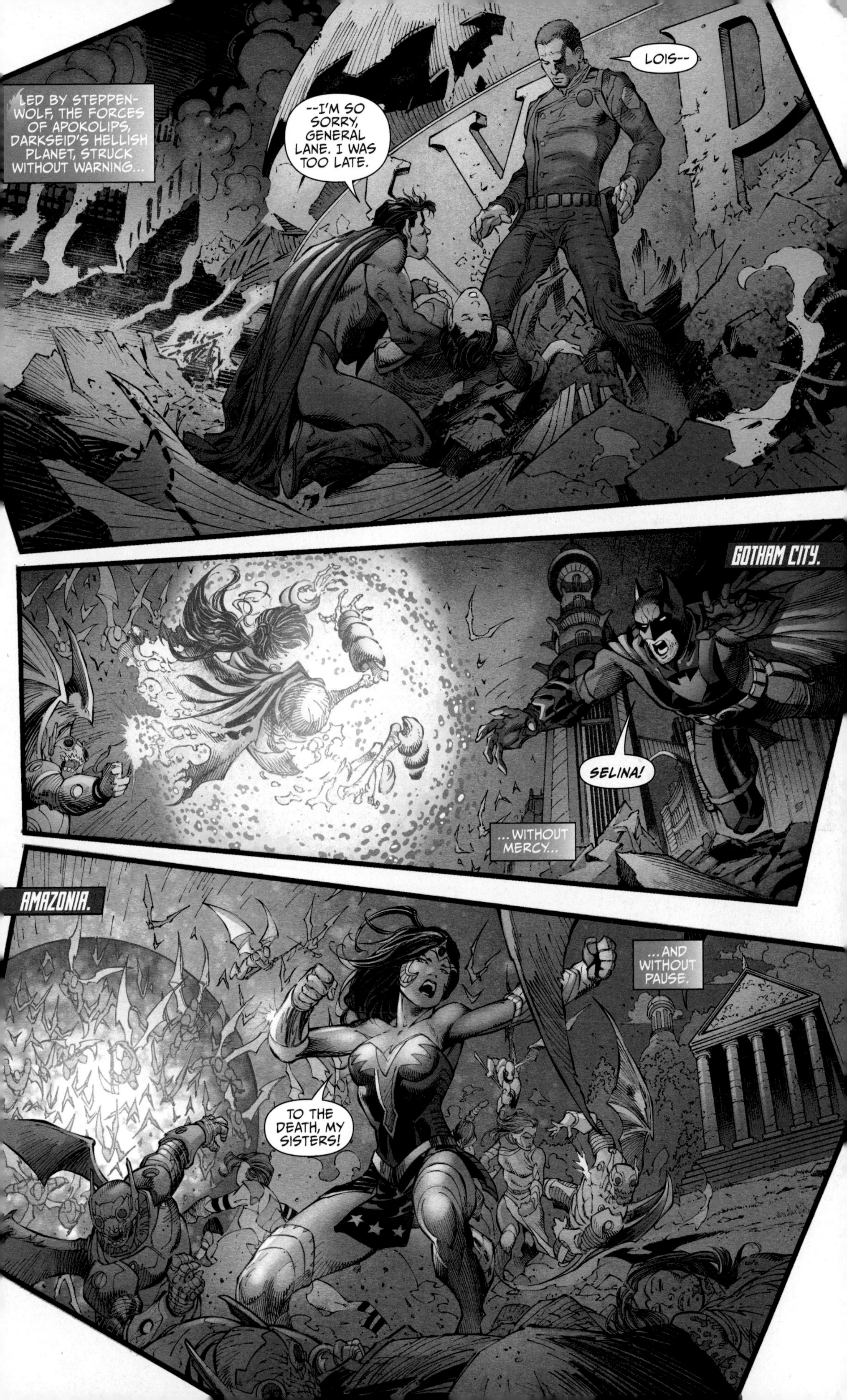
LED BY STEPPENWOLF, THE FORCES OF APOKOLIPS, DARKSEID'S HELLISH PLANET, STRUCK WITHOUT WARNING...
--I'M SO SORRY, GENERAL LANE. I WAS TOO LATE.
LOIS--
GOTHAM CITY.
SELINA!
...WITHOUT MERCY...
AMAZONIA.
...AND WITHOUT PAUSE.
TO THE DEATH, MY SISTERS!

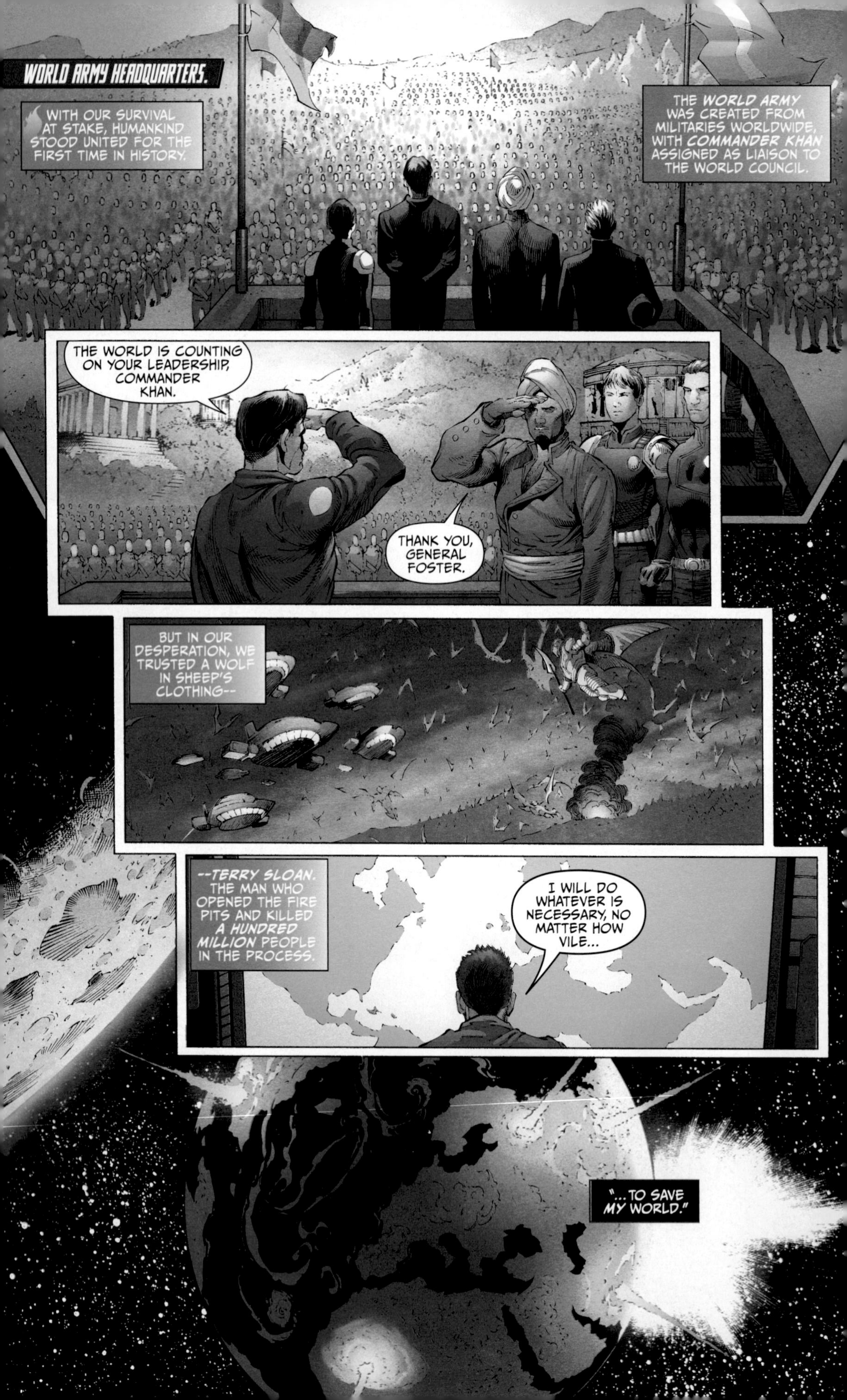
WORLD ARMY HEADQUARTERS.
WITH OUR SURVIVAL AT STAKE, HUMANKIND STOOD UNITED FOR THE FIRST TIME IN HISTORY.
THE WORLD ARMY WAS CREATED FROM MILITARIES WORLDWIDE, WITH COMMANDER KHAN ASSIGNED AS LIAISON TO THE WORLD COUNCIL.
THE WORLD IS COUNTING ON YOUR LEADERSHIP, COMMANDER KHAN.
THANK YOU, GENERAL FOSTER.
BUT IN OUR DESPERATION, WE TRUSTED A WOLF IN SHEEP'S CLOTHING--
--TERRY SLOAN. THE MAN WHO OPENED THE FIRE PITS AND KILLED A HUNDRED MILLION PEOPLE IN THE PROCESS.
I WILL DO WHATEVER IS NECESSARY, NO MATTER HOW VILE...
"...TO SAVE MY WORLD."

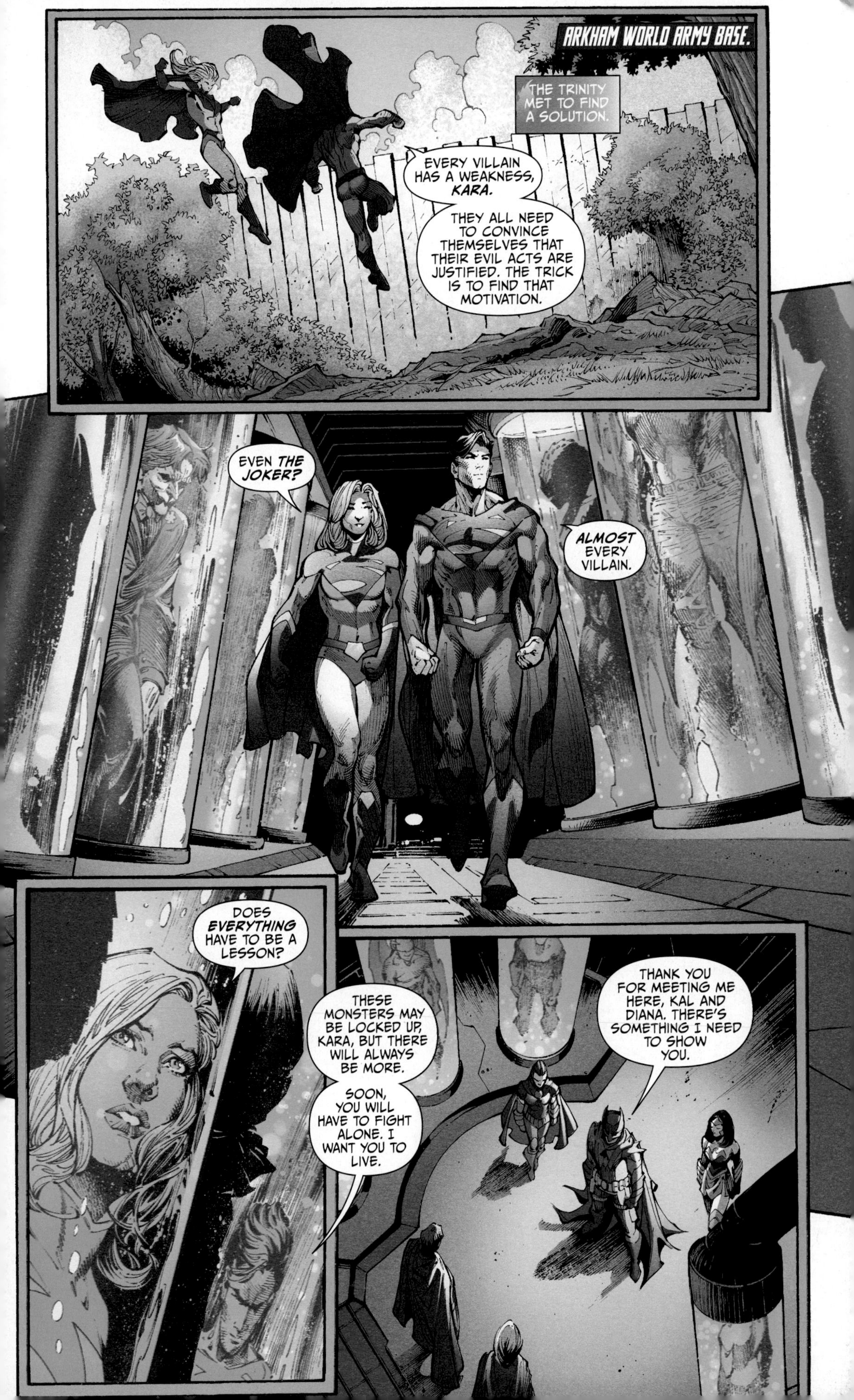
ARKHAM WORLD ARMY BASE.
THE TRINITY MET TO FIND A SOLUTION.
EVERY VILLAIN HAS A WEAKNESS, KARA.
THEY ALL NEED TO CONVINCE THEMSELVES THAT THEIR EVIL ACTS ARE JUSTIFIED. THE TRICK IS TO FIND THAT MOTIVATION.
EVEN THE JOKER?
ALMOST EVERY VILLAIN.
DOES EVERYTHING HAVE TO BE A LESSON?
THESE MONSTERS MAY BE LOCKED UP, KARA, BUT THERE WILL ALWAYS BE MORE.
SOON, YOU WILL HAVE TO FIGHT ALONE. I WANT YOU TO LIVE.
THANK YOU FOR MEETING ME HERE, KAL AND DIANA. THERE'S SOMETHING I NEED TO SHOW YOU.

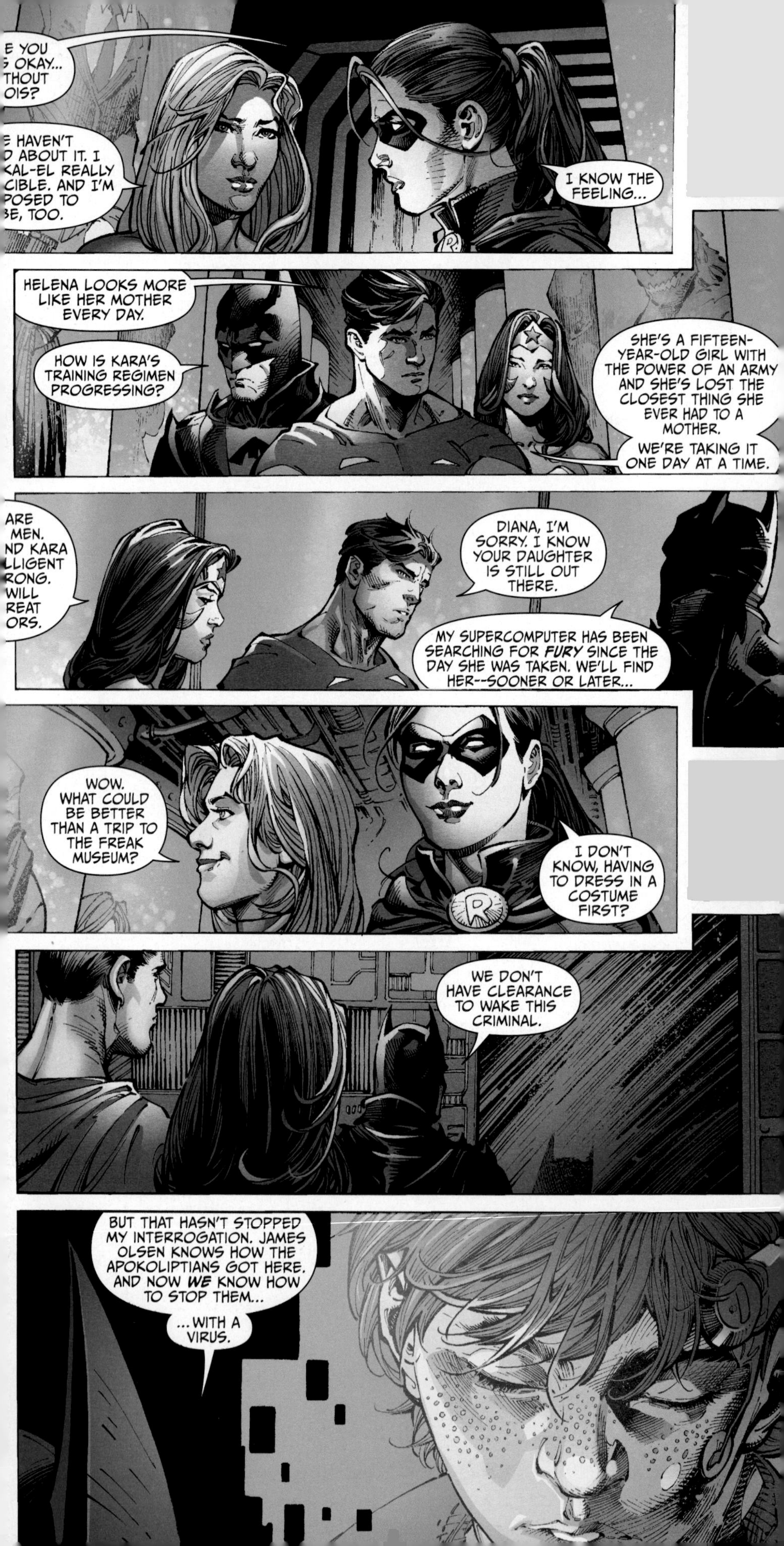
E YOU S OKAY... THOUT OIS?
E HAVEN'T D ABOUT IT. I KAL-EL REALLY CIBLE. AND I'M POSED TO BE, TOO.
I KNOW THE FEELING...
HELENA LOOKS MORE LIKE HER MOTHER EVERY DAY.
HOW IS KARA'S TRAINING REGIMEN PROGRESSING?
SHE'S A FIFTEEN-YEAR-OLD GIRL WITH THE POWER OF AN ARMY AND SHE'S LOST THE CLOSEST THING SHE EVER HAD TO A MOTHER.
WE'RE TAKING IT ONE DAY AT A TIME.
ARE MEN. ND KARA LLIGENT RONG. WILL REAT ORS.
DIANA, I'M SORRY. I KNOW YOUR DAUGHTER IS STILL OUT THERE.
MY SUPERCOMPUTER HAS BEEN SEARCHING FOR FURY SINCE THE DAY SHE WAS TAKEN. WE'LL FIND HER--SOONER OR LATER...
WOW. WHAT COULD BE BETTER THAN A TRIP TO THE FREAK MUSEUM?
I DON'T KNOW, HAVING TO DRESS IN A COSTUME FIRST?
WE DON'T HAVE CLEARANCE TO WAKE THIS CRIMINAL.
BUT THAT HASN'T STOPPED MY INTERROGATION. JAMES OLSEN KNOWS HOW THE APOKOLIPTIANS GOT HERE. AND NOW WE KNOW HOW TO STOP THEM...
...WITH A VIRUS.

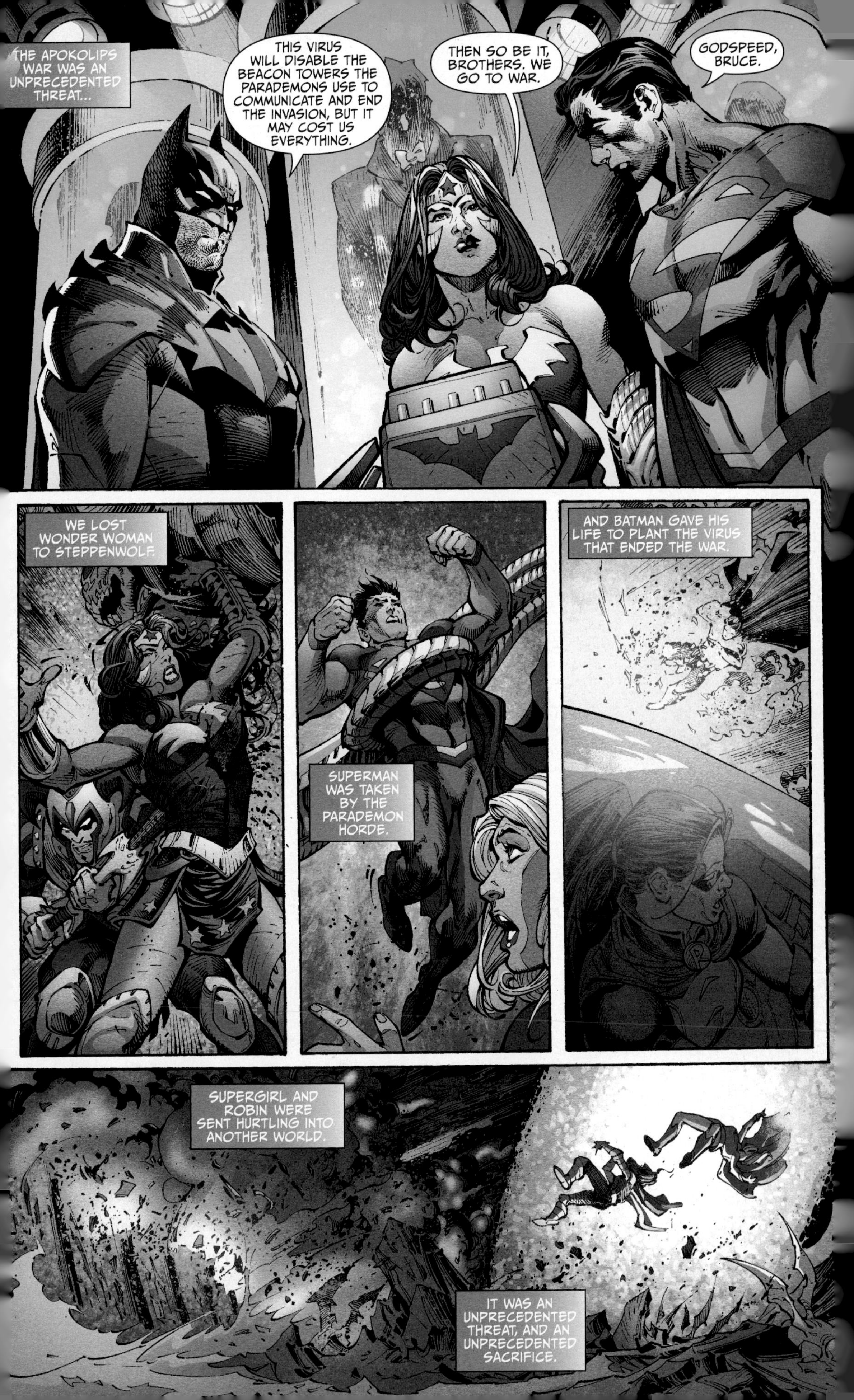
THE APOKOLIPS WAR WAS AN UNPRECEDENTED THREAT...
THIS VIRUS WILL DISABLE THE BEACON TOWERS THE PARADEMONS USE TO COMMUNICATE AND END THE INVASION, BUT IT MAY COST US EVERYTHING.
THEN SO BE IT, BROTHERS. WE GO TO WAR.
GODSPEED, BRUCE.
WE LOST WONDER WOMAN TO STEPPENWOLF.
SUPERMAN WAS TAKEN BY THE PARADEMON HORDE.
AND BATMAN GAVE HIS LIFE TO PLANT THE VIRUS THAT ENDED THE WAR.
SUPERGIRL AND ROBIN WERE SENT HURTLING INTO ANOTHER WORLD.
IT WAS AN UNPRECEDENTED THREAT, AND AN UNPRECEDENTED SACRIFICE.

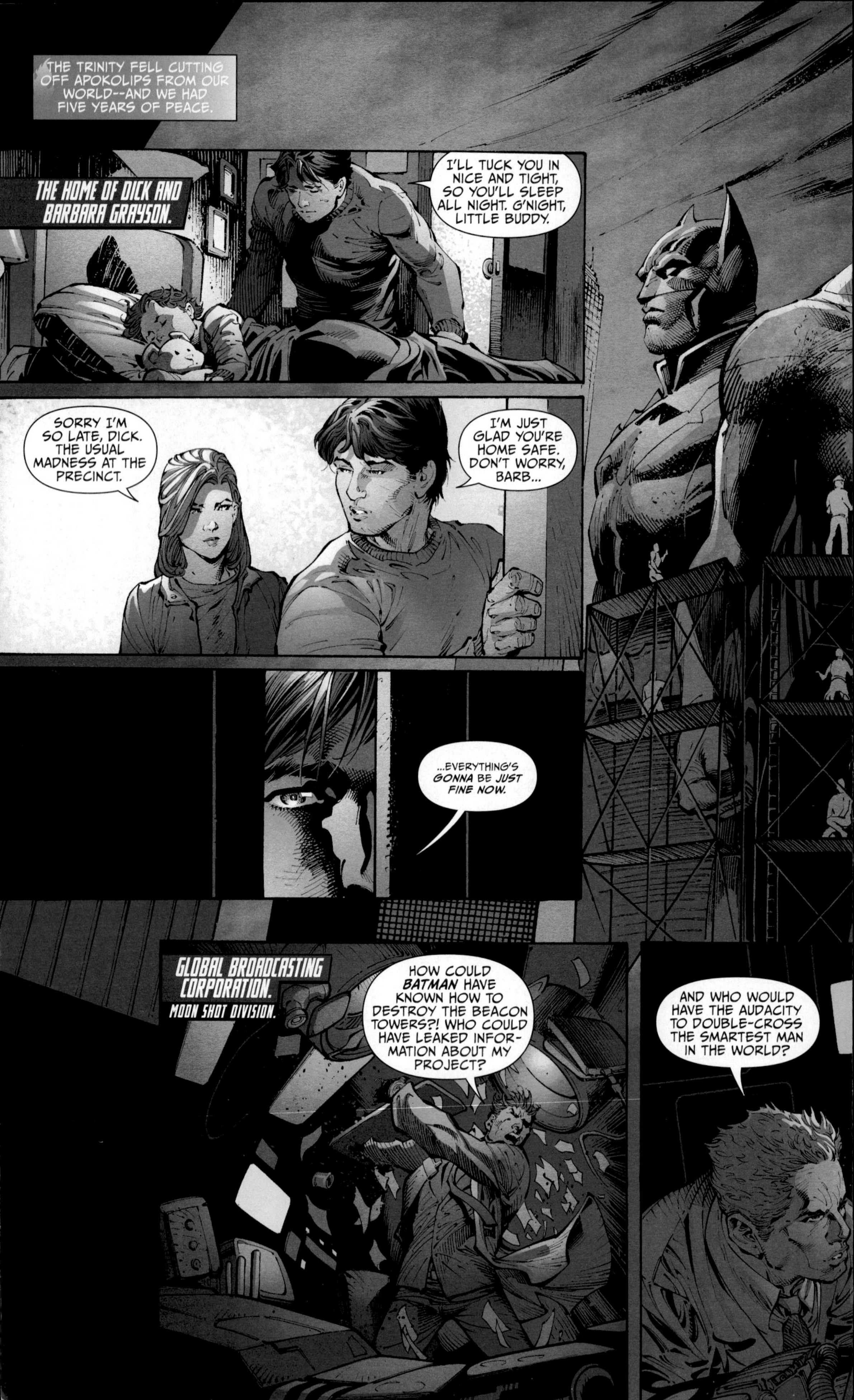
THE TRINITY FELL CUTTING OFF APOKOLIPS FROM OUR WORLD--AND WE HAD FIVE YEARS OF PEACE.
THE HOME OF DICK AND BARBARA GRAYSON.
I'LL TUCK YOU IN NICE AND TIGHT, SO YOU'LL SLEEP ALL NIGHT. G'NIGHT, LITTLE BUDDY.
SORRY I'M SO LATE, DICK. THE USUAL MADNESS AT THE PRECINCT.
I'M JUST GLAD YOU'RE HOME SAFE. DON'T WORRY, BARB...
...EVERYTHING'S GONNA BE JUST FINE NOW.
GLOBAL BROADCASTING CORPORATION.
MOON SHOT DIVISION.
HOW COULD BATMAN HAVE KNOWN HOW TO DESTROY THE BEACON TOWERS?! WHO COULD HAVE LEAKED INFORMATION ABOUT MY PROJECT?
AND WHO WOULD HAVE THE AUDACITY TO DOUBLE-CROSS THE SMARTEST MAN IN THE WORLD?

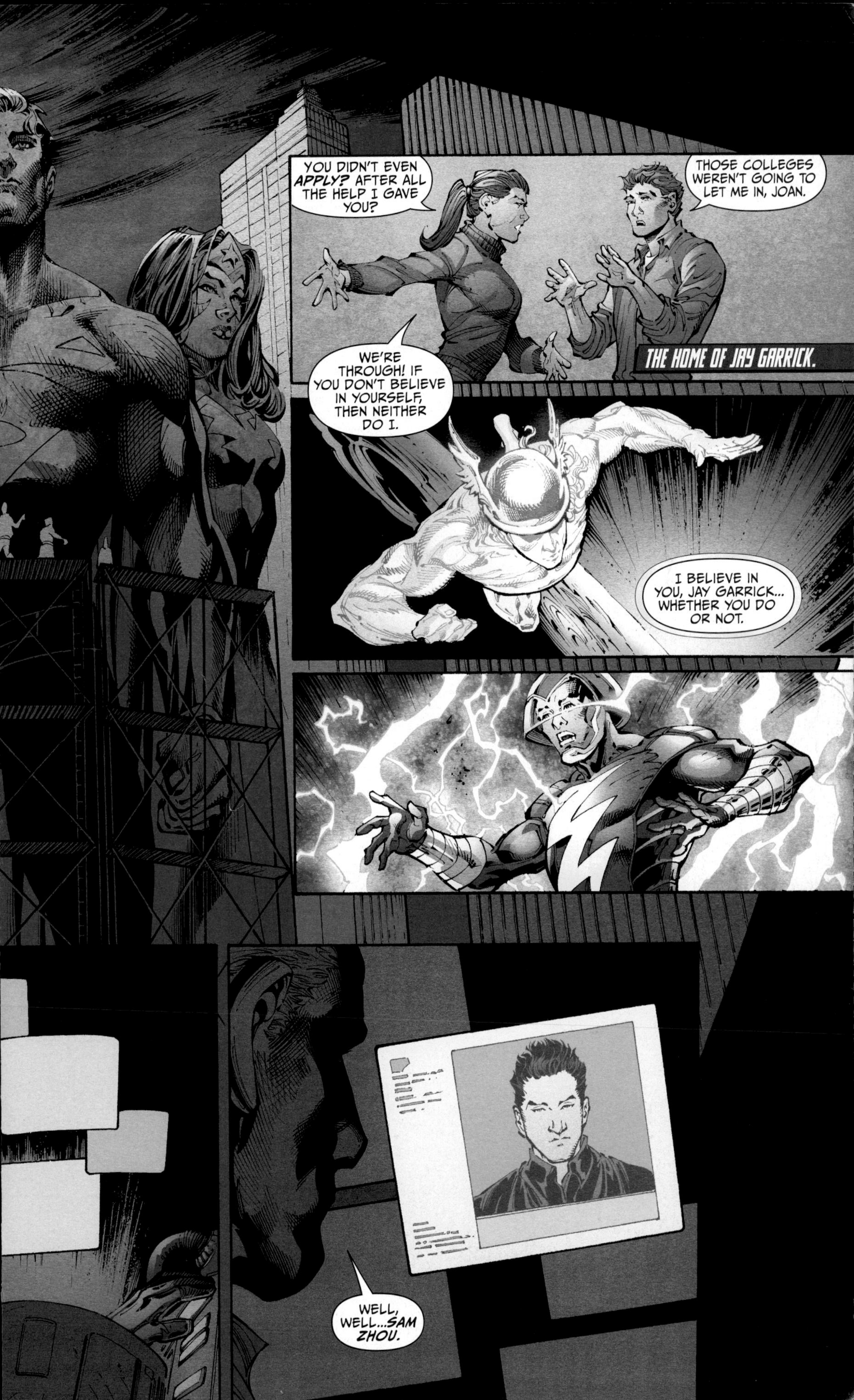
YOU DIDN'T EVEN APPLY? AFTER ALL THE HELP I GAVE YOU?
THOSE COLLEGES WEREN'T GOING TO LET ME IN, JOAN.
THE HOME OF JAY GARRICK.
WE'RE THROUGH! IF YOU DON'T BELIEVE IN YOURSELF, THEN NEITHER DO I.
I BELIEVE IN YOU, JAY GARRICK... WHETHER YOU DO OR NOT.
WELL, WELL...SAM ZHOU.

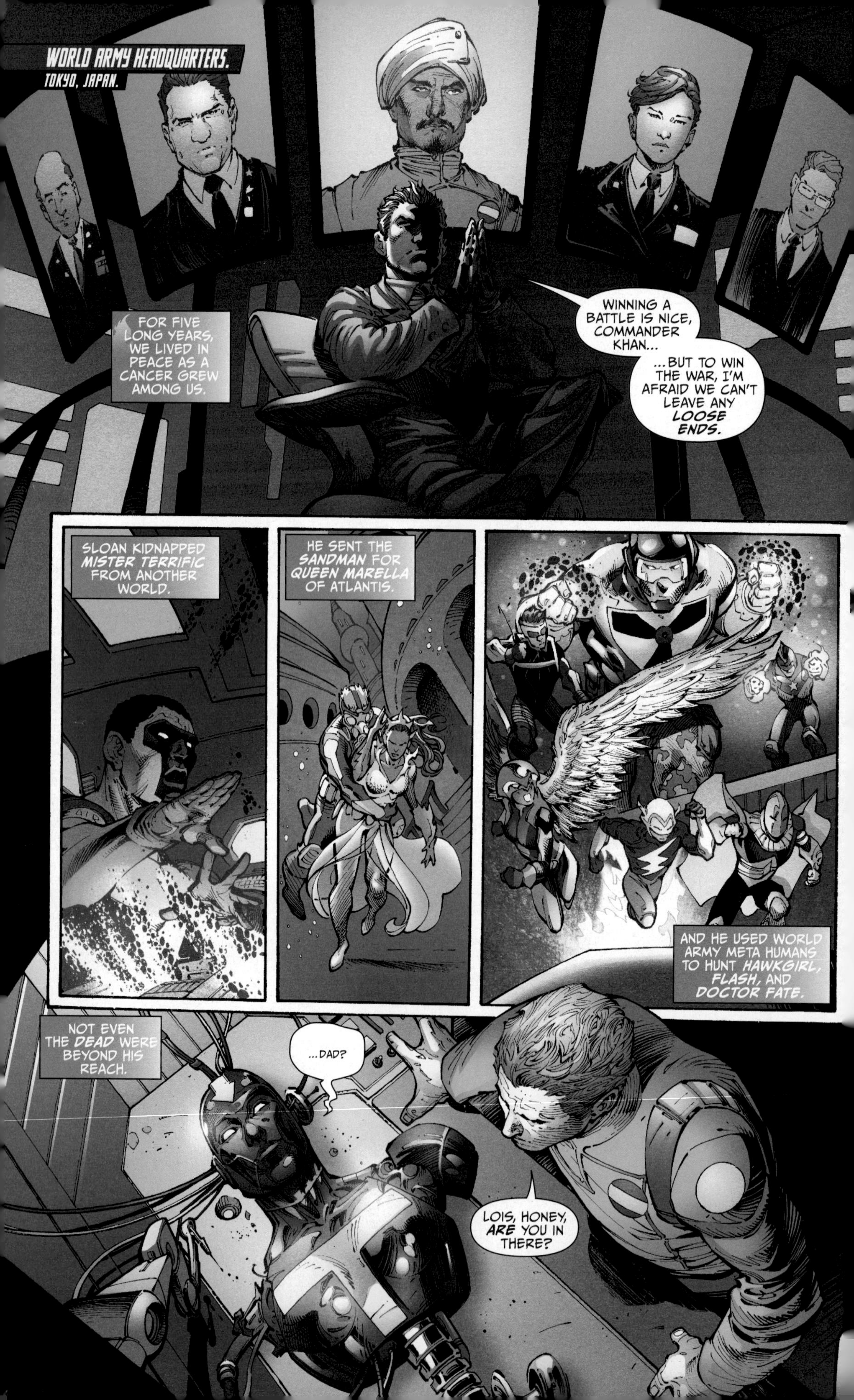
WORLD ARMY HEADQUARTERS.
TOKYO, JAPAN.
FOR FIVE LONG YEARS, WE LIVED IN PEACE AS A CANCER GREW AMONG US.
WINNING A BATTLE IS NICE, COMMANDER KHAN...
...BUT TO WIN THE WAR, I'M AFRAID WE CAN'T LEAVE ANY *LOOSE ENDS.*
SLOAN KIDNAPPED *MISTER TERRIFIC* FROM ANOTHER WORLD.
HE SENT THE *SANDMAN* FOR *QUEEN MARELLA* OF ATLANTIS.
AND HE USED WORLD ARMY META HUMANS TO HUNT *HAWKGIRL, FLASH,* AND *DOCTOR FATE.*
NOT EVEN THE *DEAD* WERE BEYOND HIS REACH.
...DAD?
LOIS, HONEY, *ARE* YOU IN THERE?

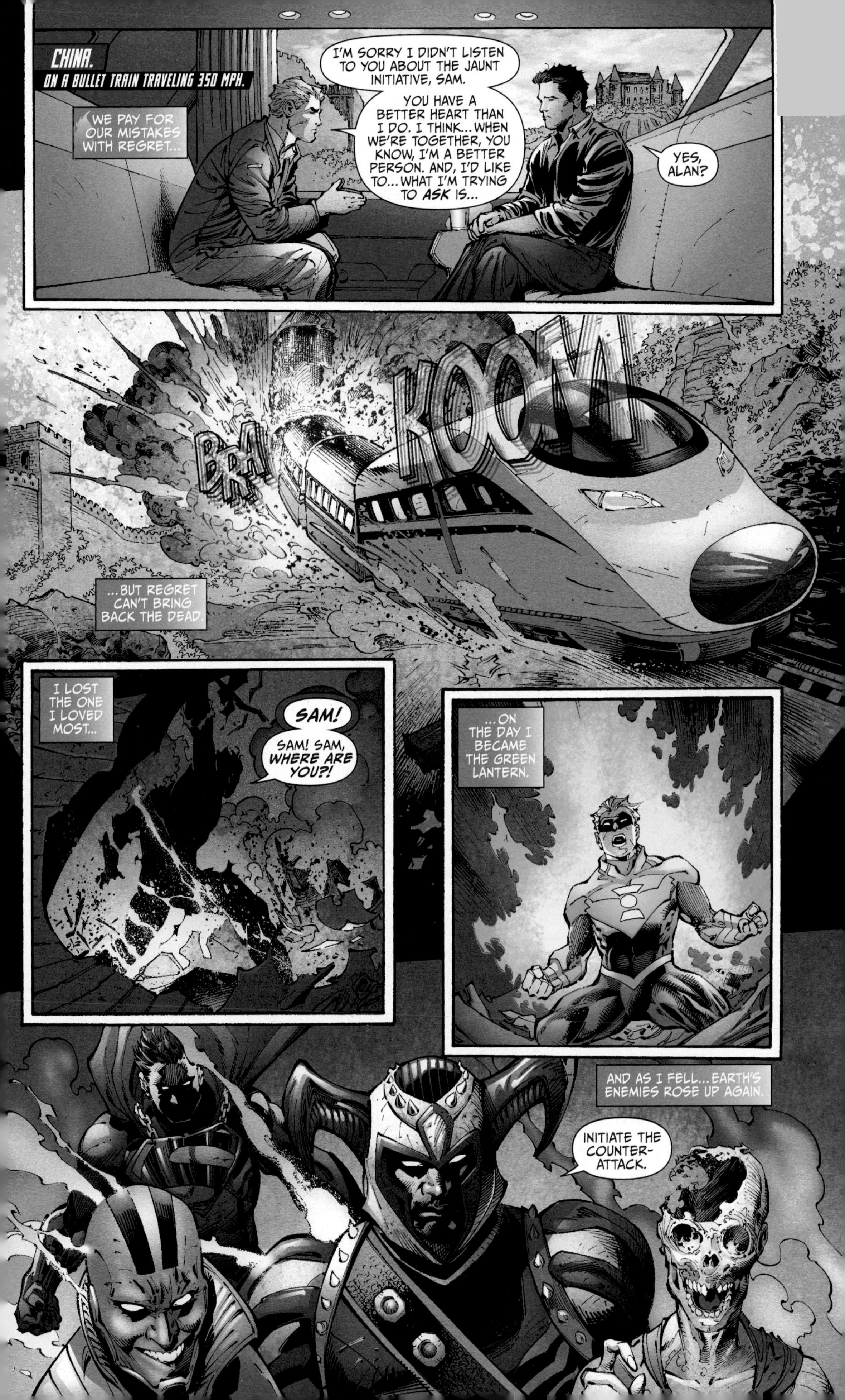
CHINA.
ON A BULLET TRAIN TRAVELING 350 MPH.
WE PAY FOR OUR MISTAKES WITH REGRET...
I'M SORRY I DIDN'T LISTEN TO YOU ABOUT THE JAUNT INITIATIVE, SAM.
YOU HAVE A BETTER HEART THAN I DO. I THINK... WHEN WE'RE TOGETHER, YOU KNOW, I'M A BETTER PERSON. AND, I'D LIKE TO... WHAT I'M TRYING TO ASK IS...
YES, ALAN?
BRA
KOOM
...BUT REGRET CAN'T BRING BACK THE DEAD.
I LOST THE ONE I LOVED MOST...
SAM!
SAM! SAM, WHERE ARE YOU?!
...ON THE DAY I BECAME THE GREEN LANTERN.
AND AS I FELL... EARTH'S ENEMIES ROSE UP AGAIN.
INITIATE THE COUNTER-ATTACK.

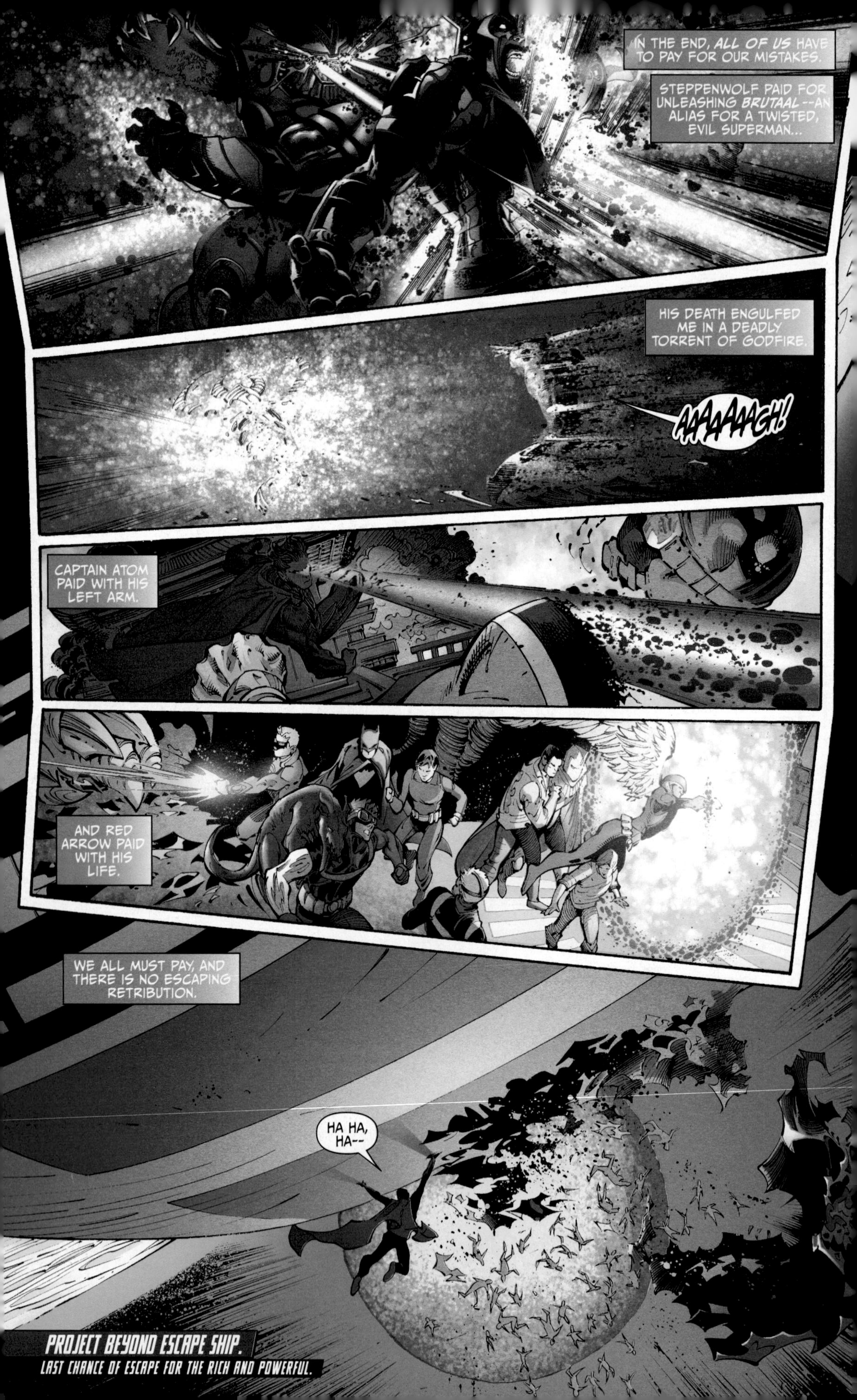
IN THE END, ALL OF US HAVE TO PAY FOR OUR MISTAKES.
STEPPENWOLF PAID FOR UNLEASHING BRUTAAL--AN ALIAS FOR A TWISTED, EVIL SUPERMAN...
HIS DEATH ENGULFED ME IN A DEADLY TORRENT OF GODFIRE.
AAAAAAAGH!
CAPTAIN ATOM PAID WITH HIS LEFT ARM.
AND RED ARROW PAID WITH HIS LIFE.
WE ALL MUST PAY, AND THERE IS NO ESCAPING RETRIBUTION.
HA HA, HA--
PROJECT BEYOND ESCAPE SHIP.
LAST CHANCE OF ESCAPE FOR THE RICH AND POWERFUL.

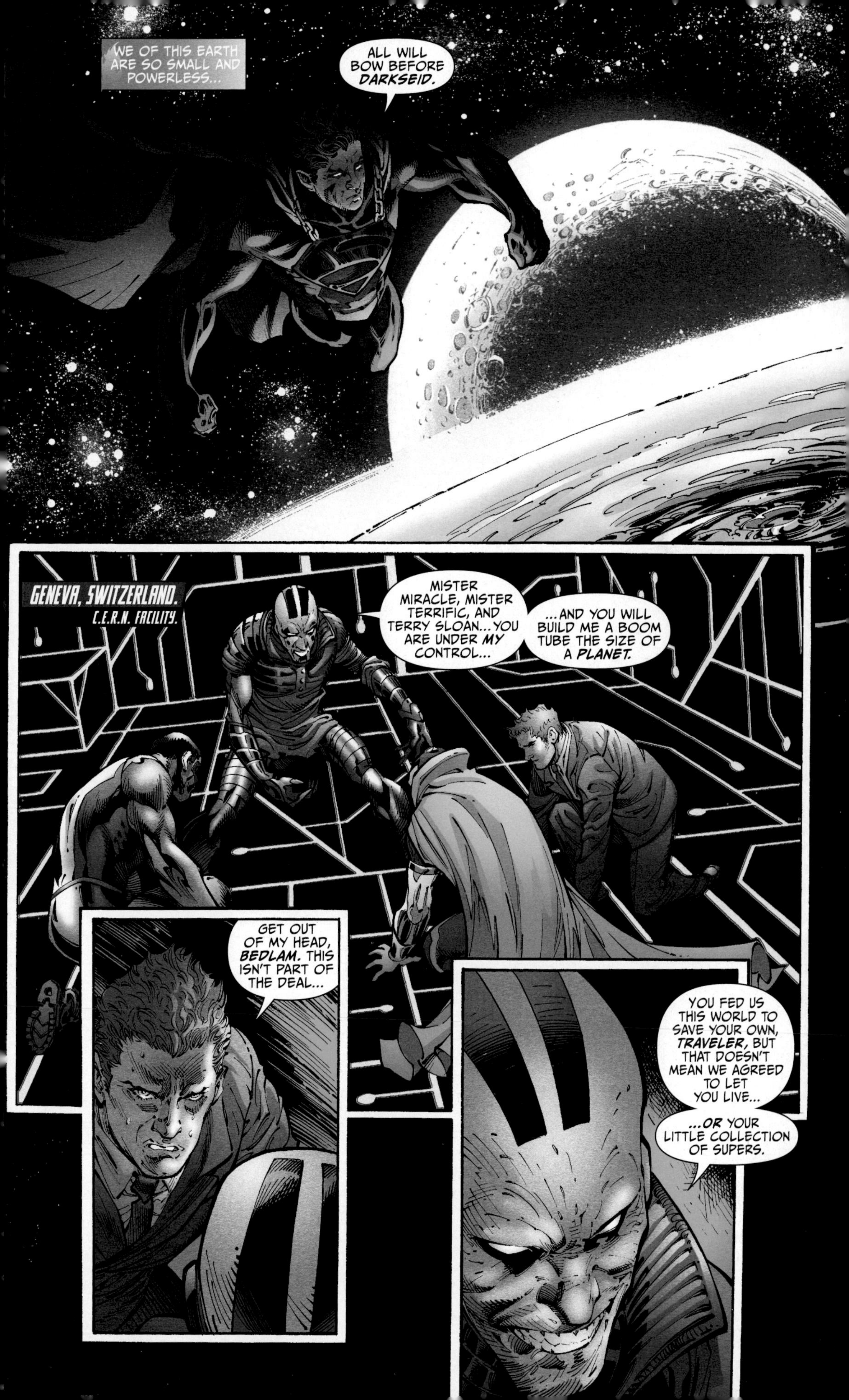
WE OF THIS EARTH ARE SO SMALL AND POWERLESS...
ALL WILL BOW BEFORE DARKSEID.
GENEVA, SWITZERLAND.
C.E.R.N. FACILITY.
MISTER MIRACLE, MISTER TERRIFIC, AND TERRY SLOAN... YOU ARE UNDER MY CONTROL...
...AND YOU WILL BUILD ME A BOOM TUBE THE SIZE OF A PLANET.
GET OUT OF MY HEAD, BEDLAM. THIS ISN'T PART OF THE DEAL...
YOU FED US THIS WORLD TO SAVE YOUR OWN, TRAVELER, BUT THAT DOESN'T MEAN WE AGREED TO LET YOU LIVE...
...OR YOUR LITTLE COLLECTION OF SUPERS.

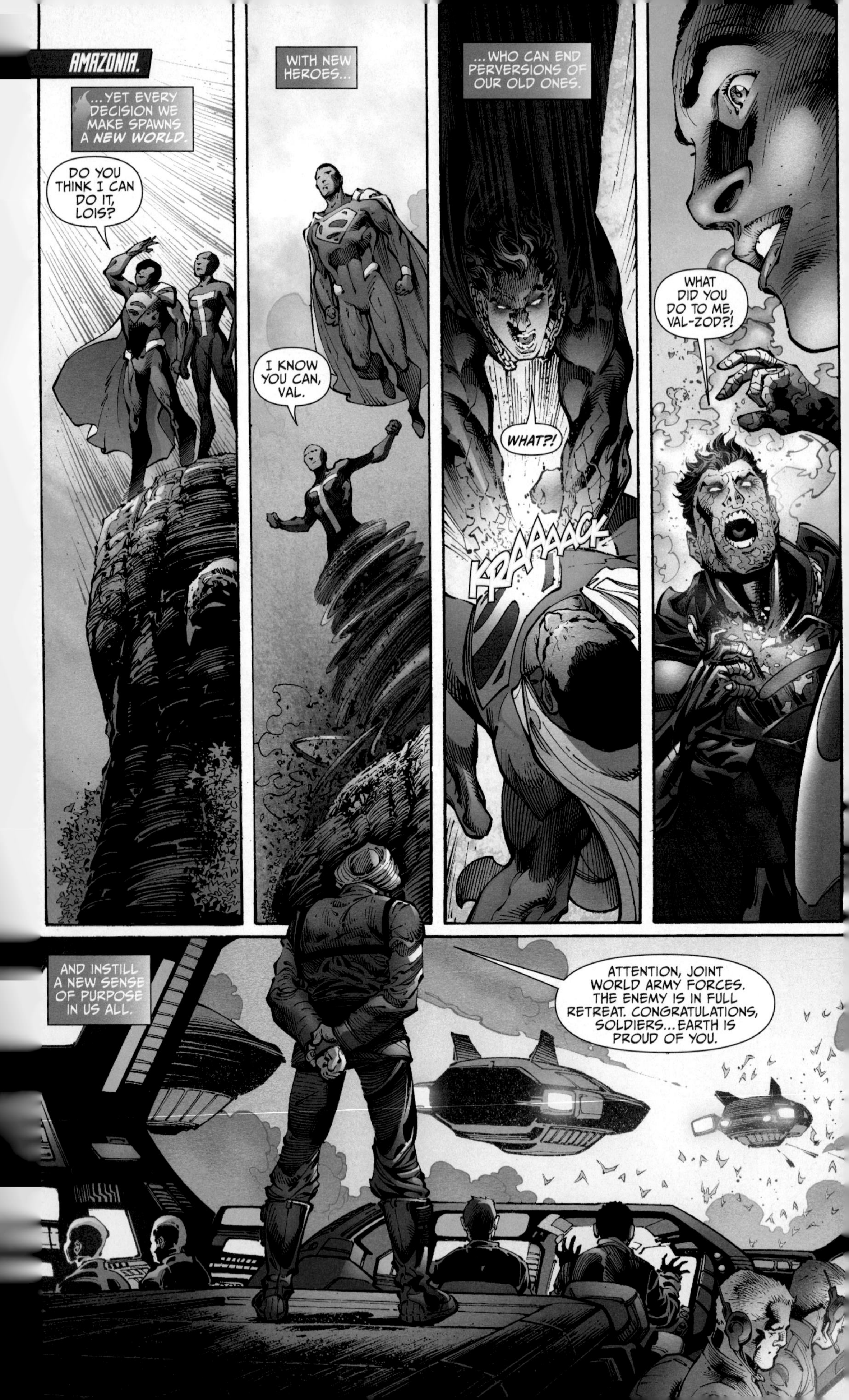
AMAZONIA.
...YET EVERY DECISION WE MAKE SPAWNS A NEW WORLD.
DO YOU THINK I CAN DO IT, LOIS?
WITH NEW HEROES...
I KNOW YOU CAN, VAL.
...WHO CAN END PERVERSIONS OF OUR OLD ONES.
WHAT?!
KRAAAACK
WHAT DID YOU DO TO ME, VAL-ZOD?!
AND INSTILL A NEW SENSE OF PURPOSE IN US ALL.
ATTENTION, JOINT WORLD ARMY FORCES. THE ENEMY IS IN FULL RETREAT. CONGRATULATIONS, SOLDIERS... EARTH IS PROUD OF YOU.

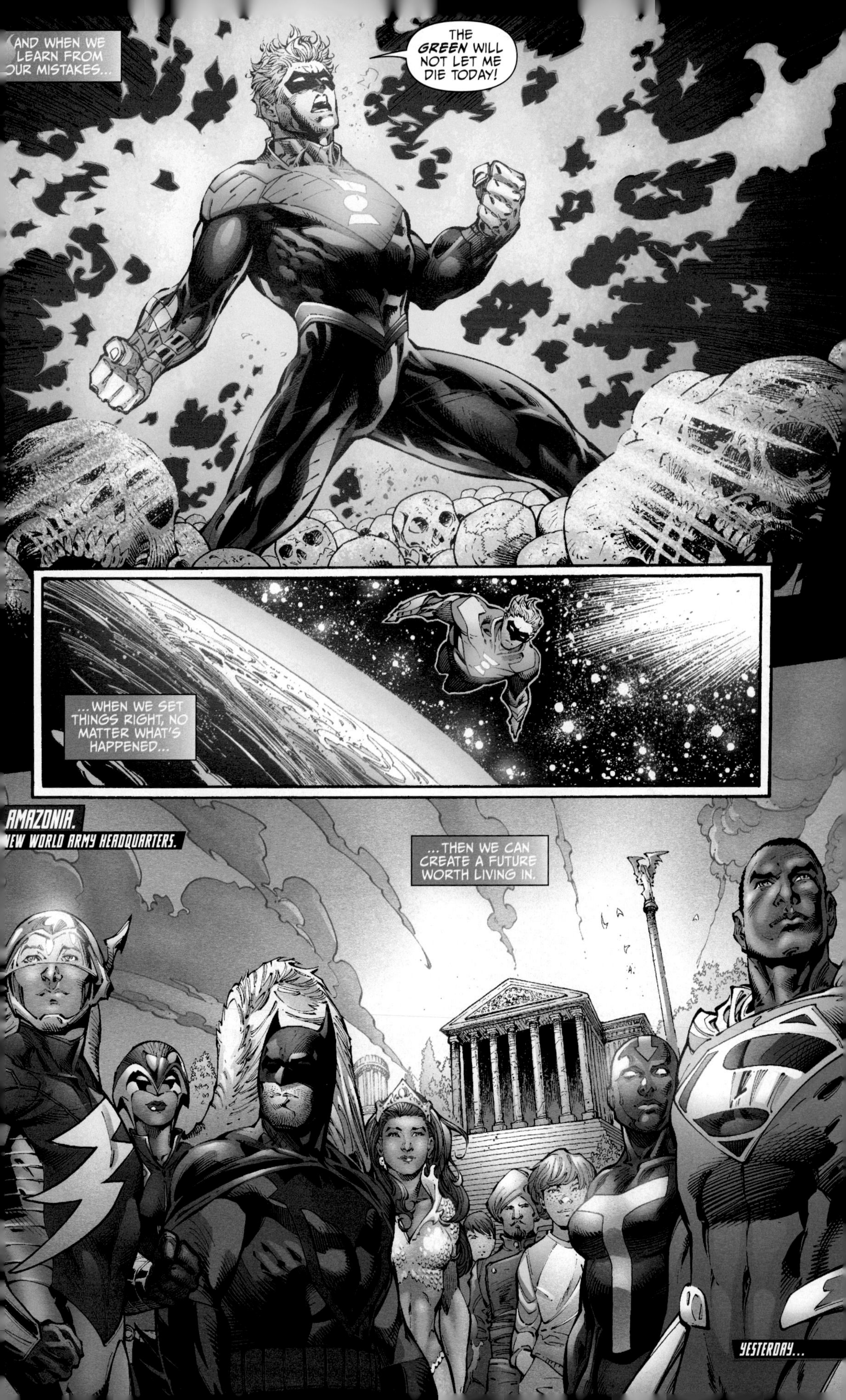
AND WHEN WE LEARN FROM OUR MISTAKES...
THE GREEN WILL NOT LET ME DIE TODAY!
...WHEN WE SET THINGS RIGHT, NO MATTER WHAT'S HAPPENED...
AMAZONIA.
NEW WORLD ARMY HEADQUARTERS.
...THEN WE CAN CREATE A FUTURE WORTH LIVING IN.
YESTERDAY...

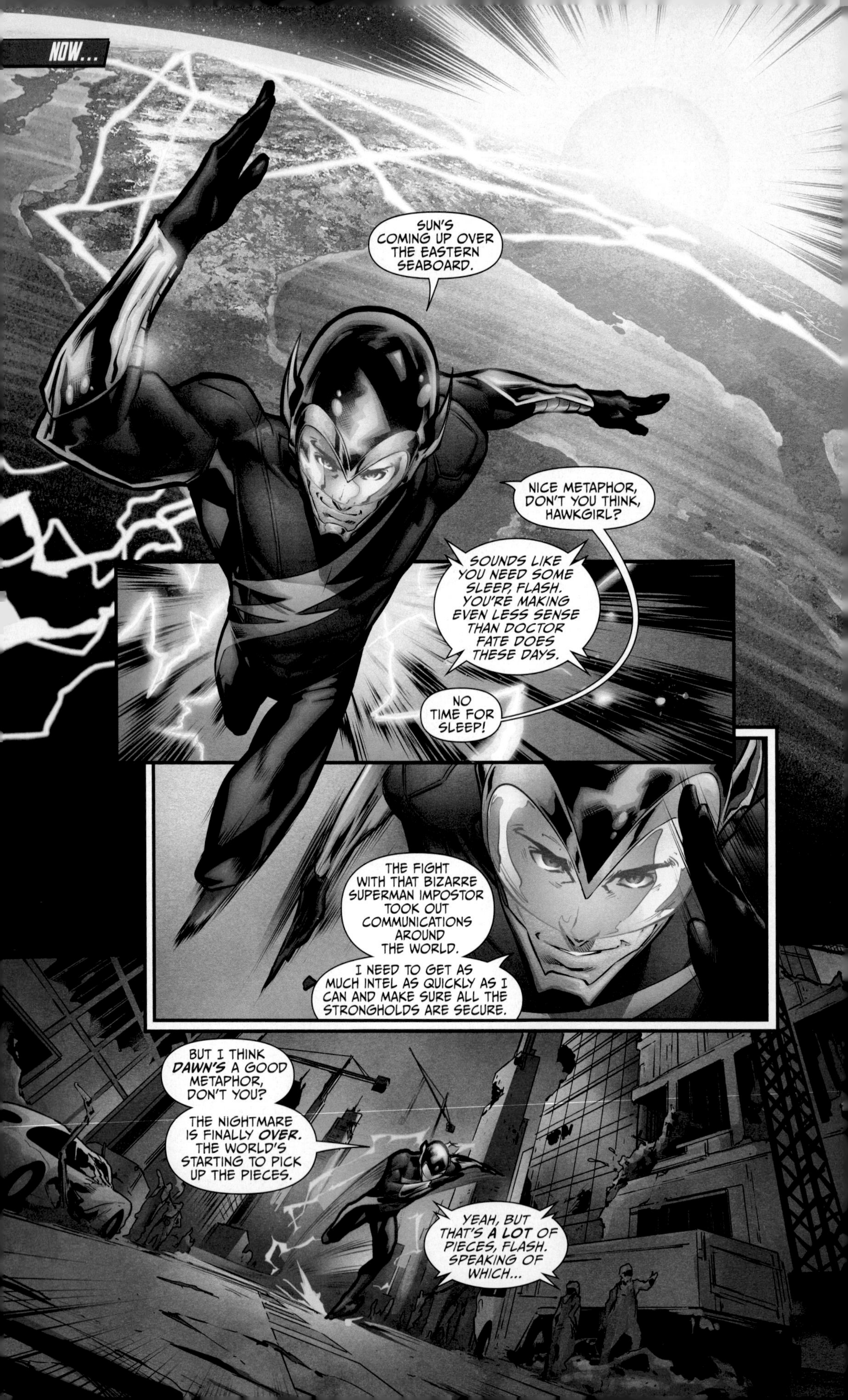
NOW...
SUN'S COMING UP OVER THE EASTERN SEABOARD.
NICE METAPHOR, DON'T YOU THINK, HAWKGIRL?
SOUNDS LIKE YOU NEED SOME SLEEP, FLASH. YOU'RE MAKING EVEN LESS SENSE THAN DOCTOR FATE DOES THESE DAYS.
NO TIME FOR SLEEP!
THE FIGHT WITH THAT BIZARRE SUPERMAN IMPOSTOR TOOK OUT COMMUNICATIONS AROUND THE WORLD.
I NEED TO GET AS MUCH INTEL AS QUICKLY AS I CAN AND MAKE SURE ALL THE STRONGHOLDS ARE SECURE.
BUT I THINK DAWN'S A GOOD METAPHOR, DON'T YOU?
THE NIGHTMARE IS FINALLY OVER. THE WORLD'S STARTING TO PICK UP THE PIECES.
YEAH, BUT THAT'S A LOT OF PIECES, FLASH. SPEAKING OF WHICH...

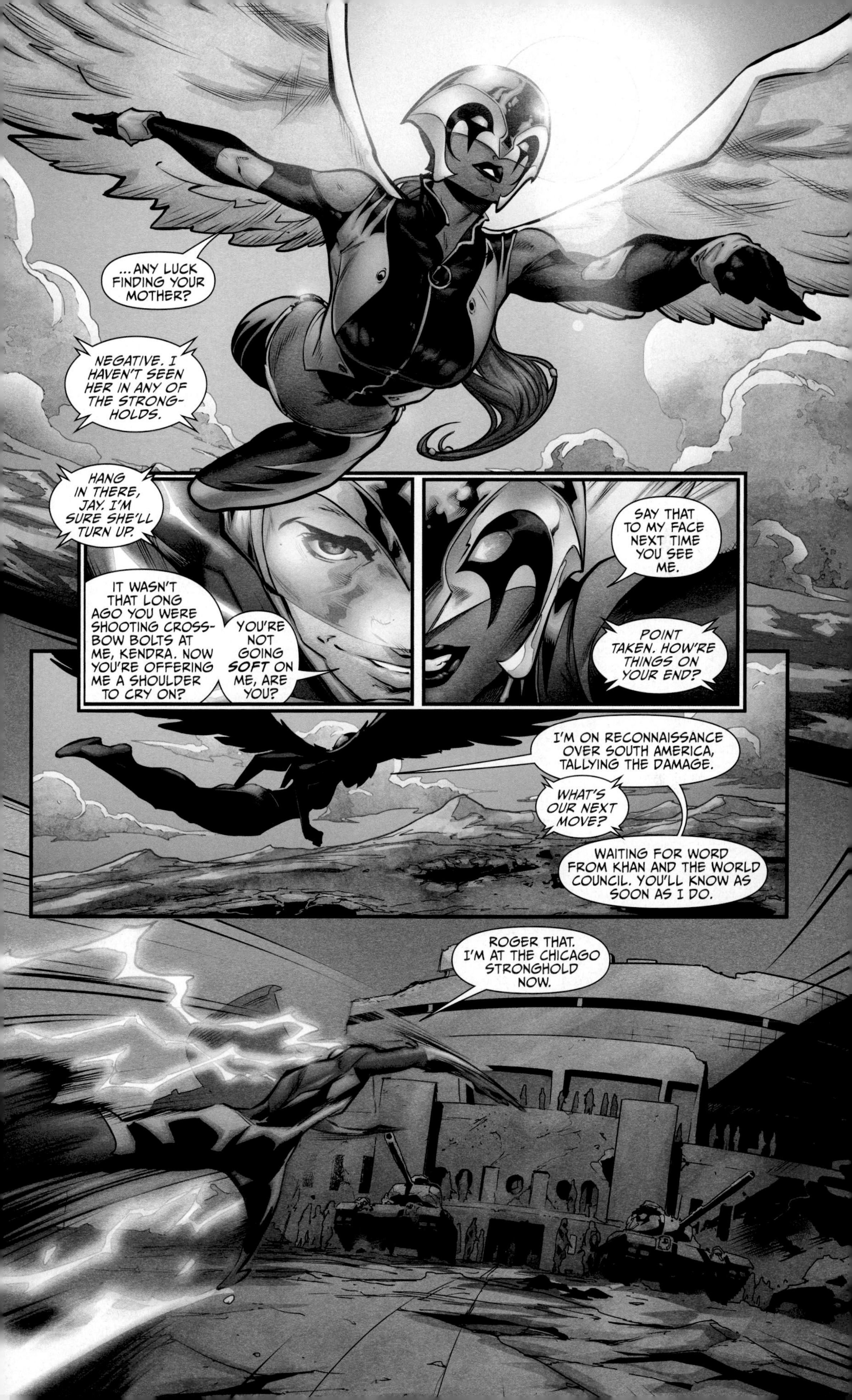
...ANY LUCK FINDING YOUR MOTHER?
NEGATIVE. I HAVEN'T SEEN HER IN ANY OF THE STRONG-HOLDS.
HANG IN THERE, JAY. I'M SURE SHE'LL TURN UP.
IT WASN'T THAT LONG AGO YOU WERE SHOOTING CROSS-BOW BOLTS AT ME, KENDRA. NOW YOU'RE OFFERING ME A SHOULDER TO CRY ON?
YOU'RE NOT GOING SOFT ON ME, ARE YOU?
SAY THAT TO MY FACE NEXT TIME YOU SEE ME.
POINT TAKEN. HOW'RE THINGS ON YOUR END?
I'M ON RECONNAISSANCE OVER SOUTH AMERICA, TALLYING THE DAMAGE.
WHAT'S OUR NEXT MOVE?
WAITING FOR WORD FROM KHAN AND THE WORLD COUNCIL. YOU'LL KNOW AS SOON AS I DO.
ROGER THAT. I'M AT THE CHICAGO STRONGHOLD NOW.

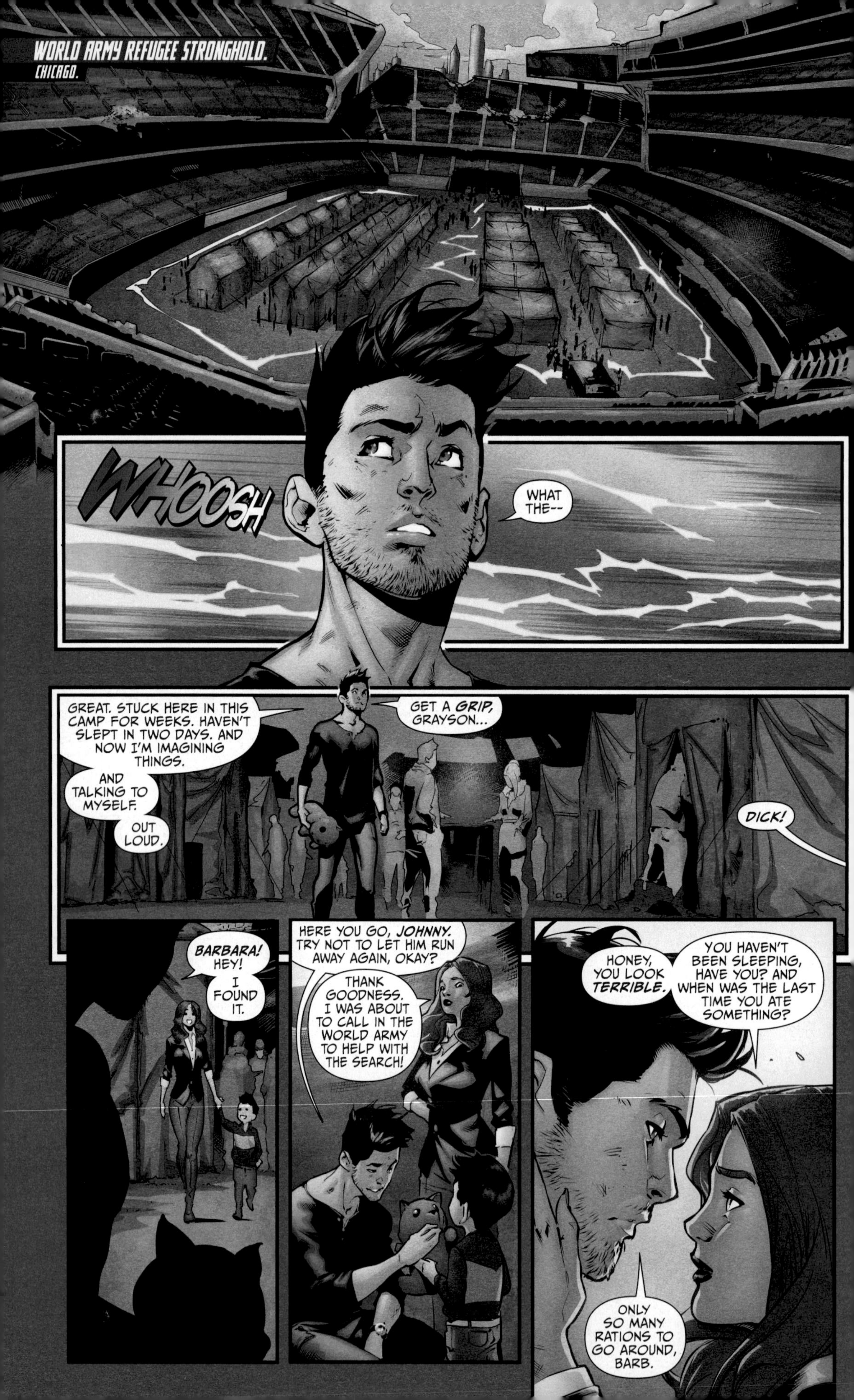
WORLD ARMY REFUGEE STRONGHOLD.
CHICAGO.
WHOOSH
WHAT THE--
GREAT. STUCK HERE IN THIS CAMP FOR WEEKS. HAVEN'T SLEPT IN TWO DAYS. AND NOW I'M IMAGINING THINGS.
AND TALKING TO MYSELF.
OUT LOUD.
GET A GRIP, GRAYSON...
DICK!
BARBARA! HEY!
I FOUND IT.
HERE YOU GO, JOHNNY. TRY NOT TO LET HIM RUN AWAY AGAIN, OKAY?
THANK GOODNESS. I WAS ABOUT TO CALL IN THE WORLD ARMY TO HELP WITH THE SEARCH!
HONEY, YOU LOOK TERRIBLE.
YOU HAVEN'T BEEN SLEEPING, HAVE YOU? AND WHEN WAS THE LAST TIME YOU ATE SOMETHING?
ONLY SO MANY RATIONS TO GO AROUND, BARB.

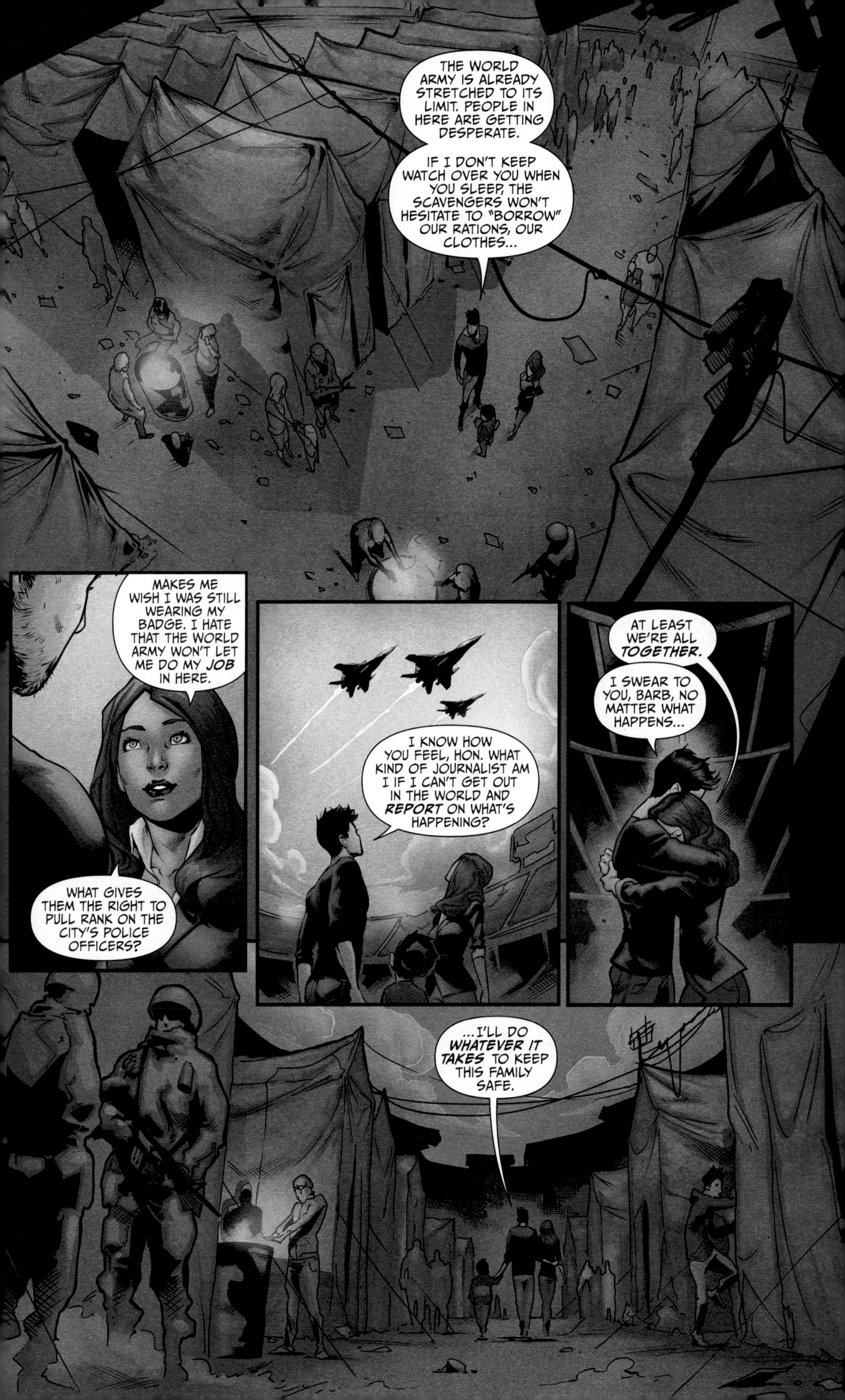
THE WORLD ARMY IS ALREADY STRETCHED TO ITS LIMIT. PEOPLE IN HERE ARE GETTING DESPERATE.
IF I DON'T KEEP WATCH OVER YOU WHEN YOU SLEEP, THE SCAVENGERS WON'T HESITATE TO "BORROW" OUR RATIONS, OUR CLOTHES...
MAKES ME WISH I WAS STILL WEARING MY BADGE. I HATE THAT THE WORLD ARMY WON'T LET ME DO MY *JOB* IN HERE.
WHAT GIVES THEM THE RIGHT TO PULL RANK ON THE CITY'S POLICE OFFICERS?
I KNOW HOW YOU FEEL, HON. WHAT KIND OF JOURNALIST AM I IF I CAN'T GET OUT IN THE WORLD AND *REPORT* ON WHAT'S HAPPENING?
AT LEAST WE'RE ALL *TOGETHER.*
I SWEAR TO YOU, BARB, NO MATTER WHAT HAPPENS...
...I'LL DO *WHATEVER IT TAKES* TO KEEP THIS FAMILY SAFE.

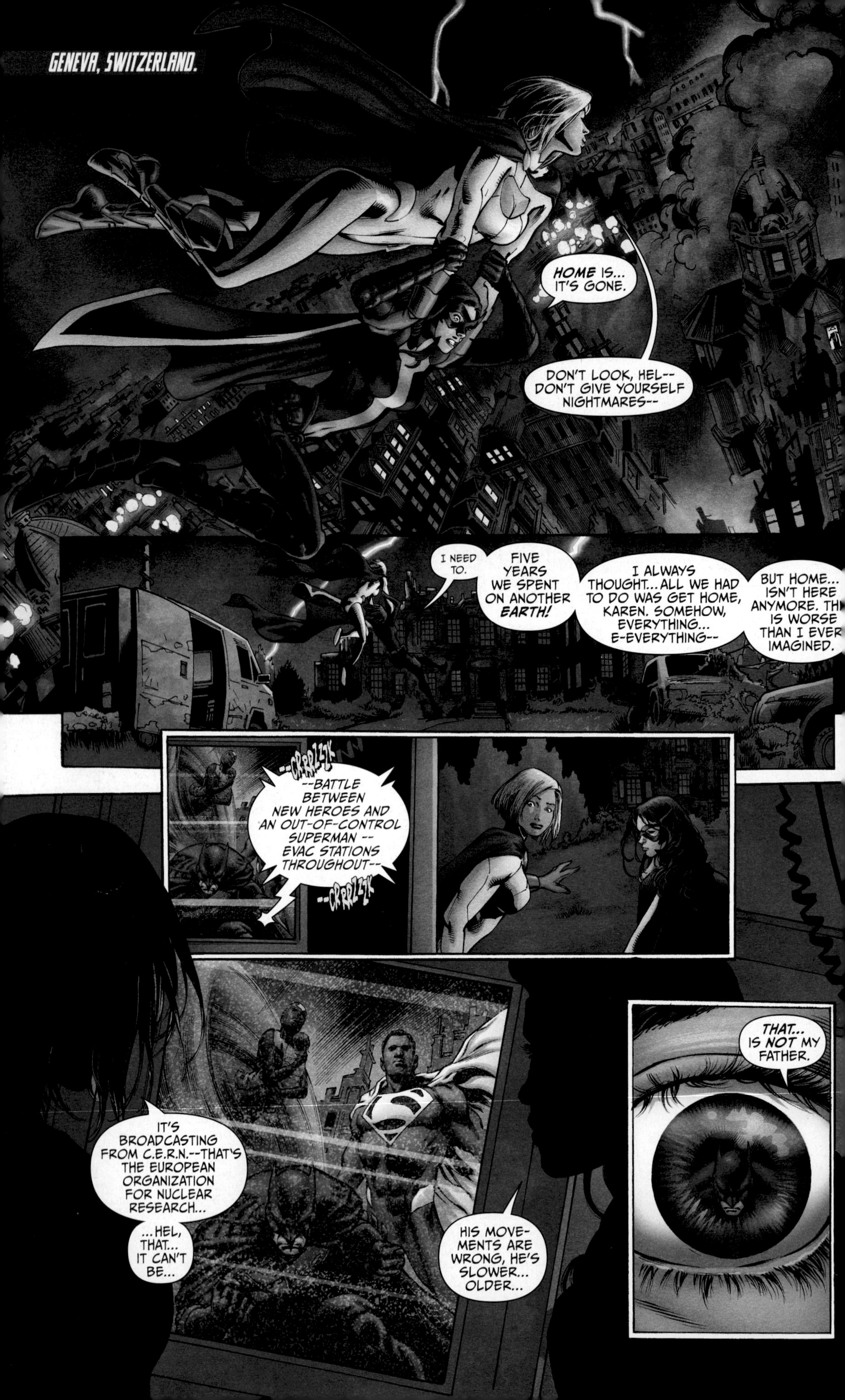
GENEVA, SWITZERLAND.
HOME IS... IT'S GONE.
DON'T LOOK, HEL-- DON'T GIVE YOURSELF NIGHTMARES--
I NEED TO.
FIVE YEARS WE SPENT ON ANOTHER EARTH!
I ALWAYS THOUGHT...ALL WE HAD TO DO WAS GET HOME, KAREN. SOMEHOW, EVERYTHING... E-EVERYTHING--
BUT HOME... ISN'T HERE ANYMORE. THI IS WORSE THAN I EVER IMAGINED.
--CRRZZZK
--BATTLE BETWEEN NEW HEROES AND AN OUT-OF-CONTROL SUPERMAN -- EVAC STATIONS THROUGHOUT--
--CRRZZZK
IT'S BROADCASTING FROM C.E.R.N.--THAT'S THE EUROPEAN ORGANIZATION FOR NUCLEAR RESEARCH...
...HEL, THAT... IT CAN'T BE...
HIS MOVE-MENTS ARE WRONG, HE'S SLOWER... OLDER...
THAT... IS NOT MY FATHER.

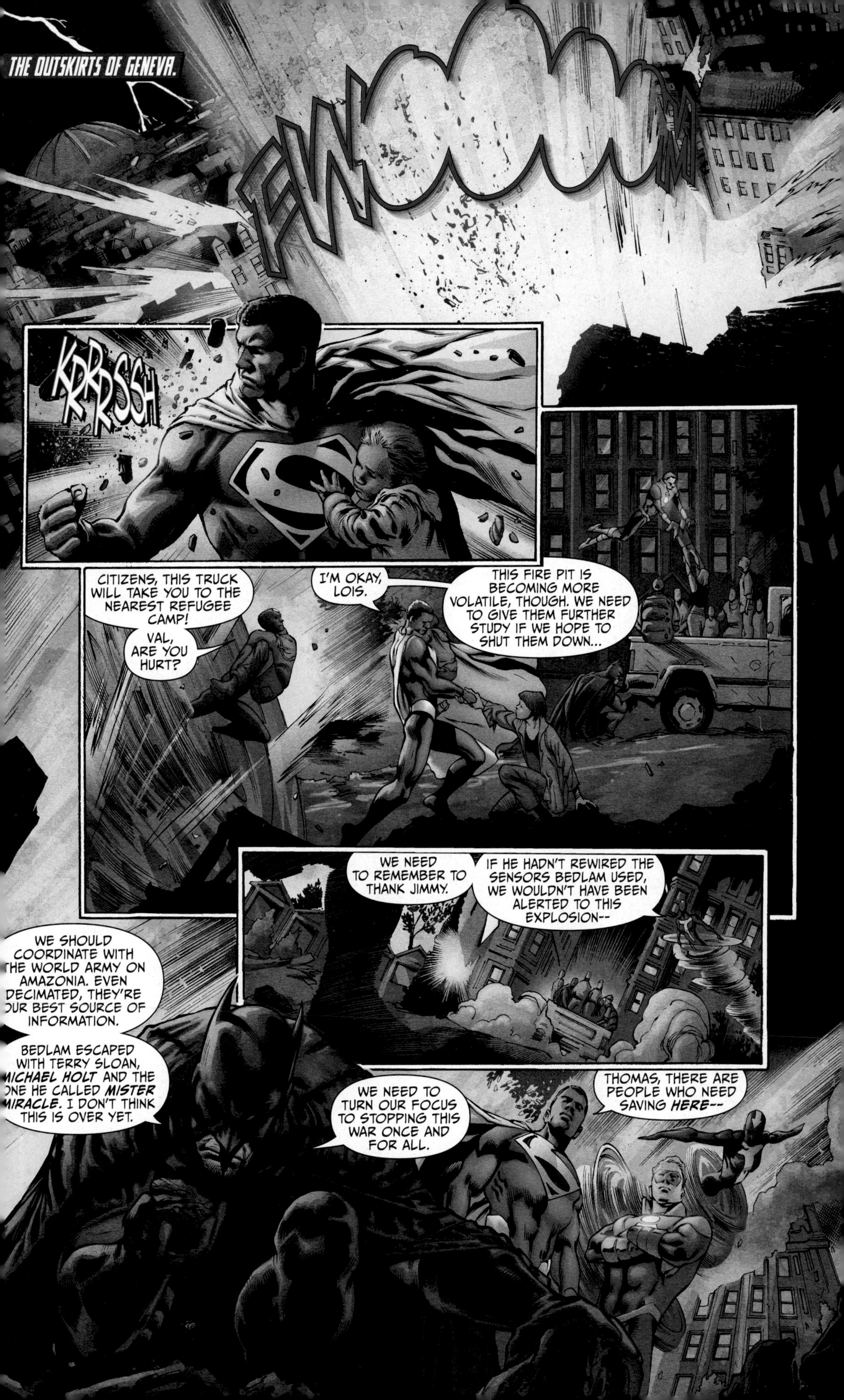
THE OUTSKIRTS OF GENEVA.
FWOOOOOM
KRRRSSH
CITIZENS, THIS TRUCK WILL TAKE YOU TO THE NEAREST REFUGEE CAMP!
VAL, ARE YOU HURT?
I'M OKAY, LOIS.
THIS FIRE PIT IS BECOMING MORE VOLATILE, THOUGH. WE NEED TO GIVE THEM FURTHER STUDY IF WE HOPE TO SHUT THEM DOWN...
WE NEED TO REMEMBER TO THANK JIMMY.
IF HE HADN'T REWIRED THE SENSORS BEDLAM USED, WE WOULDN'T HAVE BEEN ALERTED TO THIS EXPLOSION--
WE SHOULD COORDINATE WITH THE WORLD ARMY ON AMAZONIA. EVEN DECIMATED, THEY'RE OUR BEST SOURCE OF INFORMATION.
BEDLAM ESCAPED WITH TERRY SLOAN, MICHAEL HOLT AND THE ONE HE CALLED MISTER MIRACLE. I DON'T THINK THIS IS OVER YET.
WE NEED TO TURN OUR FOCUS TO STOPPING THIS WAR ONCE AND FOR ALL.
THOMAS, THERE ARE PEOPLE WHO NEED SAVING HERE--

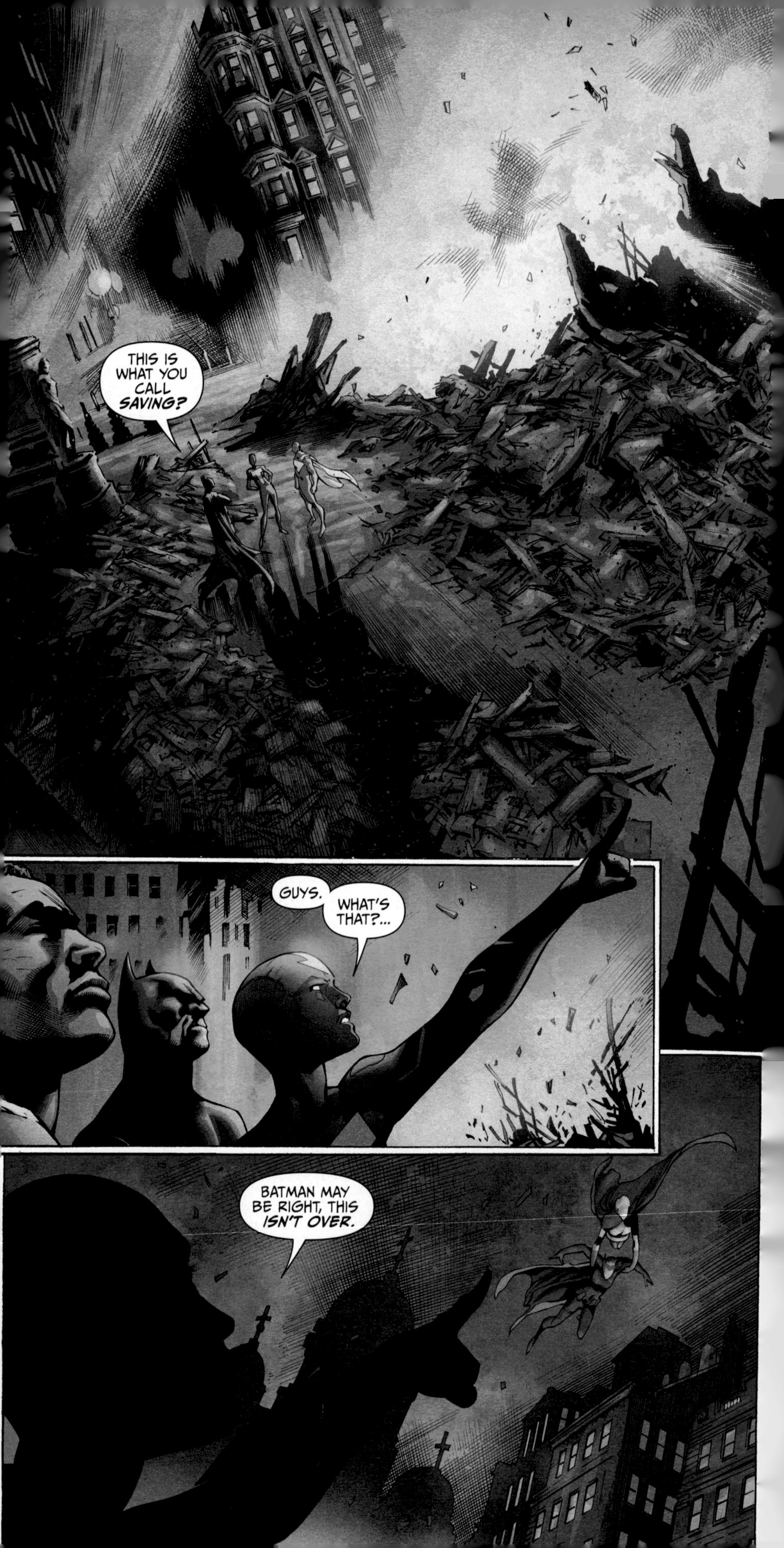
THIS IS WHAT YOU CALL SAVING?
GUYS.
WHAT'S THAT?...
BATMAN MAY BE RIGHT, THIS ISN'T OVER.

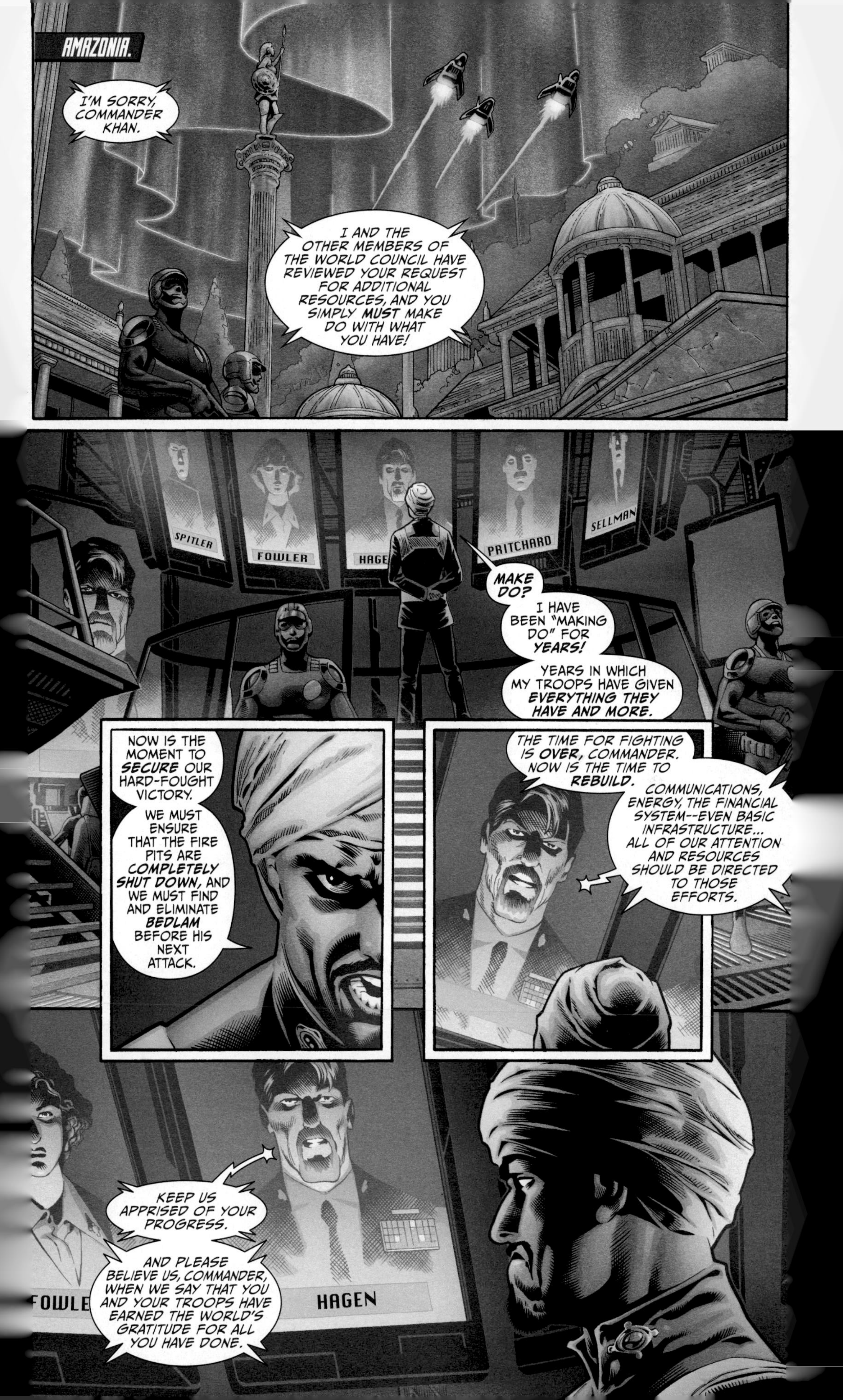
AMAZONIA.
I'M SORRY, COMMANDER KHAN.
I AND THE OTHER MEMBERS OF THE WORLD COUNCIL HAVE REVIEWED YOUR REQUEST FOR ADDITIONAL RESOURCES, AND YOU SIMPLY MUST MAKE DO WITH WHAT YOU HAVE!
SPITLER
FOWLER
HAGE
PRITCHARD
SELLMAN
MAKE DO? I HAVE BEEN "MAKING DO" FOR YEARS!
YEARS IN WHICH MY TROOPS HAVE GIVEN EVERYTHING THEY HAVE AND MORE.
NOW IS THE MOMENT TO SECURE OUR HARD-FOUGHT VICTORY.
WE MUST ENSURE THAT THE FIRE PITS ARE COMPLETELY SHUT DOWN, AND WE MUST FIND AND ELIMINATE BEDLAM BEFORE HIS NEXT ATTACK.
THE TIME FOR FIGHTING IS OVER, COMMANDER. NOW IS THE TIME TO REBUILD.
COMMUNICATIONS, ENERGY, THE FINANCIAL SYSTEM--EVEN BASIC INFRASTRUCTURE... ALL OF OUR ATTENTION AND RESOURCES SHOULD BE DIRECTED TO THOSE EFFORTS.
KEEP US APPRISED OF YOUR PROGRESS.
AND PLEASE BELIEVE US, COMMANDER, WHEN WE SAY THAT YOU AND YOUR TROOPS HAVE EARNED THE WORLD'S GRATITUDE FOR ALL YOU HAVE DONE.
FOWLE
HAGEN

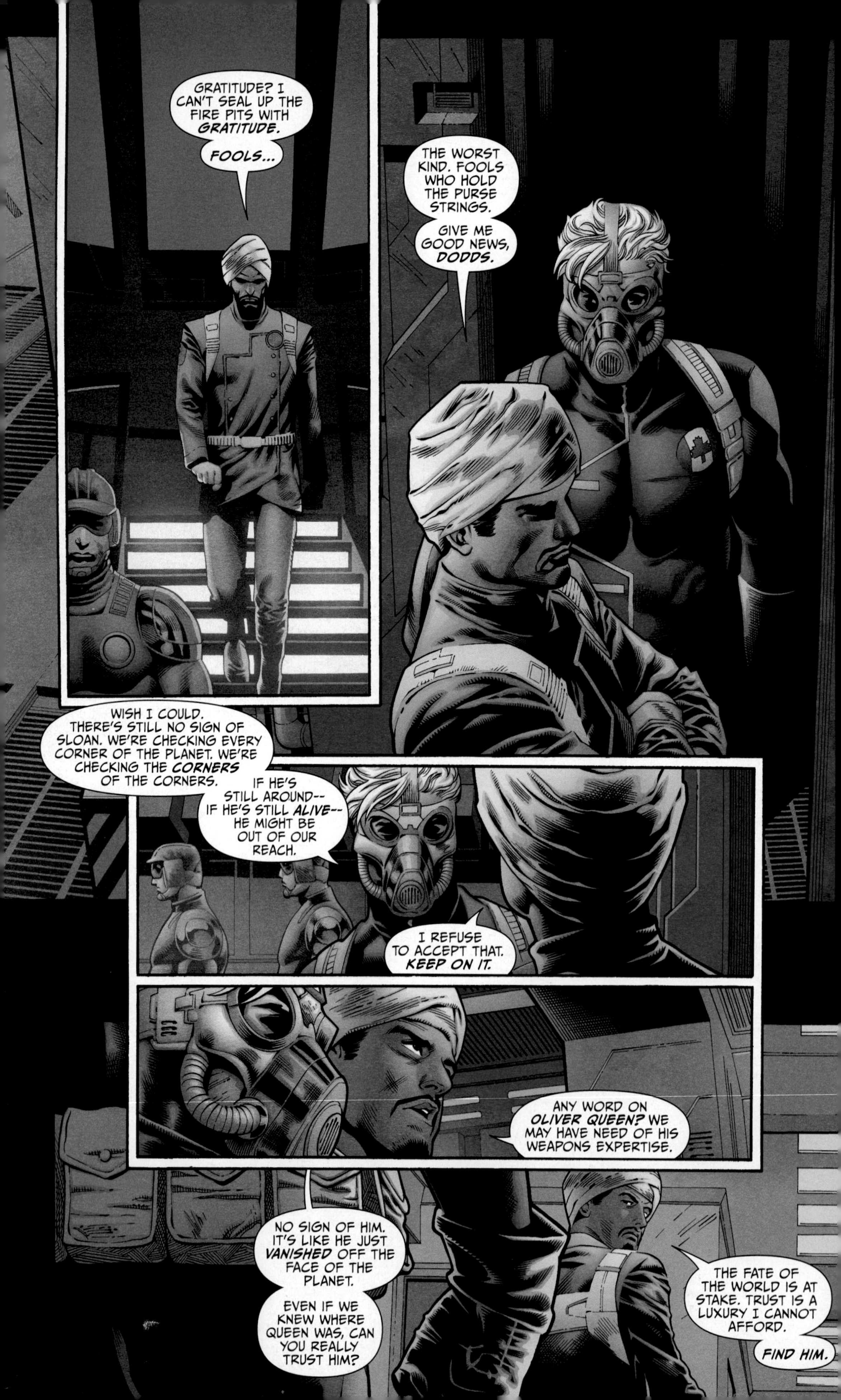
GRATITUDE? I CAN'T SEAL UP THE FIRE PITS WITH *GRATITUDE.*
FOOLS...
THE WORST KIND. FOOLS WHO HOLD THE PURSE STRINGS.
GIVE ME GOOD NEWS, *DODDS.*
WISH I COULD. THERE'S STILL NO SIGN OF SLOAN. WE'RE CHECKING EVERY CORNER OF THE PLANET. WE'RE CHECKING THE *CORNERS* OF THE CORNERS.
IF HE'S STILL AROUND-- IF HE'S STILL *ALIVE*-- HE MIGHT BE OUT OF OUR REACH.
I REFUSE TO ACCEPT THAT. *KEEP ON IT.*
ANY WORD ON *OLIVER QUEEN?* WE MAY HAVE NEED OF HIS WEAPONS EXPERTISE.
NO SIGN OF HIM. IT'S LIKE HE JUST *VANISHED* OFF THE FACE OF THE PLANET.
EVEN IF WE KNEW WHERE QUEEN WAS, CAN YOU REALLY TRUST HIM?
THE FATE OF THE WORLD IS AT STAKE. TRUST IS A LUXURY I CANNOT AFFORD.
FIND HIM.

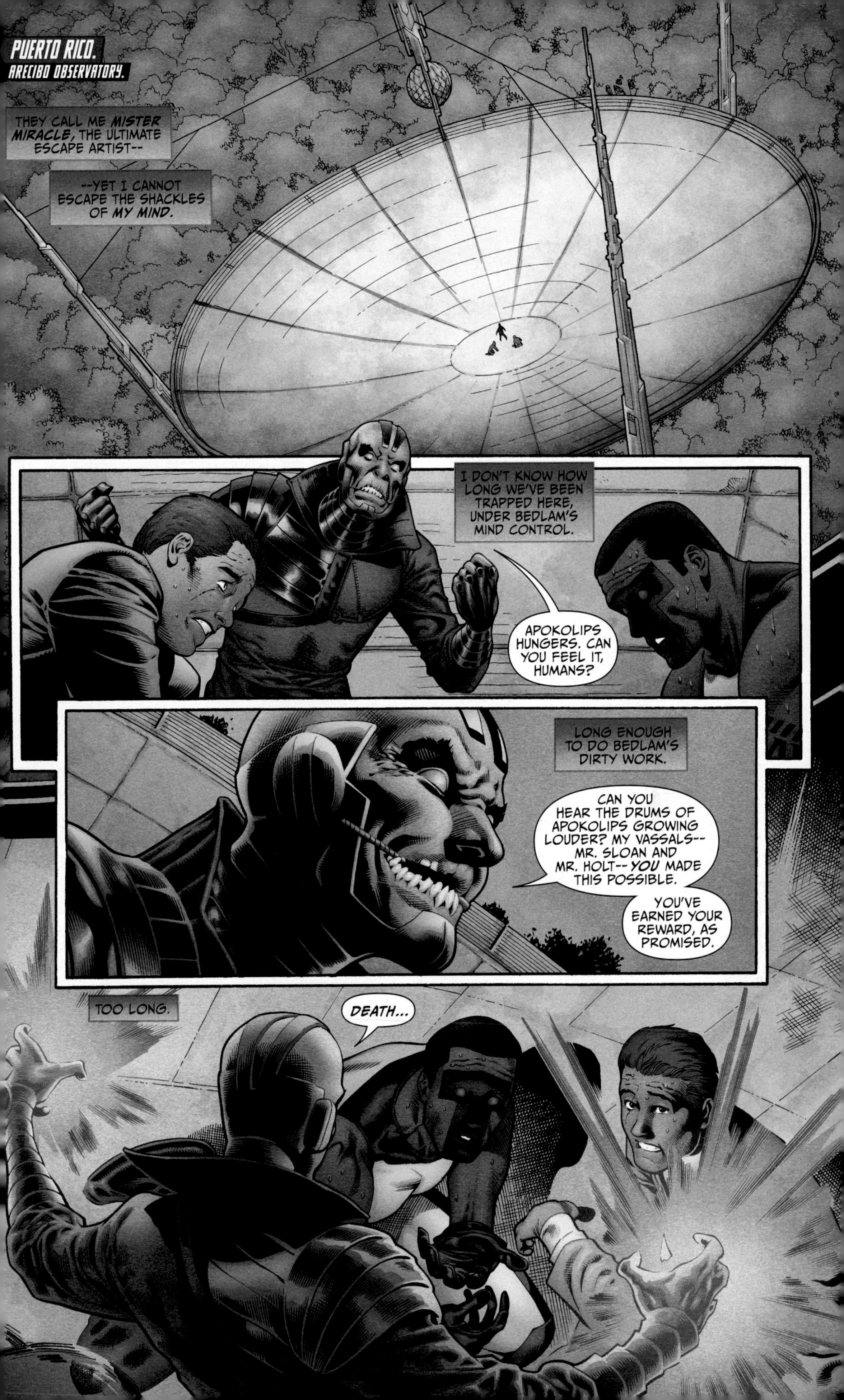
PUERTO RICO.
ARECIBO OBSERVATORY.
THEY CALL ME MISTER MIRACLE, THE ULTIMATE ESCAPE ARTIST--
--YET I CANNOT ESCAPE THE SHACKLES OF MY MIND.
I DON'T KNOW HOW LONG WE'VE BEEN TRAPPED HERE, UNDER BEDLAM'S MIND CONTROL.
APOKOLIPS HUNGERS. CAN YOU FEEL IT, HUMANS?
LONG ENOUGH TO DO BEDLAM'S DIRTY WORK.
CAN YOU HEAR THE DRUMS OF APOKOLIPS GROWING LOUDER? MY VASSALS-- MR. SLOAN AND MR. HOLT--YOU MADE THIS POSSIBLE.
YOU'VE EARNED YOUR REWARD, AS PROMISED.
TOO LONG.
DEATH...

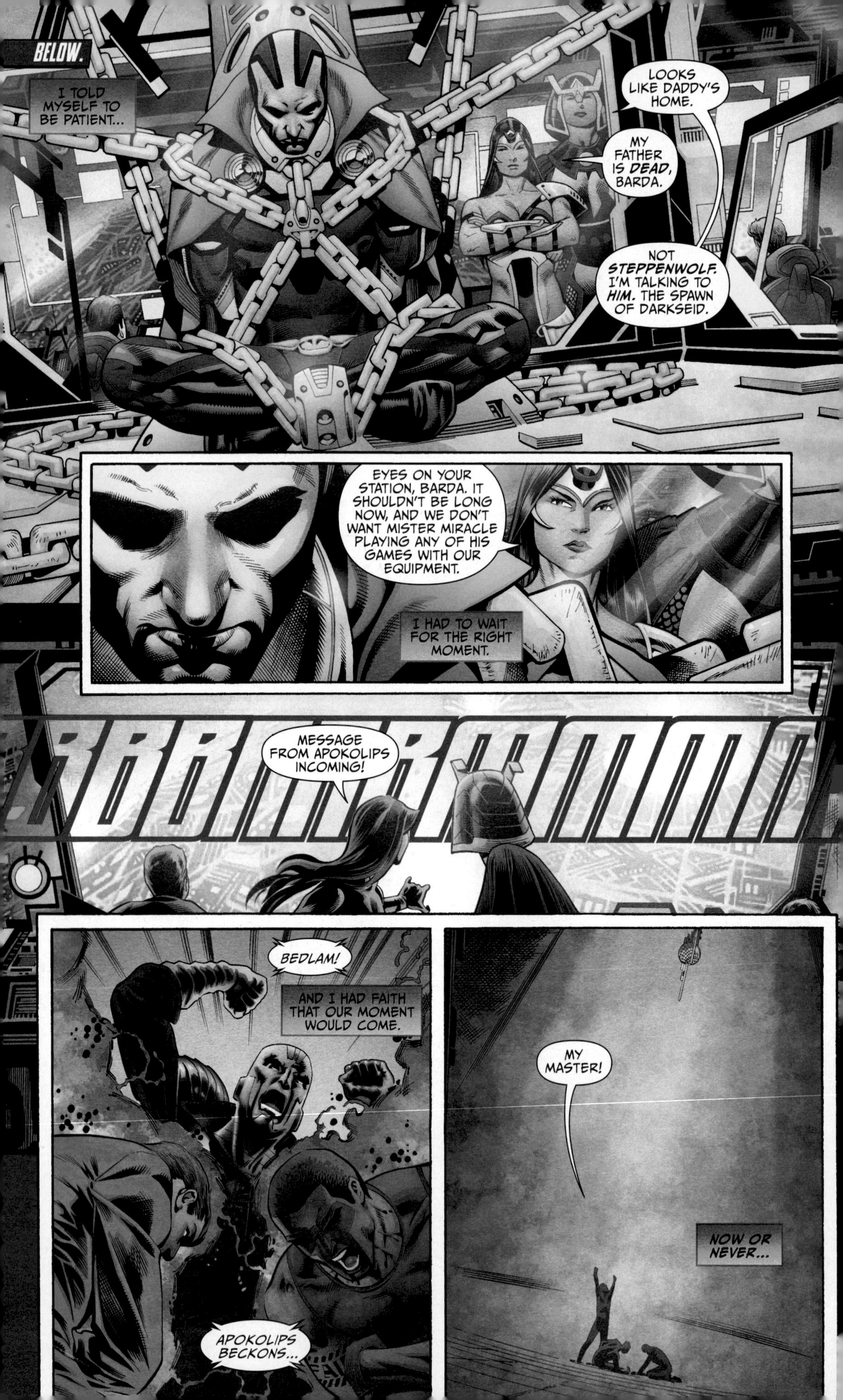
BELOW.
I TOLD MYSELF TO BE PATIENT...
LOOKS LIKE DADDY'S HOME.
MY FATHER IS DEAD, BARDA.
NOT STEPPENWOLF. I'M TALKING TO HIM. THE SPAWN OF DARKSEID.
EYES ON YOUR STATION, BARDA. IT SHOULDN'T BE LONG NOW, AND WE DON'T WANT MISTER MIRACLE PLAYING ANY OF HIS GAMES WITH OUR EQUIPMENT.
I HAD TO WAIT FOR THE RIGHT MOMENT.
MESSAGE FROM APOKOLIPS INCOMING!
BEDLAM!
AND I HAD FAITH THAT OUR MOMENT WOULD COME.
APOKOLIPS BECKONS...
MY MASTER!
NOW OR NEVER...

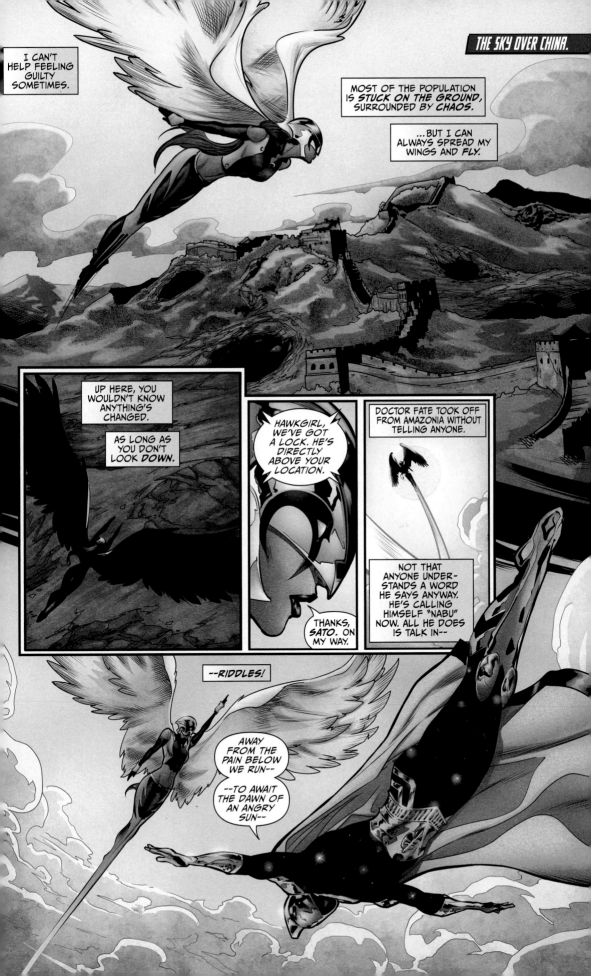

I CAN'T HELP FEELING GUILTY SOMETIMES.

MOST OF THE POPULATION IS *STUCK ON THE GROUND,* SURROUNDED BY *CHAOS.*

...BUT I CAN ALWAYS SPREAD MY WINGS AND *FLY.*

UP HERE, YOU WOULDN'T KNOW ANYTHING'S CHANGED.

AS LONG AS YOU DON'T LOOK *DOWN.*

HAWKGIRL, WE'VE GOT A LOCK. HE'S DIRECTLY ABOVE YOUR LOCATION.

DOCTOR FATE TOOK OFF FROM AMAZONIA WITHOUT TELLING ANYONE.

NOT THAT ANYONE UNDERSTANDS A WORD HE SAYS ANYWAY. HE'S CALLING HIMSELF "NABU" NOW. ALL HE DOES IS TALK IN--

THANKS, SATO. ON MY WAY.

--RIDDLES!

AWAY FROM THE PAIN BELOW WE RUN--

--TO AWAIT THE DAWN OF AN ANGRY SUN--

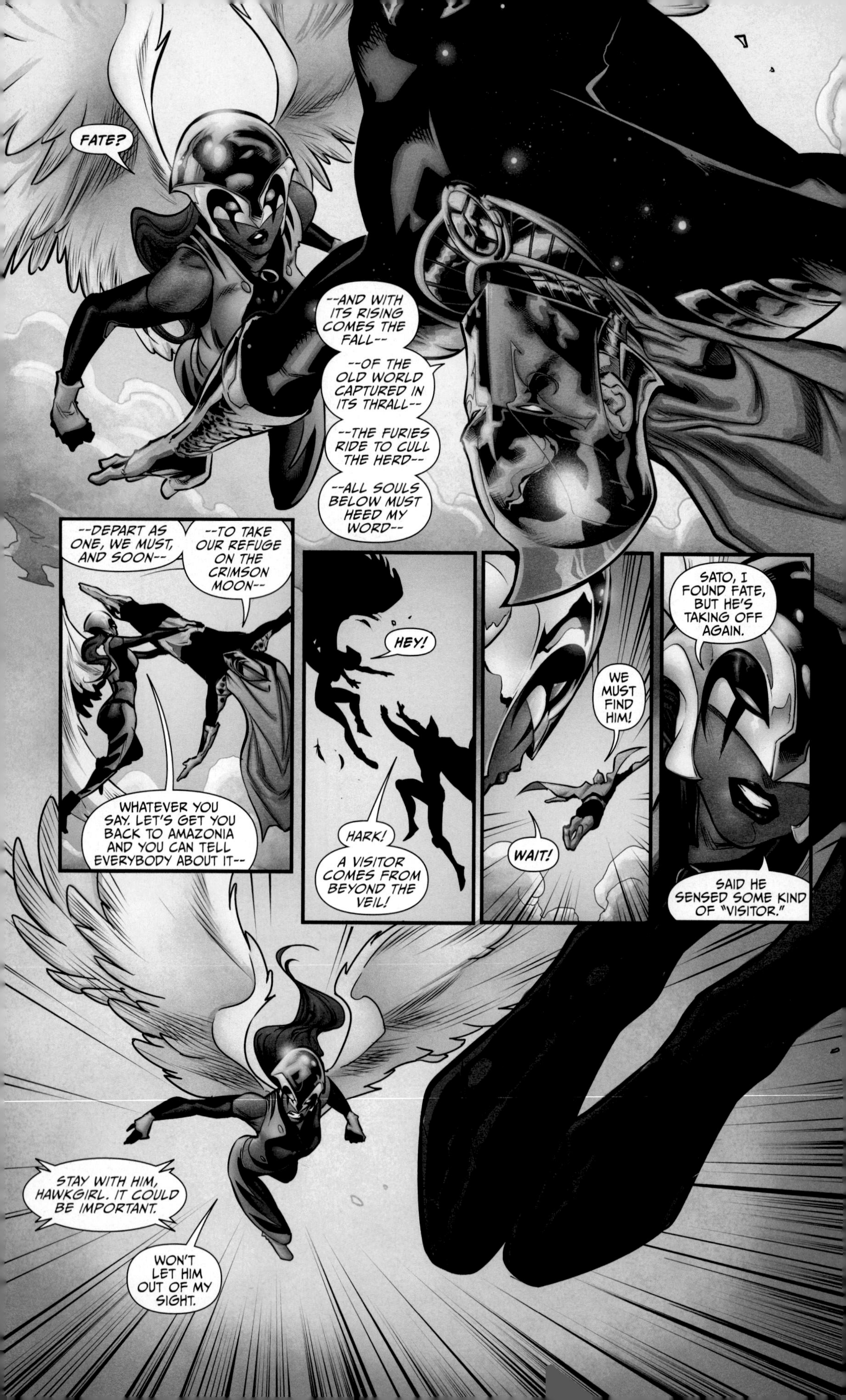
FATE?
--AND WITH ITS RISING COMES THE FALL--
--OF THE OLD WORLD CAPTURED IN ITS THRALL--
--THE FURIES RIDE TO CULL THE HERD--
--ALL SOULS BELOW MUST HEED MY WORD--
--DEPART AS ONE, WE MUST, AND SOON--
--TO TAKE OUR REFUGE ON THE CRIMSON MOON--
WHATEVER YOU SAY. LET'S GET YOU BACK TO AMAZONIA AND YOU CAN TELL EVERYBODY ABOUT IT--
HEY!
HARK!
A VISITOR COMES FROM BEYOND THE VEIL!
WE MUST FIND HIM!
WAIT!
SATO, I FOUND FATE, BUT HE'S TAKING OFF AGAIN.
SAID HE SENSED SOME KIND OF "VISITOR."
STAY WITH HIM, HAWKGIRL. IT COULD BE IMPORTANT.
WON'T LET HIM OUT OF MY SIGHT.

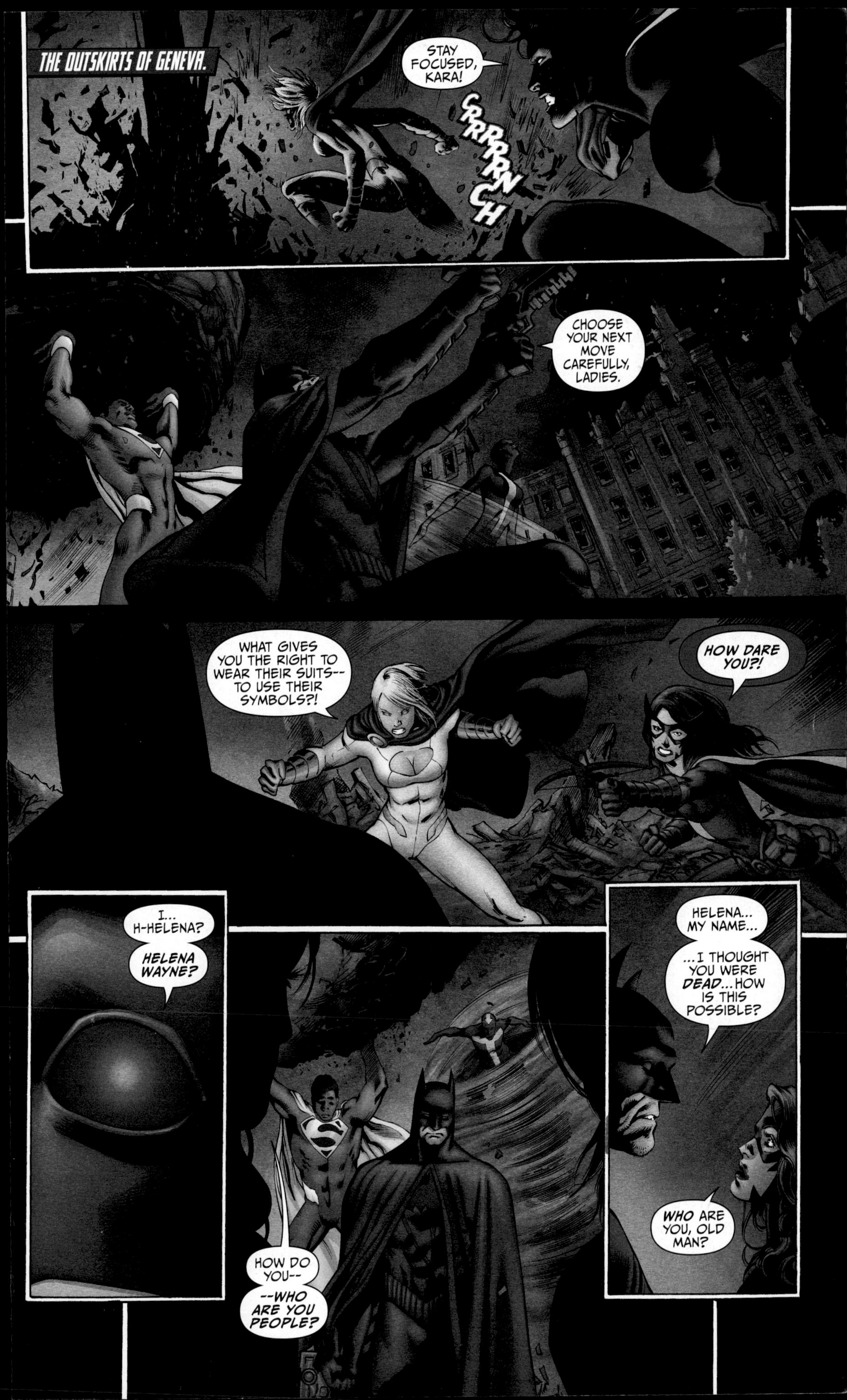
THE OUTSKIRTS OF GENEVA.
STAY FOCUSED, KARA!
CRRRRNCH
CHOOSE YOUR NEXT MOVE CAREFULLY, LADIES.
WHAT GIVES YOU THE RIGHT TO WEAR THEIR SUITS-- TO USE THEIR SYMBOLS?!
HOW DARE YOU?!
I... H-HELENA?
HELENA WAYNE?
HOW DO YOU--
--WHO ARE YOU PEOPLE?
HELENA... MY NAME...
...I THOUGHT YOU WERE DEAD...HOW IS THIS POSSIBLE?
WHO ARE YOU, OLD MAN?

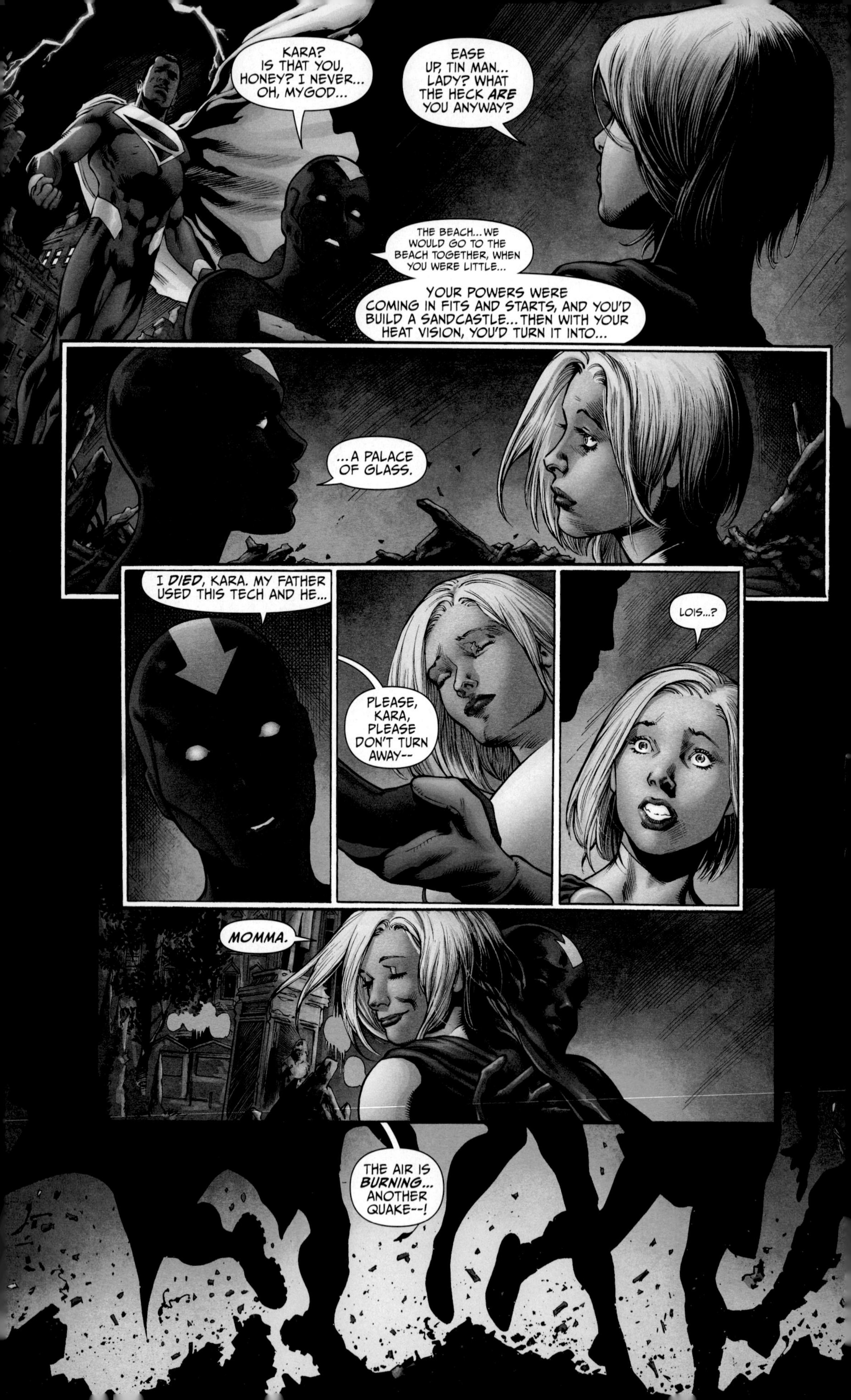
KARA? IS THAT YOU, HONEY? I NEVER... OH, MYGOD...
EASE UP, TIN MAN... LADY? WHAT THE HECK *ARE* YOU ANYWAY?
THE BEACH...WE WOULD GO TO THE BEACH TOGETHER, WHEN YOU WERE LITTLE...
YOUR POWERS WERE COMING IN FITS AND STARTS, AND YOU'D BUILD A SANDCASTLE...THEN WITH YOUR HEAT VISION, YOU'D TURN IT INTO...
...A PALACE OF GLASS.
I *DIED*, KARA. MY FATHER USED THIS TECH AND HE...
PLEASE, KARA, PLEASE DON'T TURN AWAY--
LOIS...?
MOMMA.
THE AIR IS *BURNING...* ANOTHER QUAKE--!

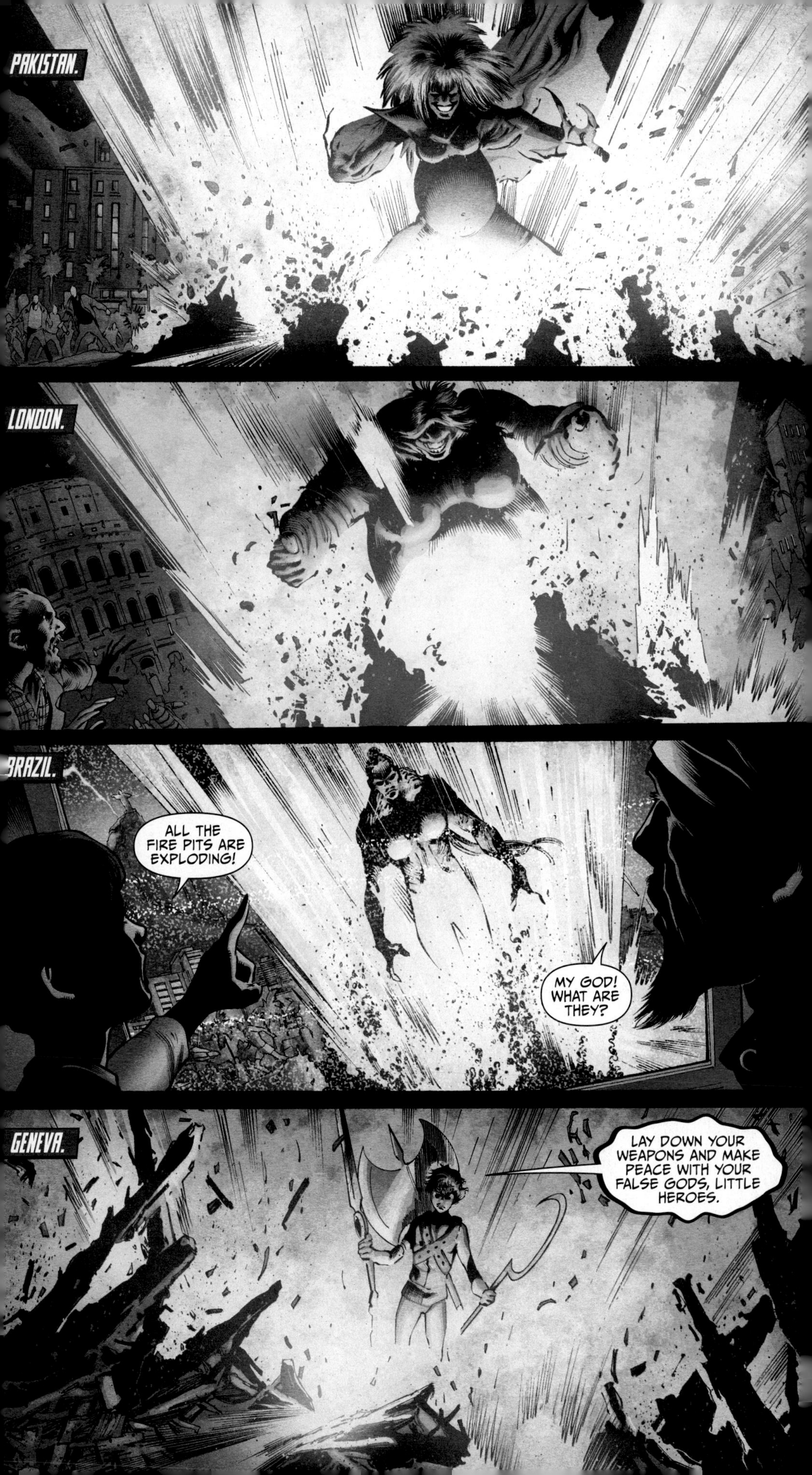
PAKISTAN.
LONDON.
BRAZIL.
ALL THE FIRE PITS ARE EXPLODING!
MY GOD! WHAT ARE THEY?
GENEVA.
LAY DOWN YOUR WEAPONS AND MAKE PEACE WITH YOUR FALSE GODS, LITTLE HEROES.

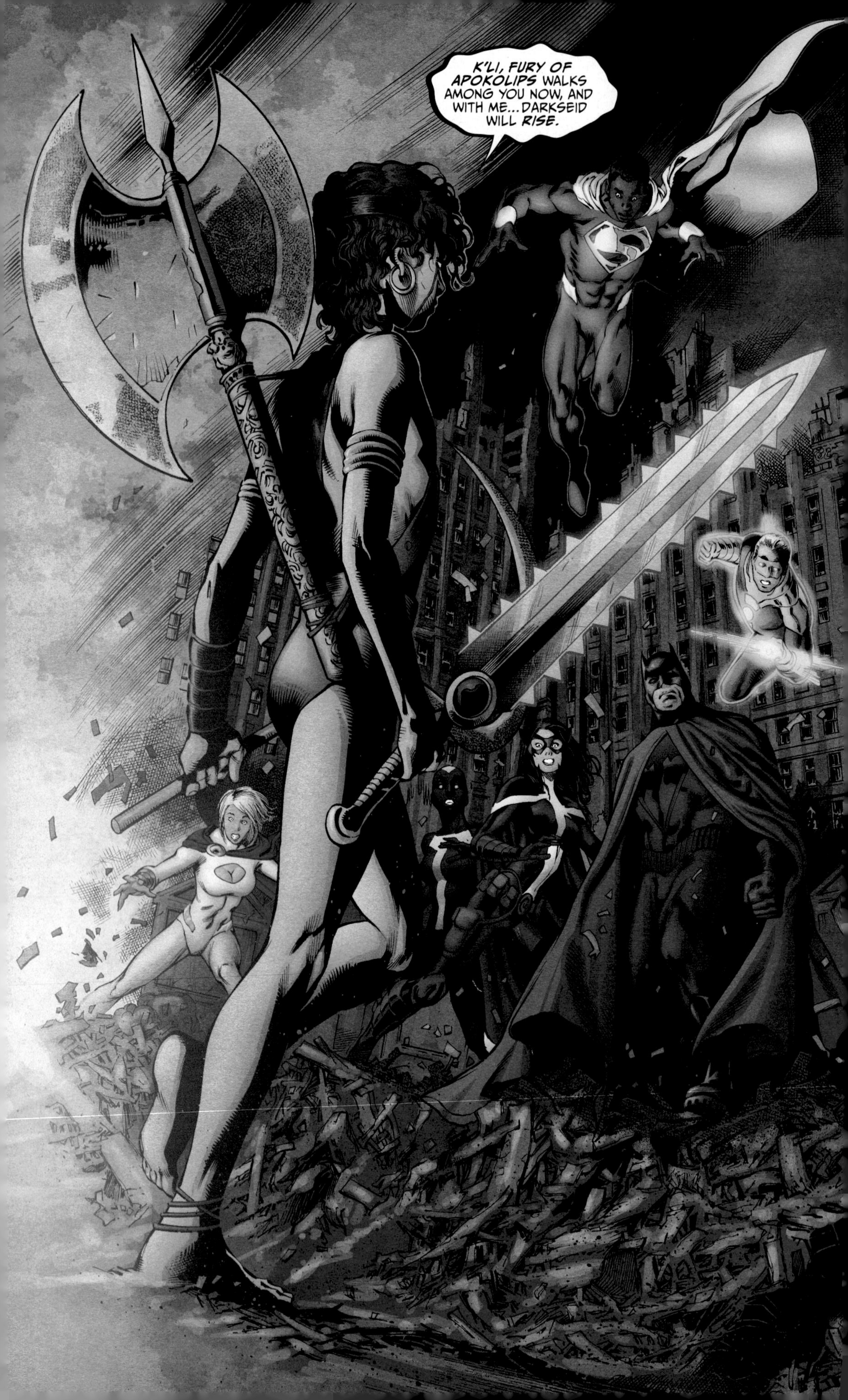
K'LI, FURY OF APOKOLIPS WALKS AMONG YOU NOW, AND WITH ME... DARKSEID WILL RISE.

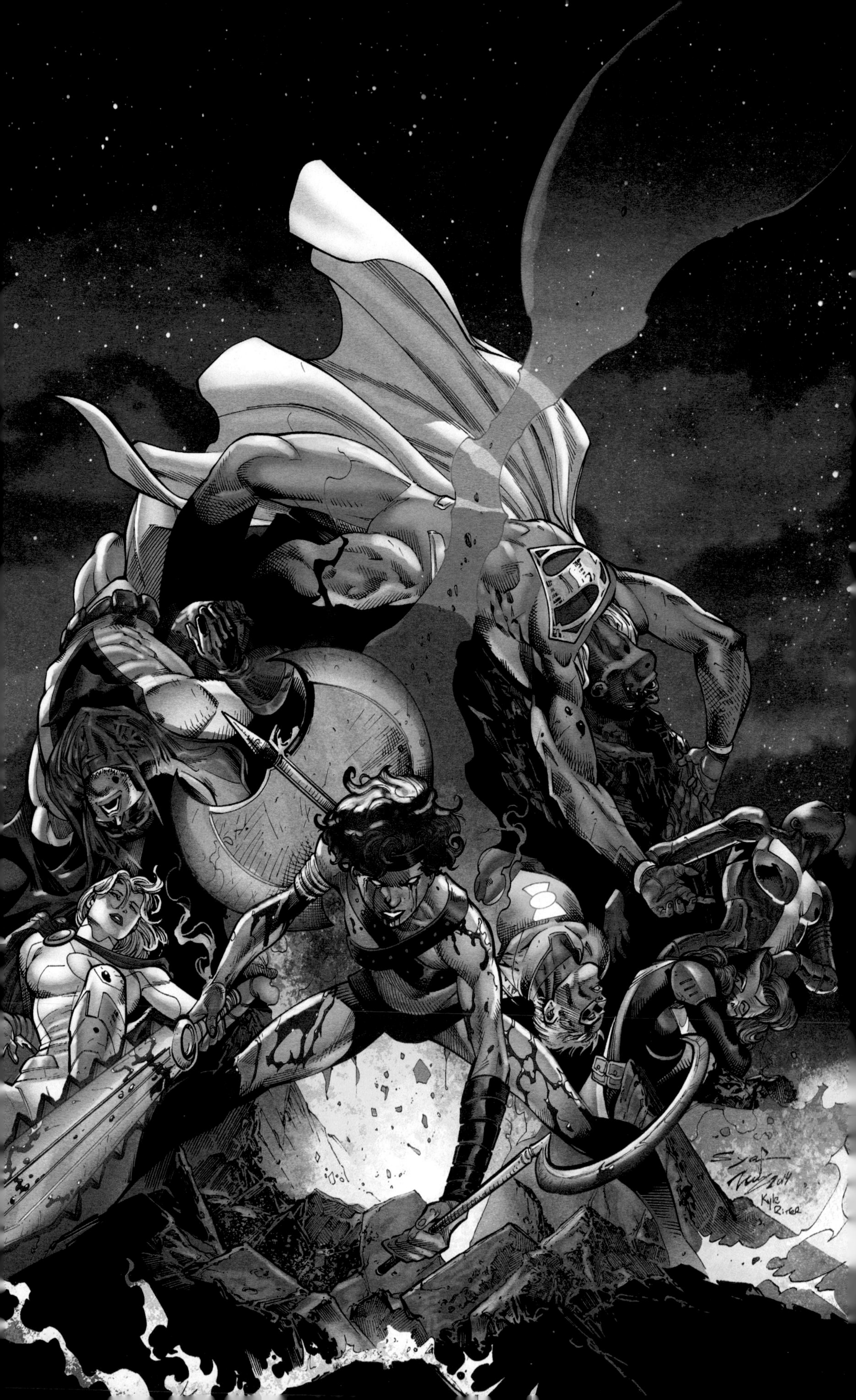

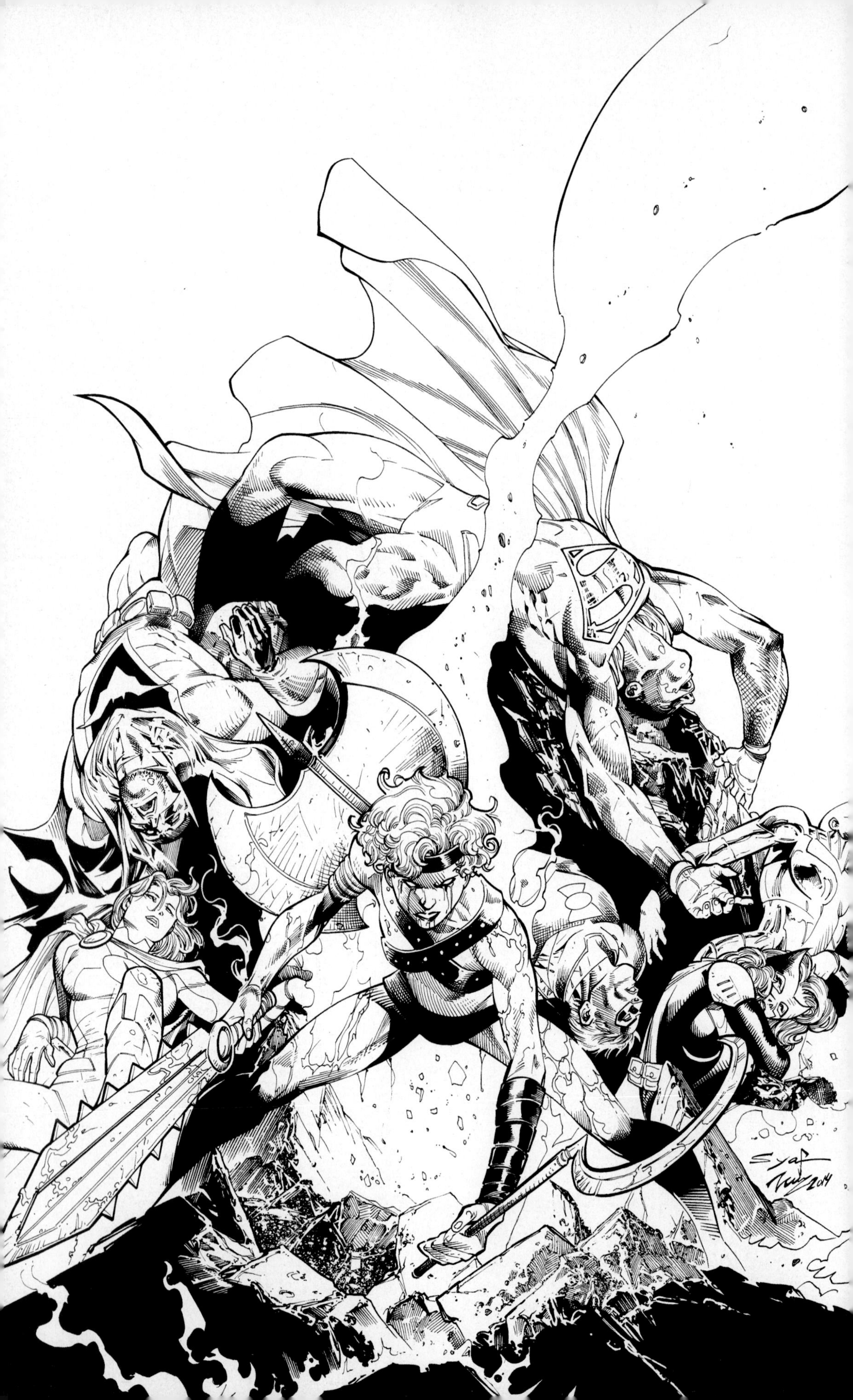

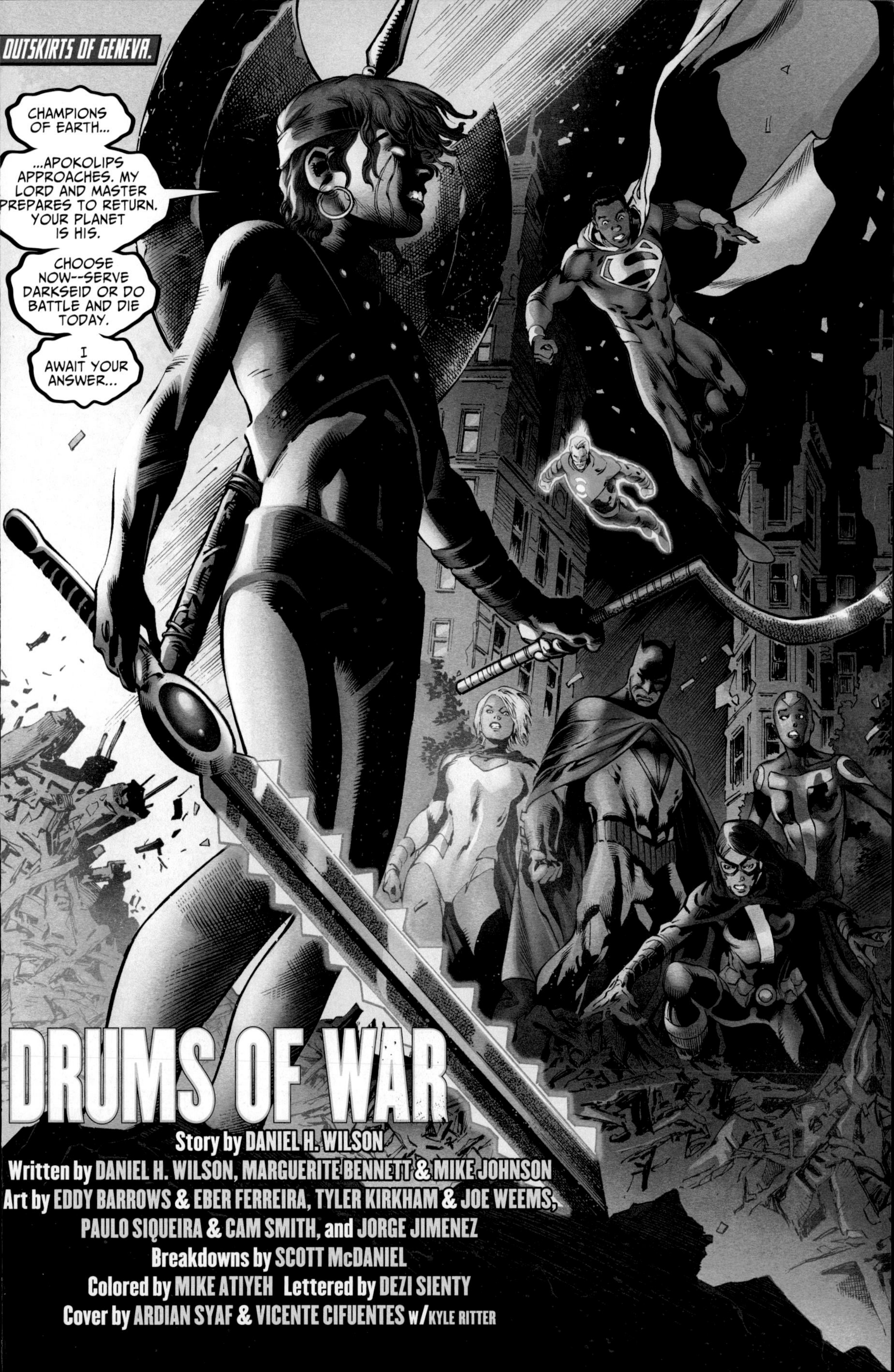
OUTSKIRTS OF GENEVA.
CHAMPIONS OF EARTH...
...APOKOLIPS APPROACHES. MY LORD AND MASTER PREPARES TO RETURN. YOUR PLANET IS HIS.
CHOOSE NOW--SERVE DARKSEID OR DO BATTLE AND DIE TODAY.
I AWAIT YOUR ANSWER...
DRUMS OF WAR
Story by DANIEL H. WILSON
Written by DANIEL H. WILSON, MARGUERITE BENNETT & MIKE JOHNSON
Art by EDDY BARROWS & EBER FERREIRA, TYLER KIRKHAM & JOE WEEMS, PAULO SIQUEIRA & CAM SMITH, and JORGE JIMENEZ
Breakdowns by SCOTT McDANIEL
Colored by MIKE ATIYEH Lettered by DEZI SIENTY
Cover by ARDIAN SYAF & VICENTE CIFUENTES w/KYLE RITTER

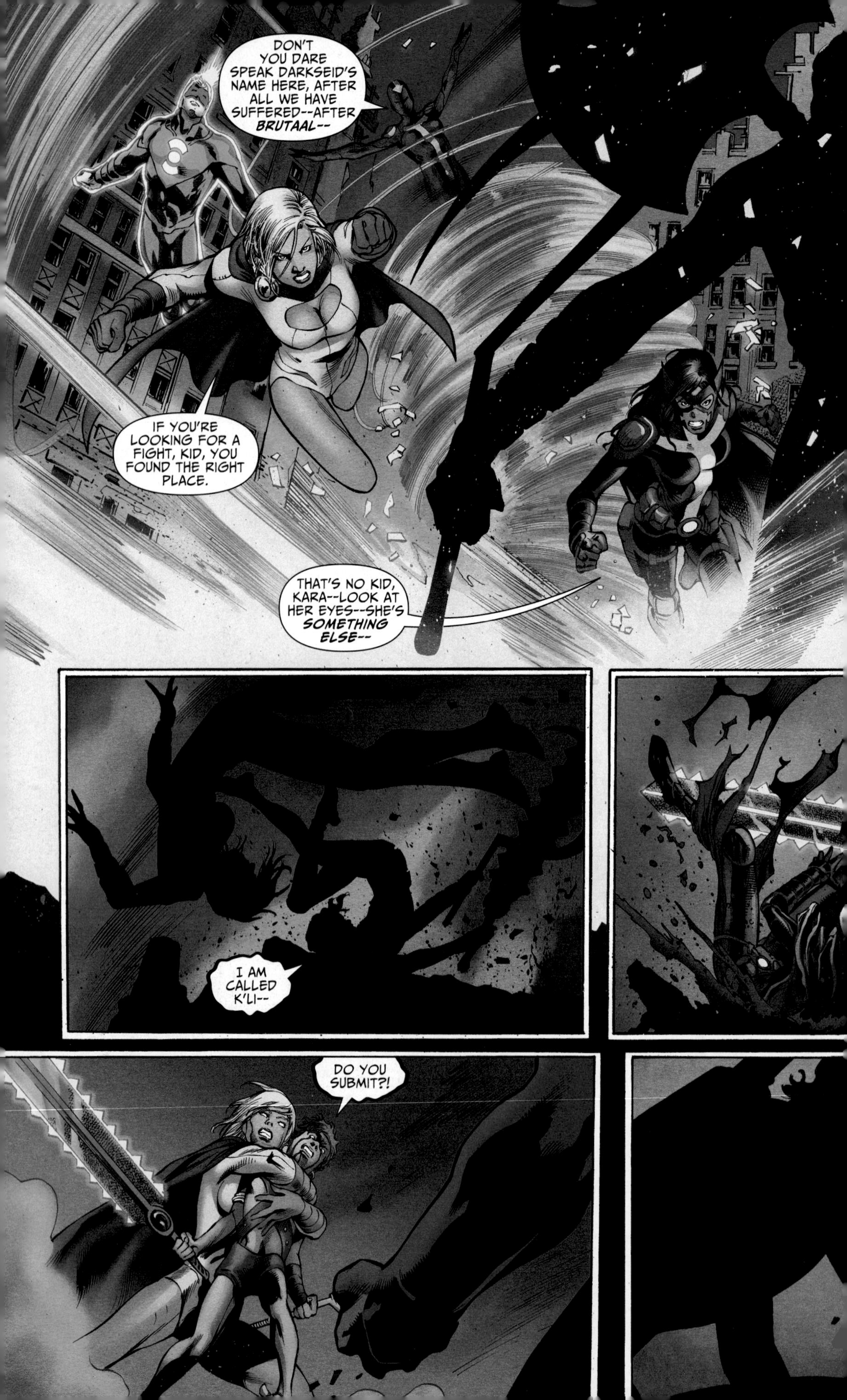
DON'T YOU DARE SPEAK DARKSEID'S NAME HERE, AFTER ALL WE HAVE SUFFERED--AFTER BRUTAAL--
IF YOU'RE LOOKING FOR A FIGHT, KID, YOU FOUND THE RIGHT PLACE.
THAT'S NO KID, KARA--LOOK AT HER EYES--SHE'S SOMETHING ELSE--
I AM CALLED K'LI--
DO YOU SUBMIT?!

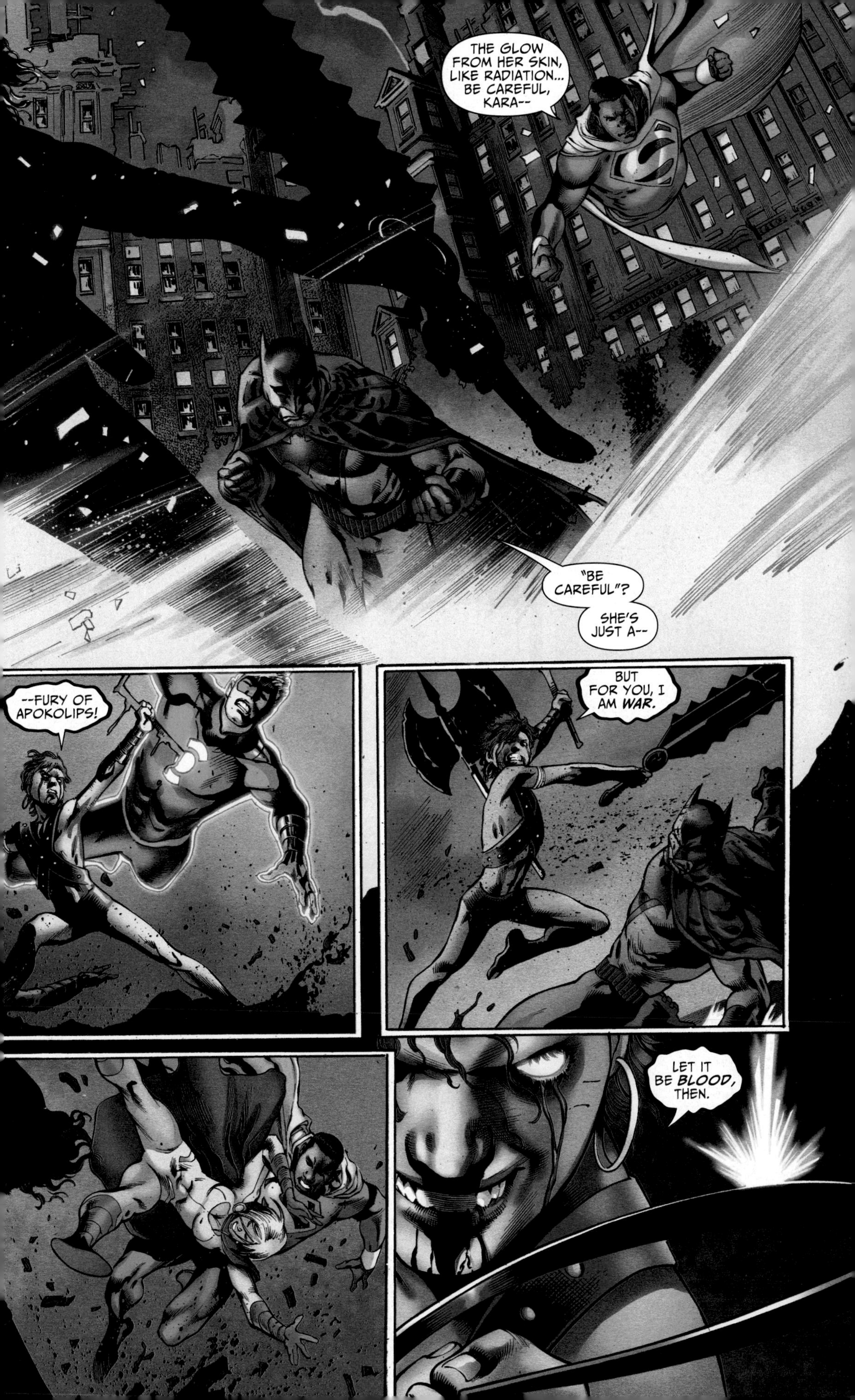
THE GLOW FROM HER SKIN, LIKE RADIATION... BE CAREFUL, KARA--
"BE CAREFUL"?
SHE'S JUST A--
--FURY OF APOKOLIPS!
BUT FOR YOU, I AM WAR.
LET IT BE BLOOD, THEN.

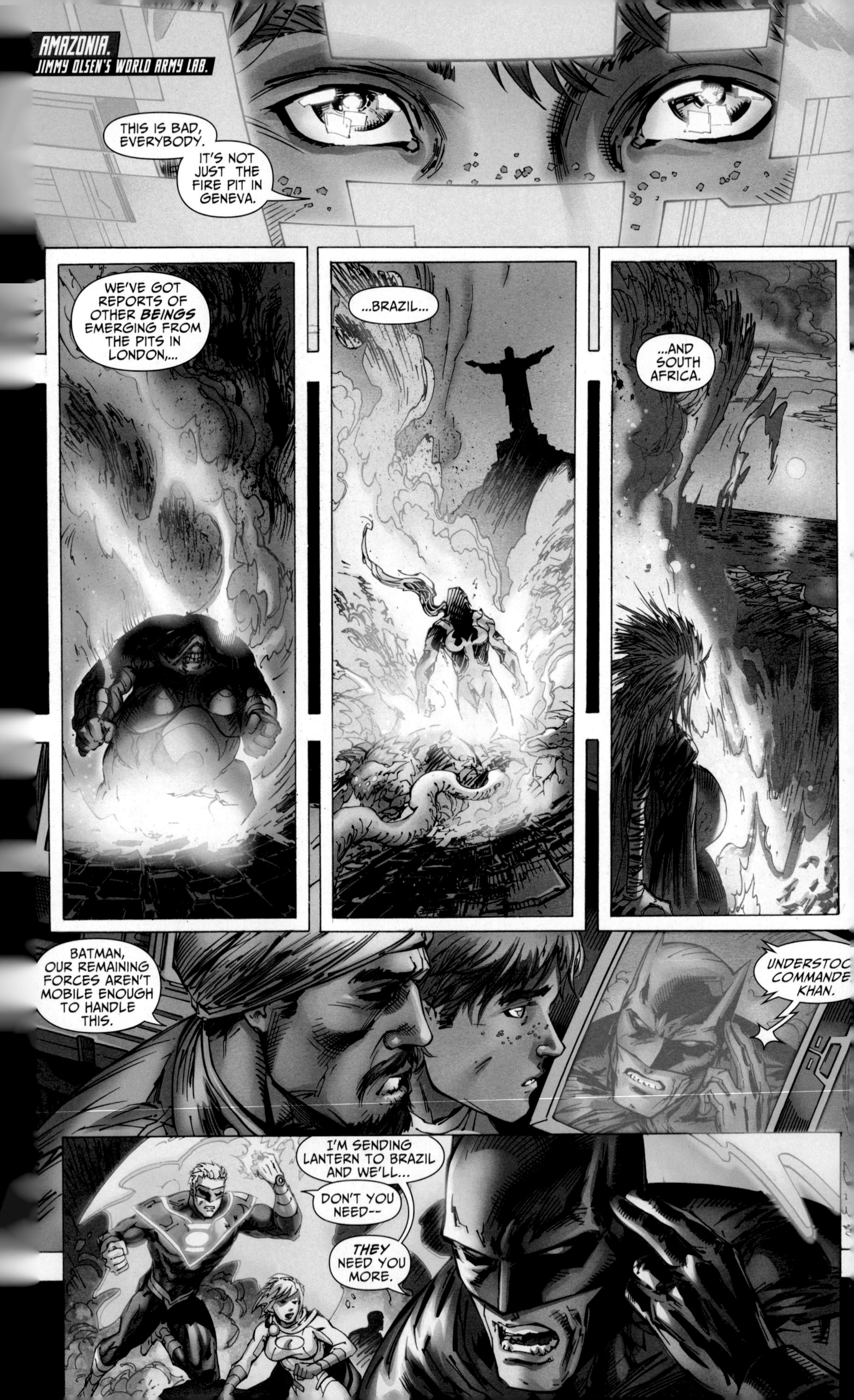
AMAZONIA.
JIMMY OLSEN'S WORLD ARMY LAB.
THIS IS BAD, EVERYBODY.
IT'S NOT JUST THE FIRE PIT IN GENEVA.
WE'VE GOT REPORTS OF OTHER BEINGS EMERGING FROM THE PITS IN LONDON,...
...BRAZIL...
...AND SOUTH AFRICA.
BATMAN, OUR REMAINING FORCES AREN'T MOBILE ENOUGH TO HANDLE THIS.
UNDERSTOO COMMANDE KHAN.
I'M SENDING LANTERN TO BRAZIL AND WE'LL...
DON'T YOU NEED--
THEY NEED YOU MORE.

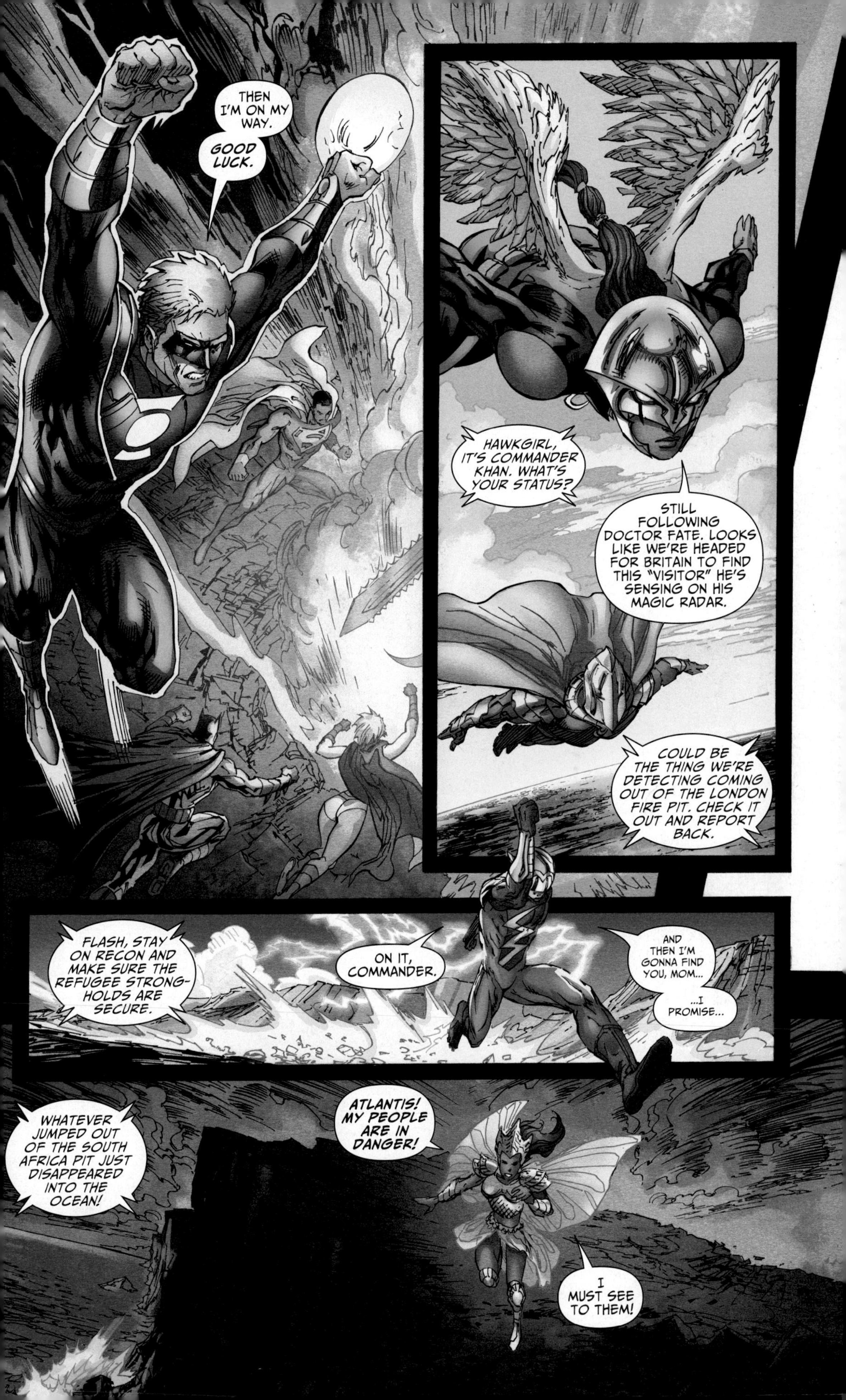
THEN I'M ON MY WAY.
GOOD LUCK.
HAWKGIRL, IT'S COMMANDER KHAN. WHAT'S YOUR STATUS?
STILL FOLLOWING DOCTOR FATE. LOOKS LIKE WE'RE HEADED FOR BRITAIN TO FIND THIS "VISITOR" HE'S SENSING ON HIS MAGIC RADAR.
COULD BE THE THING WE'RE DETECTING COMING OUT OF THE LONDON FIRE PIT. CHECK IT OUT AND REPORT BACK.
FLASH, STAY ON RECON AND MAKE SURE THE REFUGEE STRONG-HOLDS ARE SECURE.
ON IT, COMMANDER.
AND THEN I'M GONNA FIND YOU, MOM...
...I PROMISE...
WHATEVER JUMPED OUT OF THE SOUTH AFRICA PIT JUST DISAPPEARED INTO THE OCEAN!
ATLANTIS! MY PEOPLE ARE IN DANGER!
I MUST SEE TO THEM!

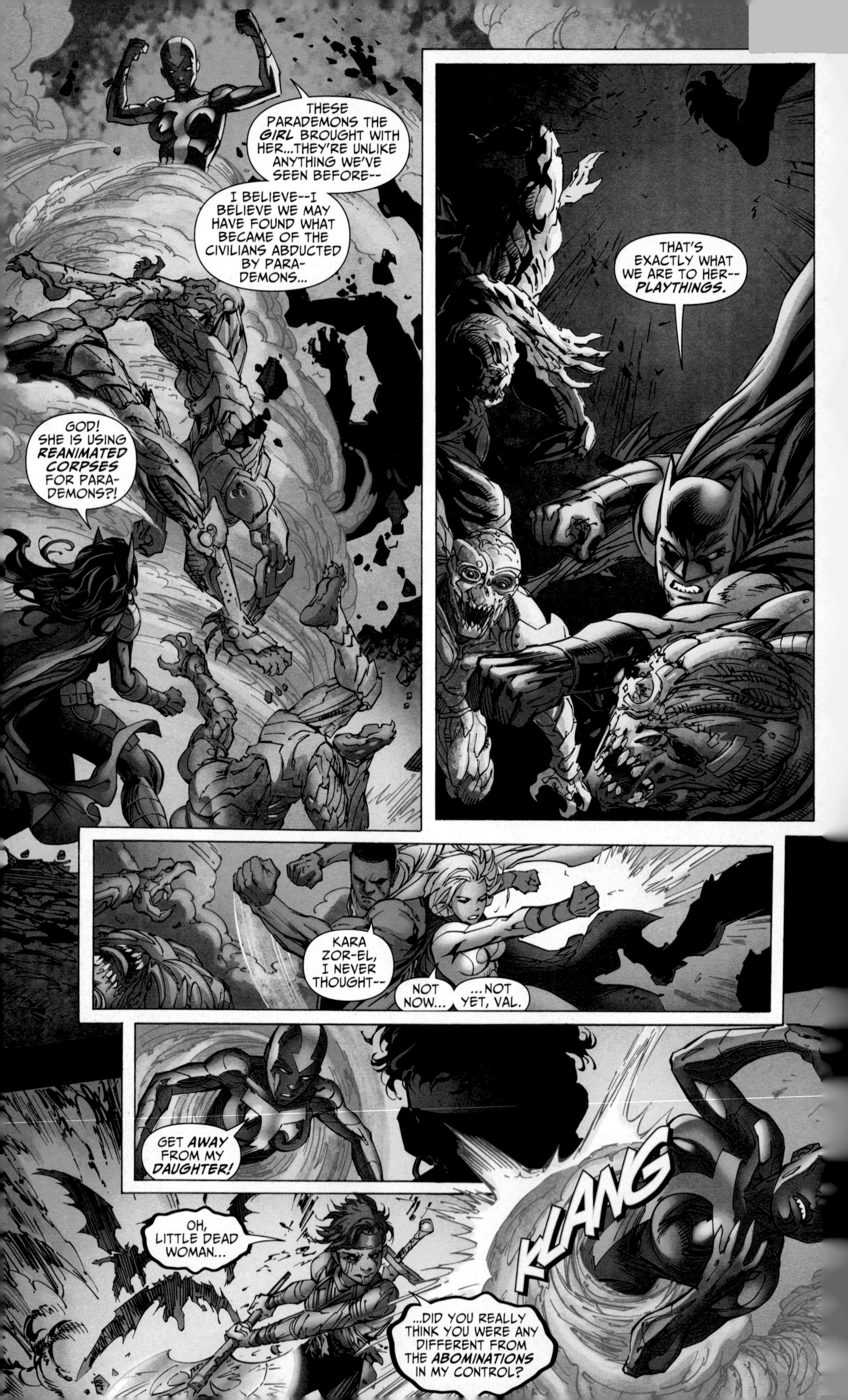
THESE PARADEMONS THE GIRL BROUGHT WITH HER...THEY'RE UNLIKE ANYTHING WE'VE SEEN BEFORE--
I BELIEVE--I BELIEVE WE MAY HAVE FOUND WHAT BECAME OF THE CIVILIANS ABDUCTED BY PARA-DEMONS...
GOD! SHE IS USING REANIMATED CORPSES FOR PARA-DEMONS?!
THAT'S EXACTLY WHAT WE ARE TO HER--PLAYTHINGS.
KARA ZOR-EL, I NEVER THOUGHT--
NOT NOW...
...NOT YET, VAL.
GET AWAY FROM MY DAUGHTER!
OH, LITTLE DEAD WOMAN...
KLANG
...DID YOU REALLY THINK YOU WERE ANY DIFFERENT FROM THE ABOMINATIONS IN MY CONTROL?

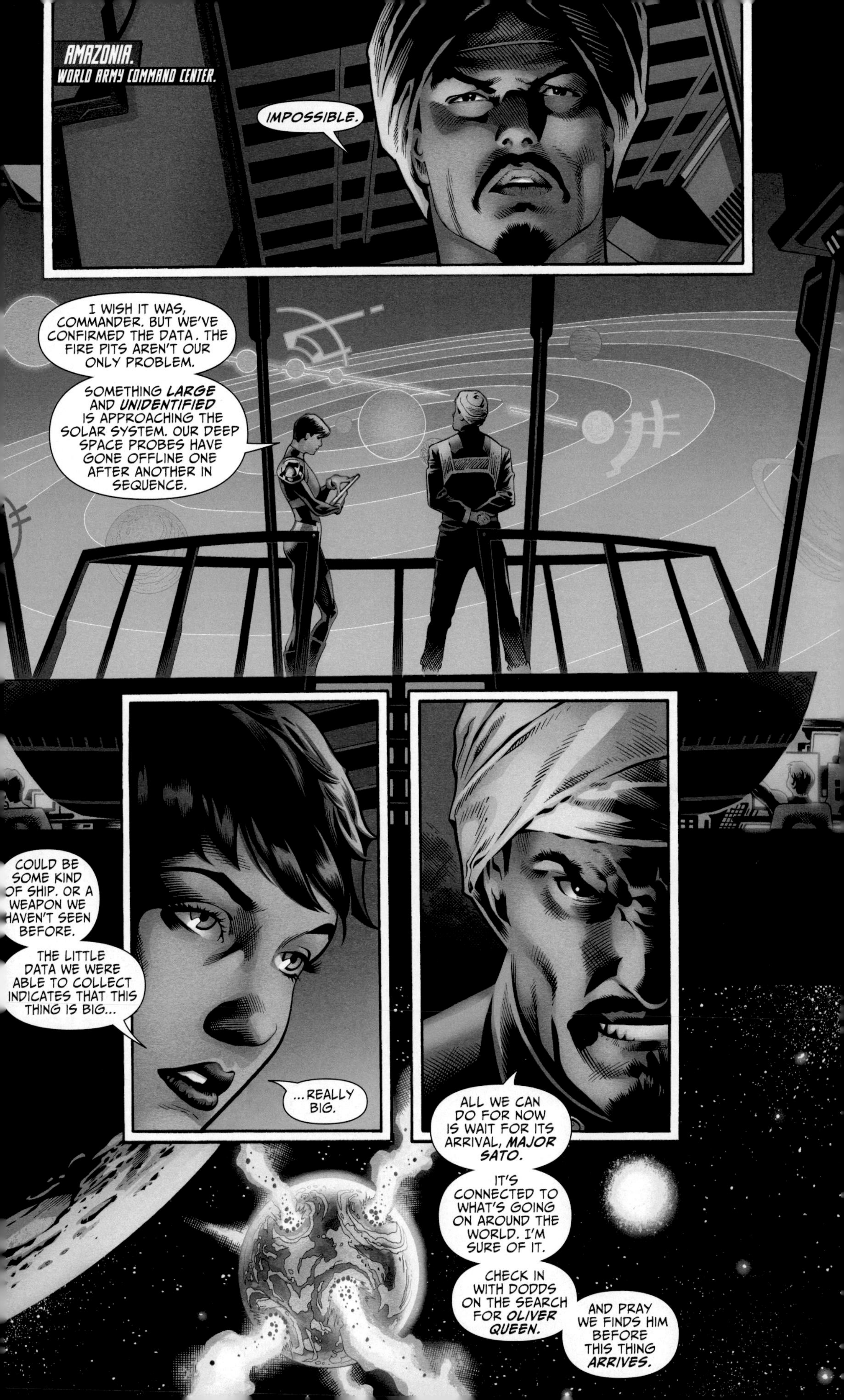
AMAZONIA.
WORLD ARMY COMMAND CENTER.
IMPOSSIBLE.
I WISH IT WAS, COMMANDER. BUT WE'VE CONFIRMED THE DATA. THE FIRE PITS AREN'T OUR ONLY PROBLEM.
SOMETHING LARGE AND UNIDENTIFIED IS APPROACHING THE SOLAR SYSTEM. OUR DEEP SPACE PROBES HAVE GONE OFFLINE ONE AFTER ANOTHER IN SEQUENCE.
COULD BE SOME KIND OF SHIP. OR A WEAPON WE HAVEN'T SEEN BEFORE.
THE LITTLE DATA WE WERE ABLE TO COLLECT INDICATES THAT THIS THING IS BIG...
...REALLY BIG.
ALL WE CAN DO FOR NOW IS WAIT FOR ITS ARRIVAL, MAJOR SATO.
IT'S CONNECTED TO WHAT'S GOING ON AROUND THE WORLD. I'M SURE OF IT.
CHECK IN WITH DODDS ON THE SEARCH FOR OLIVER QUEEN.
AND PRAY WE FINDS HIM BEFORE THIS THING ARRIVES.

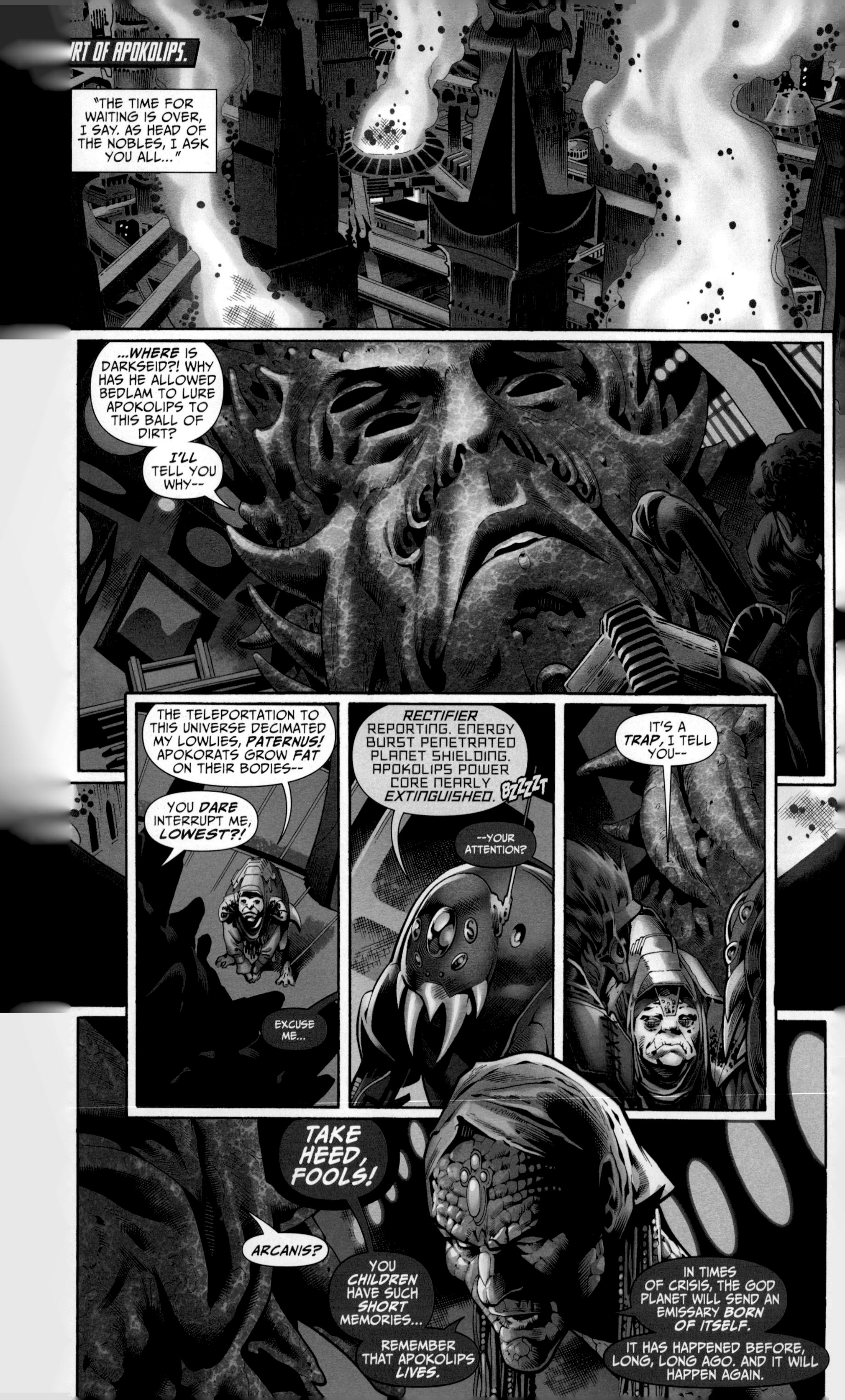

RT OF APOKOLIPS.
"THE TIME FOR WAITING IS OVER, I SAY. AS HEAD OF THE NOBLES, I ASK YOU ALL..."
...WHERE IS DARKSEID?! WHY HAS HE ALLOWED BEDLAM TO LURE APOKOLIPS TO THIS BALL OF DIRT?
I'LL TELL YOU WHY--
THE TELEPORTATION TO THIS UNIVERSE DECIMATED MY LOWLIES, PATERNUS! APOKORATS GROW FAT ON THEIR BODIES--
YOU DARE INTERRUPT ME, LOWEST?!
EXCUSE ME...
--YOUR ATTENTION?
RECTIFIER REPORTING. ENERGY BURST PENETRATED PLANET SHIELDING. APOKOLIPS POWER CORE NEARLY EXTINGUISHED.
BZZZZT
IT'S A TRAP, I TELL YOU--
TAKE HEED, FOOLS!
ARCANIS?
YOU CHILDREN HAVE SUCH SHORT MEMORIES...
REMEMBER THAT APOKOLIPS LIVES.
IN TIMES OF CRISIS, THE GOD PLANET WILL SEND AN EMISSARY BORN OF ITSELF.
IT HAS HAPPENED BEFORE, LONG, LONG AGO. AND IT WILL HAPPEN AGAIN.

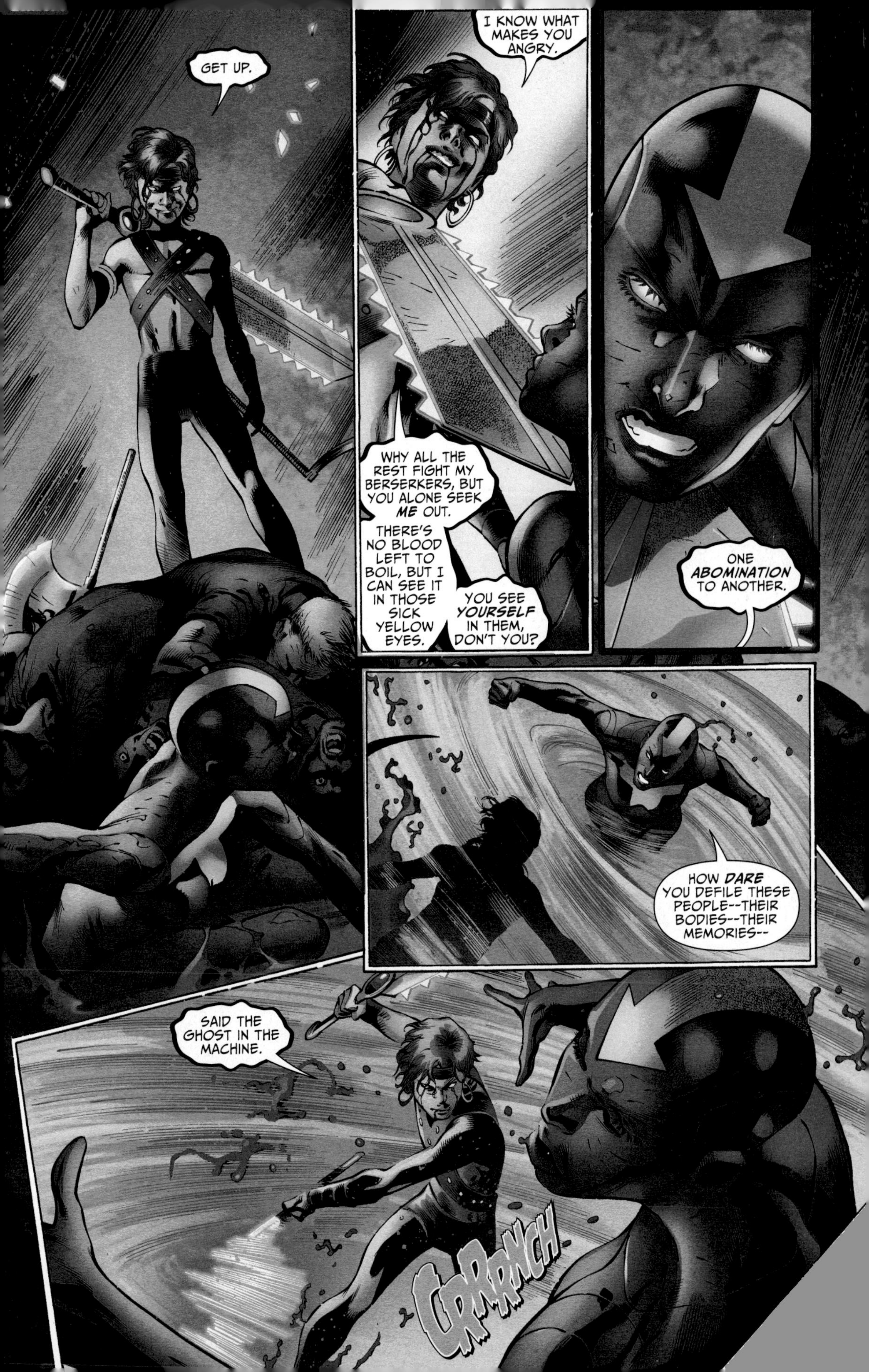
GET UP.
I KNOW WHAT MAKES YOU ANGRY.
WHY ALL THE REST FIGHT MY BERSERKERS, BUT YOU ALONE SEEK *ME* OUT.
THERE'S NO BLOOD LEFT TO BOIL, BUT I CAN SEE IT IN THOSE SICK YELLOW EYES.
YOU SEE *YOURSELF* IN THEM, DON'T YOU?
ONE *ABOMINATION* TO ANOTHER.
HOW *DARE* YOU DEFILE THESE PEOPLE--THEIR BODIES--THEIR MEMORIES--
SAID THE GHOST IN THE MACHINE.
CRRRNCH

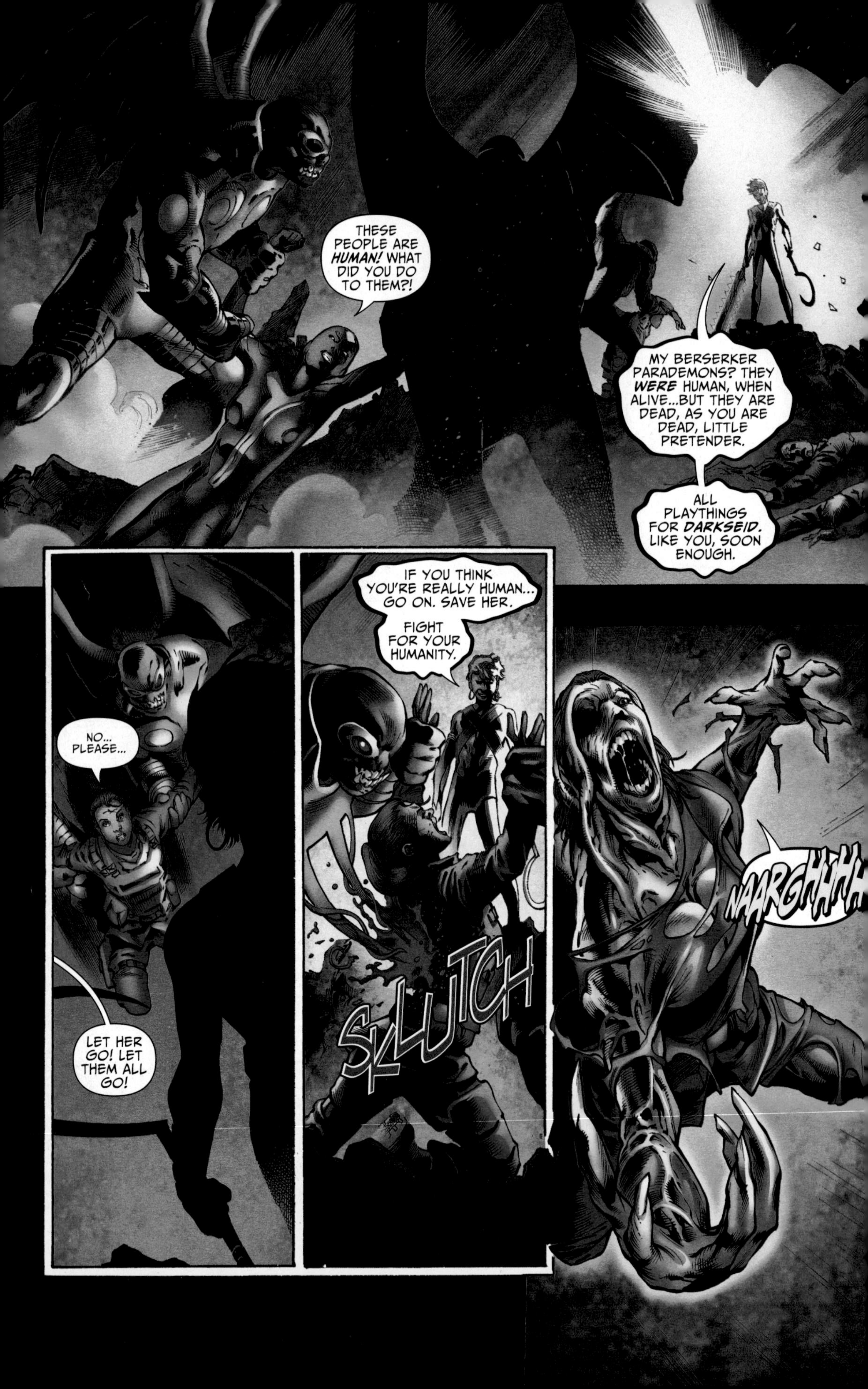

THESE PEOPLE ARE HUMAN! WHAT DID YOU DO TO THEM?!
MY BERSERKER PARADEMONS? THEY WERE HUMAN, WHEN ALIVE...BUT THEY ARE DEAD, AS YOU ARE DEAD, LITTLE PRETENDER.
ALL PLAYTHINGS FOR DARKSEID. LIKE YOU, SOON ENOUGH.
NO... PLEASE...
LET HER GO! LET THEM ALL GO!
IF YOU THINK YOU'RE REALLY HUMAN... GO ON. SAVE HER.
FIGHT FOR YOUR HUMANITY.
SKLUTCH
NAARGHHHH

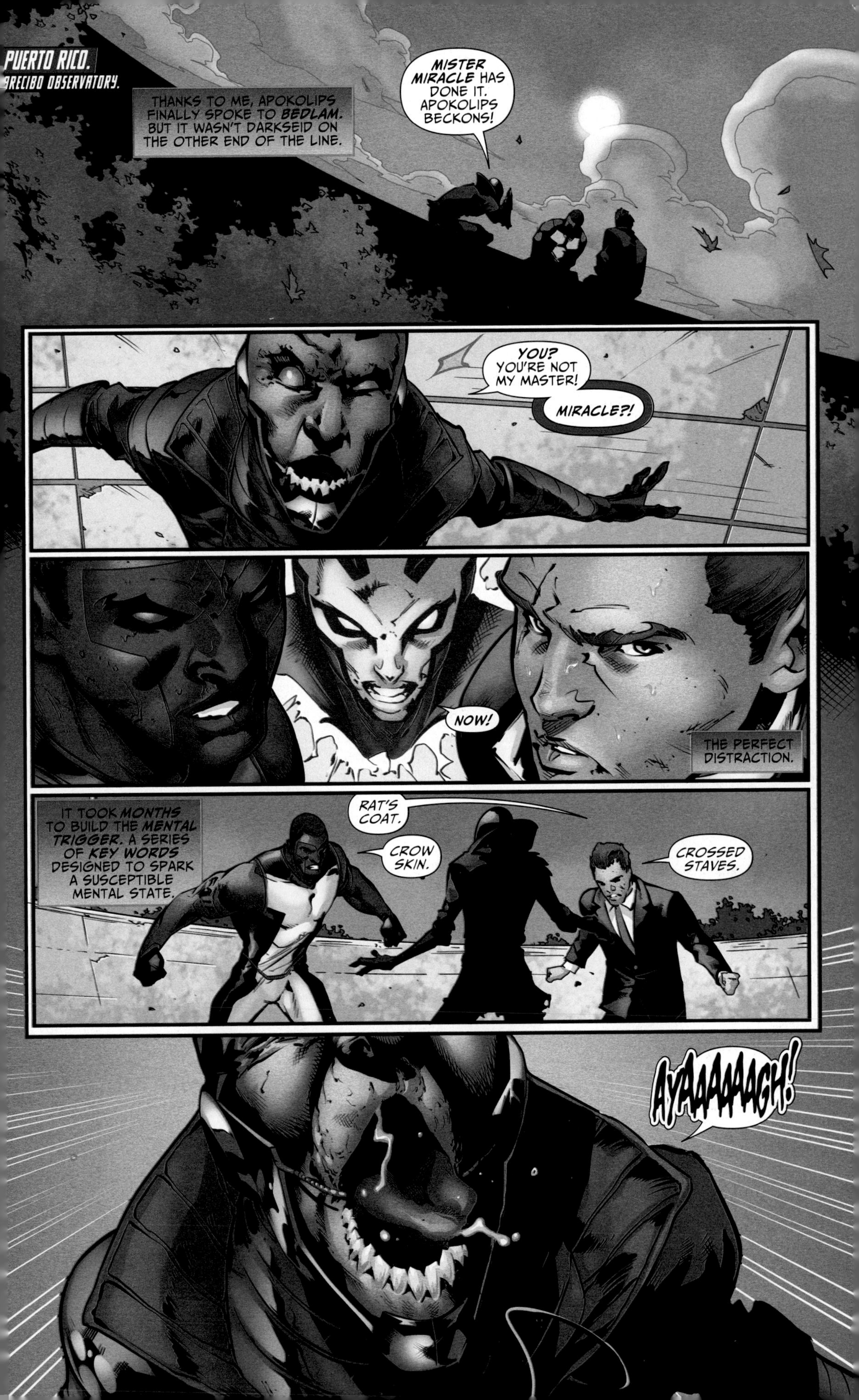
PUERTO RICO.
ARECIBO OBSERVATORY.
THANKS TO ME, APOKOLIPS FINALLY SPOKE TO BEDLAM. BUT IT WASN'T DARKSEID ON THE OTHER END OF THE LINE.
MISTER MIRACLE HAS DONE IT. APOKOLIPS BECKONS!
YOU? YOU'RE NOT MY MASTER!
MIRACLE?!
NOW!
THE PERFECT DISTRACTION.
IT TOOK MONTHS TO BUILD THE MENTAL TRIGGER. A SERIES OF KEY WORDS DESIGNED TO SPARK A SUSCEPTIBLE MENTAL STATE.
RAT'S COAT.
CROW SKIN.
CROSSED STAVES.
AYAAAAAAGH!

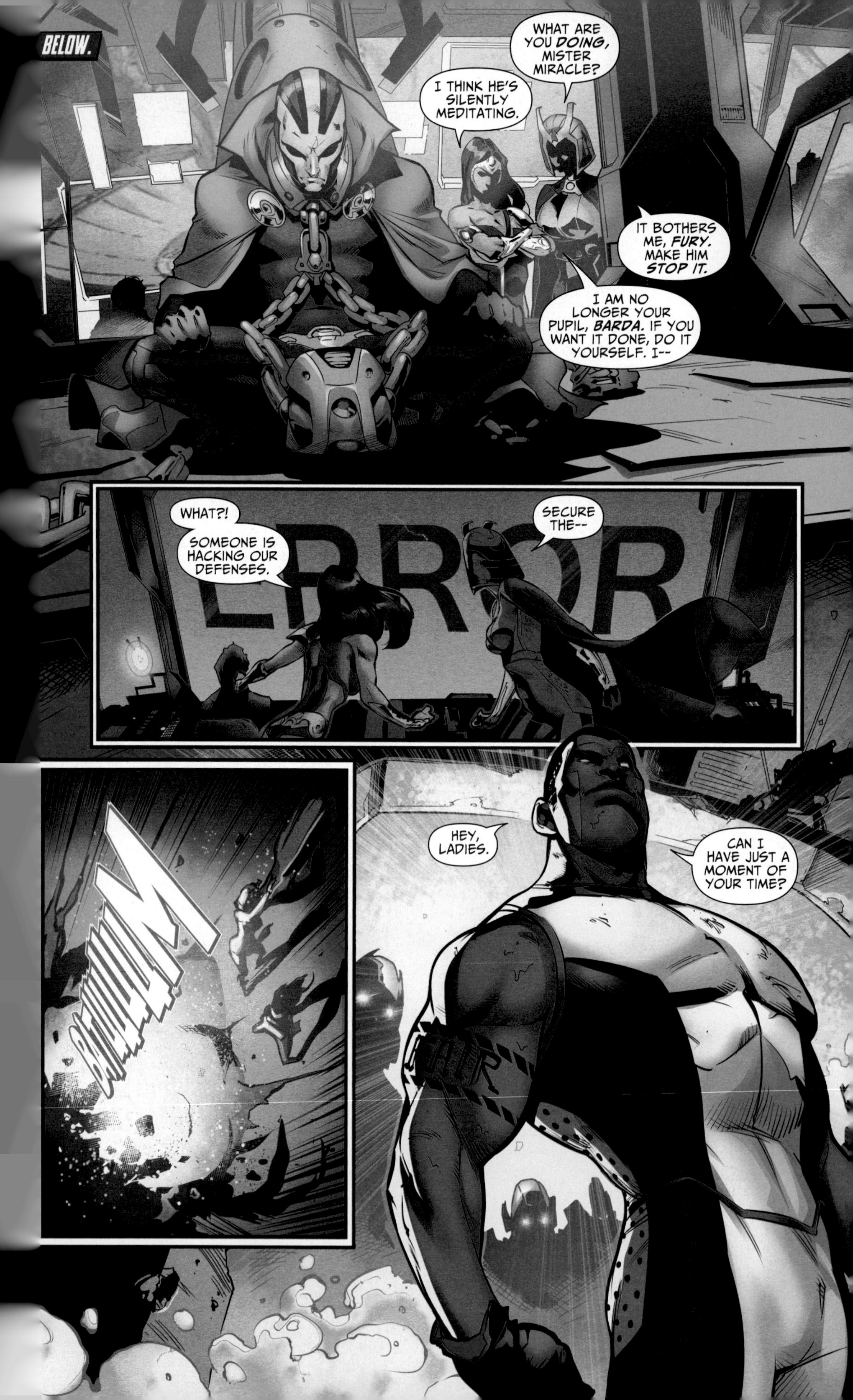
BELOW.
I THINK HE'S SILENTLY MEDITATING.
WHAT ARE YOU DOING, MISTER MIRACLE?
IT BOTHERS ME, FURY. MAKE HIM STOP IT.
I AM NO LONGER YOUR PUPIL, BARDA. IF YOU WANT IT DONE, DO IT YOURSELF. I--
WHAT?!
SOMEONE IS HACKING OUR DEFENSES.
SECURE THE--
ERROR
HEY, LADIES.
CAN I HAVE JUST A MOMENT OF YOUR TIME?

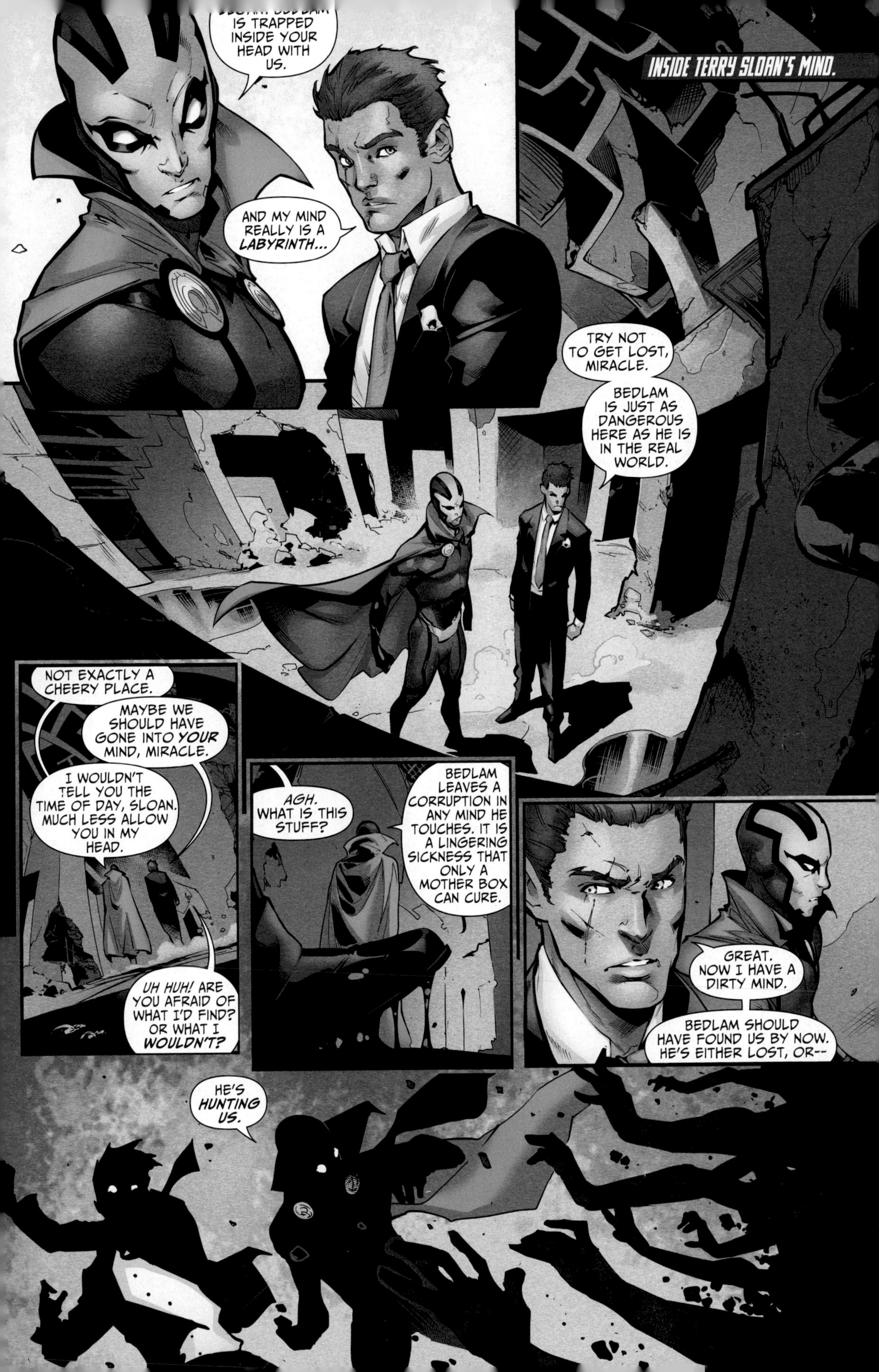
IS TRAPPED INSIDE YOUR HEAD WITH US.
AND MY MIND REALLY IS A LABYRINTH...
INSIDE TERRY SLOAN'S MIND.
TRY NOT TO GET LOST, MIRACLE.
BEDLAM IS JUST AS DANGEROUS HERE AS HE IS IN THE REAL WORLD.
NOT EXACTLY A CHEERY PLACE.
MAYBE WE SHOULD HAVE GONE INTO YOUR MIND, MIRACLE.
I WOULDN'T TELL YOU THE TIME OF DAY, SLOAN. MUCH LESS ALLOW YOU IN MY HEAD.
UH HUH! ARE YOU AFRAID OF WHAT I'D FIND? OR WHAT I WOULDN'T?
AGH. WHAT IS THIS STUFF?
BEDLAM LEAVES A CORRUPTION IN ANY MIND HE TOUCHES. IT IS A LINGERING SICKNESS THAT ONLY A MOTHER BOX CAN CURE.
GREAT. NOW I HAVE A DIRTY MIND.
BEDLAM SHOULD HAVE FOUND US BY NOW. HE'S EITHER LOST, OR--
HE'S HUNTING US.

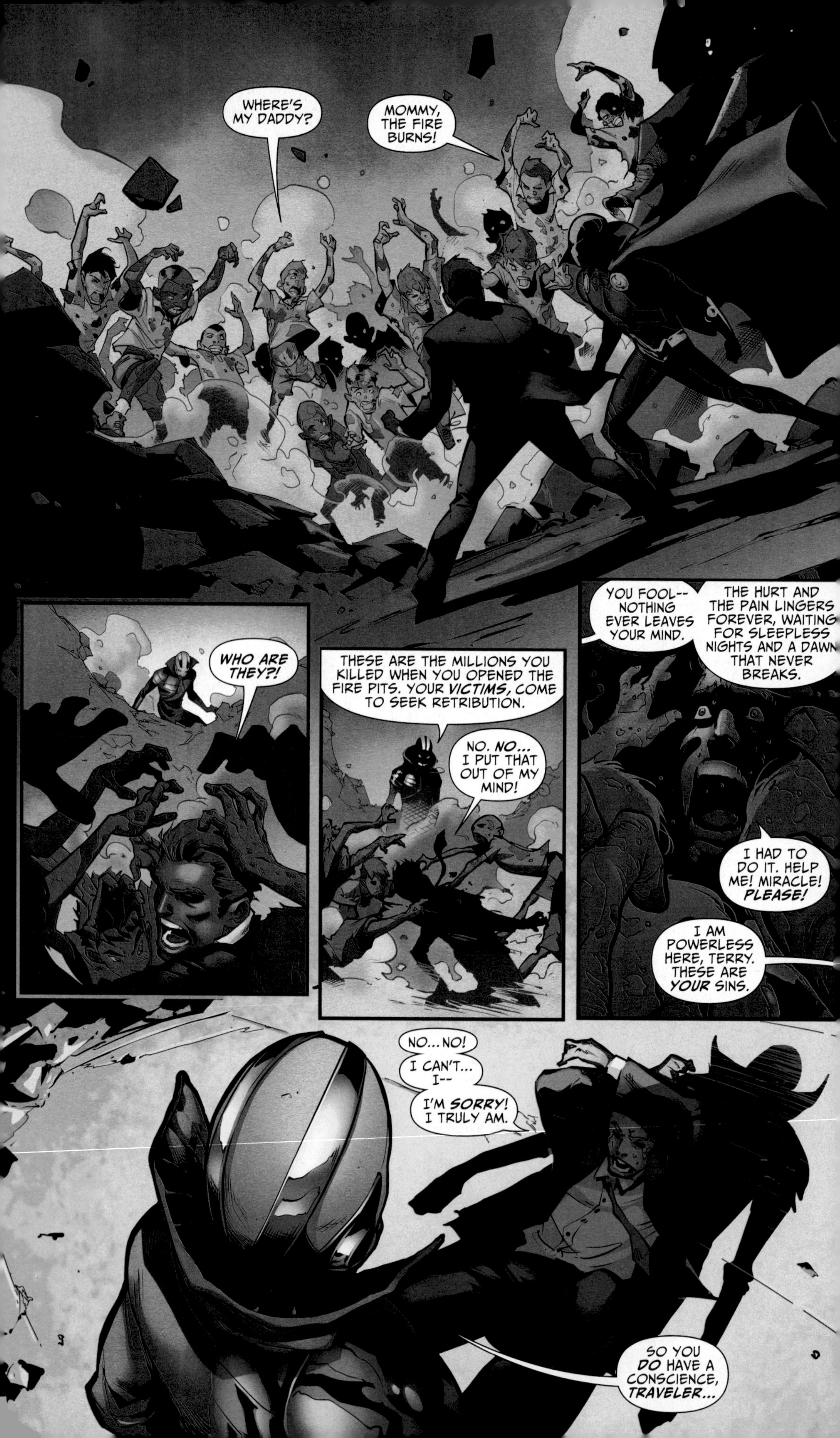
WHERE'S MY DADDY?
MOMMY, THE FIRE BURNS!
WHO ARE THEY?!
THESE ARE THE MILLIONS YOU KILLED WHEN YOU OPENED THE FIRE PITS. YOUR VICTIMS, COME TO SEEK RETRIBUTION.
NO. NO... I PUT THAT OUT OF MY MIND!
YOU FOOL-- NOTHING EVER LEAVES YOUR MIND.
THE HURT AND THE PAIN LINGERS FOREVER, WAITING FOR SLEEPLESS NIGHTS AND A DAWN THAT NEVER BREAKS.
I HAD TO DO IT. HELP ME! MIRACLE! PLEASE!
I AM POWERLESS HERE, TERRY. THESE ARE YOUR SINS.
NO...NO!
I CAN'T... I--
I'M SORRY! I TRULY AM.
SO YOU DO HAVE A CONSCIENCE, TRAVELER...

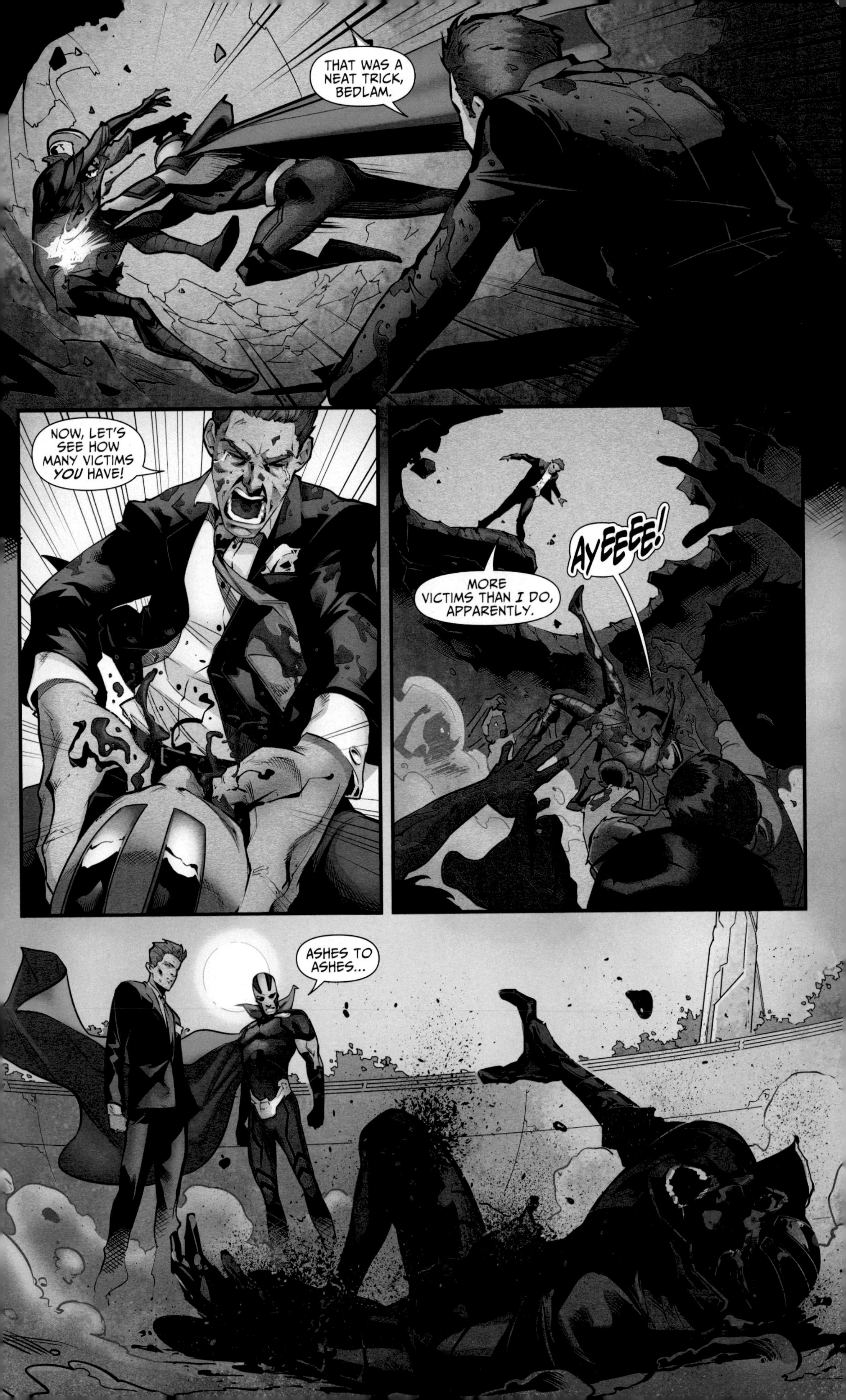
THAT WAS A NEAT TRICK, BEDLAM.
NOW, LET'S SEE HOW MANY VICTIMS *YOU* HAVE!
MORE VICTIMS THAN *I* DO, APPARENTLY.
AYEEEE!
ASHES TO ASHES...

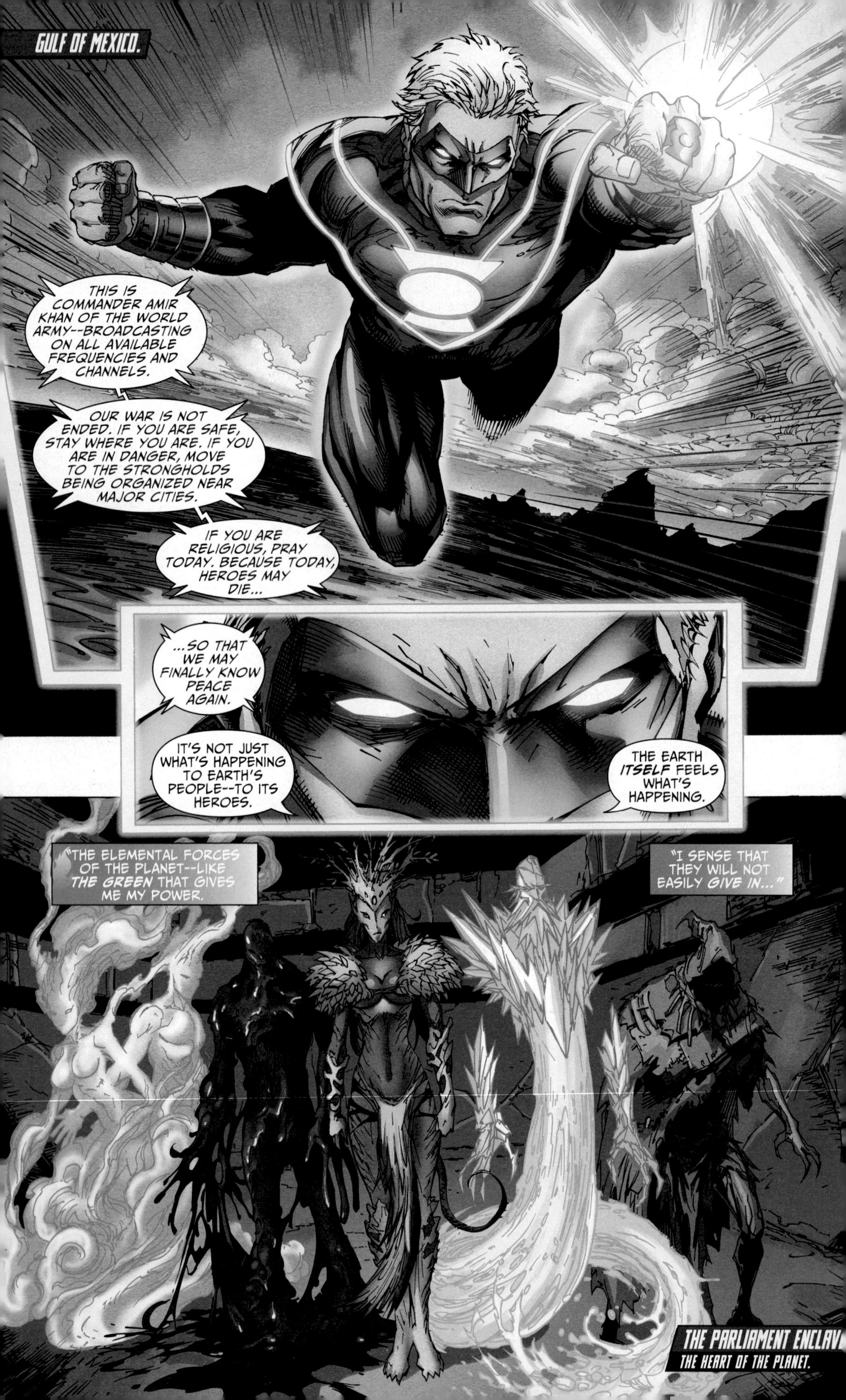

GULF OF MEXICO.
THIS IS COMMANDER AMIR KHAN OF THE WORLD ARMY--BROADCASTING ON ALL AVAILABLE FREQUENCIES AND CHANNELS.
OUR WAR IS NOT ENDED. IF YOU ARE SAFE, STAY WHERE YOU ARE. IF YOU ARE IN DANGER, MOVE TO THE STRONGHOLDS BEING ORGANIZED NEAR MAJOR CITIES.
IF YOU ARE RELIGIOUS, PRAY TODAY. BECAUSE TODAY, HEROES MAY DIE...
...SO THAT WE MAY FINALLY KNOW PEACE AGAIN.
IT'S NOT JUST WHAT'S HAPPENING TO EARTH'S PEOPLE--TO ITS HEROES.
THE EARTH *ITSELF* FEELS WHAT'S HAPPENING.
"THE ELEMENTAL FORCES OF THE PLANET--LIKE *THE GREEN* THAT GIVES ME MY POWER.
"I SENSE THAT THEY WILL NOT EASILY *GIVE IN*..."
THE PARLIAMENT ENCLAVE
THE HEART OF THE PLANET.

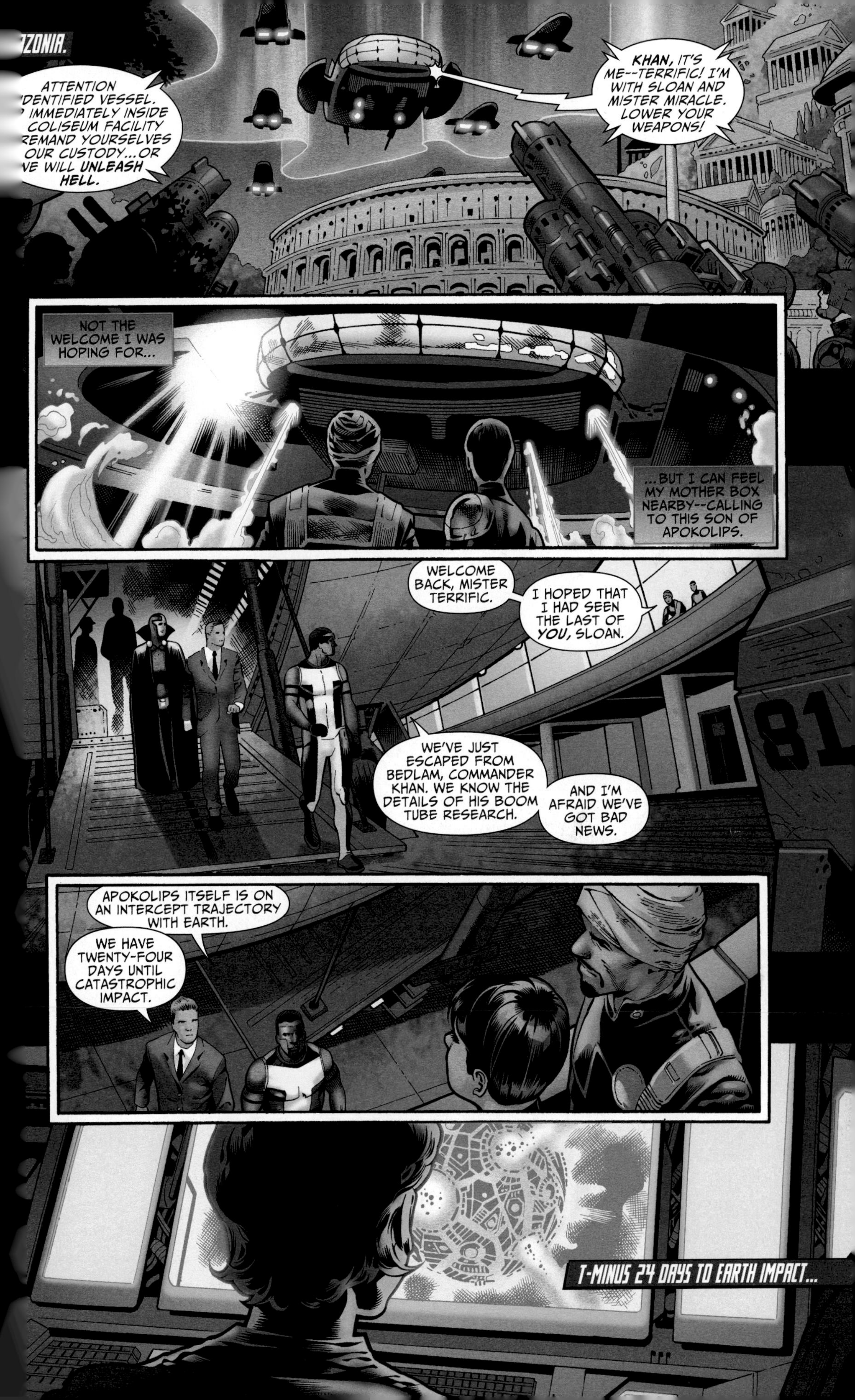

ZONIA.
ATTENTION
IDENTIFIED VESSEL.
P IMMEDIATELY INSIDE
COLISEUM FACILITY
REMAND YOURSELVES
OUR CUSTODY...OR
VE WILL UNLEASH
HELL.
KHAN, IT'S ME--TERRIFIC! I'M WITH SLOAN AND MISTER MIRACLE. LOWER YOUR WEAPONS!
NOT THE WELCOME I WAS HOPING FOR...
...BUT I CAN FEEL MY MOTHER BOX NEARBY--CALLING TO THIS SON OF APOKOLIPS.
WELCOME BACK, MISTER TERRIFIC.
I HOPED THAT I HAD SEEN THE LAST OF YOU, SLOAN.
WE'VE JUST ESCAPED FROM BEDLAM, COMMANDER KHAN. WE KNOW THE DETAILS OF HIS BOOM TUBE RESEARCH.
AND I'M AFRAID WE'VE GOT BAD NEWS.
APOKOLIPS ITSELF IS ON AN INTERCEPT TRAJECTORY WITH EARTH.
WE HAVE TWENTY-FOUR DAYS UNTIL CATASTROPHIC IMPACT.
T-MINUS 24 DAYS TO EARTH IMPACT...

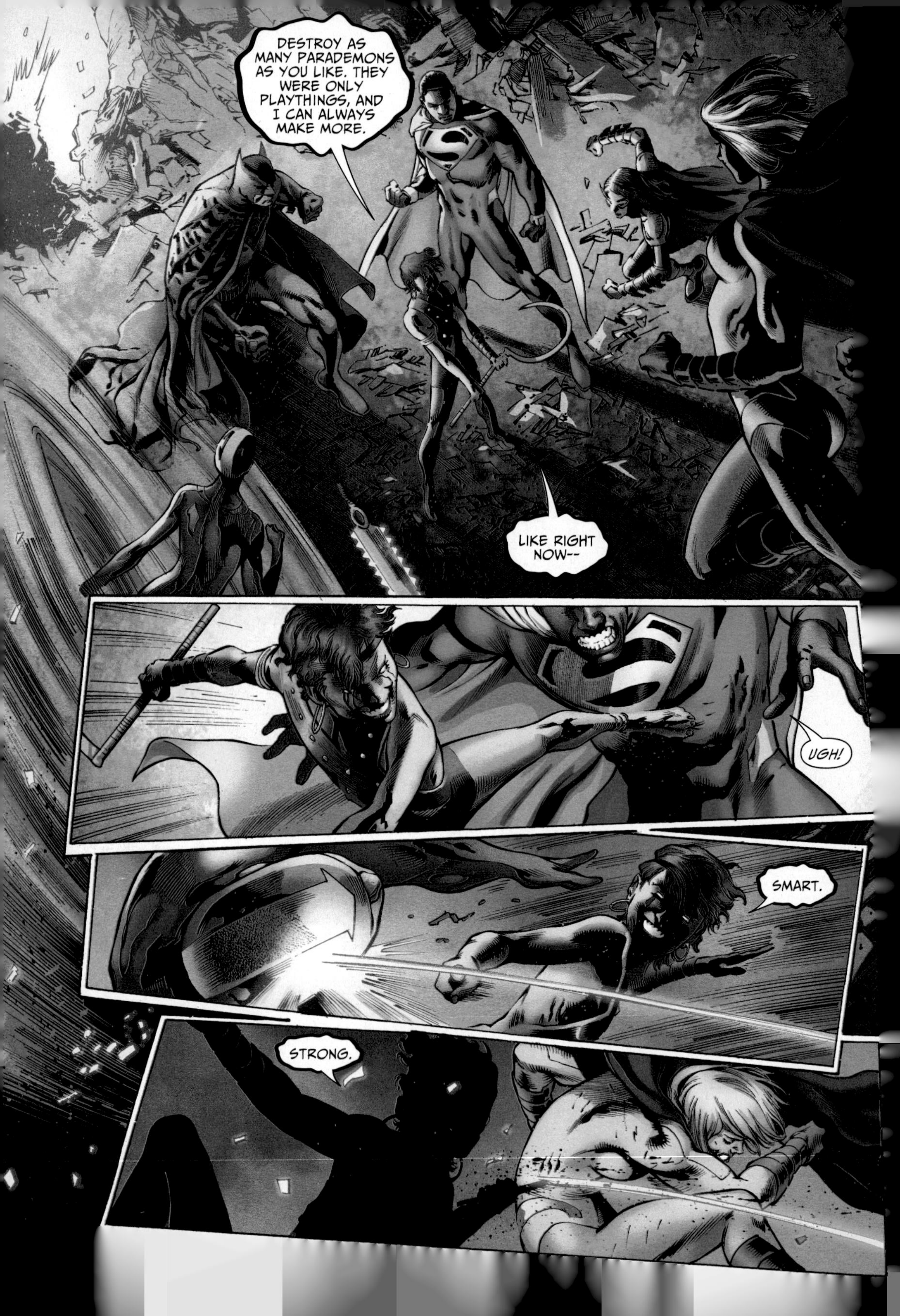
DESTROY AS MANY PARADEMONS AS YOU LIKE. THEY WERE ONLY PLAYTHINGS, AND I CAN ALWAYS MAKE MORE.
LIKE RIGHT NOW--
UGH!
SMART.
STRONG.

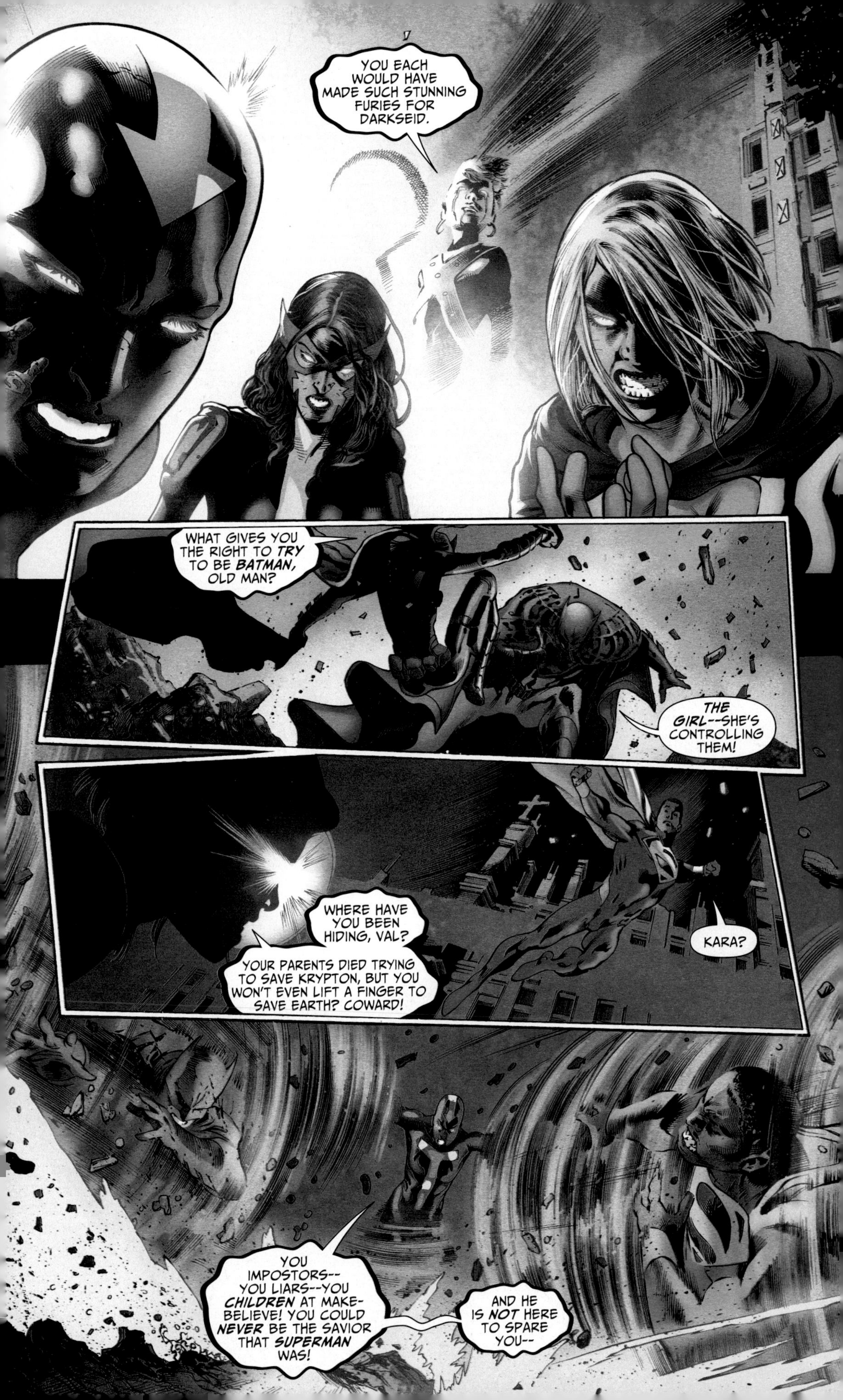
YOU EACH WOULD HAVE MADE SUCH STUNNING FURIES FOR DARKSEID.
WHAT GIVES YOU THE RIGHT TO *TRY* TO BE *BATMAN*, OLD MAN?
THE GIRL--SHE'S CONTROLLING THEM!
WHERE HAVE YOU BEEN HIDING, VAL?
YOUR PARENTS DIED TRYING TO SAVE KRYPTON, BUT YOU WON'T EVEN LIFT A FINGER TO SAVE EARTH? COWARD!
KARA?
YOU IMPOSTORS-- YOU LIARS--YOU *CHILDREN* AT MAKE-BELIEVE! YOU COULD *NEVER* BE THE SAVIOR THAT *SUPERMAN* WAS!
AND HE IS *NOT* HERE TO SPARE YOU--

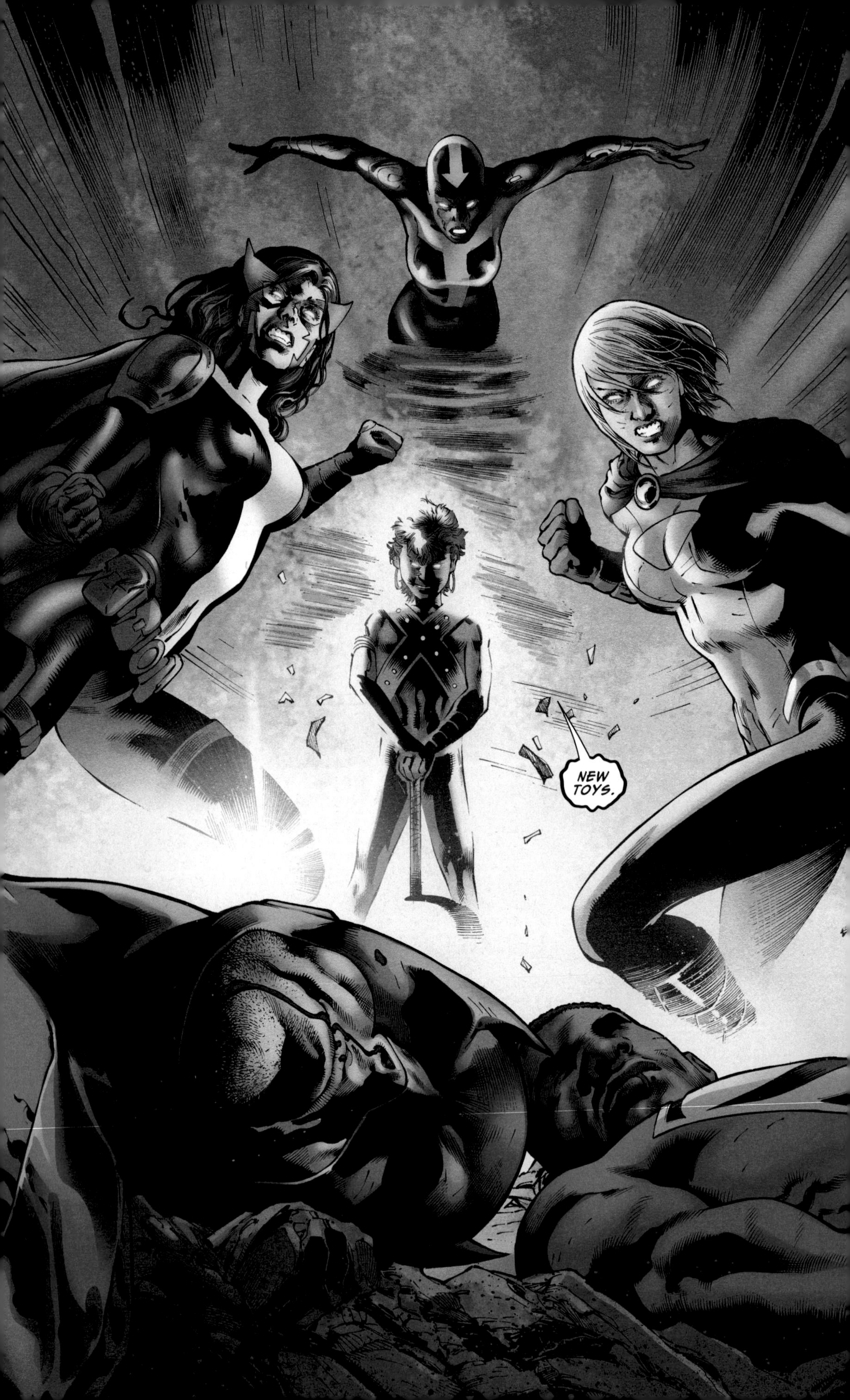
NEW TOYS.

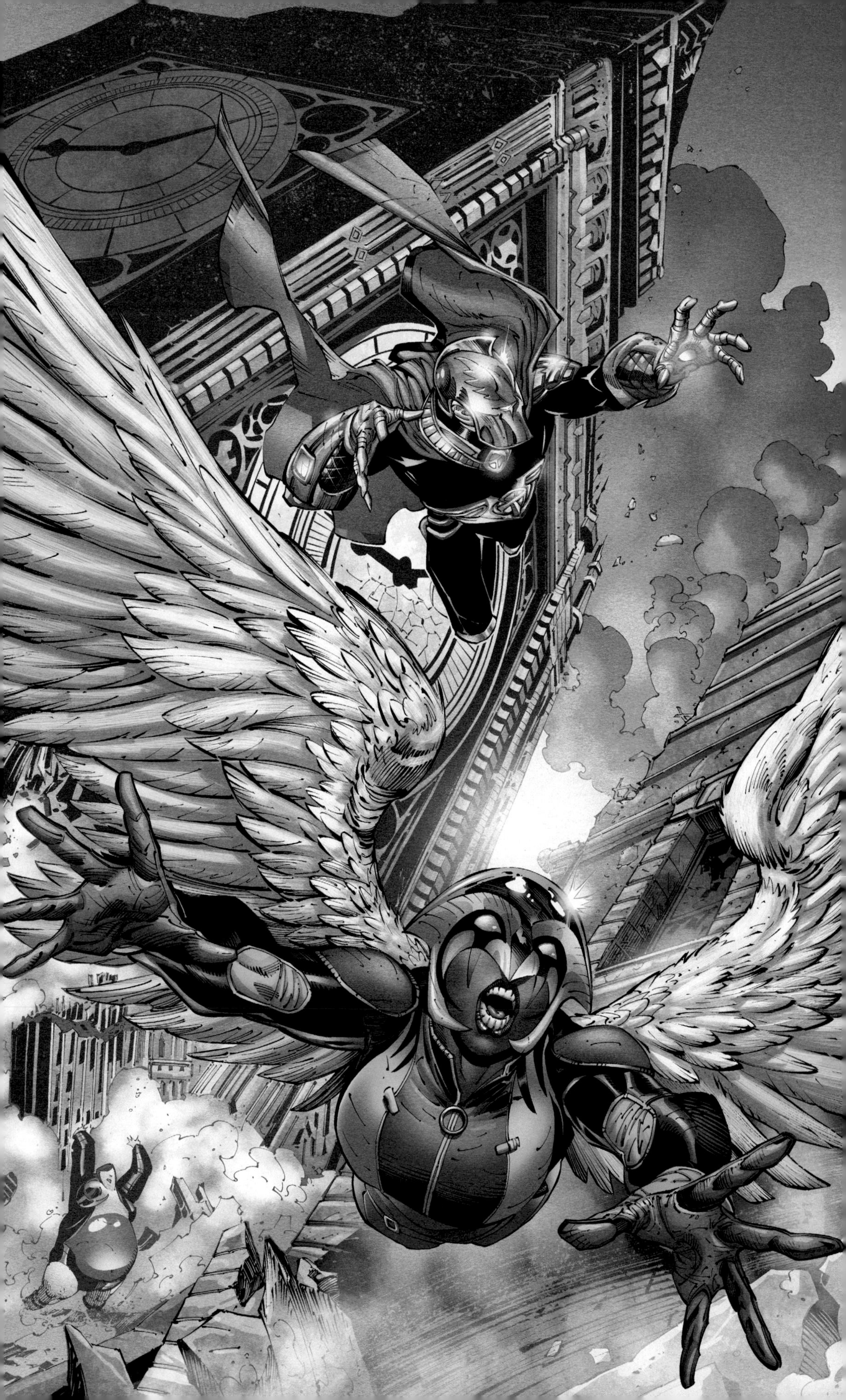

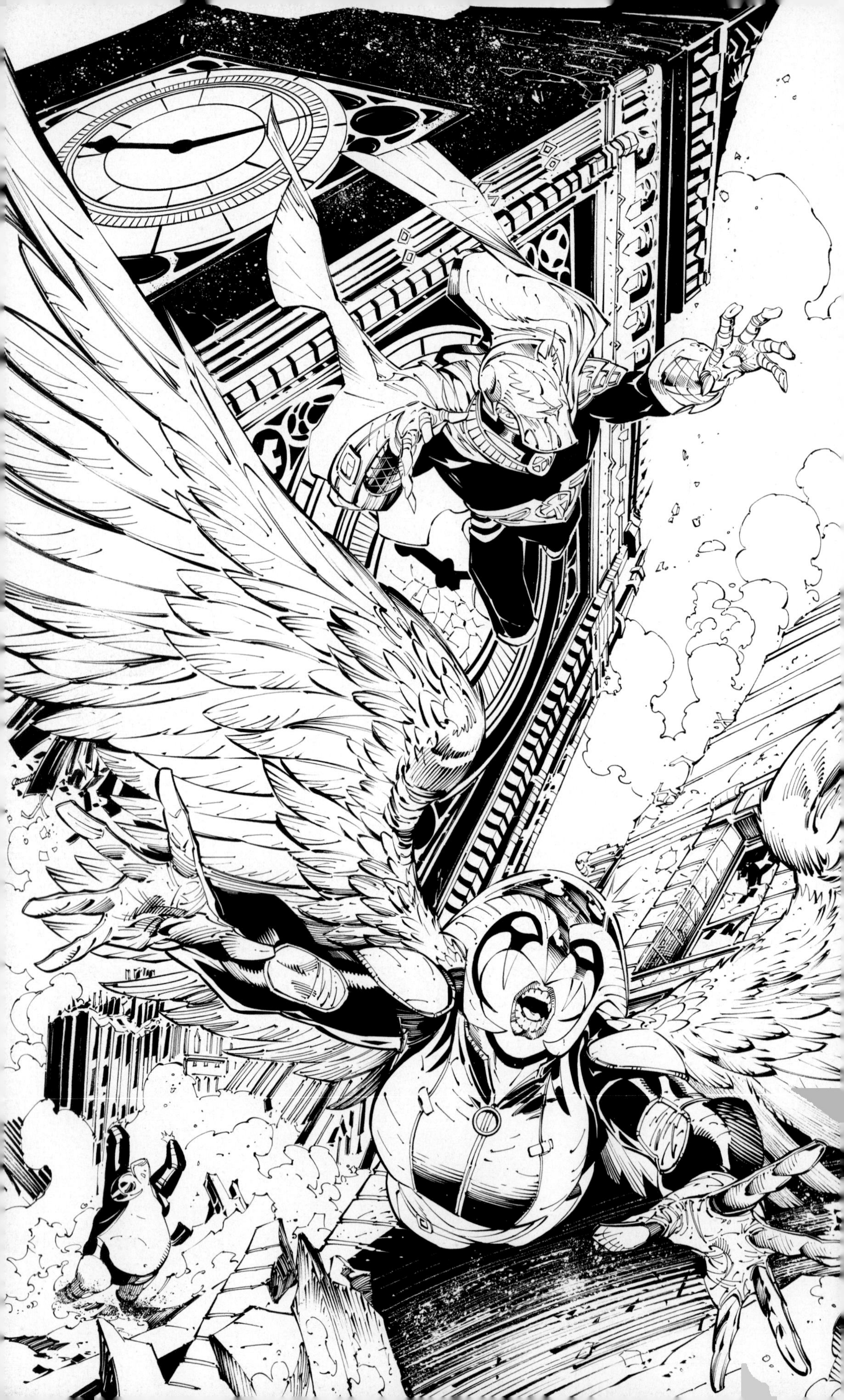

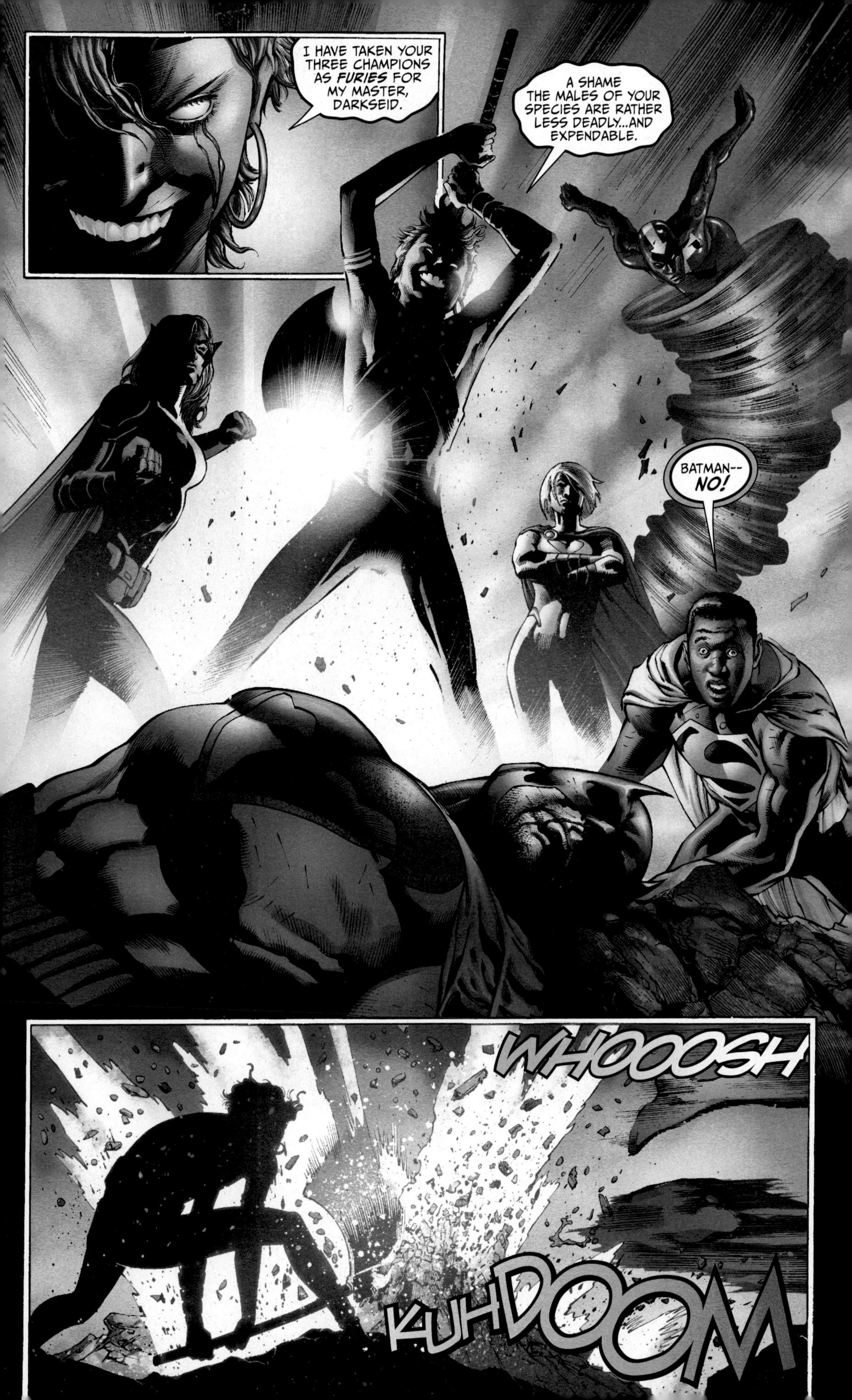
I HAVE TAKEN YOUR THREE CHAMPIONS AS FURIES FOR MY MASTER, DARKSEID.
A SHAME THE MALES OF YOUR SPECIES ARE RATHER LESS DEADLY...AND EXPENDABLE.
BATMAN-- NO!
WHOOOSH
KUHDOOM

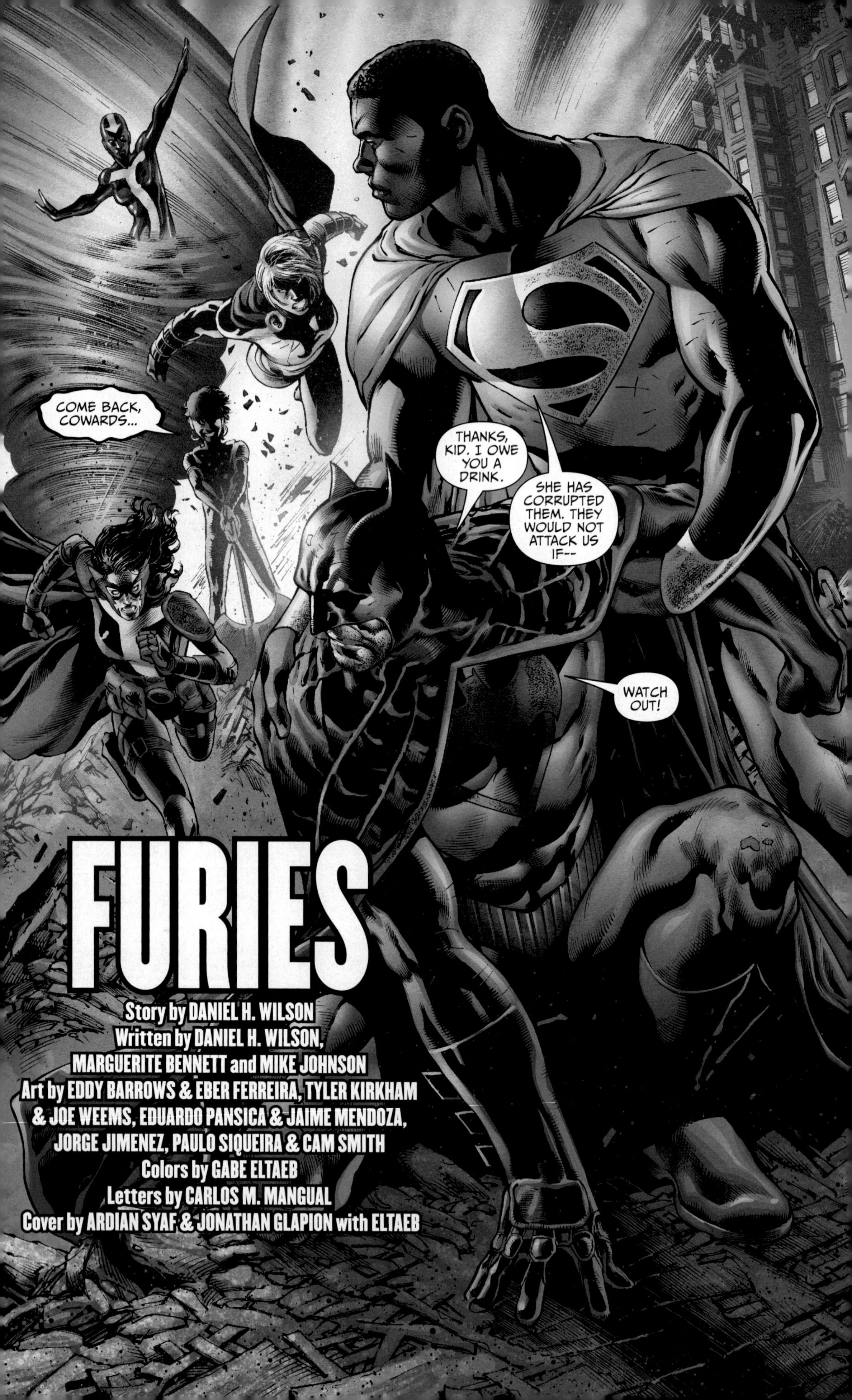
COME BACK, COWARDS...
THANKS, KID. I OWE YOU A DRINK.
SHE HAS CORRUPTED THEM. THEY WOULD NOT ATTACK US IF--
WATCH OUT!
FURIES
Story by DANIEL H. WILSON
Written by DANIEL H. WILSON, MARGUERITE BENNETT and MIKE JOHNSON
Art by EDDY BARROWS & EBER FERREIRA, TYLER KIRKHAM & JOE WEEMS, EDUARDO PANSICA & JAIME MENDOZA, JORGE JIMENEZ, PAULO SIQUEIRA & CAM SMITH
Colors by GABE ELTAEB
Letters by CARLOS M. MANGUAL
Cover by ARDIAN SYAF & JONATHAN GLAPION with ELTAEB

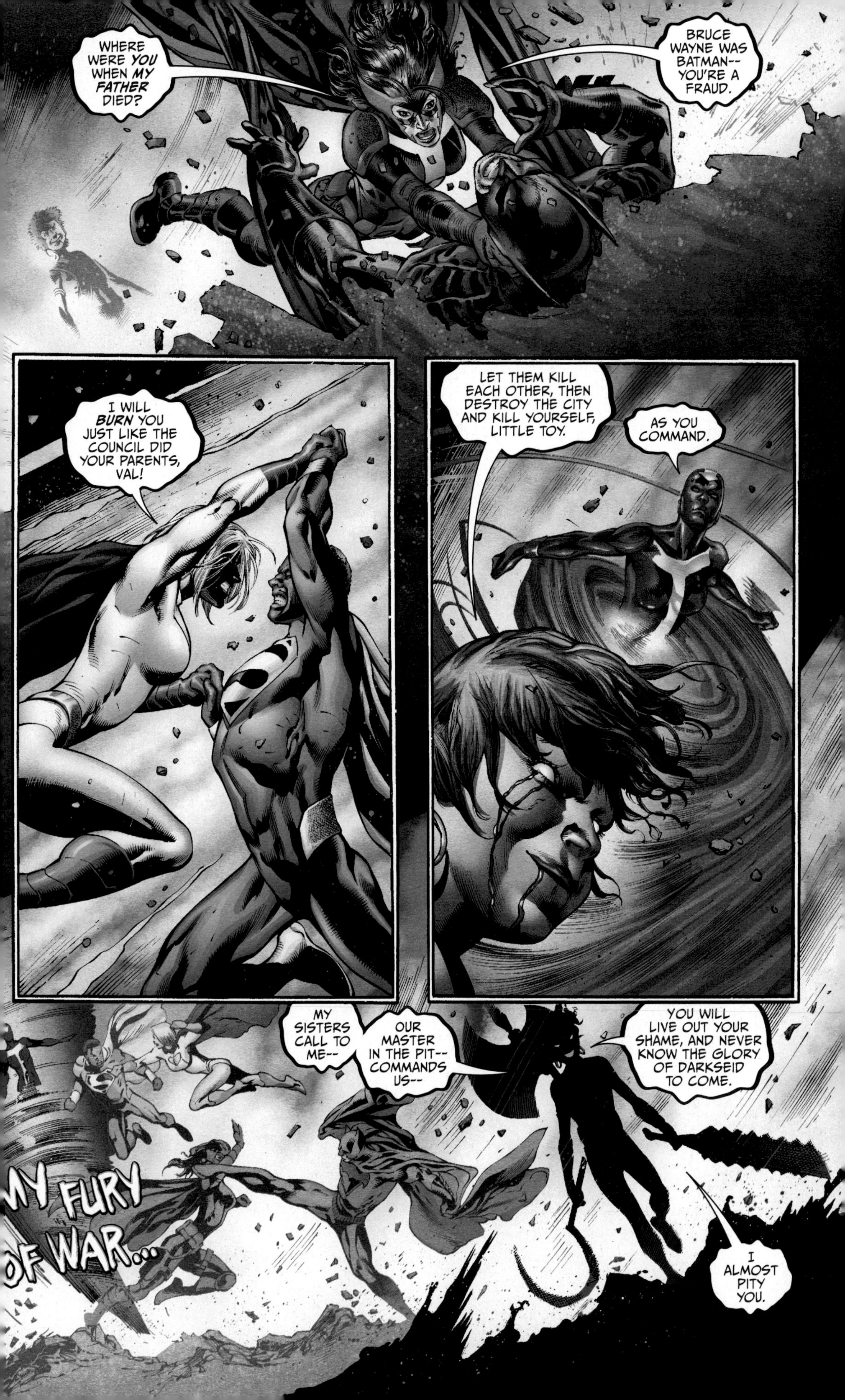
WHERE WERE *YOU* WHEN *MY FATHER* DIED?
BRUCE WAYNE WAS BATMAN-- YOU'RE A FRAUD.
I WILL *BURN* YOU JUST LIKE THE COUNCIL DID YOUR PARENTS, VAL!
LET THEM KILL EACH OTHER, THEN DESTROY THE CITY AND KILL YOURSELF, LITTLE TOY.
AS YOU COMMAND.
MY SISTERS CALL TO ME--
OUR MASTER IN THE PIT-- COMMANDS US--
YOU WILL LIVE OUT YOUR SHAME, AND NEVER KNOW THE GLORY OF DARKSEID TO COME.
MY FURY OF WAR...
I ALMOST PITY YOU.

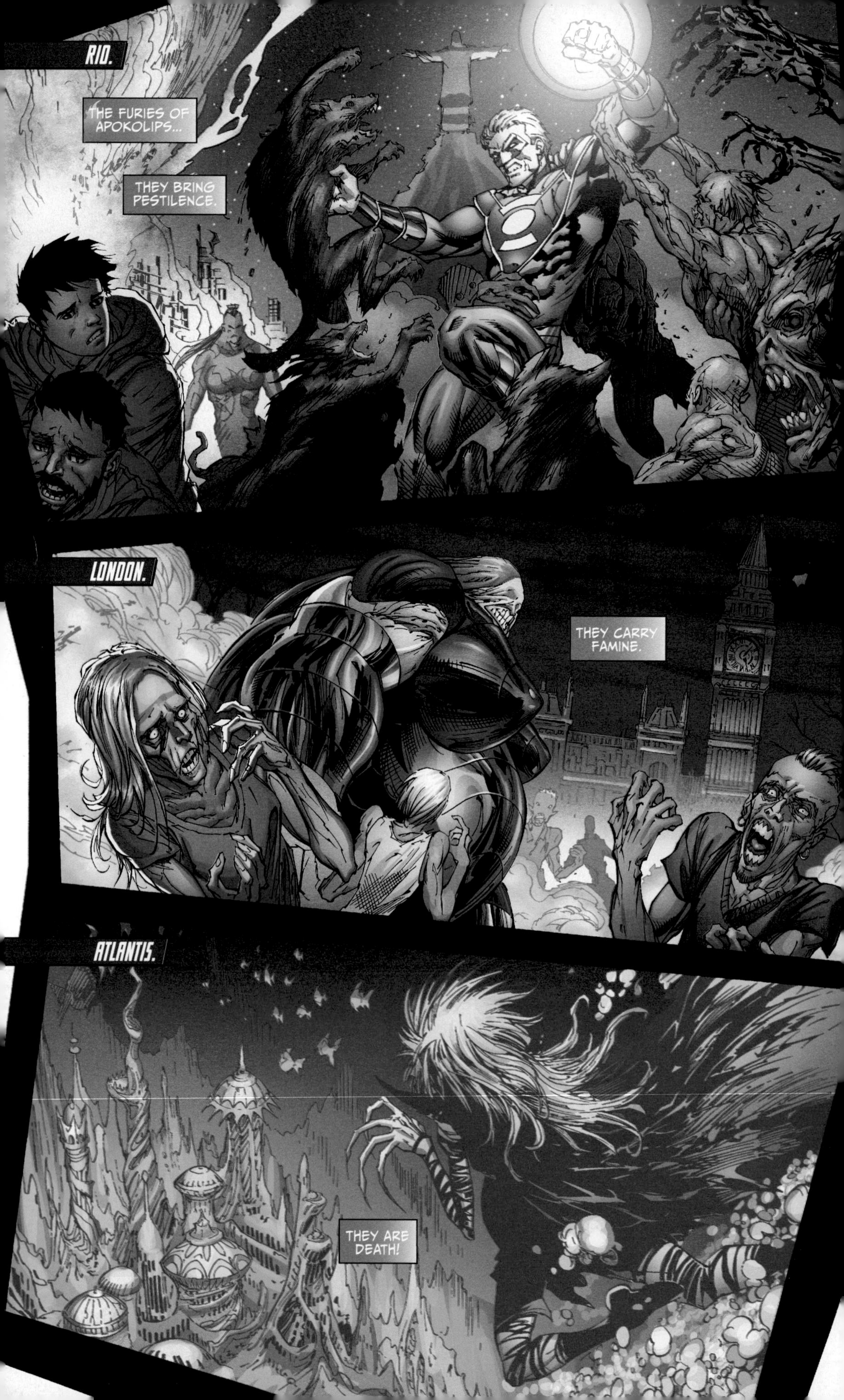
RIO.
THE FURIES OF APOKOLIPS...
THEY BRING PESTILENCE.
LONDON.
THEY CARRY FAMINE.
ATLANTIS.
THEY ARE DEATH!

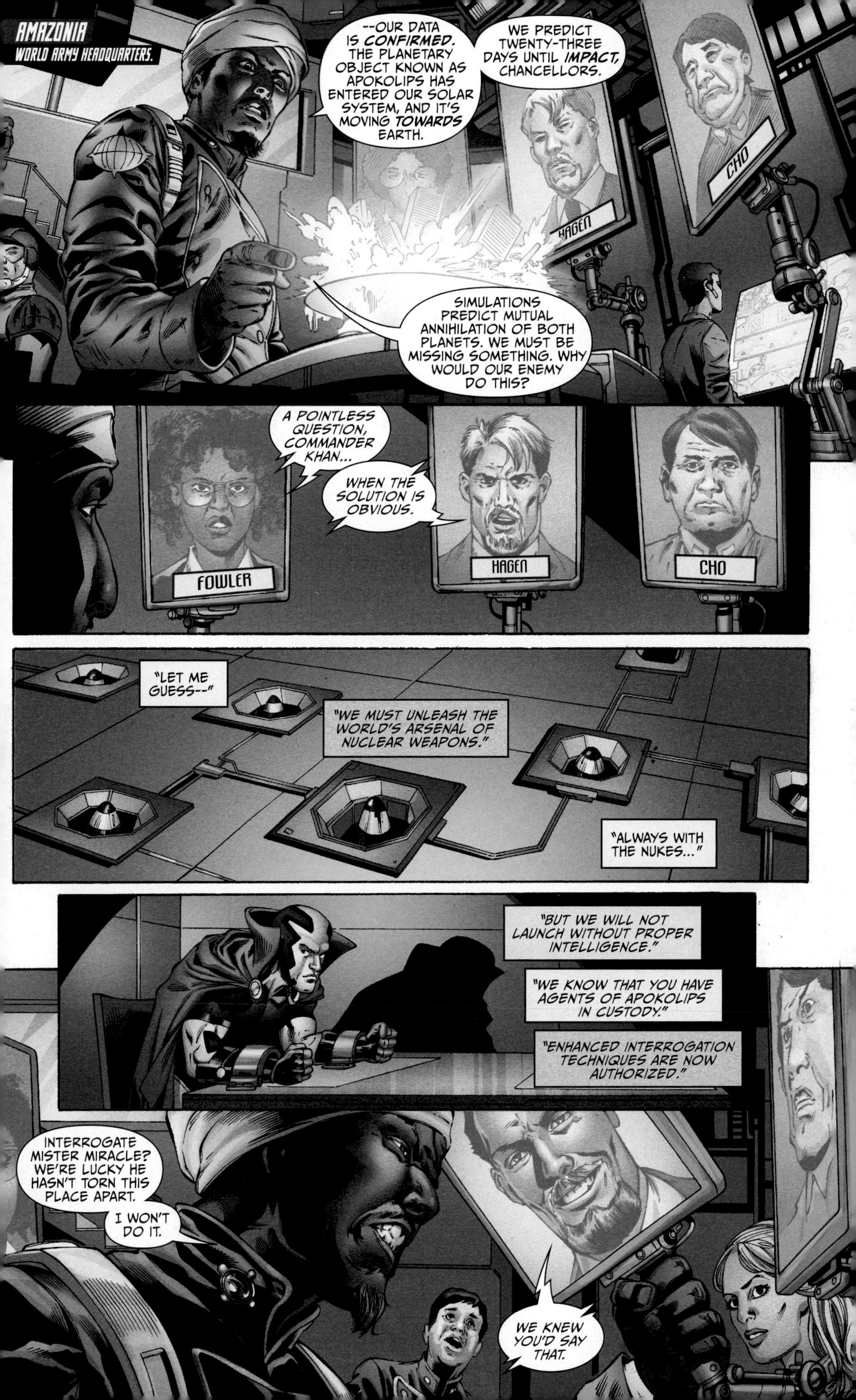
AMAZONIA
WORLD ARMY HEADQUARTERS.
--OUR DATA IS CONFIRMED. THE PLANETARY OBJECT KNOWN AS APOKOLIPS HAS ENTERED OUR SOLAR SYSTEM, AND IT'S MOVING TOWARDS EARTH.
WE PREDICT TWENTY-THREE DAYS UNTIL IMPACT, CHANCELLORS.
CHO
HAGEN
SIMULATIONS PREDICT MUTUAL ANNIHILATION OF BOTH PLANETS. WE MUST BE MISSING SOMETHING. WHY WOULD OUR ENEMY DO THIS?
A POINTLESS QUESTION, COMMANDER KHAN...
WHEN THE SOLUTION IS OBVIOUS.
FOWLER
HAGEN
CHO
"LET ME GUESS--"
"WE MUST UNLEASH THE WORLD'S ARSENAL OF NUCLEAR WEAPONS."
"ALWAYS WITH THE NUKES..."
"BUT WE WILL NOT LAUNCH WITHOUT PROPER INTELLIGENCE."
"WE KNOW THAT YOU HAVE AGENTS OF APOKOLIPS IN CUSTODY."
"ENHANCED INTERROGATION TECHNIQUES ARE NOW AUTHORIZED."
INTERROGATE MISTER MIRACLE? WE'RE LUCKY HE HASN'T TORN THIS PLACE APART.
I WON'T DO IT.
WE KNEW YOU'D SAY THAT.

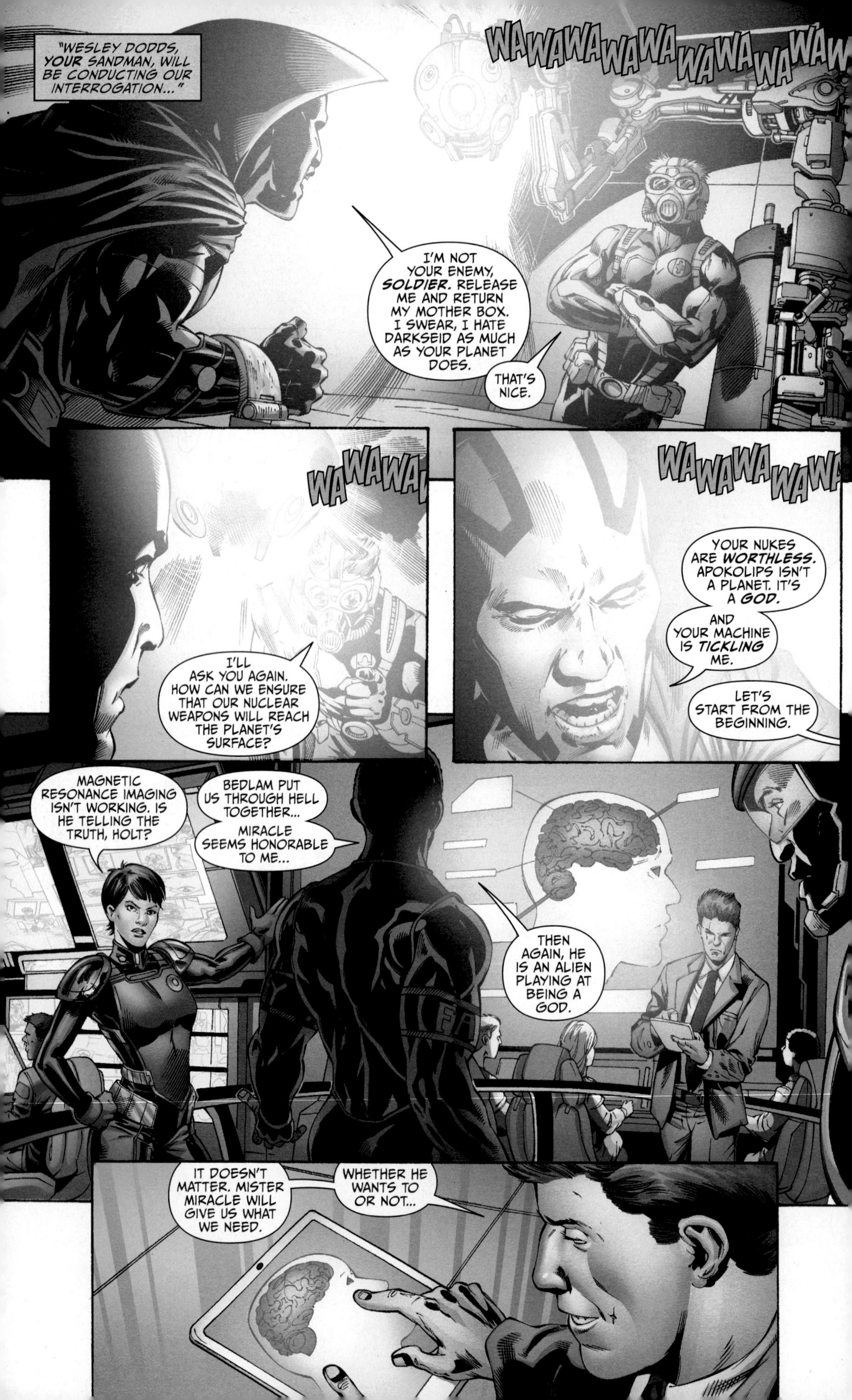
"WESLEY DODDS, YOUR SANDMAN, WILL BE CONDUCTING OUR INTERROGATION..."
WAWAWAWAWAWAWAWAWAWAWAW
I'M NOT YOUR ENEMY, SOLDIER. RELEASE ME AND RETURN MY MOTHER BOX. I SWEAR, I HATE DARKSEID AS MUCH AS YOUR PLANET DOES.
THAT'S NICE.
WAWAWAW
I'LL ASK YOU AGAIN. HOW CAN WE ENSURE THAT OUR NUCLEAR WEAPONS WILL REACH THE PLANET'S SURFACE?
WAWAWAWAWAW
YOUR NUKES ARE WORTHLESS. APOKOLIPS ISN'T A PLANET. IT'S A GOD.
AND YOUR MACHINE IS TICKLING ME.
LET'S START FROM THE BEGINNING.
MAGNETIC RESONANCE IMAGING ISN'T WORKING. IS HE TELLING THE TRUTH, HOLT?
BEDLAM PUT US THROUGH HELL TOGETHER...
MIRACLE SEEMS HONORABLE TO ME...
THEN AGAIN, HE IS AN ALIEN PLAYING AT BEING A GOD.
IT DOESN'T MATTER. MISTER MIRACLE WILL GIVE US WHAT WE NEED.
WHETHER HE WANTS TO OR NOT...

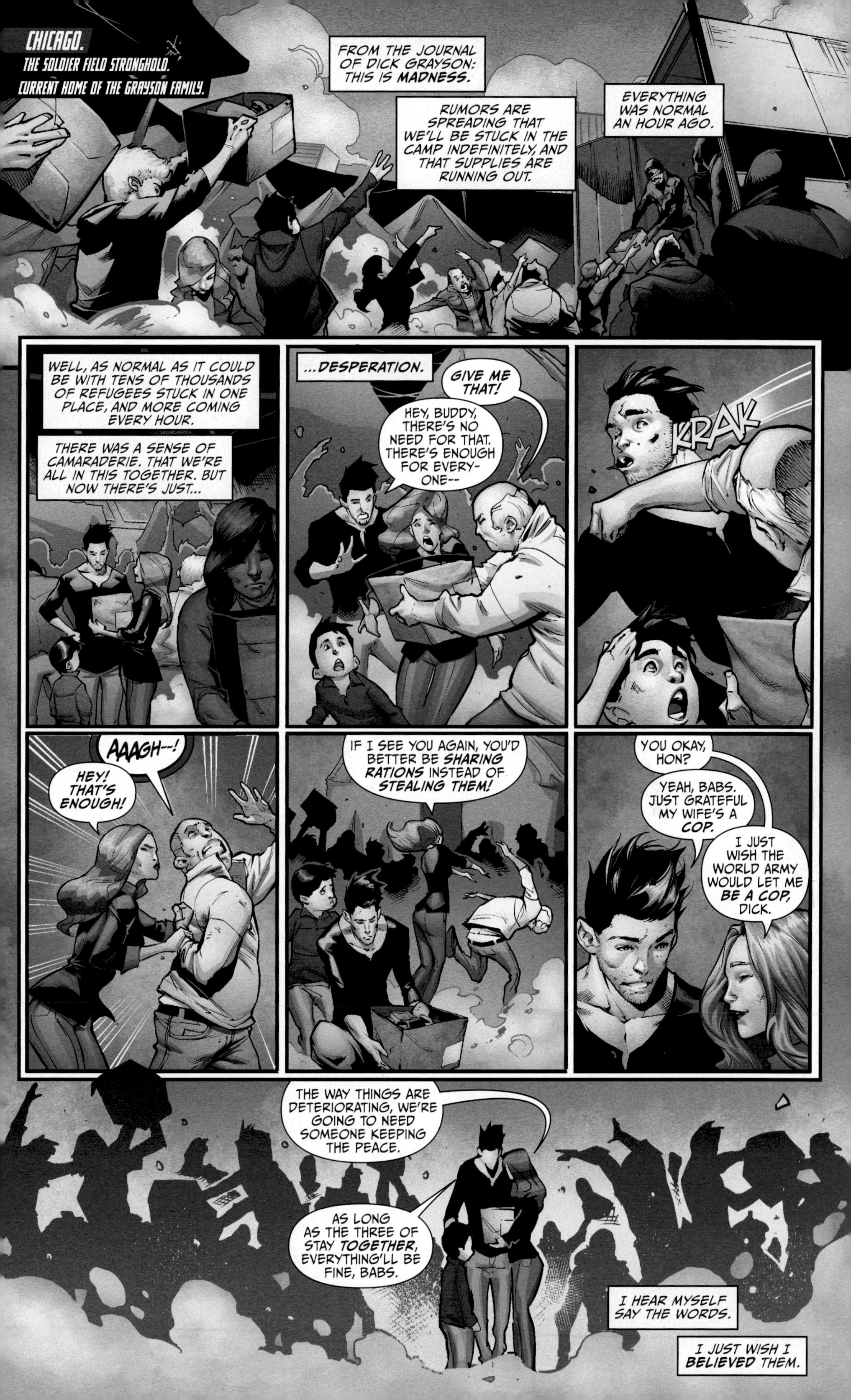
CHICAGO.
THE SOLDIER FIELD STRONGHOLD.
CURRENT HOME OF THE GRAYSON FAMILY.
FROM THE JOURNAL OF DICK GRAYSON: THIS IS MADNESS.
RUMORS ARE SPREADING THAT WE'LL BE STUCK IN THE CAMP INDEFINITELY, AND THAT SUPPLIES ARE RUNNING OUT.
EVERYTHING WAS NORMAL AN HOUR AGO.
WELL, AS NORMAL AS IT COULD BE WITH TENS OF THOUSANDS OF REFUGEES STUCK IN ONE PLACE, AND MORE COMING EVERY HOUR.
THERE WAS A SENSE OF CAMARADERIE. THAT WE'RE ALL IN THIS TOGETHER. BUT NOW THERE'S JUST...
...DESPERATION.
GIVE ME THAT!
HEY, BUDDY, THERE'S NO NEED FOR THAT. THERE'S ENOUGH FOR EVERY-ONE--
KRAK
AAAGH--!
HEY! THAT'S ENOUGH!
IF I SEE YOU AGAIN, YOU'D BETTER BE SHARING RATIONS INSTEAD OF STEALING THEM!
YOU OKAY, HON?
YEAH, BABS. JUST GRATEFUL MY WIFE'S A COP.
I JUST WISH THE WORLD ARMY WOULD LET ME BE A COP, DICK.
THE WAY THINGS ARE DETERIORATING, WE'RE GOING TO NEED SOMEONE KEEPING THE PEACE.
AS LONG AS THE THREE OF STAY TOGETHER, EVERYTHING'LL BE FINE, BABS.
I HEAR MYSELF SAY THE WORDS.
I JUST WISH I BELIEVED THEM.

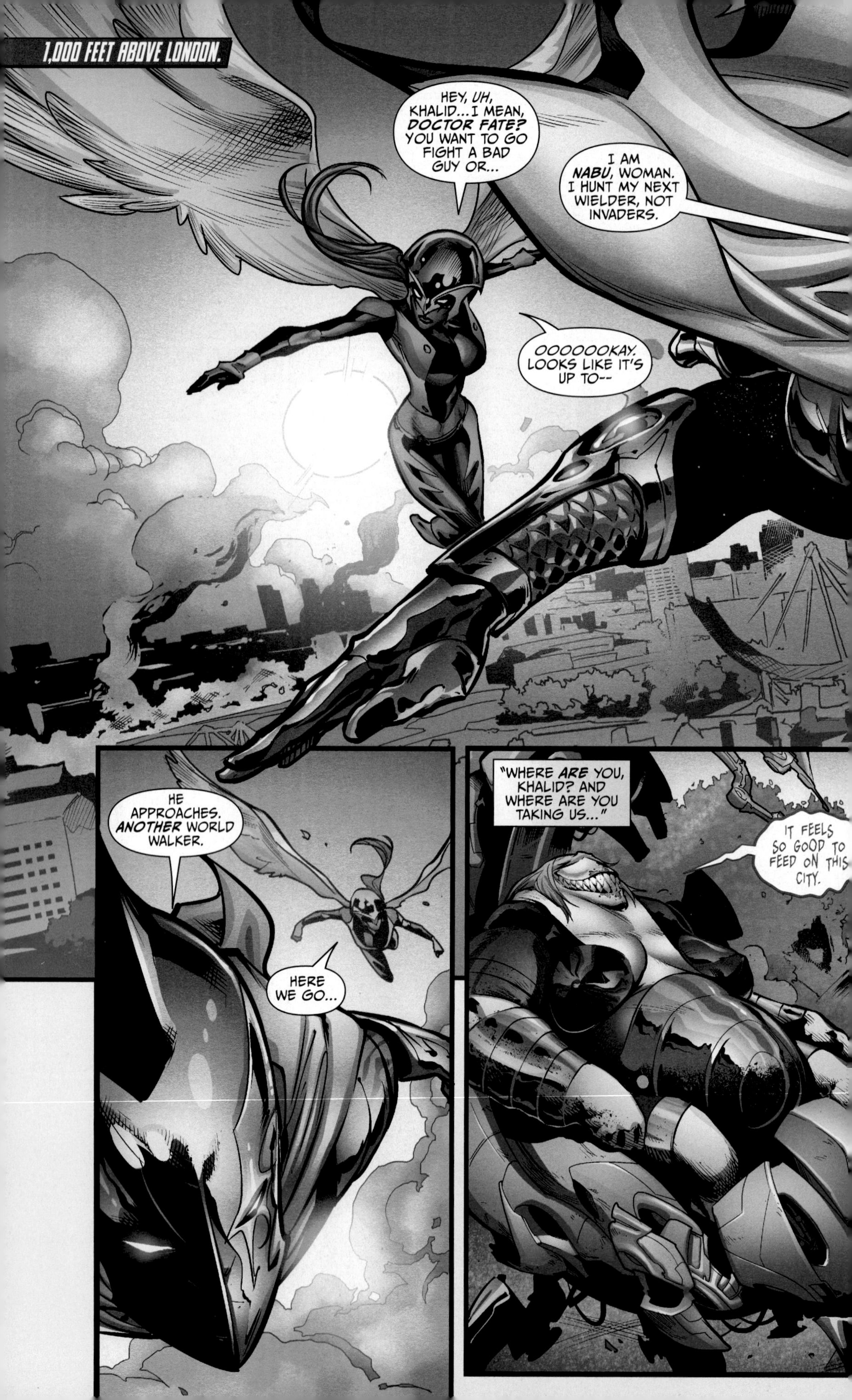
1,000 FEET ABOVE LONDON.
HEY, UH, KHALID...I MEAN, DOCTOR FATE? YOU WANT TO GO FIGHT A BAD GUY OR...
I AM NABU, WOMAN. I HUNT MY NEXT WIELDER, NOT INVADERS.
OOOOOOKAY. LOOKS LIKE IT'S UP TO--
HE APPROACHES. ANOTHER WORLD WALKER.
HERE WE GO...
"WHERE ARE YOU, KHALID? AND WHERE ARE YOU TAKING US..."
IT FEELS SO GOOD TO FEED ON THIS CITY.

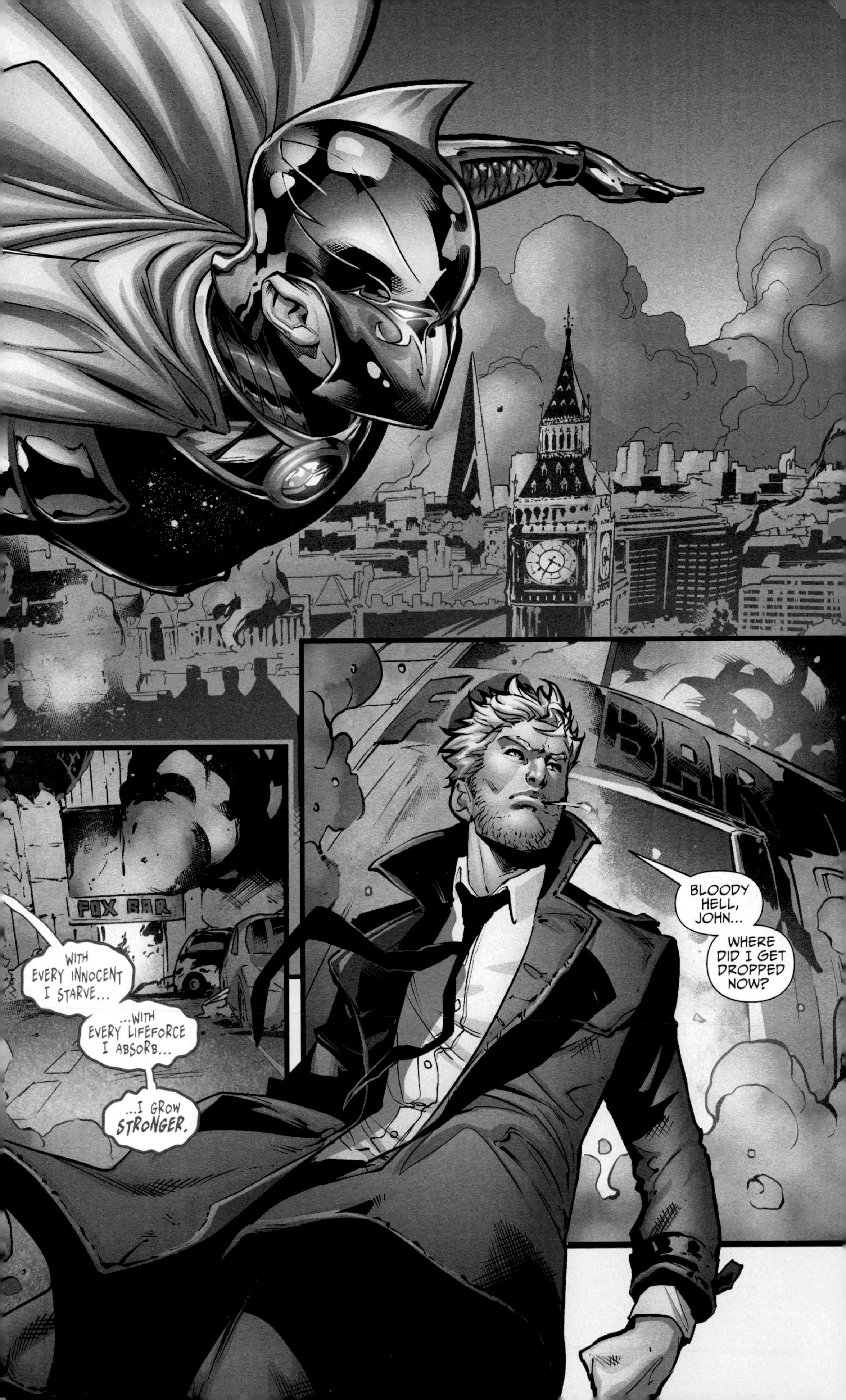
FOX BAR
WITH EVERY INNOCENT I STARVE...
...WITH EVERY LIFEFORCE I ABSORB...
...I GROW STRONGER.
BLOODY HELL, JOHN...
WHERE DID I GET DROPPED NOW?

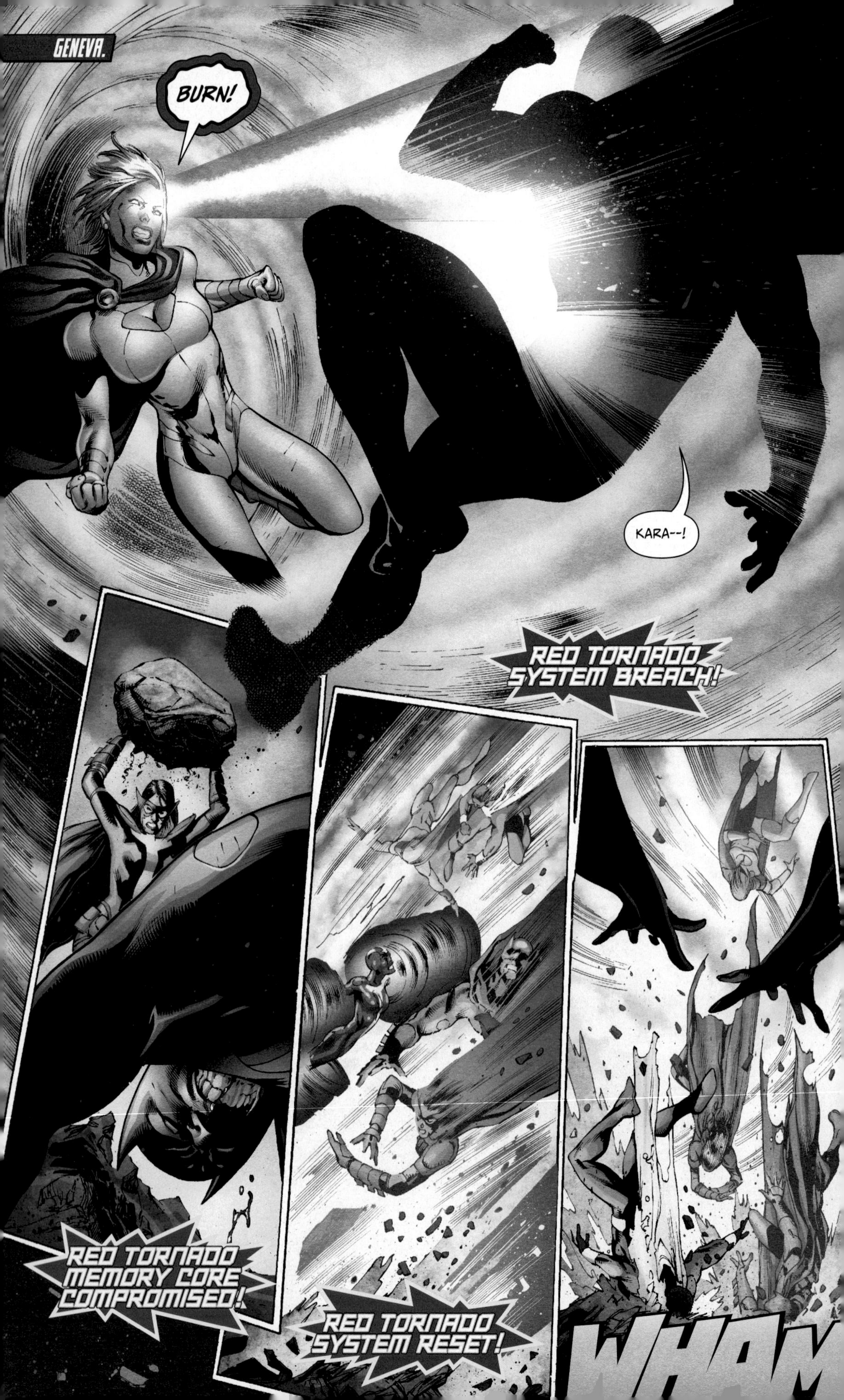

GENEVA.
BURN!
KARA--!
RED TORNADO SYSTEM BREACH!
RED TORNADO MEMORY CORE COMPROMISED!
RED TORNADO SYSTEM RESET!
WHAM

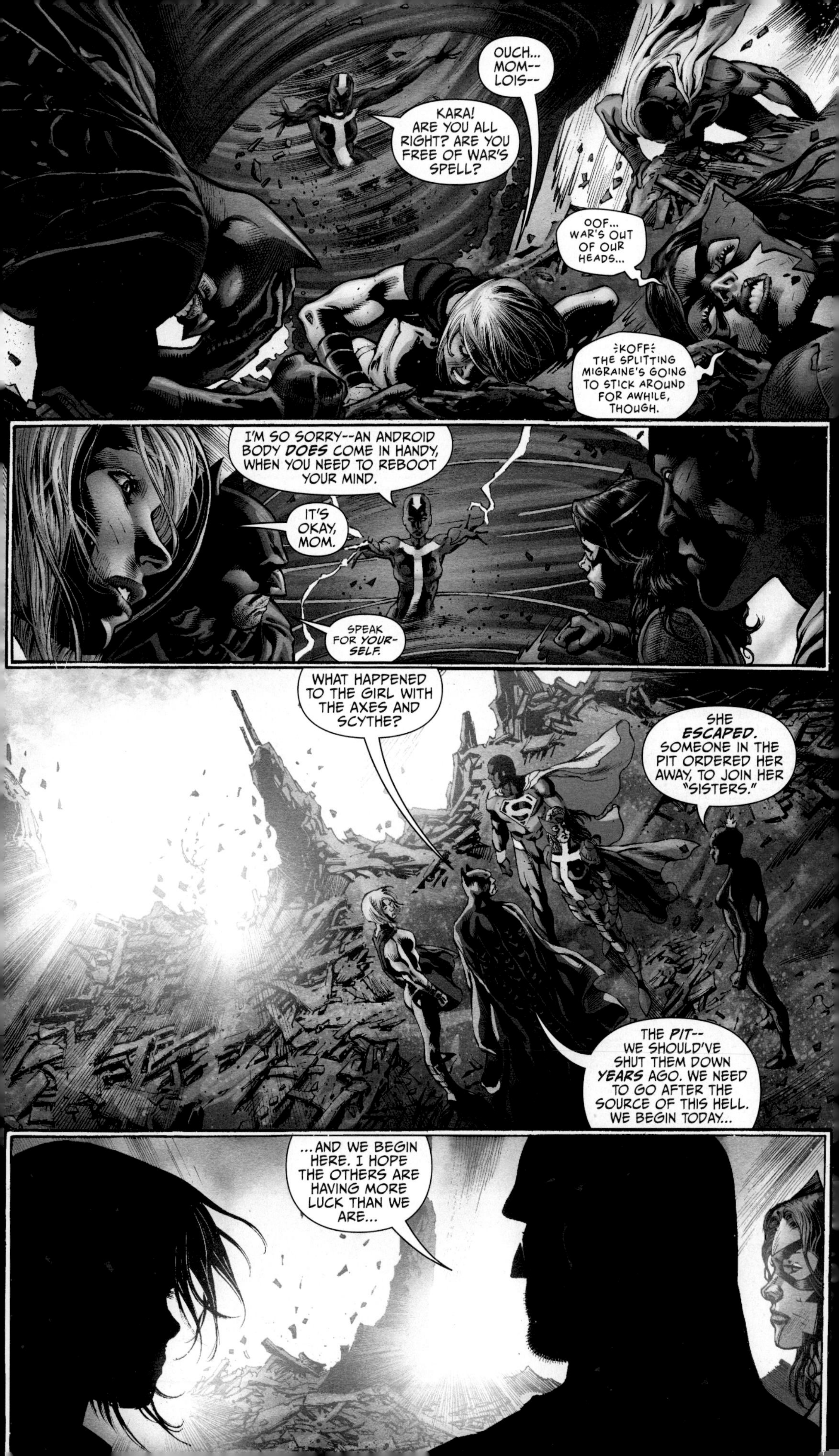
OUCH... MOM-- LOIS--
KARA! ARE YOU ALL RIGHT? ARE YOU FREE OF WAR'S SPELL?
OOF... WAR'S OUT OF OUR HEADS...
≷KOFF≶ THE SPLITTING MIGRAINE'S GOING TO STICK AROUND FOR AWHILE, THOUGH.
I'M SO SORRY--AN ANDROID BODY DOES COME IN HANDY, WHEN YOU NEED TO REBOOT YOUR MIND.
IT'S OKAY, MOM.
SPEAK FOR YOURSELF.
WHAT HAPPENED TO THE GIRL WITH THE AXES AND SCYTHE?
SHE ESCAPED. SOMEONE IN THE PIT ORDERED HER AWAY, TO JOIN HER "SISTERS."
THE PIT-- WE SHOULD'VE SHUT THEM DOWN YEARS AGO. WE NEED TO GO AFTER THE SOURCE OF THIS HELL. WE BEGIN TODAY...
...AND WE BEGIN HERE. I HOPE THE OTHERS ARE HAVING MORE LUCK THAN WE ARE...

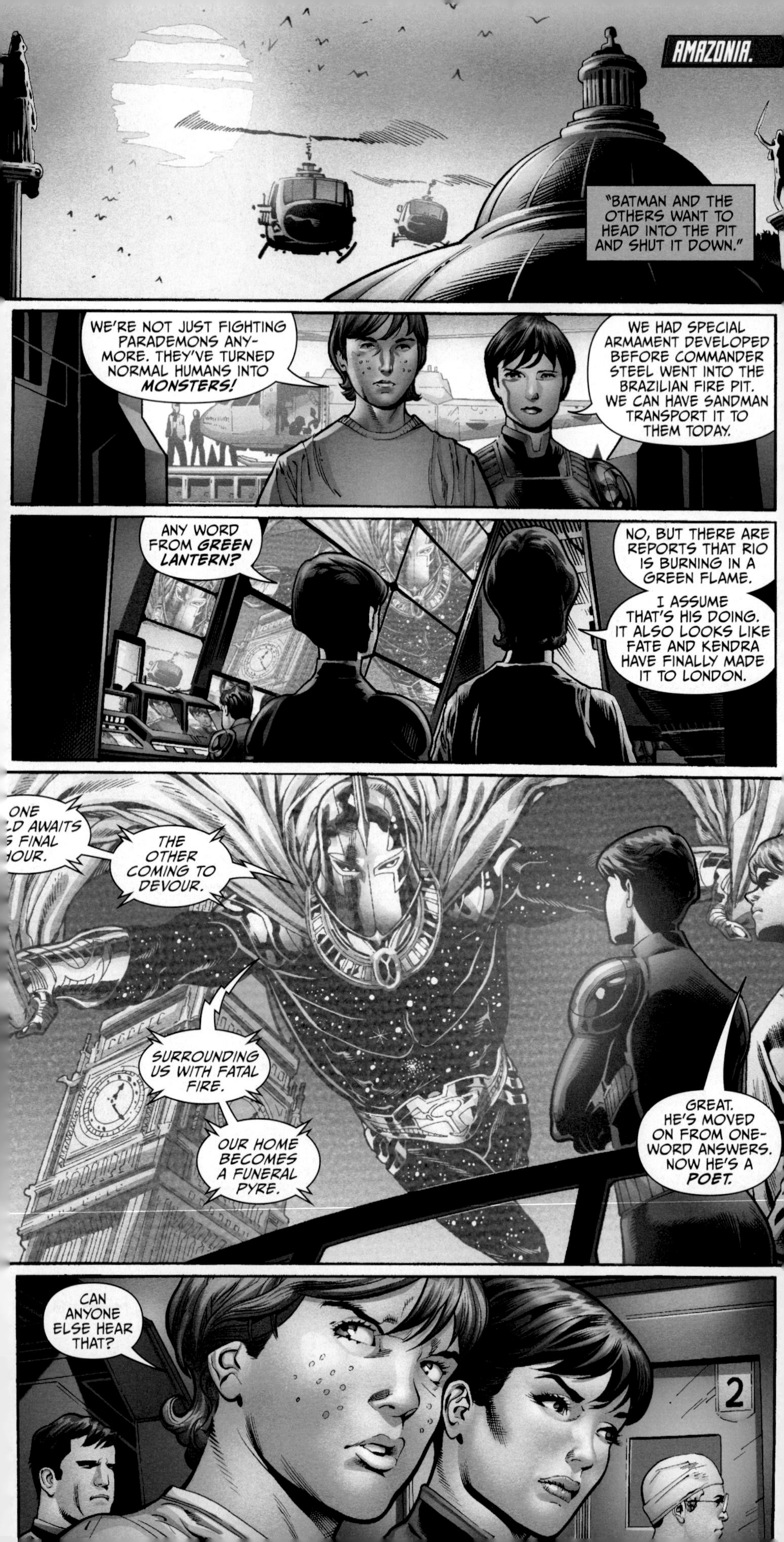

AMAZONIA.
"BATMAN AND THE OTHERS WANT TO HEAD INTO THE PIT AND SHUT IT DOWN."
WE'RE NOT JUST FIGHTING PARADEMONS ANYMORE. THEY'VE TURNED NORMAL HUMANS INTO MONSTERS!
WE HAD SPECIAL ARMAMENT DEVELOPED BEFORE COMMANDER STEEL WENT INTO THE BRAZILIAN FIRE PIT. WE CAN HAVE SANDMAN TRANSPORT IT TO THEM TODAY.
ANY WORD FROM GREEN LANTERN?
NO, BUT THERE ARE REPORTS THAT RIO IS BURNING IN A GREEN FLAME.
I ASSUME THAT'S HIS DOING. IT ALSO LOOKS LIKE FATE AND KENDRA HAVE FINALLY MADE IT TO LONDON.
ONE AWAITS FINAL HOUR.
THE OTHER COMING TO DEVOUR.
SURROUNDING US WITH FATAL FIRE.
OUR HOME BECOMES A FUNERAL PYRE.
GREAT. HE'S MOVED ON FROM ONE-WORD ANSWERS. NOW HE'S A POET.
CAN ANYONE ELSE HEAR THAT?
2

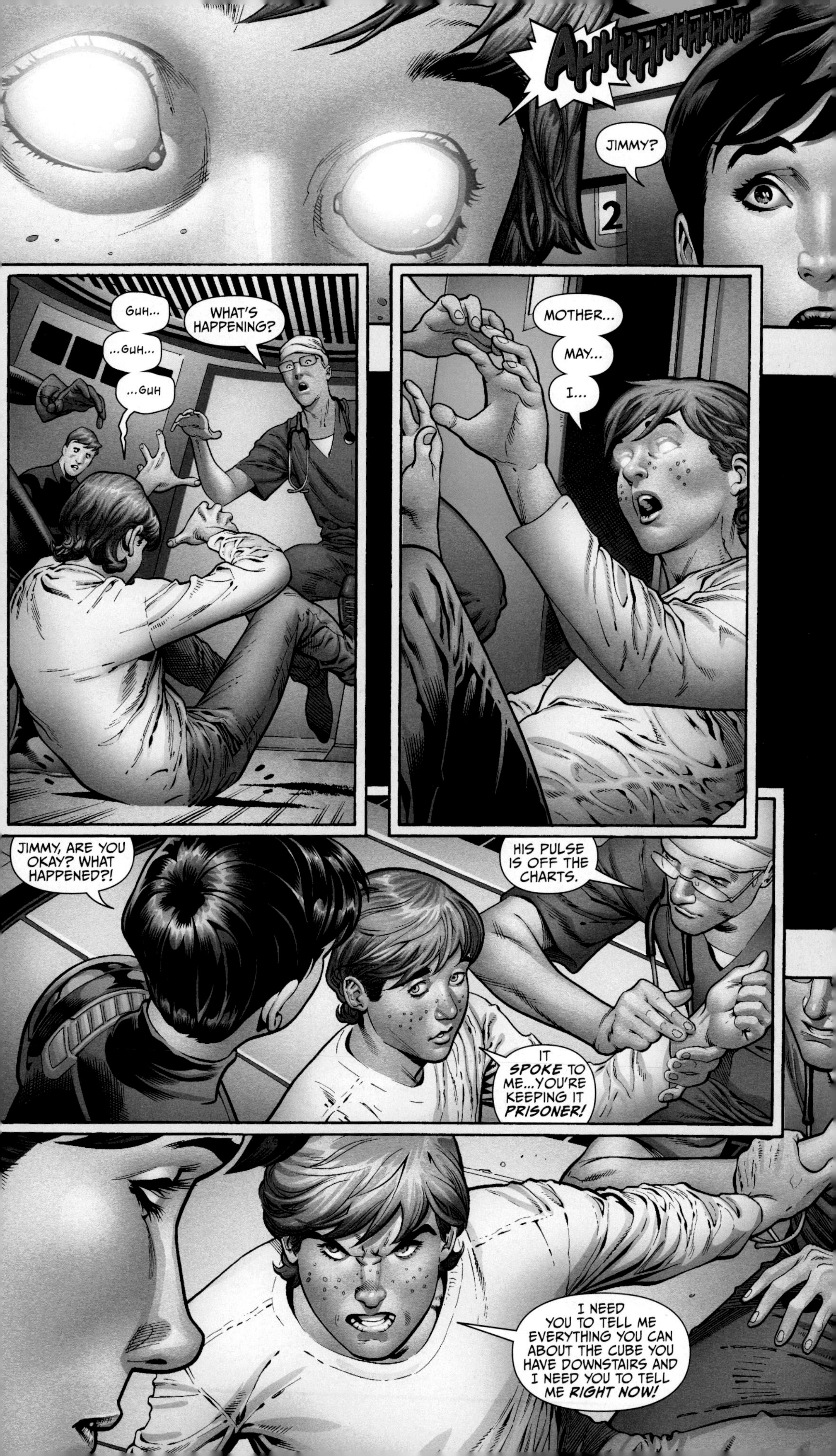
AHHHHHHHHHHHH
JIMMY?
2
GUH...
...GUH...
...GUH
WHAT'S HAPPENING?
MOTHER...
MAY...
I...
JIMMY, ARE YOU OKAY? WHAT HAPPENED?!
HIS PULSE IS OFF THE CHARTS.
IT SPOKE TO ME...YOU'RE KEEPING IT PRISONER!
I NEED YOU TO TELL ME EVERYTHING YOU CAN ABOUT THE CUBE YOU HAVE DOWNSTAIRS AND I NEED YOU TO TELL ME RIGHT NOW!

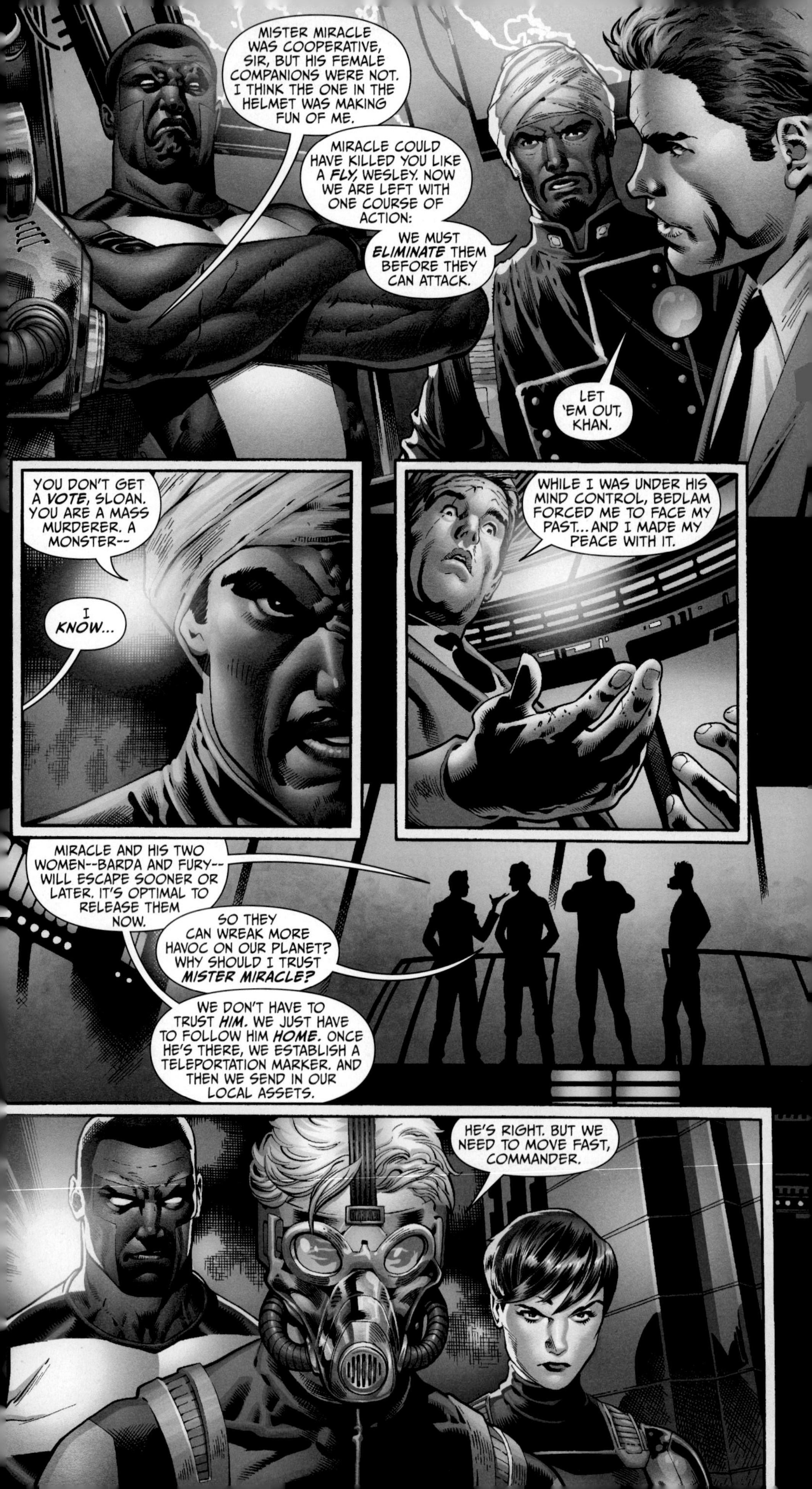
MISTER MIRACLE WAS COOPERATIVE, SIR, BUT HIS FEMALE COMPANIONS WERE NOT. I THINK THE ONE IN THE HELMET WAS MAKING FUN OF ME.
MIRACLE COULD HAVE KILLED YOU LIKE A FLY, WESLEY. NOW WE ARE LEFT WITH ONE COURSE OF ACTION:
WE MUST ELIMINATE THEM BEFORE THEY CAN ATTACK.
LET 'EM OUT, KHAN.
YOU DON'T GET A VOTE, SLOAN. YOU ARE A MASS MURDERER. A MONSTER--
I KNOW...
WHILE I WAS UNDER HIS MIND CONTROL, BEDLAM FORCED ME TO FACE MY PAST...AND I MADE MY PEACE WITH IT.
MIRACLE AND HIS TWO WOMEN--BARDA AND FURY--WILL ESCAPE SOONER OR LATER. IT'S OPTIMAL TO RELEASE THEM NOW.
SO THEY CAN WREAK MORE HAVOC ON OUR PLANET? WHY SHOULD I TRUST MISTER MIRACLE?
WE DON'T HAVE TO TRUST HIM. WE JUST HAVE TO FOLLOW HIM HOME. ONCE HE'S THERE, WE ESTABLISH A TELEPORTATION MARKER. AND THEN WE SEND IN OUR LOCAL ASSETS.
HE'S RIGHT. BUT WE NEED TO MOVE FAST, COMMANDER.

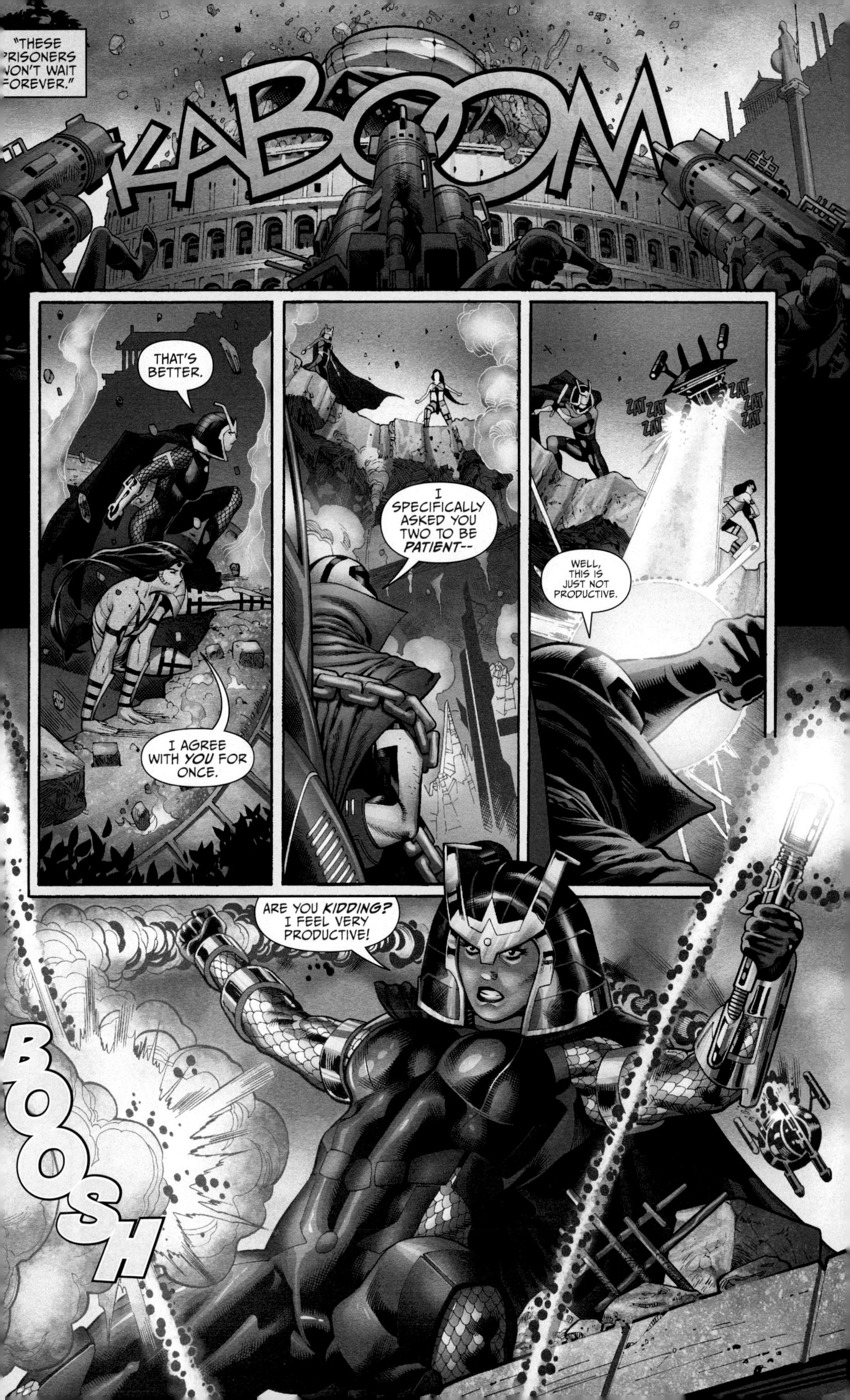
"THESE PRISONERS WON'T WAIT FOREVER."
KABOOM
THAT'S BETTER.
I AGREE WITH *YOU* FOR ONCE.
I SPECIFICALLY ASKED YOU TWO TO BE *PATIENT*--
ZAT ZAT ZAT
ZAT ZAT ZAT
WELL, THIS IS JUST NOT PRODUCTIVE.
ARE YOU *KIDDING?* I FEEL VERY PRODUCTIVE!
BOOOSH

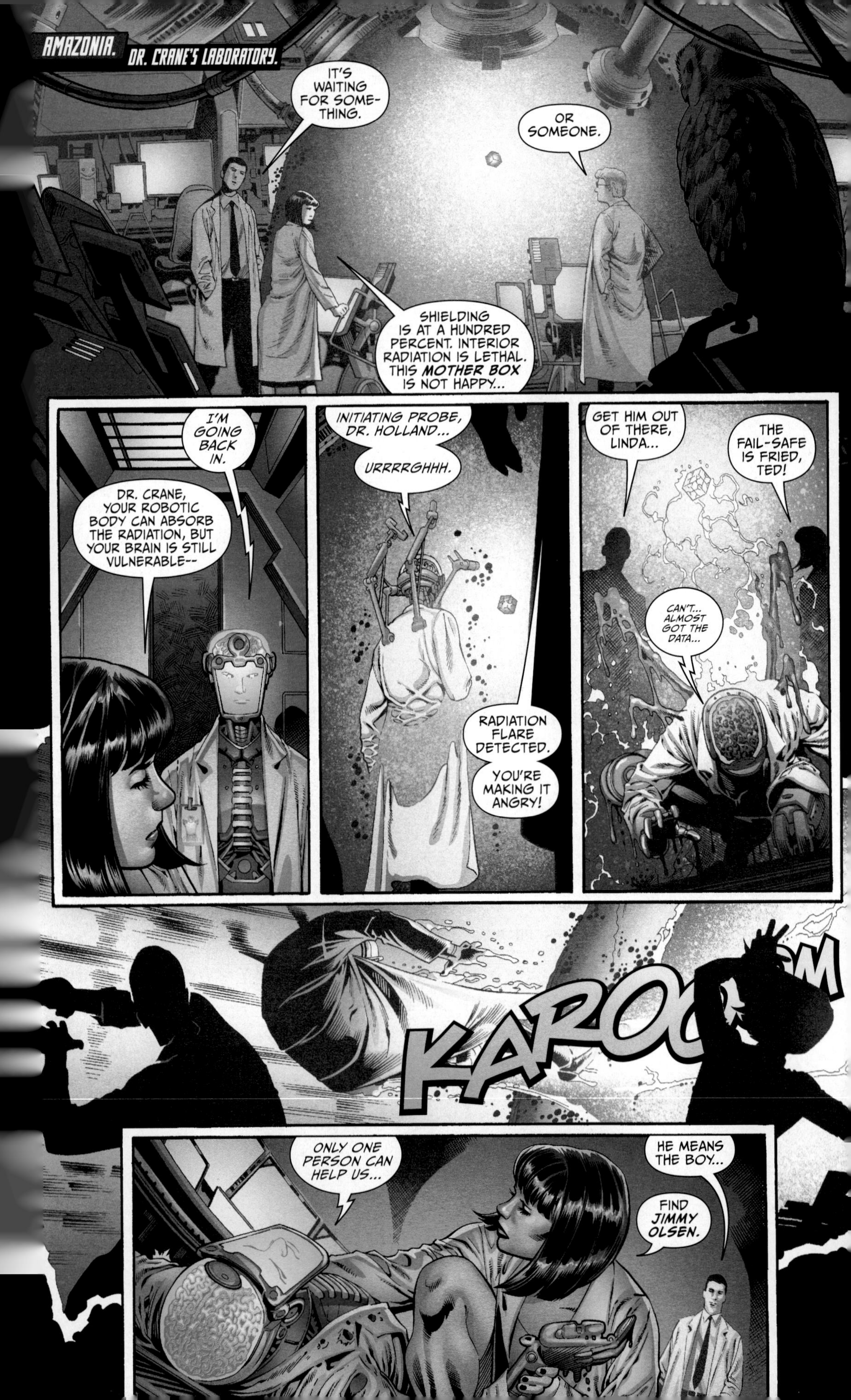
AMAZONIA.
DR. CRANE'S LABORATORY.
IT'S WAITING FOR SOME-THING.
OR SOMEONE.
SHIELDING IS AT A HUNDRED PERCENT. INTERIOR RADIATION IS LETHAL. THIS MOTHER BOX IS NOT HAPPY...
I'M GOING BACK IN.
DR. CRANE, YOUR ROBOTIC BODY CAN ABSORB THE RADIATION, BUT YOUR BRAIN IS STILL VULNERABLE--
INITIATING PROBE, DR. HOLLAND...
URRRRGHHH.
RADIATION FLARE DETECTED.
YOU'RE MAKING IT ANGRY!
GET HIM OUT OF THERE, LINDA...
THE FAIL-SAFE IS FRIED, TED!
CAN'T... ALMOST GOT THE DATA...
KAROOOOM
ONLY ONE PERSON CAN HELP US...
HE MEANS THE BOY...
FIND JIMMY OLSEN.

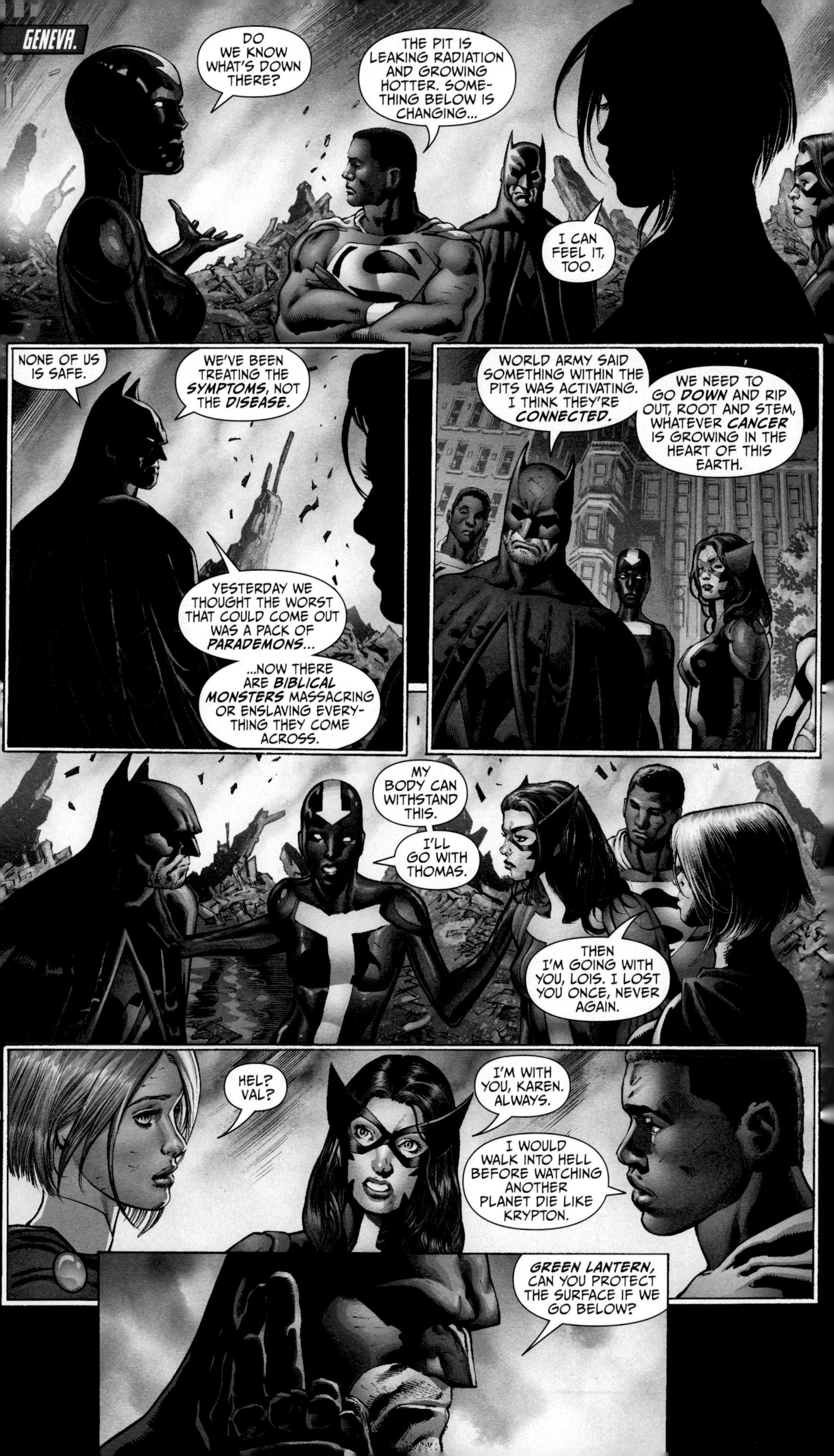
GENEVA.
DO WE KNOW WHAT'S DOWN THERE?
THE PIT IS LEAKING RADIATION AND GROWING HOTTER. SOMETHING BELOW IS CHANGING...
I CAN FEEL IT, TOO.
NONE OF US IS SAFE.
WE'VE BEEN TREATING THE SYMPTOMS, NOT THE DISEASE.
YESTERDAY WE THOUGHT THE WORST THAT COULD COME OUT WAS A PACK OF PARADEMONS...
...NOW THERE ARE BIBLICAL MONSTERS MASSACRING OR ENSLAVING EVERYTHING THEY COME ACROSS.
WORLD ARMY SAID SOMETHING WITHIN THE PITS WAS ACTIVATING. I THINK THEY'RE CONNECTED.
WE NEED TO GO DOWN AND RIP OUT, ROOT AND STEM, WHATEVER CANCER IS GROWING IN THE HEART OF THIS EARTH.
MY BODY CAN WITHSTAND THIS.
I'LL GO WITH THOMAS.
THEN I'M GOING WITH YOU, LOIS. I LOST YOU ONCE, NEVER AGAIN.
HEL? VAL?
I'M WITH YOU, KAREN. ALWAYS.
I WOULD WALK INTO HELL BEFORE WATCHING ANOTHER PLANET DIE LIKE KRYPTON.
GREEN LANTERN, CAN YOU PROTECT THE SURFACE IF WE GO BELOW?

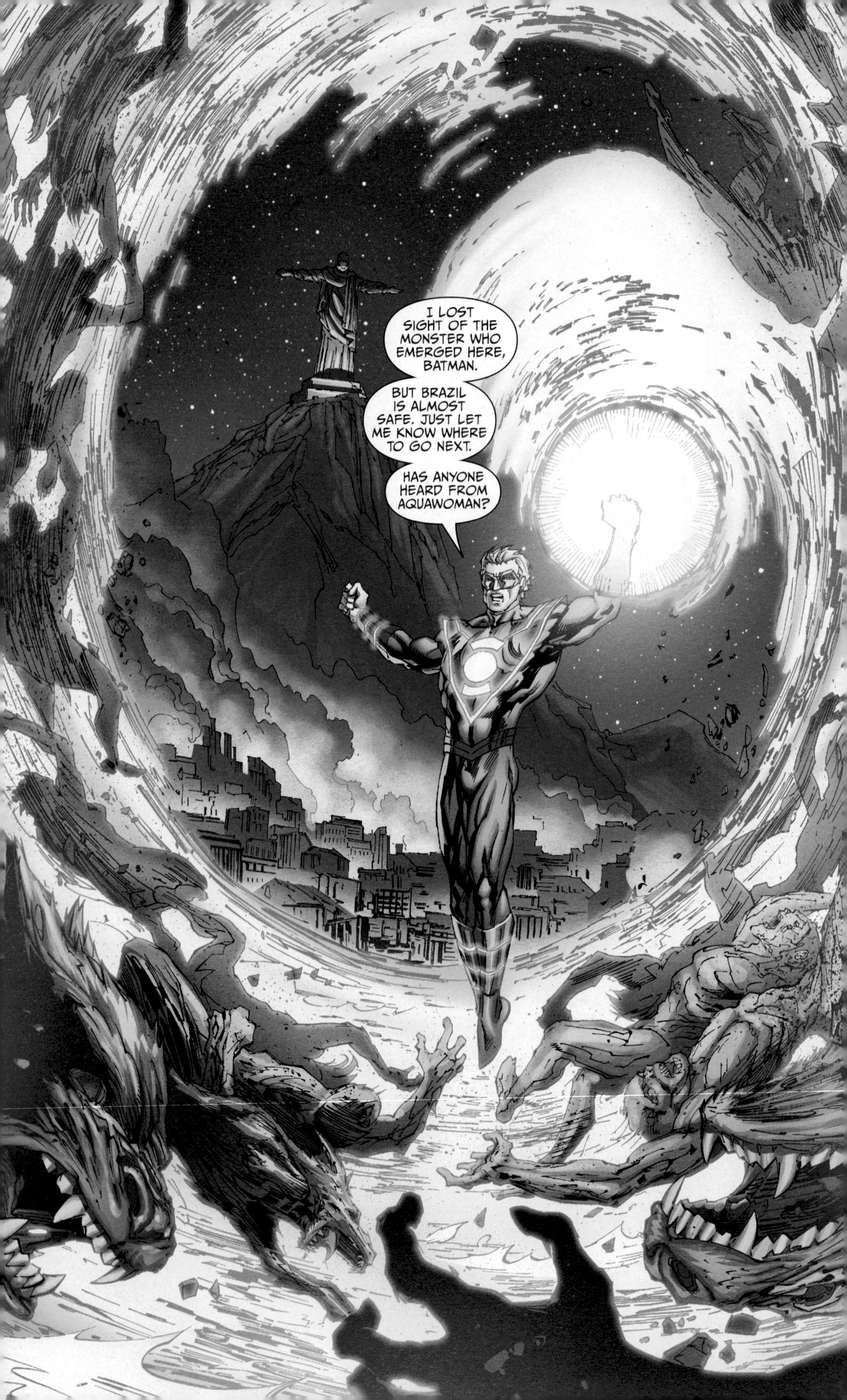
I LOST SIGHT OF THE MONSTER WHO EMERGED HERE, BATMAN.
BUT BRAZIL IS ALMOST SAFE. JUST LET ME KNOW WHERE TO GO NEXT.
HAS ANYONE HEARD FROM AQUAWOMAN?

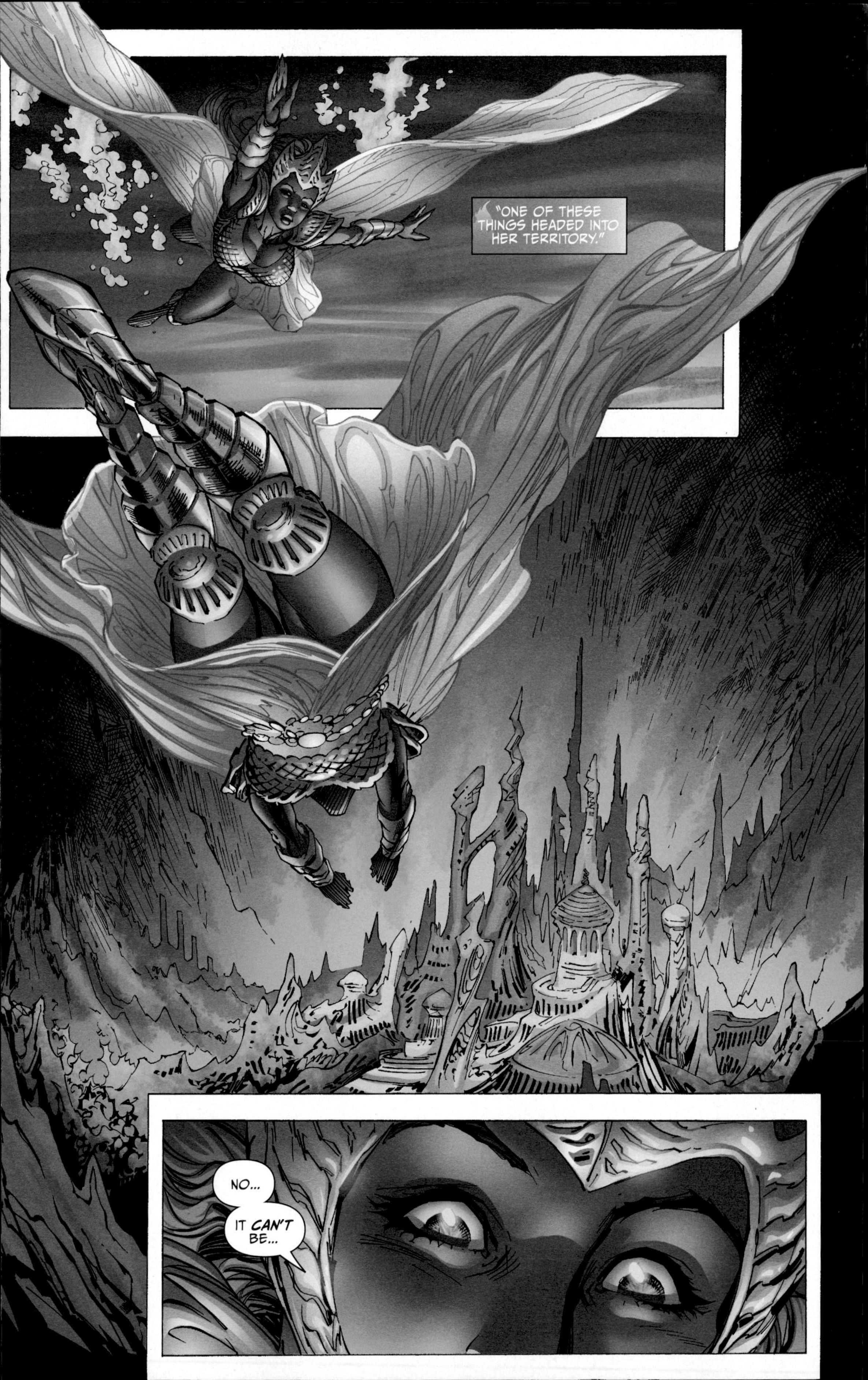
"ONE OF THESE THINGS HEADED INTO HER TERRITORY."
NO...
IT CAN'T BE...

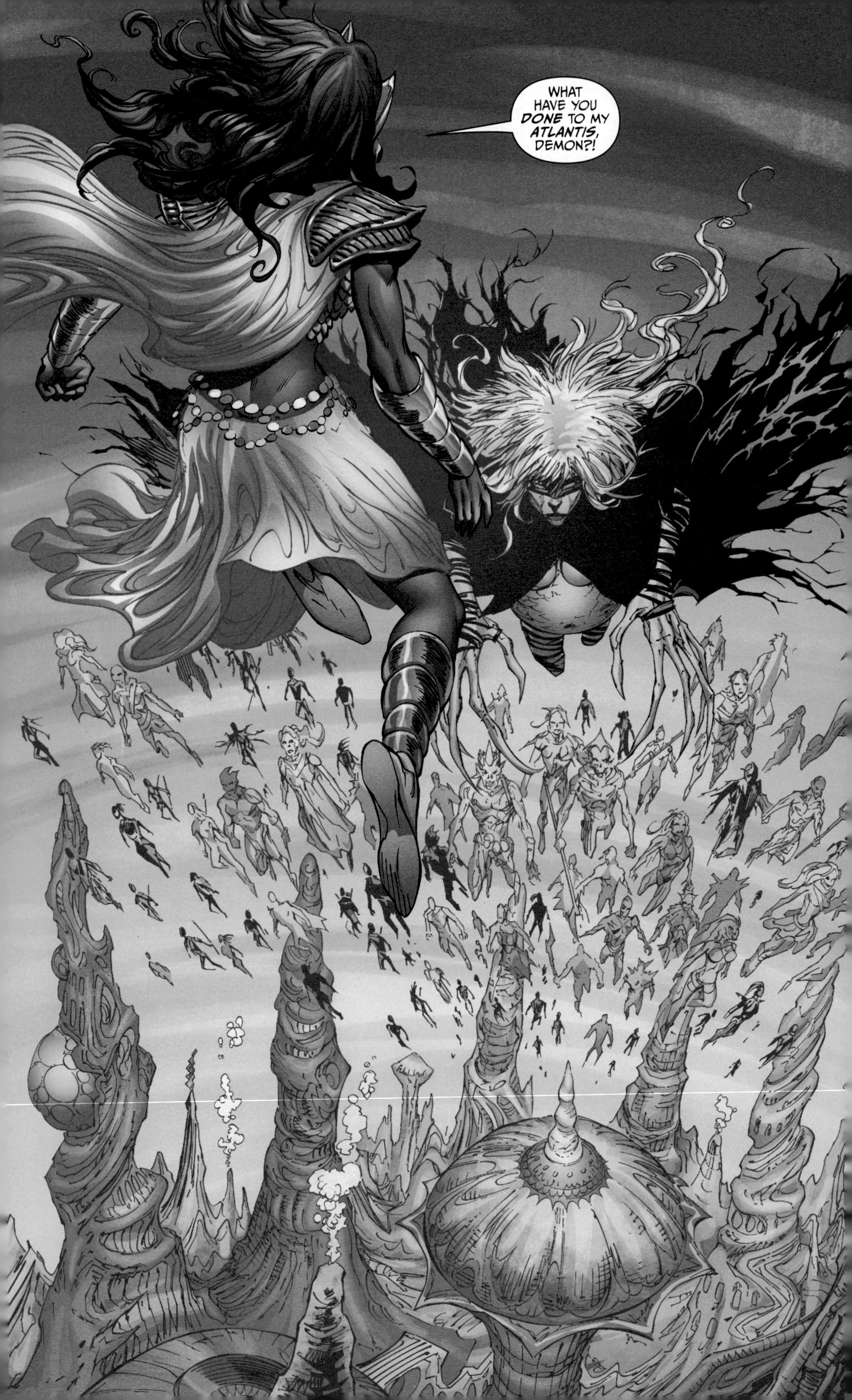
WHAT HAVE YOU DONE TO MY ATLANTIS, DEMON?!

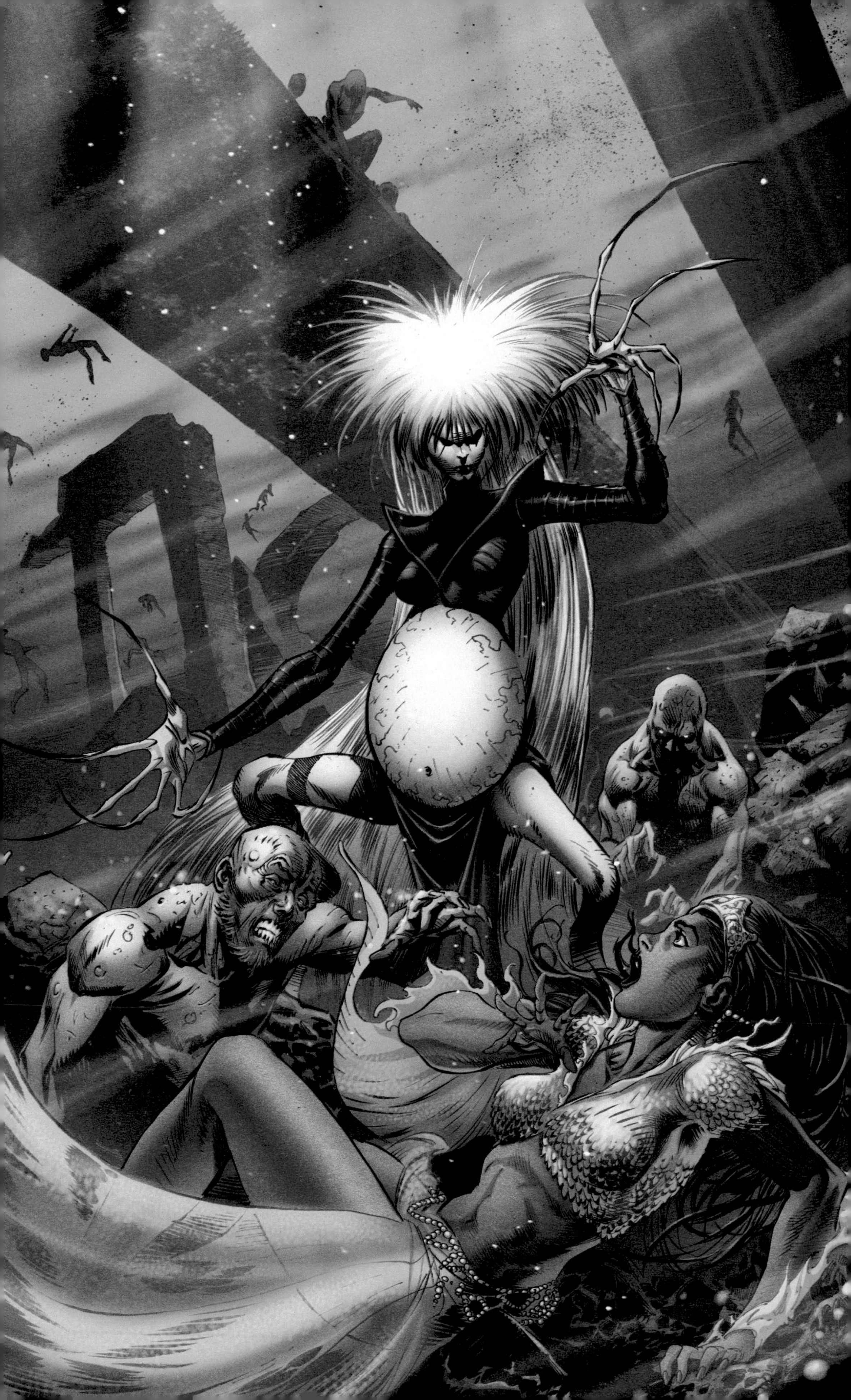

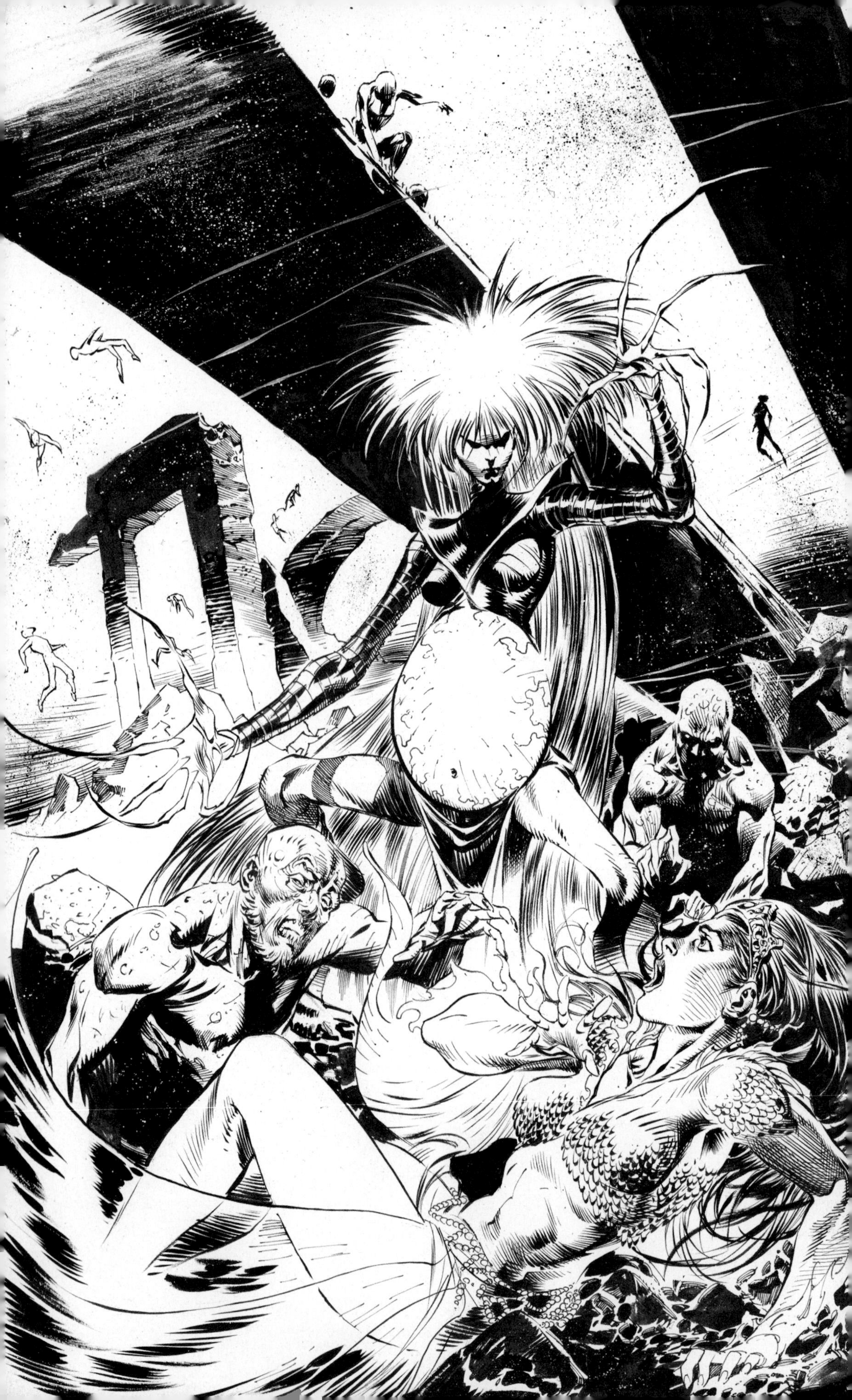

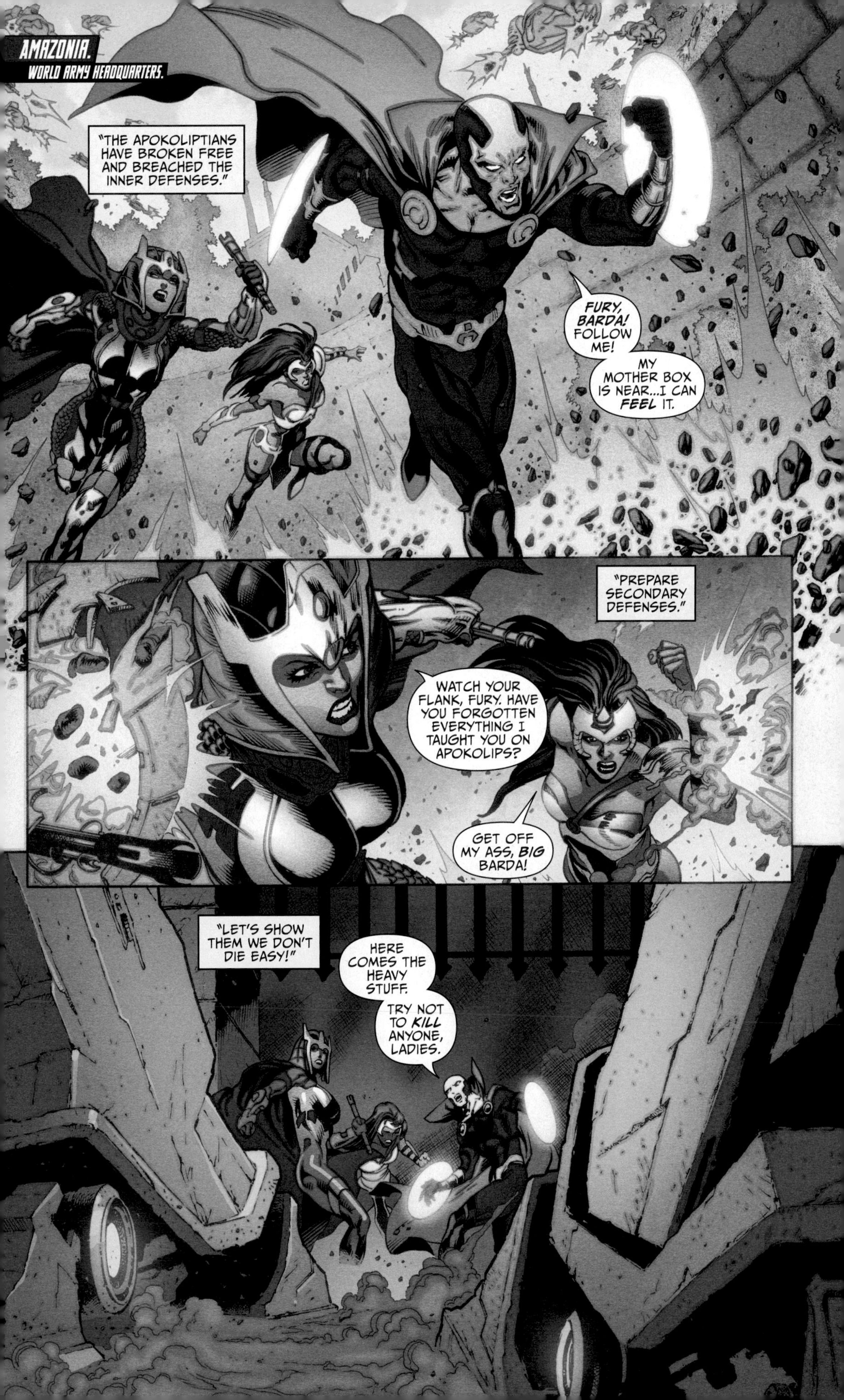

AMAZONIA.
WORLD ARMY HEADQUARTERS.
"THE APOKOLIPTIANS HAVE BROKEN FREE AND BREACHED THE INNER DEFENSES."
FURY, BARDA! FOLLOW ME!
MY MOTHER BOX IS NEAR...I CAN FEEL IT.
"PREPARE SECONDARY DEFENSES."
WATCH YOUR FLANK, FURY. HAVE YOU FORGOTTEN EVERYTHING I TAUGHT YOU ON APOKOLIPS?
GET OFF MY ASS, BIG BARDA!
"LET'S SHOW THEM WE DON'T DIE EASY!"
HERE COMES THE HEAVY STUFF.
TRY NOT TO KILL ANYONE, LADIES.

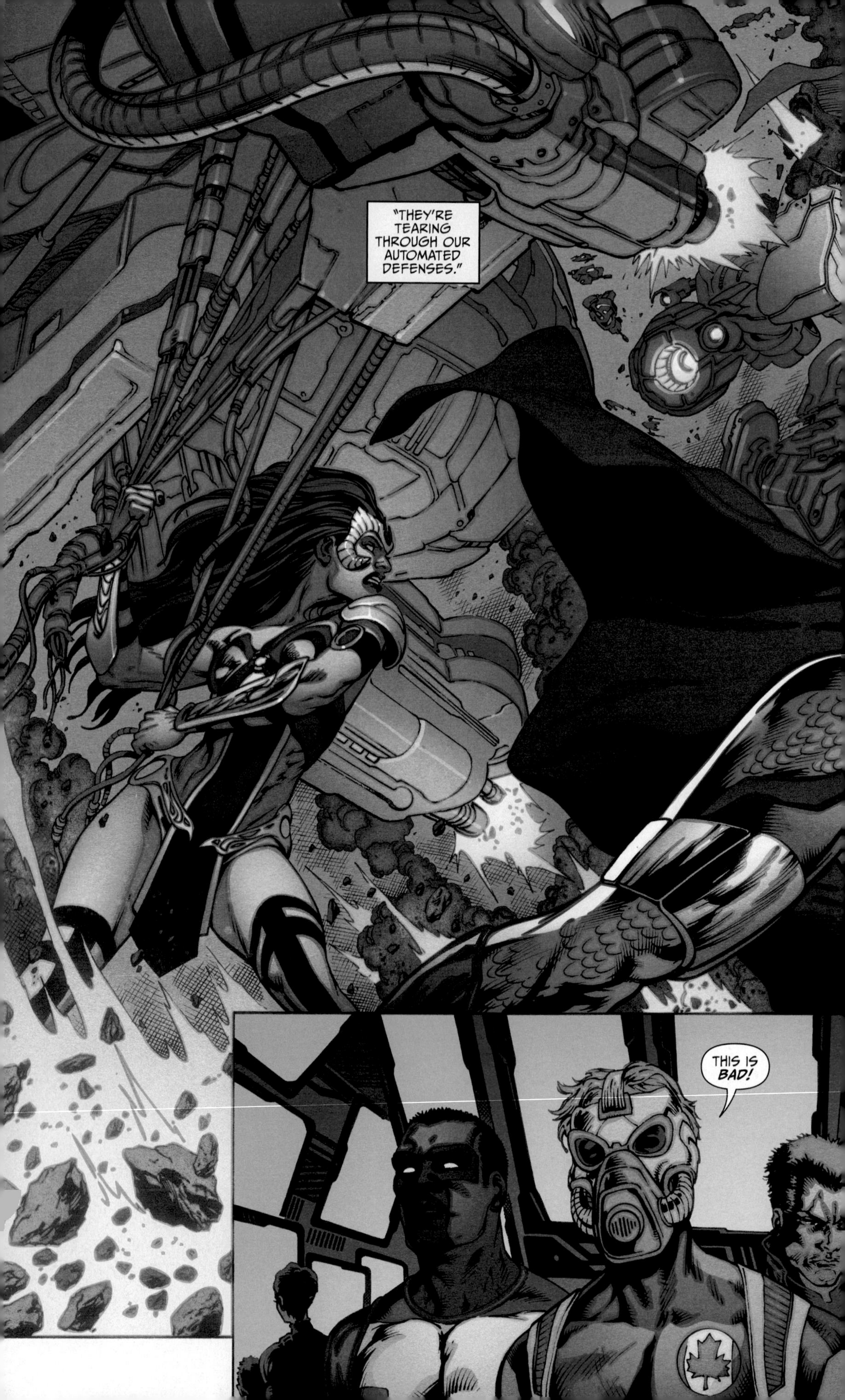
"THEY'RE TEARING THROUGH OUR AUTOMATED DEFENSES."
THIS IS BAD!

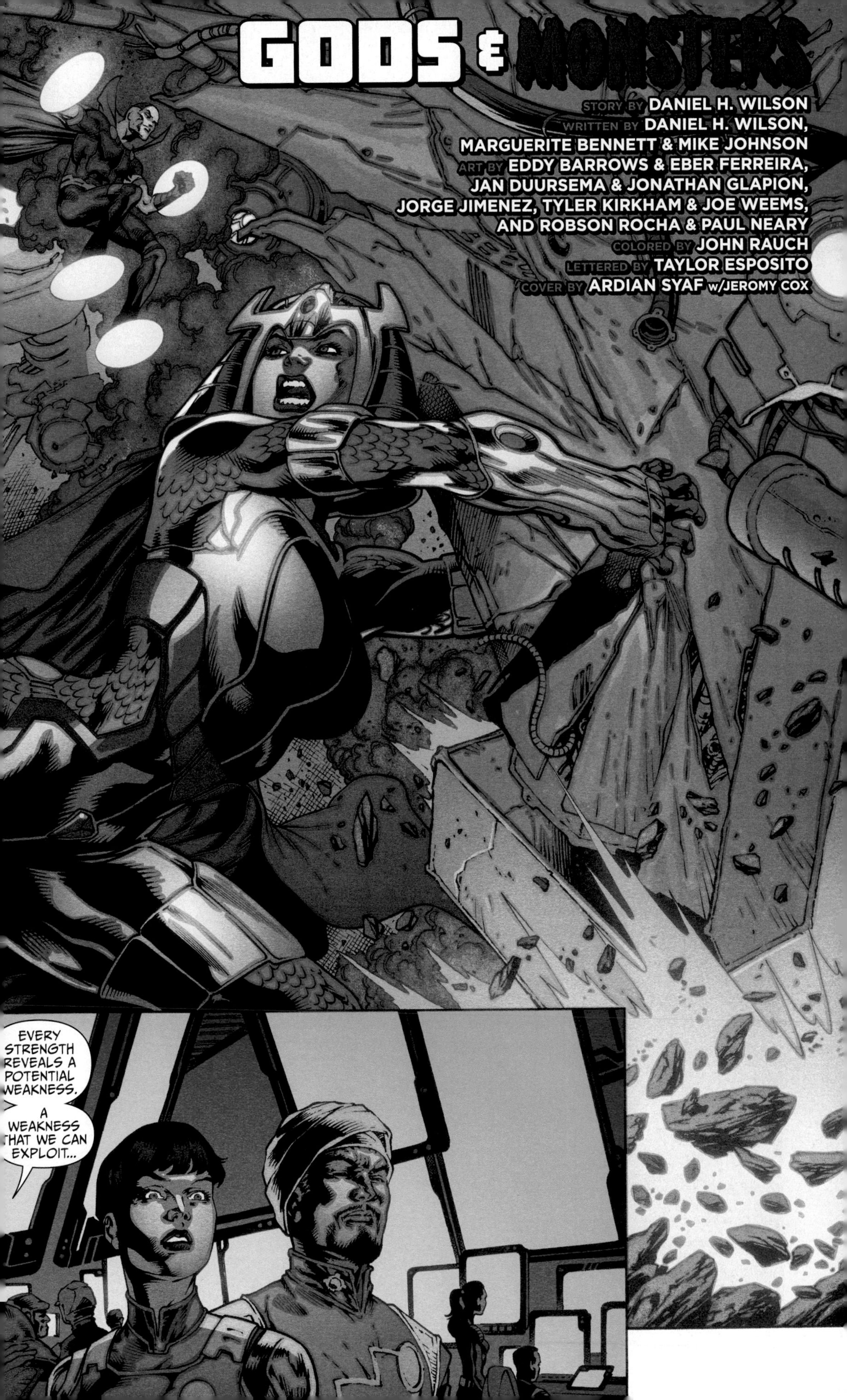
GODS & MONSTERS
STORY BY DANIEL H. WILSON
WRITTEN BY DANIEL H. WILSON, MARGUERITE BENNETT & MIKE JOHNSON
ART BY EDDY BARROWS & EBER FERREIRA, JAN DUURSEMA & JONATHAN GLAPION, JORGE JIMENEZ, TYLER KIRKHAM & JOE WEEMS, AND ROBSON ROCHA & PAUL NEARY
COLORED BY JOHN RAUCH
LETTERED BY TAYLOR ESPOSITO
COVER BY ARDIAN SYAF w/JEROMY COX
EVERY STRENGTH REVEALS A POTENTIAL WEAKNESS.
A WEAKNESS THAT WE CAN EXPLOIT...

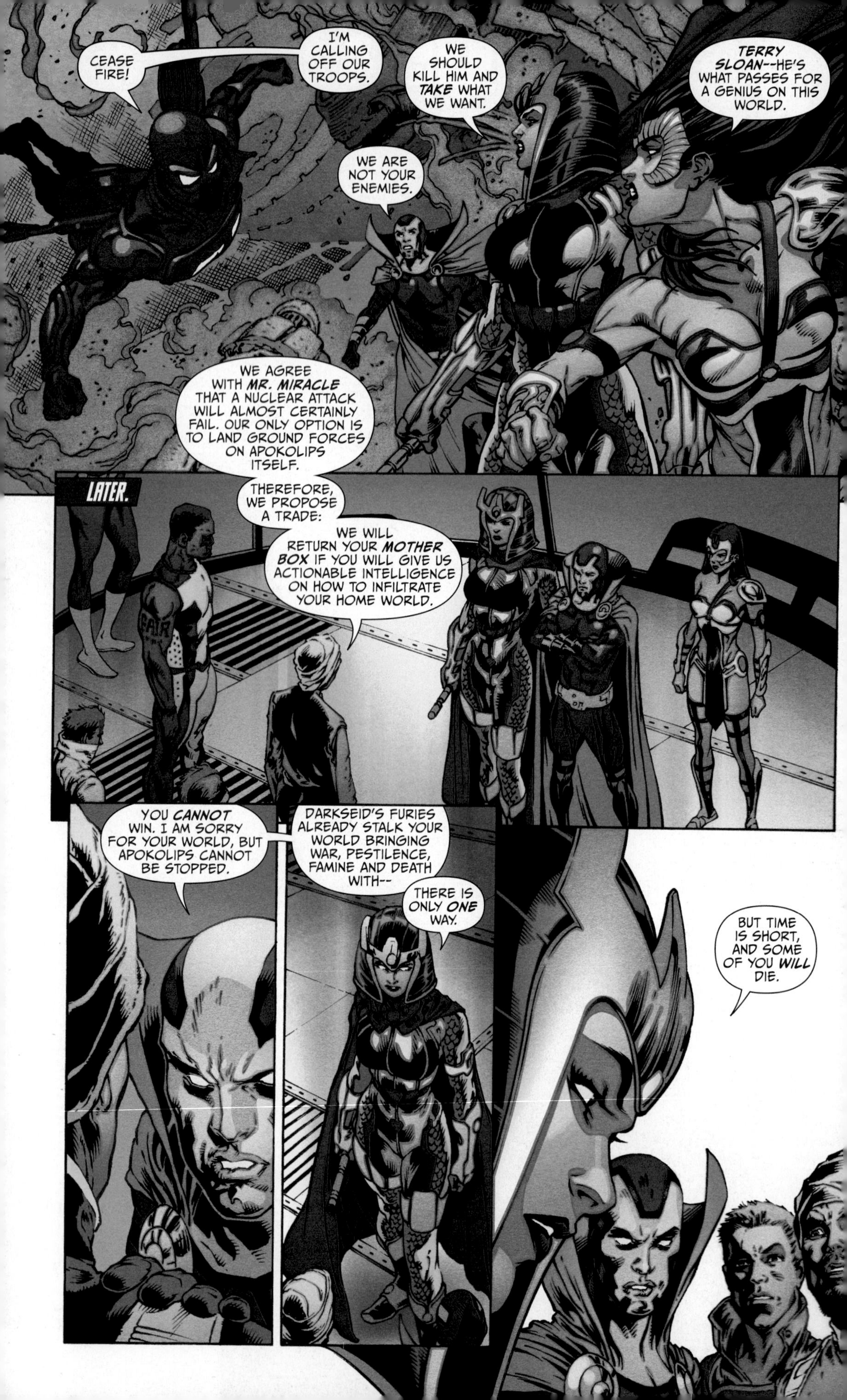
CEASE FIRE!
I'M CALLING OFF OUR TROOPS.
WE SHOULD KILL HIM AND TAKE WHAT WE WANT.
TERRY SLOAN--HE'S WHAT PASSES FOR A GENIUS ON THIS WORLD.
WE ARE NOT YOUR ENEMIES.
WE AGREE WITH MR. MIRACLE THAT A NUCLEAR ATTACK WILL ALMOST CERTAINLY FAIL. OUR ONLY OPTION IS TO LAND GROUND FORCES ON APOKOLIPS ITSELF.
LATER.
THEREFORE, WE PROPOSE A TRADE:
WE WILL RETURN YOUR MOTHER BOX IF YOU WILL GIVE US ACTIONABLE INTELLIGENCE ON HOW TO INFILTRATE YOUR HOME WORLD.
YOU CANNOT WIN. I AM SORRY FOR YOUR WORLD, BUT APOKOLIPS CANNOT BE STOPPED.
DARKSEID'S FURIES ALREADY STALK YOUR WORLD BRINGING WAR, PESTILENCE, FAMINE AND DEATH WITH--
THERE IS ONLY ONE WAY.
BUT TIME IS SHORT, AND SOME OF YOU WILL DIE.

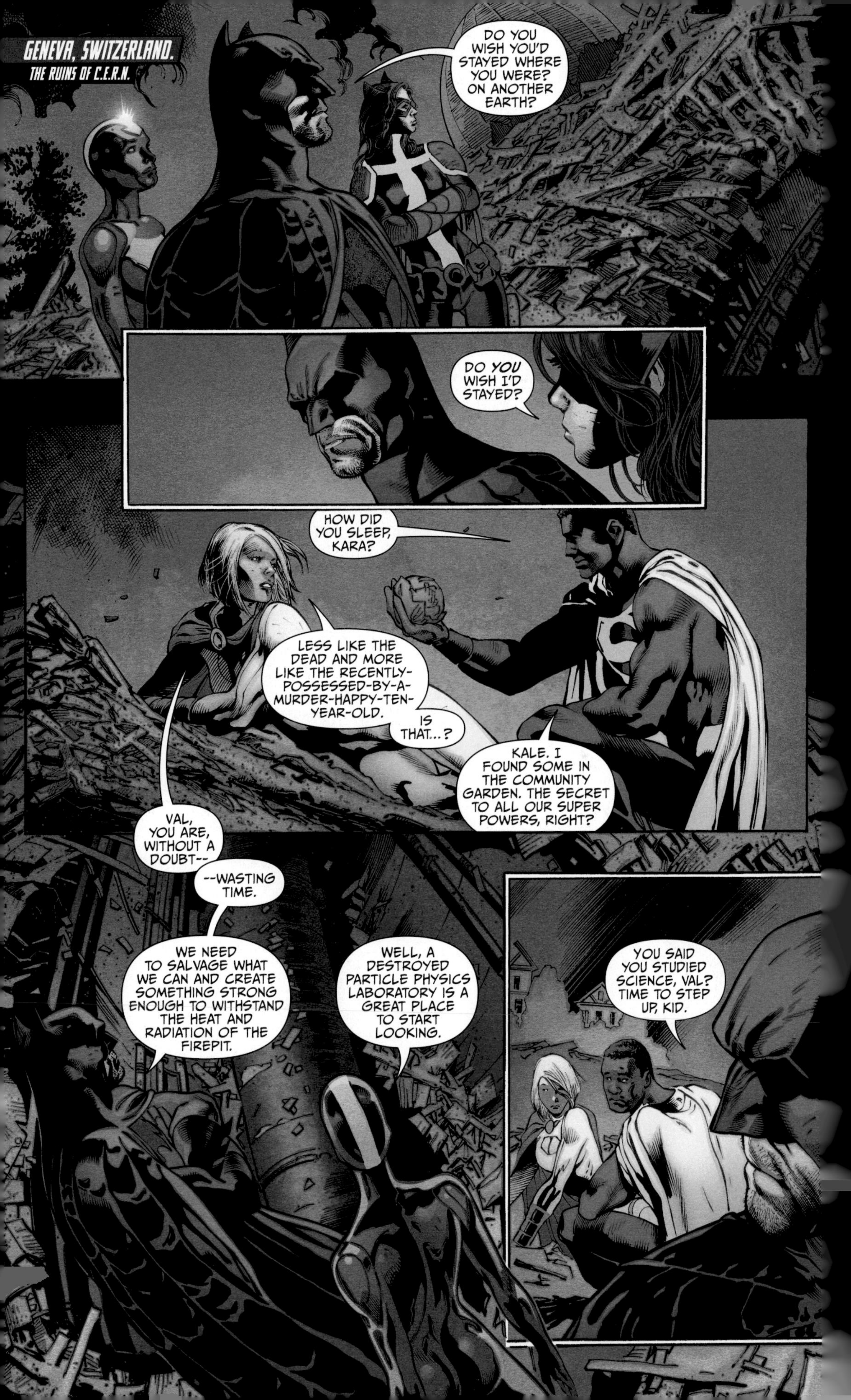
GENEVA, SWITZERLAND.
THE RUINS OF C.E.R.N.
DO YOU WISH YOU'D STAYED WHERE YOU WERE? ON ANOTHER EARTH?
DO *YOU* WISH I'D STAYED?
HOW DID YOU SLEEP, KARA?
LESS LIKE THE DEAD AND MORE LIKE THE RECENTLY-POSSESSED-BY-A-MURDER-HAPPY-TEN-YEAR-OLD.
IS THAT...?
KALE. I FOUND SOME IN THE COMMUNITY GARDEN. THE SECRET TO ALL OUR SUPER POWERS, RIGHT?
VAL, YOU ARE, WITHOUT A DOUBT--
--WASTING TIME.
WE NEED TO SALVAGE WHAT WE CAN AND CREATE SOMETHING STRONG ENOUGH TO WITHSTAND THE HEAT AND RADIATION OF THE FIREPIT.
WELL, A DESTROYED PARTICLE PHYSICS LABORATORY IS A GREAT PLACE TO START LOOKING.
YOU SAID YOU STUDIED SCIENCE, VAL? TIME TO STEP UP, KID.

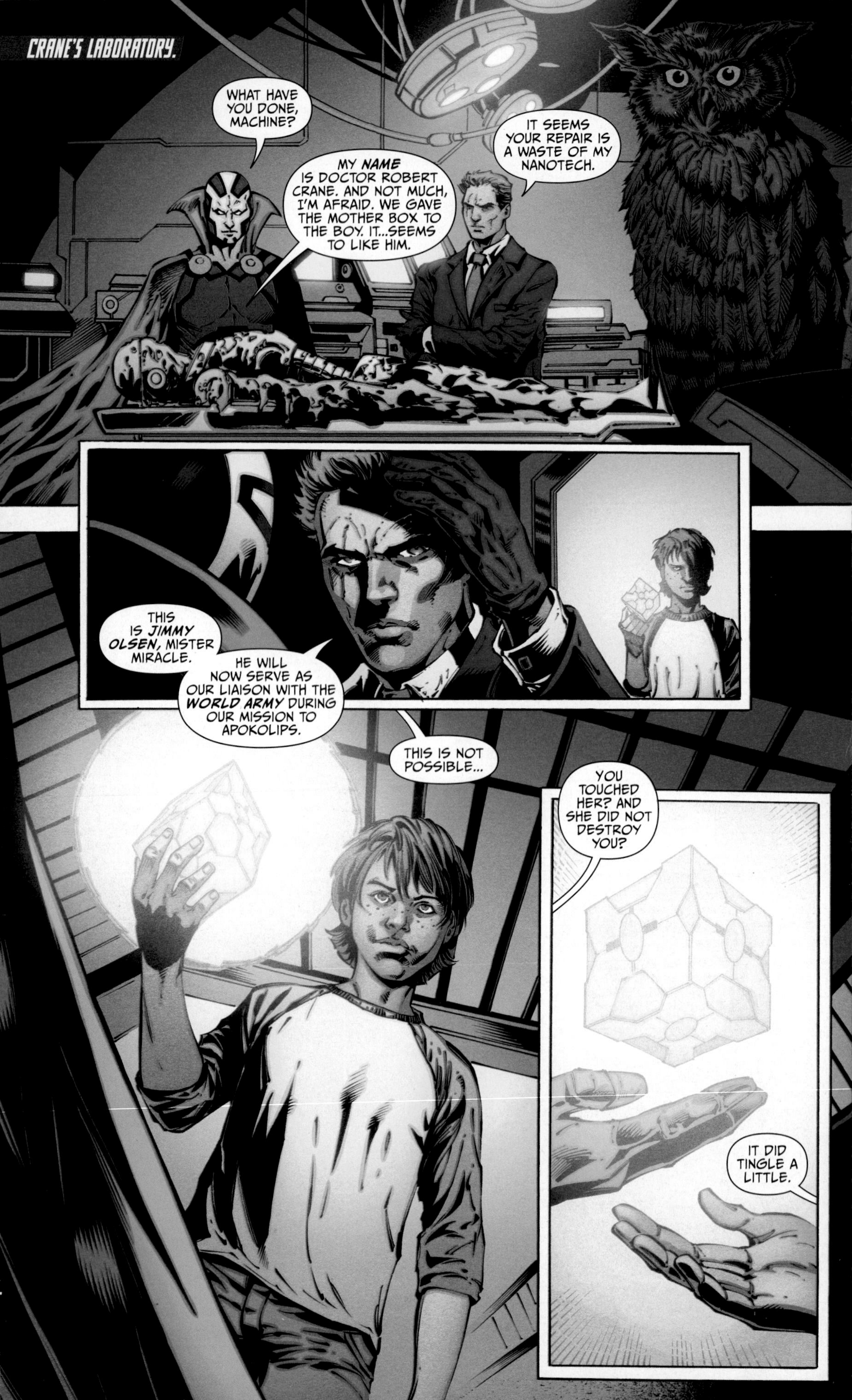
CRANE'S LABORATORY.
WHAT HAVE YOU DONE, MACHINE?
MY NAME IS DOCTOR ROBERT CRANE. AND NOT MUCH, I'M AFRAID. WE GAVE THE MOTHER BOX TO THE BOY. IT...SEEMS TO LIKE HIM.
IT SEEMS YOUR REPAIR IS A WASTE OF MY NANOTECH.
THIS IS JIMMY OLSEN, MISTER MIRACLE.
HE WILL NOW SERVE AS OUR LIAISON WITH THE WORLD ARMY DURING OUR MISSION TO APOKOLIPS.
THIS IS NOT POSSIBLE...
YOU TOUCHED HER? AND SHE DID NOT DESTROY YOU?
IT DID TINGLE A LITTLE.

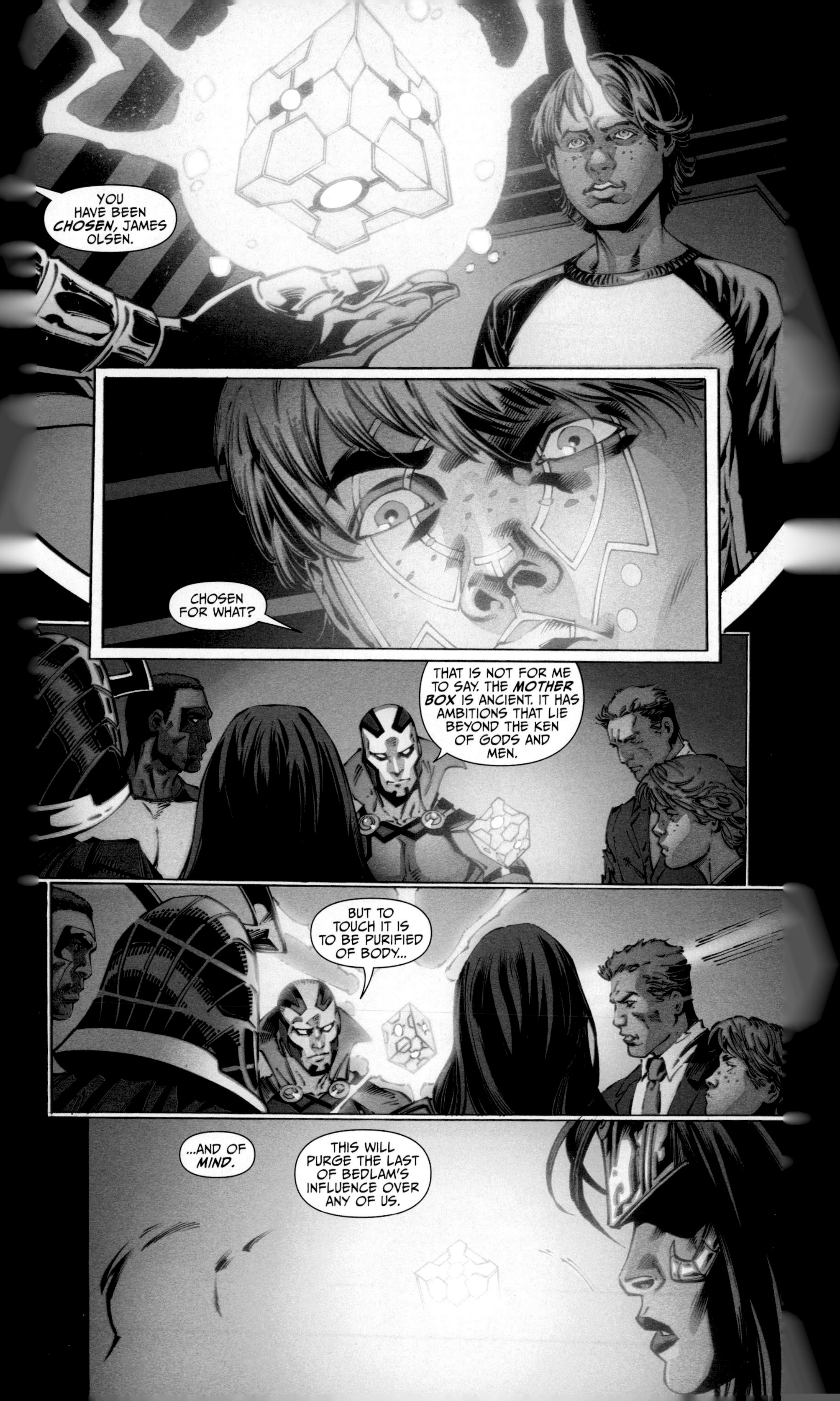

YOU HAVE BEEN CHOSEN, JAMES OLSEN.
CHOSEN FOR WHAT?
THAT IS NOT FOR ME TO SAY. THE MOTHER BOX IS ANCIENT. IT HAS AMBITIONS THAT LIE BEYOND THE KEN OF GODS AND MEN.
BUT TO TOUCH IT IS TO BE PURIFIED OF BODY...
...AND OF MIND.
THIS WILL PURGE THE LAST OF BEDLAM'S INFLUENCE OVER ANY OF US.

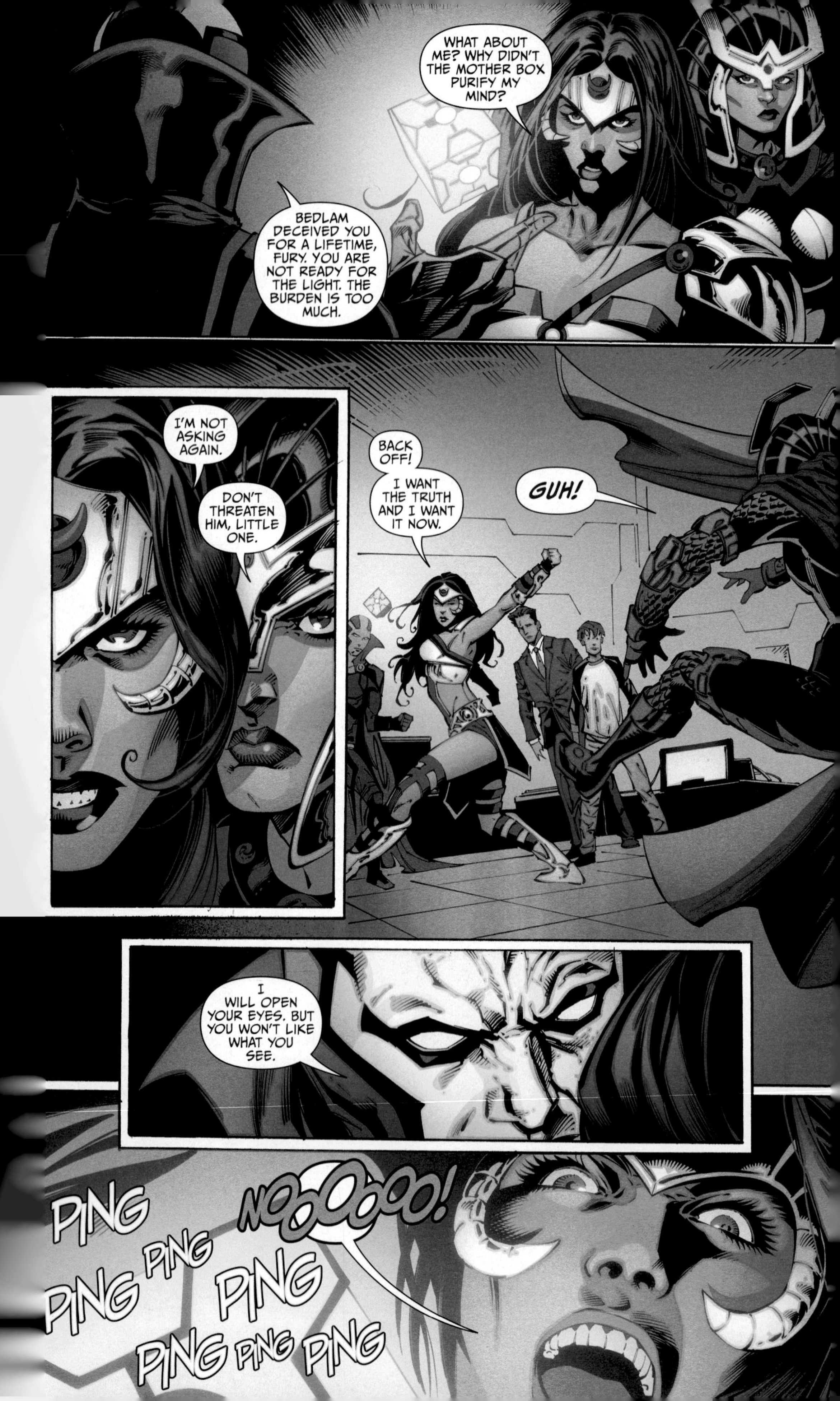
WHAT ABOUT ME? WHY DIDN'T THE MOTHER BOX PURIFY MY MIND?
BEDLAM DECEIVED YOU FOR A LIFETIME, FURY. YOU ARE NOT READY FOR THE LIGHT. THE BURDEN IS TOO MUCH.
I'M NOT ASKING AGAIN.
DON'T THREATEN HIM, LITTLE ONE.
BACK OFF!
I WANT THE TRUTH AND I WANT IT NOW.
GUH!
I WILL OPEN YOUR EYES. BUT YOU WON'T LIKE WHAT YOU SEE.
NOOOOOOO!
PING PING PING PING PING PING PING PING

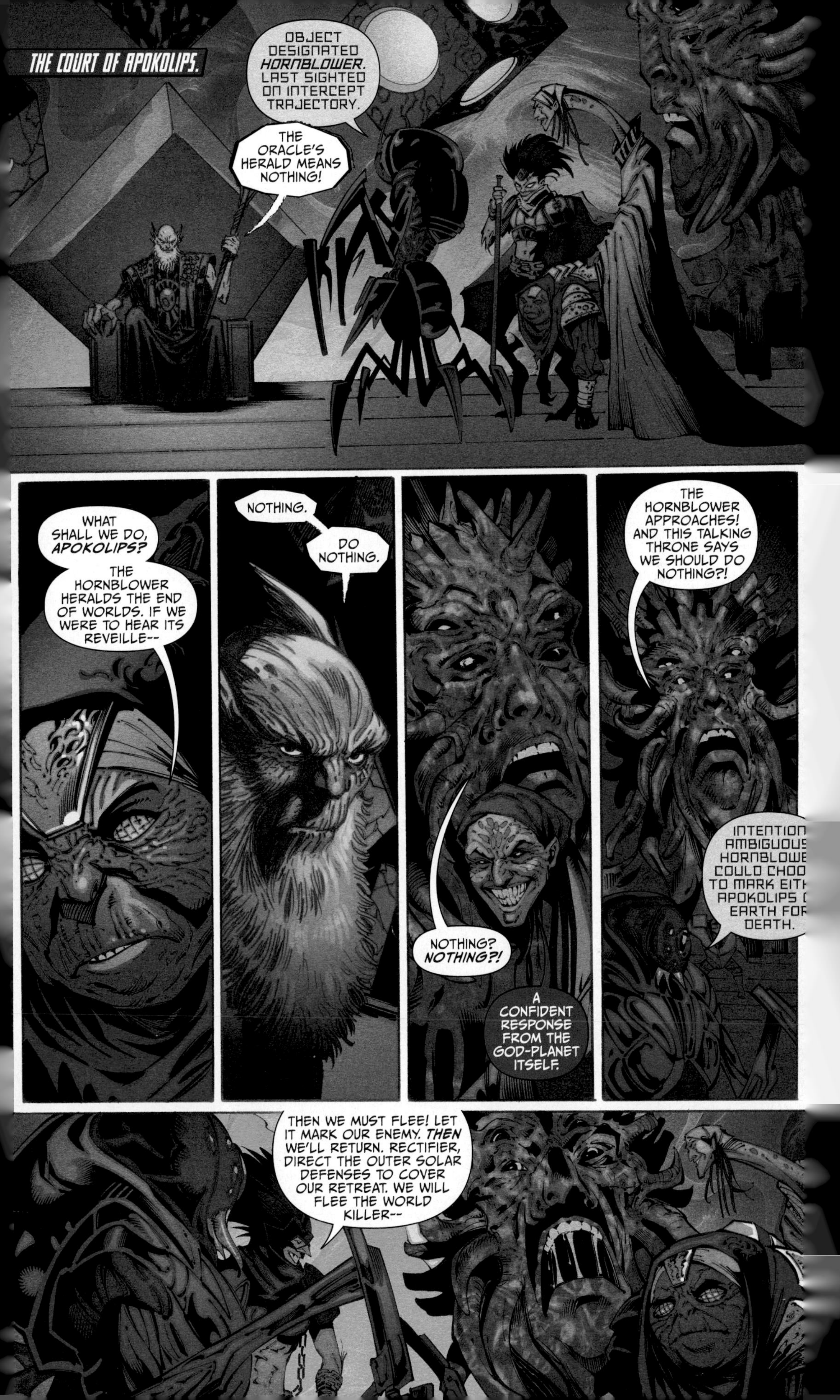
THE COURT OF APOKOLIPS.
OBJECT DESIGNATED HORNBLOWER. LAST SIGHTED ON INTERCEPT TRAJECTORY.
THE ORACLE'S HERALD MEANS NOTHING!
WHAT SHALL WE DO, APOKOLIPS?
THE HORNBLOWER HERALDS THE END OF WORLDS. IF WE WERE TO HEAR ITS REVEILLE--
NOTHING.
DO NOTHING.
NOTHING? NOTHING?!
A CONFIDENT RESPONSE FROM THE GOD-PLANET ITSELF.
THE HORNBLOWER APPROACHES! AND THIS TALKING THRONE SAYS WE SHOULD DO NOTHING?!
INTENTION AMBIGUOUS. HORNBLOWER COULD CHOOSE TO MARK EITHER APOKOLIPS OR EARTH FOR DEATH.
THEN WE MUST FLEE! LET IT MARK OUR ENEMY. THEN WE'LL RETURN. RECTIFIER, DIRECT THE OUTER SOLAR DEFENSES TO COVER OUR RETREAT. WE WILL FLEE THE WORLD KILLER--

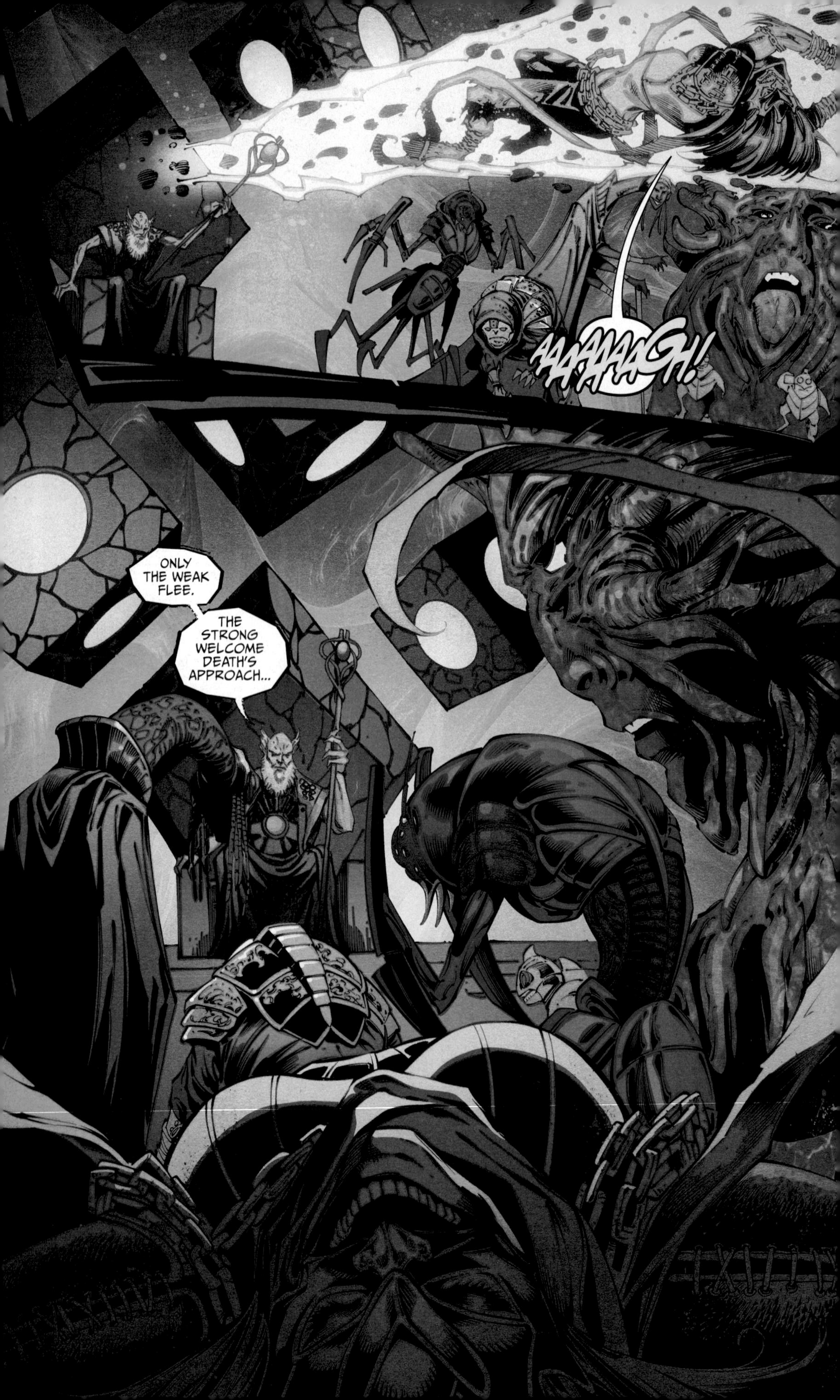
AAAAAAAAGH!
ONLY THE WEAK FLEE.
THE STRONG WELCOME DEATH'S APPROACH...

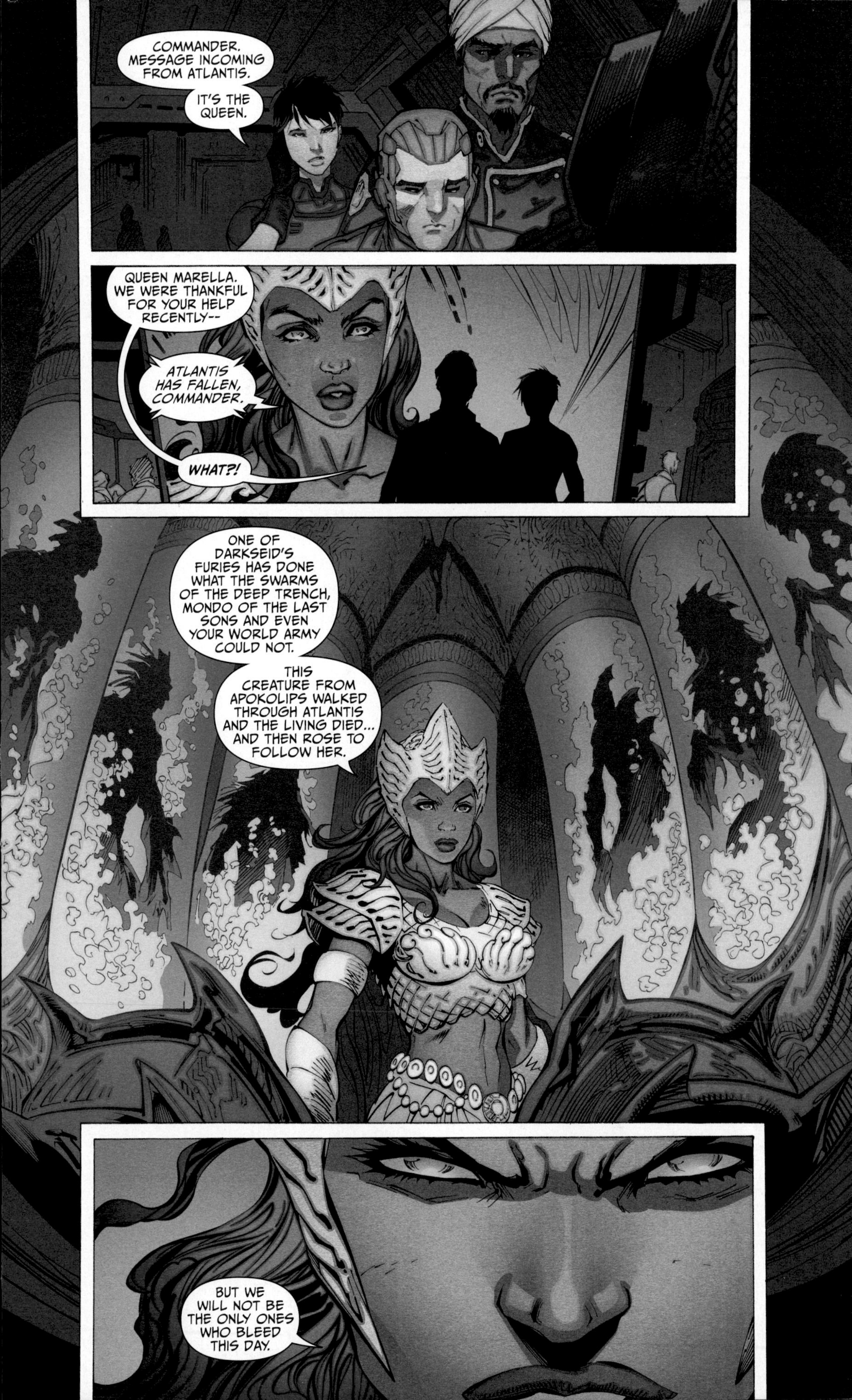
COMMANDER. MESSAGE INCOMING FROM ATLANTIS.
IT'S THE QUEEN.
QUEEN MARELLA. WE WERE THANKFUL FOR YOUR HELP RECENTLY--
ATLANTIS HAS FALLEN, COMMANDER.
WHAT?!
ONE OF DARKSEID'S FURIES HAS DONE WHAT THE SWARMS OF THE DEEP TRENCH, MONDO OF THE LAST SONS AND EVEN YOUR WORLD ARMY COULD NOT.
THIS CREATURE FROM APOKOLIPS WALKED THROUGH ATLANTIS AND THE LIVING DIED... AND THEN ROSE TO FOLLOW HER.
BUT WE WILL NOT BE THE ONLY ONES WHO BLEED THIS DAY.

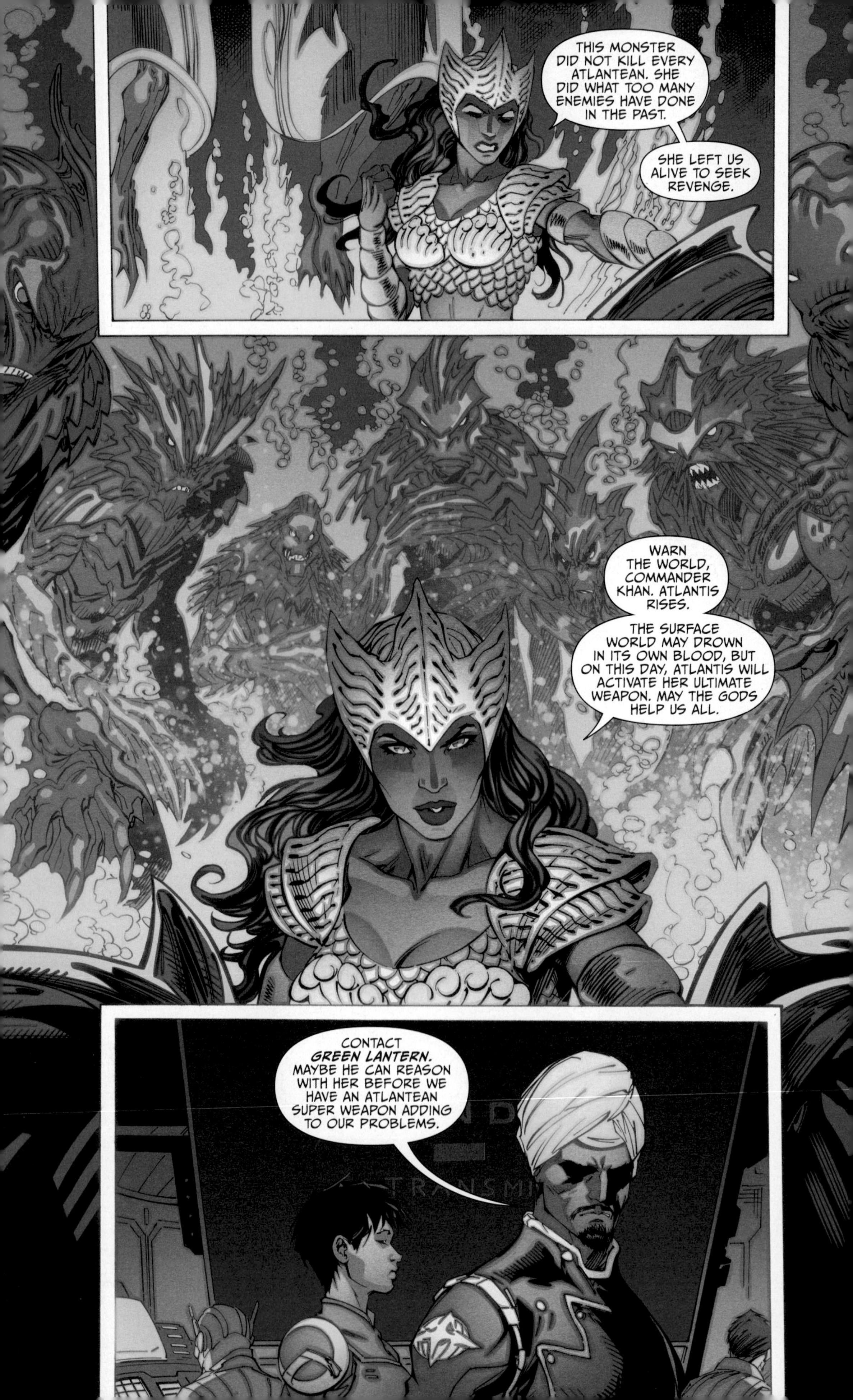
THIS MONSTER DID NOT KILL EVERY ATLANTEAN. SHE DID WHAT TOO MANY ENEMIES HAVE DONE IN THE PAST.
SHE LEFT US ALIVE TO SEEK REVENGE.
WARN THE WORLD, COMMANDER KHAN. ATLANTIS RISES.
THE SURFACE WORLD MAY DROWN IN ITS OWN BLOOD, BUT ON THIS DAY, ATLANTIS WILL ACTIVATE HER ULTIMATE WEAPON. MAY THE GODS HELP US ALL.
CONTACT *GREEN LANTERN.* MAYBE HE CAN REASON WITH HER BEFORE WE HAVE AN ATLANTEAN SUPER WEAPON ADDING TO OUR PROBLEMS.

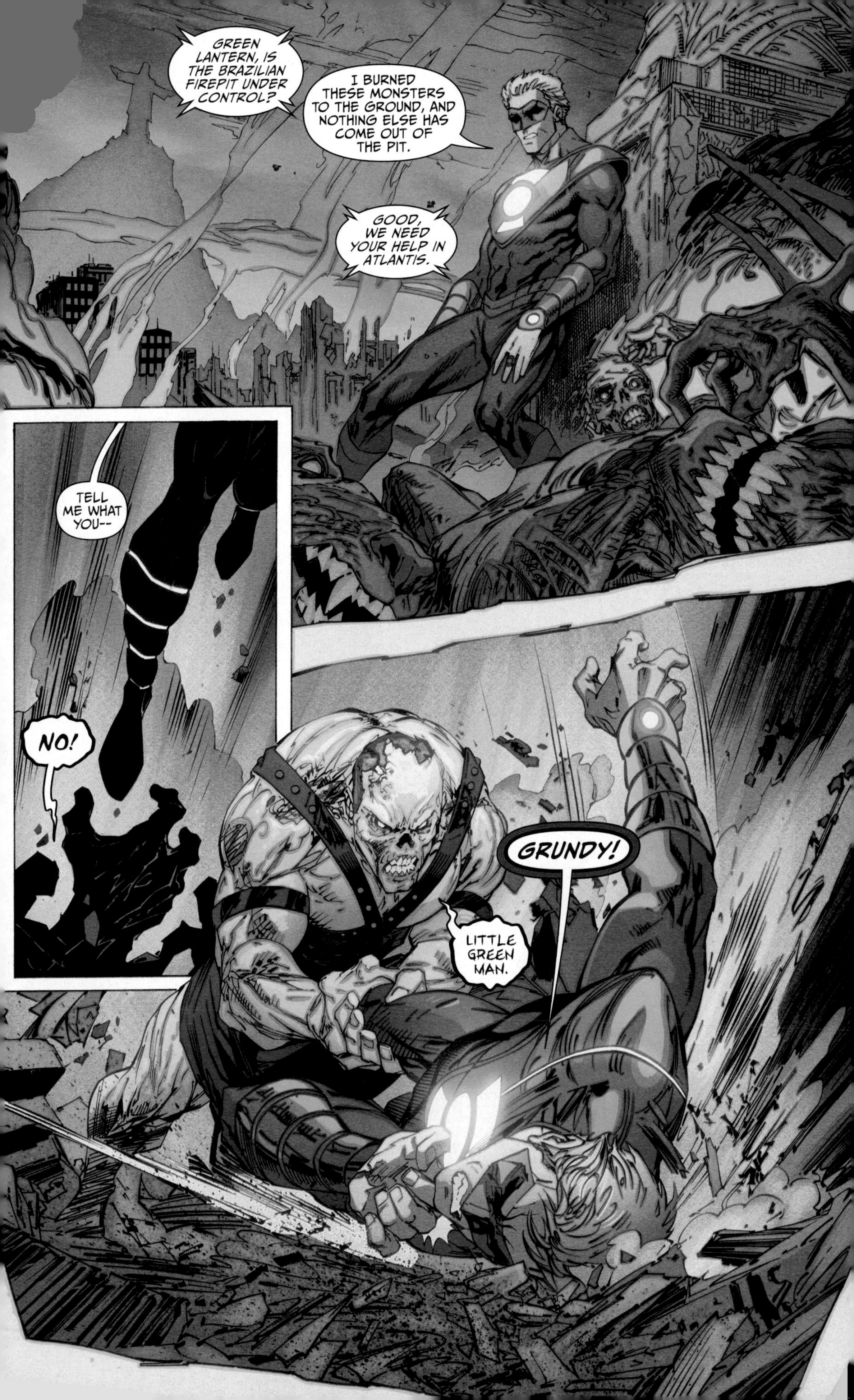
GREEN LANTERN, IS THE BRAZILIAN FIREPIT UNDER CONTROL?
I BURNED THESE MONSTERS TO THE GROUND, AND NOTHING ELSE HAS COME OUT OF THE PIT.
GOOD, WE NEED YOUR HELP IN ATLANTIS.
TELL ME WHAT YOU--
NO!
GRUNDY!
LITTLE GREEN MAN.

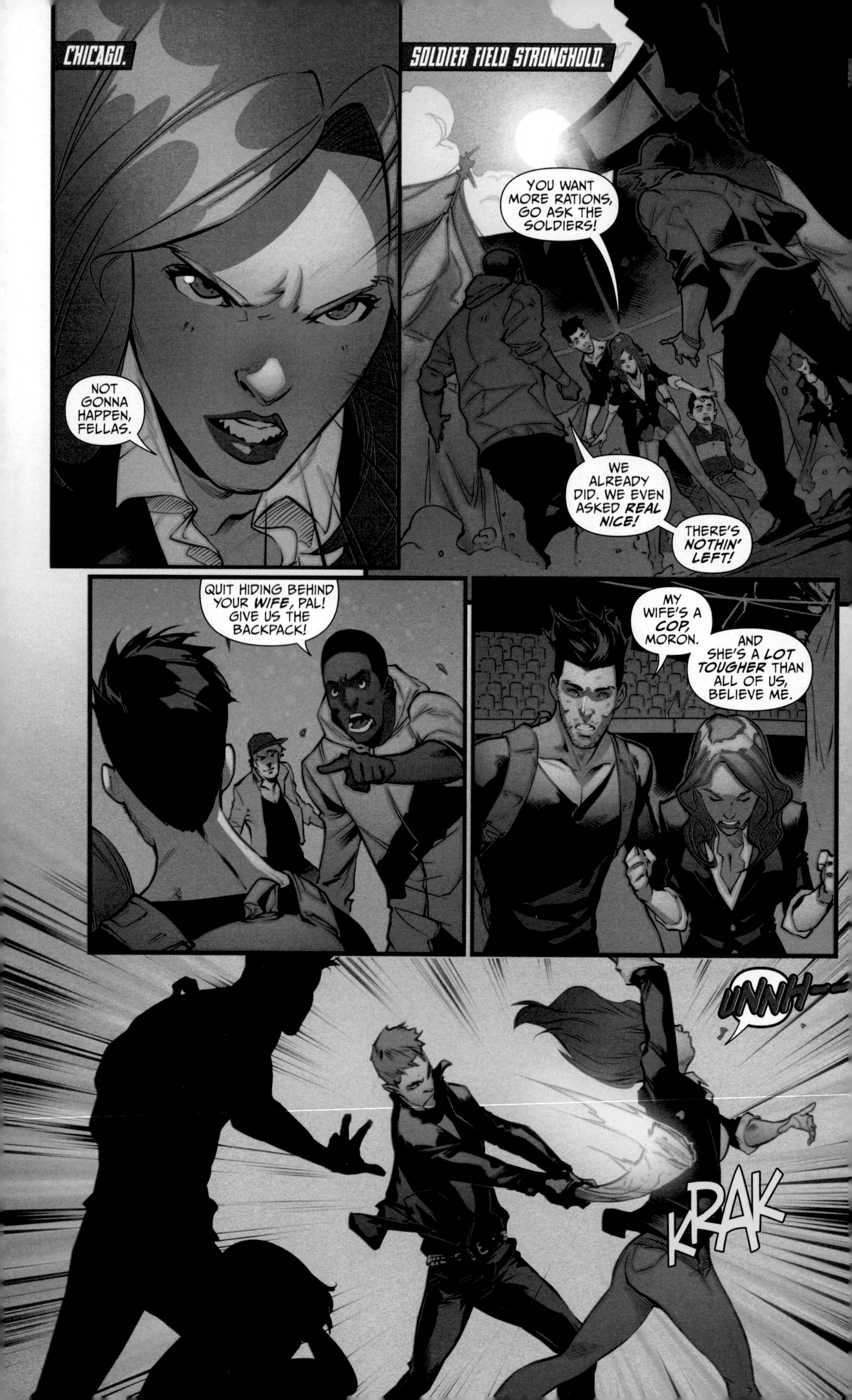
CHICAGO.
NOT GONNA HAPPEN, FELLAS.
SOLDIER FIELD STRONGHOLD.
YOU WANT MORE RATIONS, GO ASK THE SOLDIERS!
WE ALREADY DID. WE EVEN ASKED REAL NICE!
THERE'S NOTHIN' LEFT!
QUIT HIDING BEHIND YOUR WIFE, PAL! GIVE US THE BACKPACK!
MY WIFE'S A COP, MORON.
AND SHE'S A LOT TOUGHER THAN ALL OF US, BELIEVE ME.
UNNH--
KRAK

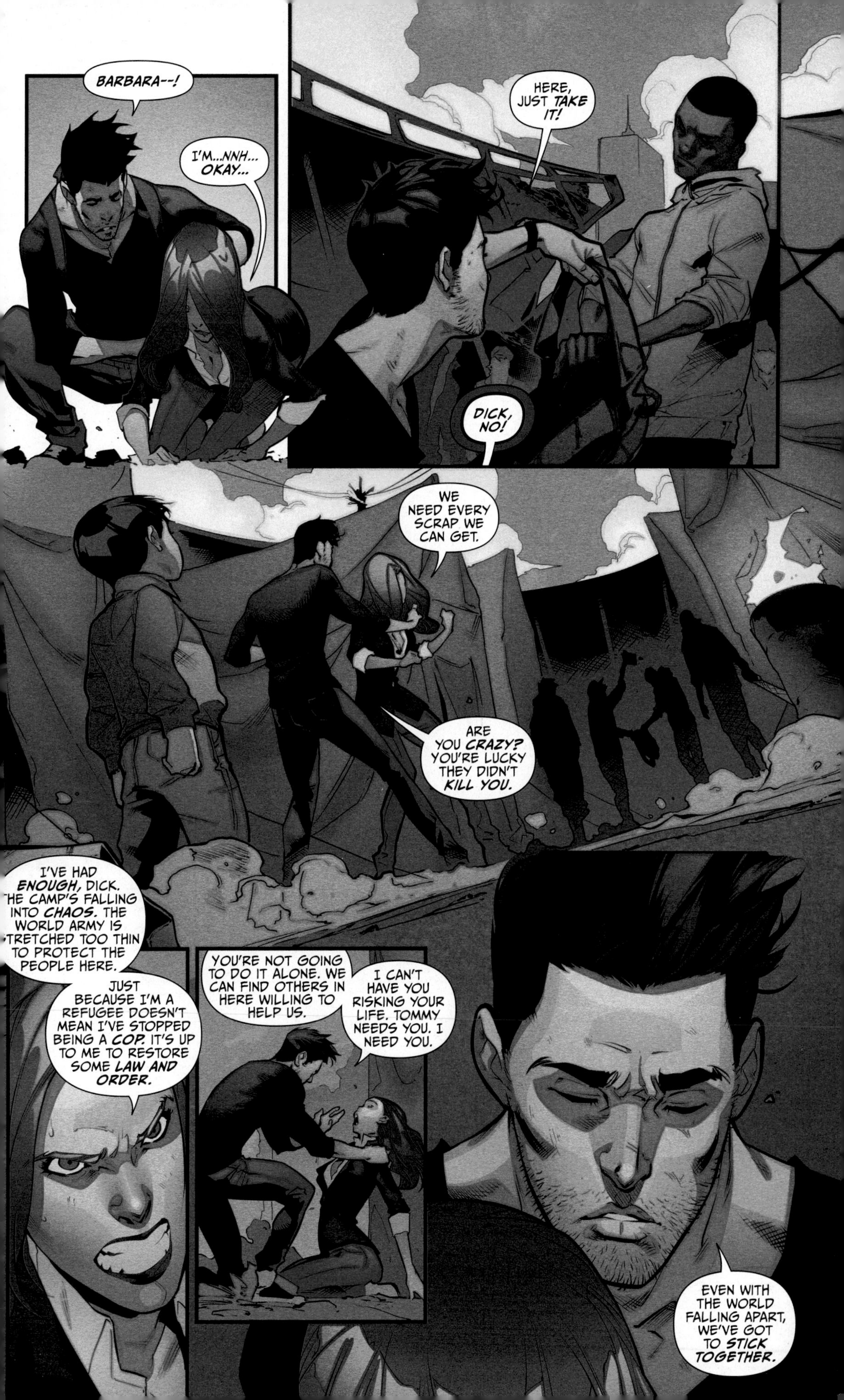
BARBARA--!
I'M...NNH... OKAY...
HERE, JUST TAKE IT!
DICK, NO!
WE NEED EVERY SCRAP WE CAN GET.
ARE YOU CRAZY? YOU'RE LUCKY THEY DIDN'T KILL YOU.
I'VE HAD ENOUGH, DICK. THE CAMP'S FALLING INTO CHAOS. THE WORLD ARMY IS STRETCHED TOO THIN TO PROTECT THE PEOPLE HERE.
JUST BECAUSE I'M A REFUGEE DOESN'T MEAN I'VE STOPPED BEING A COP. IT'S UP TO ME TO RESTORE SOME LAW AND ORDER.
YOU'RE NOT GOING TO DO IT ALONE. WE CAN FIND OTHERS IN HERE WILLING TO HELP US.
I CAN'T HAVE YOU RISKING YOUR LIFE. TOMMY NEEDS YOU. I NEED YOU.
EVEN WITH THE WORLD FALLING APART, WE'VE GOT TO STICK TOGETHER.

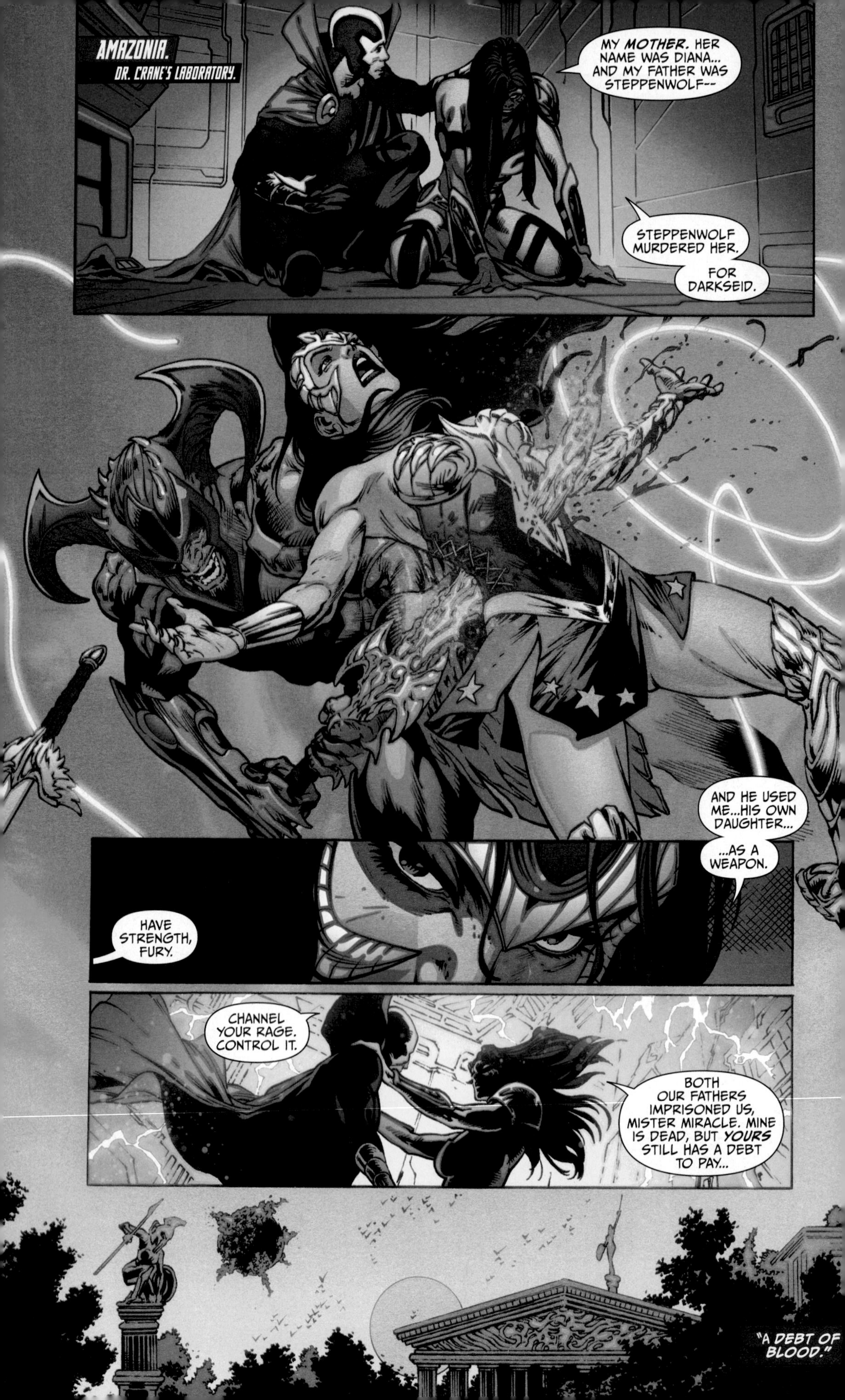
AMAZONIA.
DR. CRANE'S LABORATORY.
MY MOTHER. HER NAME WAS DIANA... AND MY FATHER WAS STEPPENWOLF--
STEPPENWOLF MURDERED HER.
FOR DARKSEID.
AND HE USED ME...HIS OWN DAUGHTER...
...AS A WEAPON.
HAVE STRENGTH, FURY.
CHANNEL YOUR RAGE. CONTROL IT.
BOTH OUR FATHERS IMPRISONED US, MISTER MIRACLE. MINE IS DEAD, BUT YOURS STILL HAS A DEBT TO PAY...
"A DEBT OF BLOOD."

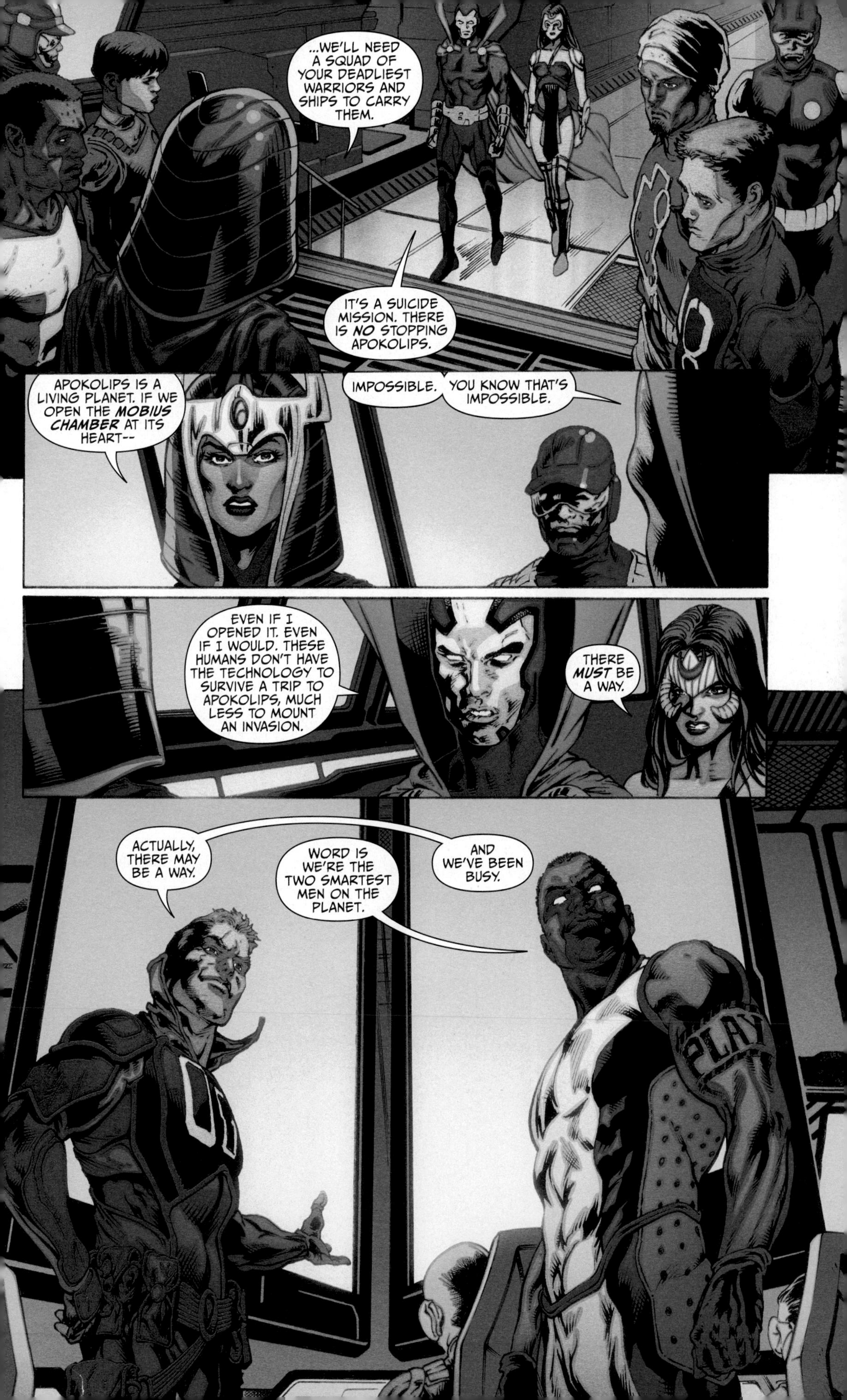
...WE'LL NEED A SQUAD OF YOUR DEADLIEST WARRIORS AND SHIPS TO CARRY THEM.
IT'S A SUICIDE MISSION. THERE IS *NO* STOPPING APOKOLIPS.
APOKOLIPS IS A LIVING PLANET. IF WE OPEN THE *MOBIUS CHAMBER* AT ITS HEART--
IMPOSSIBLE.
YOU KNOW THAT'S IMPOSSIBLE.
EVEN IF I OPENED IT. EVEN IF I WOULD. THESE HUMANS DON'T HAVE THE TECHNOLOGY TO SURVIVE A TRIP TO APOKOLIPS, MUCH LESS TO MOUNT AN INVASION.
THERE *MUST* BE A WAY.
ACTUALLY, THERE MAY BE A WAY.
AND WE'VE BEEN BUSY.
WORD IS WE'RE THE TWO SMARTEST MEN ON THE PLANET.
PLAY

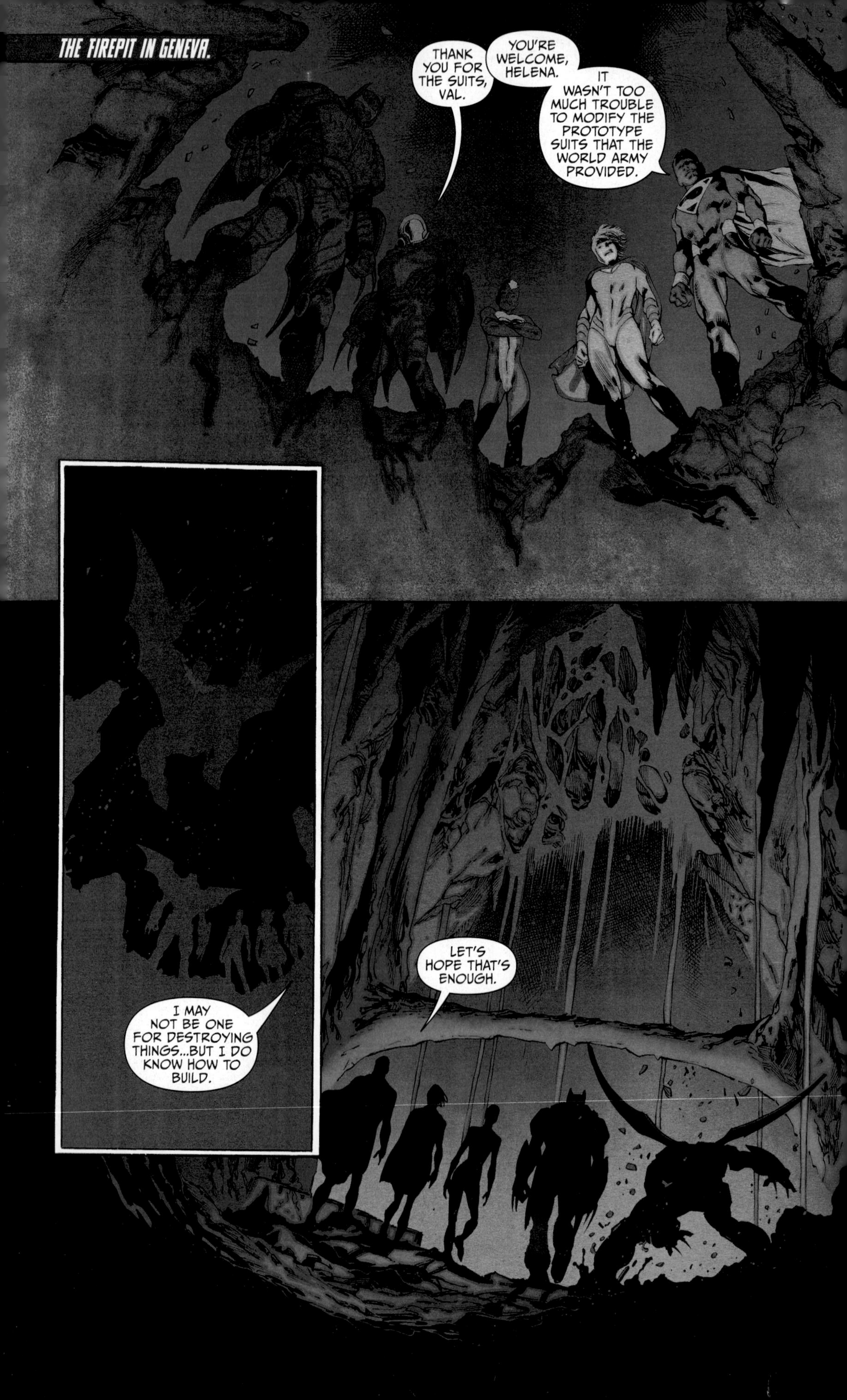
THE FIREPIT IN GENEVA.
THANK YOU FOR THE SUITS, VAL.
YOU'RE WELCOME, HELENA.
IT WASN'T TOO MUCH TROUBLE TO MODIFY THE PROTOTYPE SUITS THAT THE WORLD ARMY PROVIDED.
I MAY NOT BE ONE FOR DESTROYING THINGS...BUT I DO KNOW HOW TO BUILD.
LET'S HOPE THAT'S ENOUGH.

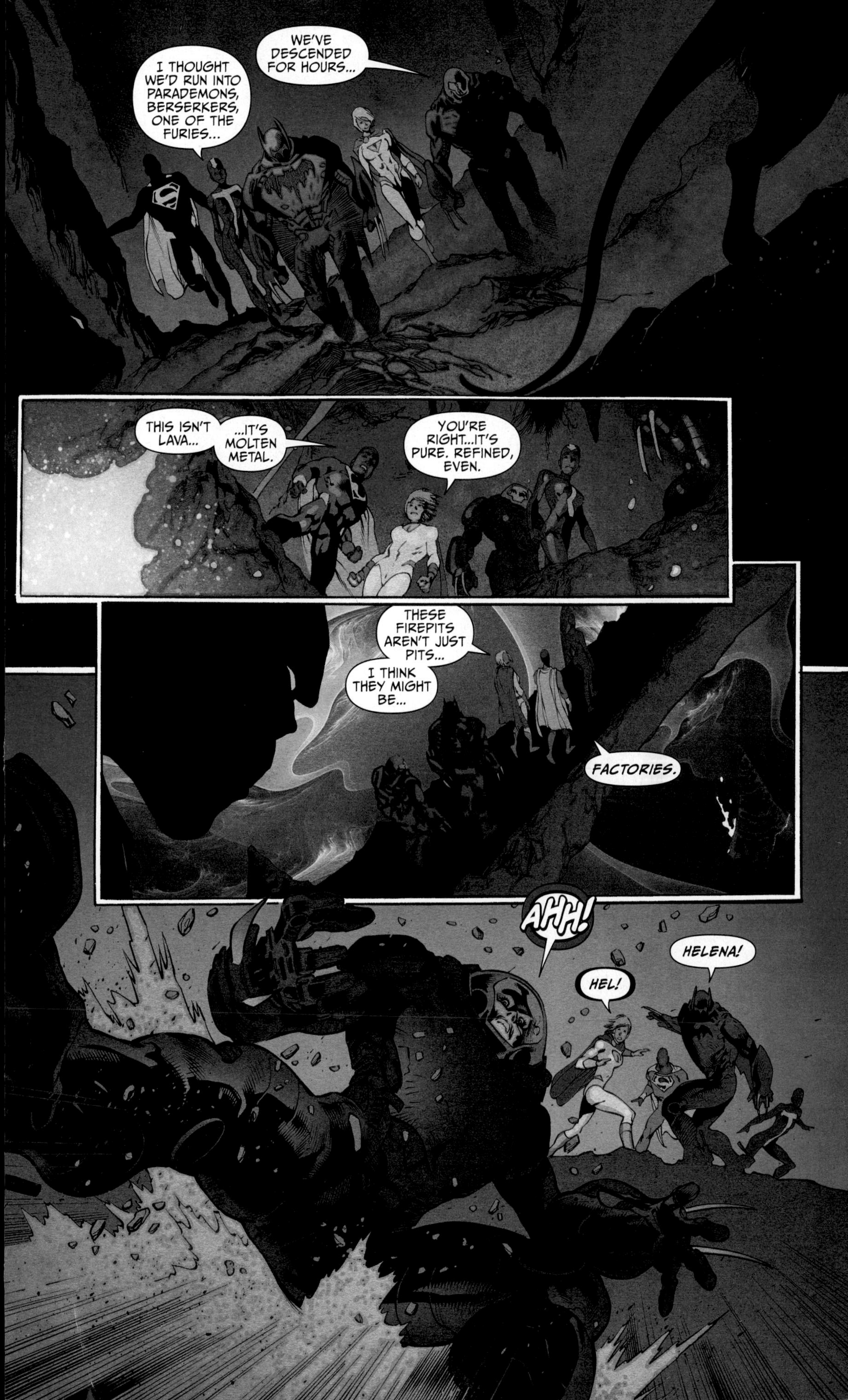

I THOUGHT WE'D RUN INTO PARADEMONS, BERSERKERS, ONE OF THE FURIES...
WE'VE DESCENDED FOR HOURS...
THIS ISN'T LAVA...
...IT'S MOLTEN METAL.
YOU'RE RIGHT...IT'S PURE. REFINED, EVEN.
THESE FIREPITS AREN'T JUST PITS...
I THINK THEY MIGHT BE...
FACTORIES.
AHH!
HELENA!
HEL!

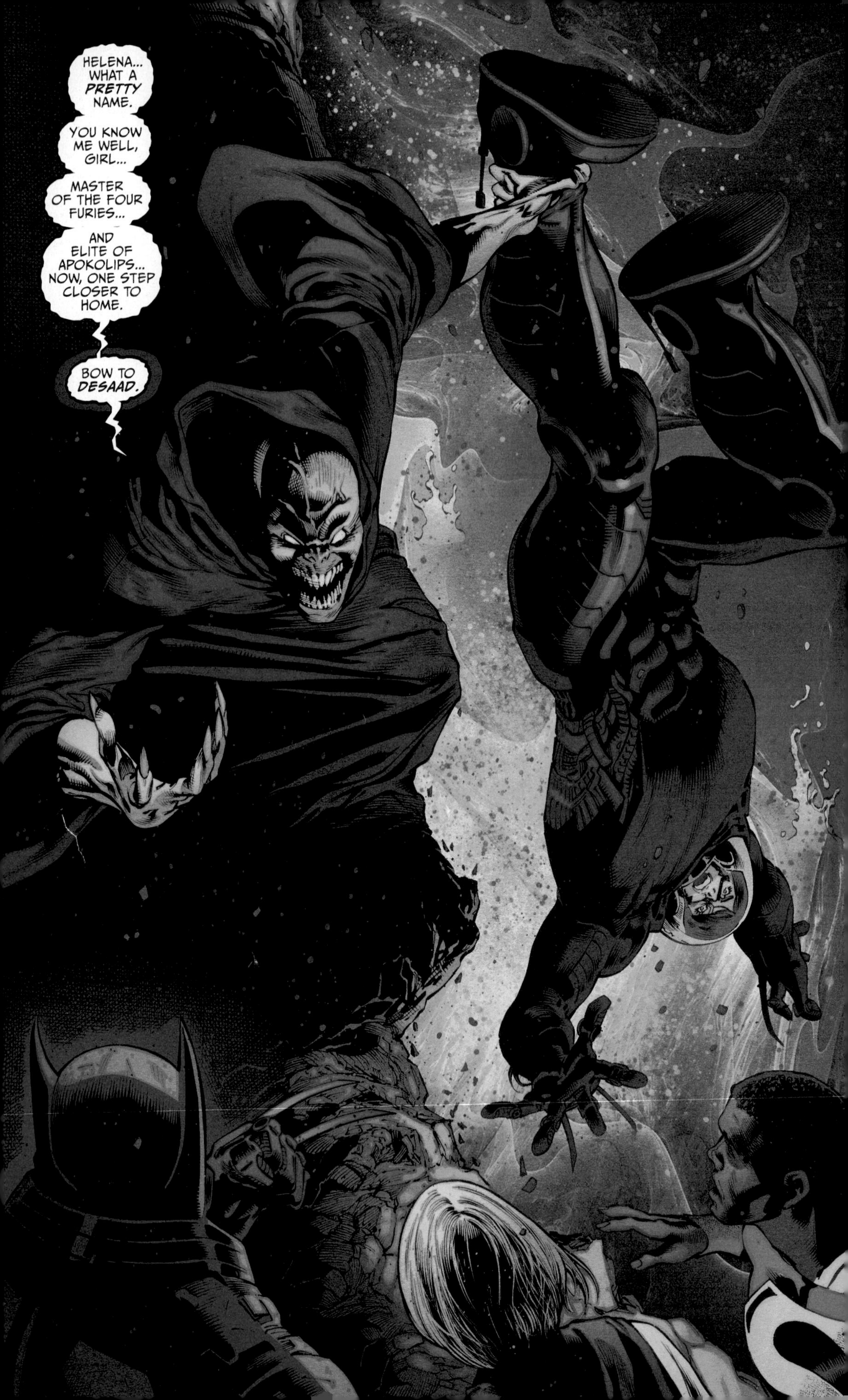
HELENA... WHAT A *PRETTY* NAME.
YOU KNOW ME WELL, GIRL...
MASTER OF THE FOUR FURIES...
AND ELITE OF APOKOLIPS... NOW, ONE STEP CLOSER TO HOME.
BOW TO *DESAAD.*

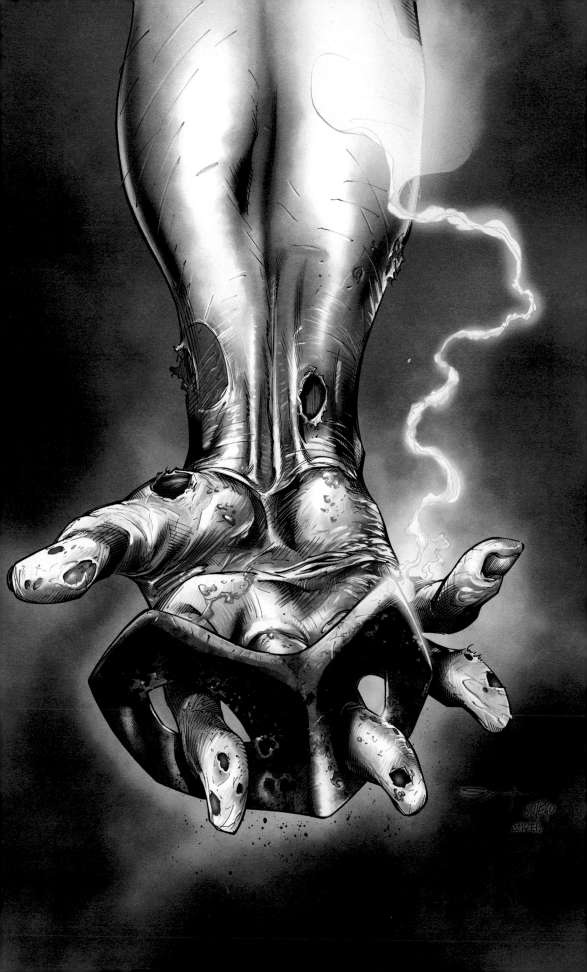

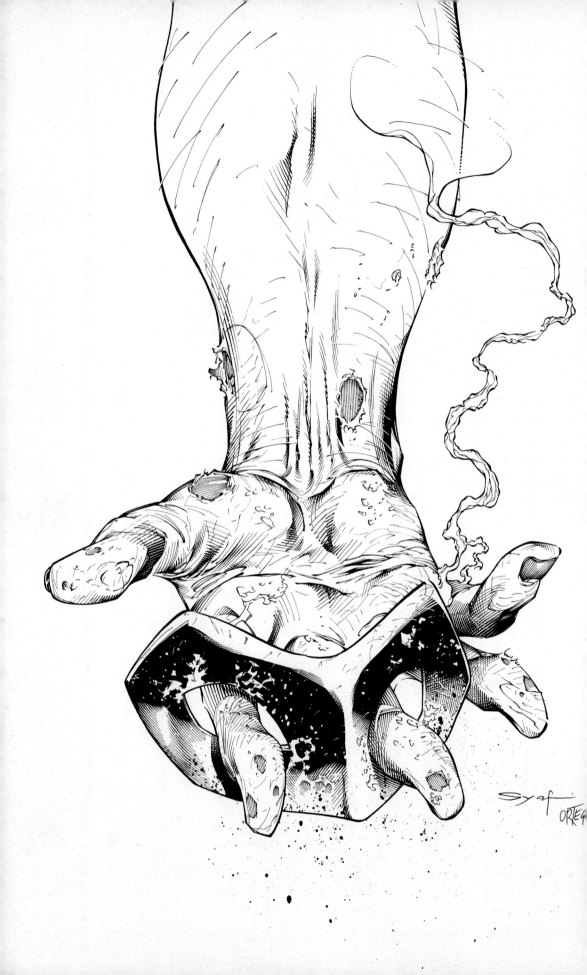

THE SMELL IS THE WORST PART.

SOLOMON GRUNDY'S PUNCHES I CAN HANDLE. HIS ROTTING TENDRILS I CAN DEAL WITH.

BUT I DON'T HAVE A DEFENSE AGAINST THE STINK OF DEATH AND DECAY THAT SURROUNDS HIM.

HERE IN THE RUINS OF RIO DE JANEIRO WHERE SO MANY HAVE ALREADY LOST THEIR LIVES...

...I CAN'T HELP BUT THINK THAT GRUNDY FEELS RIGHT AT HOME!

EMERALD QUEST

Story by DANIEL H. WILSON Written by DANIEL H. WILSON, MARGUERITE BENNETT & MIKE JOHNSON
Art by JAN DUURSEMA & JONATHAN GLAPION, TYLER KIRKHAM & JOE WEEMS,
EDUARDO PANSICA & JAIME MENDOZA, EDDY BARROWS & EBER FERREIRA
Colors by MIKE ATIYEH Letters by CARLOS M. MANGUAL
Cover by ARDIAN SYAF & GUILLERMO ORTEGO with ATIYEH

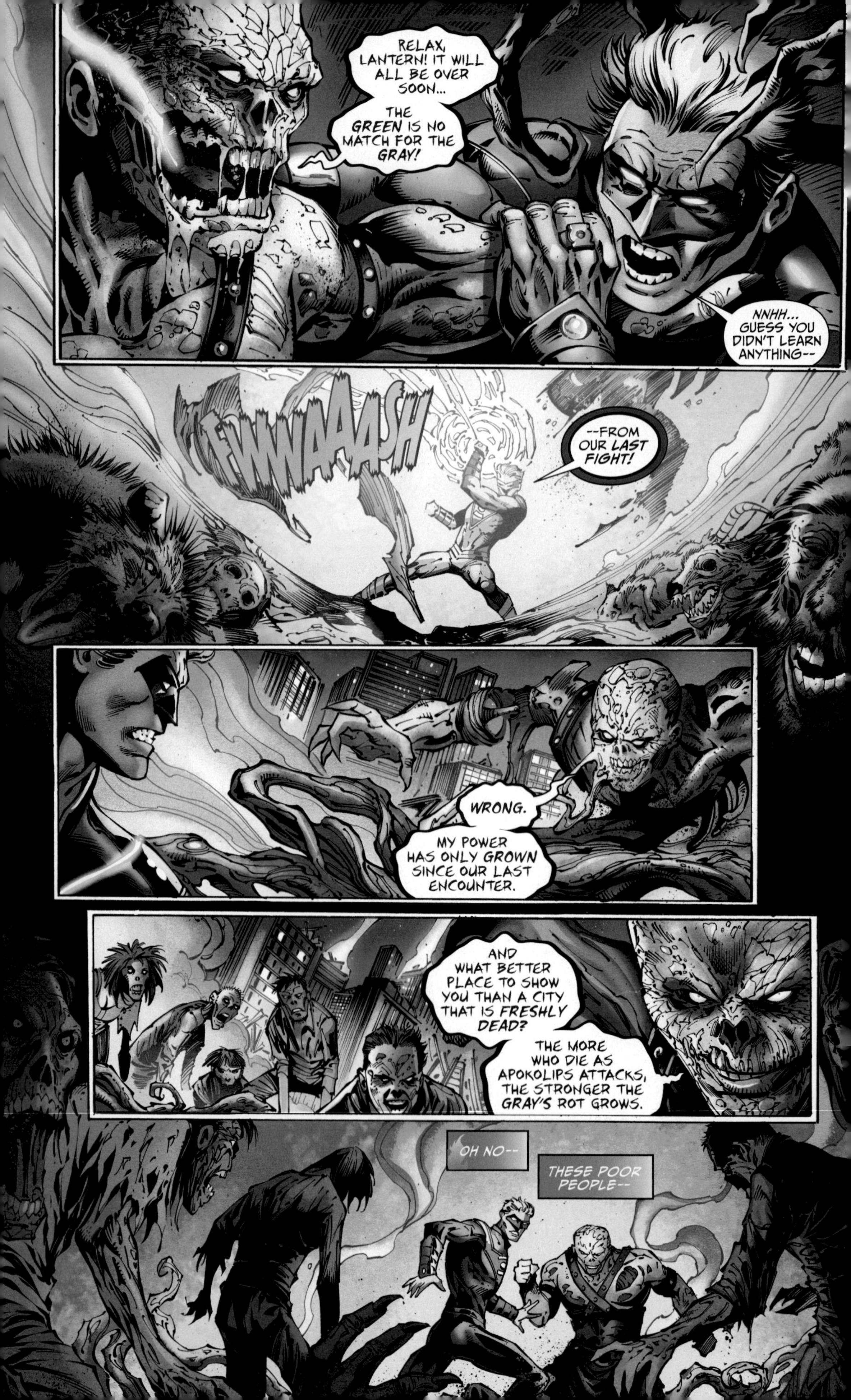
RELAX, LANTERN! IT WILL ALL BE OVER SOON...
THE GREEN IS NO MATCH FOR THE GRAY!
NNHH... GUESS YOU DIDN'T LEARN ANYTHING--
FWWAAASH
--FROM OUR LAST FIGHT!
WRONG.
MY POWER HAS ONLY GROWN SINCE OUR LAST ENCOUNTER.
AND WHAT BETTER PLACE TO SHOW YOU THAN A CITY THAT IS FRESHLY DEAD?
THE MORE WHO DIE AS APOKOLIPS ATTACKS, THE STRONGER THE GRAY'S ROT GROWS.
OH NO--
THESE POOR PEOPLE--

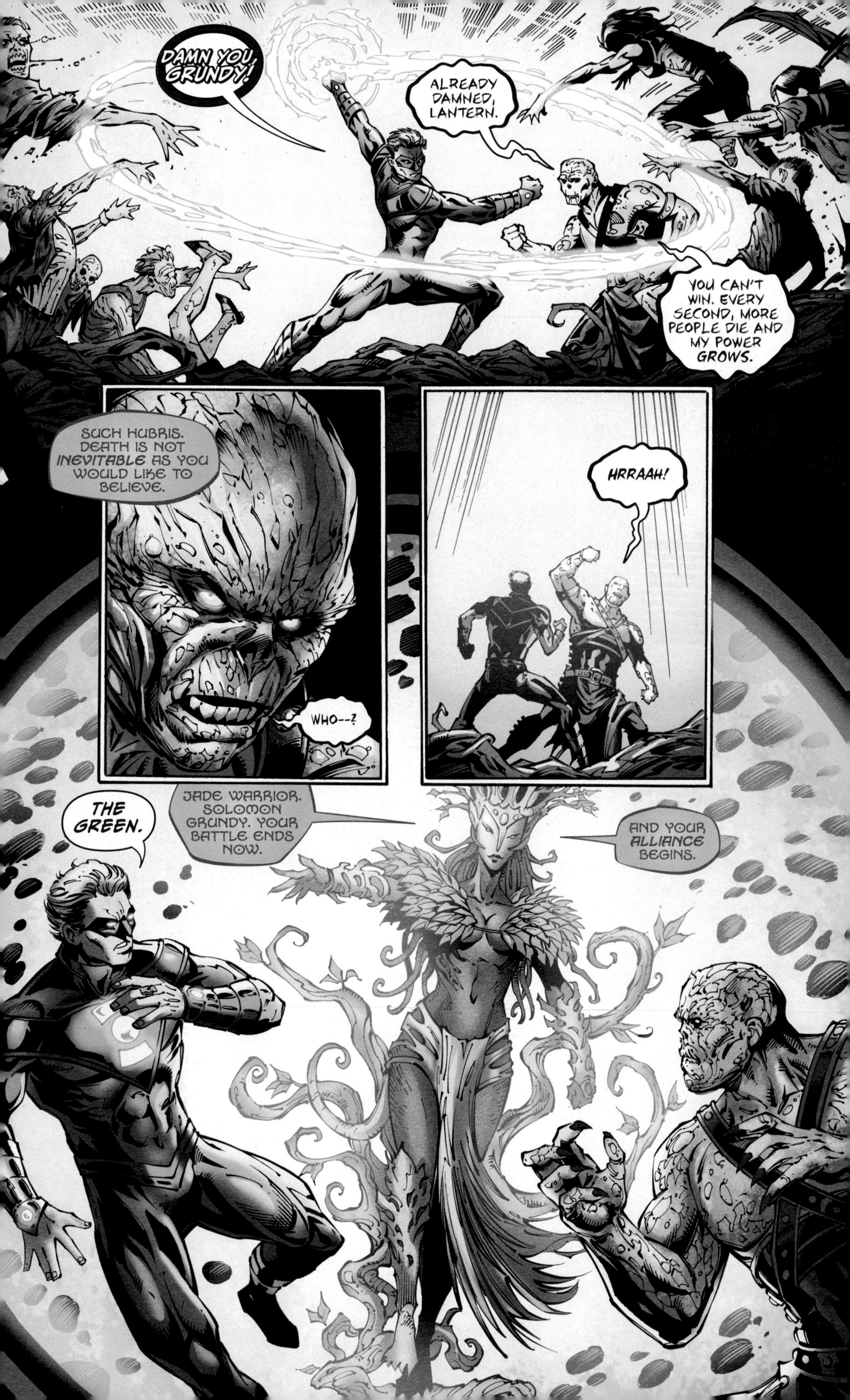
DAMN YOU, GRUNDY!
ALREADY DAMNED, LANTERN.
YOU CAN'T WIN. EVERY SECOND, MORE PEOPLE DIE AND MY POWER GROWS.
SUCH HUBRIS. DEATH IS NOT INEVITABLE AS YOU WOULD LIKE TO BELIEVE.
WHO--?
HRRAAH!
THE GREEN.
JADE WARRIOR. SOLOMON GRUNDY. YOUR BATTLE ENDS NOW.
AND YOUR ALLIANCE BEGINS.

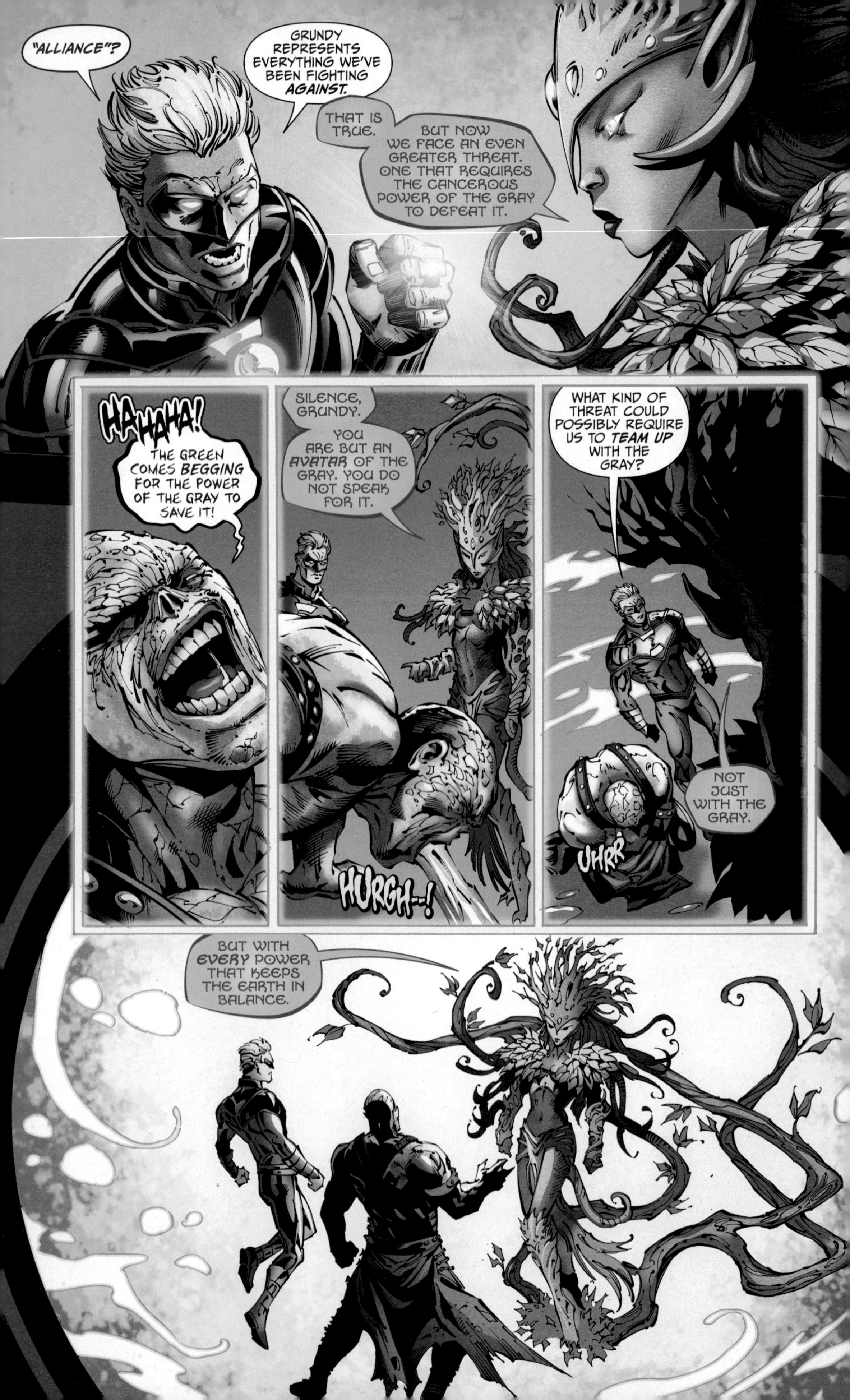
"ALLIANCE"?
GRUNDY REPRESENTS EVERYTHING WE'VE BEEN FIGHTING AGAINST.
THAT IS TRUE.
BUT NOW WE FACE AN EVEN GREATER THREAT. ONE THAT REQUIRES THE CANCEROUS POWER OF THE GRAY TO DEFEAT IT.
HAHAHA!
THE GREEN COMES BEGGING FOR THE POWER OF THE GRAY TO SAVE IT!
SILENCE, GRUNDY.
YOU ARE BUT AN AVATAR OF THE GRAY. YOU DO NOT SPEAK FOR IT.
HURGH--!
WHAT KIND OF THREAT COULD POSSIBLY REQUIRE US TO TEAM UP WITH THE GRAY?
NOT JUST WITH THE GRAY.
UHRR
BUT WITH EVERY POWER THAT KEEPS THE EARTH IN BALANCE.

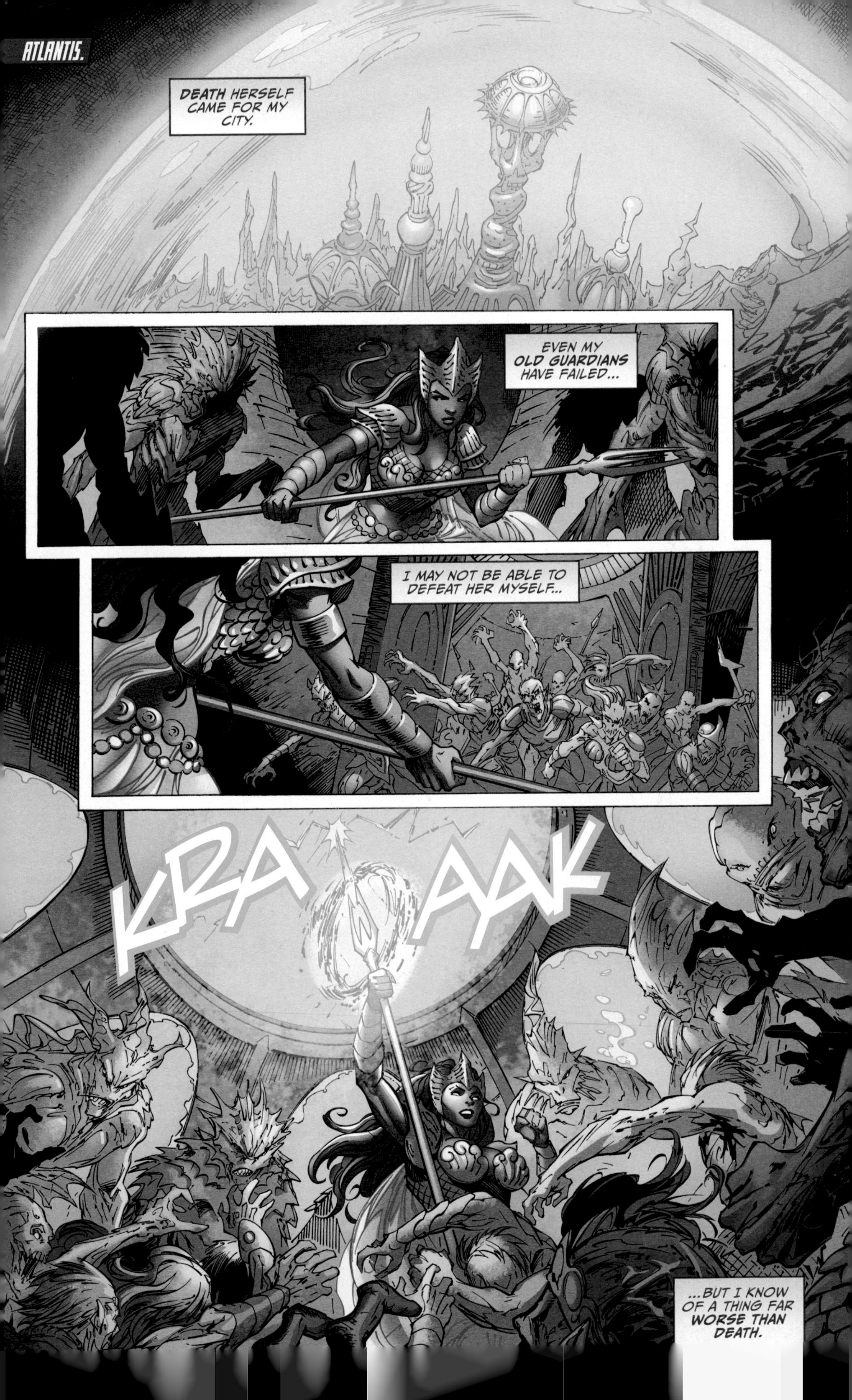
ATLANTIS.
DEATH HERSELF CAME FOR MY CITY.
EVEN MY OLD GUARDIANS HAVE FAILED...
I MAY NOT BE ABLE TO DEFEAT HER MYSELF...
KRA AAK
...BUT I KNOW OF A THING FAR WORSE THAN DEATH.

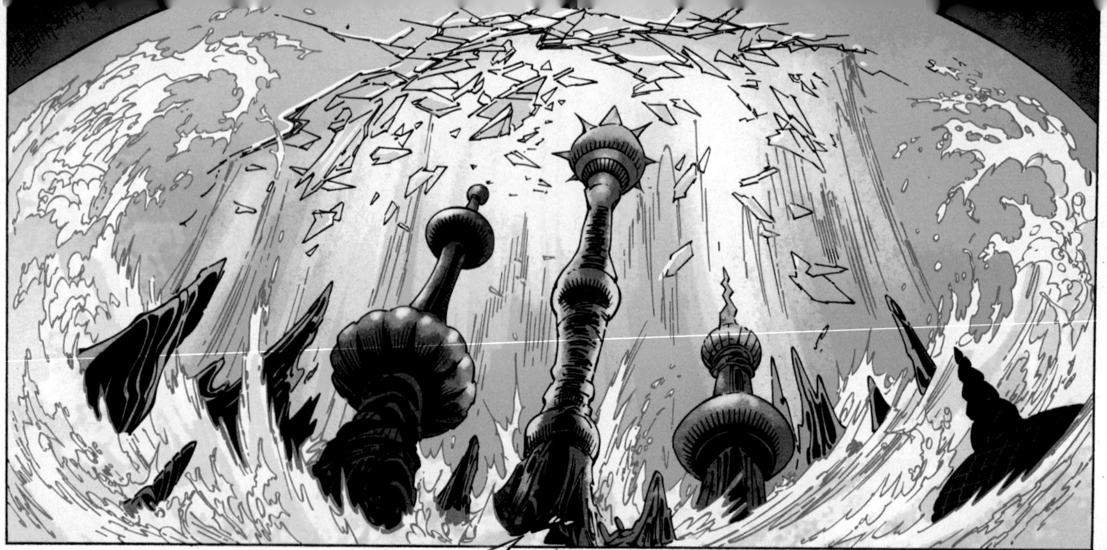

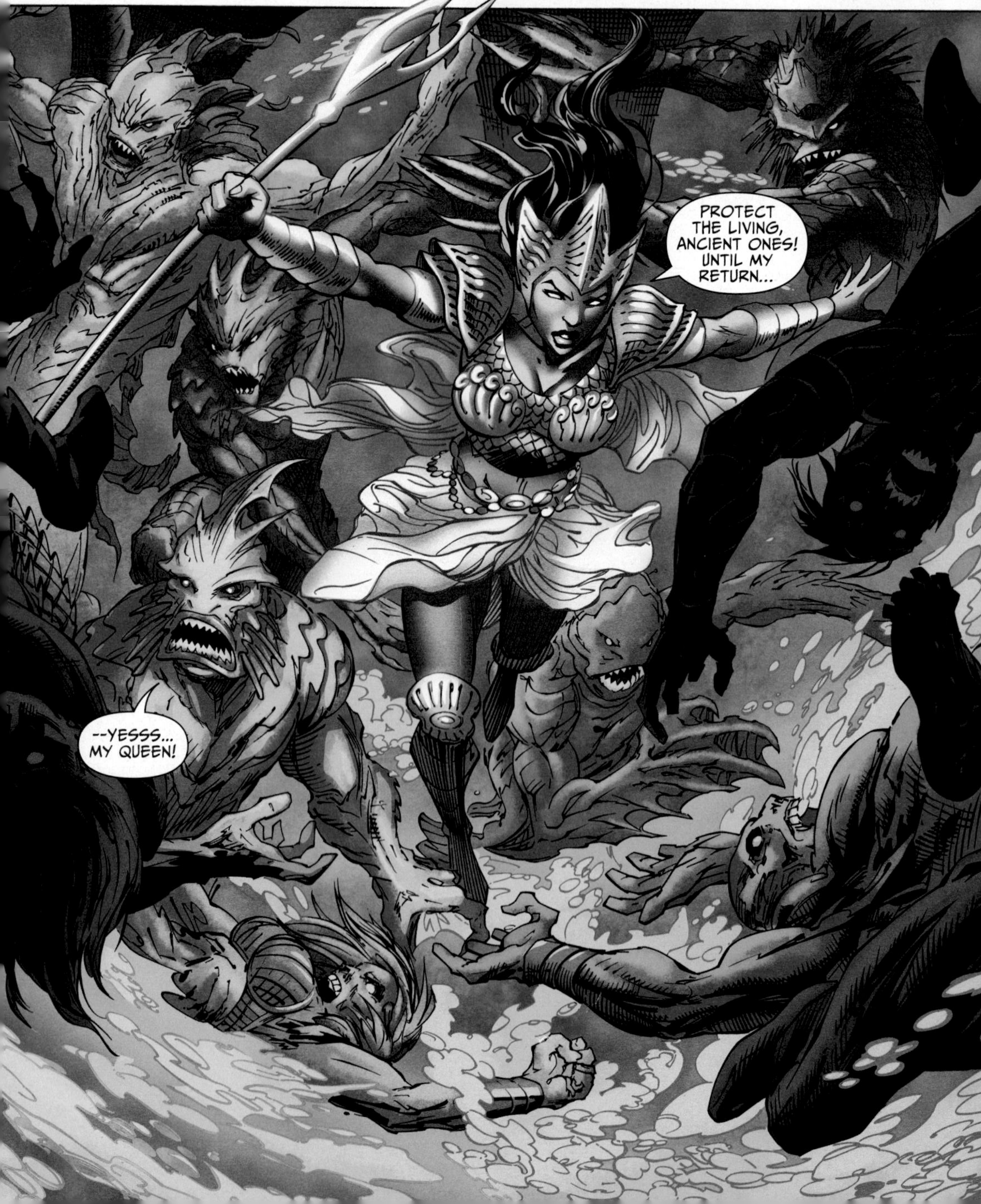
PROTECT THE LIVING, ANCIENT ONES! UNTIL MY RETURN...
--YESSS... MY QUEEN!

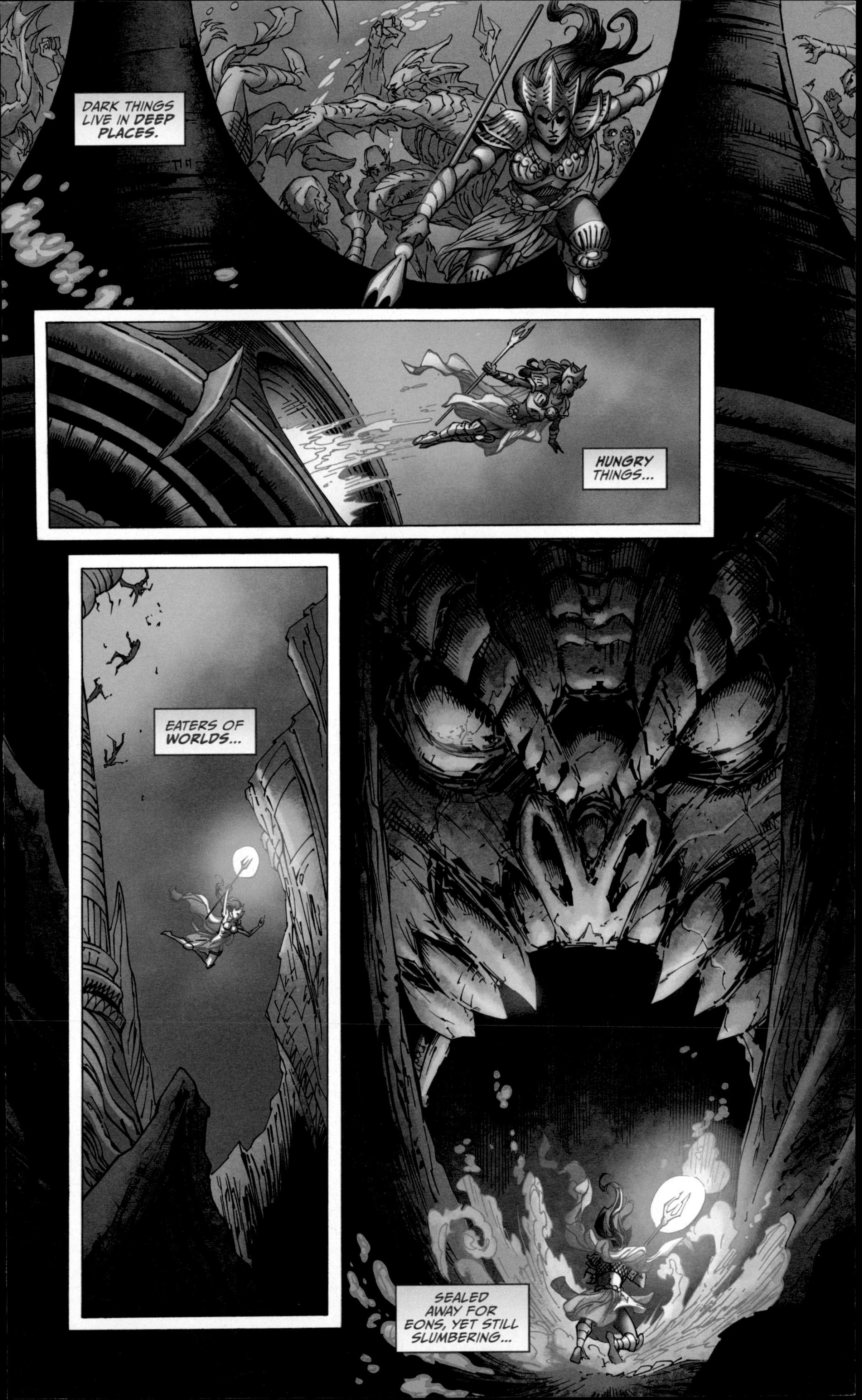
DARK THINGS LIVE IN DEEP PLACES.
HUNGRY THINGS...
EATERS OF WORLDS...
SEALED AWAY FOR EONS, YET STILL SLUMBERING...

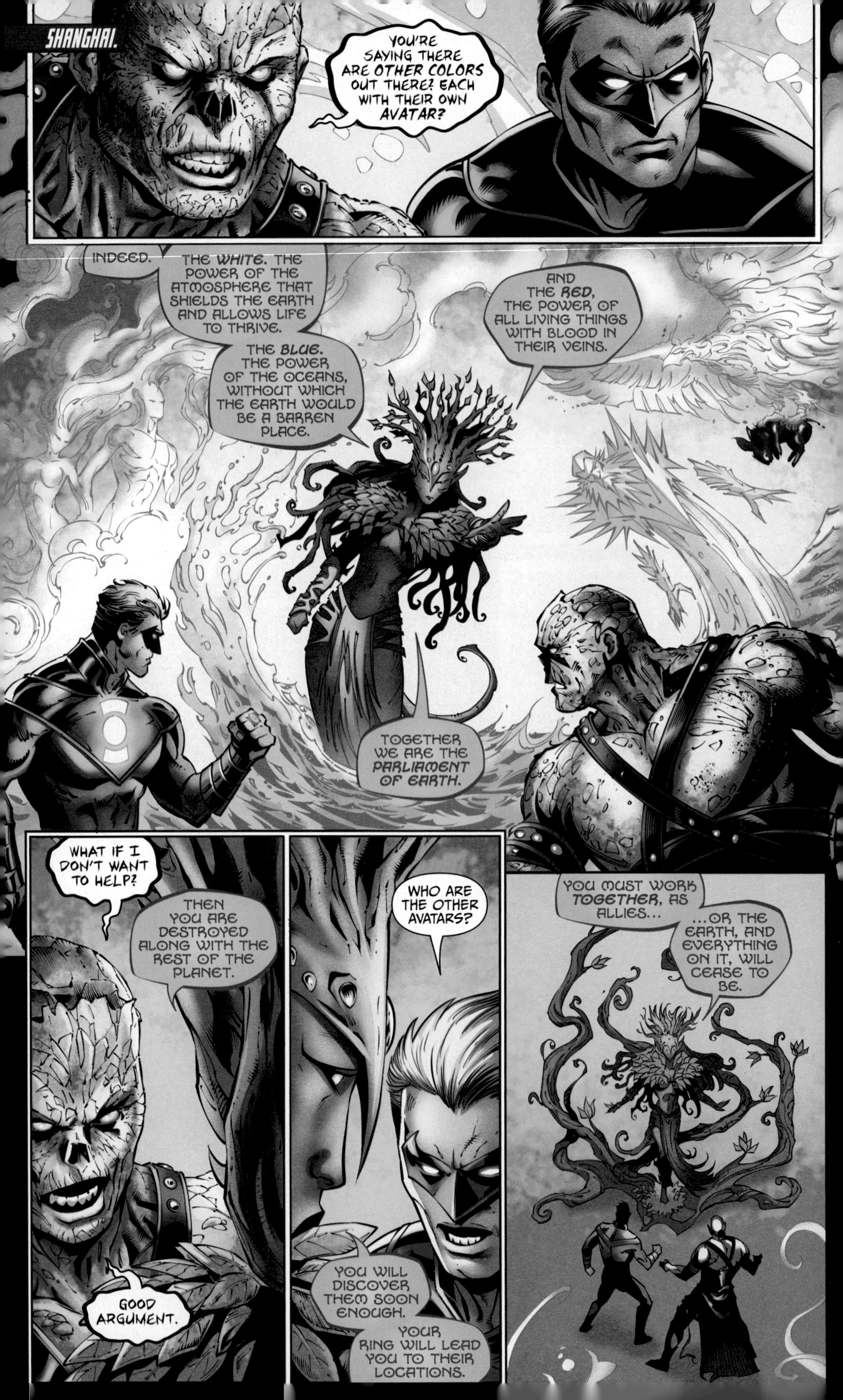
SHANGHAI.
YOU'RE SAYING THERE ARE OTHER COLORS OUT THERE? EACH WITH THEIR OWN AVATAR?
INDEED.
THE WHITE. THE POWER OF THE ATMOSPHERE THAT SHIELDS THE EARTH AND ALLOWS LIFE TO THRIVE.
THE BLUE. THE POWER OF THE OCEANS, WITHOUT WHICH THE EARTH WOULD BE A BARREN PLACE.
AND THE RED, THE POWER OF ALL LIVING THINGS WITH BLOOD IN THEIR VEINS.
TOGETHER WE ARE THE PARLIAMENT OF EARTH.
WHAT IF I DON'T WANT TO HELP?
THEN YOU ARE DESTROYED ALONG WITH THE REST OF THE PLANET.
GOOD ARGUMENT.
WHO ARE THE OTHER AVATARS?
YOU WILL DISCOVER THEM SOON ENOUGH.
YOUR RING WILL LEAD YOU TO THEIR LOCATIONS.
YOU MUST WORK TOGETHER, AS ALLIES...
...OR THE EARTH, AND EVERYTHING ON IT, WILL CEASE TO BE.

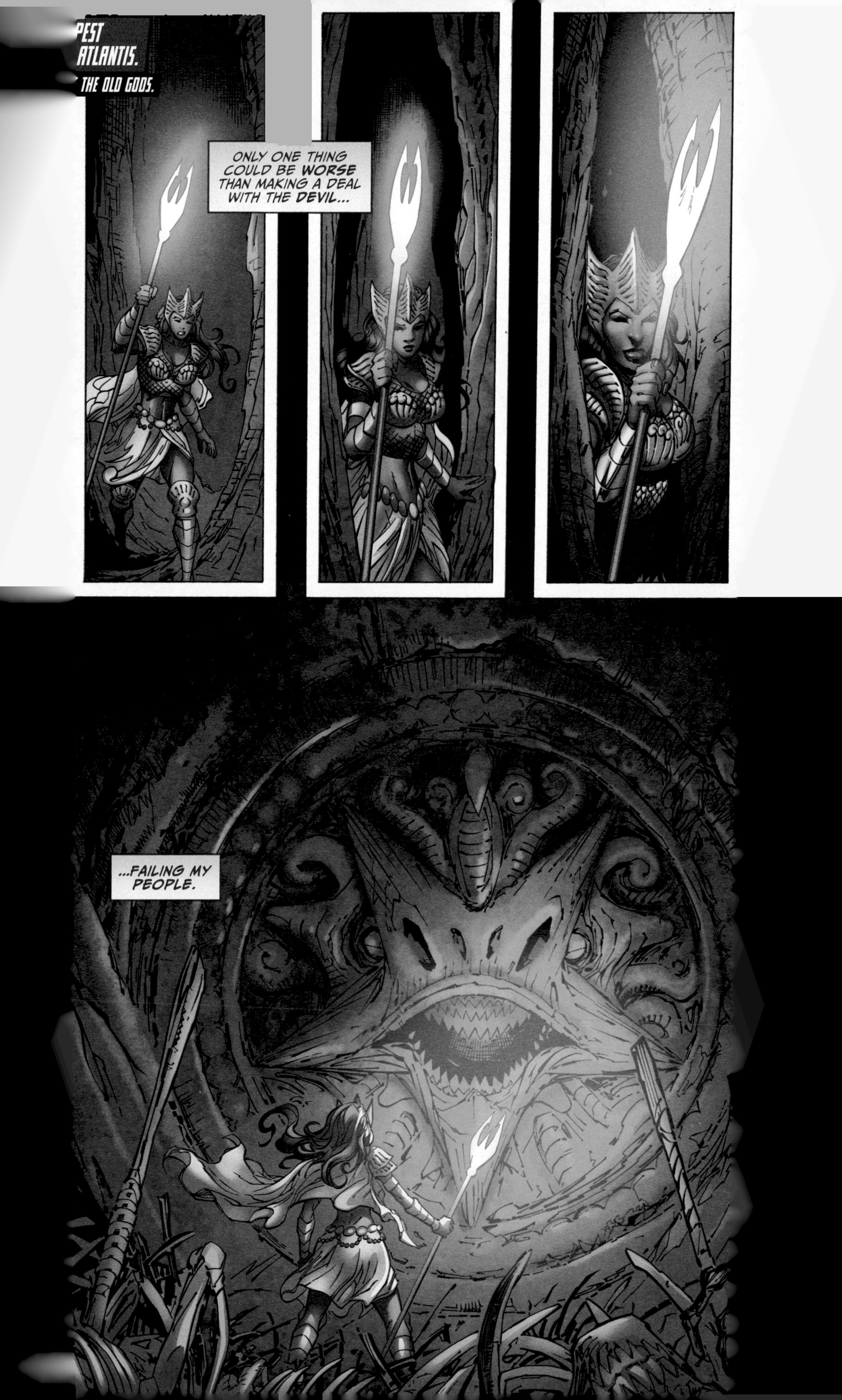

PEST
ATLANTIS.
THE OLD GODS.
ONLY ONE THING COULD BE WORSE THAN MAKING A DEAL WITH THE DEVIL...
...FAILING MY PEOPLE.

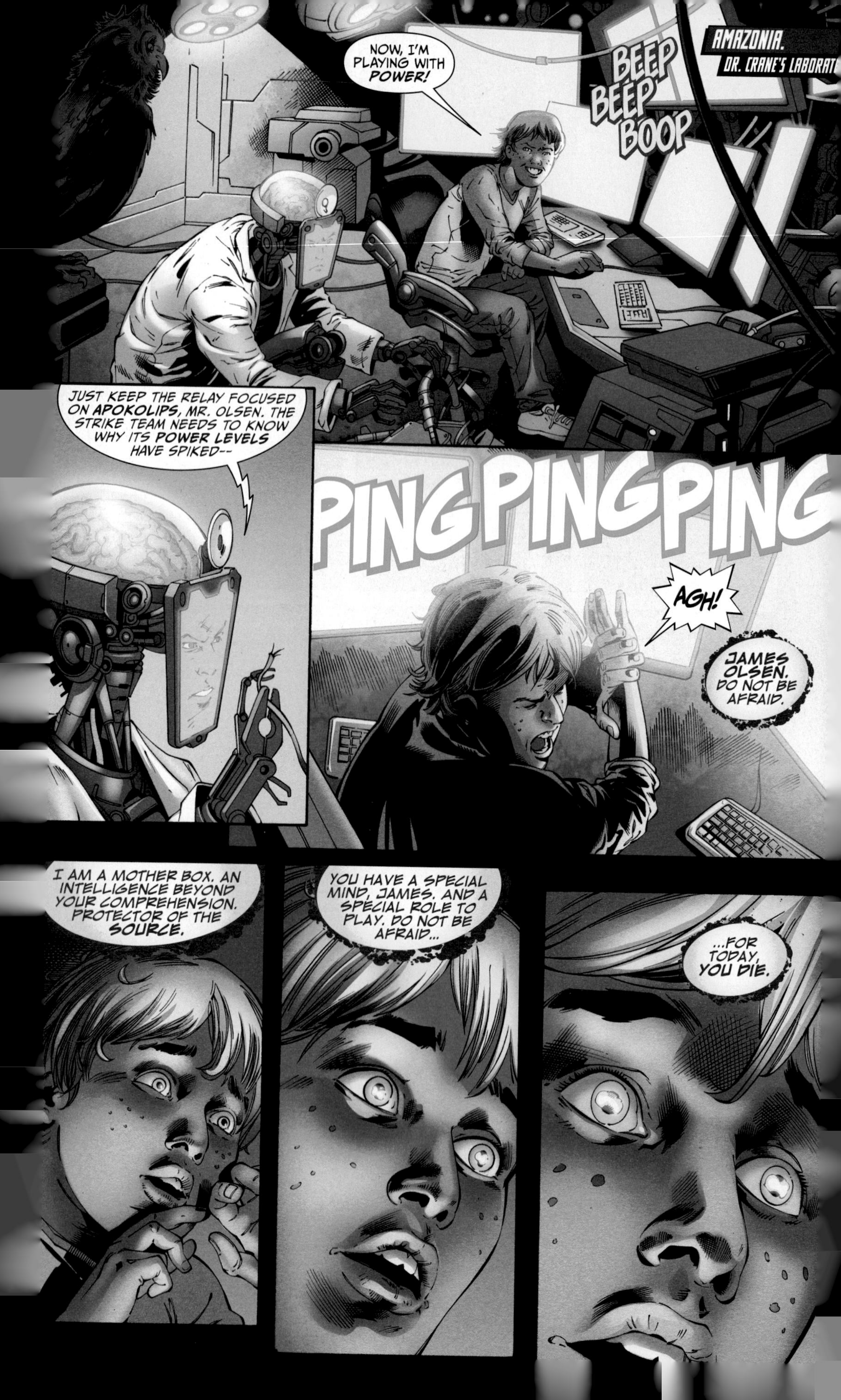
AMAZONIA.
DR. CRANE'S LABORAT
NOW, I'M PLAYING WITH POWER!
BEEP BEEP BOOP
JUST KEEP THE RELAY FOCUSED ON APOKOLIPS, MR. OLSEN. THE STRIKE TEAM NEEDS TO KNOW WHY ITS POWER LEVELS HAVE SPIKED--
PINGPINGPING
AGH!
JAMES OLSEN. DO NOT BE AFRAID.
I AM A MOTHER BOX. AN INTELLIGENCE BEYOND YOUR COMPREHENSION. PROTECTOR OF THE SOURCE.
YOU HAVE A SPECIAL MIND, JAMES. AND A SPECIAL ROLE TO PLAY. DO NOT BE AFRAID...
...FOR TODAY, YOU DIE.

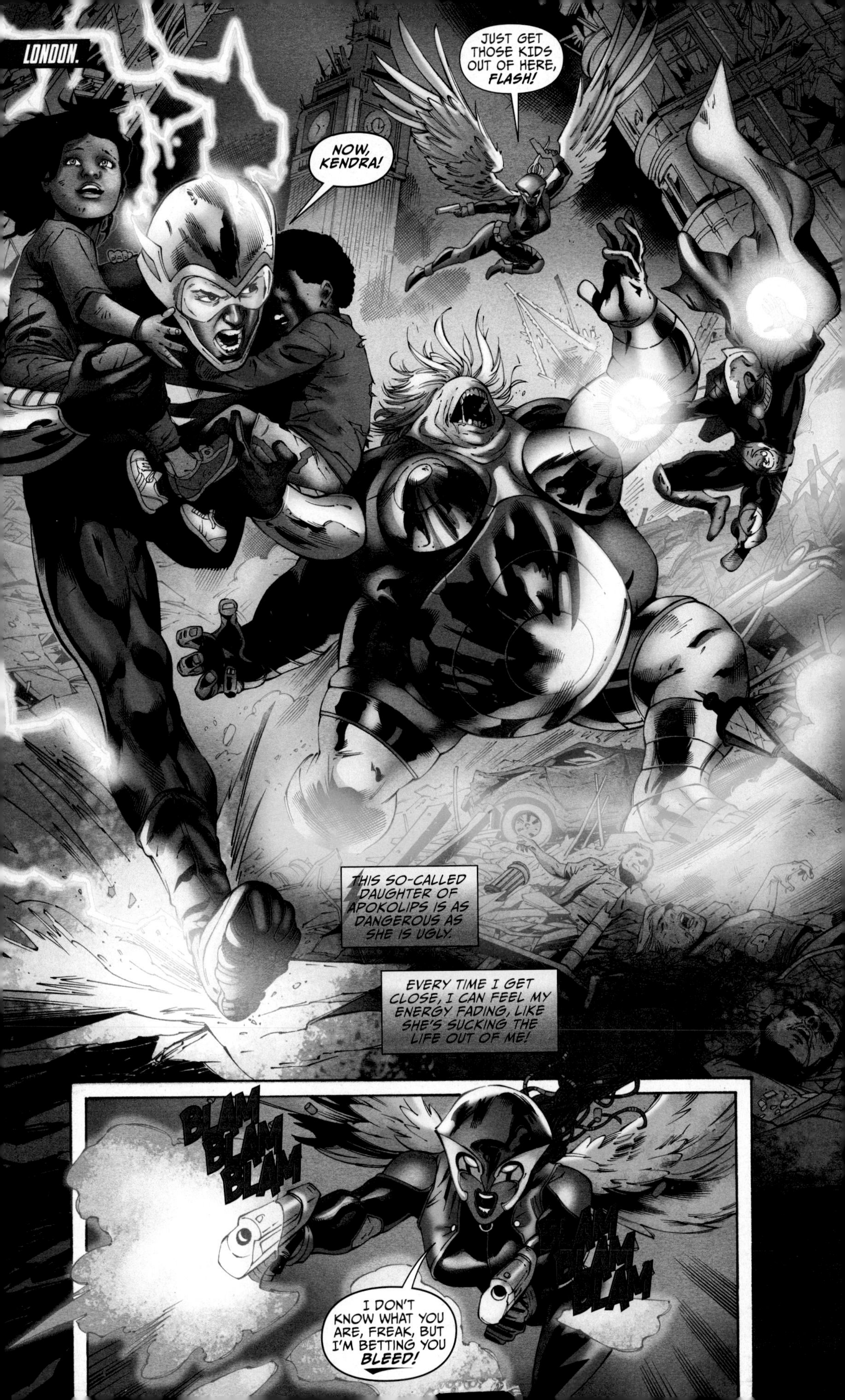
LONDON.
NOW, KENDRA!
JUST GET THOSE KIDS OUT OF HERE, FLASH!
THIS SO-CALLED DAUGHTER OF APOKOLIPS IS AS DANGEROUS AS SHE IS UGLY.
EVERY TIME I GET CLOSE, I CAN FEEL MY ENERGY FADING, LIKE SHE'S SUCKING THE LIFE OUT OF ME!
BLAM BLAM BLAM
BLAM BLAM BLAM
I DON'T KNOW WHAT YOU ARE, FREAK, BUT I'M BETTING YOU BLEED!

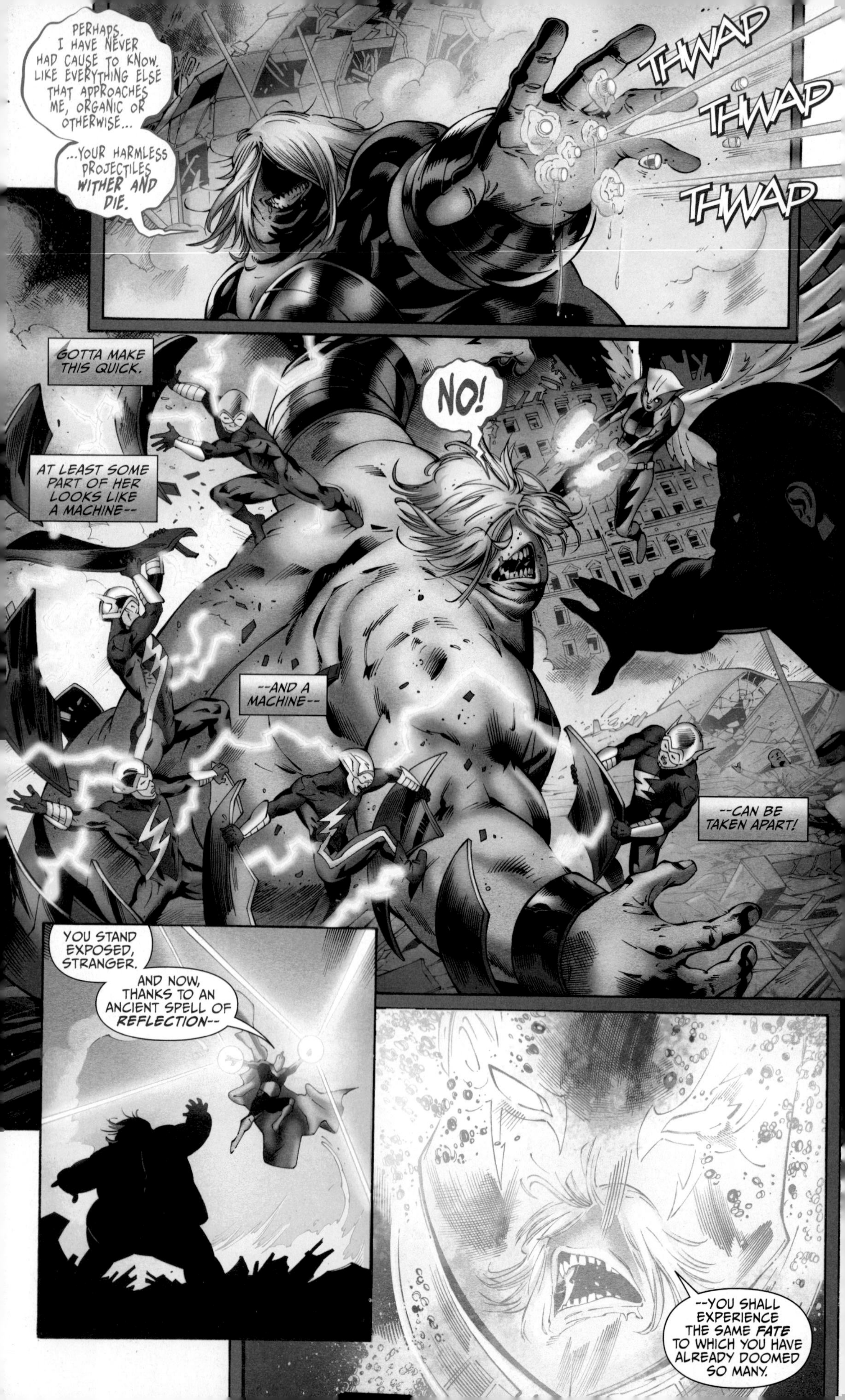
PERHAPS. I HAVE NEVER HAD CAUSE TO KNOW. LIKE EVERYTHING ELSE THAT APPROACHES ME, ORGANIC OR OTHERWISE...
...YOUR HARMLESS PROJECTILES WITHER AND DIE.
THWAP
THWAP
THWAP
GOTTA MAKE THIS QUICK.
NO!
AT LEAST SOME PART OF HER LOOKS LIKE A MACHINE--
--AND A MACHINE--
--CAN BE TAKEN APART!
YOU STAND EXPOSED, STRANGER.
AND NOW, THANKS TO AN ANCIENT SPELL OF REFLECTION--
--YOU SHALL EXPERIENCE THE SAME FATE TO WHICH YOU HAVE ALREADY DOOMED SO MANY.

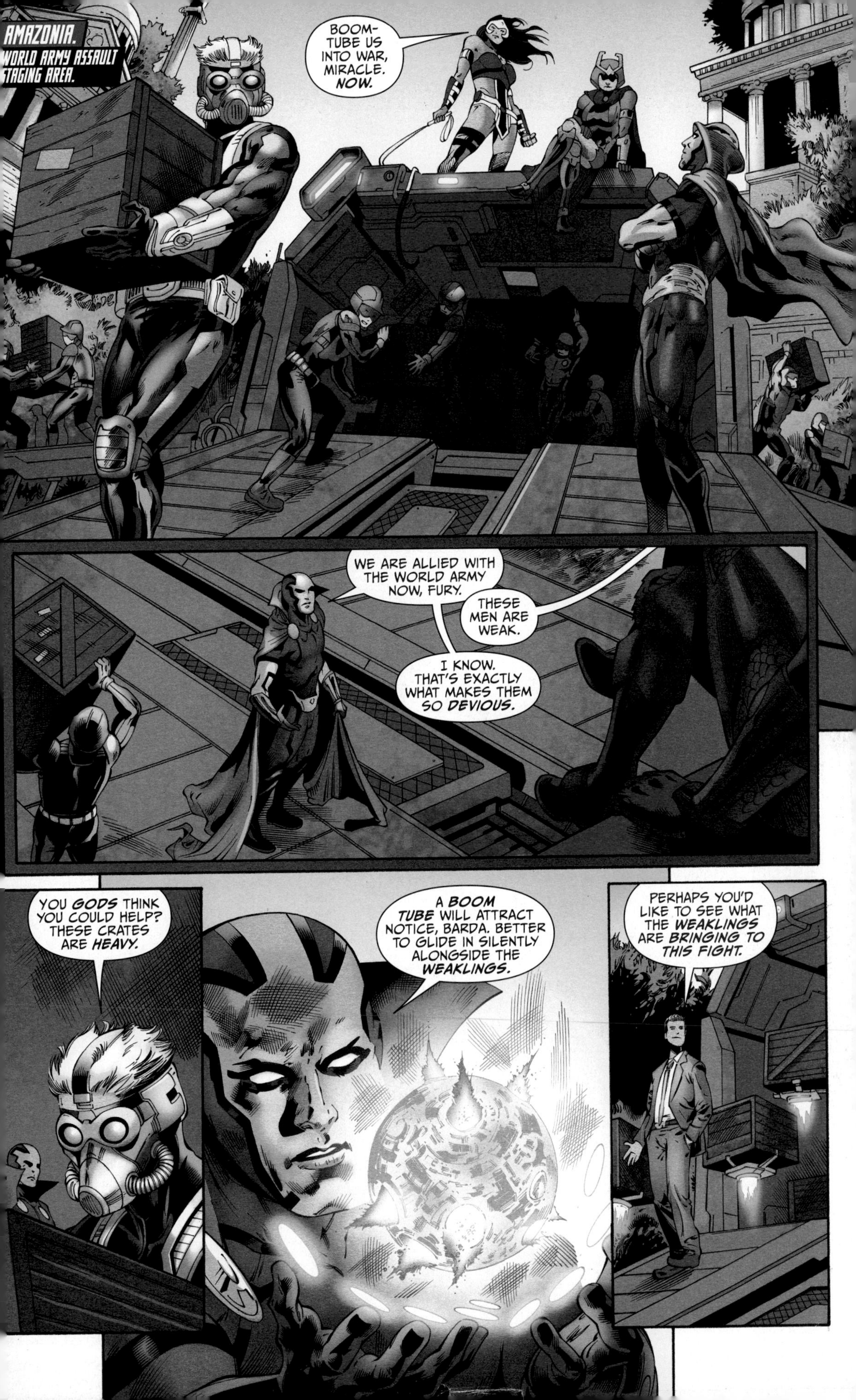
AMAZONIA.
WORLD ARMY ASSAULT STAGING AREA.
BOOM-TUBE US INTO WAR, MIRACLE. NOW.
WE ARE ALLIED WITH THE WORLD ARMY NOW, FURY.
THESE MEN ARE WEAK.
I KNOW. THAT'S EXACTLY WHAT MAKES THEM SO DEVIOUS.
YOU GODS THINK YOU COULD HELP? THESE CRATES ARE HEAVY.
A BOOM TUBE WILL ATTRACT NOTICE, BARDA. BETTER TO GLIDE IN SILENTLY ALONGSIDE THE WEAKLINGS.
PERHAPS YOU'D LIKE TO SEE WHAT THE WEAKLINGS ARE BRINGING TO THIS FIGHT.

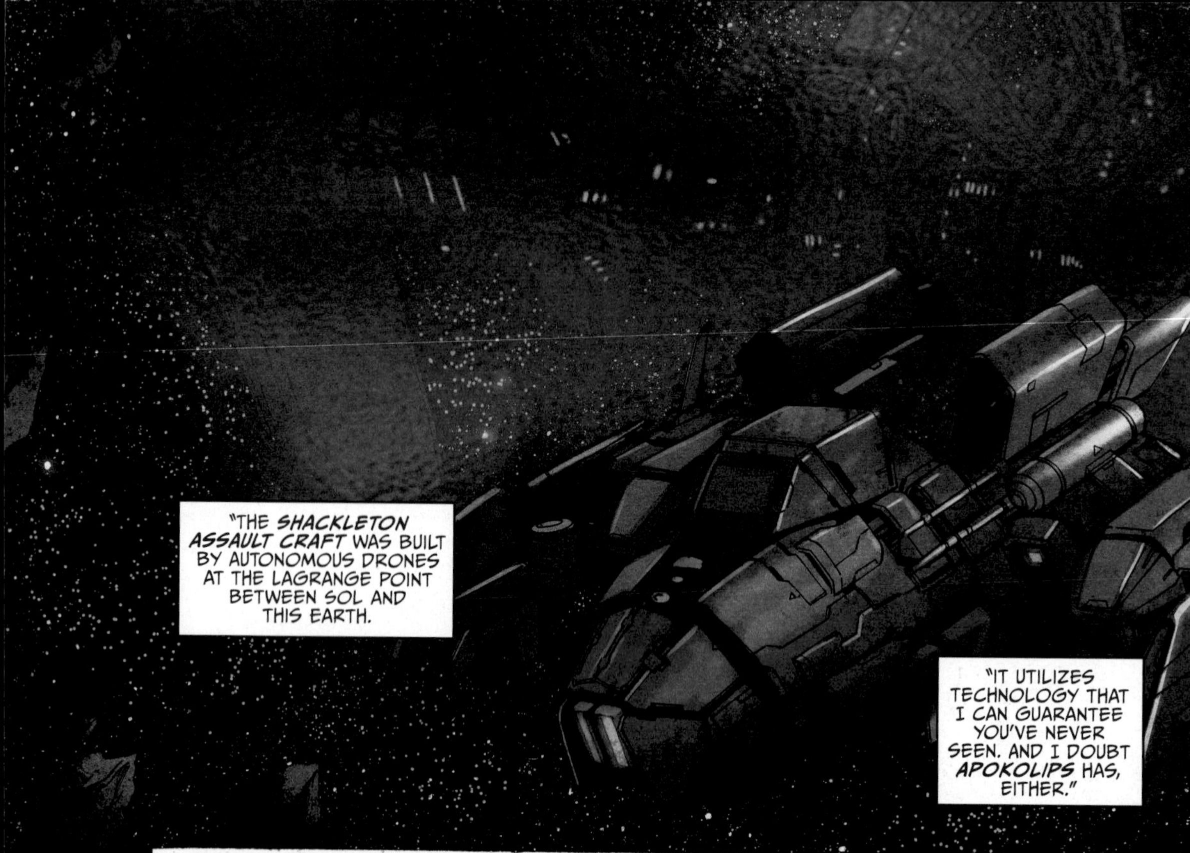
"THE SHACKLETON ASSAULT CRAFT WAS BUILT BY AUTONOMOUS DRONES AT THE LAGRANGE POINT BETWEEN SOL AND THIS EARTH.
"IT UTILIZES TECHNOLOGY THAT I CAN GUARANTEE YOU'VE NEVER SEEN. AND I DOUBT APOKOLIPS HAS, EITHER."

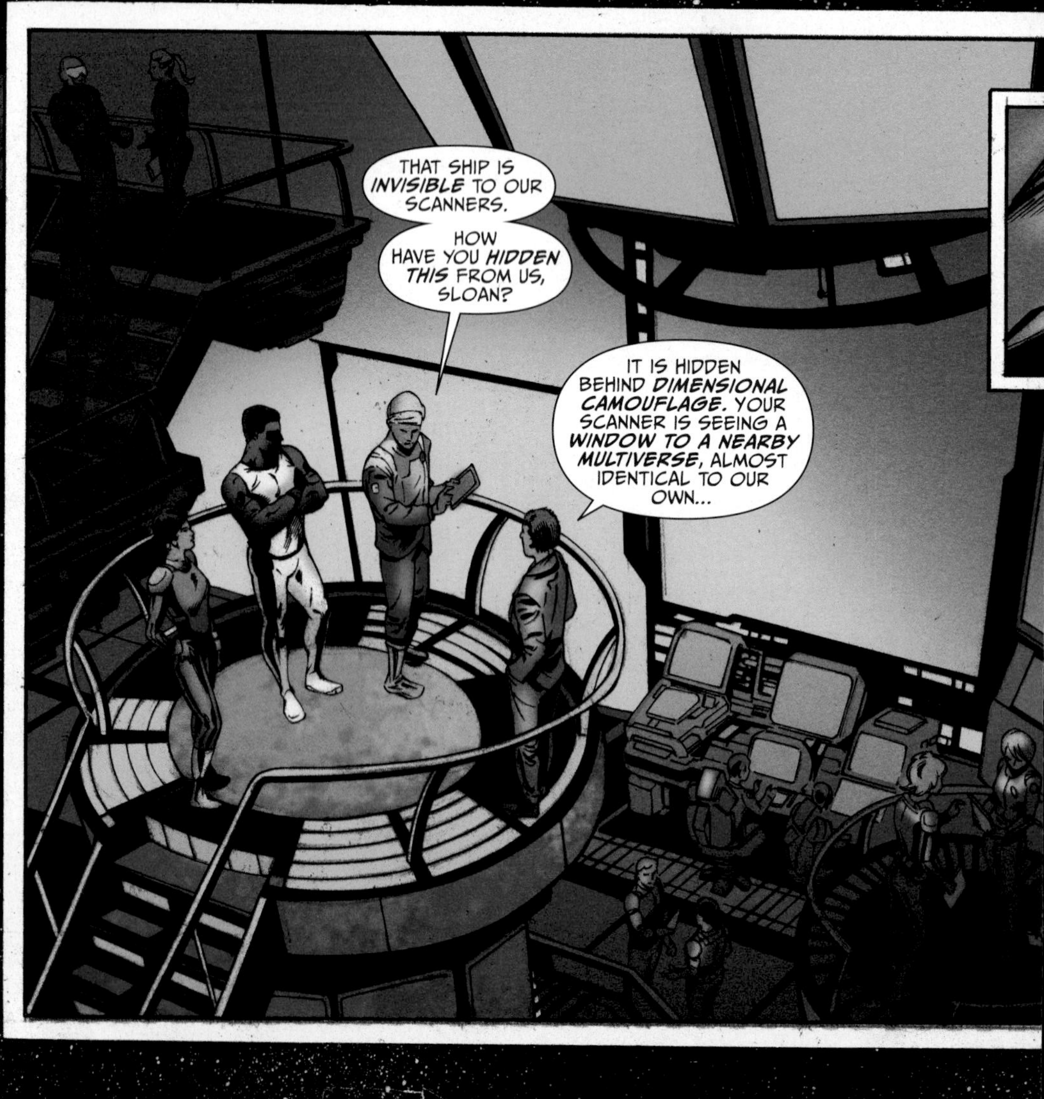
THAT SHIP IS INVISIBLE TO OUR SCANNERS.
HOW HAVE YOU HIDDEN THIS FROM US, SLOAN?
IT IS HIDDEN BEHIND DIMENSIONAL CAMOUFLAGE. YOUR SCANNER IS SEEING A WINDOW TO A NEARBY MULTIVERSE, ALMOST IDENTICAL TO OUR OWN...

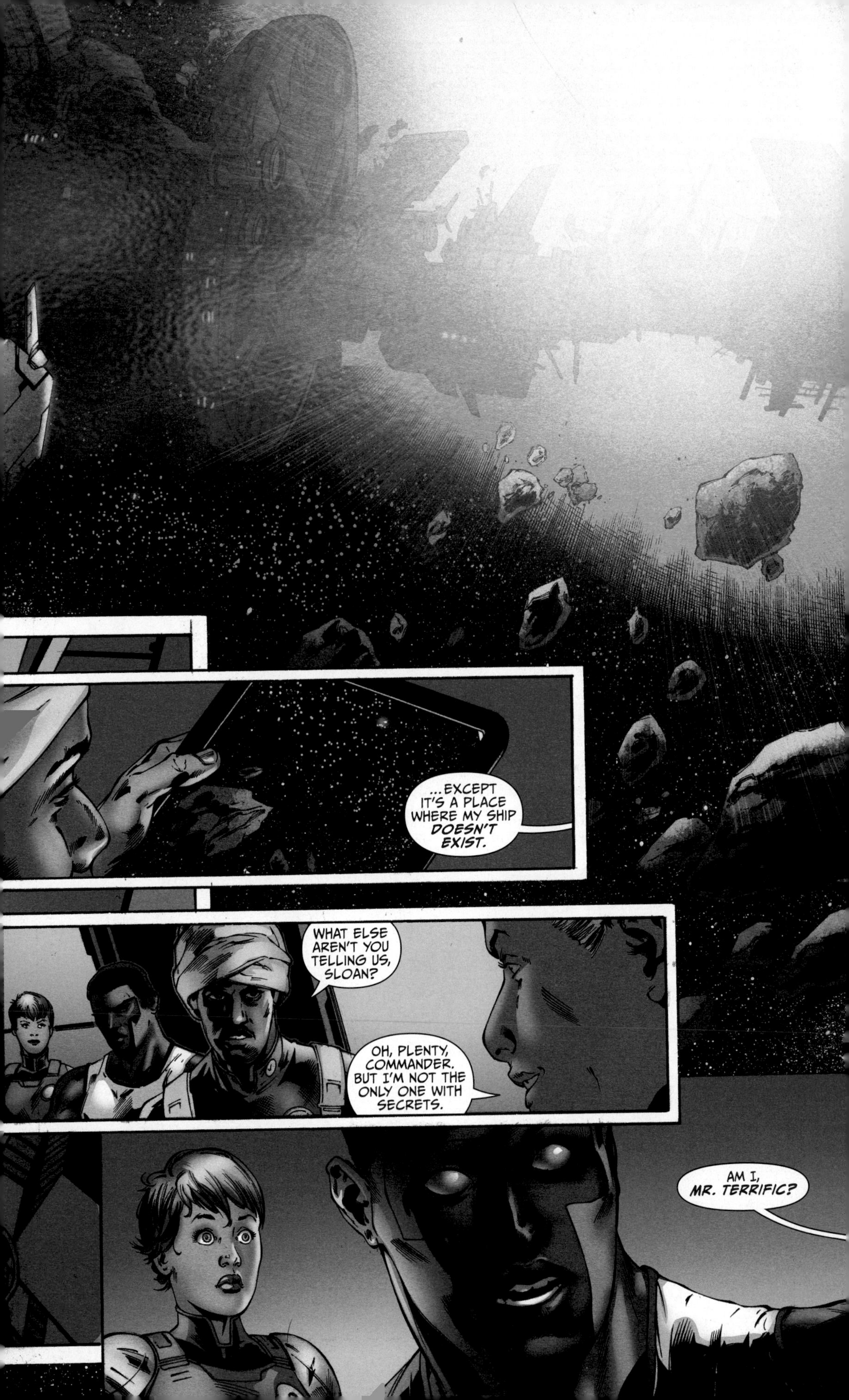
...EXCEPT IT'S A PLACE WHERE MY SHIP DOESN'T EXIST.
WHAT ELSE AREN'T YOU TELLING US, SLOAN?
OH, PLENTY, COMMANDER. BUT I'M NOT THE ONLY ONE WITH SECRETS.
AM I, MR. TERRIFIC?

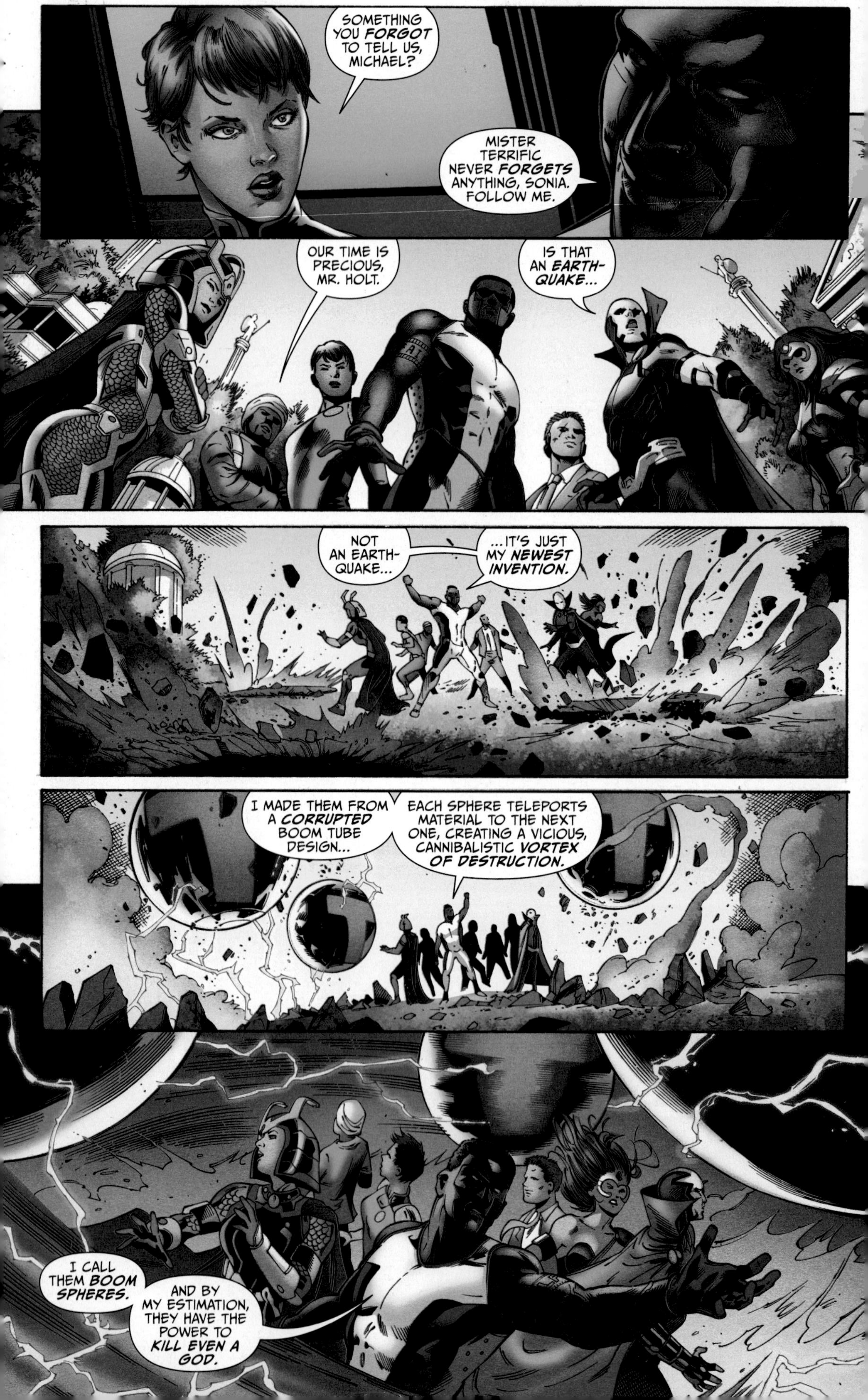
SOMETHING YOU FORGOT TO TELL US, MICHAEL?
MISTER TERRIFIC NEVER FORGETS ANYTHING, SONIA. FOLLOW ME.
OUR TIME IS PRECIOUS, MR. HOLT.
IS THAT AN EARTH-QUAKE...
NOT AN EARTH-QUAKE...
...IT'S JUST MY NEWEST INVENTION.
I MADE THEM FROM A CORRUPTED BOOM TUBE DESIGN...
EACH SPHERE TELEPORTS MATERIAL TO THE NEXT ONE, CREATING A VICIOUS, CANNIBALISTIC VORTEX OF DESTRUCTION.
I CALL THEM BOOM SPHERES.
AND BY MY ESTIMATION, THEY HAVE THE POWER TO KILL EVEN A GOD.

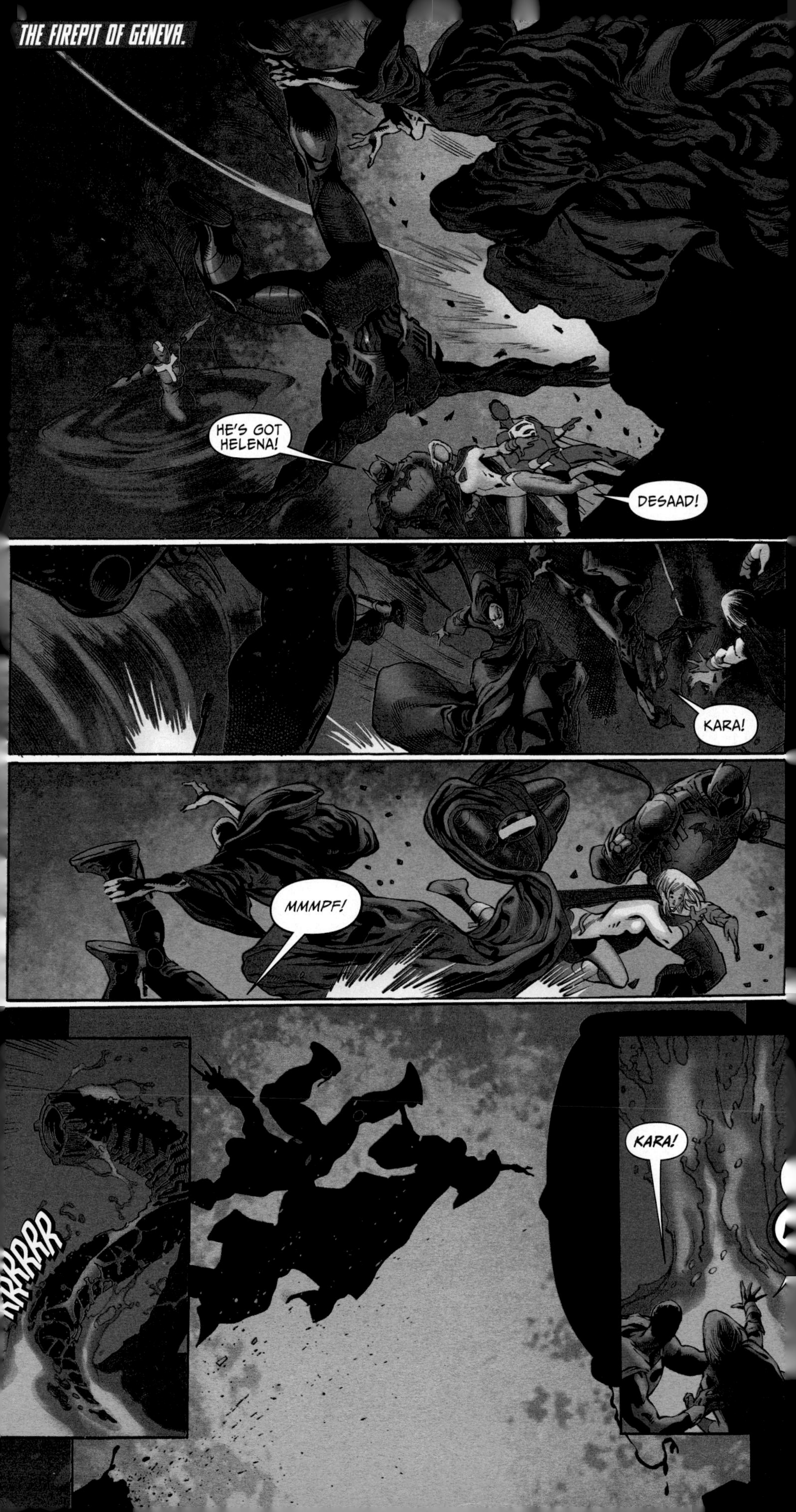
THE FIREPIT OF GENEVA.
HE'S GOT HELENA!
DESAAD!
KARA!
MMMPF!
KRRRR
KARA!

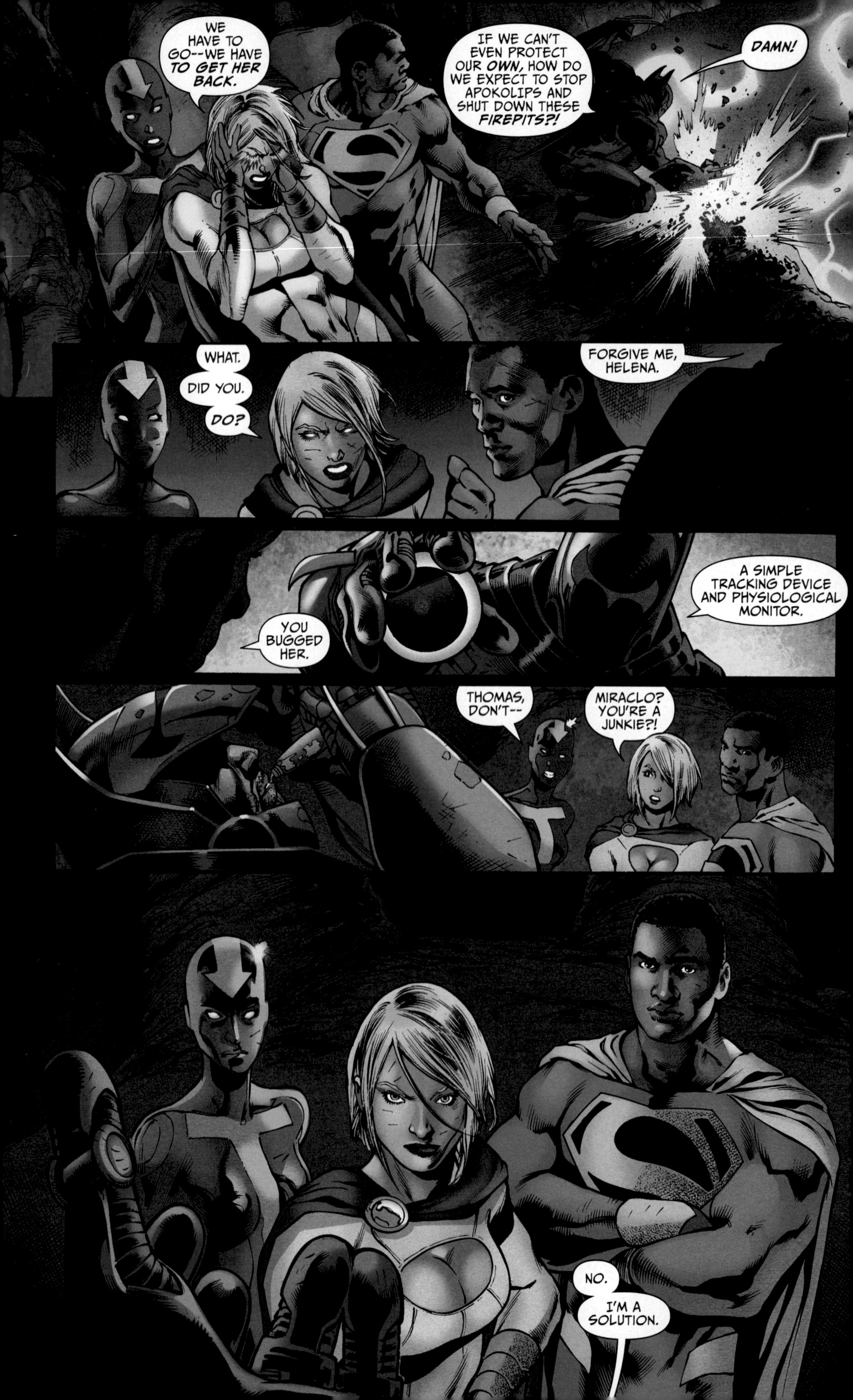
WE HAVE TO GO--WE HAVE TO GET HER BACK.
IF WE CAN'T EVEN PROTECT OUR OWN, HOW DO WE EXPECT TO STOP APOKOLIPS AND SHUT DOWN THESE FIREPITS?!
DAMN!
WHAT.
DID YOU.
DO?
FORGIVE ME, HELENA.
YOU BUGGED HER.
A SIMPLE TRACKING DEVICE AND PHYSIOLOGICAL MONITOR.
THOMAS, DON'T--
MIRACLO? YOU'RE A JUNKIE?!
NO.
I'M A SOLUTION.

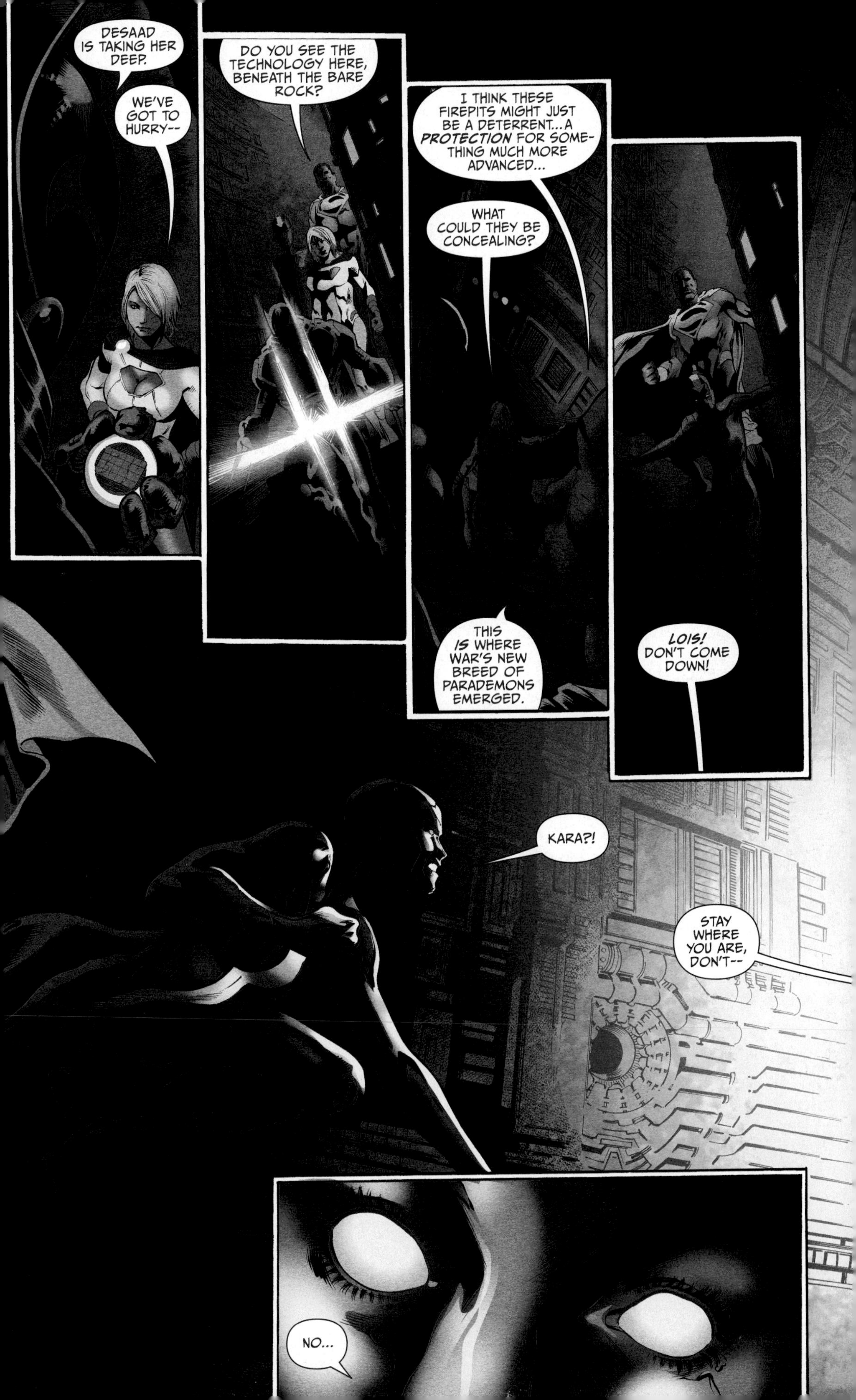
DESAAD IS TAKING HER DEEP.
WE'VE GOT TO HURRY--
DO YOU SEE THE TECHNOLOGY HERE, BENEATH THE BARE ROCK?
I THINK THESE FIREPITS MIGHT JUST BE A DETERRENT...A PROTECTION FOR SOMETHING MUCH MORE ADVANCED...
WHAT COULD THEY BE CONCEALING?
THIS IS WHERE WAR'S NEW BREED OF PARADEMONS EMERGED.
LOIS! DON'T COME DOWN!
KARA?!
STAY WHERE YOU ARE, DON'T--
NO...

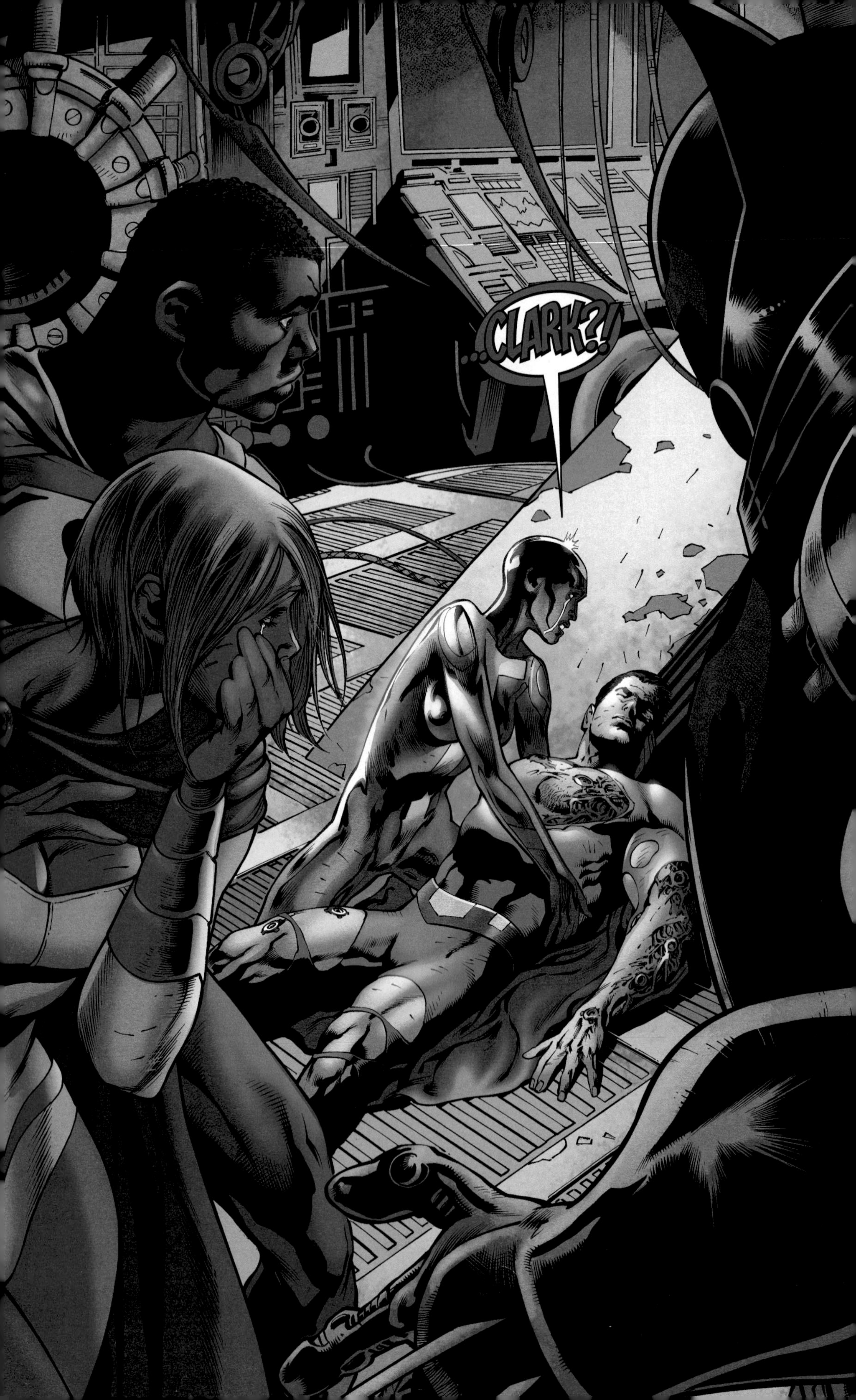
...CLARK?!

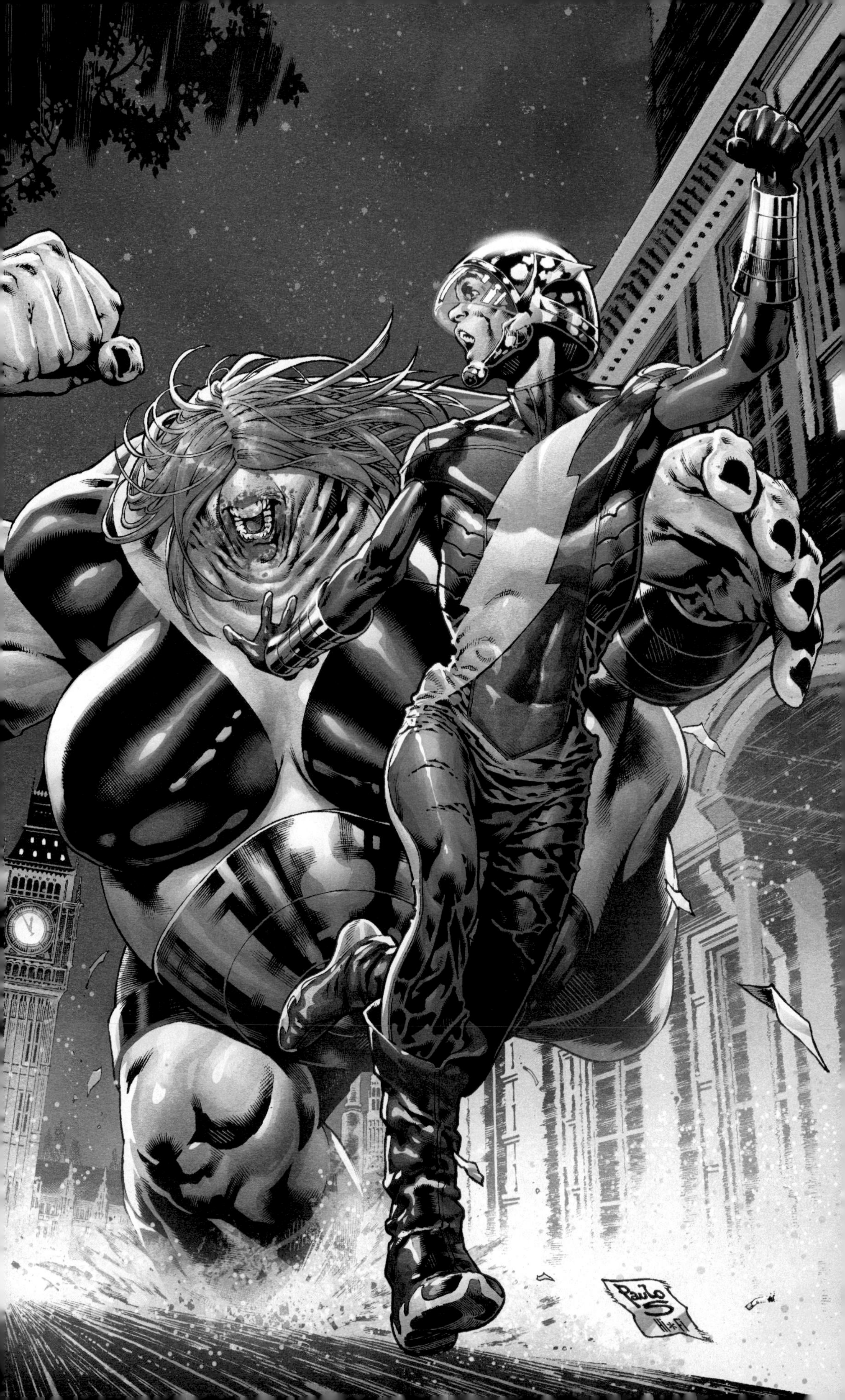

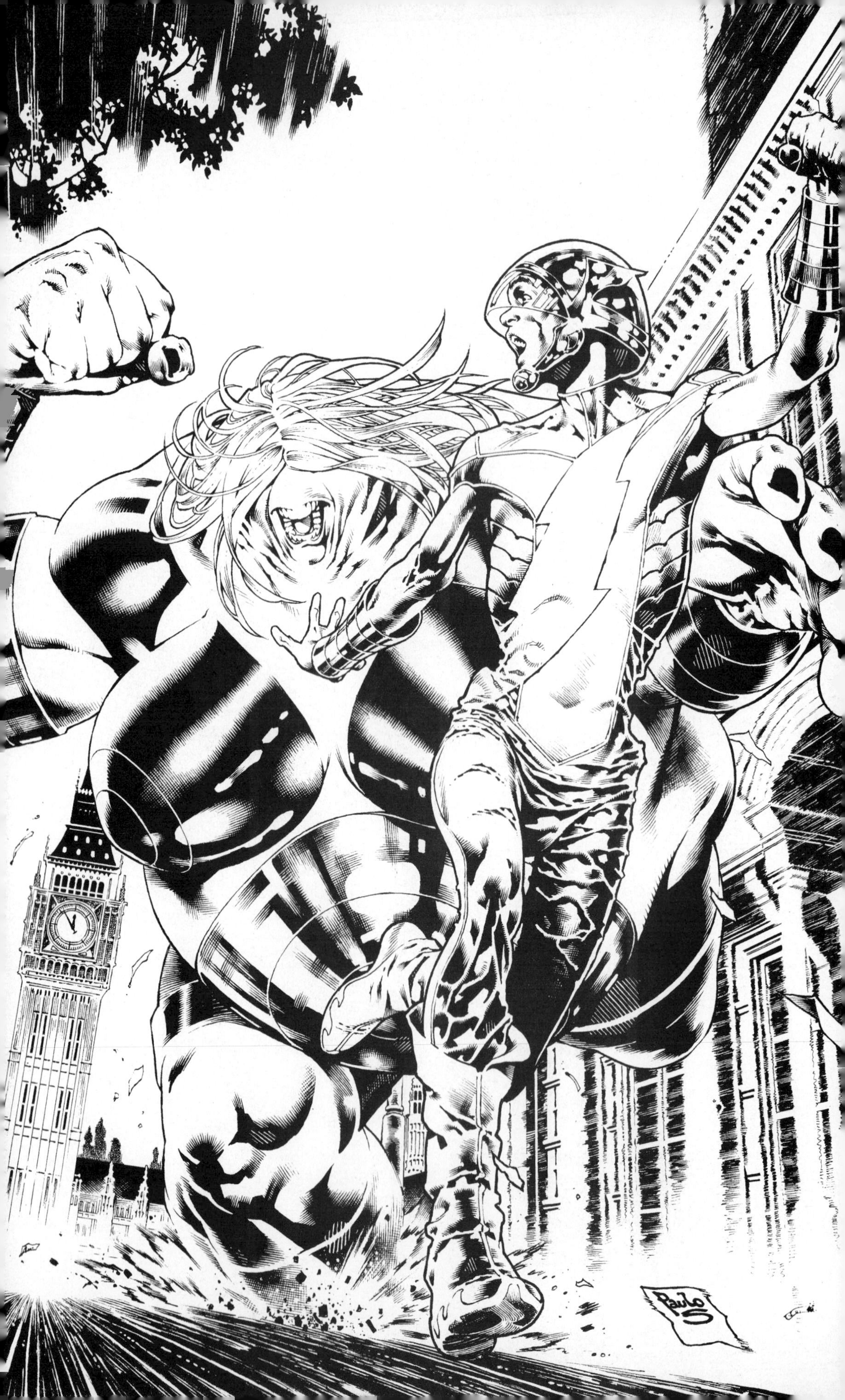

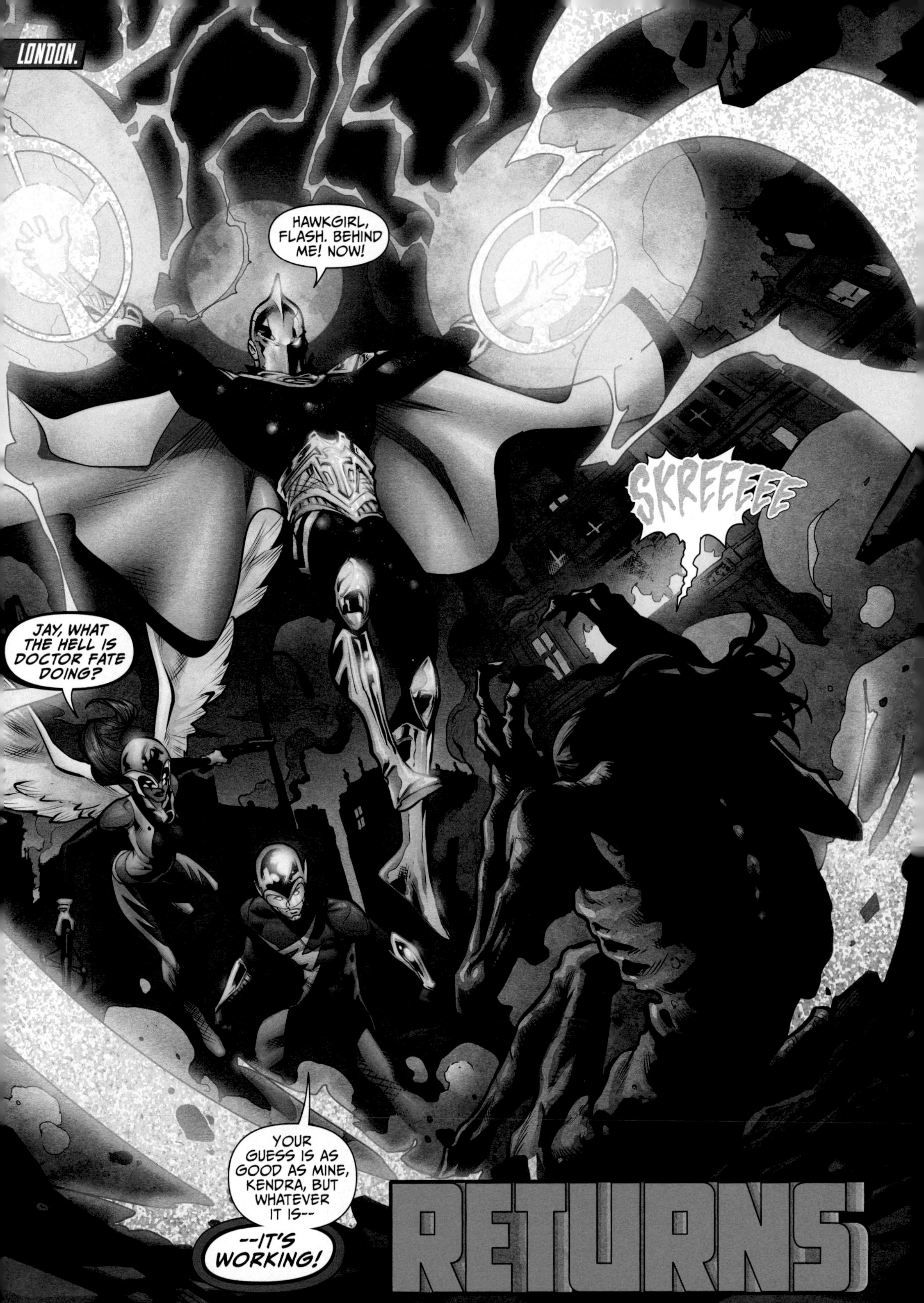

LONDON.
HAWKGIRL, FLASH. BEHIND ME! NOW!
SKREEEEEE
JAY, WHAT THE HELL IS DOCTOR FATE DOING?
YOUR GUESS IS AS GOOD AS MINE, KENDRA, BUT WHATEVER IT IS--
--IT'S WORKING!
RETURNS

STORY BY DANIEL H. WILSON
WRITTEN BY DANIEL H. WILSON, MARGUERITE BENNETT & MIKE JOHNSON
ART BY JORGE JIMENEZ , TYLER KIRKHAM & JOE WEEMS, EDDY BARROWS & EBER FERREIRA, JAN DUURSEMA & DREW GERACI, EDUARDO PANSICA & WALDEN WONG W/JAIME MENDOZA
COLORED BY ALLEN PASSALAQUA LETTERED BY TAYLOR ESPOSITO COVER BY PAULO SIQUEIRA W/ HI-FI

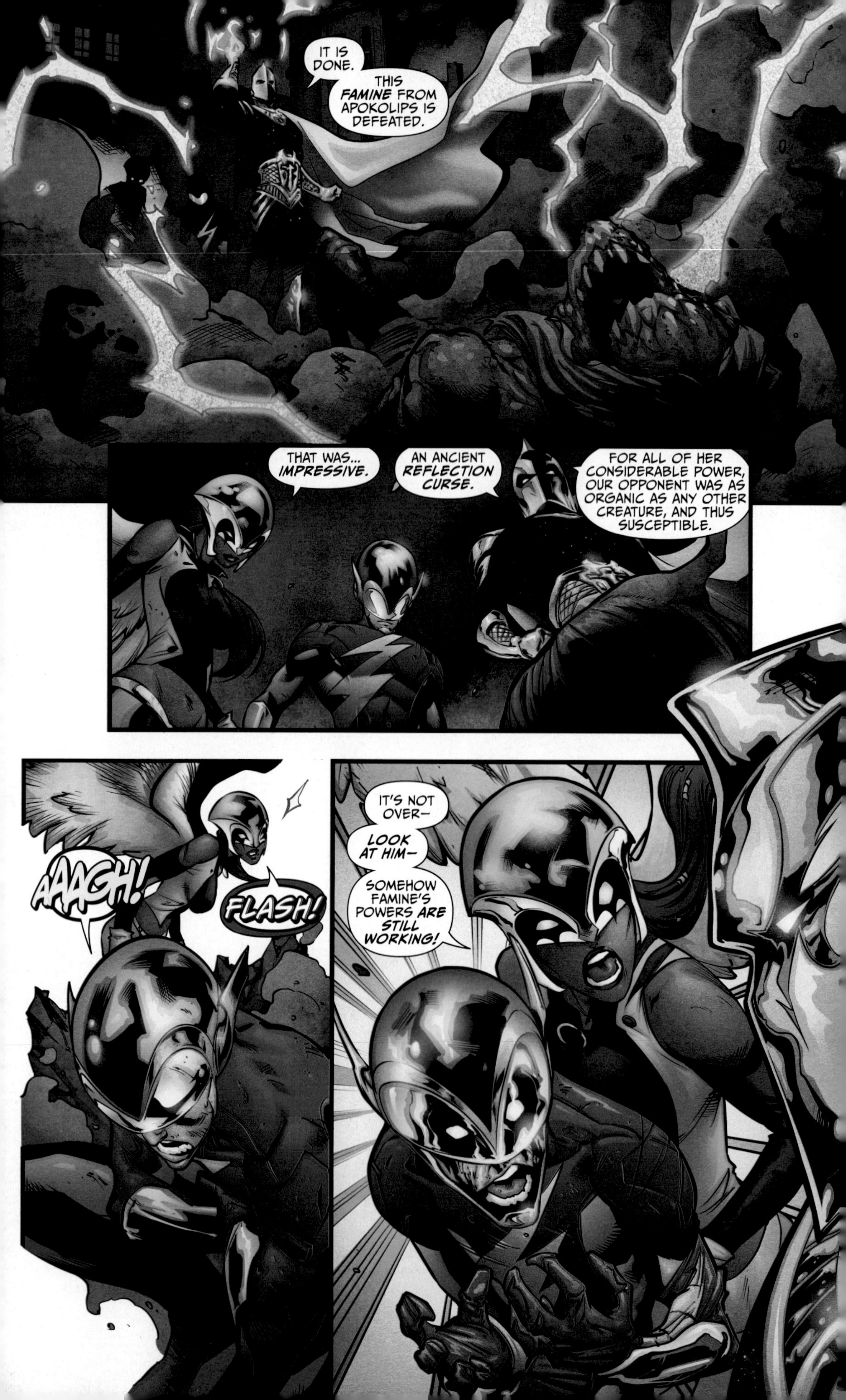
IT IS DONE.
THIS *FAMINE* FROM APOKOLIPS IS DEFEATED.
THAT WAS... *IMPRESSIVE.*
AN ANCIENT *REFLECTION CURSE.*
FOR ALL OF HER CONSIDERABLE POWER, OUR OPPONENT WAS AS ORGANIC AS ANY OTHER CREATURE, AND THUS SUSCEPTIBLE.
AAAGH!
FLASH!
IT'S NOT OVER--
LOOK AT HIM--
SOMEHOW FAMINE'S POWERS *ARE STILL WORKING!*

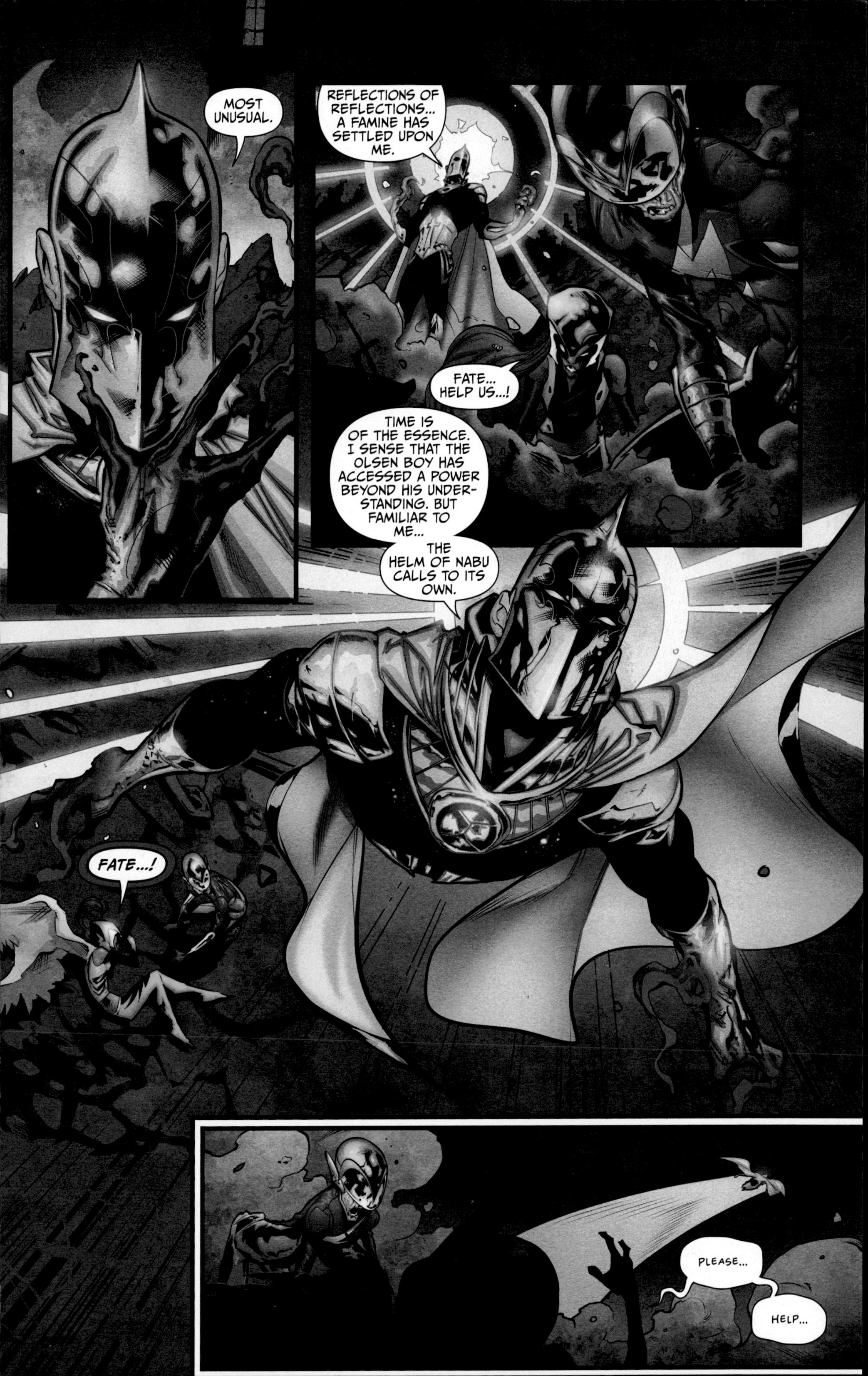

MOST UNUSUAL.
REFLECTIONS OF REFLECTIONS... A FAMINE HAS SETTLED UPON ME.
FATE... HELP US...!
TIME IS OF THE ESSENCE. I SENSE THAT THE OLSEN BOY HAS ACCESSED A POWER BEYOND HIS UNDER-STANDING. BUT FAMILIAR TO ME...
THE HELM OF NABU CALLS TO ITS OWN.
FATE...!
PLEASE...
HELP...

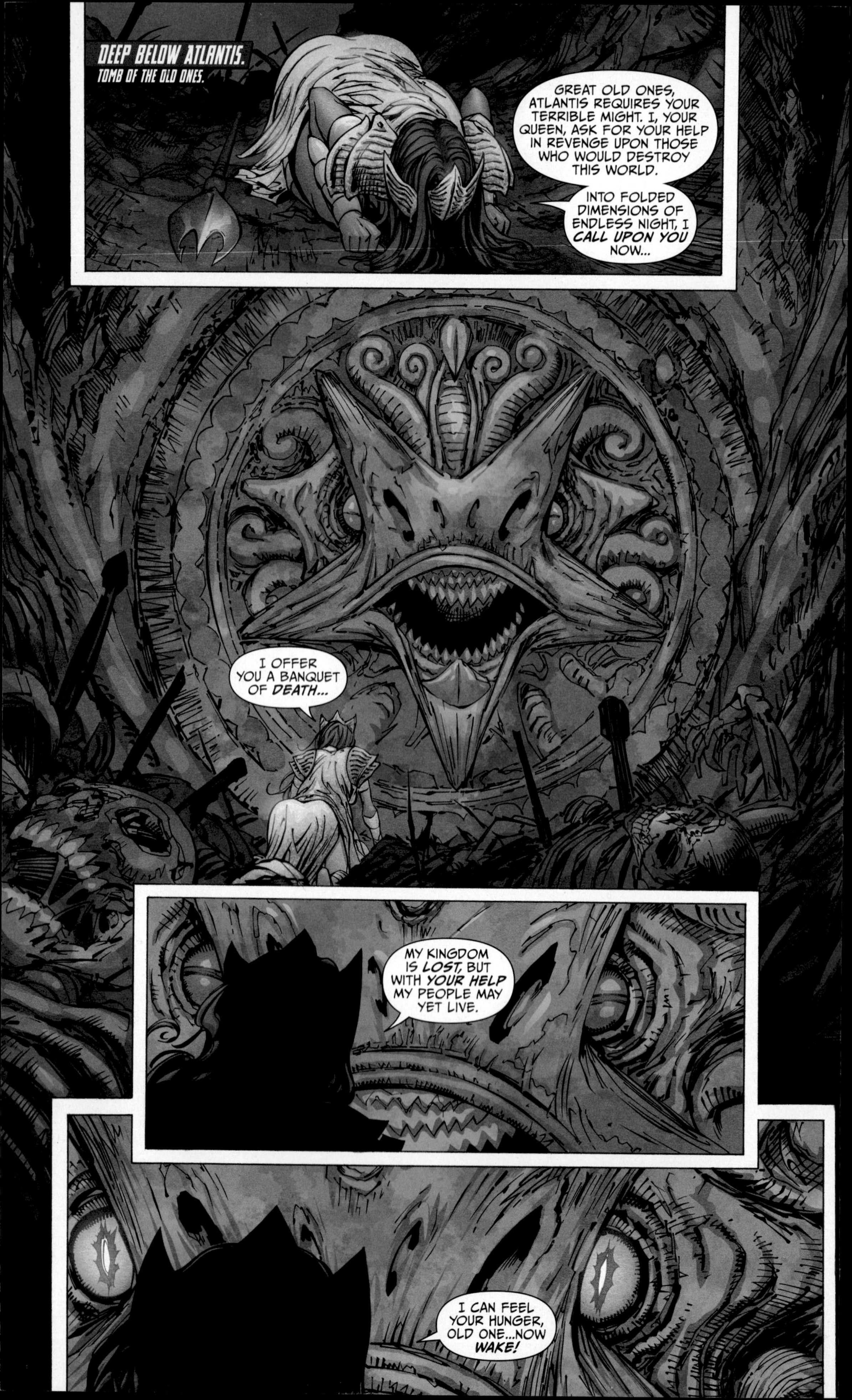
DEEP BELOW ATLANTIS.
TOMB OF THE OLD ONES.
GREAT OLD ONES, ATLANTIS REQUIRES YOUR TERRIBLE MIGHT. I, YOUR QUEEN, ASK FOR YOUR HELP IN REVENGE UPON THOSE WHO WOULD DESTROY THIS WORLD.
INTO FOLDED DIMENSIONS OF ENDLESS NIGHT, I *CALL UPON YOU* NOW...
I OFFER YOU A BANQUET OF *DEATH...*
MY KINGDOM IS *LOST,* BUT WITH *YOUR HELP* MY PEOPLE MAY YET LIVE.
I CAN FEEL YOUR HUNGER, OLD ONE...NOW *WAKE!*

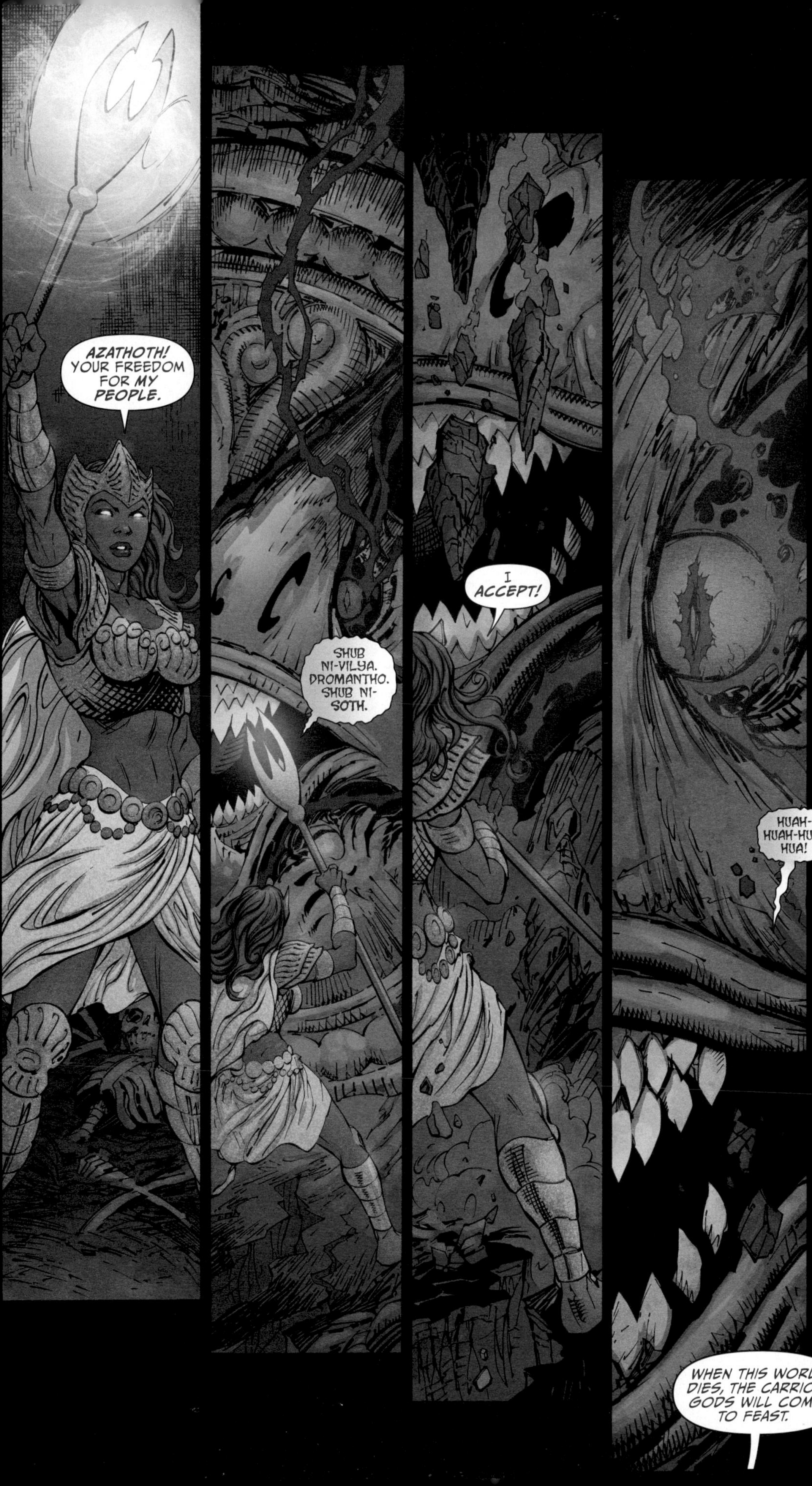
AZATHOTH! YOUR FREEDOM FOR MY PEOPLE.
SHUB NI-VILYA. DROMANTHO. SHUB NI-SOTH.
I ACCEPT!
HUAH-HUAH-HUA-HUA!
WHEN THIS WORLD DIES, THE CARRION GODS WILL COME TO FEAST.

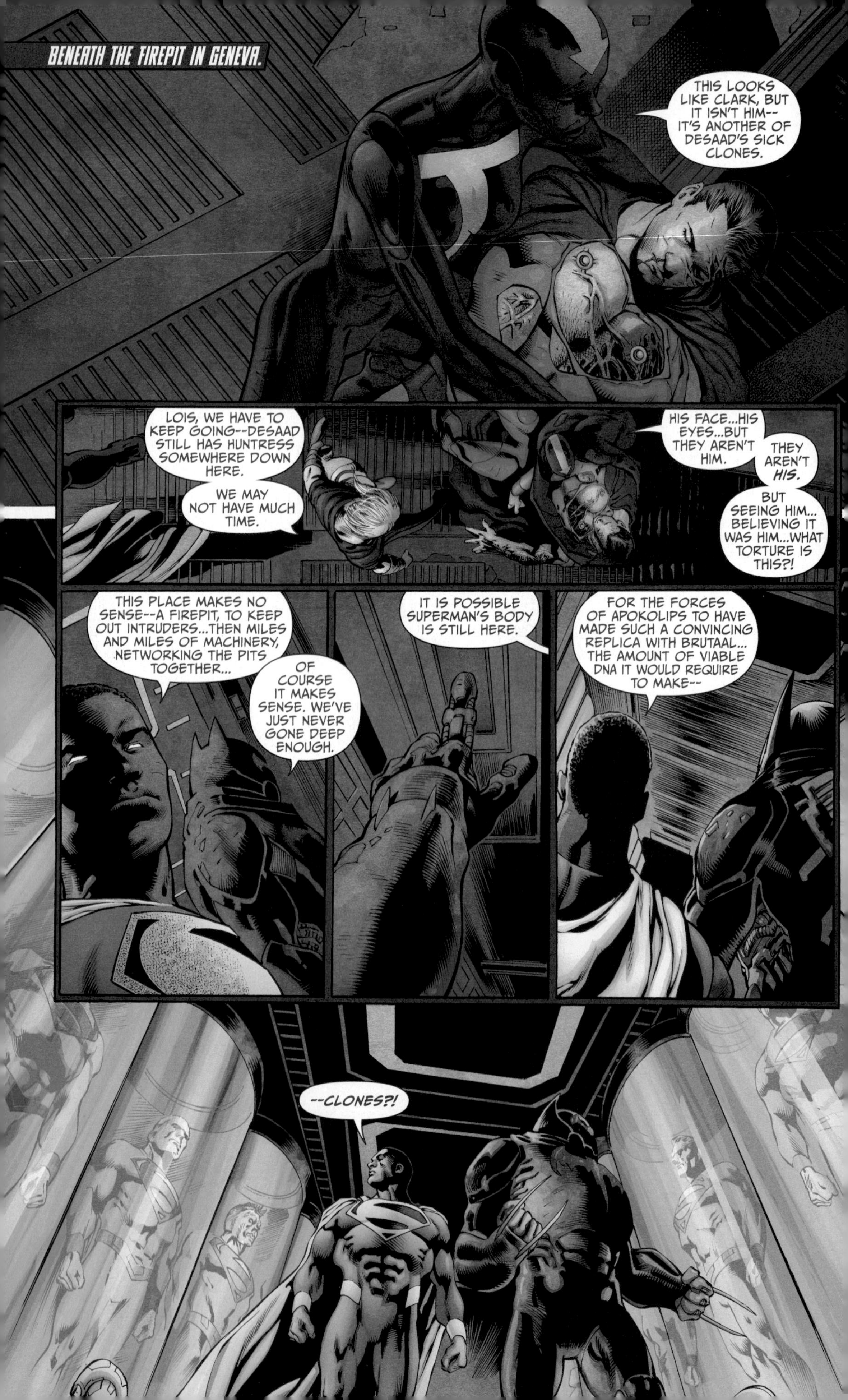
BENEATH THE FIREPIT IN GENEVA.
THIS LOOKS LIKE CLARK, BUT IT ISN'T HIM-- IT'S ANOTHER OF DESAAD'S SICK CLONES.
LOIS, WE HAVE TO KEEP GOING--DESAAD STILL HAS HUNTRESS SOMEWHERE DOWN HERE.
WE MAY NOT HAVE MUCH TIME.
HIS FACE...HIS EYES...BUT THEY AREN'T HIM.
THEY AREN'T *HIS.*
BUT SEEING HIM... BELIEVING IT WAS HIM...WHAT TORTURE IS THIS?!
THIS PLACE MAKES NO SENSE--A FIREPIT, TO KEEP OUT INTRUDERS...THEN MILES AND MILES OF MACHINERY, NETWORKING THE PITS TOGETHER...
OF COURSE IT MAKES SENSE. WE'VE JUST NEVER GONE DEEP ENOUGH.
IT IS POSSIBLE SUPERMAN'S BODY IS STILL HERE.
FOR THE FORCES OF APOKOLIPS TO HAVE MADE SUCH A CONVINCING REPLICA WITH BRUTAAL... THE AMOUNT OF VIABLE DNA IT WOULD REQUIRE TO MAKE--
--CLONES?!

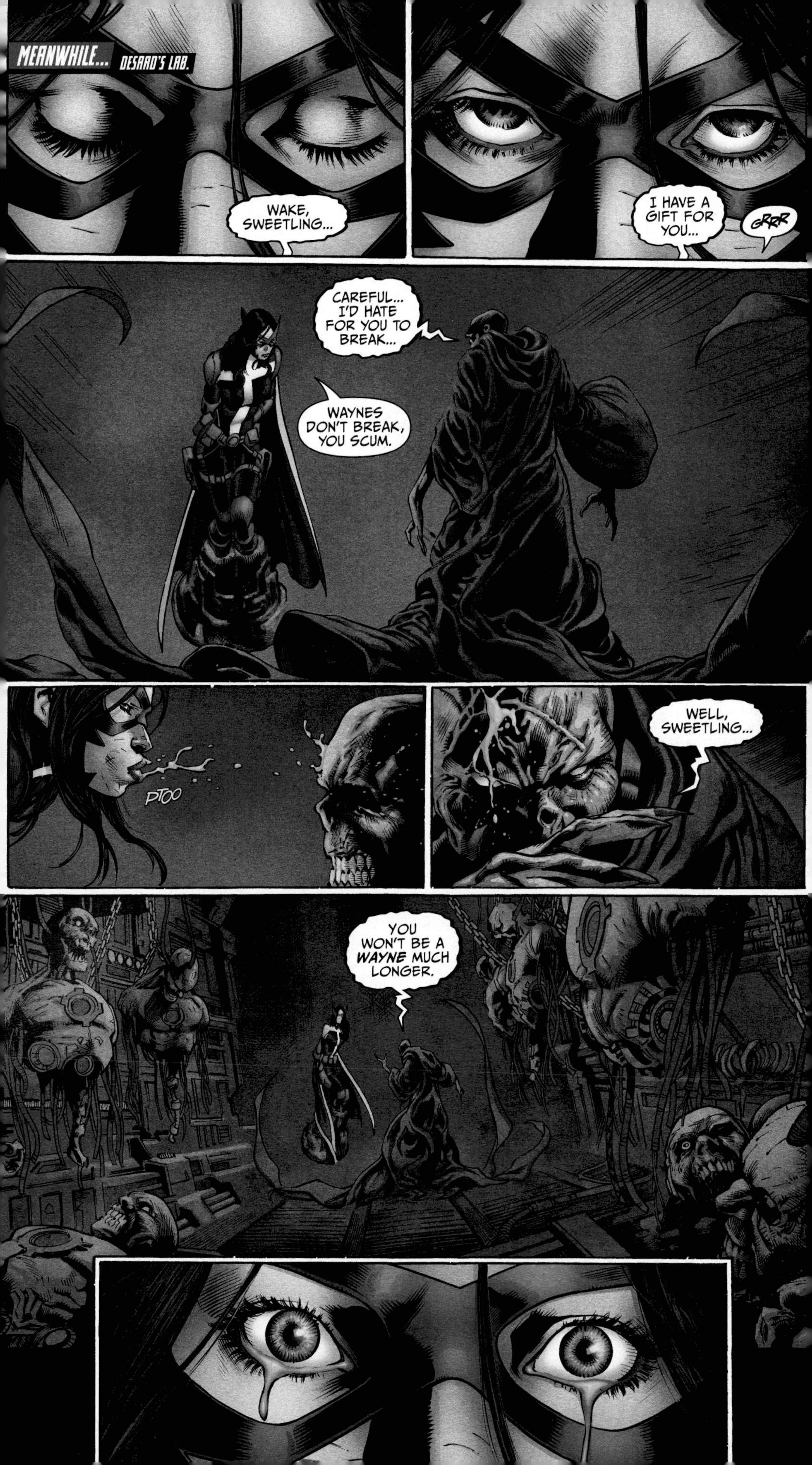
MEANWHILE... DESARD'S LAB.
WAKE, SWEETLING...
I HAVE A GIFT FOR YOU...
GRRR
CAREFUL... I'D HATE FOR YOU TO BREAK...
WAYNES DON'T BREAK, YOU SCUM.
PTOO
WELL, SWEETLING...
YOU WON'T BE A WAYNE MUCH LONGER.

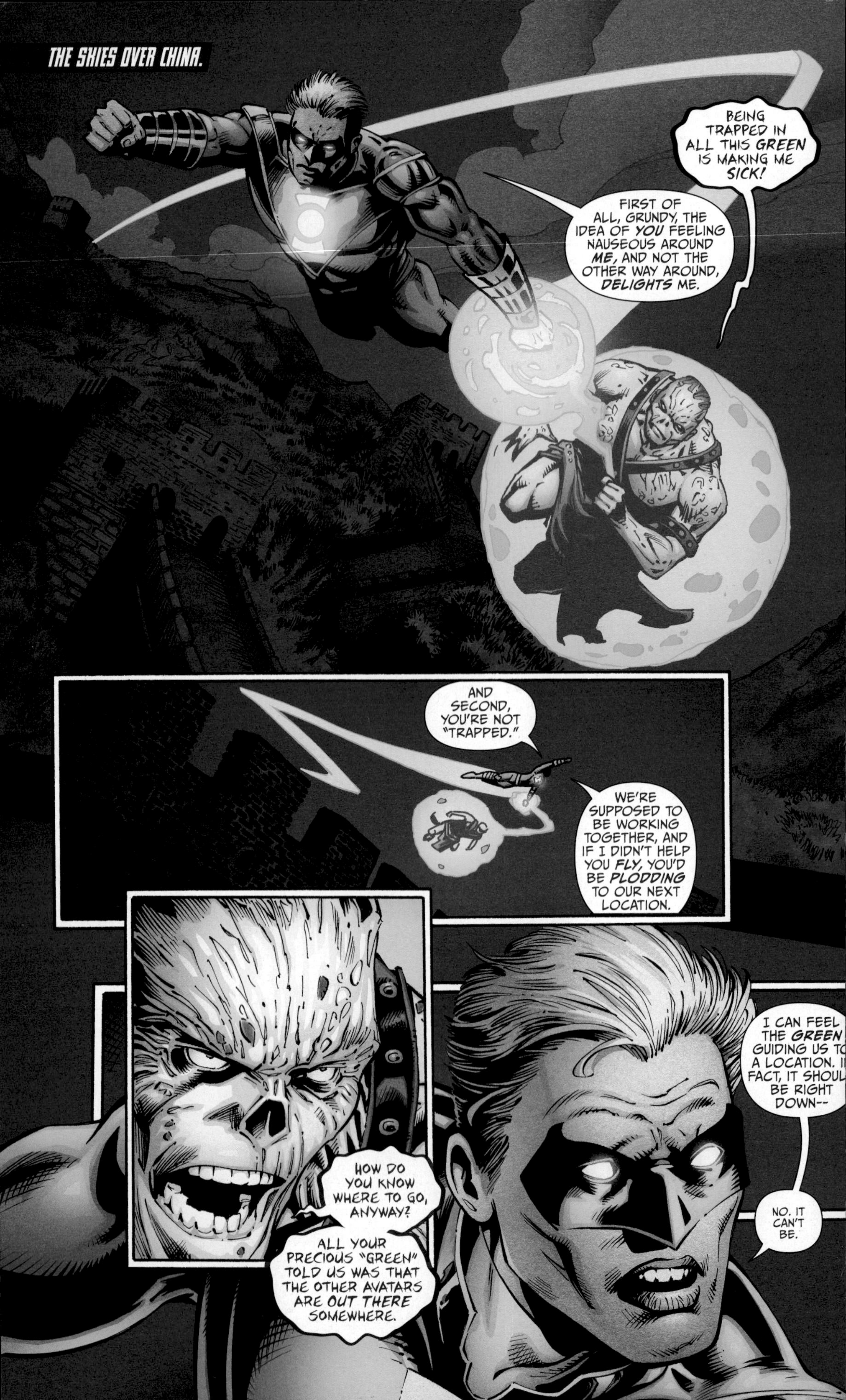
THE SKIES OVER CHINA.
BEING TRAPPED IN ALL THIS GREEN IS MAKING ME SICK!
FIRST OF ALL, GRUNDY, THE IDEA OF YOU FEELING NAUSEOUS AROUND ME, AND NOT THE OTHER WAY AROUND, DELIGHTS ME.
AND SECOND, YOU'RE NOT "TRAPPED."
WE'RE SUPPOSED TO BE WORKING TOGETHER, AND IF I DIDN'T HELP YOU FLY, YOU'D BE PLODDING TO OUR NEXT LOCATION.
HOW DO YOU KNOW WHERE TO GO, ANYWAY?
ALL YOUR PRECIOUS "GREEN" TOLD US WAS THAT THE OTHER AVATARS ARE OUT THERE SOMEWHERE.
I CAN FEEL THE GREEN GUIDING US TO A LOCATION. IN FACT, IT SHOUL BE RIGHT DOWN--
NO. IT CAN'T BE.

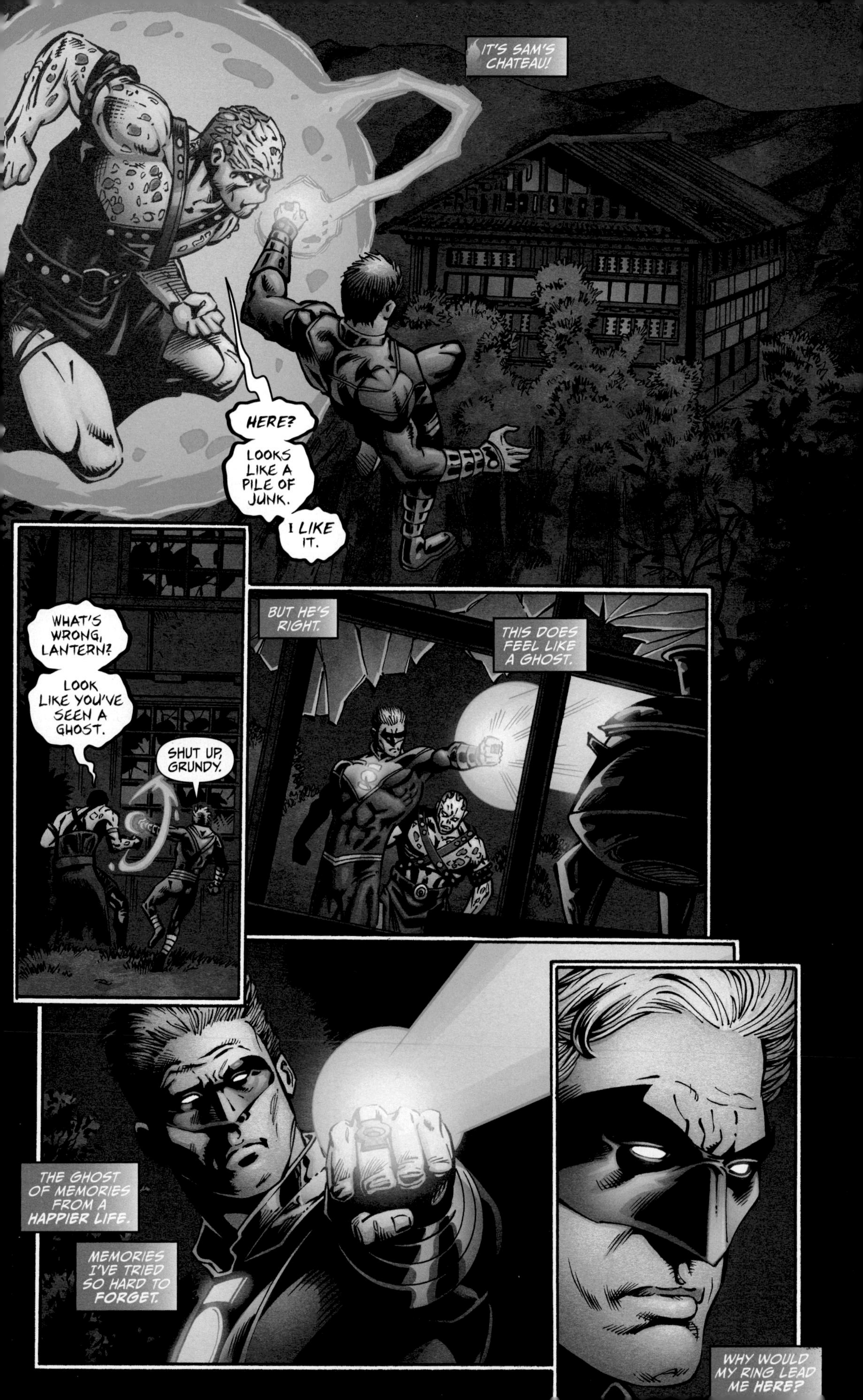
IT'S SAM'S CHATEAU!
HERE?
LOOKS LIKE A PILE OF JUNK.
I LIKE IT.
WHAT'S WRONG, LANTERN?
LOOK LIKE YOU'VE SEEN A GHOST.
SHUT UP, GRUNDY.
BUT HE'S RIGHT.
THIS DOES FEEL LIKE A GHOST.
THE GHOST OF MEMORIES FROM A HAPPIER LIFE.
MEMORIES I'VE TRIED SO HARD TO FORGET.
WHY WOULD MY RING LEAD ME HERE?

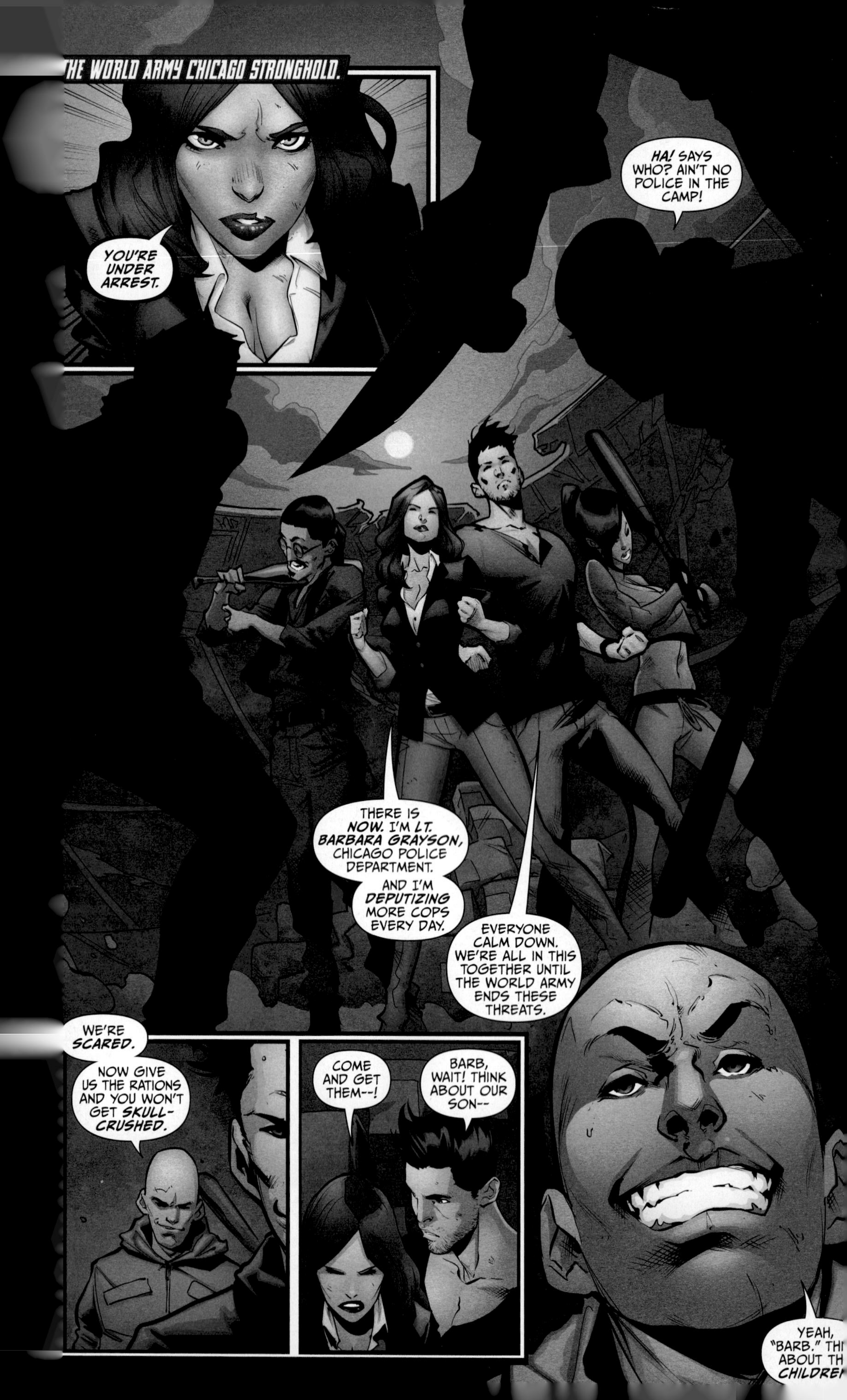
THE WORLD ARMY CHICAGO STRONGHOLD.
YOU'RE UNDER ARREST.
HA! SAYS WHO? AIN'T NO POLICE IN THE CAMP!
THERE IS NOW. I'M LT. BARBARA GRAYSON, CHICAGO POLICE DEPARTMENT.
AND I'M DEPUTIZING MORE COPS EVERY DAY.
EVERYONE CALM DOWN. WE'RE ALL IN THIS TOGETHER UNTIL THE WORLD ARMY ENDS THESE THREATS.
WE'RE SCARED.
NOW GIVE US THE RATIONS AND YOU WON'T GET SKULL-CRUSHED.
COME AND GET THEM--!
BARB, WAIT! THINK ABOUT OUR SON--
YEAH, "BARB." THI ABOUT TH CHILDRE

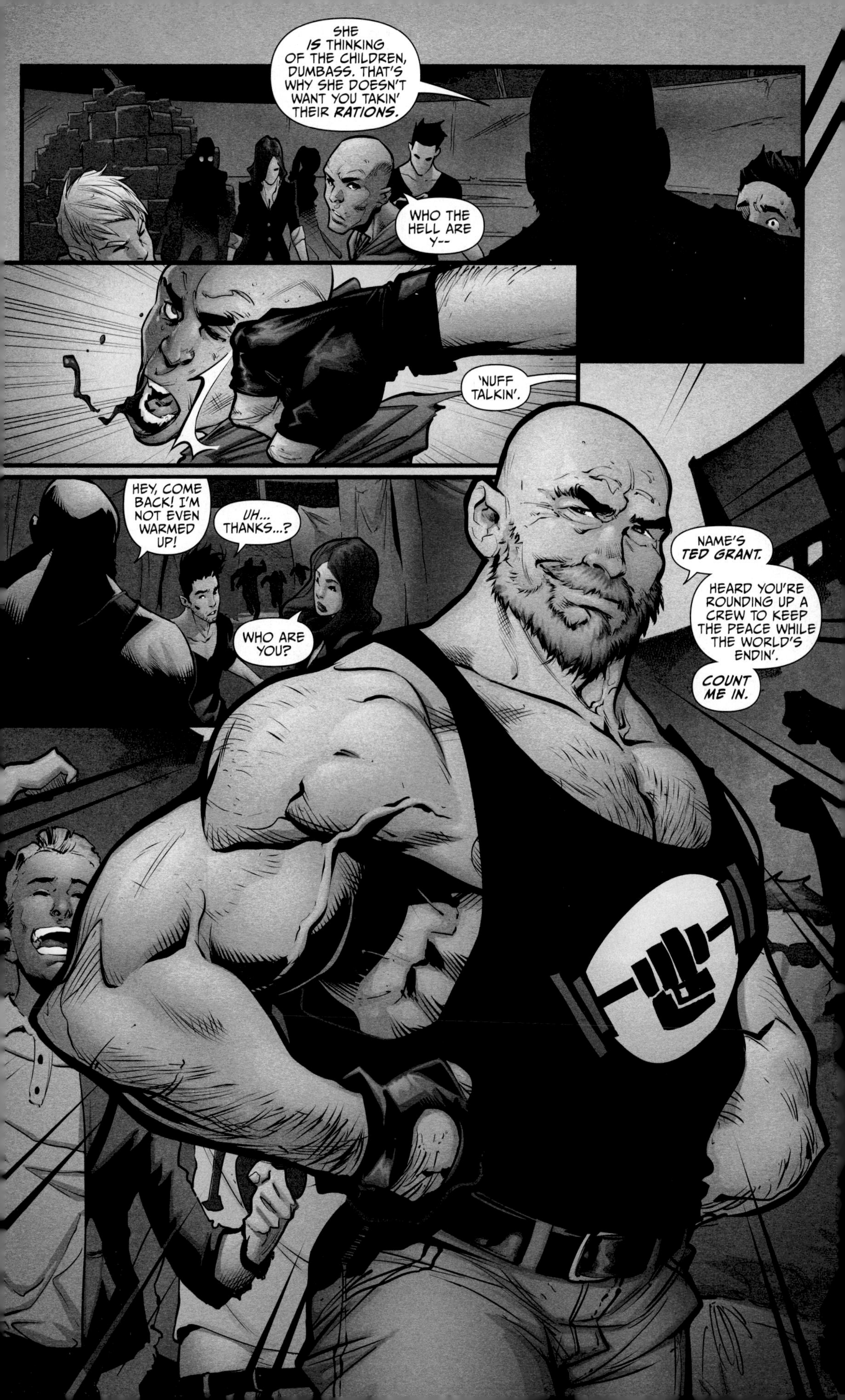
SHE IS THINKING OF THE CHILDREN, DUMBASS. THAT'S WHY SHE DOESN'T WANT YOU TAKIN' THEIR RATIONS.
WHO THE HELL ARE Y--
'NUFF TALKIN'.
HEY, COME BACK! I'M NOT EVEN WARMED UP!
UH... THANKS...?
WHO ARE YOU?
NAME'S TED GRANT.
HEARD YOU'RE ROUNDING UP A CREW TO KEEP THE PEACE WHILE THE WORLD'S ENDIN'.
COUNT ME IN.

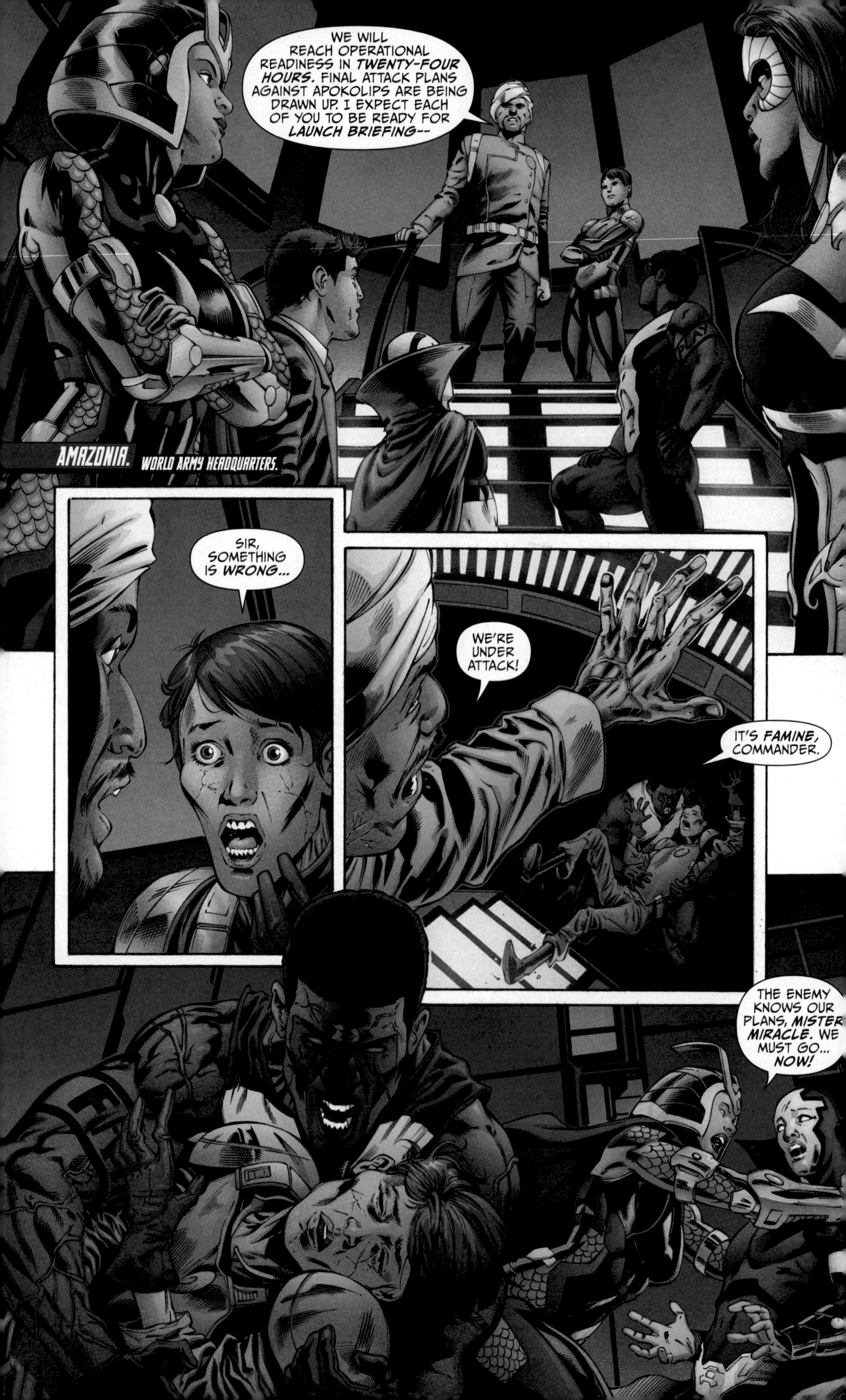
WE WILL REACH OPERATIONAL READINESS IN TWENTY-FOUR HOURS. FINAL ATTACK PLANS AGAINST APOKOLIPS ARE BEING DRAWN UP. I EXPECT EACH OF YOU TO BE READY FOR LAUNCH BRIEFING--
AMAZONIA. WORLD ARMY HEADQUARTERS.
SIR, SOMETHING IS WRONG...
WE'RE UNDER ATTACK!
IT'S FAMINE, COMMANDER.
THE ENEMY KNOWS OUR PLANS, MISTER MIRACLE. WE MUST GO... NOW!

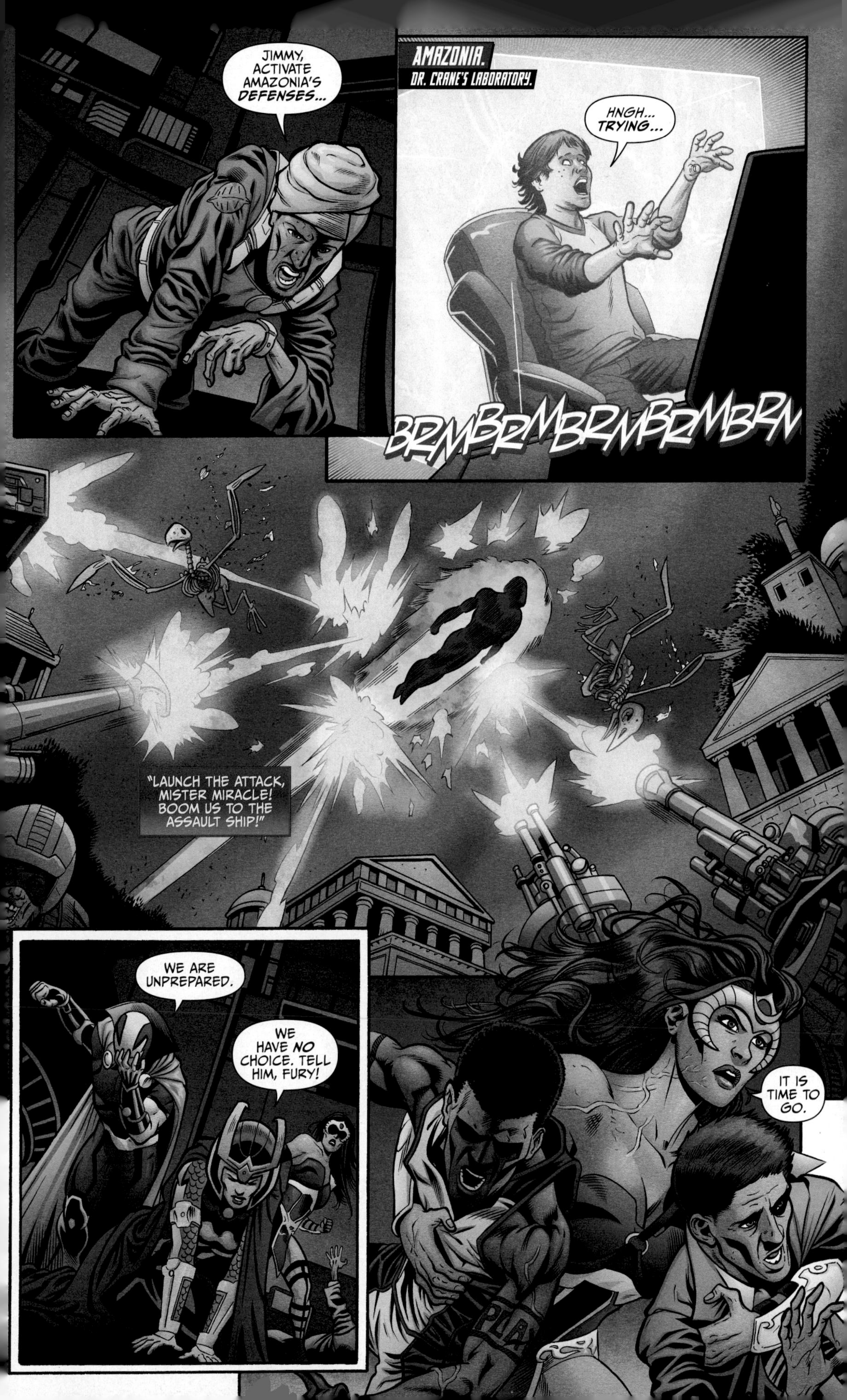
JIMMY, ACTIVATE AMAZONIA'S DEFENSES...
AMAZONIA.
DR. CRANE'S LABORATORY.
HNGH... TRYING...
BRMBRMBRMBRMBRMBRN
"LAUNCH THE ATTACK, MISTER MIRACLE! BOOM US TO THE ASSAULT SHIP!"
WE ARE UNPREPARED.
WE HAVE NO CHOICE. TELL HIM, FURY!
IT IS TIME TO GO.

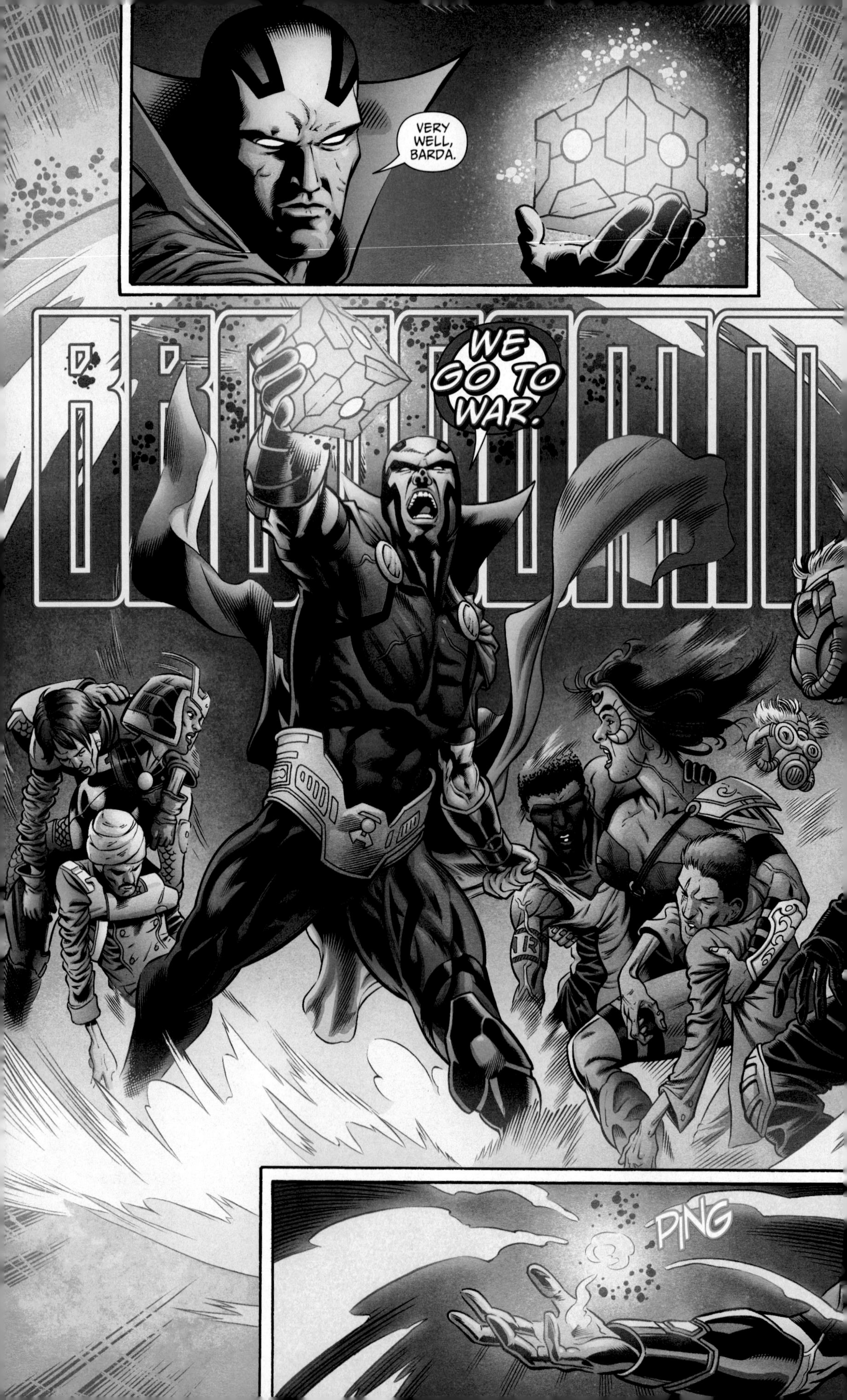
VERY WELL, BARDA.
WE GO TO WAR.
PING

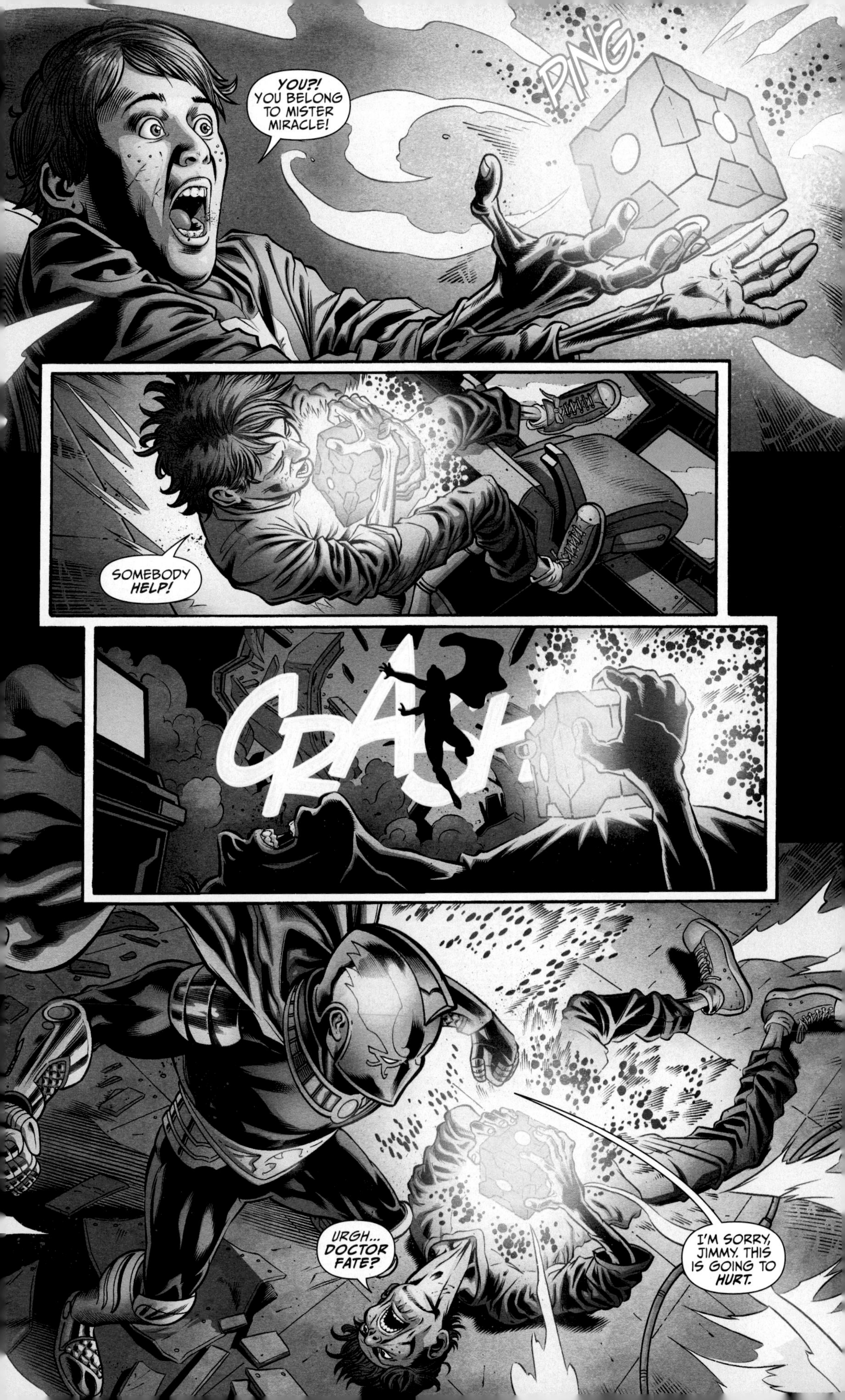
PING
YOU?! YOU BELONG TO MISTER MIRACLE!
SOMEBODY HELP!
CRASH
URGH... DOCTOR FATE?
I'M SORRY, JIMMY. THIS IS GOING TO HURT.

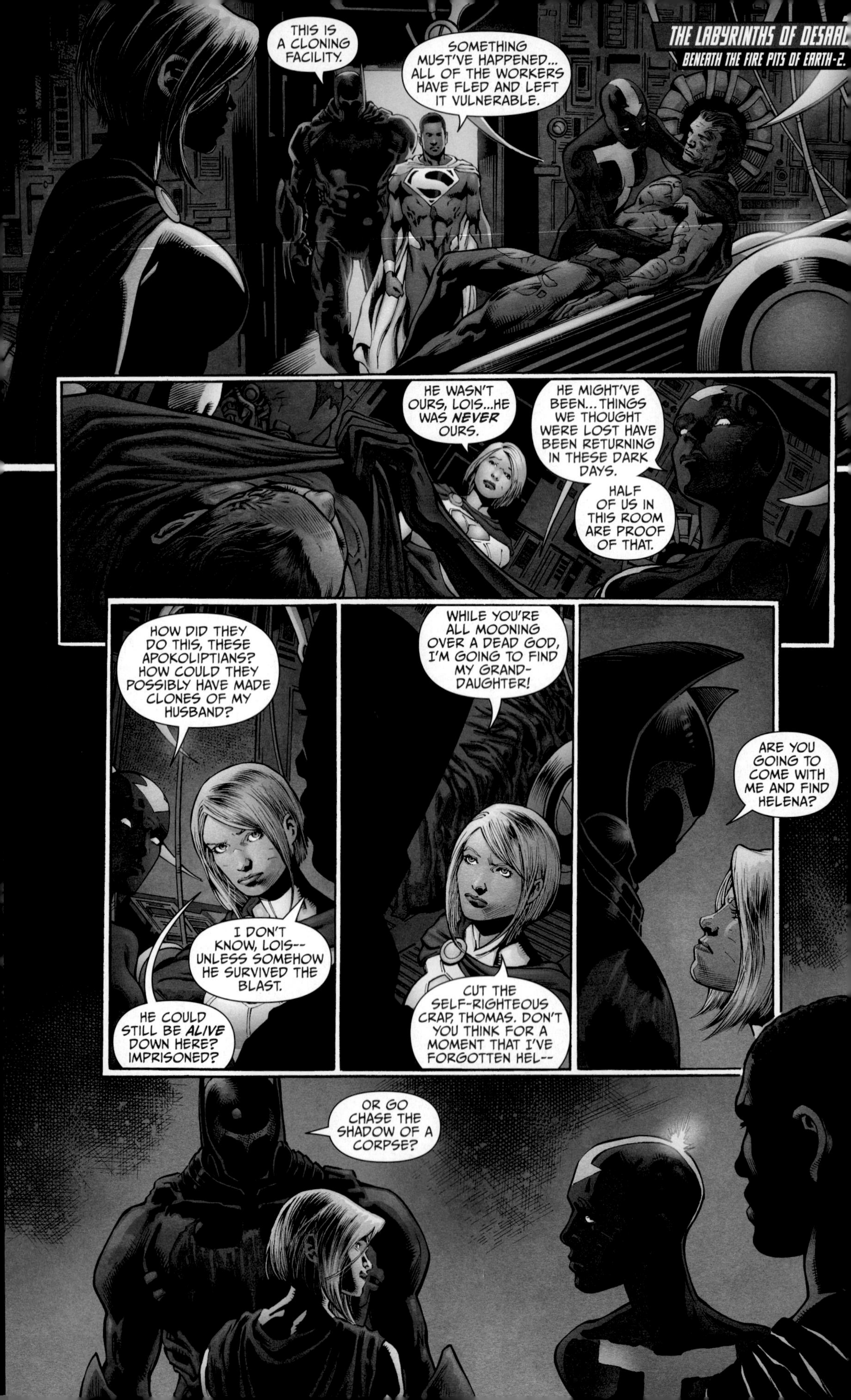

THE LABYRINTHS OF DESAAD
BENEATH THE FIRE PITS OF EARTH-2.
THIS IS A CLONING FACILITY.
SOMETHING MUST'VE HAPPENED... ALL OF THE WORKERS HAVE FLED AND LEFT IT VULNERABLE.
HE WASN'T OURS, LOIS...HE WAS NEVER OURS.
HE MIGHT'VE BEEN... THINGS WE THOUGHT WERE LOST HAVE BEEN RETURNING IN THESE DARK DAYS.
HALF OF US IN THIS ROOM ARE PROOF OF THAT.
HOW DID THEY DO THIS, THESE APOKOLIPTIANS? HOW COULD THEY POSSIBLY HAVE MADE CLONES OF MY HUSBAND?
I DON'T KNOW, LOIS-- UNLESS SOMEHOW HE SURVIVED THE BLAST.
HE COULD STILL BE ALIVE DOWN HERE? IMPRISONED?
WHILE YOU'RE ALL MOONING OVER A DEAD GOD, I'M GOING TO FIND MY GRAND-DAUGHTER!
CUT THE SELF-RIGHTEOUS CRAP, THOMAS. DON'T YOU THINK FOR A MOMENT THAT I'VE FORGOTTEN HEL--
ARE YOU GOING TO COME WITH ME AND FIND HELENA?
OR GO CHASE THE SHADOW OF A CORPSE?

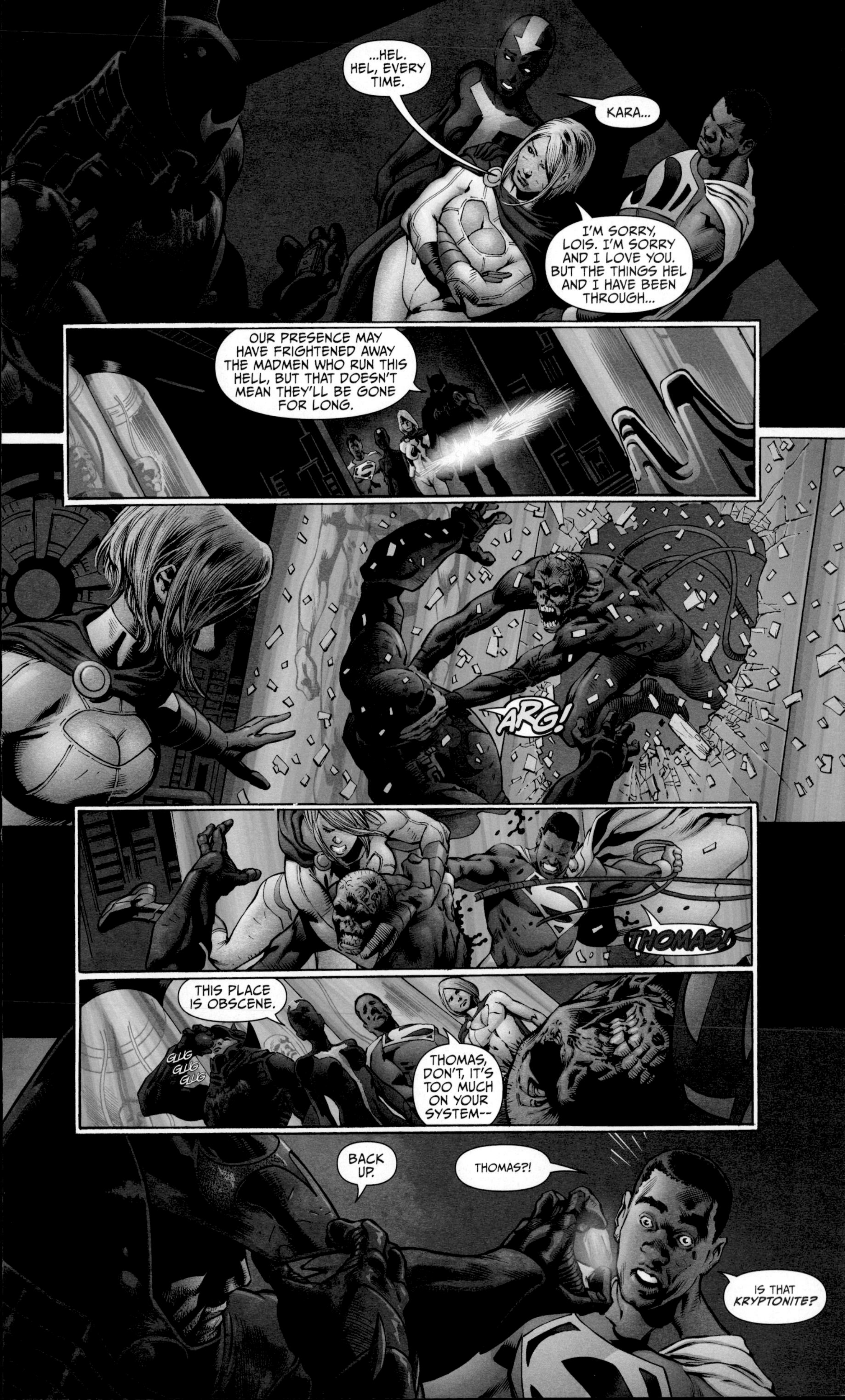

...HEL. HEL, EVERY TIME.
KARA...
I'M SORRY, LOIS. I'M SORRY AND I LOVE YOU. BUT THE THINGS HEL AND I HAVE BEEN THROUGH...
OUR PRESENCE MAY HAVE FRIGHTENED AWAY THE MADMEN WHO RUN THIS HELL, BUT THAT DOESN'T MEAN THEY'LL BE GONE FOR LONG.
ARG!
THOMAS!
THIS PLACE IS OBSCENE.
GLUG GLUG GLUG
THOMAS, DON'T, IT'S TOO MUCH ON YOUR SYSTEM--
BACK UP.
THOMAS?!
IS THAT KRYPTONITE?

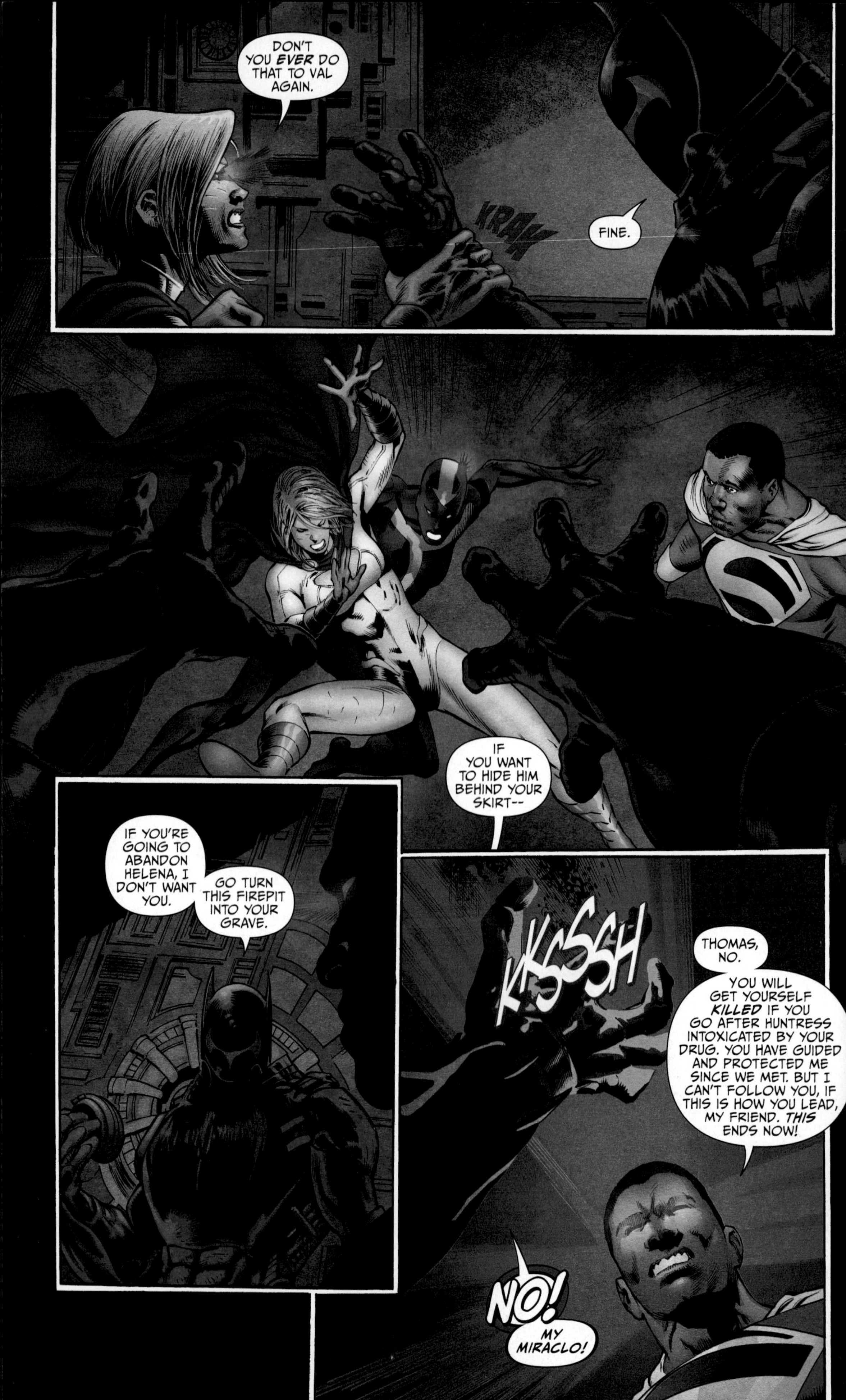

DON'T YOU **EVER** DO THAT TO VAL AGAIN.
KRAK
FINE.
IF YOU WANT TO HIDE HIM BEHIND YOUR SKIRT--
IF YOU'RE GOING TO ABANDON HELENA, I DON'T WANT YOU.
GO TURN THIS FIREPIT INTO YOUR GRAVE.
KKSSSH
THOMAS, NO.
YOU WILL GET YOURSELF **KILLED** IF YOU GO AFTER HUNTRESS INTOXICATED BY YOUR DRUG. YOU HAVE GUIDED AND PROTECTED ME SINCE WE MET. BUT I CAN'T FOLLOW YOU, IF THIS IS HOW YOU LEAD, MY FRIEND. ***THIS*** ENDS NOW!
NO! MY MIRACLO!

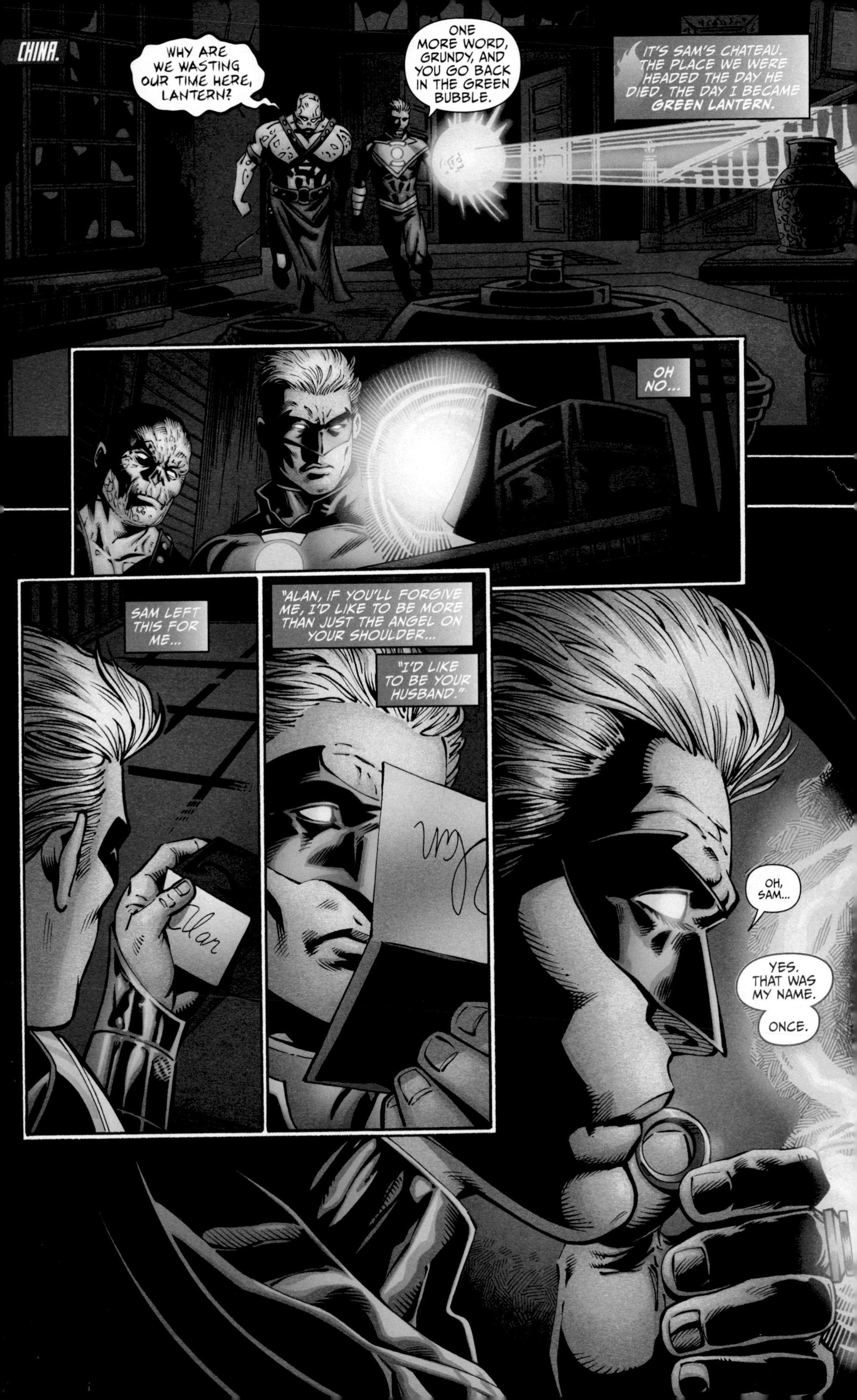
CHINA.
WHY ARE WE WASTING OUR TIME HERE, LANTERN?
ONE MORE WORD, GRUNDY, AND YOU GO BACK IN THE GREEN BUBBLE.
IT'S SAM'S CHATEAU. THE PLACE WE WERE HEADED THE DAY HE DIED. THE DAY I BECAME GREEN LANTERN.
OH NO...
SAM LEFT THIS FOR ME...
Alan
"ALAN, IF YOU'LL FORGIVE ME, I'D LIKE TO BE MORE THAN JUST THE ANGEL ON YOUR SHOULDER...
"I'D LIKE TO BE YOUR HUSBAND."
OH, SAM...
YES. THAT WAS MY NAME.
ONCE.

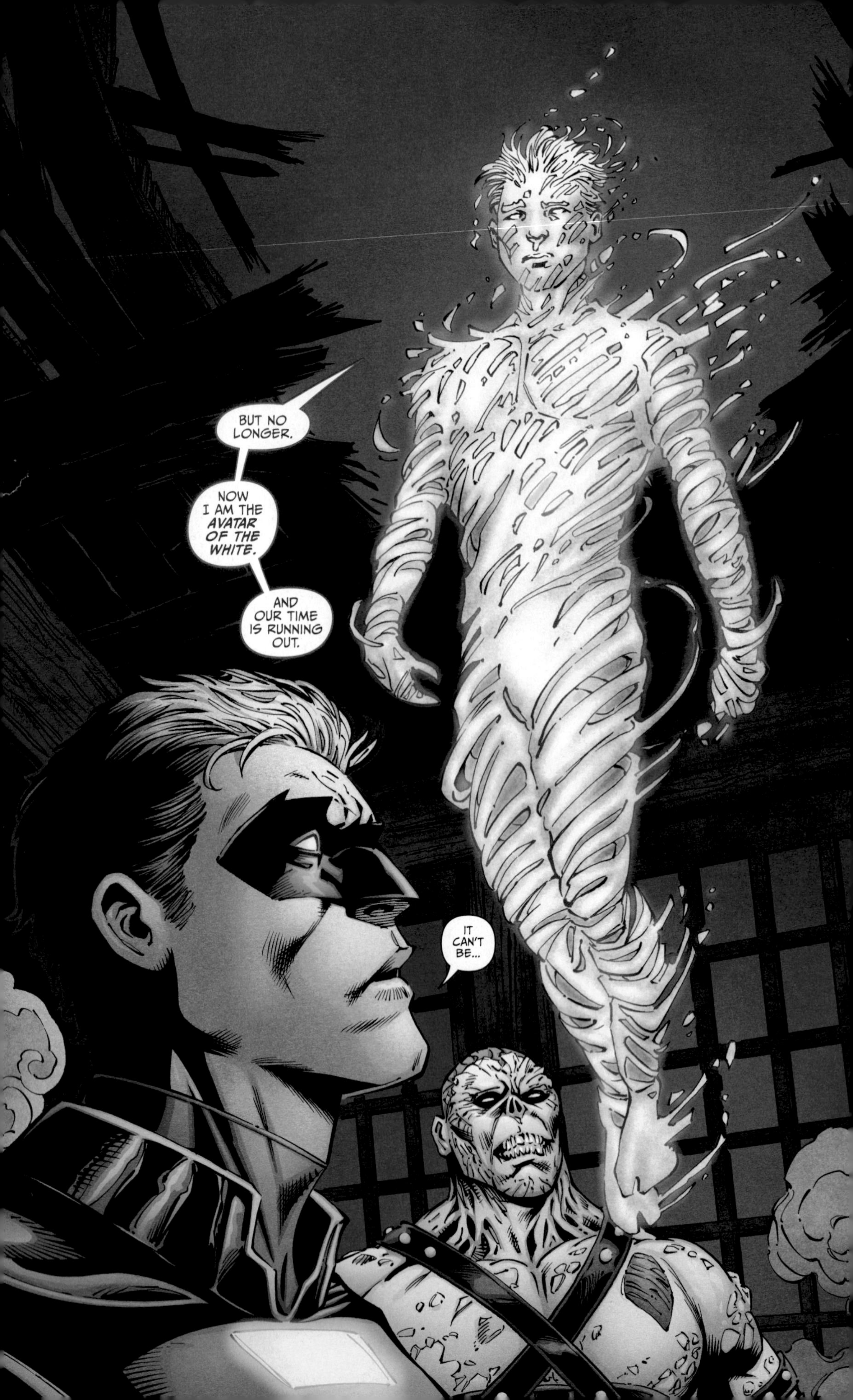
BUT NO LONGER.
NOW I AM THE *AVATAR OF THE WHITE.*
AND OUR TIME IS RUNNING OUT.
IT CAN'T BE...

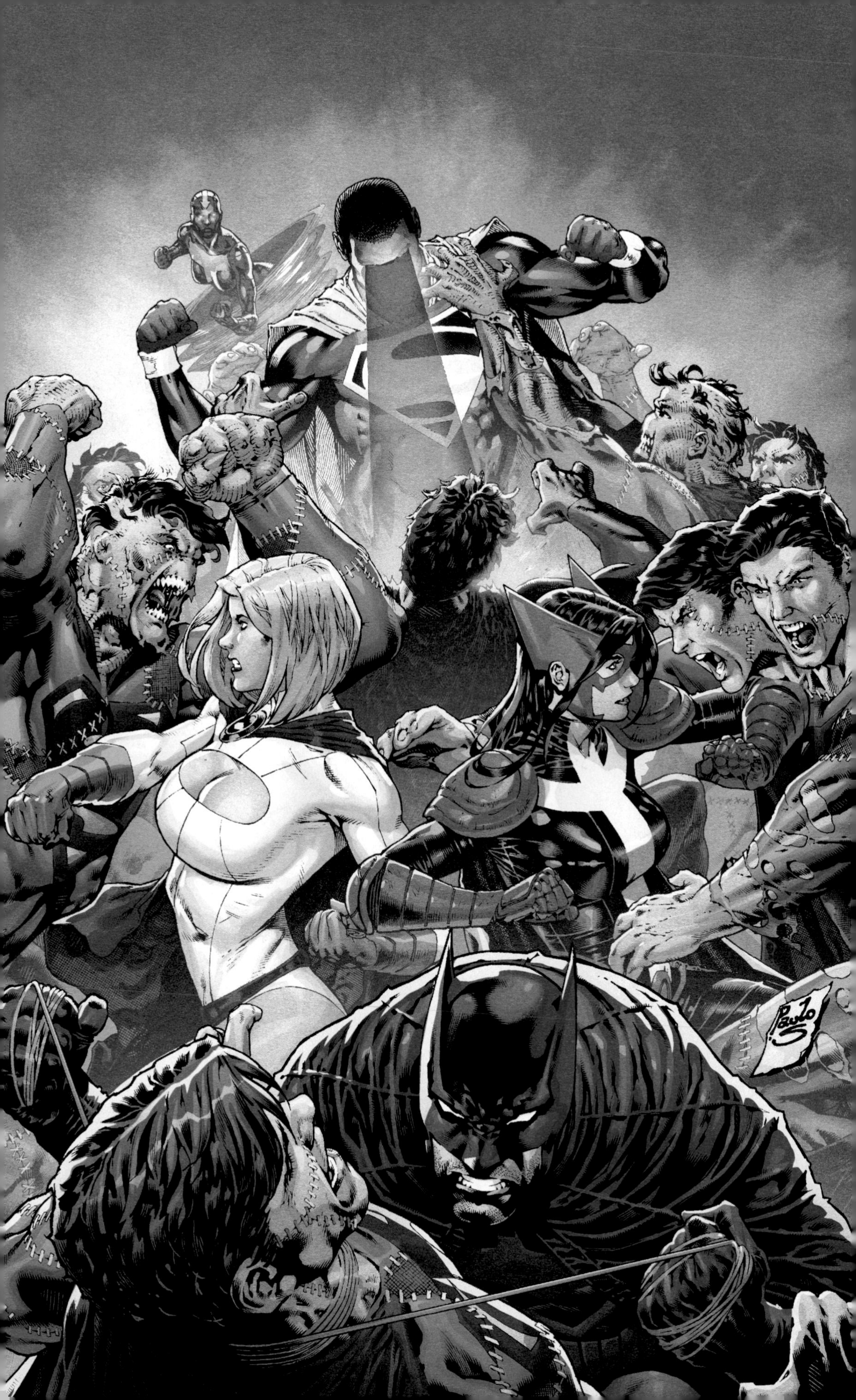

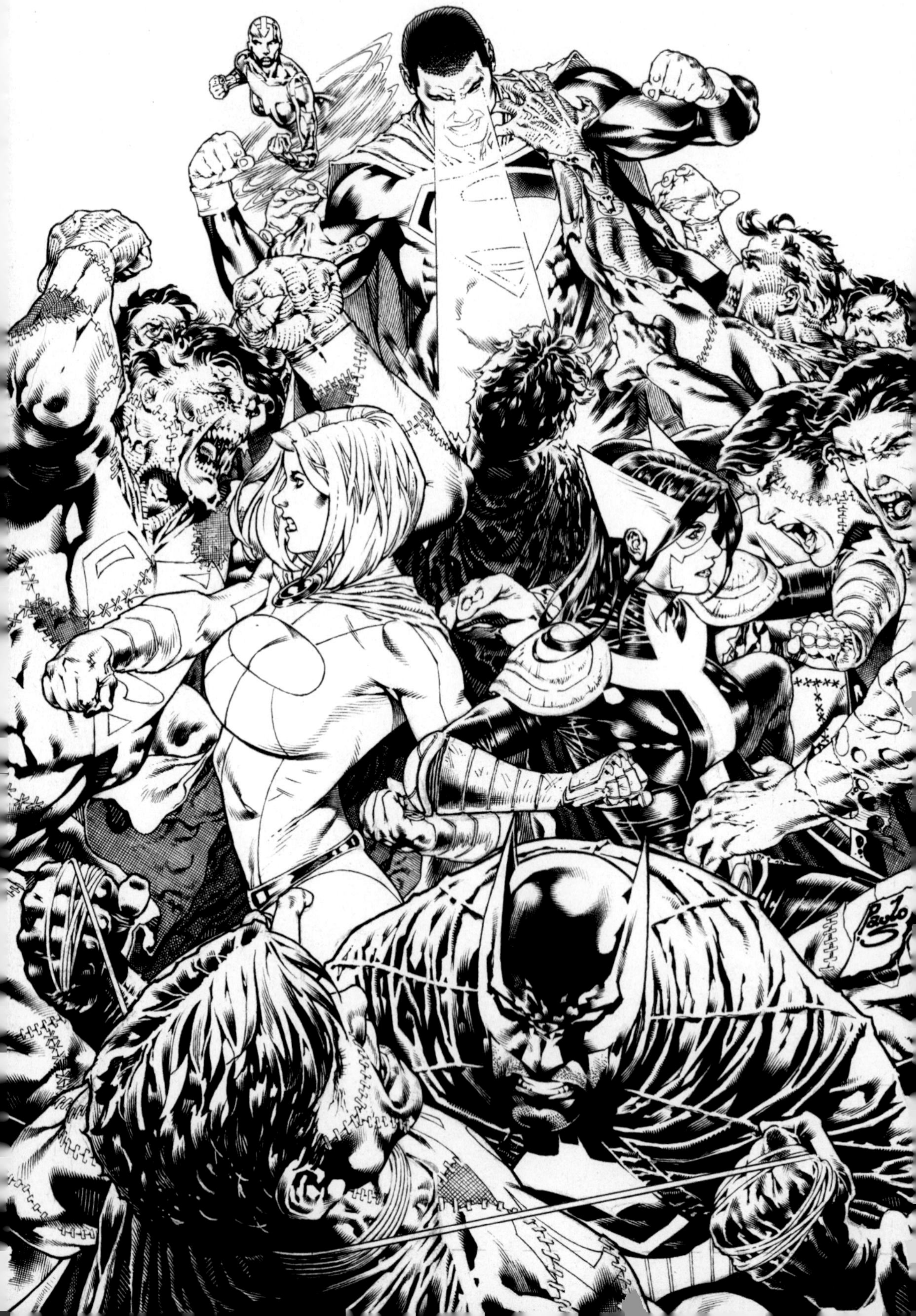
Paulo

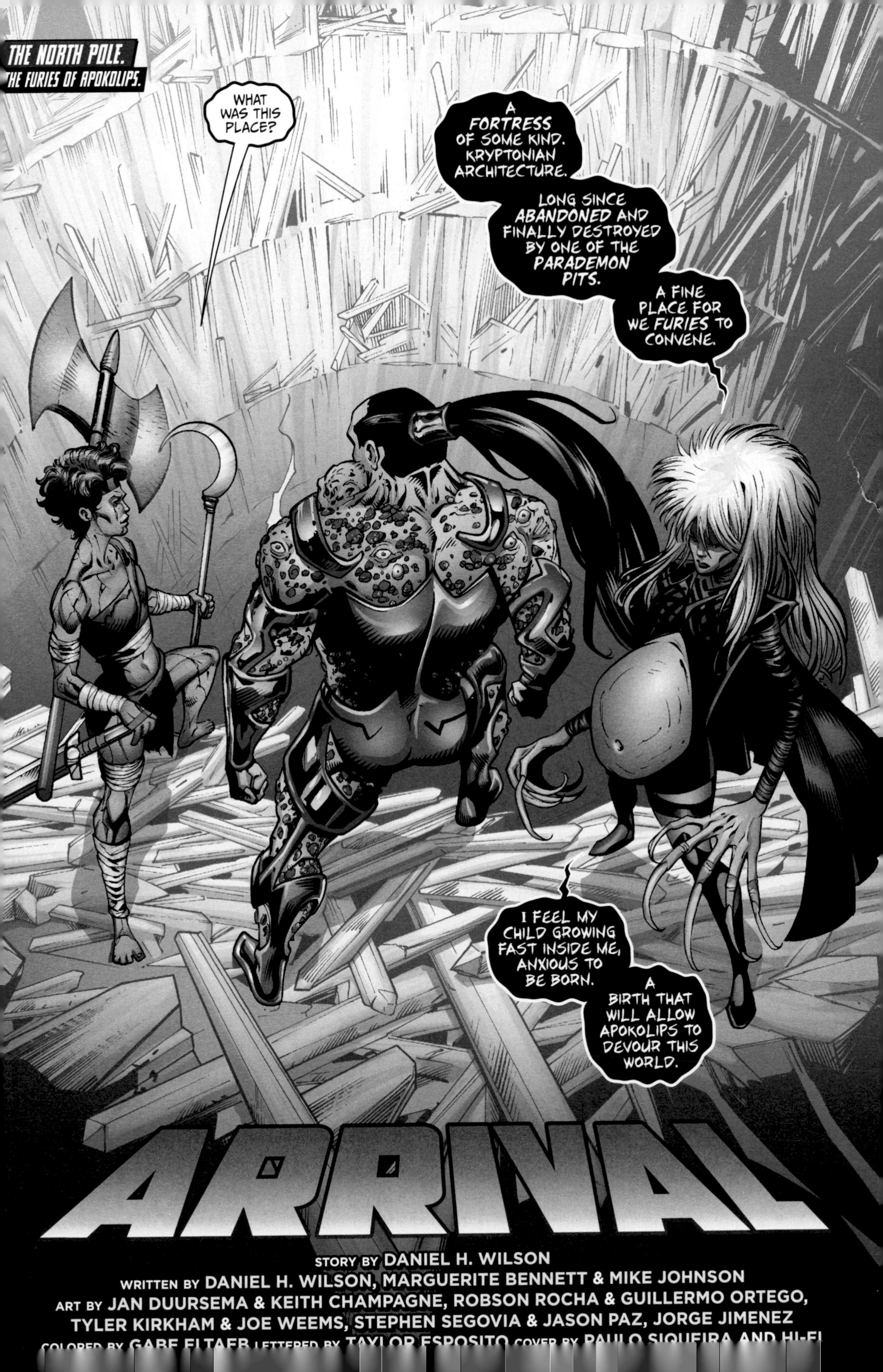
THE NORTH POLE.
THE FURIES OF APOKOLIPS.
WHAT WAS THIS PLACE?
A FORTRESS OF SOME KIND. KRYPTONIAN ARCHITECTURE.
LONG SINCE ABANDONED AND FINALLY DESTROYED BY ONE OF THE PARADEMON PITS.
A FINE PLACE FOR WE FURIES TO CONVENE.
I FEEL MY CHILD GROWING FAST INSIDE ME, ANXIOUS TO BE BORN.
A BIRTH THAT WILL ALLOW APOKOLIPS TO DEVOUR THIS WORLD.
ARRIVAL
STORY BY DANIEL H. WILSON
WRITTEN BY DANIEL H. WILSON, MARGUERITE BENNETT & MIKE JOHNSON
ART BY JAN DUURSEMA & KEITH CHAMPAGNE, ROBSON ROCHA & GUILLERMO ORTEGO, TYLER KIRKHAM & JOE WEEMS, STEPHEN SEGOVIA & JASON PAZ, JORGE JIMENEZ

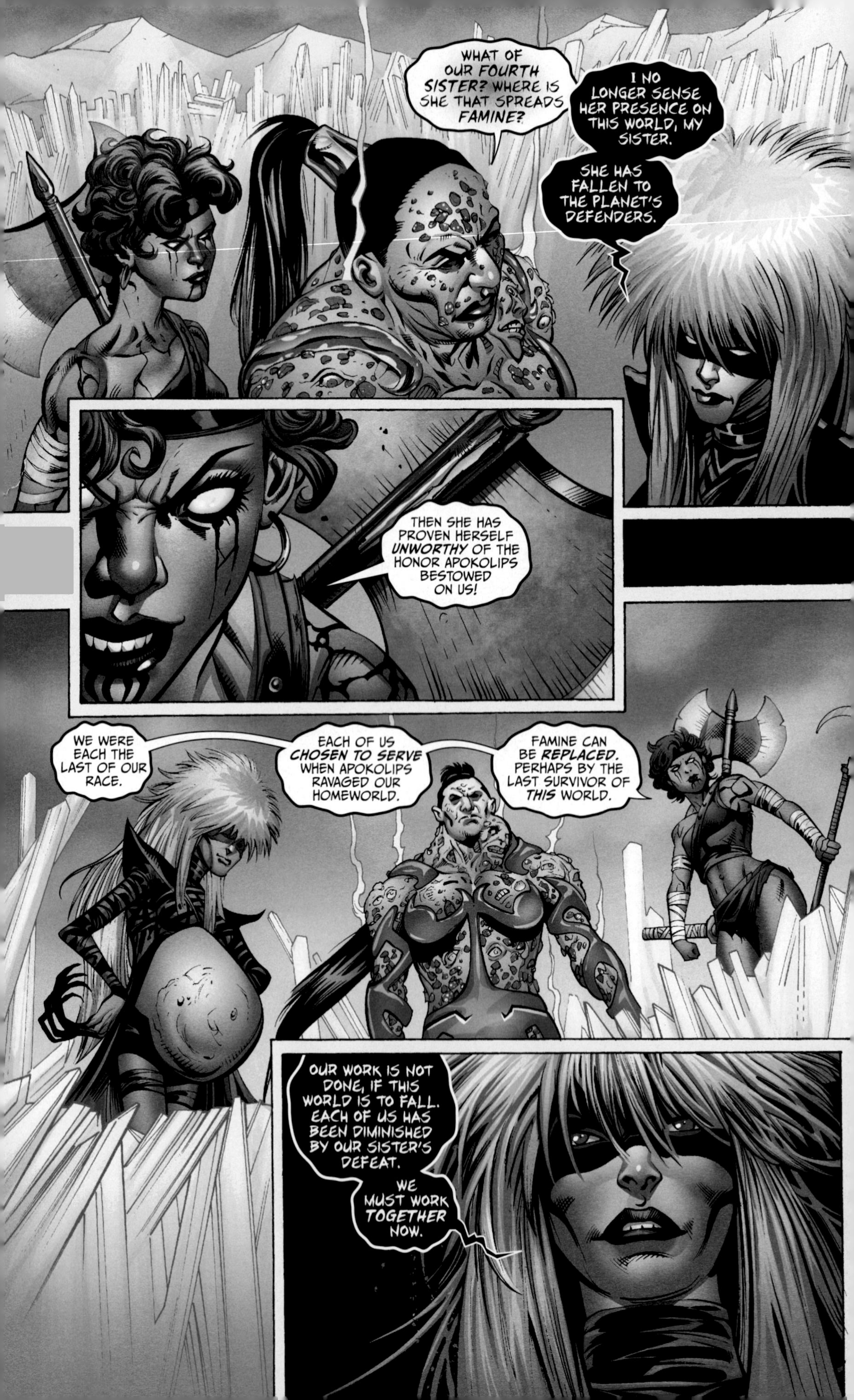
WHAT OF OUR FOURTH SISTER? WHERE IS SHE THAT SPREADS FAMINE?
I NO LONGER SENSE HER PRESENCE ON THIS WORLD, MY SISTER.
SHE HAS FALLEN TO THE PLANET'S DEFENDERS.
THEN SHE HAS PROVEN HERSELF UNWORTHY OF THE HONOR APOKOLIPS BESTOWED ON US!
WE WERE EACH THE LAST OF OUR RACE.
EACH OF US CHOSEN TO SERVE WHEN APOKOLIPS RAVAGED OUR HOMEWORLD.
FAMINE CAN BE REPLACED. PERHAPS BY THE LAST SURVIVOR OF THIS WORLD.
OUR WORK IS NOT DONE, IF THIS WORLD IS TO FALL. EACH OF US HAS BEEN DIMINISHED BY OUR SISTER'S DEFEAT.
WE MUST WORK TOGETHER NOW.

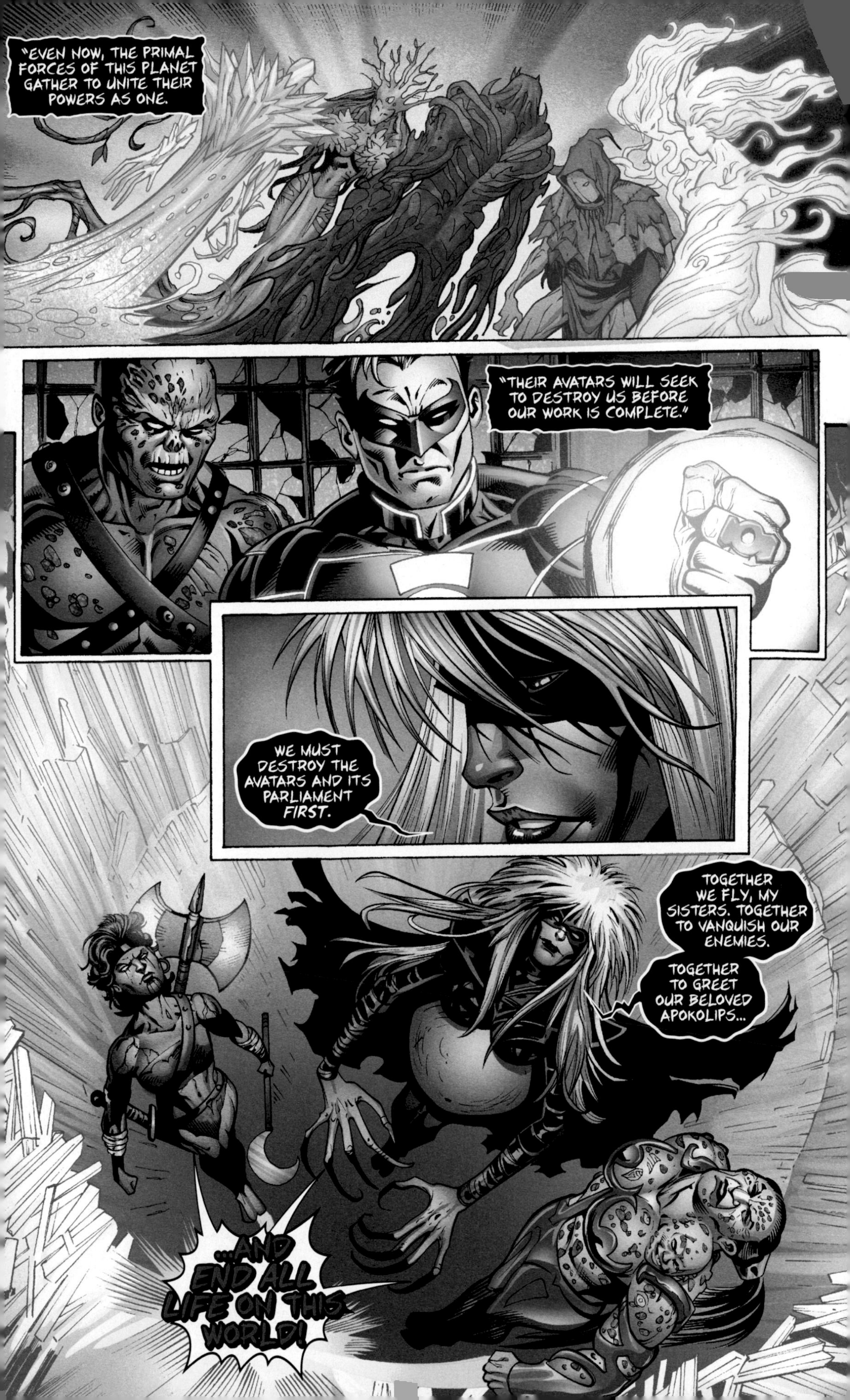
"EVEN NOW, THE PRIMAL FORCES OF THIS PLANET GATHER TO UNITE THEIR POWERS AS ONE.
"THEIR AVATARS WILL SEEK TO DESTROY US BEFORE OUR WORK IS COMPLETE."
WE MUST DESTROY THE AVATARS AND ITS PARLIAMENT FIRST.
TOGETHER WE FLY, MY SISTERS. TOGETHER TO VANQUISH OUR ENEMIES.
TOGETHER TO GREET OUR BELOVED APOKOLIPS...
...AND END ALL LIFE ON THIS WORLD!

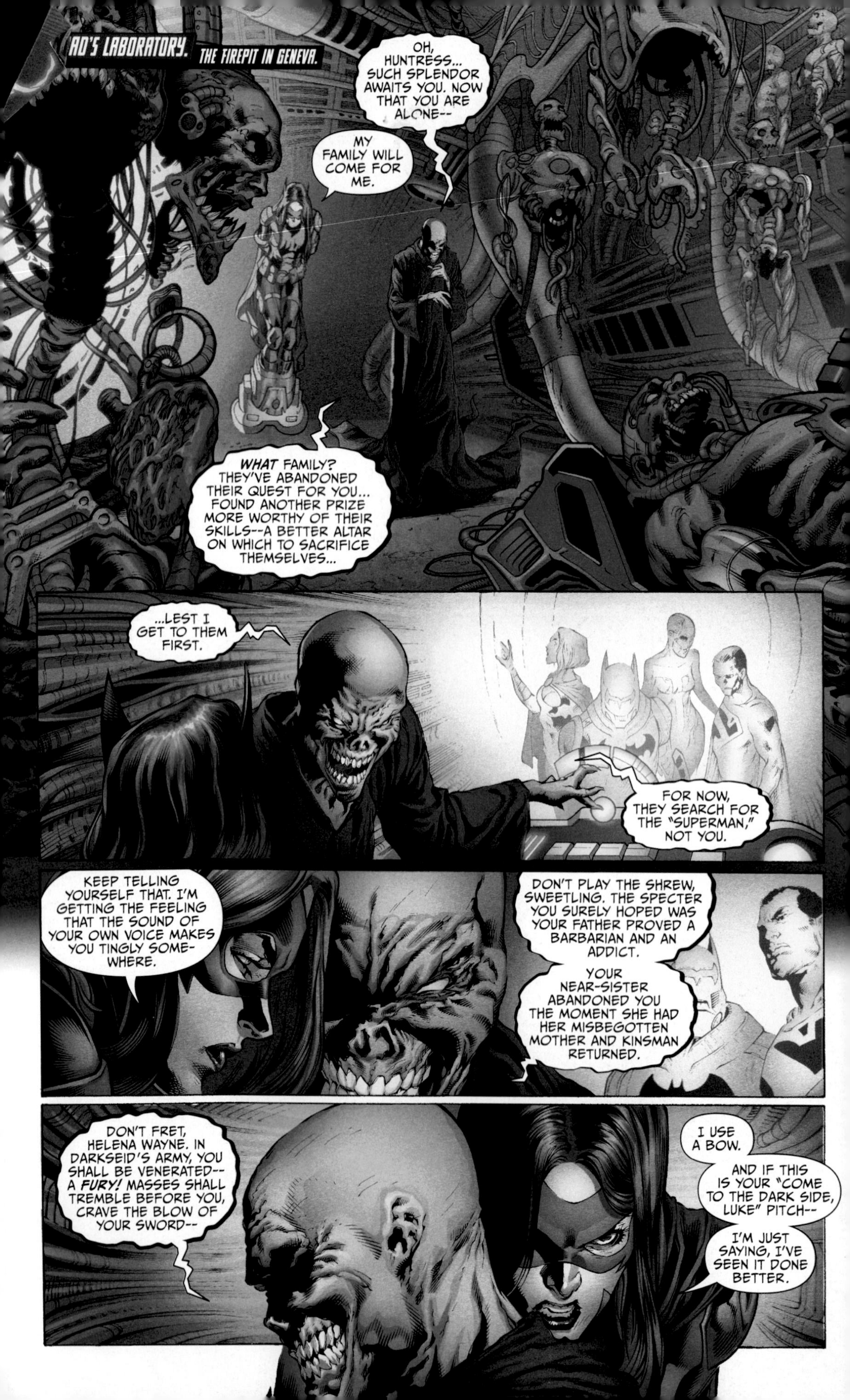
AD'S LABORATORY. THE FIREPIT IN GENEVA.
OH, HUNTRESS... SUCH SPLENDOR AWAITS YOU. NOW THAT YOU ARE ALONE--
MY FAMILY WILL COME FOR ME.
WHAT FAMILY? THEY'VE ABANDONED THEIR QUEST FOR YOU... FOUND ANOTHER PRIZE MORE WORTHY OF THEIR SKILLS--A BETTER ALTAR ON WHICH TO SACRIFICE THEMSELVES...
...LEST I GET TO THEM FIRST.
FOR NOW, THEY SEARCH FOR THE "SUPERMAN," NOT YOU.
KEEP TELLING YOURSELF THAT. I'M GETTING THE FEELING THAT THE SOUND OF YOUR OWN VOICE MAKES YOU TINGLY SOME-WHERE.
DON'T PLAY THE SHREW, SWEETLING. THE SPECTER YOU SURELY HOPED WAS YOUR FATHER PROVED A BARBARIAN AND AN ADDICT.
YOUR NEAR-SISTER ABANDONED YOU THE MOMENT SHE HAD HER MISBEGOTTEN MOTHER AND KINSMAN RETURNED.
DON'T FRET, HELENA WAYNE. IN DARKSEID'S ARMY, YOU SHALL BE VENERATED-- A FURY! MASSES SHALL TREMBLE BEFORE YOU, CRAVE THE BLOW OF YOUR SWORD--
I USE A BOW.
AND IF THIS IS YOUR "COME TO THE DARK SIDE, LUKE" PITCH--
I'M JUST SAYING, I'VE SEEN IT DONE BETTER.

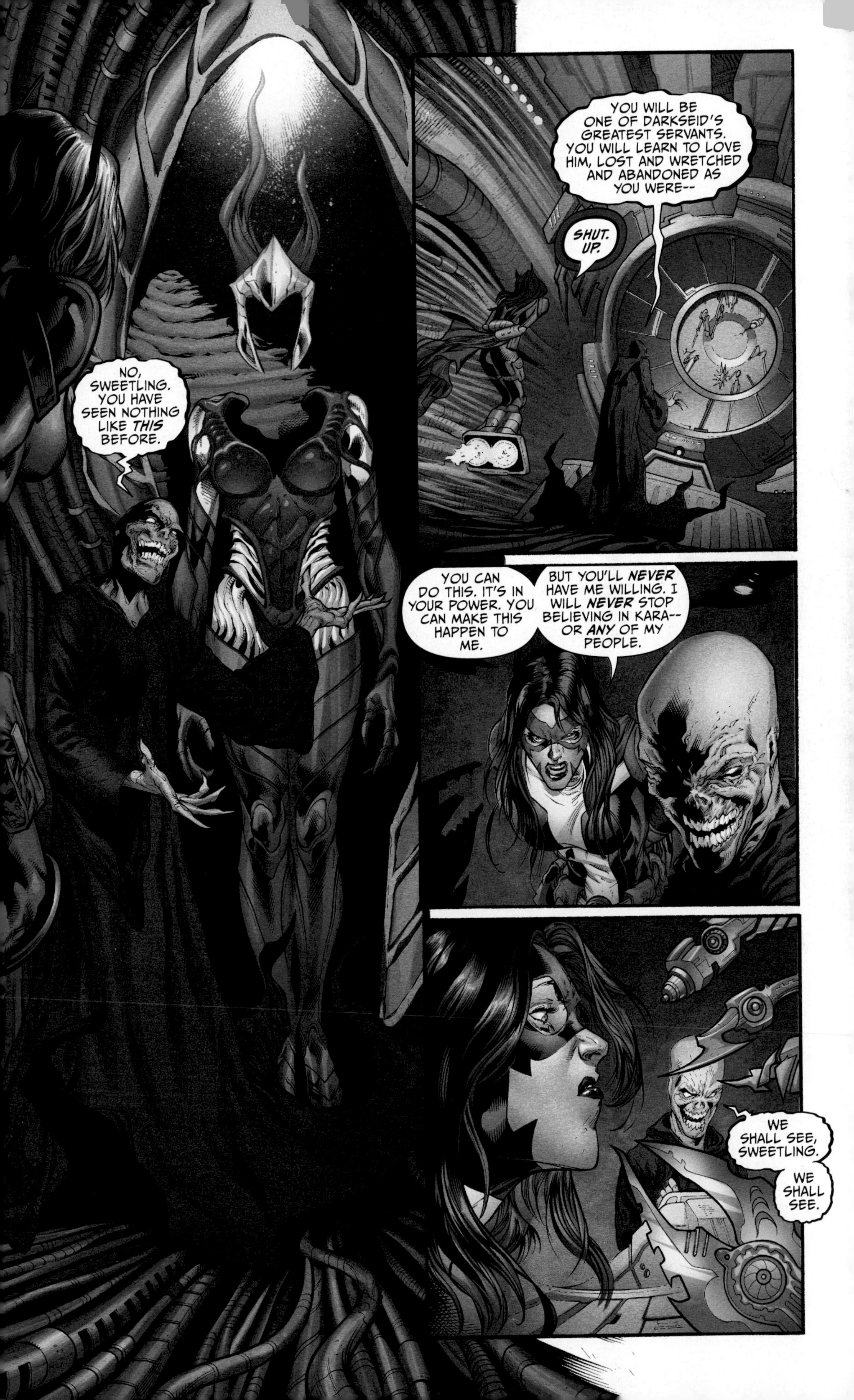
NO, SWEETLING. YOU HAVE SEEN NOTHING LIKE *THIS* BEFORE.
YOU WILL BE ONE OF DARKSEID'S GREATEST SERVANTS. YOU WILL LEARN TO LOVE HIM, LOST AND WRETCHED AND ABANDONED AS YOU WERE--
SHUT. UP.
YOU CAN DO THIS. IT'S IN YOUR POWER. YOU CAN MAKE THIS HAPPEN TO ME.
BUT YOU'LL *NEVER* HAVE ME WILLING. I WILL *NEVER* STOP BELIEVING IN KARA-- OR *ANY* OF MY PEOPLE.
WE SHALL SEE, SWEETLING.
WE SHALL SEE.

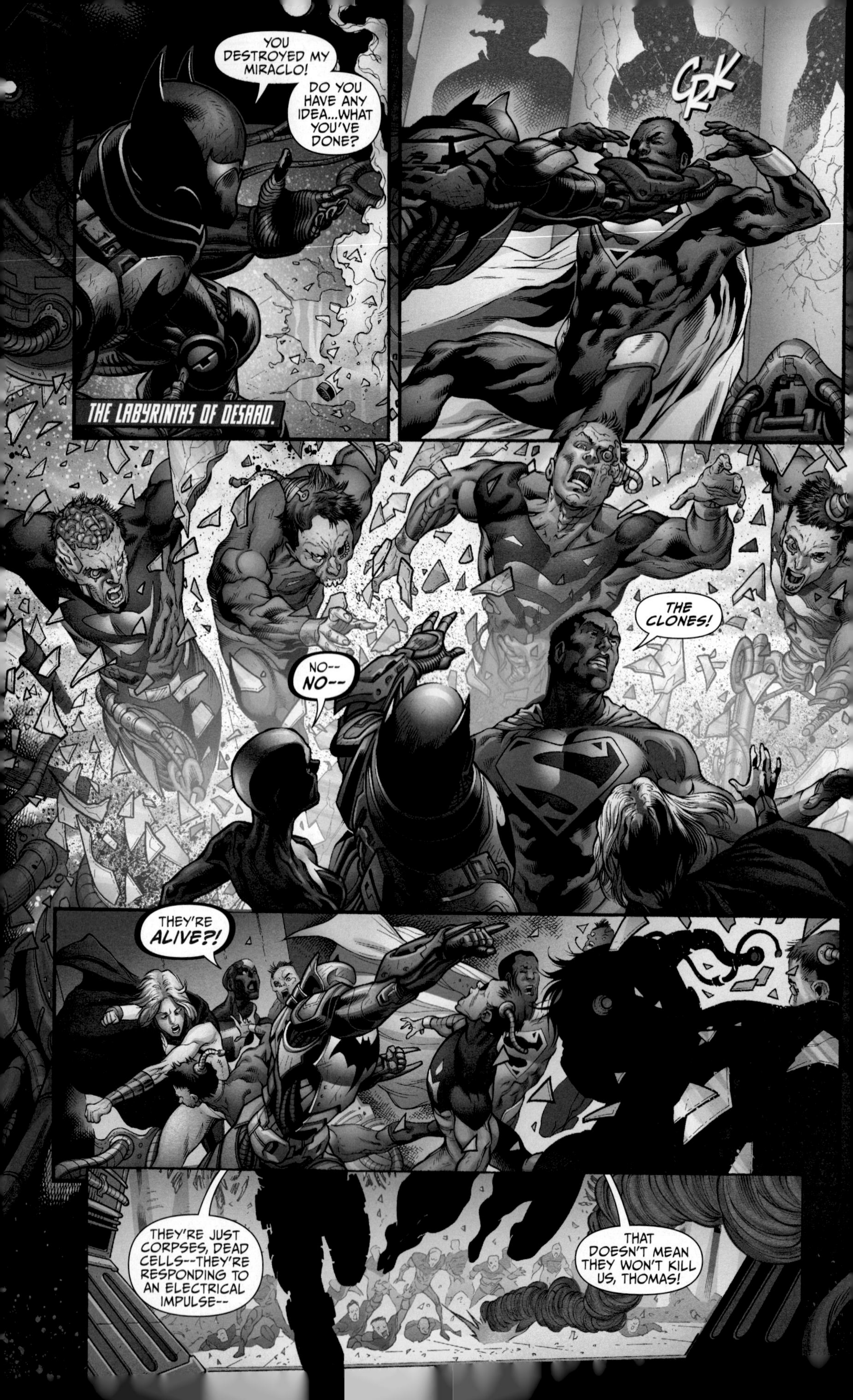
THE LABYRINTHS OF DESAAD.
YOU DESTROYED MY MIRACLO!
DO YOU HAVE ANY IDEA...WHAT YOU'VE DONE?
CRK
THE CLONES!
NO-- NO--
THEY'RE ALIVE?!
THEY'RE JUST CORPSES, DEAD CELLS--THEY'RE RESPONDING TO AN ELECTRICAL IMPULSE--
THAT DOESN'T MEAN THEY WON'T KILL US, THOMAS!

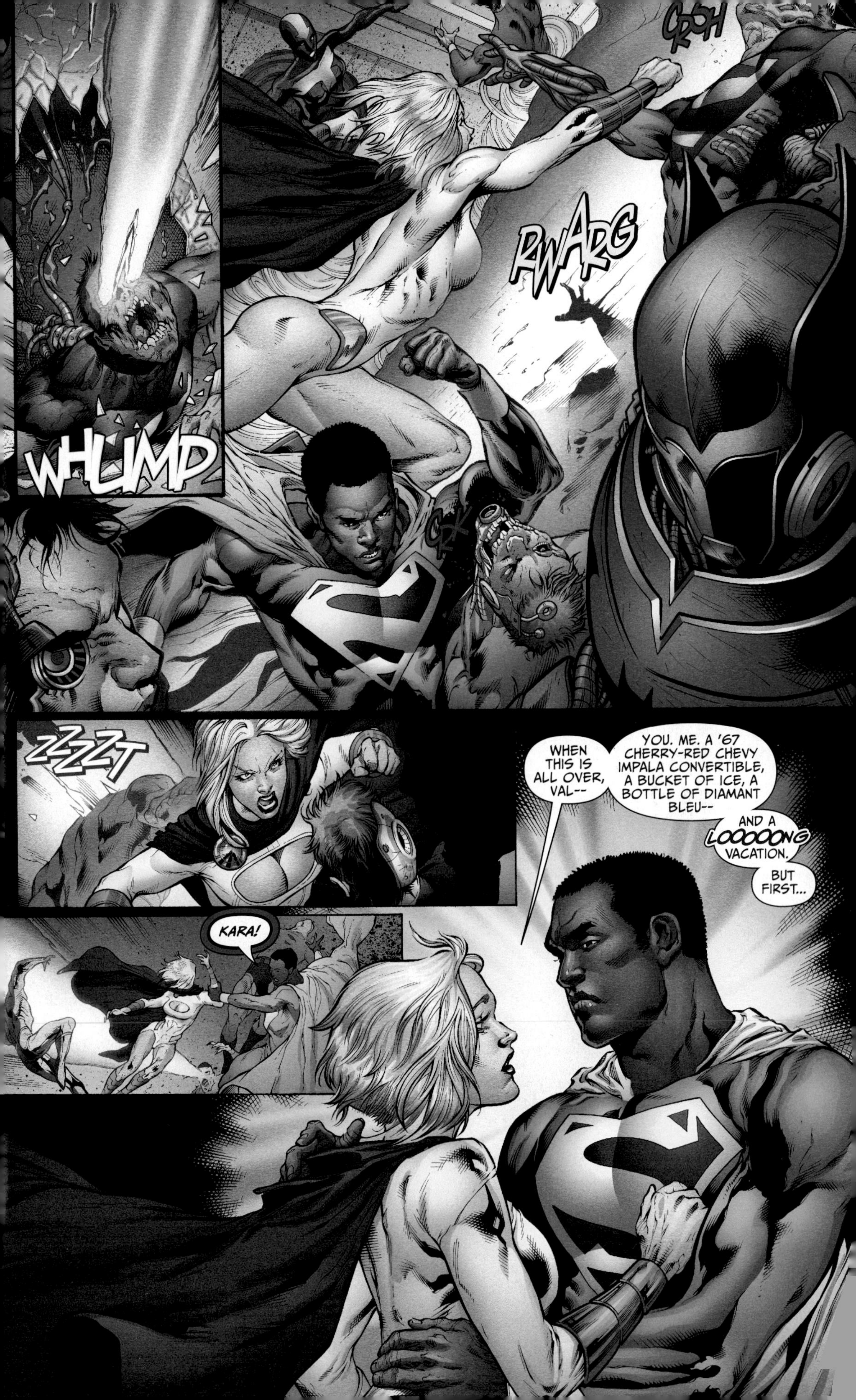
CRSH
RWARG
WHUMP
GRK
ZZZZT
WHEN THIS IS ALL OVER, VAL--
YOU. ME. A '67 CHERRY-RED CHEVY IMPALA CONVERTIBLE, A BUCKET OF ICE, A BOTTLE OF DIAMANT BLEU--
AND A LOOOOONG VACATION.
BUT FIRST...
KARA!

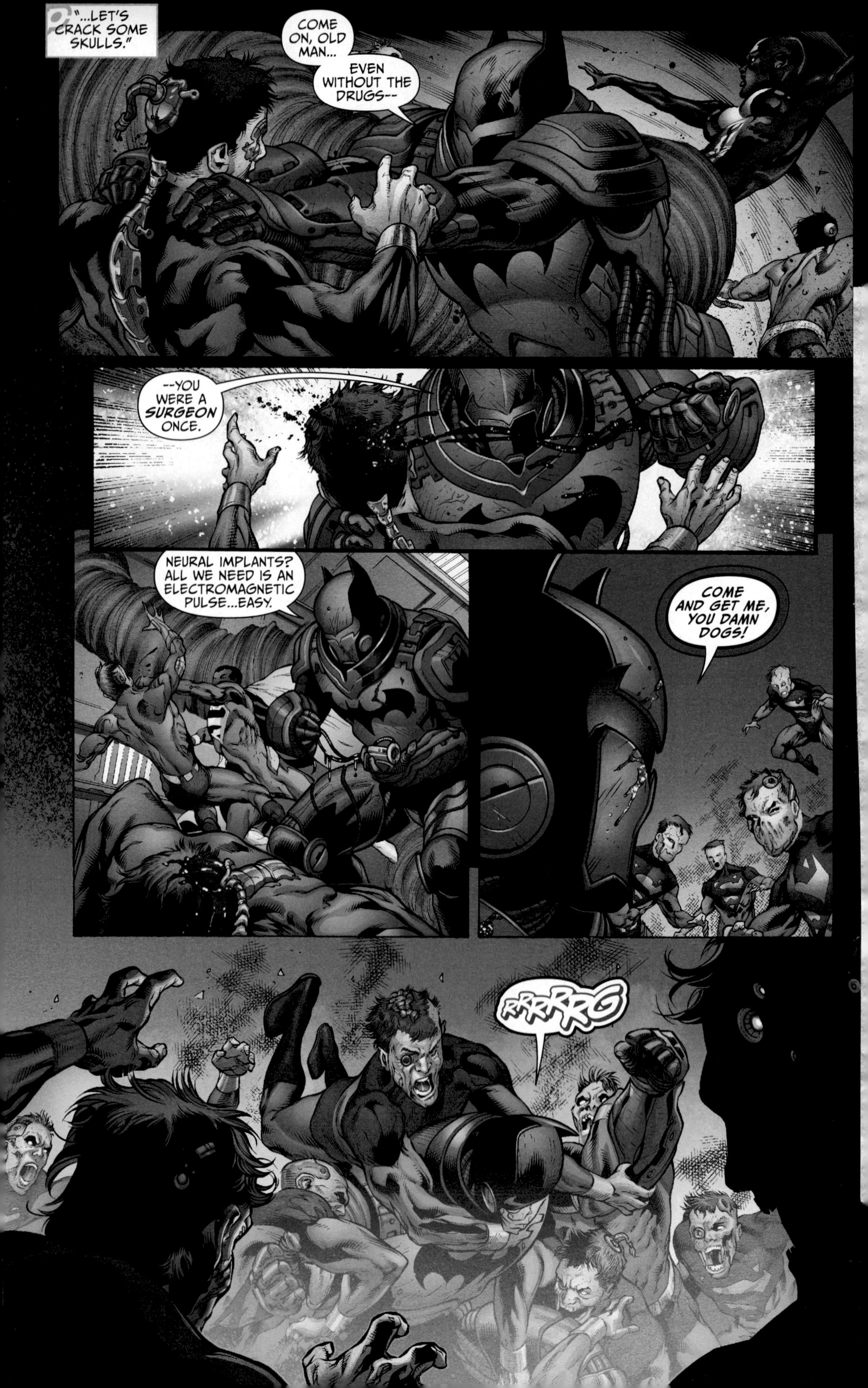
"...LET'S CRACK SOME SKULLS."
COME ON, OLD MAN...
EVEN WITHOUT THE DRUGS--
--YOU WERE A SURGEON ONCE.
NEURAL IMPLANTS? ALL WE NEED IS AN ELECTROMAGNETIC PULSE...EASY.
COME AND GET ME, YOU DAMN DOGS!
RRRRRG

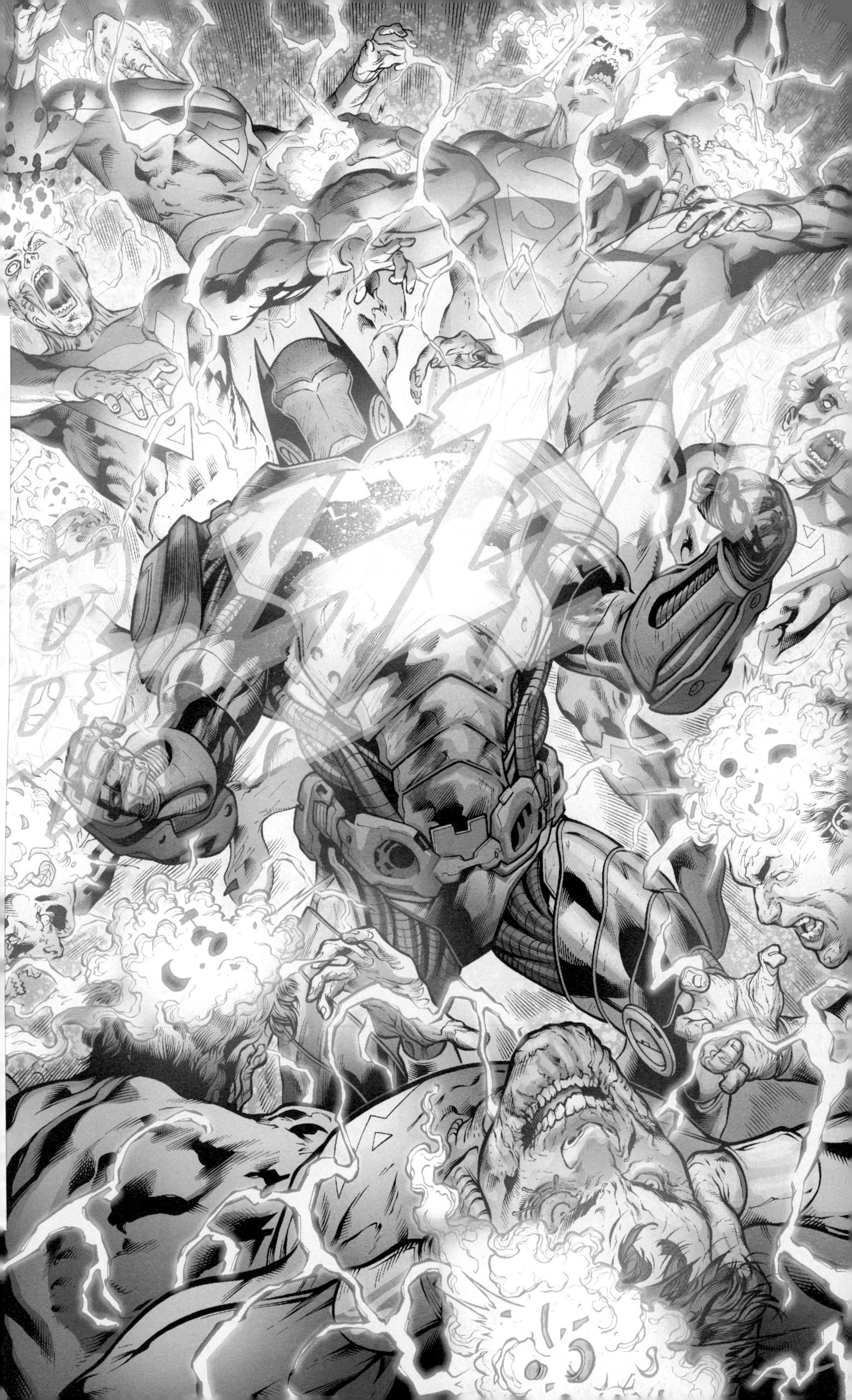

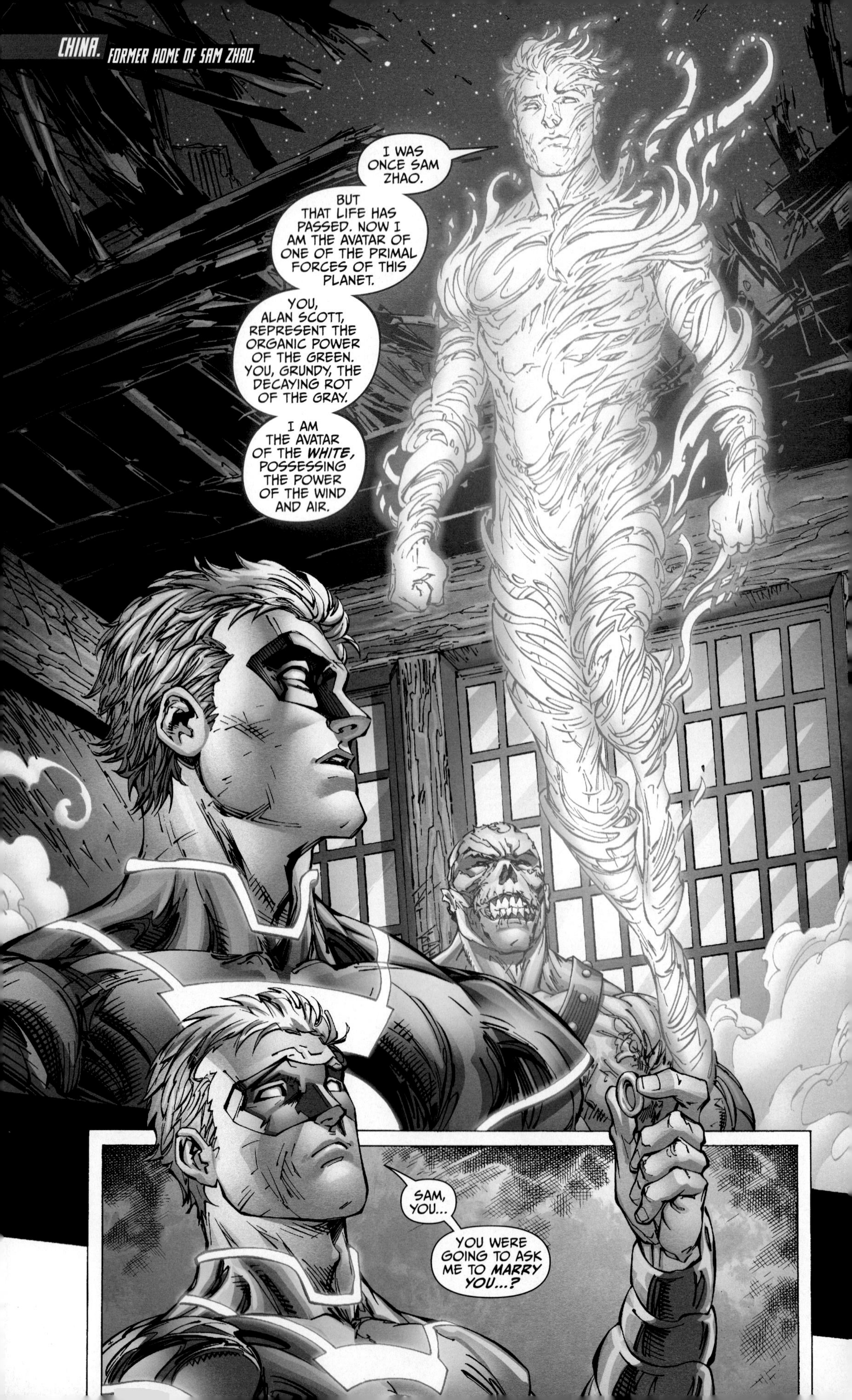
CHINA. FORMER HOME OF SAM ZHAO.
I WAS ONCE SAM ZHAO.
BUT THAT LIFE HAS PASSED. NOW I AM THE AVATAR OF ONE OF THE PRIMAL FORCES OF THIS PLANET.
YOU, ALAN SCOTT, REPRESENT THE ORGANIC POWER OF THE GREEN. YOU, GRUNDY, THE DECAYING ROT OF THE GRAY.
I AM THE AVATAR OF THE *WHITE*, POSSESSING THE POWER OF THE WIND AND AIR.
SAM, YOU...
YOU WERE GOING TO ASK ME TO *MARRY YOU*...?

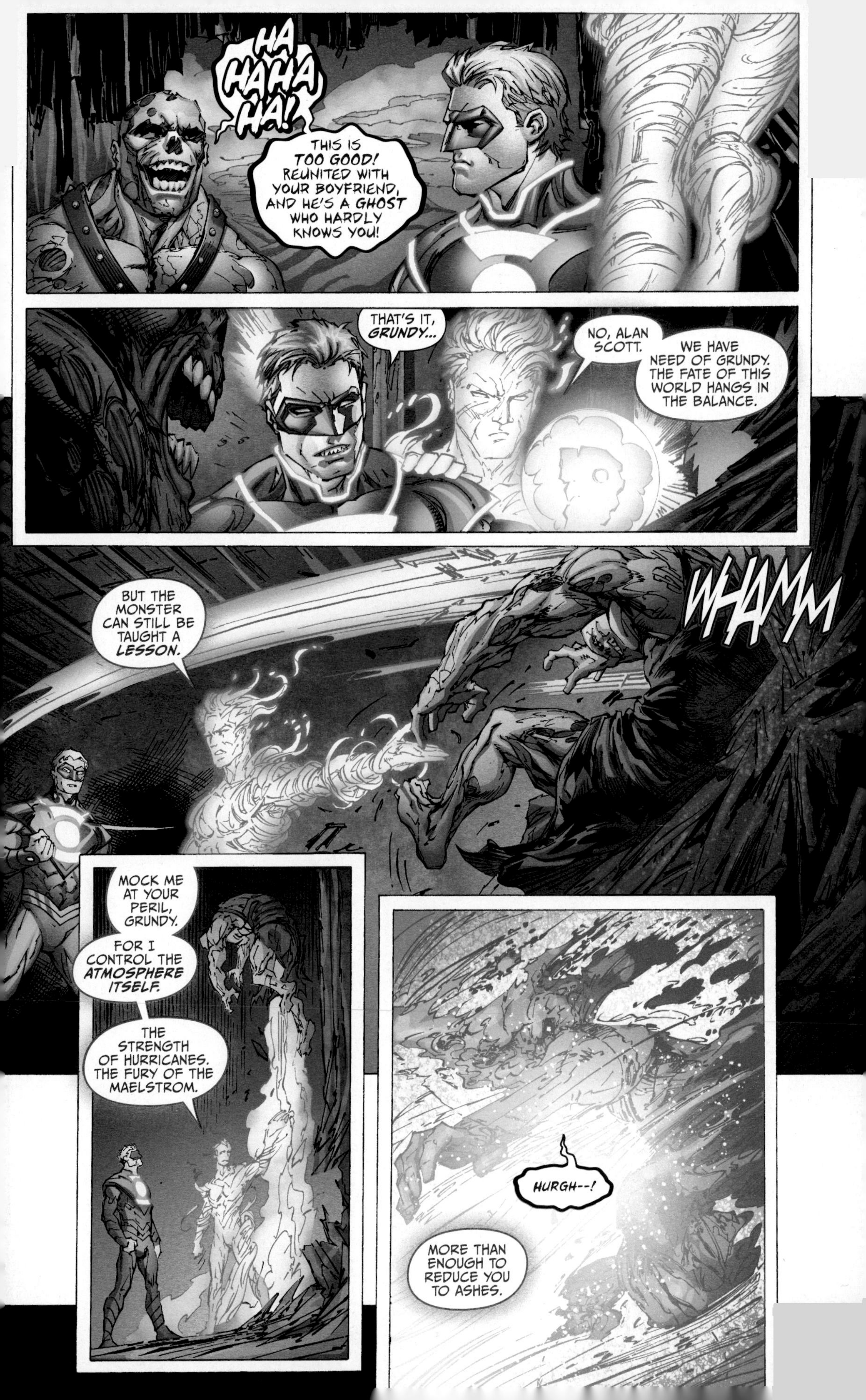
HA HAHAHA HA!
THIS IS TOO GOOD! REUNITED WITH YOUR BOYFRIEND, AND HE'S A GHOST WHO HARDLY KNOWS YOU!
THAT'S IT, GRUNDY...
NO, ALAN SCOTT.
WE HAVE NEED OF GRUNDY. THE FATE OF THIS WORLD HANGS IN THE BALANCE.
BUT THE MONSTER CAN STILL BE TAUGHT A LESSON.
WHAMM
MOCK ME AT YOUR PERIL, GRUNDY.
FOR I CONTROL THE ATMOSPHERE ITSELF.
THE STRENGTH OF HURRICANES. THE FURY OF THE MAELSTROM.
HURGH--!
MORE THAN ENOUGH TO REDUCE YOU TO ASHES.

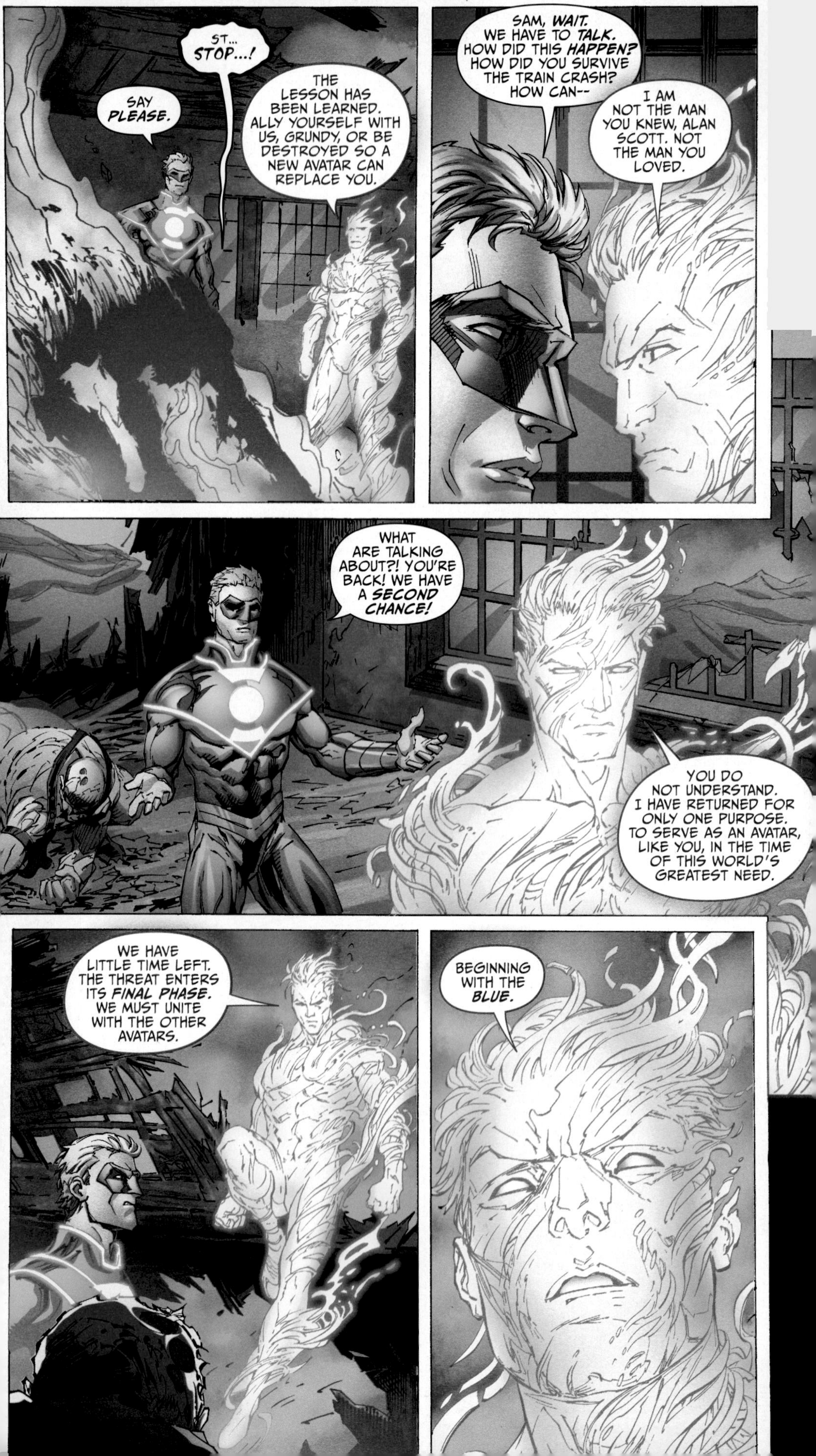

SAY PLEASE.
ST... STOP...!
THE LESSON HAS BEEN LEARNED. ALLY YOURSELF WITH US, GRUNDY, OR BE DESTROYED SO A NEW AVATAR CAN REPLACE YOU.
SAM, WAIT. WE HAVE TO TALK. HOW DID THIS HAPPEN? HOW DID YOU SURVIVE THE TRAIN CRASH? HOW CAN--
I AM NOT THE MAN YOU KNEW, ALAN SCOTT. NOT THE MAN YOU LOVED.
WHAT ARE TALKING ABOUT?! YOU'RE BACK! WE HAVE A SECOND CHANCE!
YOU DO NOT UNDERSTAND. I HAVE RETURNED FOR ONLY ONE PURPOSE. TO SERVE AS AN AVATAR, LIKE YOU, IN THE TIME OF THIS WORLD'S GREATEST NEED.
WE HAVE LITTLE TIME LEFT. THE THREAT ENTERS ITS FINAL PHASE. WE MUST UNITE WITH THE OTHER AVATARS.
BEGINNING WITH THE BLUE.

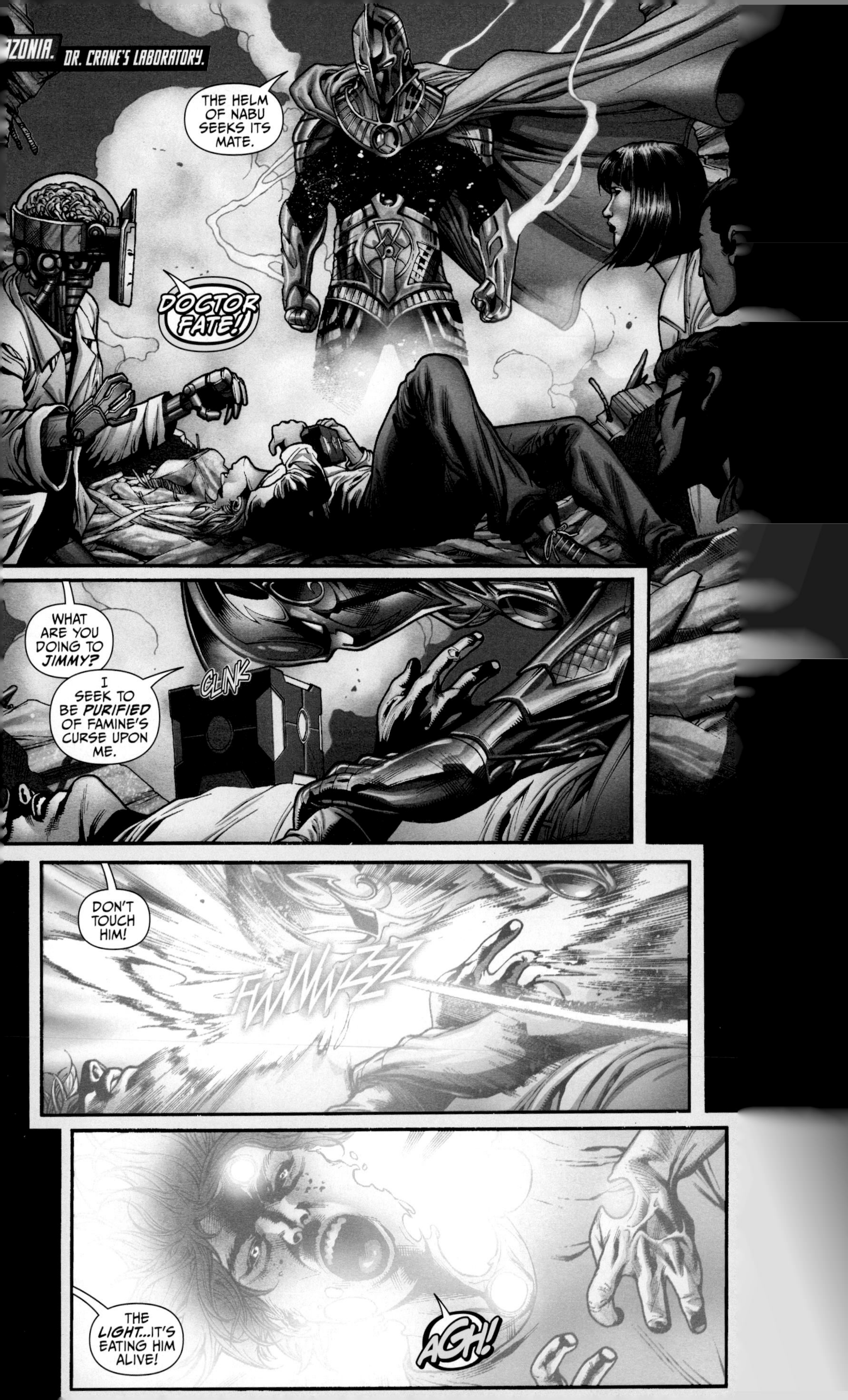

ZONIA.
DR. CRANE'S LABORATORY.
THE HELM OF NABU SEEKS ITS MATE.
DOCTOR FATE!
WHAT ARE YOU DOING TO JIMMY?
I SEEK TO BE PURIFIED OF FAMINE'S CURSE UPON ME.
CLINK
DON'T TOUCH HIM!
FWMMZZZ
THE LIGHT...IT'S EATING HIM ALIVE!
AGH!

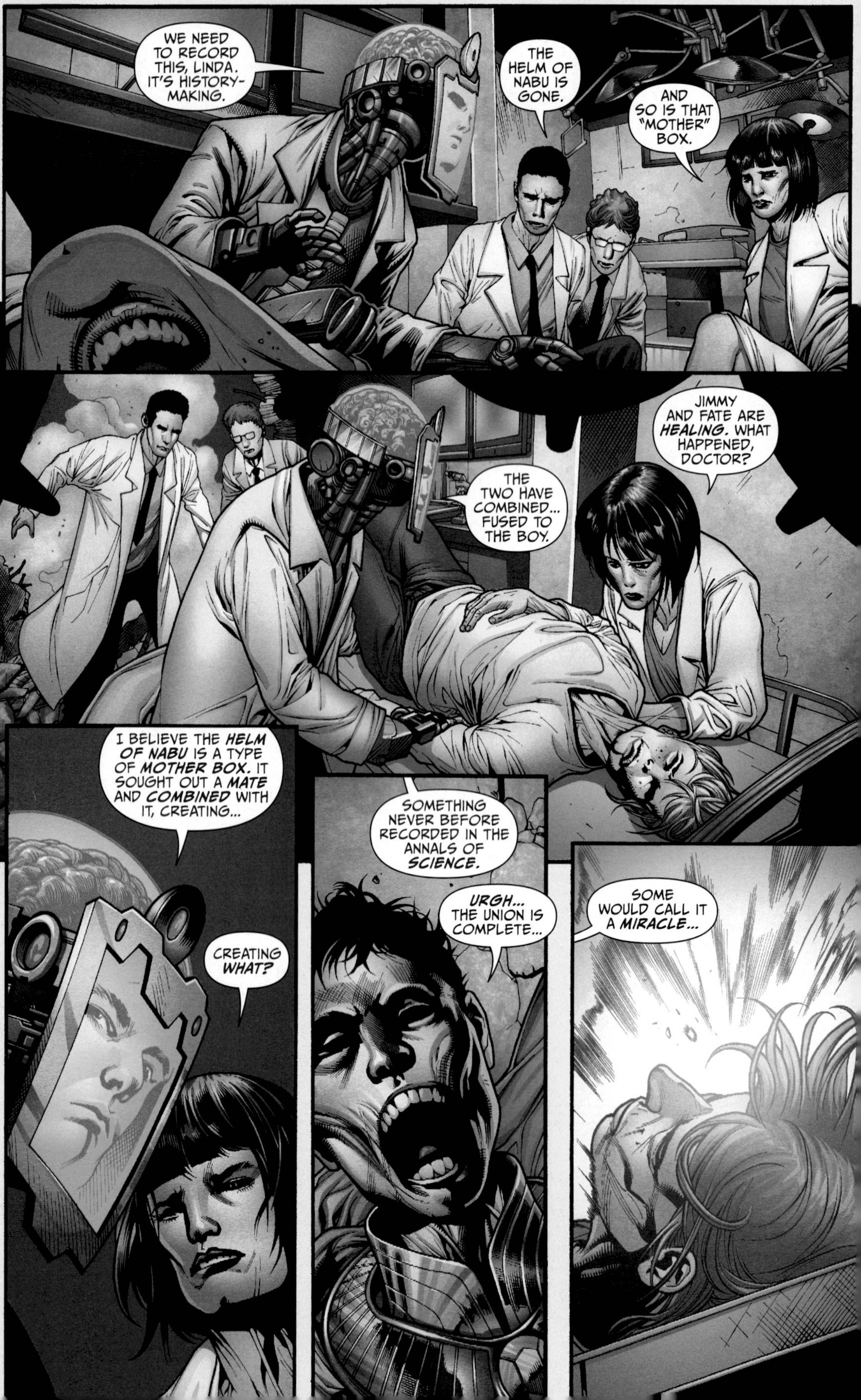
WE NEED TO RECORD THIS, LINDA. IT'S HISTORY-MAKING.
THE HELM OF NABU IS GONE.
AND SO IS THAT "MOTHER" BOX.
JIMMY AND FATE ARE *HEALING.* WHAT HAPPENED, DOCTOR?
THE TWO HAVE COMBINED... FUSED TO THE BOY.
I BELIEVE THE *HELM OF NABU* IS A TYPE OF *MOTHER BOX.* IT SOUGHT OUT A *MATE* AND *COMBINED* WITH IT, CREATING...
CREATING *WHAT?*
SOMETHING NEVER BEFORE RECORDED IN THE ANNALS OF *SCIENCE.*
URGH... THE UNION IS COMPLETE...
SOME WOULD CALL IT A *MIRACLE...*

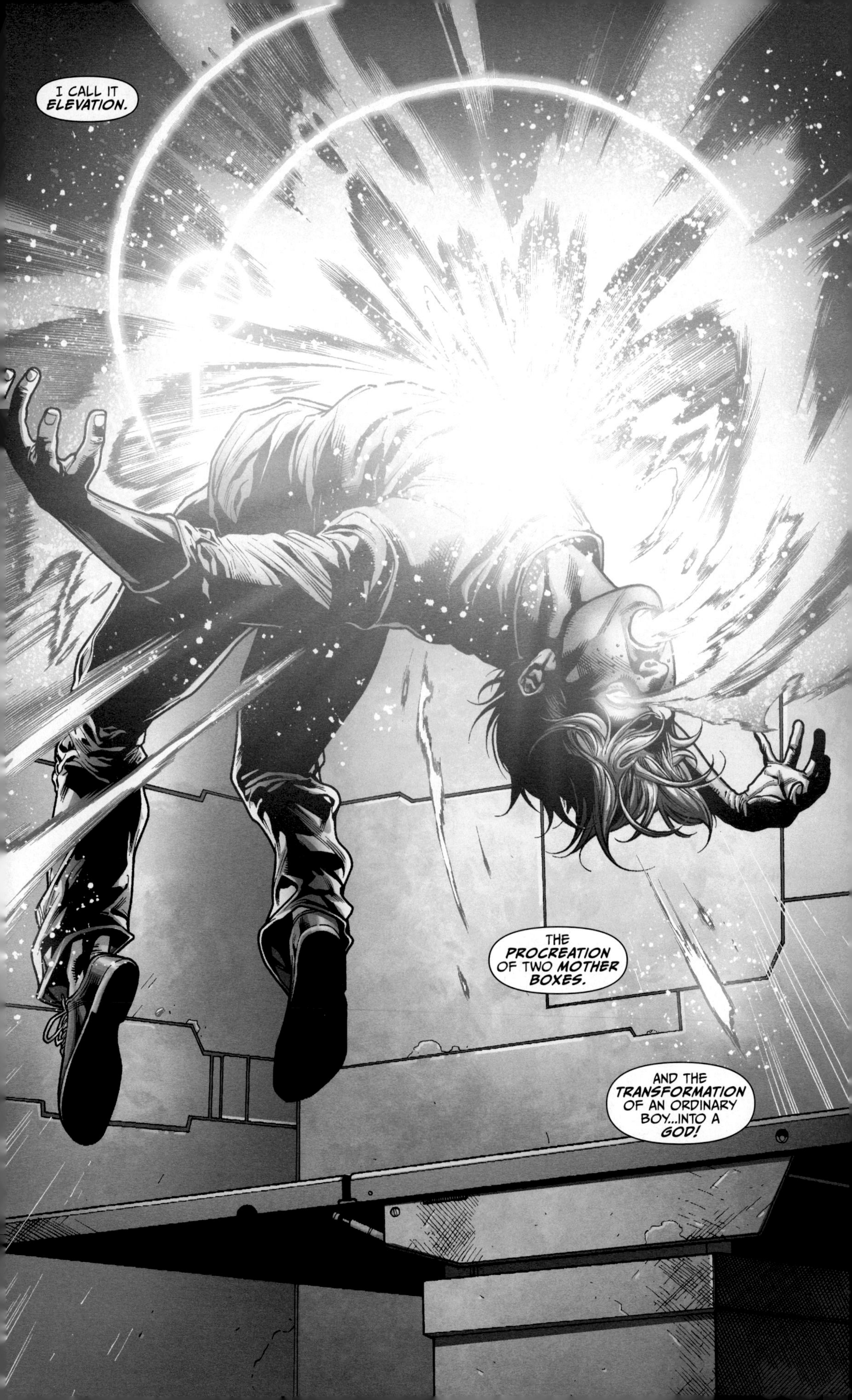
I CALL IT ELEVATION.
THE PROCREATION OF TWO MOTHER BOXES.
AND THE TRANSFORMATION OF AN ORDINARY BOY...INTO A GOD!

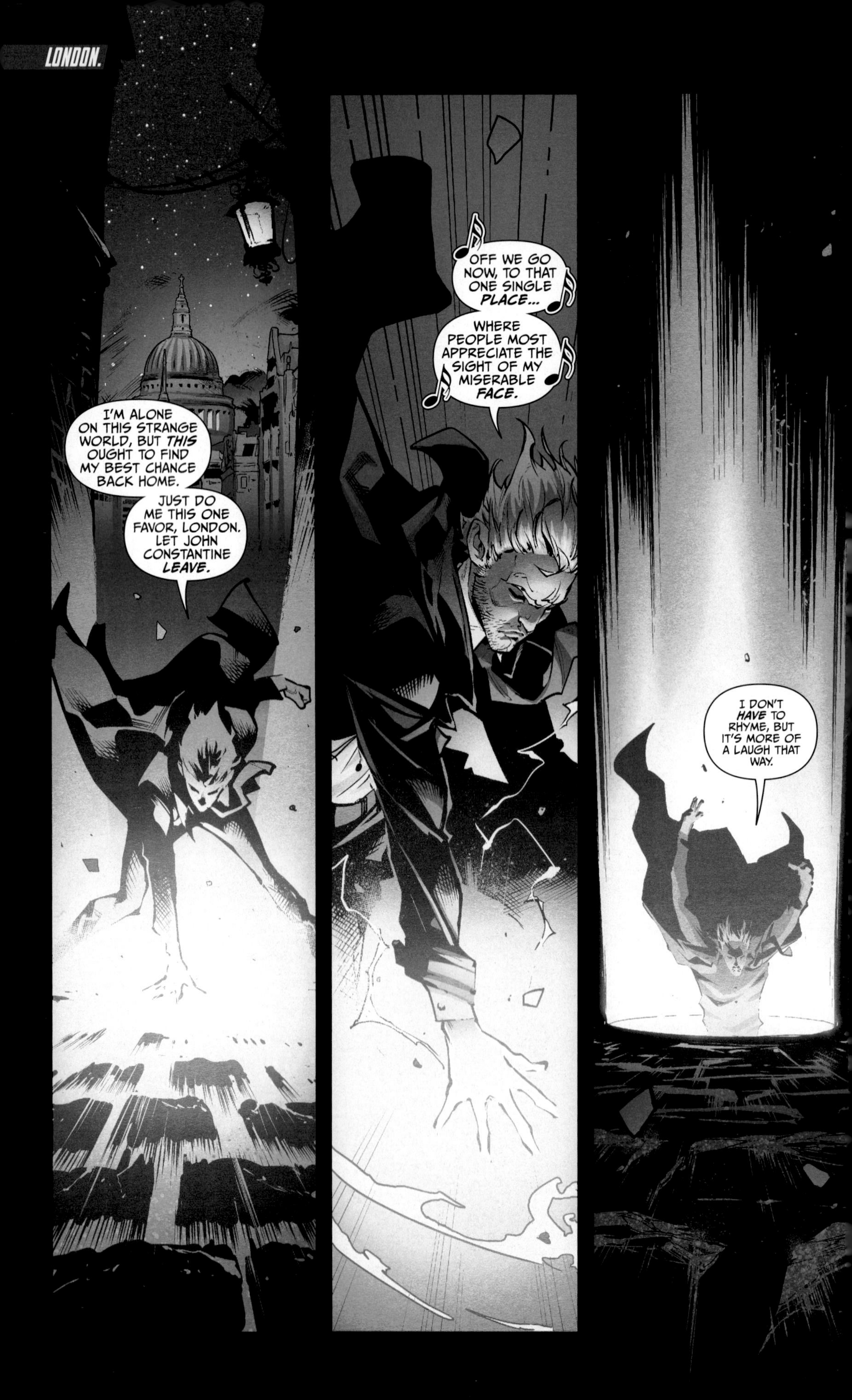
LONDON.
I'M ALONE ON THIS STRANGE WORLD, BUT THIS OUGHT TO FIND MY BEST CHANCE BACK HOME.
JUST DO ME THIS ONE FAVOR, LONDON. LET JOHN CONSTANTINE LEAVE.
OFF WE GO NOW, TO THAT ONE SINGLE PLACE...
WHERE PEOPLE MOST APPRECIATE THE SIGHT OF MY MISERABLE FACE.
I DON'T HAVE TO RHYME, BUT IT'S MORE OF A LAUGH THAT WAY.

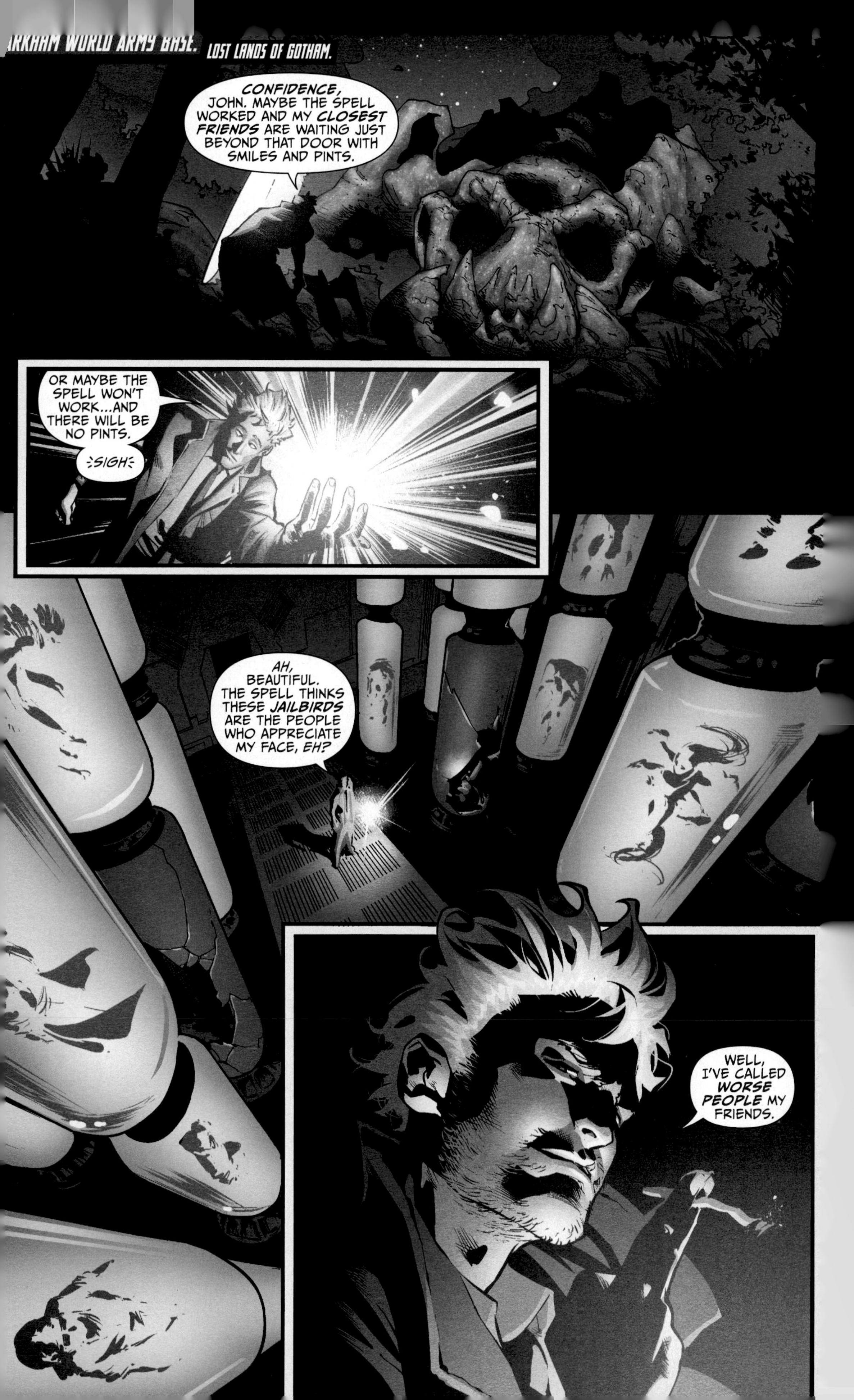
ARKHAM WORLD ARMY BASE.
LOST LANDS OF GOTHAM.
CONFIDENCE, JOHN. MAYBE THE SPELL WORKED AND MY CLOSEST FRIENDS ARE WAITING JUST BEYOND THAT DOOR WITH SMILES AND PINTS.
OR MAYBE THE SPELL WON'T WORK...AND THERE WILL BE NO PINTS.
SIGH
AH, BEAUTIFUL. THE SPELL THINKS THESE JAILBIRDS ARE THE PEOPLE WHO APPRECIATE MY FACE, EH?
WELL, I'VE CALLED WORSE PEOPLE MY FRIENDS.

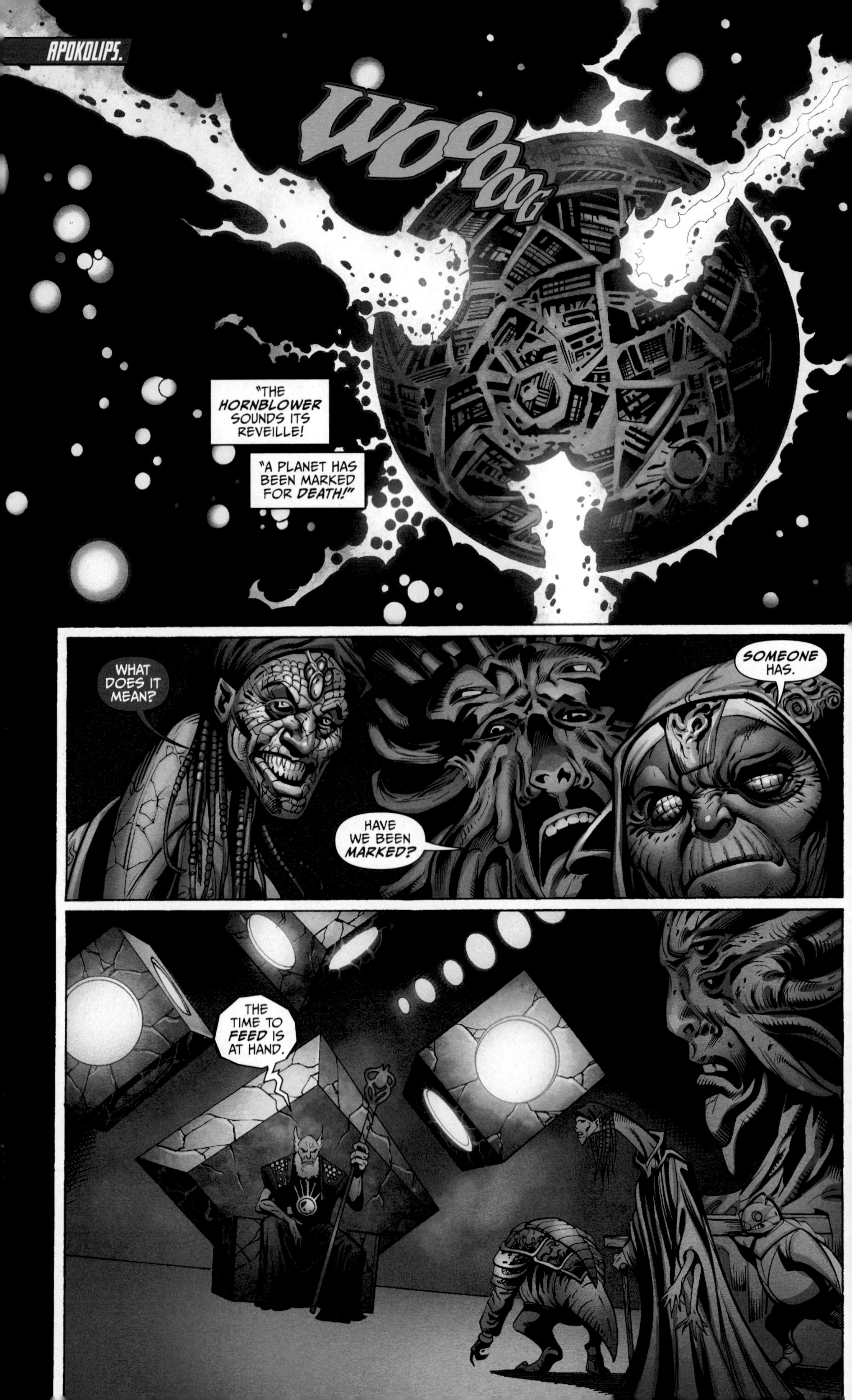
APOKOLIPS.
WOOOOOG
"THE HORNBLOWER SOUNDS ITS REVEILLE!
"A PLANET HAS BEEN MARKED FOR DEATH!"
WHAT DOES IT MEAN?
HAVE WE BEEN MARKED?
SOMEONE HAS.
THE TIME TO FEED IS AT HAND.

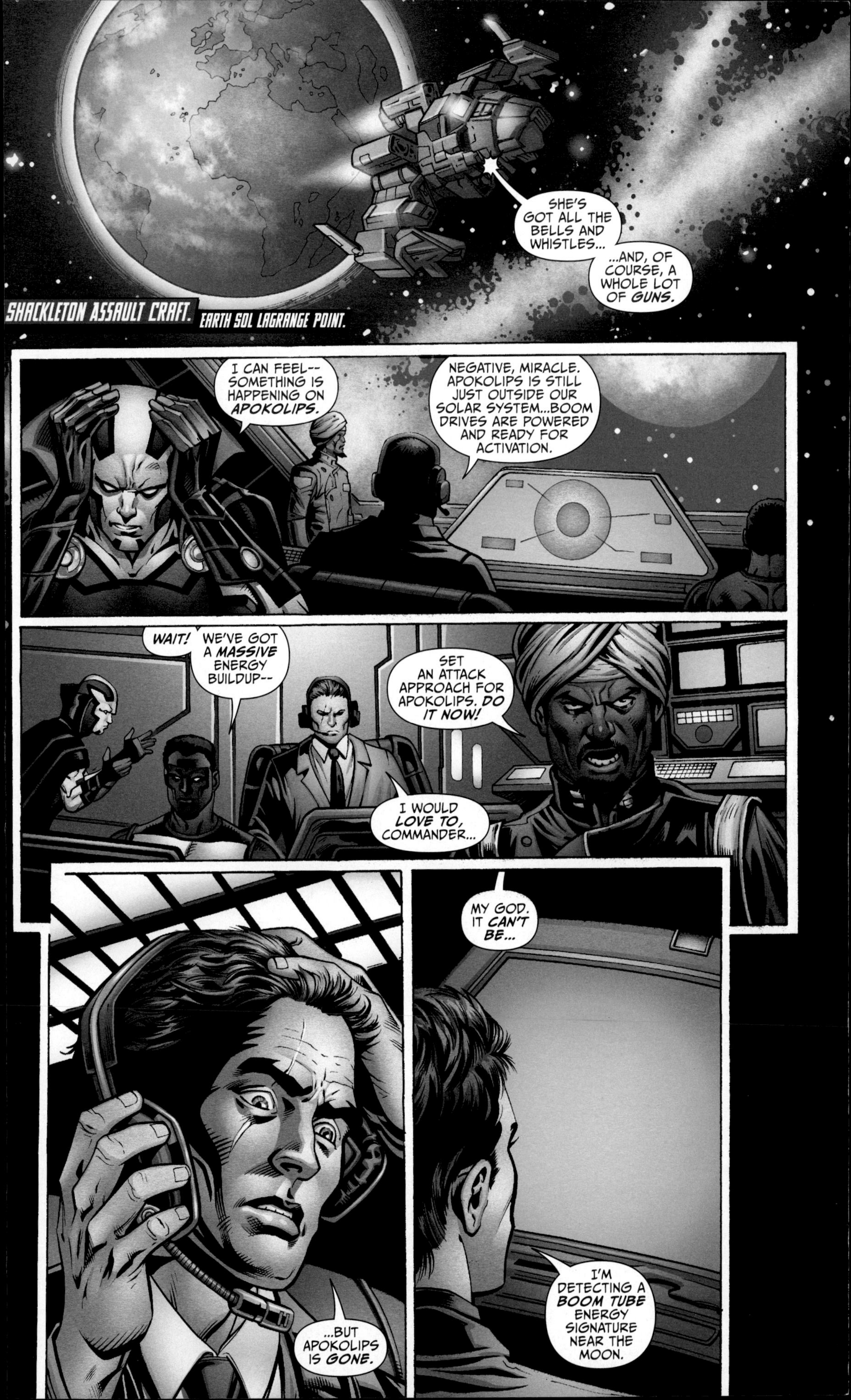
SHE'S GOT ALL THE BELLS AND WHISTLES...
...AND, OF COURSE, A WHOLE LOT OF GUNS.
SHACKLETON ASSAULT CRAFT.
EARTH SOL LAGRANGE POINT.
I CAN FEEL-- SOMETHING IS HAPPENING ON APOKOLIPS.
NEGATIVE, MIRACLE. APOKOLIPS IS STILL JUST OUTSIDE OUR SOLAR SYSTEM...BOOM DRIVES ARE POWERED AND READY FOR ACTIVATION.
WAIT!
WE'VE GOT A MASSIVE ENERGY BUILDUP--
SET AN ATTACK APPROACH FOR APOKOLIPS. DO IT NOW!
I WOULD LOVE TO, COMMANDER...
...BUT APOKOLIPS IS GONE.
MY GOD. IT CAN'T BE...
I'M DETECTING A BOOM TUBE ENERGY SIGNATURE NEAR THE MOON.

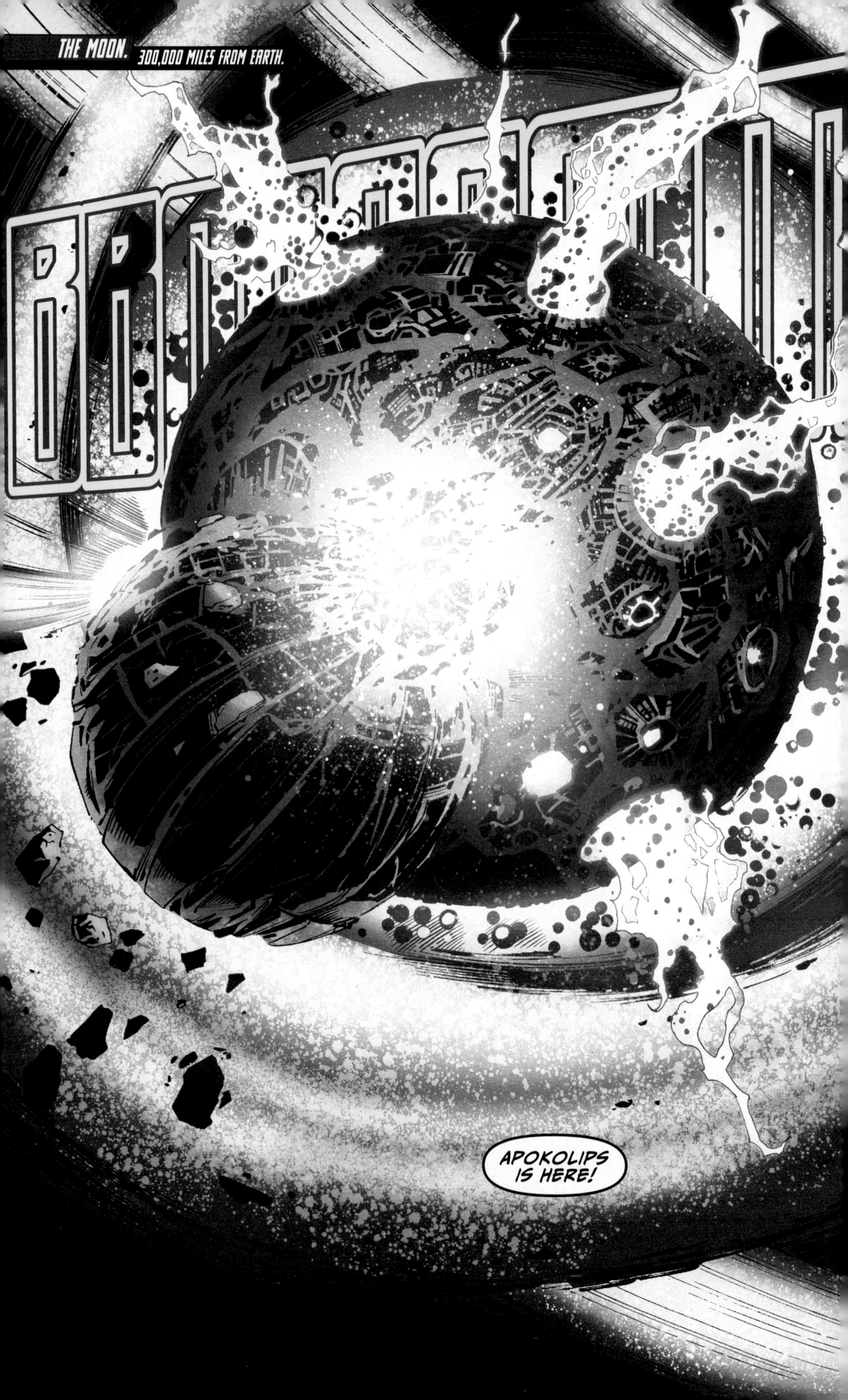
THE MOON.
300,000 MILES FROM EARTH.
APOKOLIPS IS HERE!

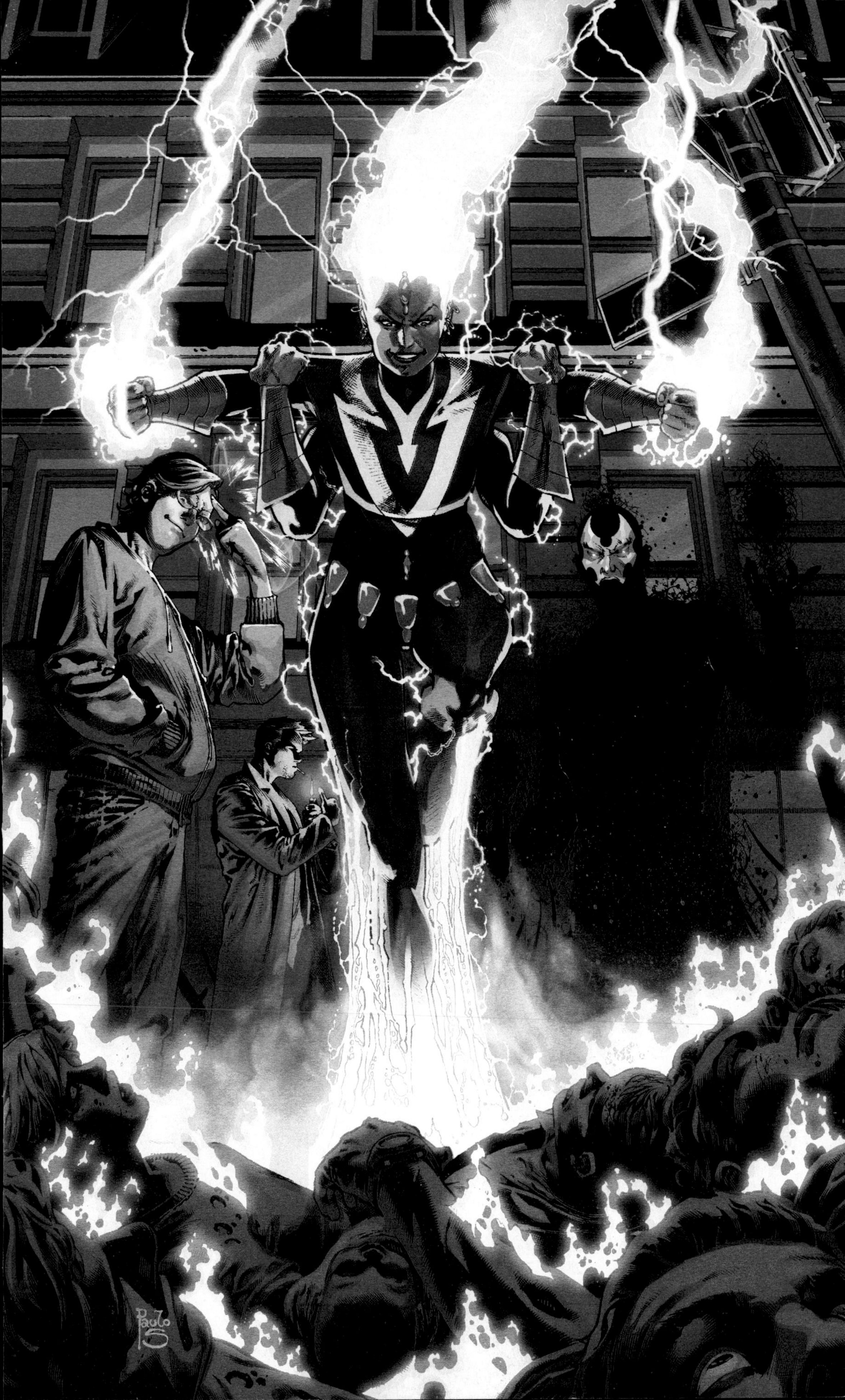

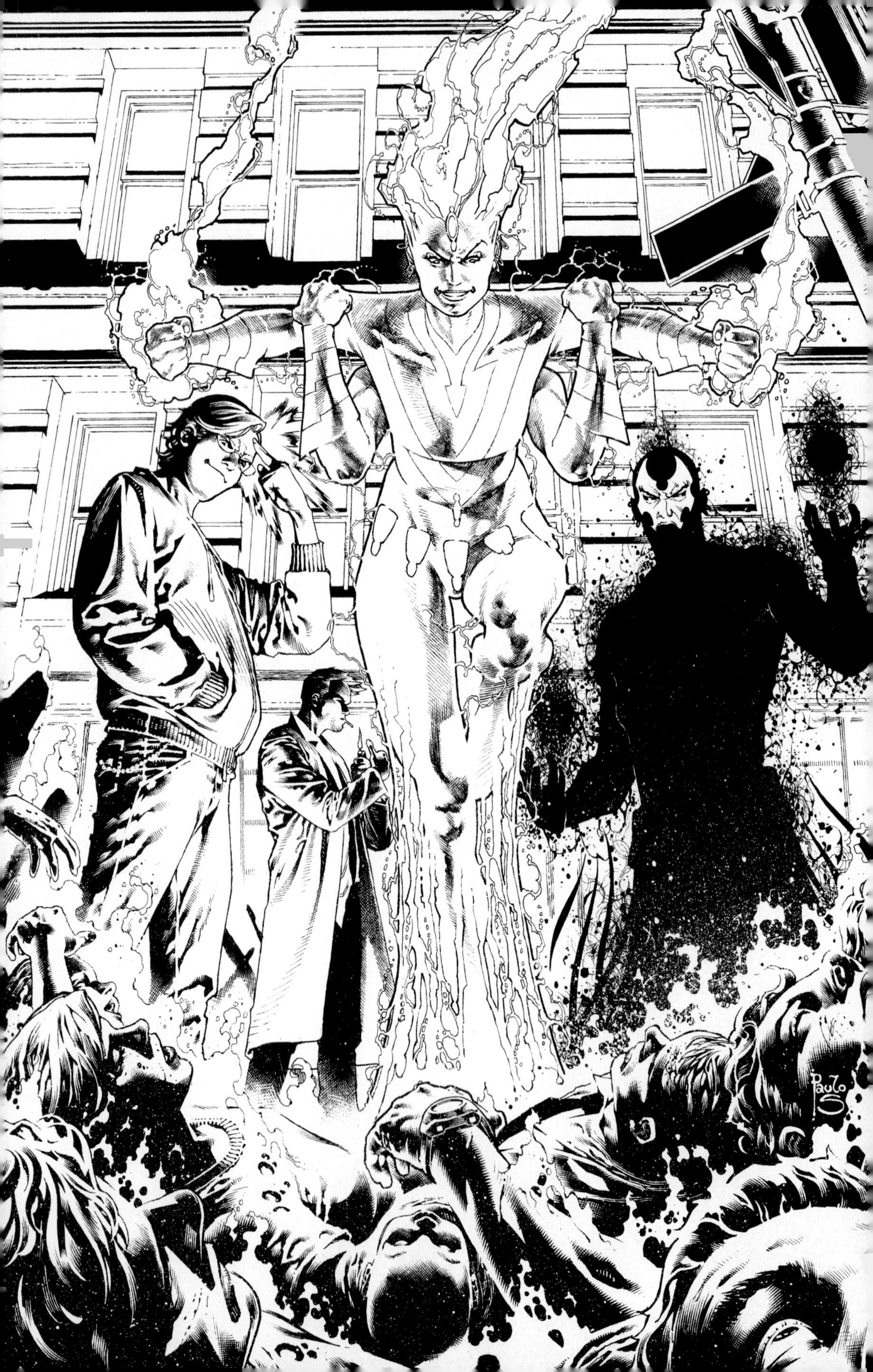

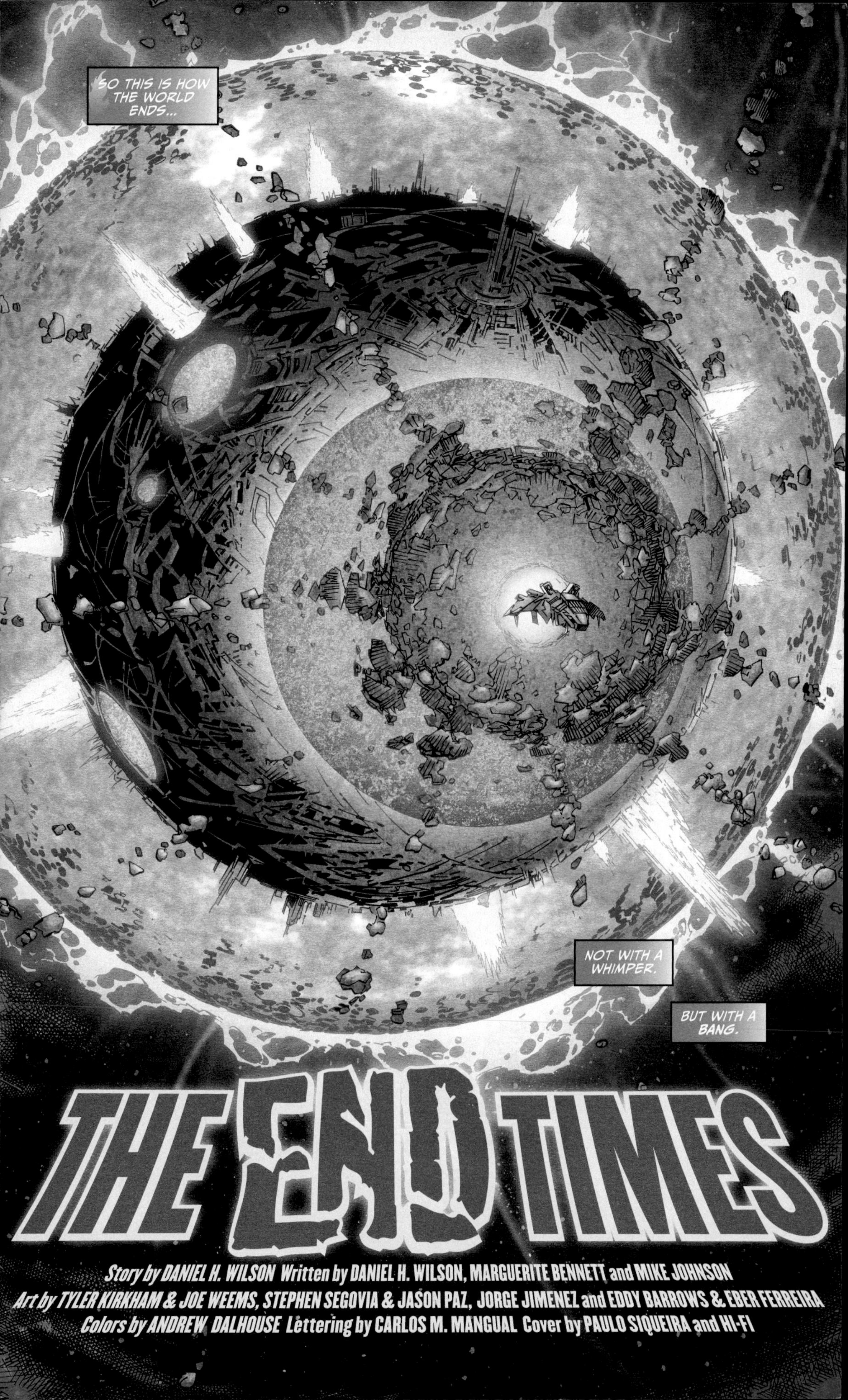
SO THIS IS HOW THE WORLD ENDS...
NOT WITH A WHIMPER.
BUT WITH A BANG.
THE END TIMES
Story by DANIEL H. WILSON Written by DANIEL H. WILSON, MARGUERITE BENNETT and MIKE JOHNSON
Art by TYLER KIRKHAM & JOE WEEMS, STEPHEN SEGOVIA & JASON PAZ, JORGE JIMENEZ and EDDY BARROWS & EBER FERREIRA
Colors by ANDREW DALHOUSE Lettering by CARLOS M. MANGUAL Cover by PAULO SIQUEIRA and HI-FI

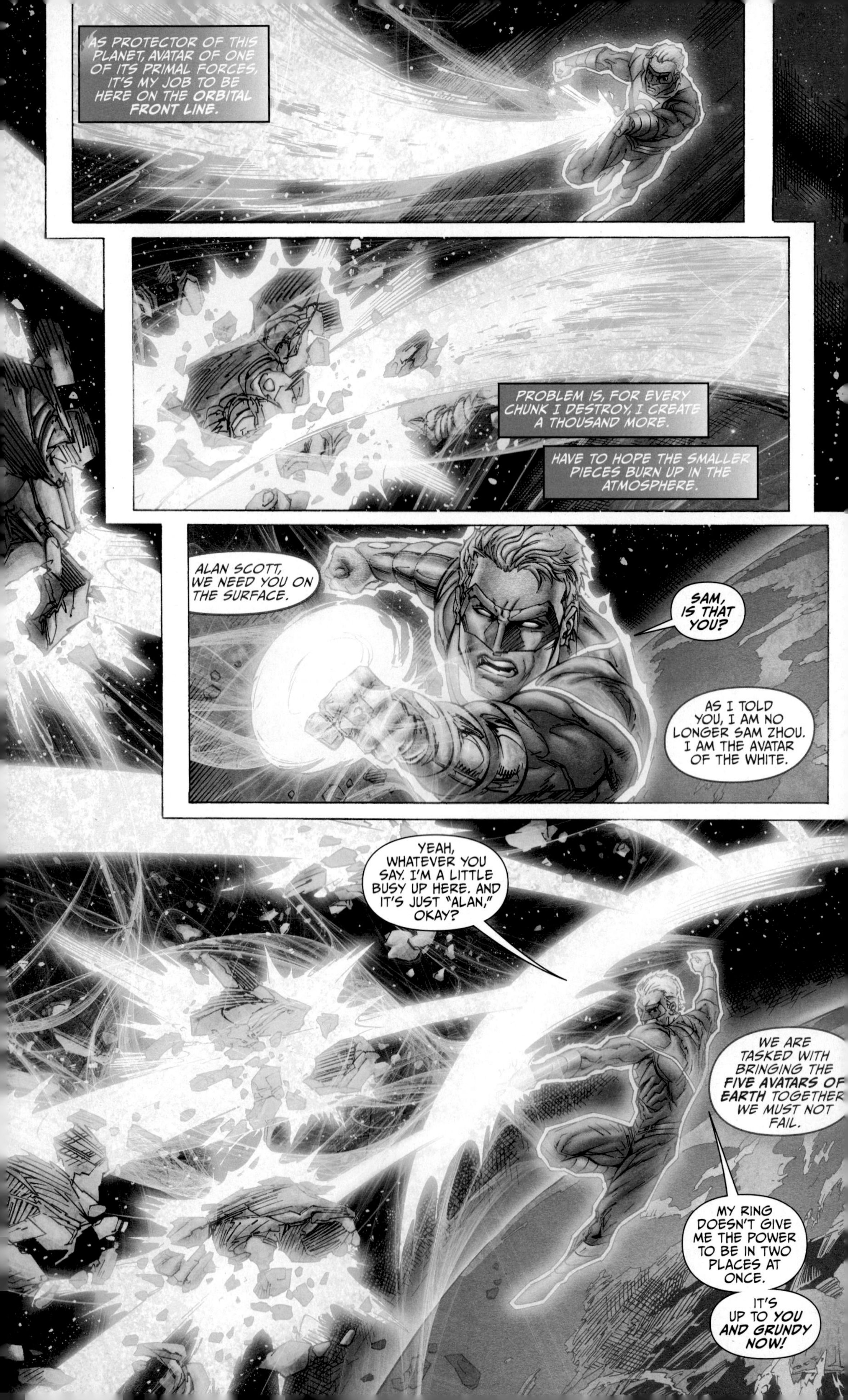
AS PROTECTOR OF THIS PLANET, AVATAR OF ONE OF ITS PRIMAL FORCES, IT'S MY JOB TO BE HERE ON THE ORBITAL FRONT LINE.
PROBLEM IS, FOR EVERY CHUNK I DESTROY, I CREATE A THOUSAND MORE.
HAVE TO HOPE THE SMALLER PIECES BURN UP IN THE ATMOSPHERE.
ALAN SCOTT, WE NEED YOU ON THE SURFACE.
SAM, IS THAT YOU?
AS I TOLD YOU, I AM NO LONGER SAM ZHOU. I AM THE AVATAR OF THE WHITE.
YEAH, WHATEVER YOU SAY. I'M A LITTLE BUSY UP HERE. AND IT'S JUST "ALAN," OKAY?
WE ARE TASKED WITH BRINGING THE FIVE AVATARS OF EARTH TOGETHER. WE MUST NOT FAIL.
MY RING DOESN'T GIVE ME THE POWER TO BE IN TWO PLACES AT ONCE.
IT'S UP TO YOU AND GRUNDY NOW!

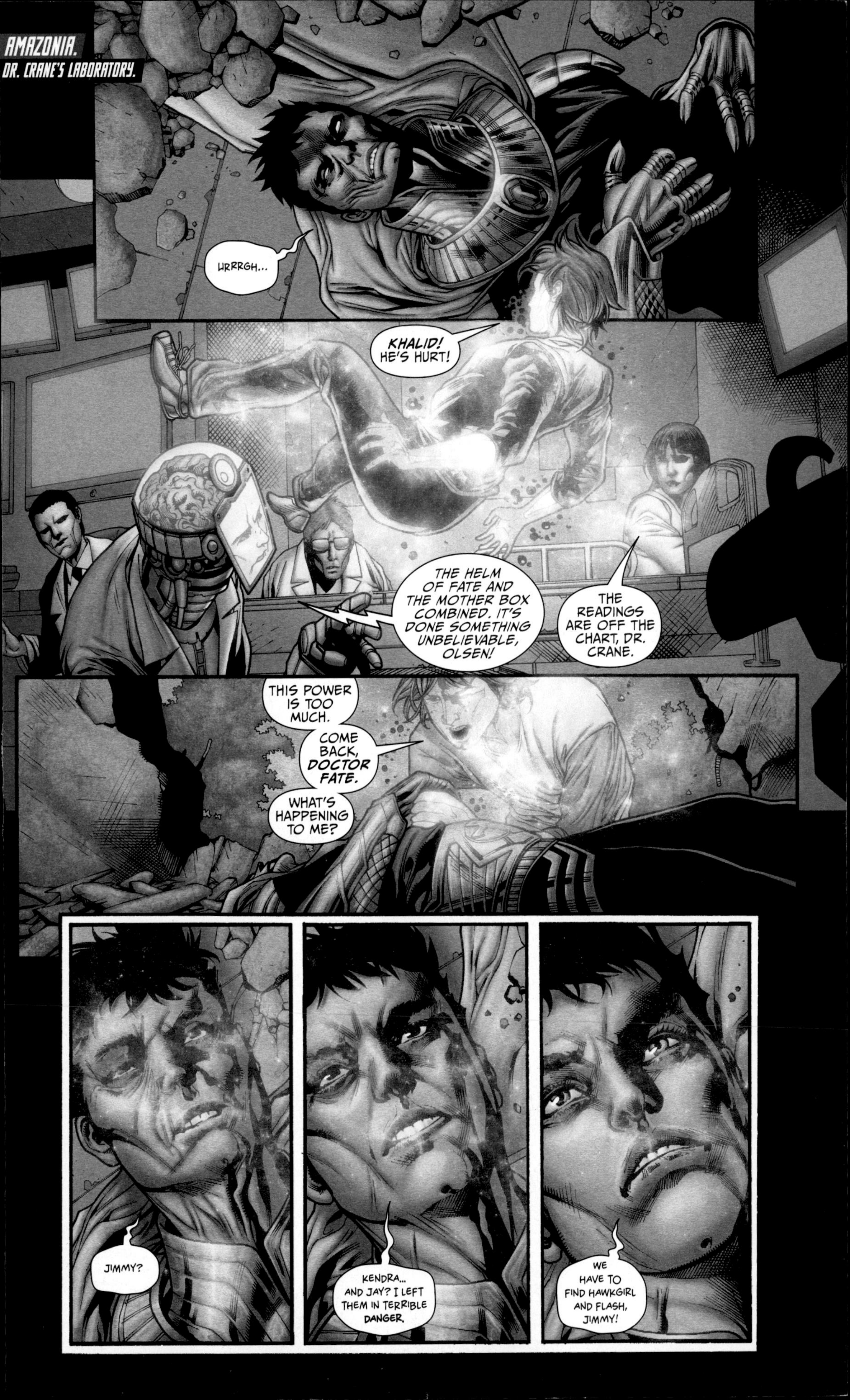
AMAZONIA.
DR. CRANE'S LABORATORY.
URRRGH...
KHALID! HE'S HURT!
THE HELM OF FATE AND THE MOTHER BOX COMBINED. IT'S DONE SOMETHING UNBELIEVABLE, OLSEN!
THE READINGS ARE OFF THE CHART, DR. CRANE.
THIS POWER IS TOO MUCH.
COME BACK, DOCTOR FATE.
WHAT'S HAPPENING TO ME?
JIMMY?
KENDRA... AND JAY? I LEFT THEM IN TERRIBLE DANGER.
WE HAVE TO FIND HAWKGIRL AND FLASH, JIMMY!

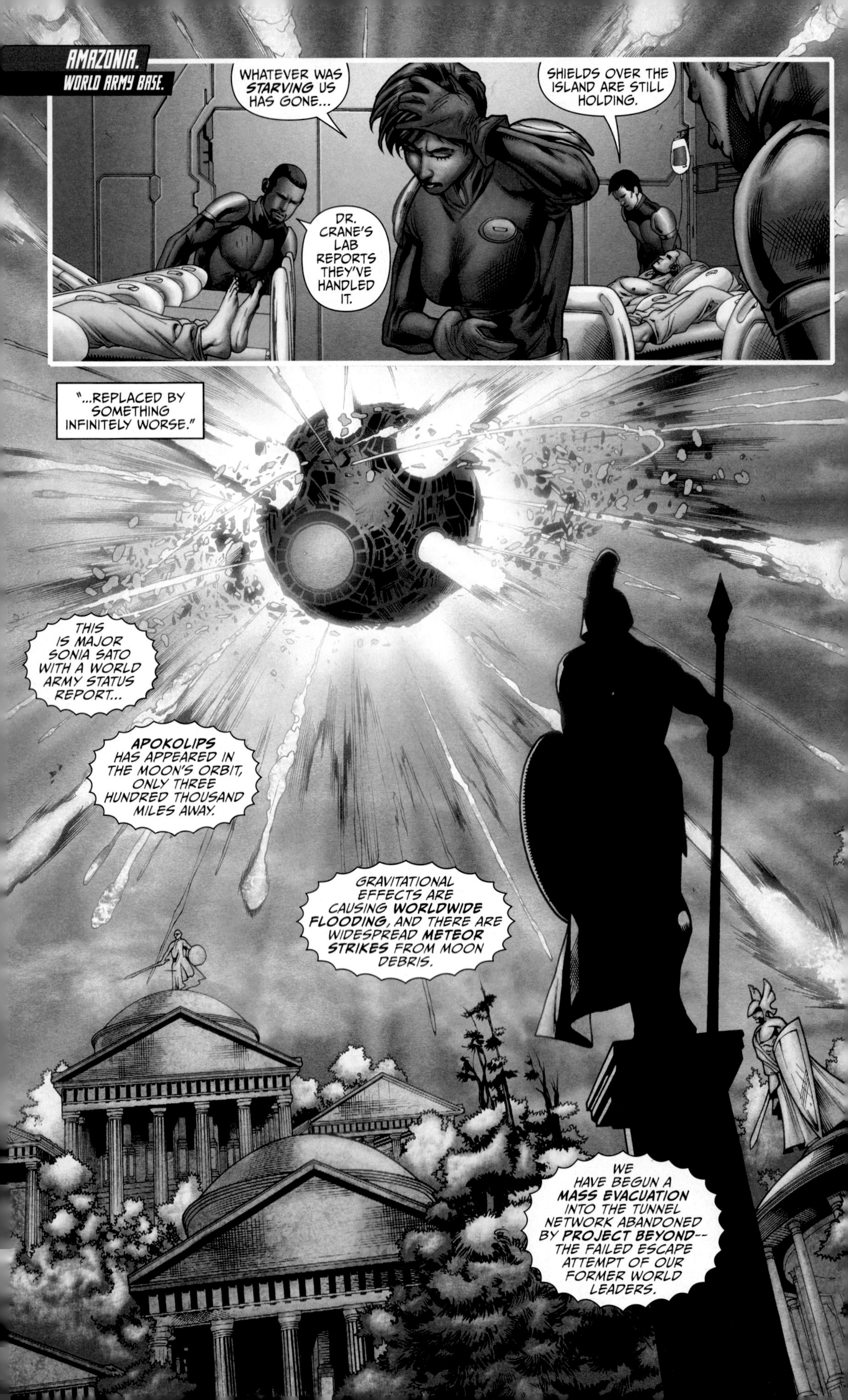
AMAZONIA.
WORLD ARMY BASE.
WHATEVER WAS STARVING US HAS GONE...
SHIELDS OVER THE ISLAND ARE STILL HOLDING.
DR. CRANE'S LAB REPORTS THEY'VE HANDLED IT.
"...REPLACED BY SOMETHING INFINITELY WORSE."
THIS IS MAJOR SONIA SATO WITH A WORLD ARMY STATUS REPORT...
APOKOLIPS HAS APPEARED IN THE MOON'S ORBIT, ONLY THREE HUNDRED THOUSAND MILES AWAY.
GRAVITATIONAL EFFECTS ARE CAUSING WORLDWIDE FLOODING, AND THERE ARE WIDESPREAD METEOR STRIKES FROM MOON DEBRIS.
WE HAVE BEGUN A MASS EVACUATION INTO THE TUNNEL NETWORK ABANDONED BY PROJECT BEYOND-- THE FAILED ESCAPE ATTEMPT OF OUR FORMER WORLD LEADERS.

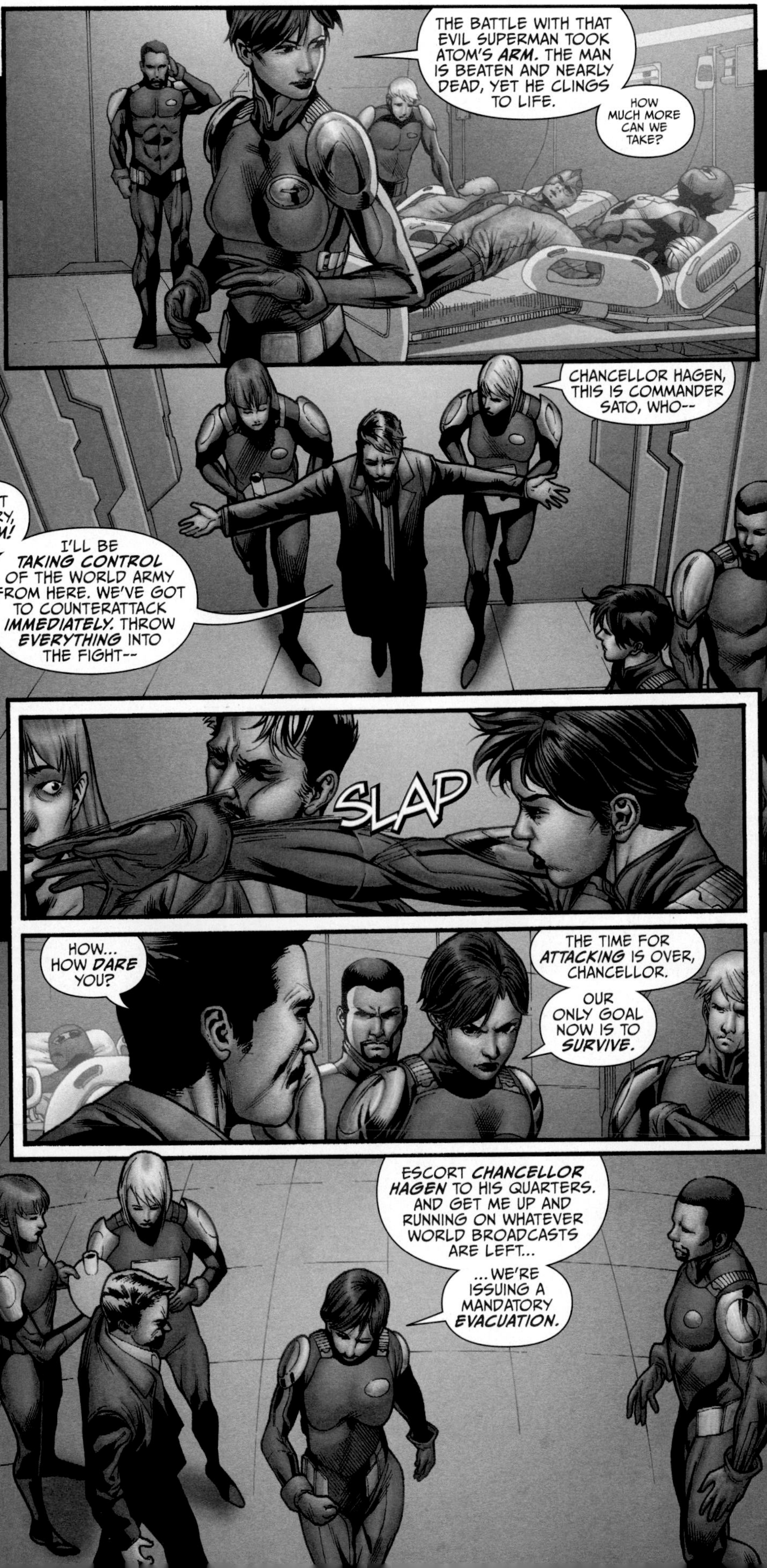
THE BATTLE WITH THAT EVIL SUPERMAN TOOK ATOM'S ARM. THE MAN IS BEATEN AND NEARLY DEAD, YET HE CLINGS TO LIFE.
HOW MUCH MORE CAN WE TAKE?
CHANCELLOR HAGEN, THIS IS COMMANDER SATO, WHO--
DON'T WORRY, MA'AM!
I'LL BE TAKING CONTROL OF THE WORLD ARMY FROM HERE. WE'VE GOT TO COUNTERATTACK IMMEDIATELY. THROW EVERYTHING INTO THE FIGHT--
SLAP
HOW... HOW DARE YOU?
THE TIME FOR ATTACKING IS OVER, CHANCELLOR.
OUR ONLY GOAL NOW IS TO SURVIVE.
ESCORT CHANCELLOR HAGEN TO HIS QUARTERS. AND GET ME UP AND RUNNING ON WHATEVER WORLD BROADCASTS ARE LEFT...
...WE'RE ISSUING A MANDATORY EVACUATION.

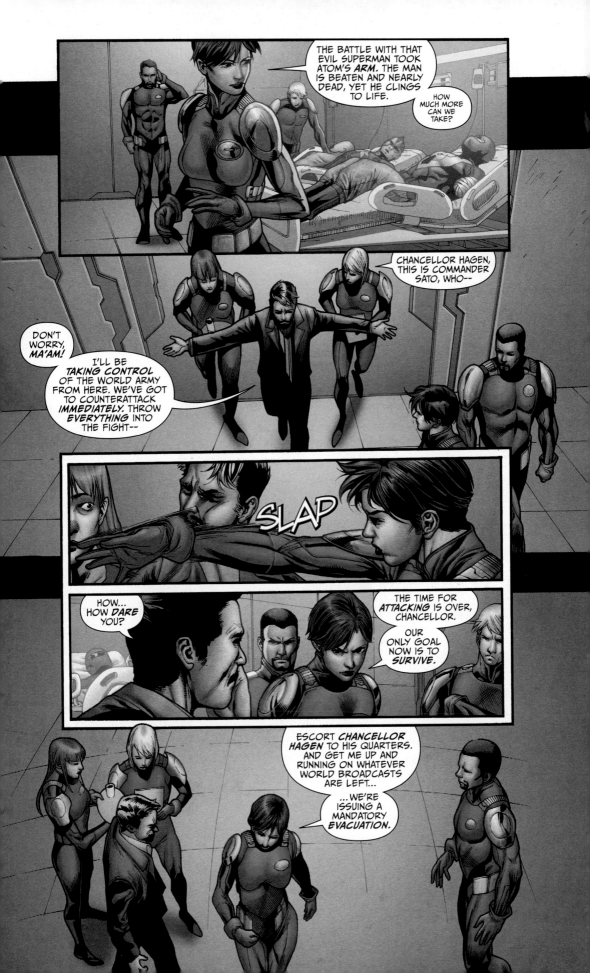

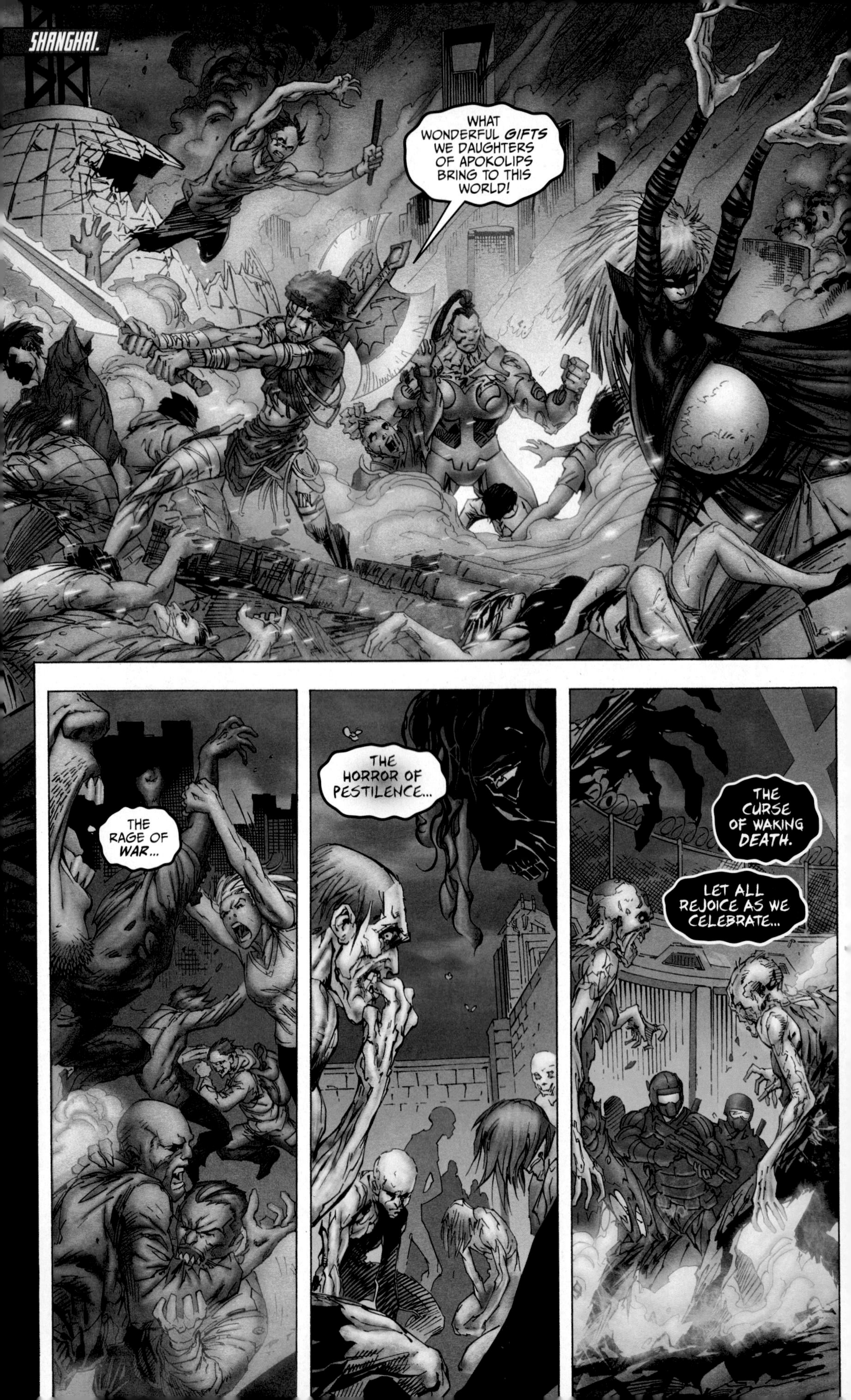
SHANGHAI.
WHAT WONDERFUL GIFTS WE DAUGHTERS OF APOKOLIPS BRING TO THIS WORLD!
THE RAGE OF WAR...
THE HORROR OF PESTILENCE...
THE CURSE OF WAKING DEATH.
LET ALL REJOICE AS WE CELEBRATE...

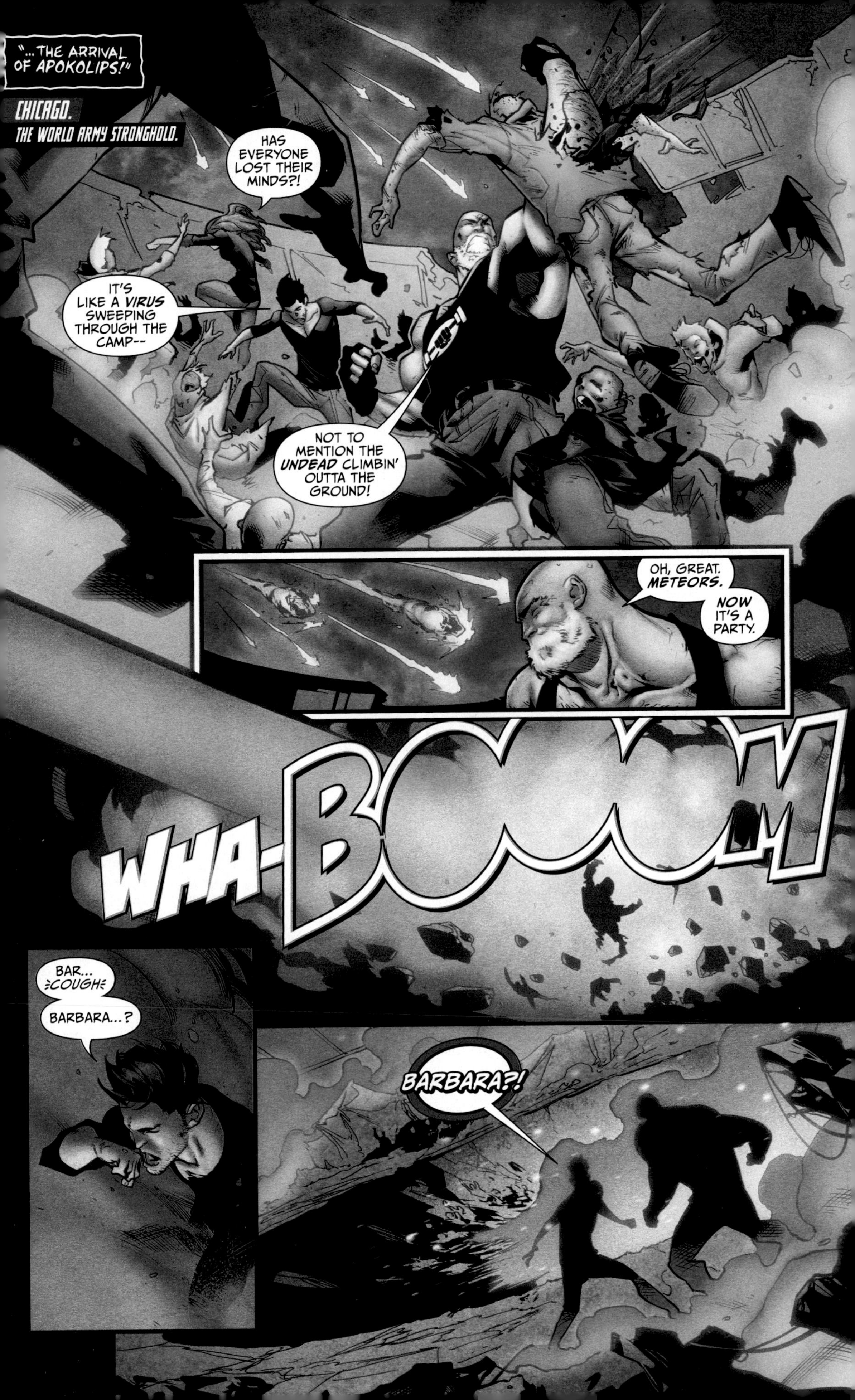

"...THE ARRIVAL OF APOKOLIPS!"
CHICAGO.
THE WORLD ARMY STRONGHOLD.
HAS EVERYONE LOST THEIR MINDS?!
IT'S LIKE A VIRUS SWEEPING THROUGH THE CAMP--
NOT TO MENTION THE UNDEAD CLIMBIN' OUTTA THE GROUND!
OH, GREAT. METEORS.
NOW IT'S A PARTY.
WHA-BOOOM
BAR... *COUGH*
BARBARA...?
BARBARA?!

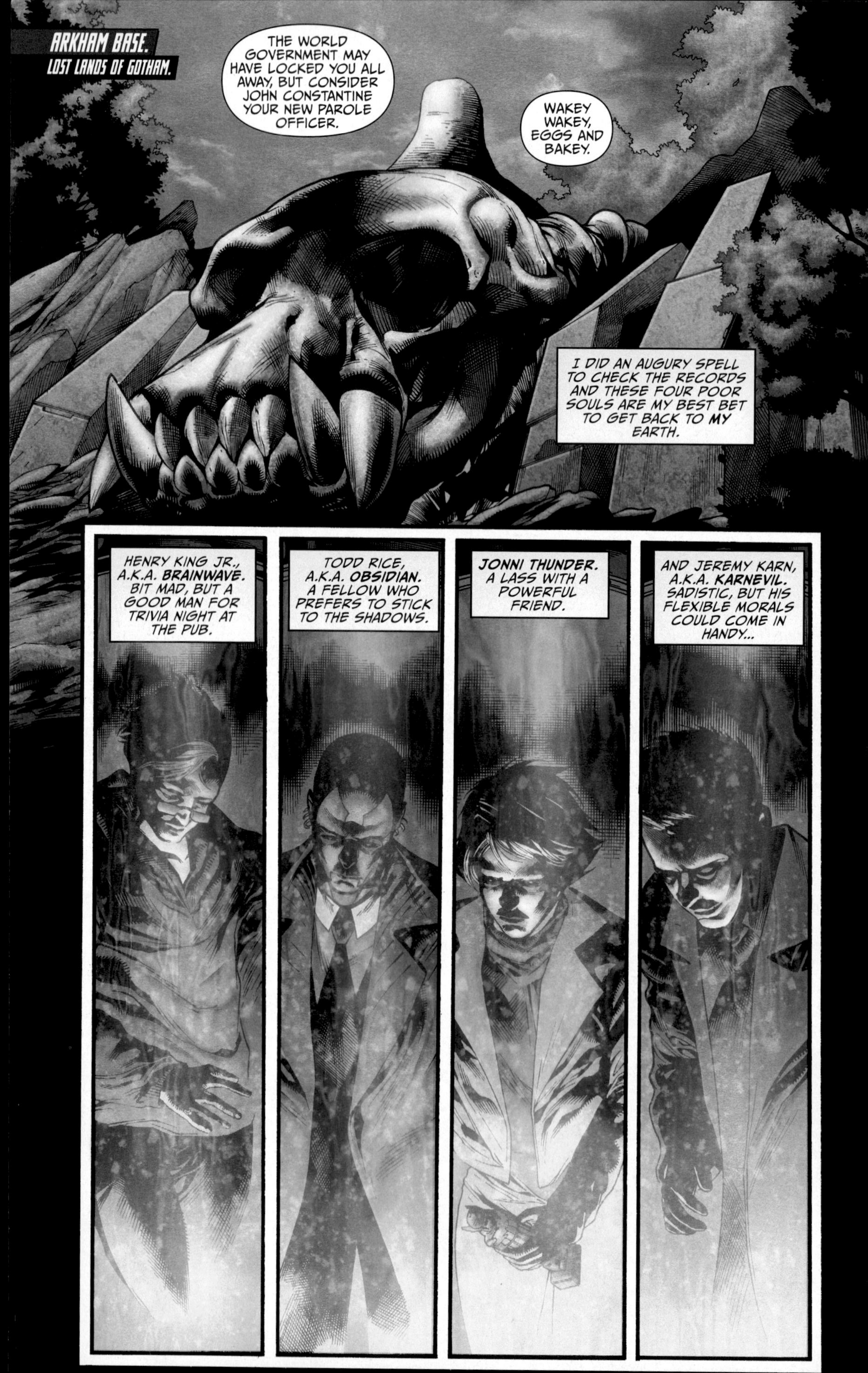
ARKHAM BASE.
LOST LANDS OF GOTHAM.
THE WORLD GOVERNMENT MAY HAVE LOCKED YOU ALL AWAY, BUT CONSIDER JOHN CONSTANTINE YOUR NEW PAROLE OFFICER.
WAKEY WAKEY, EGGS AND BAKEY.
I DID AN AUGURY SPELL TO CHECK THE RECORDS AND THESE FOUR POOR SOULS ARE MY BEST BET TO GET BACK TO MY EARTH.
HENRY KING JR., A.K.A. BRAINWAVE. BIT MAD, BUT A GOOD MAN FOR TRIVIA NIGHT AT THE PUB.
TODD RICE, A.K.A. OBSIDIAN. A FELLOW WHO PREFERS TO STICK TO THE SHADOWS.
JONNI THUNDER. A LASS WITH A POWERFUL FRIEND.
AND JEREMY KARN, A.K.A. KARNEVIL. SADISTIC, BUT HIS FLEXIBLE MORALS COULD COME IN HANDY...

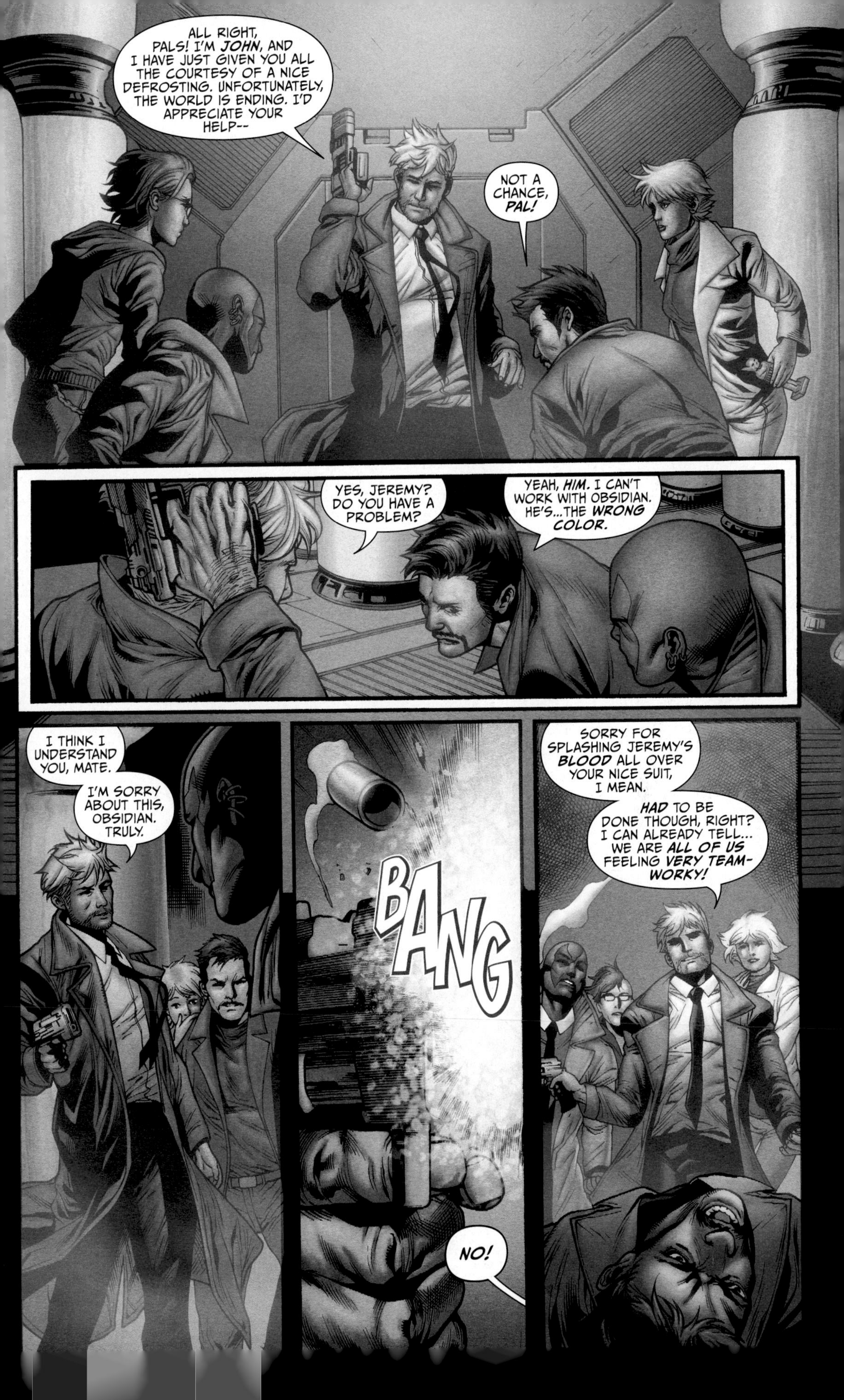
ALL RIGHT, PALS! I'M JOHN, AND I HAVE JUST GIVEN YOU ALL THE COURTESY OF A NICE DEFROSTING. UNFORTUNATELY, THE WORLD IS ENDING. I'D APPRECIATE YOUR HELP--
NOT A CHANCE, PAL!
YES, JEREMY? DO YOU HAVE A PROBLEM?
YEAH, HIM. I CAN'T WORK WITH OBSIDIAN. HE'S...THE WRONG COLOR.
I THINK I UNDERSTAND YOU, MATE.
I'M SORRY ABOUT THIS, OBSIDIAN. TRULY.
BANG
NO!
SORRY FOR SPLASHING JEREMY'S BLOOD ALL OVER YOUR NICE SUIT, I MEAN.
HAD TO BE DONE THOUGH, RIGHT? I CAN ALREADY TELL... WE ARE ALL OF US FEELING VERY TEAM-WORKY!

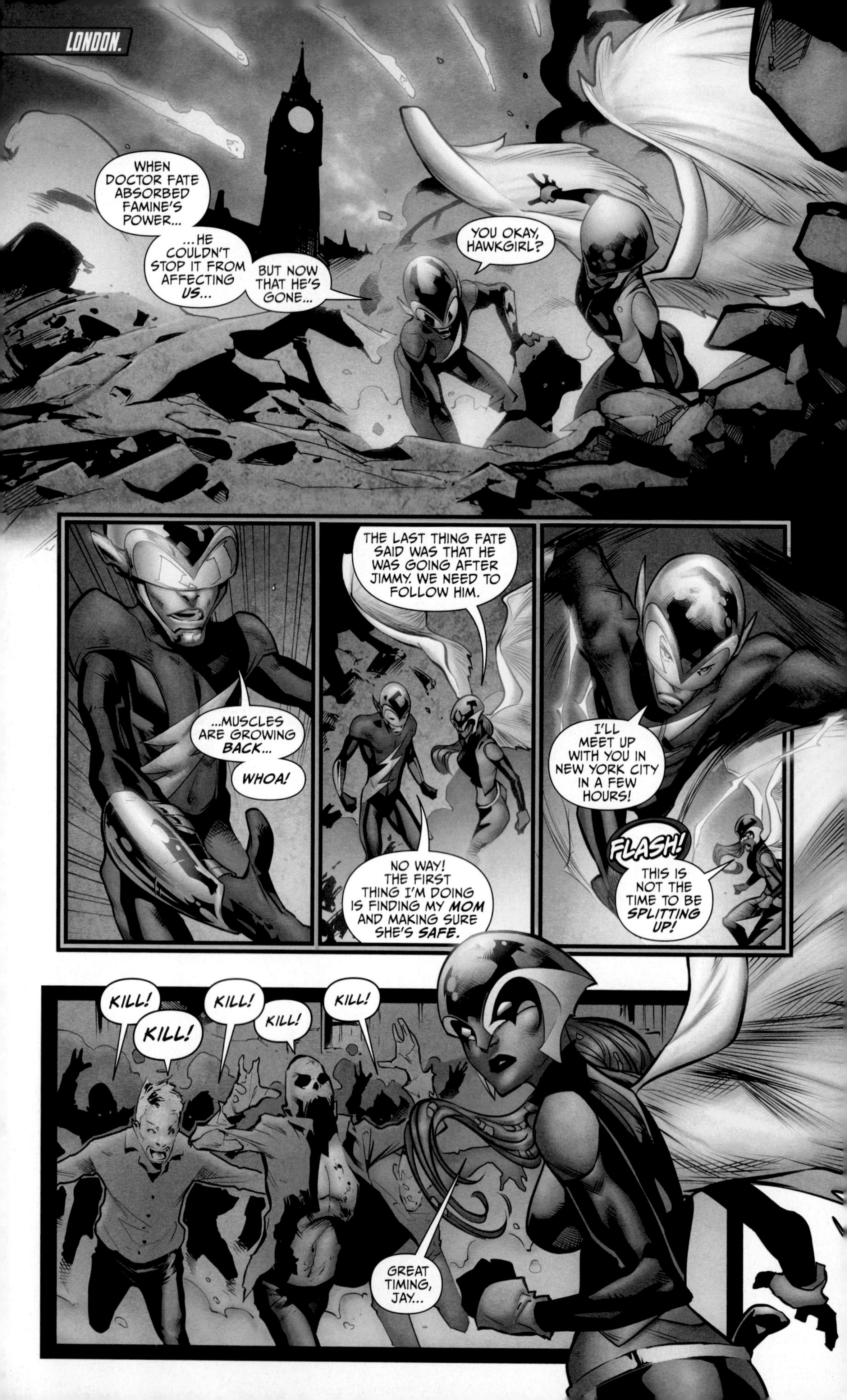
LONDON.
WHEN DOCTOR FATE ABSORBED FAMINE'S POWER...
...HE COULDN'T STOP IT FROM AFFECTING US...
BUT NOW THAT HE'S GONE...
YOU OKAY, HAWKGIRL?
...MUSCLES ARE GROWING BACK...
WHOA!
THE LAST THING FATE SAID WAS THAT HE WAS GOING AFTER JIMMY. WE NEED TO FOLLOW HIM.
NO WAY! THE FIRST THING I'M DOING IS FINDING MY MOM AND MAKING SURE SHE'S SAFE.
I'LL MEET UP WITH YOU IN NEW YORK CITY IN A FEW HOURS!
FLASH!
THIS IS NOT THE TIME TO BE SPLITTING UP!
KILL!
KILL!
KILL!
KILL!
KILL!
GREAT TIMING, JAY...

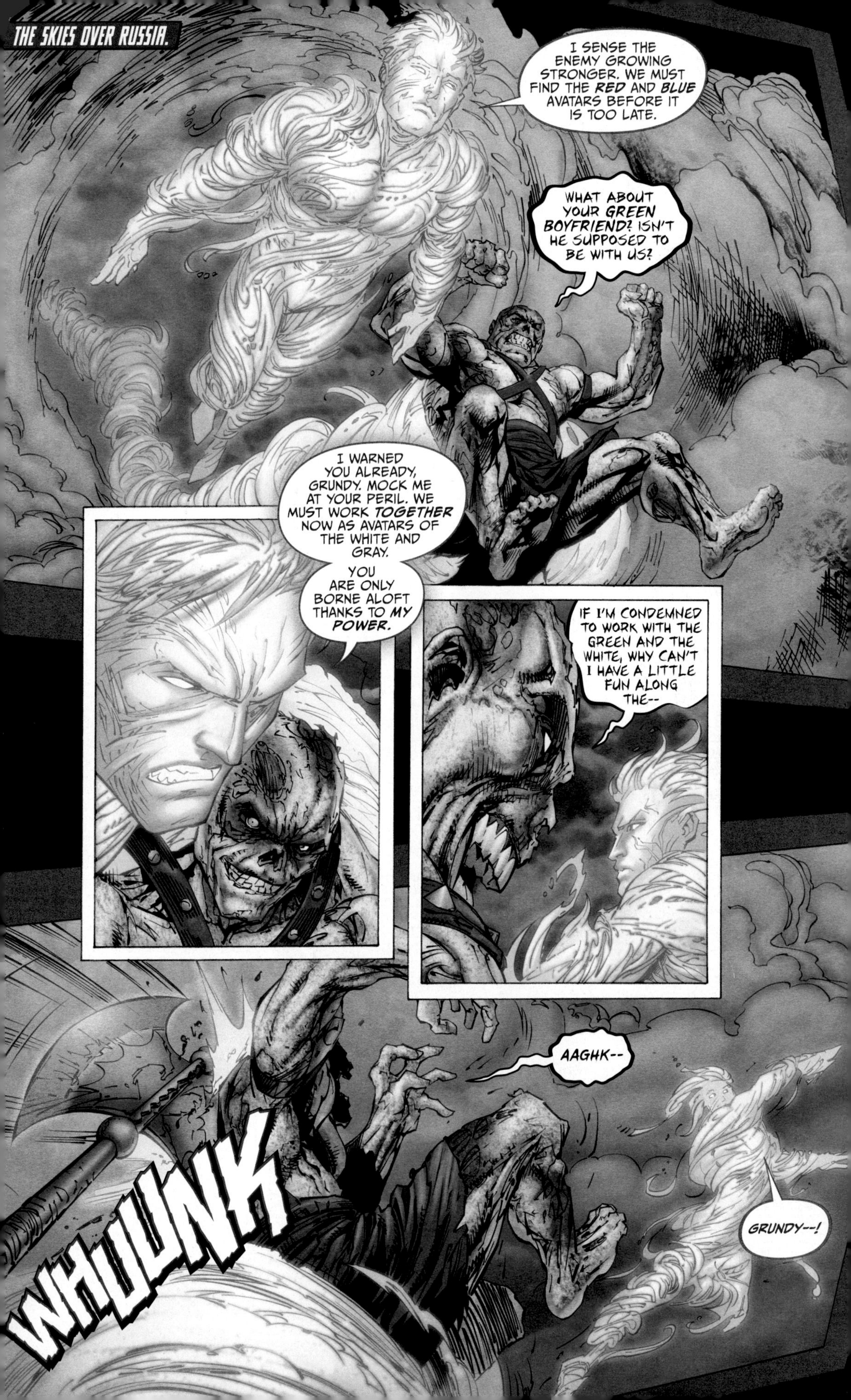
THE SKIES OVER RUSSIA.
I SENSE THE ENEMY GROWING STRONGER. WE MUST FIND THE RED AND BLUE AVATARS BEFORE IT IS TOO LATE.
WHAT ABOUT YOUR GREEN BOYFRIEND? ISN'T HE SUPPOSED TO BE WITH US?
I WARNED YOU ALREADY, GRUNDY. MOCK ME AT YOUR PERIL. WE MUST WORK TOGETHER NOW AS AVATARS OF THE WHITE AND GRAY.
YOU ARE ONLY BORNE ALOFT THANKS TO MY POWER.
IF I'M CONDEMNED TO WORK WITH THE GREEN AND THE WHITE, WHY CAN'T I HAVE A LITTLE FUN ALONG THE--
AAGHK--
WHUUNK
GRUNDY--!

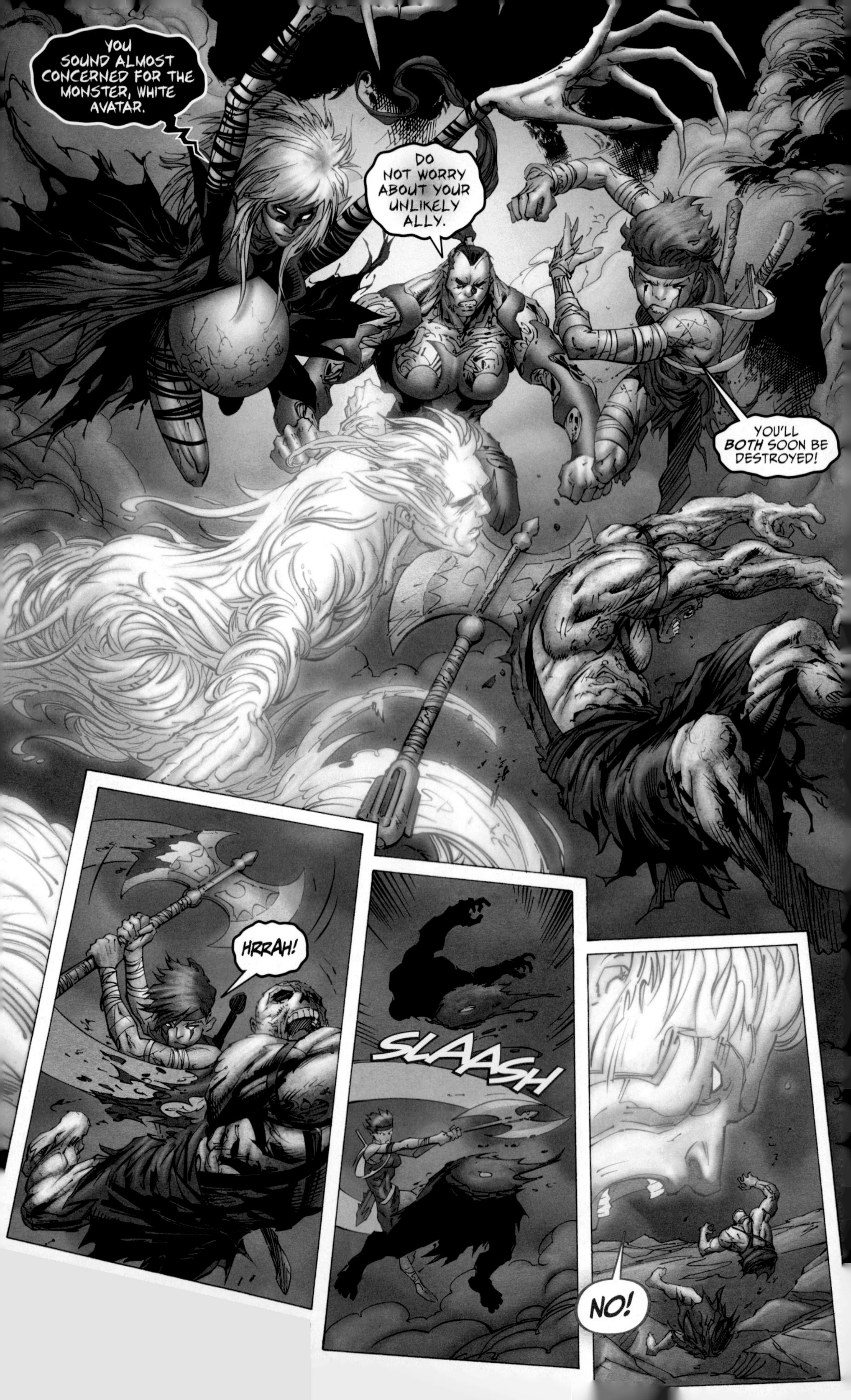
YOU SOUND ALMOST CONCERNED FOR THE MONSTER, WHITE AVATAR.
DO NOT WORRY ABOUT YOUR UNLIKELY ALLY.
YOU'LL BOTH SOON BE DESTROYED!
HRRAH!
SLAASH
NO!

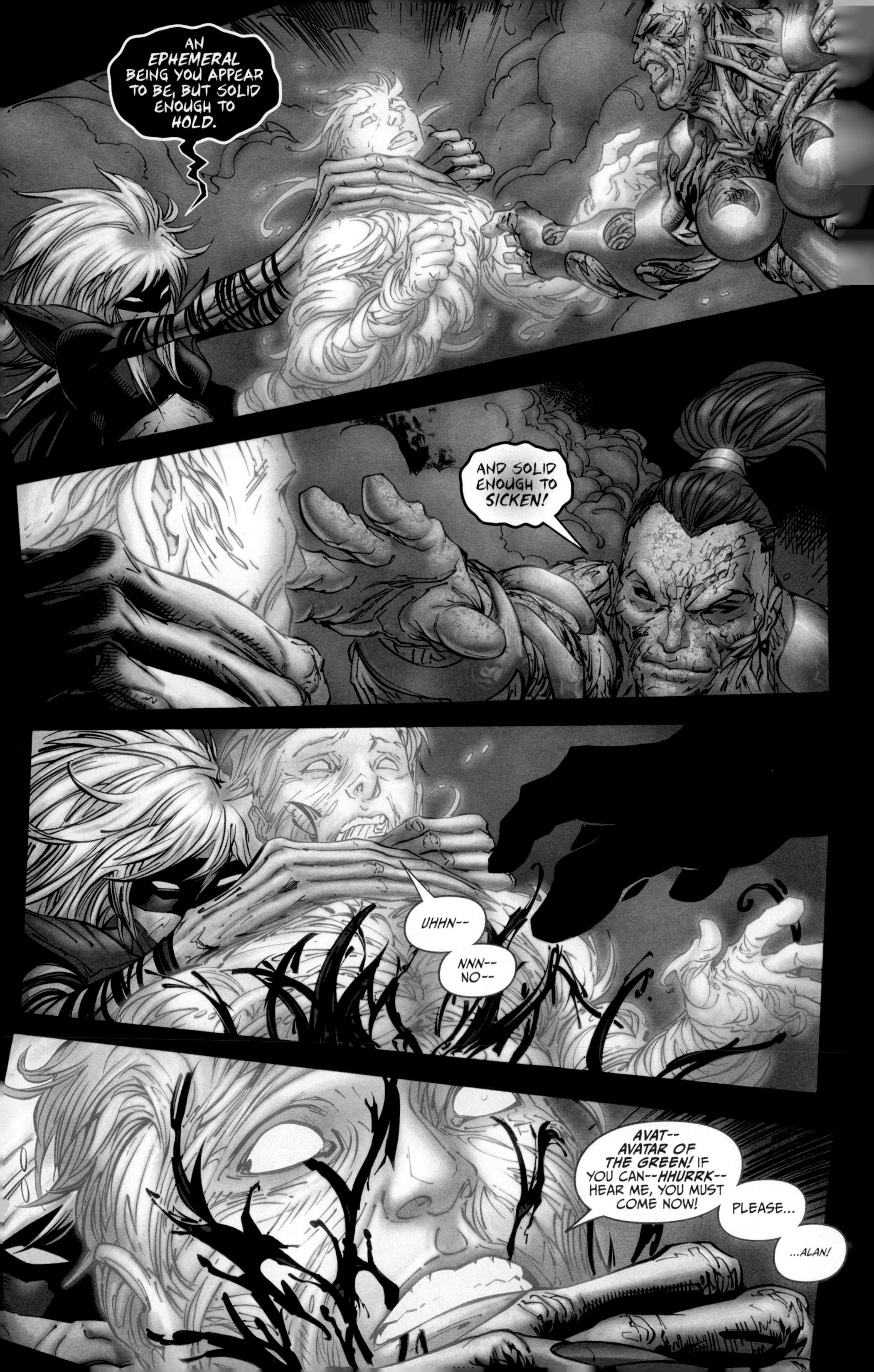
AN EPHEMERAL BEING YOU APPEAR TO BE, BUT SOLID ENOUGH TO HOLD.
AND SOLID ENOUGH TO SICKEN!
UHHN--
NNN-- NO--
AVAT-- AVATAR OF THE GREEN! IF YOU CAN--HHURRK-- HEAR ME, YOU MUST COME NOW!
PLEASE...
...ALAN!

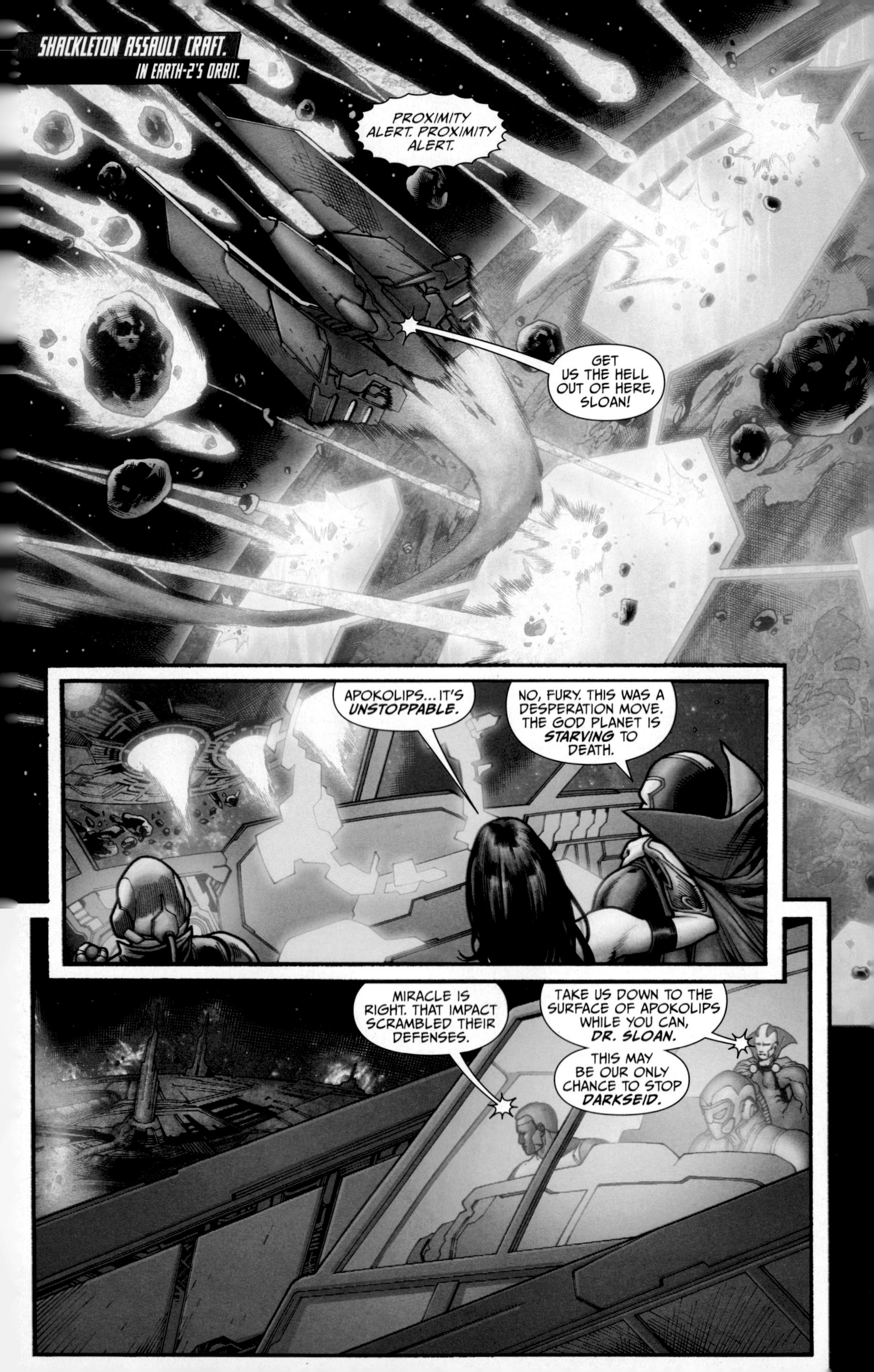
SHACKLETON ASSAULT CRAFT.
IN EARTH-2'S ORBIT.
PROXIMITY ALERT. PROXIMITY ALERT.
GET US THE HELL OUT OF HERE, SLOAN!
APOKOLIPS... IT'S UNSTOPPABLE.
NO, FURY. THIS WAS A DESPERATION MOVE. THE GOD PLANET IS STARVING TO DEATH.
MIRACLE IS RIGHT. THAT IMPACT SCRAMBLED THEIR DEFENSES.
TAKE US DOWN TO THE SURFACE OF APOKOLIPS WHILE YOU CAN, DR. SLOAN.
THIS MAY BE OUR ONLY CHANCE TO STOP DARKSEID.

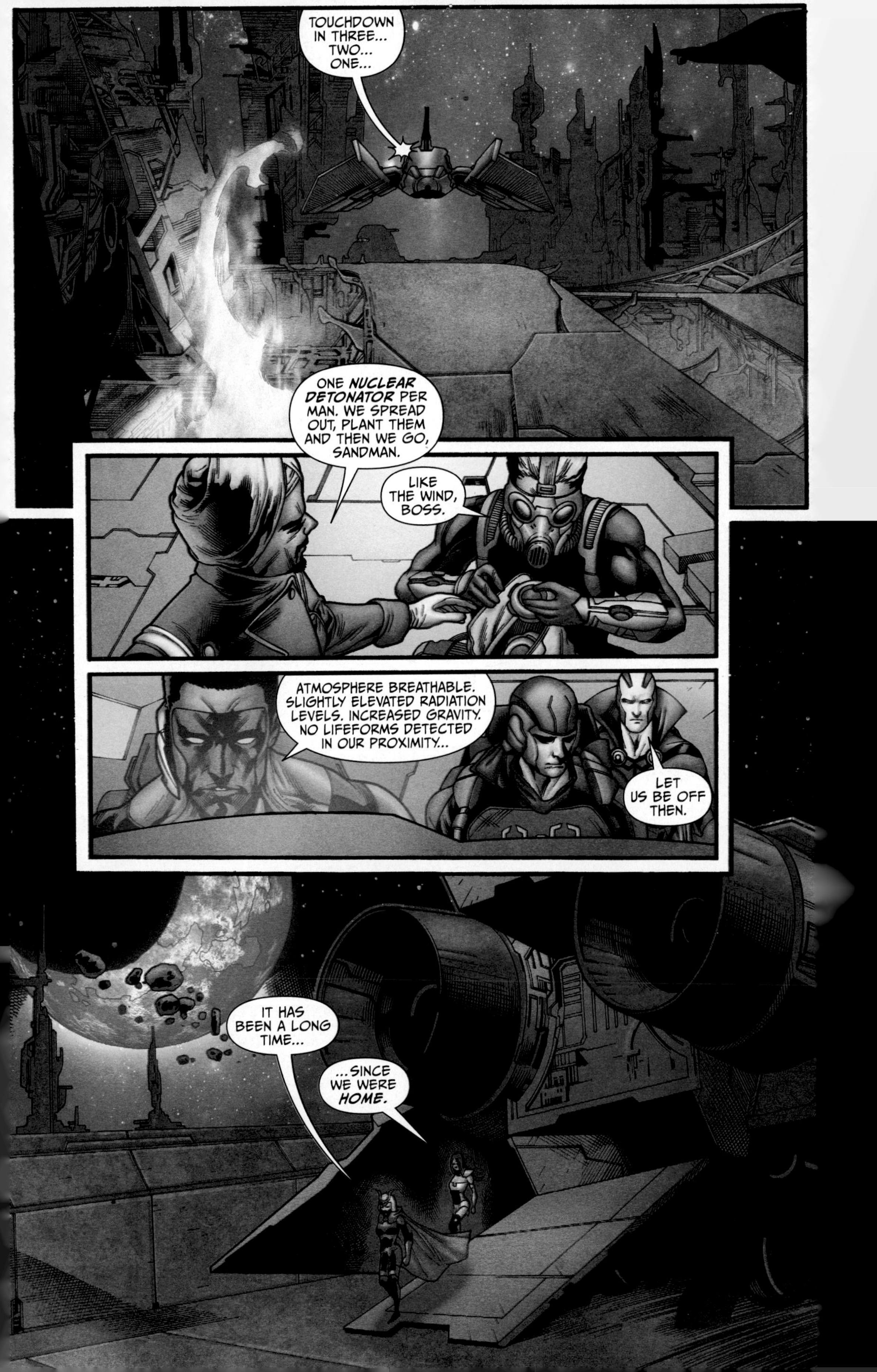
TOUCHDOWN IN THREE... TWO... ONE...
ONE NUCLEAR DETONATOR PER MAN. WE SPREAD OUT, PLANT THEM AND THEN WE GO, SANDMAN.
LIKE THE WIND, BOSS.
ATMOSPHERE BREATHABLE. SLIGHTLY ELEVATED RADIATION LEVELS. INCREASED GRAVITY. NO LIFEFORMS DETECTED IN OUR PROXIMITY...
LET US BE OFF THEN.
IT HAS BEEN A LONG TIME...
...SINCE WE WERE HOME.

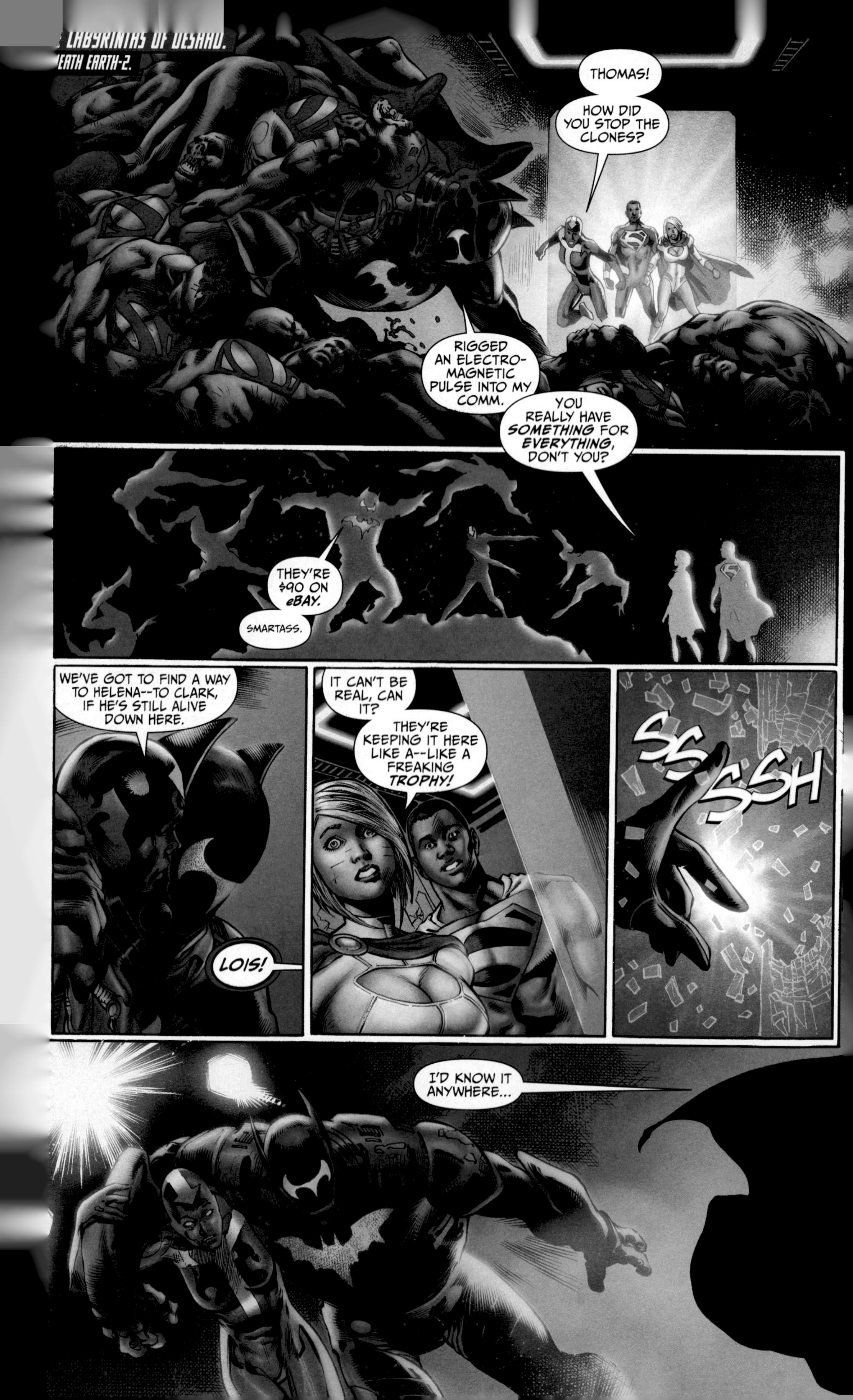
LABYRINTHS OF DESAAD.
EARTH-2.
THOMAS!
HOW DID YOU STOP THE CLONES?
RIGGED AN ELECTRO-MAGNETIC PULSE INTO MY COMM.
YOU REALLY HAVE SOMETHING FOR EVERYTHING, DON'T YOU?
THEY'RE $90 ON eBAY.
SMARTASS.
WE'VE GOT TO FIND A WAY TO HELENA--TO CLARK, IF HE'S STILL ALIVE DOWN HERE.
LOIS!
IT CAN'T BE REAL, CAN IT?
THEY'RE KEEPING IT HERE LIKE A--LIKE A FREAKING TROPHY!
SSSSH
I'D KNOW IT ANYWHERE...

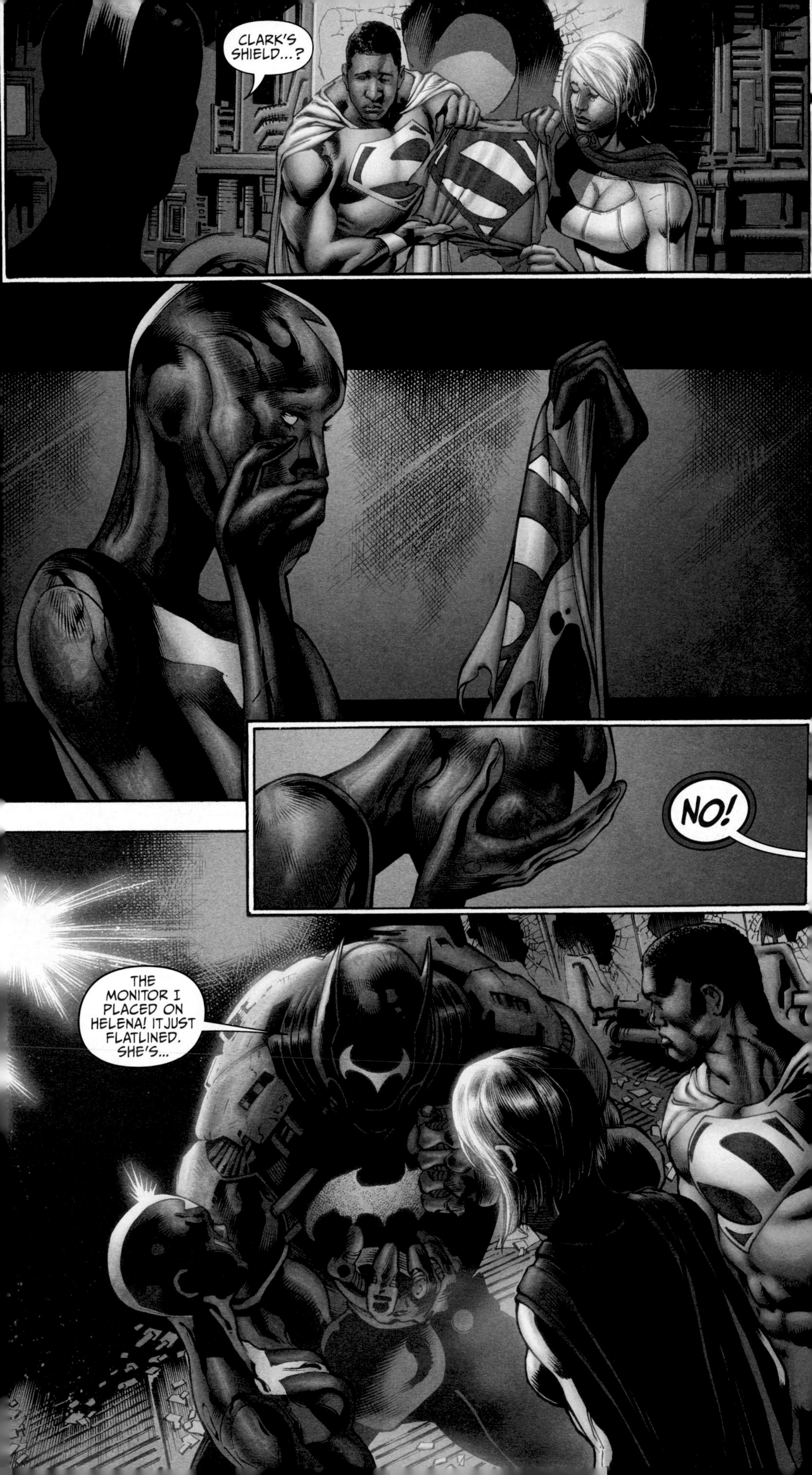
CLARK'S SHIELD...?
NO!
THE MONITOR I PLACED ON HELENA! ITJUST FLATLINED. SHE'S...

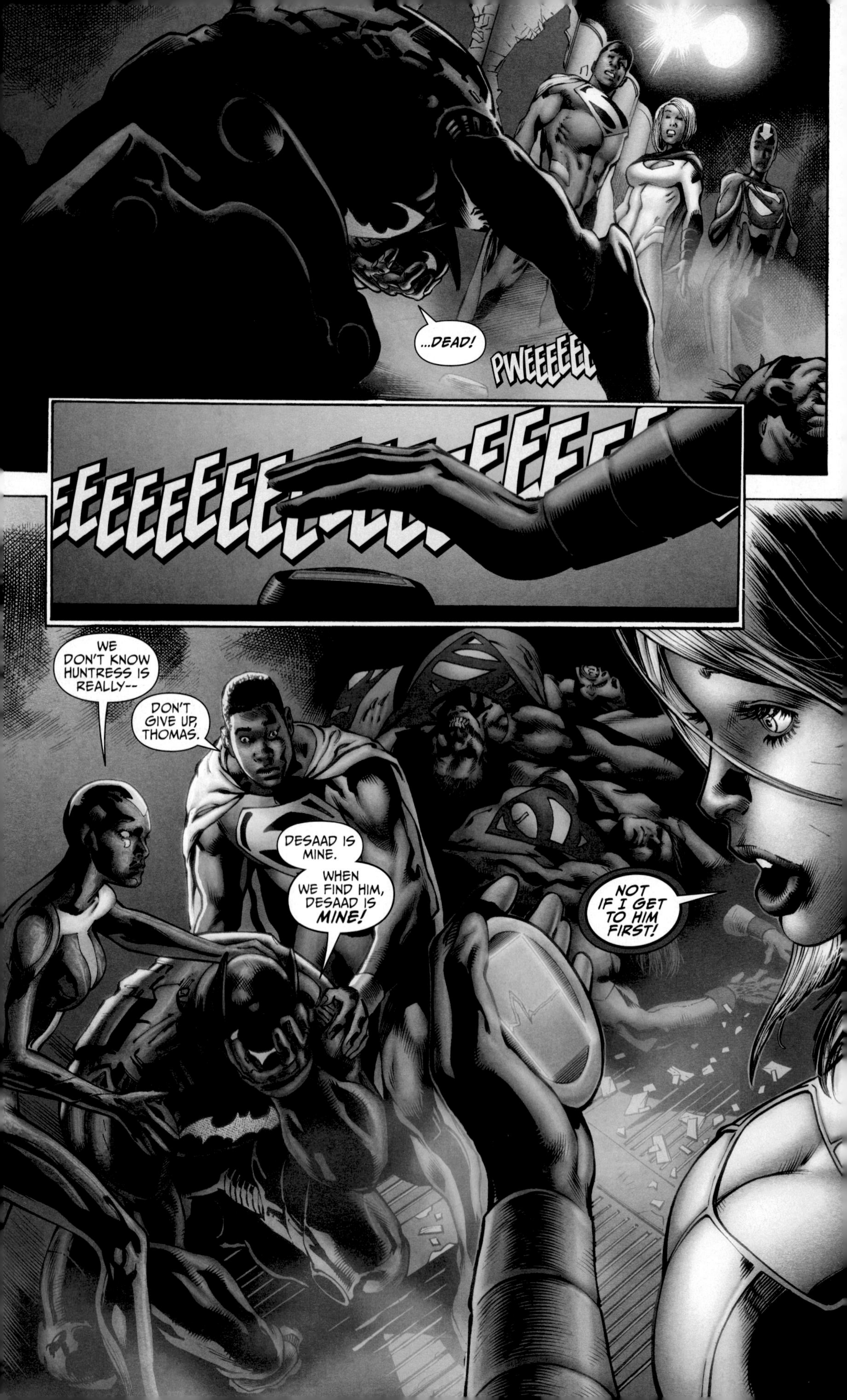
...DEAD!
PWEEEEEEEEEEEEEEEEEEEEEE
WE DON'T KNOW HUNTRESS IS REALLY--
DON'T GIVE UP, THOMAS.
DESAAD IS MINE.
WHEN WE FIND HIM, DESAAD IS MINE!
NOT IF I GET TO HIM FIRST!

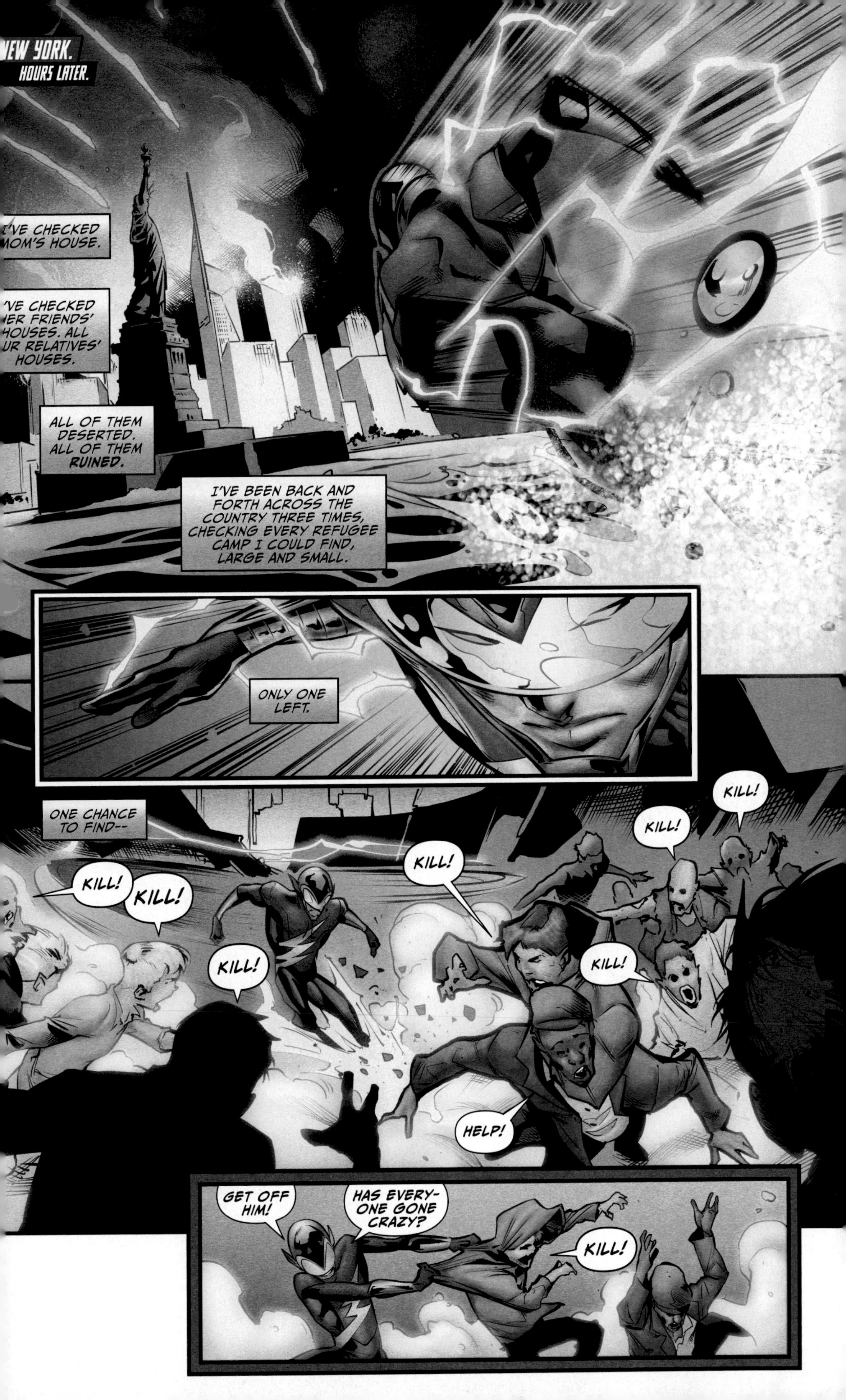

NEW YORK.
HOURS LATER.
I'VE CHECKED MOM'S HOUSE.
I'VE CHECKED HER FRIENDS' HOUSES. ALL OUR RELATIVES' HOUSES.
ALL OF THEM DESERTED. ALL OF THEM RUINED.
I'VE BEEN BACK AND FORTH ACROSS THE COUNTRY THREE TIMES, CHECKING EVERY REFUGEE CAMP I COULD FIND, LARGE AND SMALL.
ONLY ONE LEFT.
ONE CHANCE TO FIND--
KILL!
KILL!
KILL!
KILL!
KILL!
KILL!
KILL!
HELP!
GET OFF HIM!
HAS EVERY-ONE GONE CRAZY?
KILL!

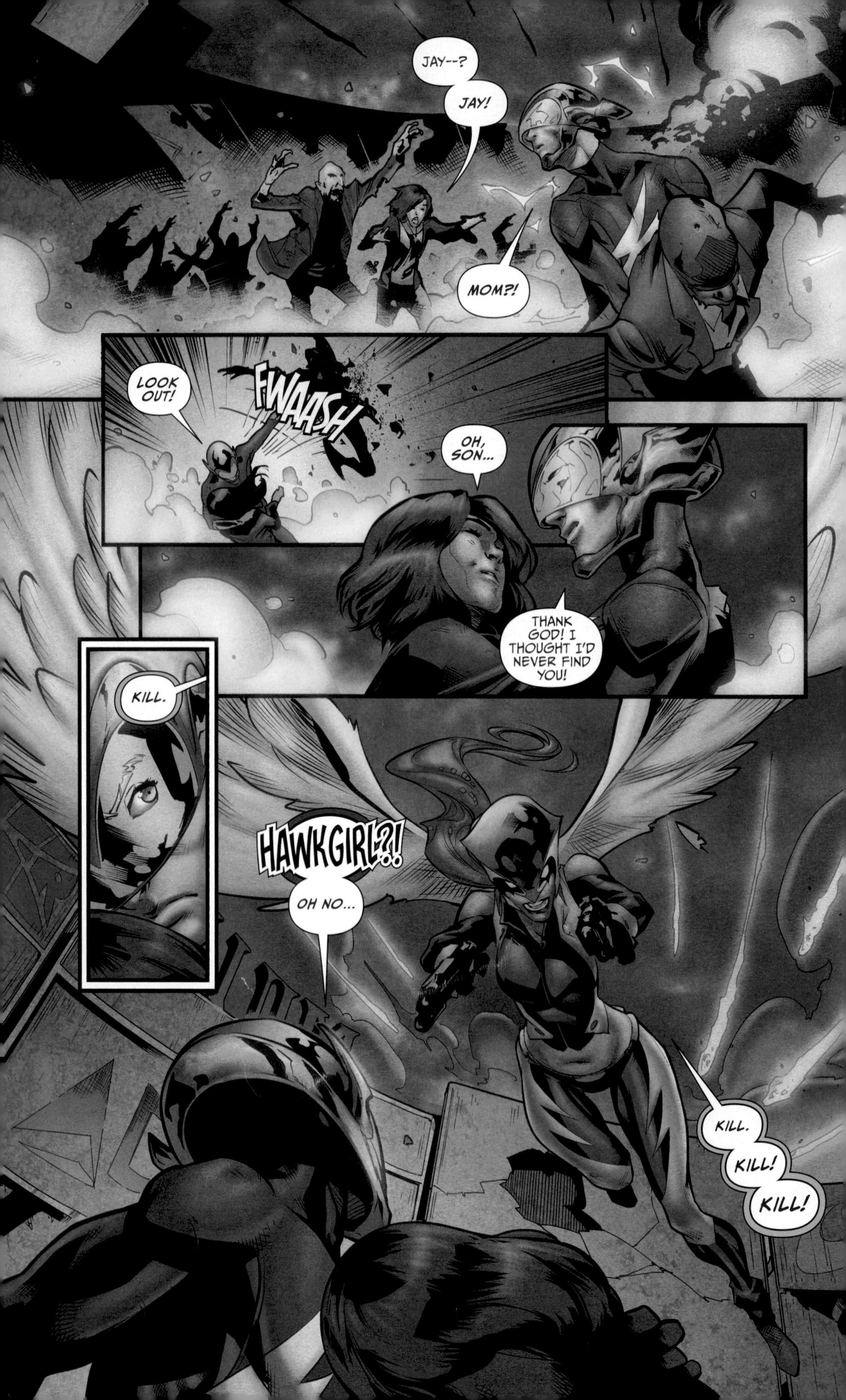
JAY--?
JAY!
MOM?!
LOOK OUT!
FWAASH
OH, SON...
THANK GOD! I THOUGHT I'D NEVER FIND YOU!
KILL.
HAWKGIRL?!
OH NO...
KILL.
KILL!
KILL!

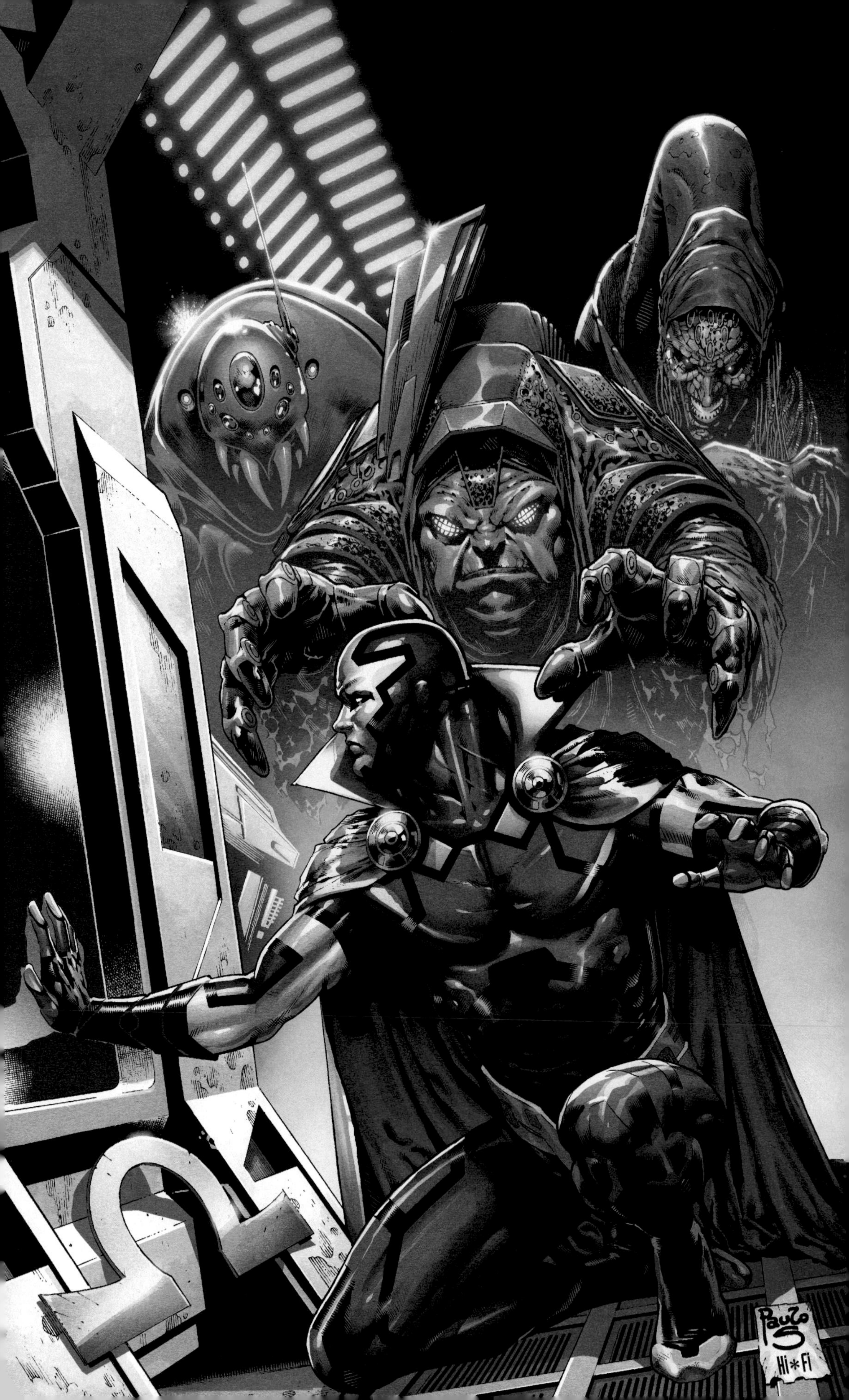
Paulo S
Hi*Fi

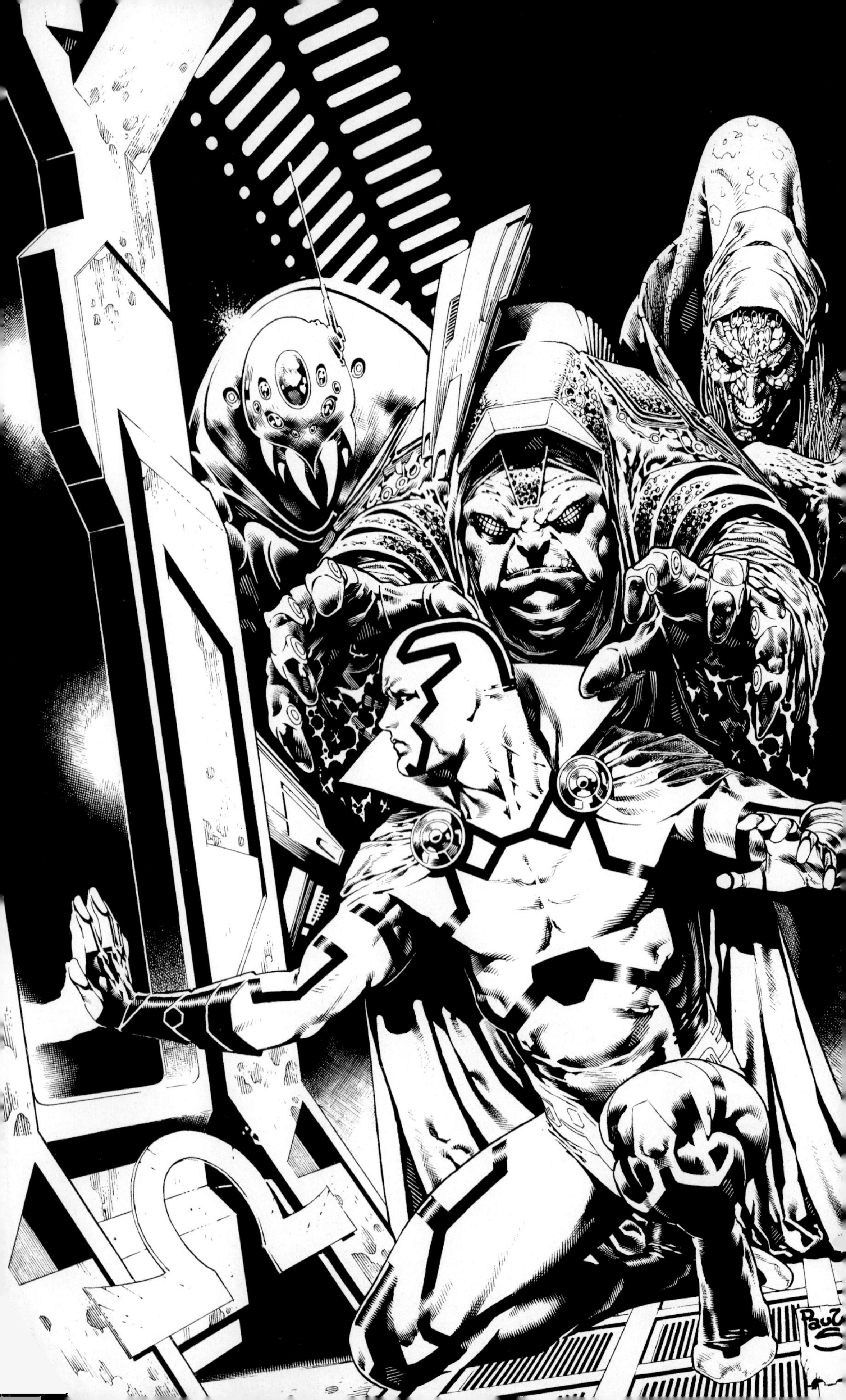

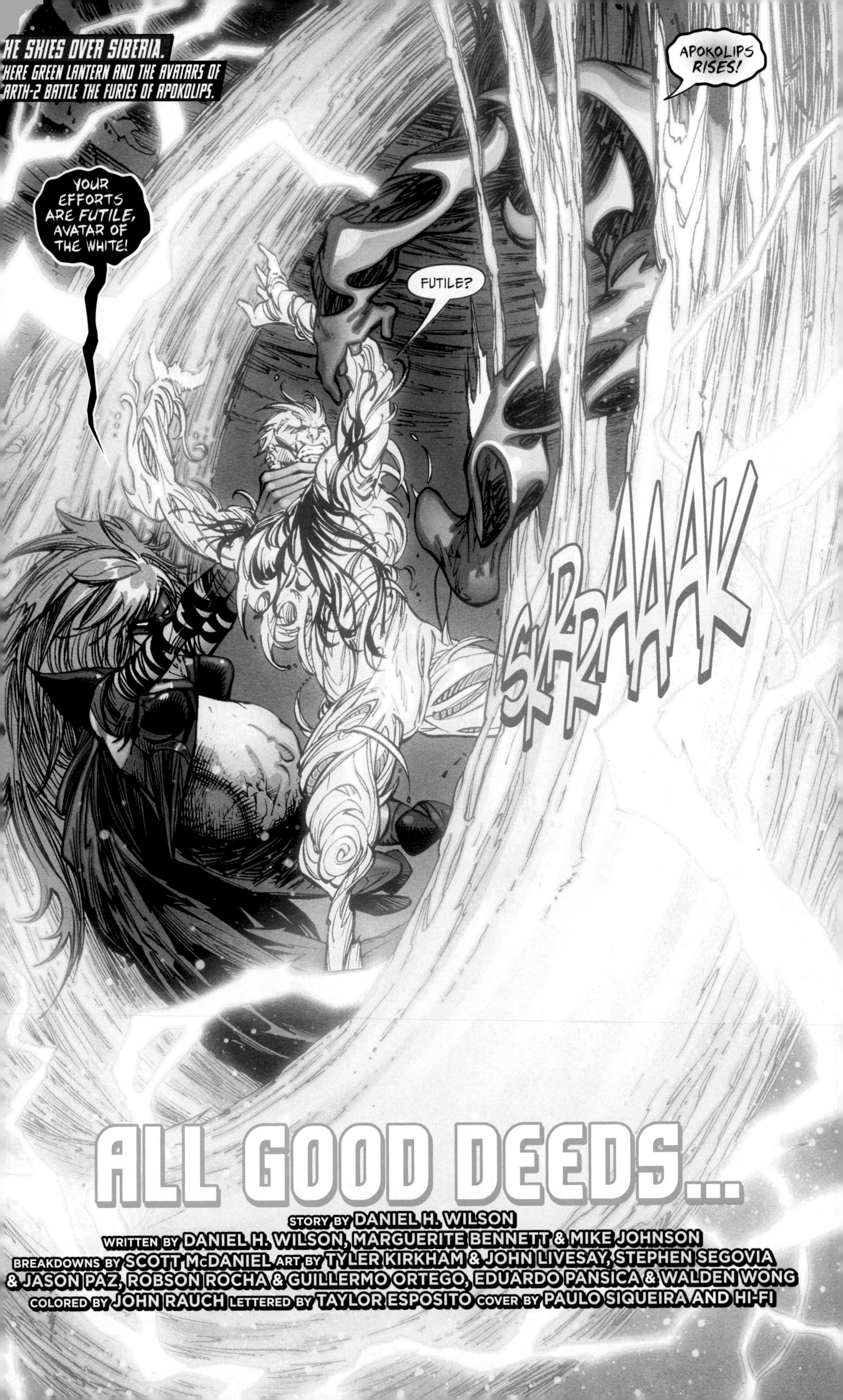
HE SKIES OVER SIBERIA.
HERE GREEN LANTERN AND THE AVATARS OF
ARTH-2 BATTLE THE FURIES OF APOKOLIPS.
APOKOLIPS RISES!
YOUR EFFORTS ARE FUTILE, AVATAR OF THE WHITE!
FUTILE?
SKRAAAK
ALL GOOD DEEDS...
STORY BY DANIEL H. WILSON
WRITTEN BY DANIEL H. WILSON, MARGUERITE BENNETT & MIKE JOHNSON
BREAKDOWNS BY SCOTT McDANIEL ART BY TYLER KIRKHAM & JOHN LIVESAY, STEPHEN SEGOVIA & JASON PAZ, ROBSON ROCHA & GUILLERMO ORTEGO, EDUARDO PANSICA & WALDEN WONG
COLORED BY JOHN RAUCH LETTERED BY TAYLOR ESPOSITO COVER BY PAULO SIQUEIRA AND HI-FI

SO LONG AS A SINGLE AVATAR OF THE EARTH REMAINS TO FIGHT YOU--

--NOTHING IS "FUTILE"!

WH**OOOSH**

AND WHEN NO AVATARS ARE LEFT?

WHAT THEN?

AAAGH--!

DON'T WORRY, SAM--

--I HEARD YOUR CALL!

SHRAAK

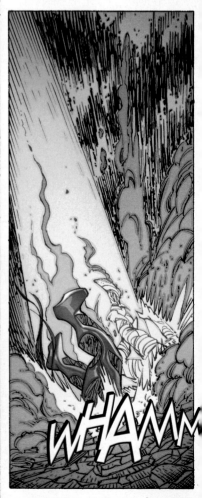

WHAMM

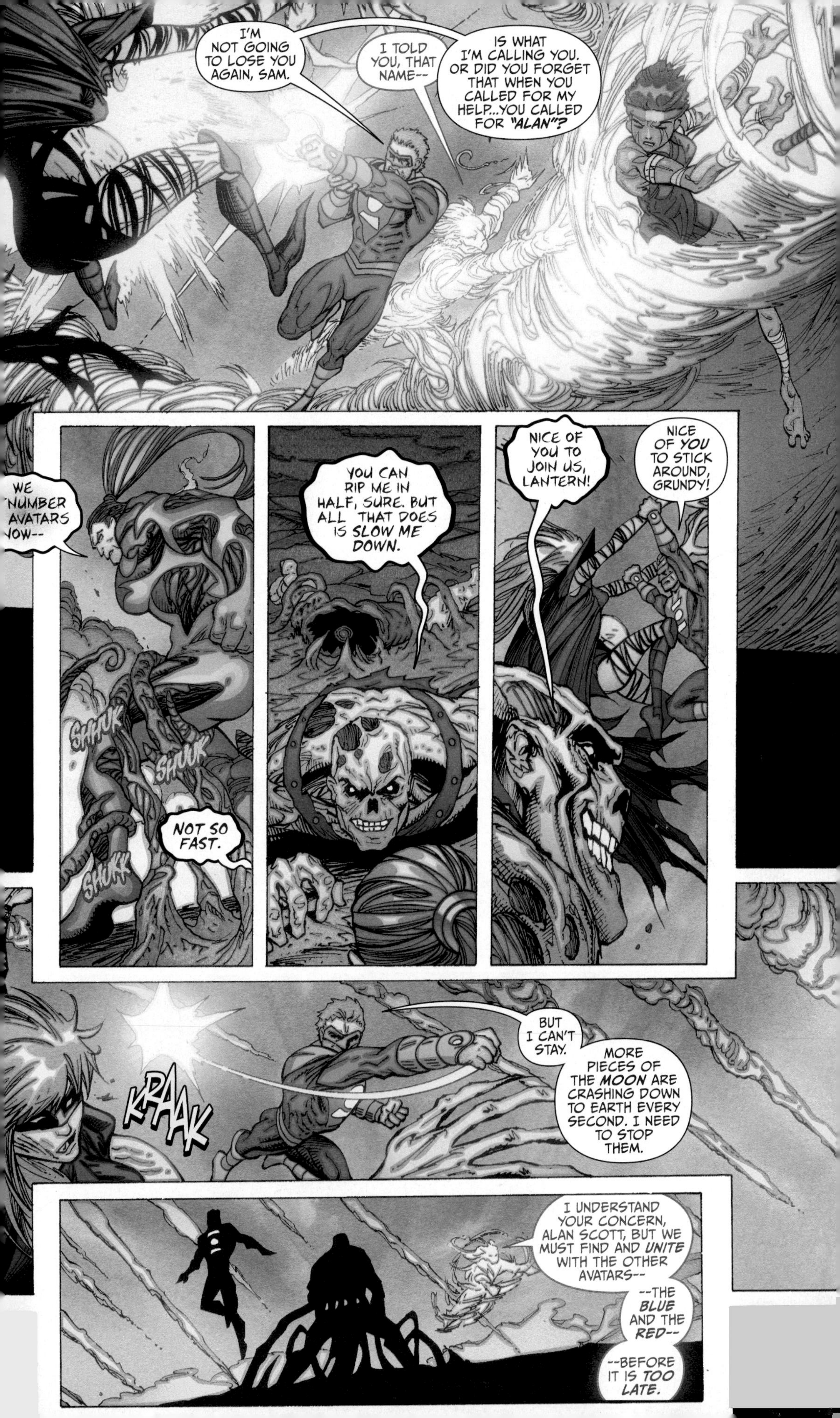
I'M NOT GOING TO LOSE YOU AGAIN, SAM.
I TOLD YOU, THAT NAME--
IS WHAT I'M CALLING YOU. OR DID YOU FORGET THAT WHEN YOU CALLED FOR MY HELP...YOU CALLED FOR "ALAN"?
WE NUMBER AVATARS NOW--
SHHUK
SHUUK
SHUKK
NOT SO FAST.
YOU CAN RIP ME IN HALF, SURE. BUT ALL THAT DOES IS SLOW ME DOWN.
NICE OF YOU TO JOIN US, LANTERN!
NICE OF YOU TO STICK AROUND, GRUNDY!
KRAAAK
BUT I CAN'T STAY.
MORE PIECES OF THE MOON ARE CRASHING DOWN TO EARTH EVERY SECOND. I NEED TO STOP THEM.
I UNDERSTAND YOUR CONCERN, ALAN SCOTT, BUT WE MUST FIND AND UNITE WITH THE OTHER AVATARS--
--THE BLUE AND THE RED--
--BEFORE IT IS TOO LATE.

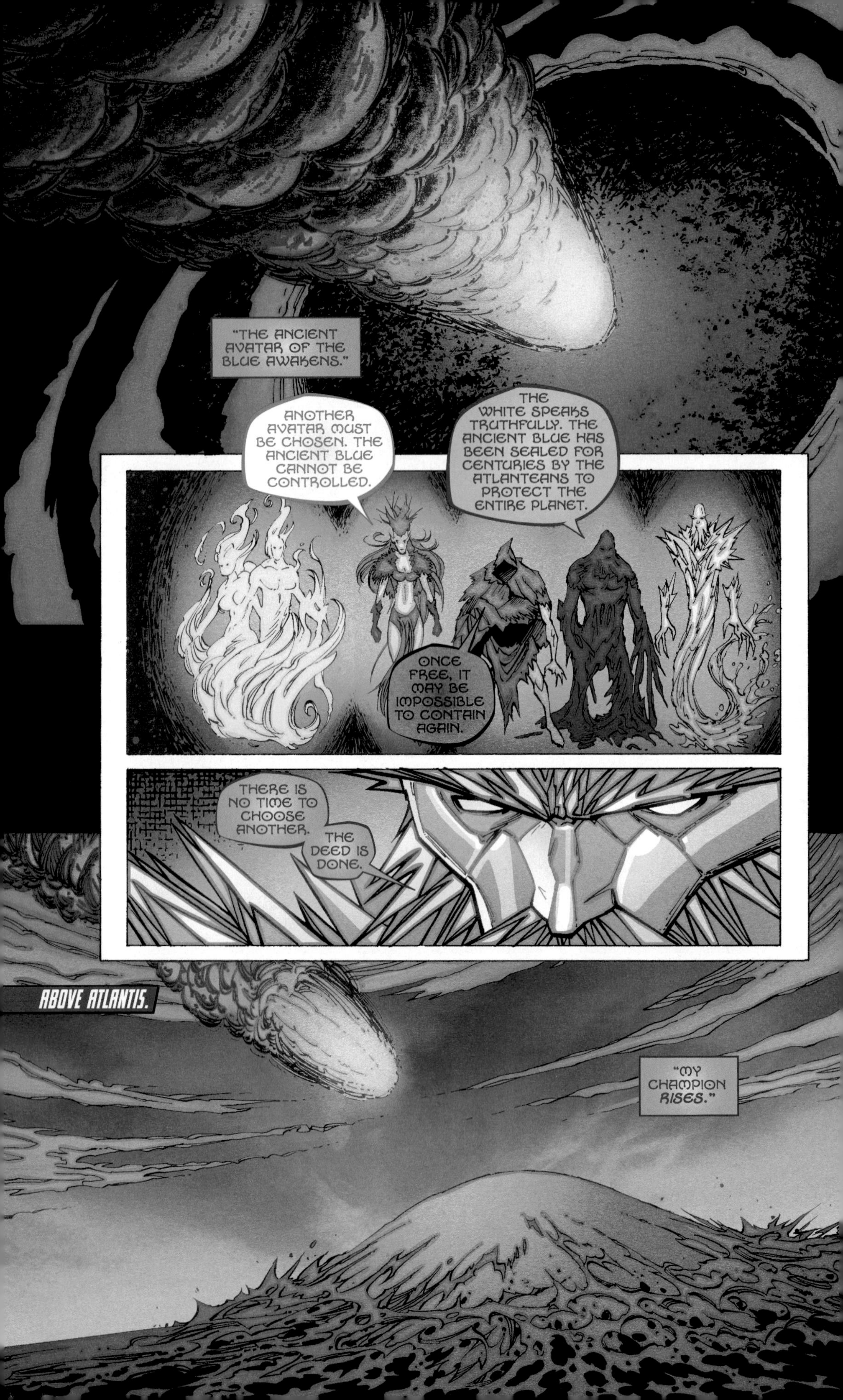
"THE ANCIENT AVATAR OF THE BLUE AWAKENS."
ANOTHER AVATAR MUST BE CHOSEN. THE ANCIENT BLUE CANNOT BE CONTROLLED.
THE WHITE SPEAKS TRUTHFULLY. THE ANCIENT BLUE HAS BEEN SEALED FOR CENTURIES BY THE ATLANTEANS TO PROTECT THE ENTIRE PLANET.
ONCE FREE, IT MAY BE IMPOSSIBLE TO CONTAIN AGAIN.
THERE IS NO TIME TO CHOOSE ANOTHER.
THE DEED IS DONE.
ABOVE ATLANTIS.
"MY CHAMPION RISES."

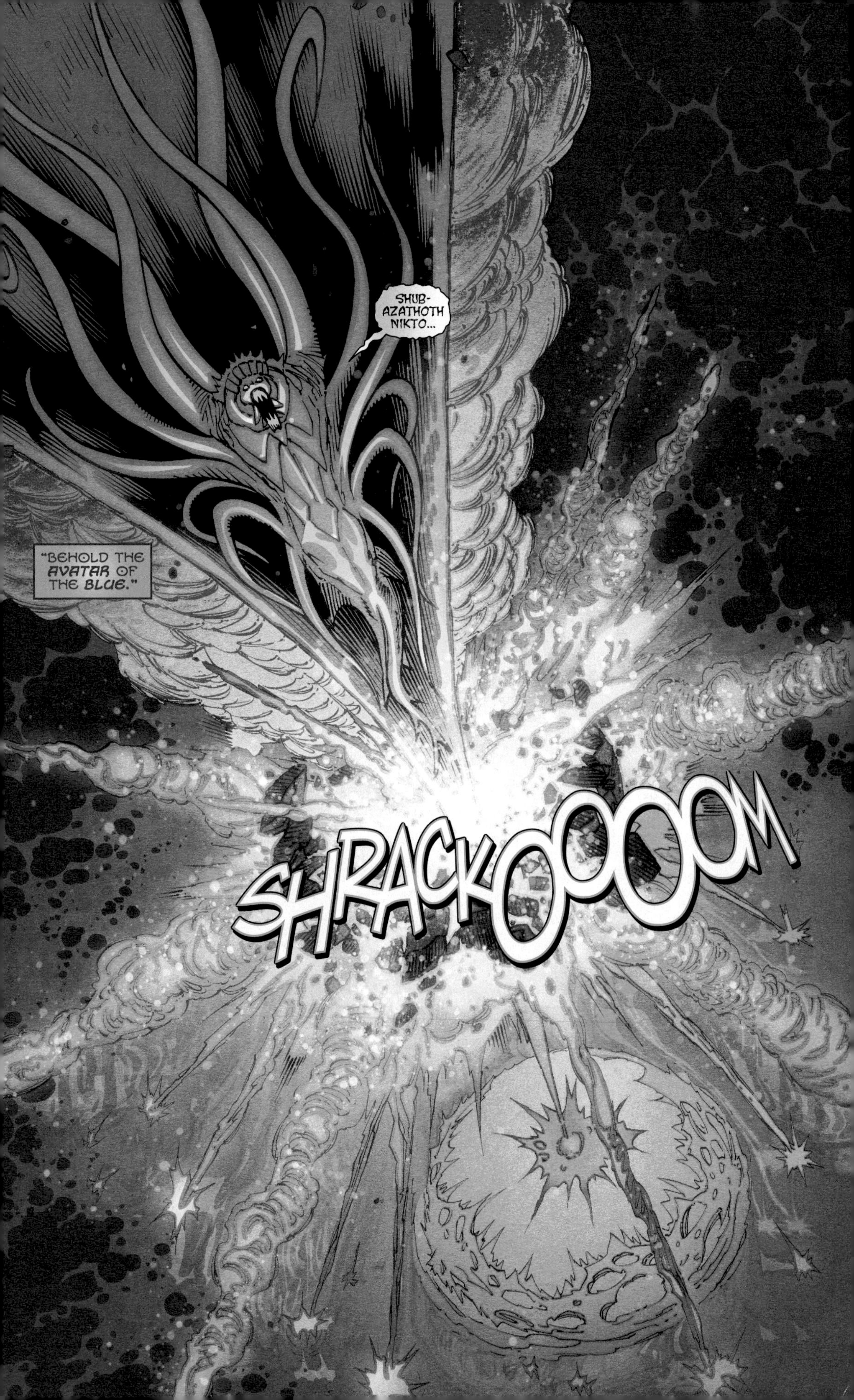
SHUB-AZATHOTH NIKTO...
"BEHOLD THE AVATAR OF THE BLUE."
SHRACKOOOOOM

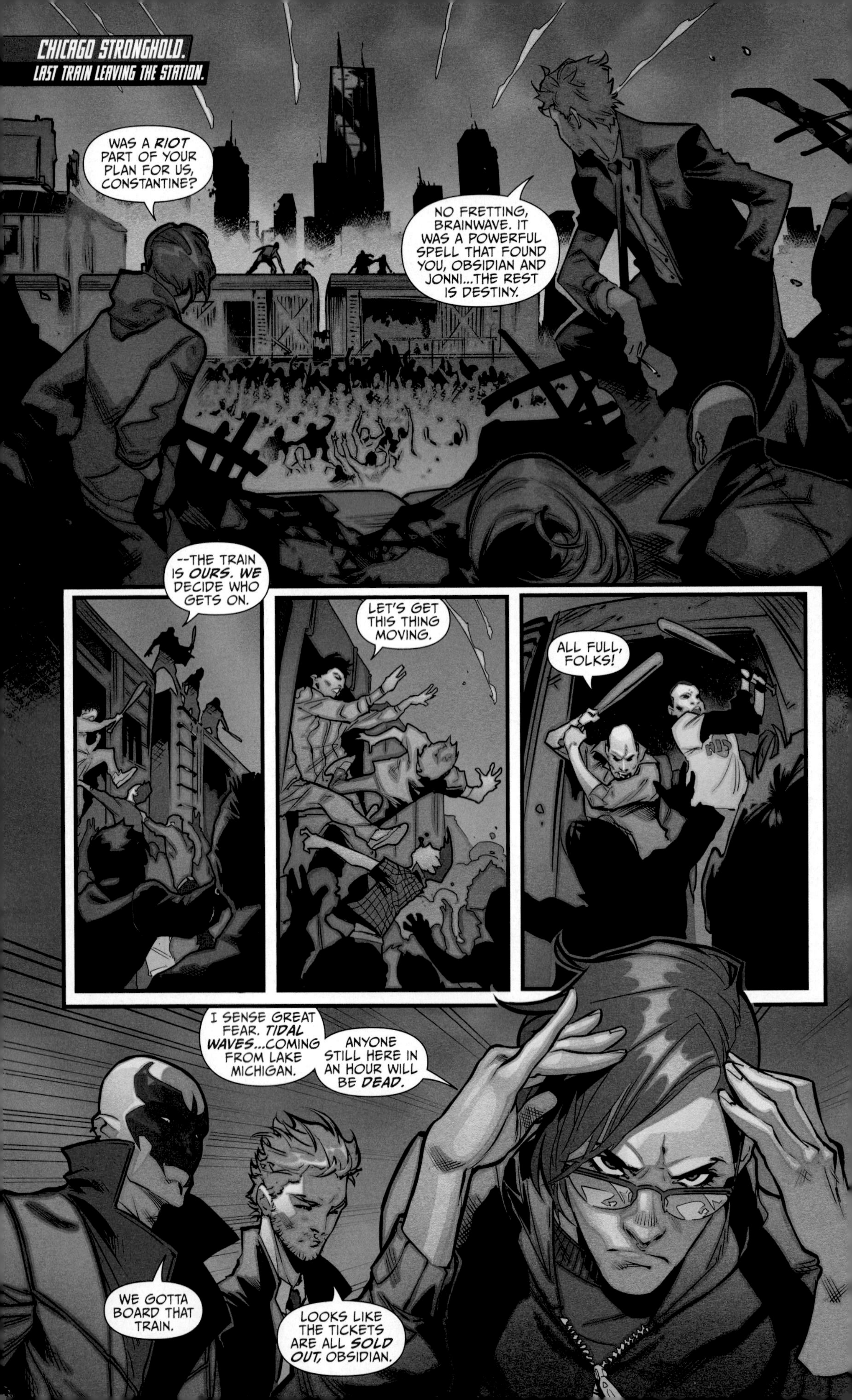
CHICAGO STRONGHOLD.
LAST TRAIN LEAVING THE STATION.
WAS A RIOT PART OF YOUR PLAN FOR US, CONSTANTINE?
NO FRETTING, BRAINWAVE. IT WAS A POWERFUL SPELL THAT FOUND YOU, OBSIDIAN AND JONNI...THE REST IS DESTINY.
--THE TRAIN IS OURS. WE DECIDE WHO GETS ON.
LET'S GET THIS THING MOVING.
ALL FULL, FOLKS!
I SENSE GREAT FEAR. TIDAL WAVES...COMING FROM LAKE MICHIGAN.
ANYONE STILL HERE IN AN HOUR WILL BE DEAD.
WE GOTTA BOARD THAT TRAIN.
LOOKS LIKE THE TICKETS ARE ALL SOLD OUT, OBSIDIAN.

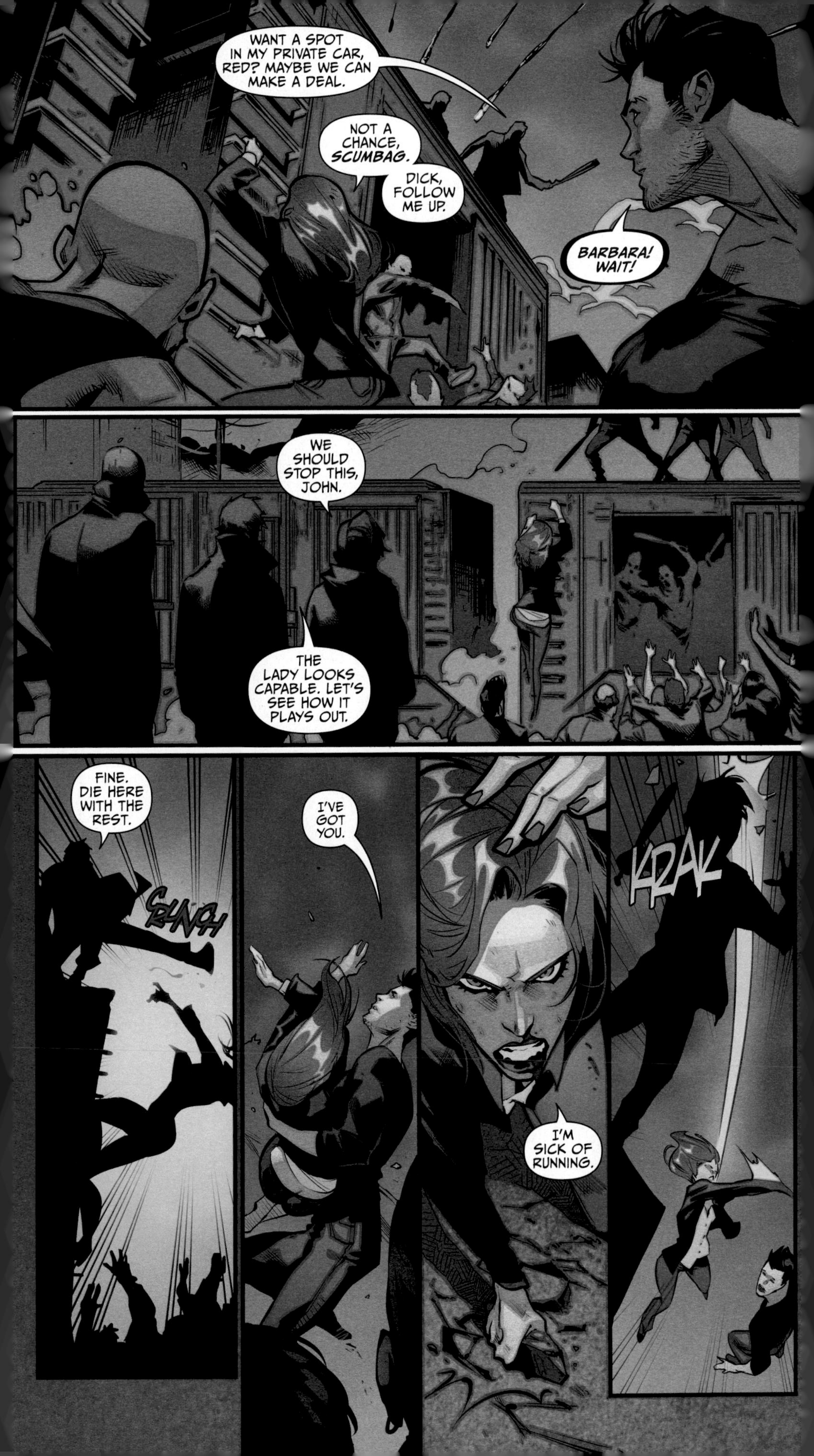

WANT A SPOT IN MY PRIVATE CAR, RED? MAYBE WE CAN MAKE A DEAL.
NOT A CHANCE, SCUMBAG.
DICK, FOLLOW ME UP.
BARBARA! WAIT!
WE SHOULD STOP THIS, JOHN.
THE LADY LOOKS CAPABLE. LET'S SEE HOW IT PLAYS OUT.
FINE. DIE HERE WITH THE REST.
CRUNCH
I'VE GOT YOU.
I'M SICK OF RUNNING.
KRAK

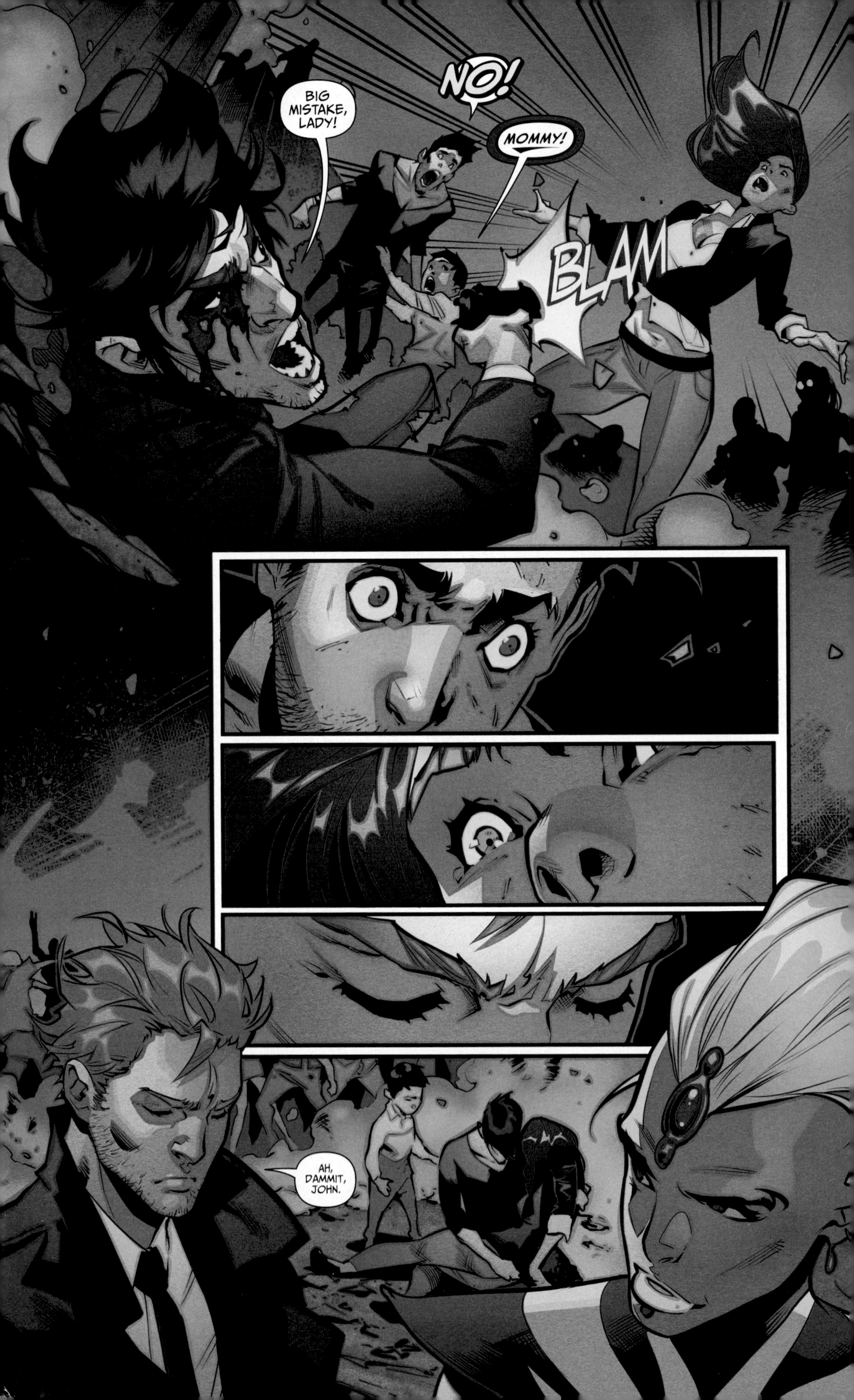
NO!
BIG MISTAKE, LADY!
MOMMY!
BLAM
AH, DAMMIT, JOHN.

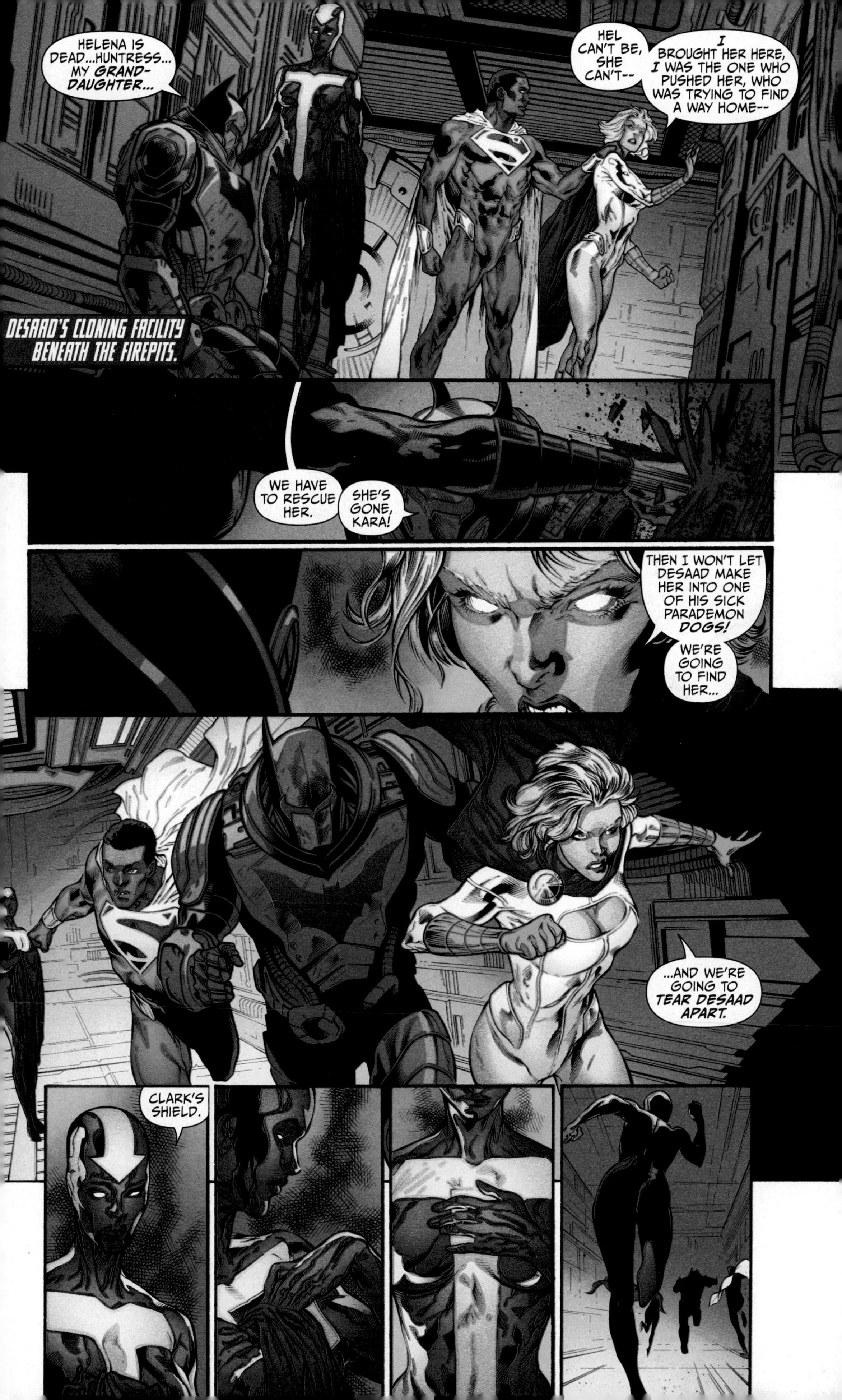
HELENA IS DEAD...HUNTRESS... MY GRAND-DAUGHTER...
HEL CAN'T BE, SHE CAN'T--
I BROUGHT HER HERE, I WAS THE ONE WHO PUSHED HER, WHO WAS TRYING TO FIND A WAY HOME--
DESAAD'S CLONING FACILITY BENEATH THE FIREPITS.
WE HAVE TO RESCUE HER.
SHE'S GONE, KARA!
THEN I WON'T LET DESAAD MAKE HER INTO ONE OF HIS SICK PARADEMON DOGS!
WE'RE GOING TO FIND HER...
...AND WE'RE GOING TO TEAR DESAAD APART.
CLARK'S SHIELD.

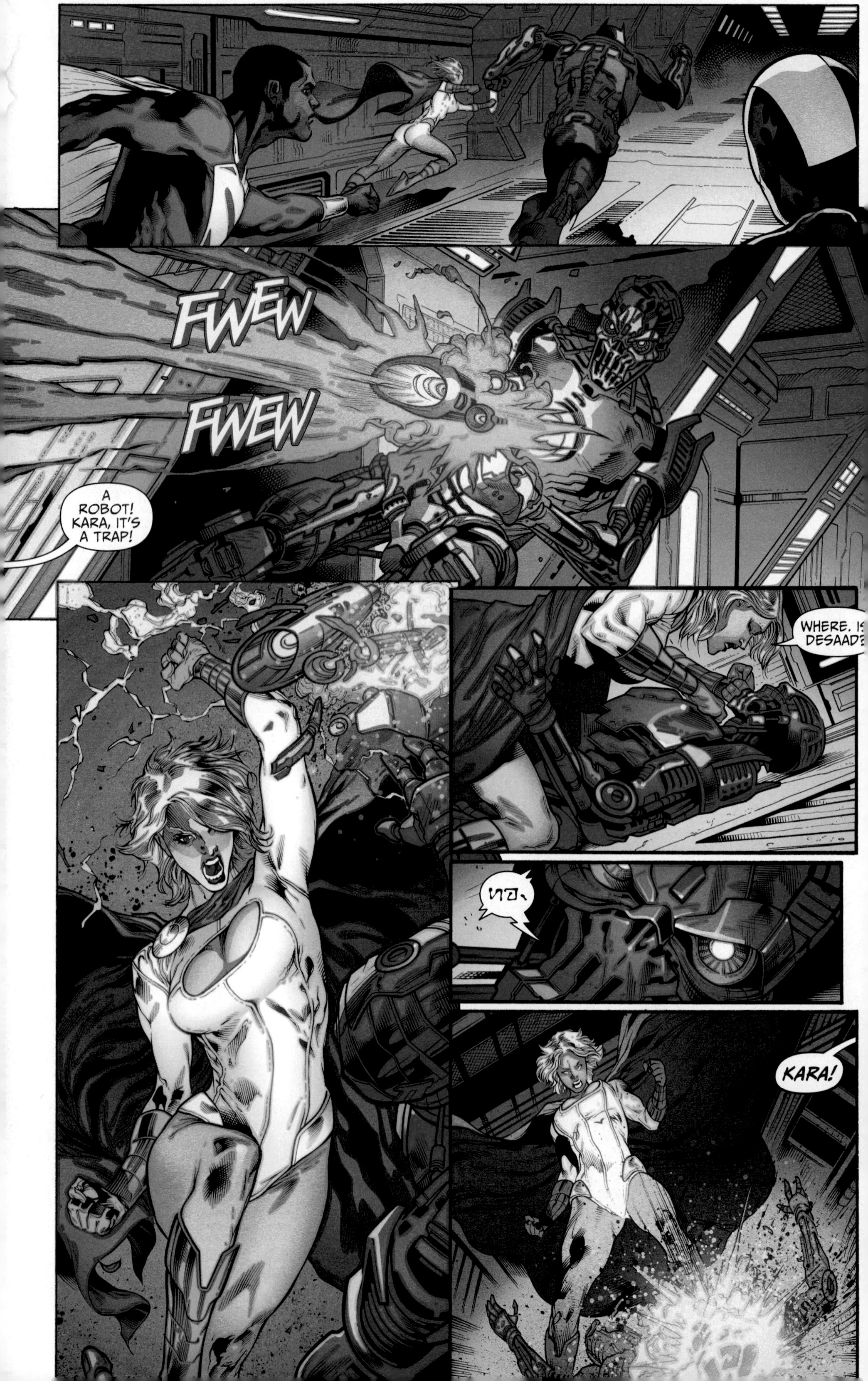
FWEW
FWEW
A ROBOT! KARA, IT'S A TRAP!
WHERE. IS DESAAD?
KARA!

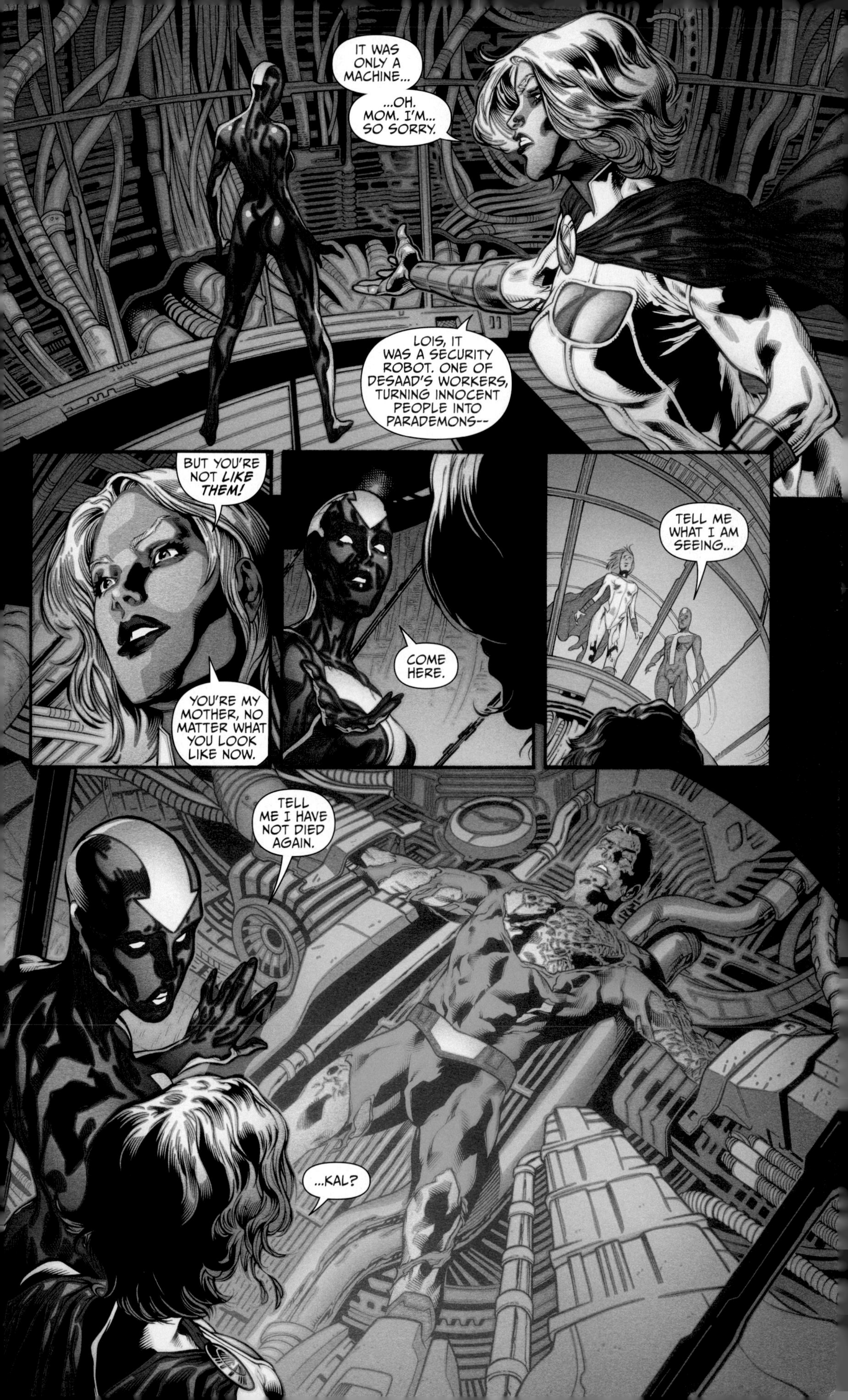
IT WAS ONLY A MACHINE...
...OH. MOM. I'M... SO SORRY.
LOIS, IT WAS A SECURITY ROBOT. ONE OF DESAAD'S WORKERS, TURNING INNOCENT PEOPLE INTO PARADEMONS--
BUT YOU'RE NOT *LIKE THEM!*
YOU'RE MY MOTHER, NO MATTER WHAT YOU LOOK LIKE NOW.
COME HERE.
TELL ME WHAT I AM SEEING...
TELL ME I HAVE NOT DIED AGAIN.
...KAL?

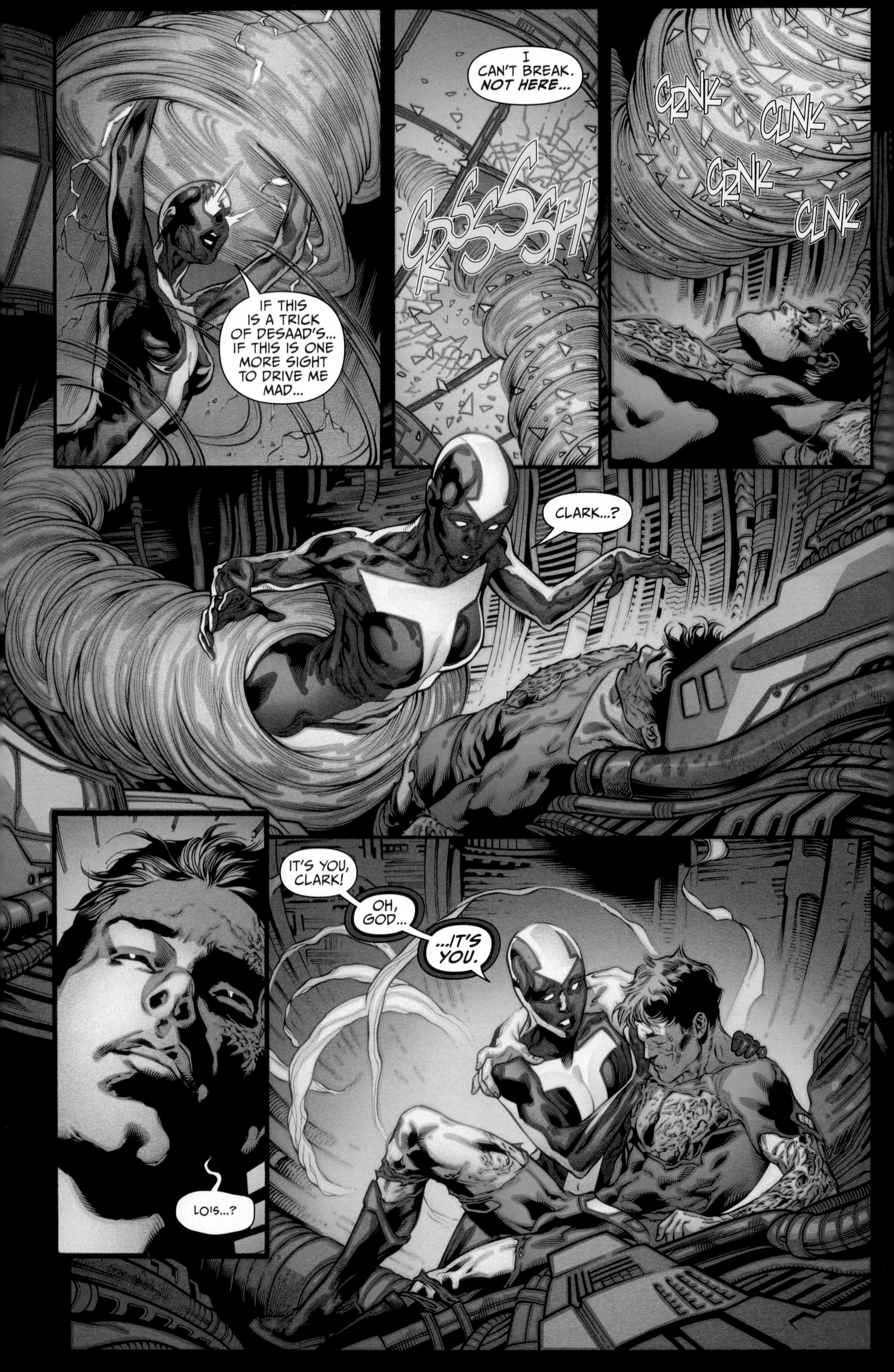
IF THIS IS A TRICK OF DESAAD'S... IF THIS IS ONE MORE SIGHT TO DRIVE ME MAD...
I CAN'T BREAK. NOT HERE...
CRSSSH
CRNK
CLNK
CRNK
CLNK
CLARK...?
LOIS...?
IT'S YOU, CLARK!
OH, GOD...
...IT'S YOU.

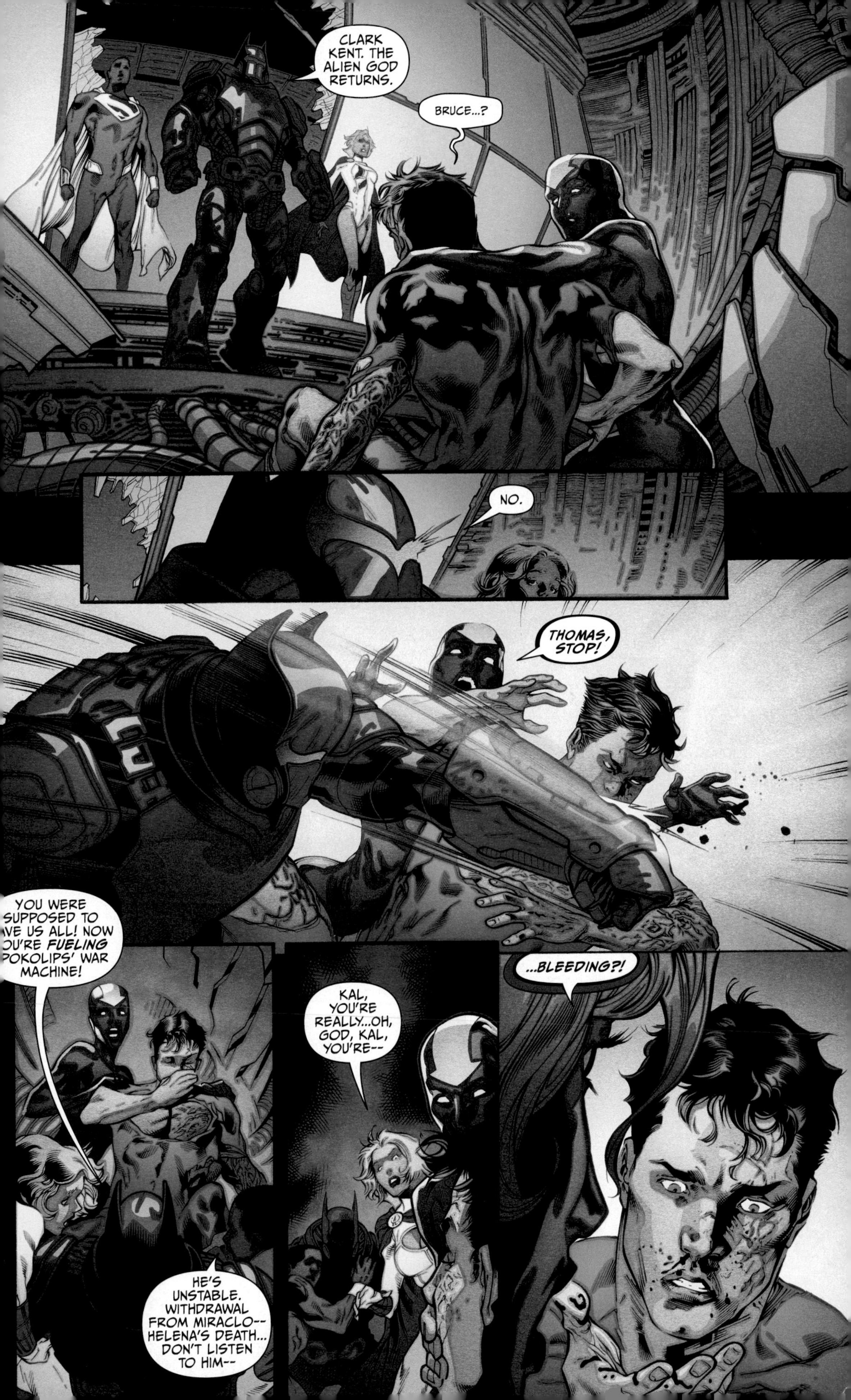
CLARK KENT. THE ALIEN GOD RETURNS.
BRUCE...?
NO.
THOMAS, STOP!
YOU WERE SUPPOSED TO VE US ALL! NOW OU'RE FUELING POKOLIPS' WAR MACHINE!
HE'S UNSTABLE. WITHDRAWAL FROM MIRACLO-- HELENA'S DEATH... DON'T LISTEN TO HIM--
KAL, YOU'RE REALLY...OH, GOD, KAL, YOU'RE--
...BLEEDING?!

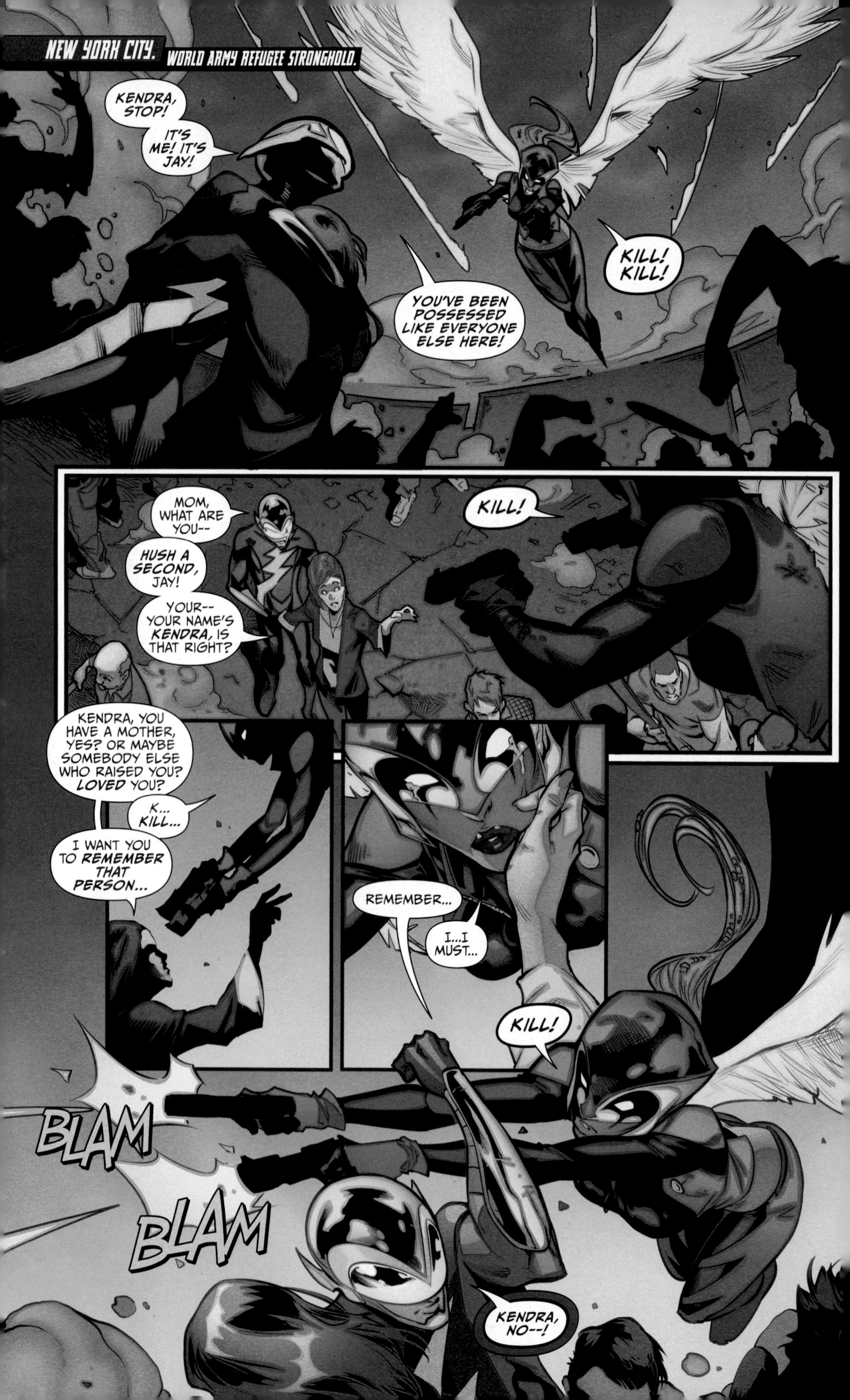
NEW YORK CITY.
WORLD ARMY REFUGEE STRONGHOLD.
KENDRA, STOP!
IT'S ME! IT'S JAY!
YOU'VE BEEN POSSESSED LIKE EVERYONE ELSE HERE!
KILL! KILL!
MOM, WHAT ARE YOU--
HUSH A SECOND, JAY!
YOUR-- YOUR NAME'S KENDRA, IS THAT RIGHT?
KILL!
KENDRA, YOU HAVE A MOTHER, YES? OR MAYBE SOMEBODY ELSE WHO RAISED YOU? LOVED YOU?
K... KILL...
I WANT YOU TO REMEMBER THAT PERSON...
REMEMBER...
I...I MUST...
KILL!
BLAM
BLAM
KENDRA, NO--!

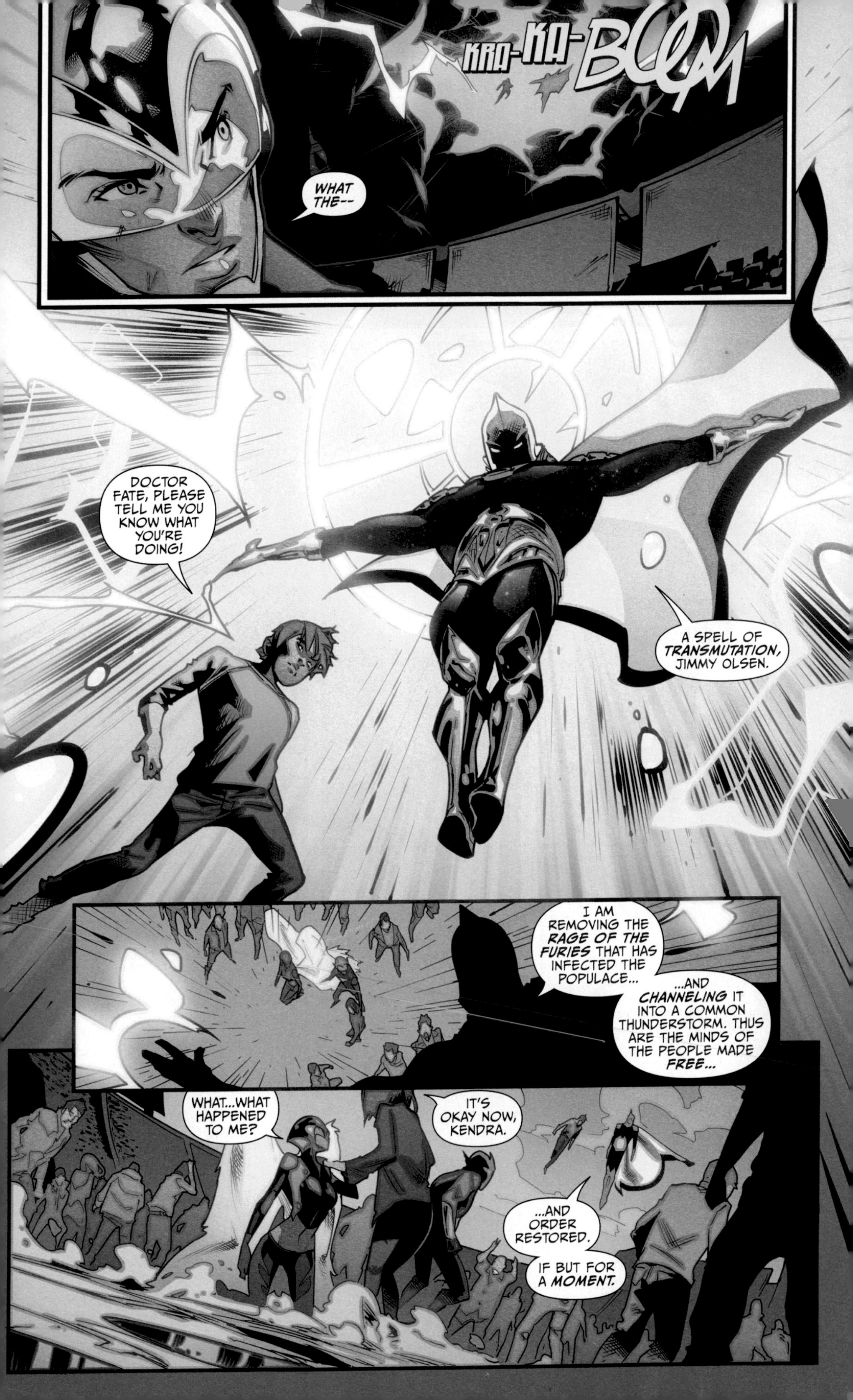
KRA-KA-BOOM
WHAT THE--
DOCTOR FATE, PLEASE TELL ME YOU KNOW WHAT YOU'RE DOING!
A SPELL OF TRANSMUTATION, JIMMY OLSEN.
I AM REMOVING THE RAGE OF THE FURIES THAT HAS INFECTED THE POPULACE...
...AND CHANNELING IT INTO A COMMON THUNDERSTORM. THUS ARE THE MINDS OF THE PEOPLE MADE FREE...
WHAT...WHAT HAPPENED TO ME?
IT'S OKAY NOW, KENDRA.
...AND ORDER RESTORED.
IF BUT FOR A MOMENT.

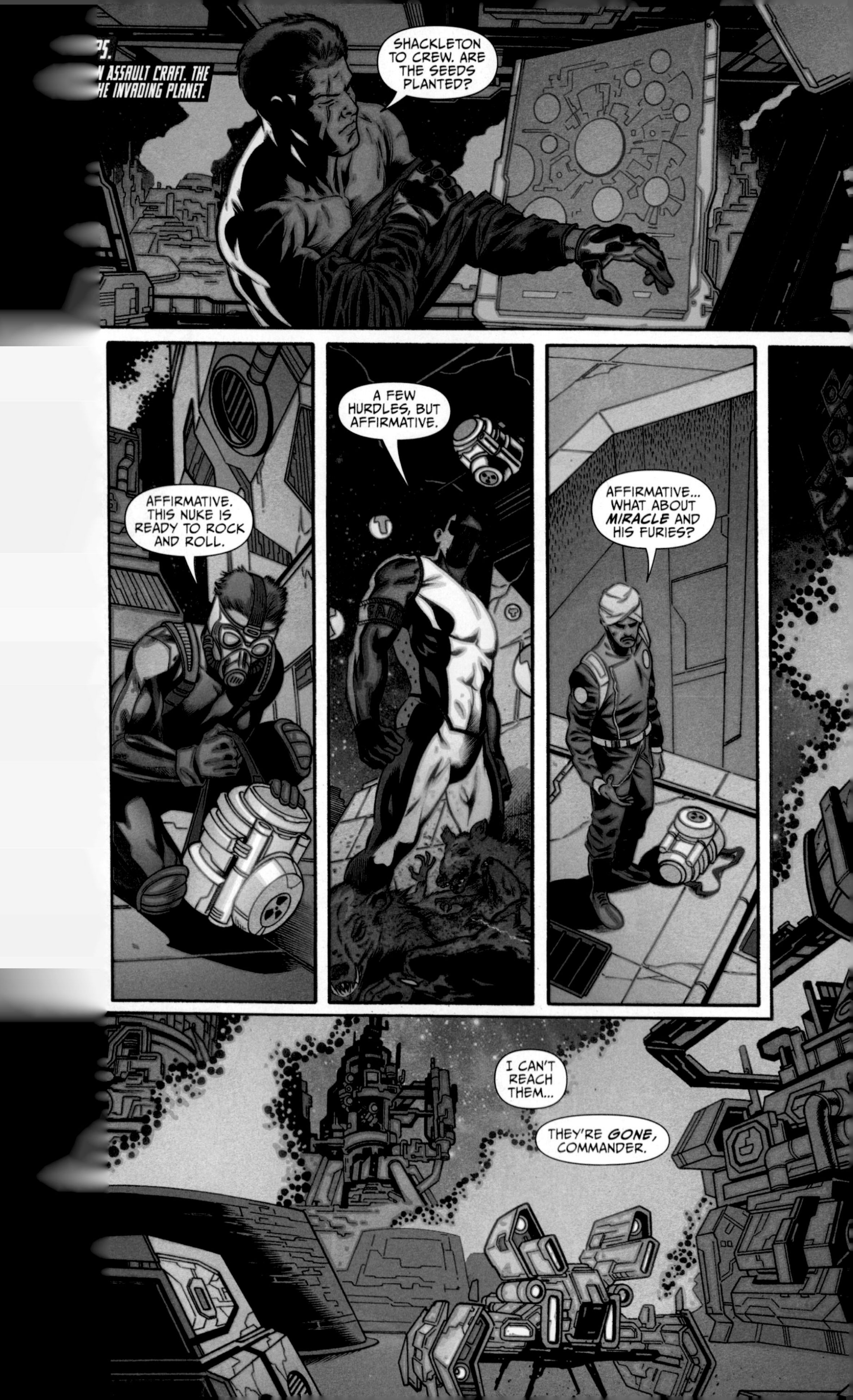
ASSAULT CRAFT. THE
INVADING PLANET.
SHACKLETON TO CREW. ARE THE SEEDS PLANTED?
AFFIRMATIVE. THIS NUKE IS READY TO ROCK AND ROLL.
A FEW HURDLES, BUT AFFIRMATIVE.
AFFIRMATIVE... WHAT ABOUT MIRACLE AND HIS FURIES?
I CAN'T REACH THEM...
THEY'RE GONE, COMMANDER.

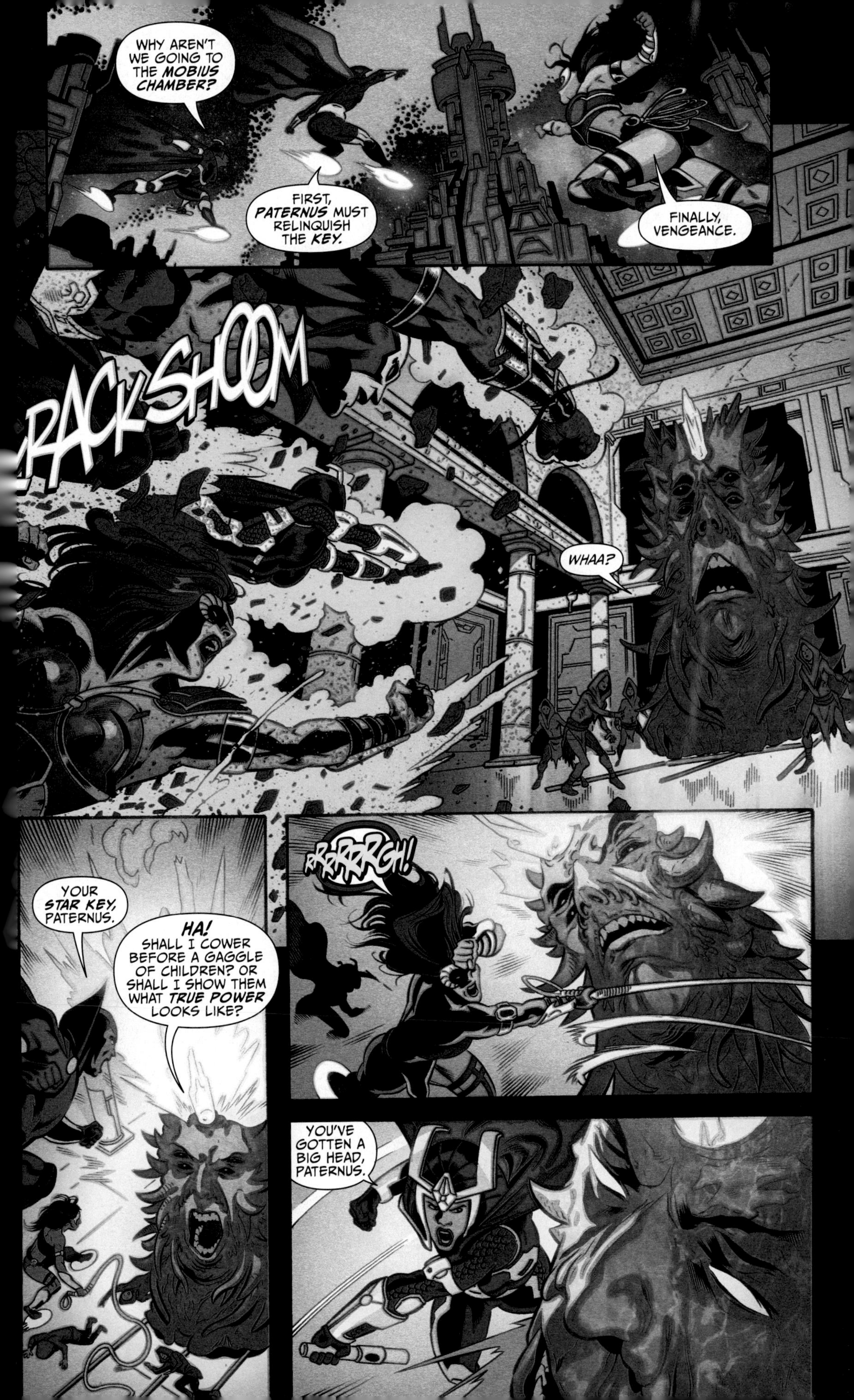
WHY AREN'T WE GOING TO THE MOBIUS CHAMBER?
FIRST, PATERNUS MUST RELINQUISH THE KEY.
FINALLY, VENGEANCE.
RACK SHOOM
WHAA?
YOUR STAR KEY, PATERNUS.
HA! SHALL I COWER BEFORE A GAGGLE OF CHILDREN? OR SHALL I SHOW THEM WHAT TRUE POWER LOOKS LIKE?
RRRRRRGH!
YOU'VE GOTTEN A BIG HEAD, PATERNUS.

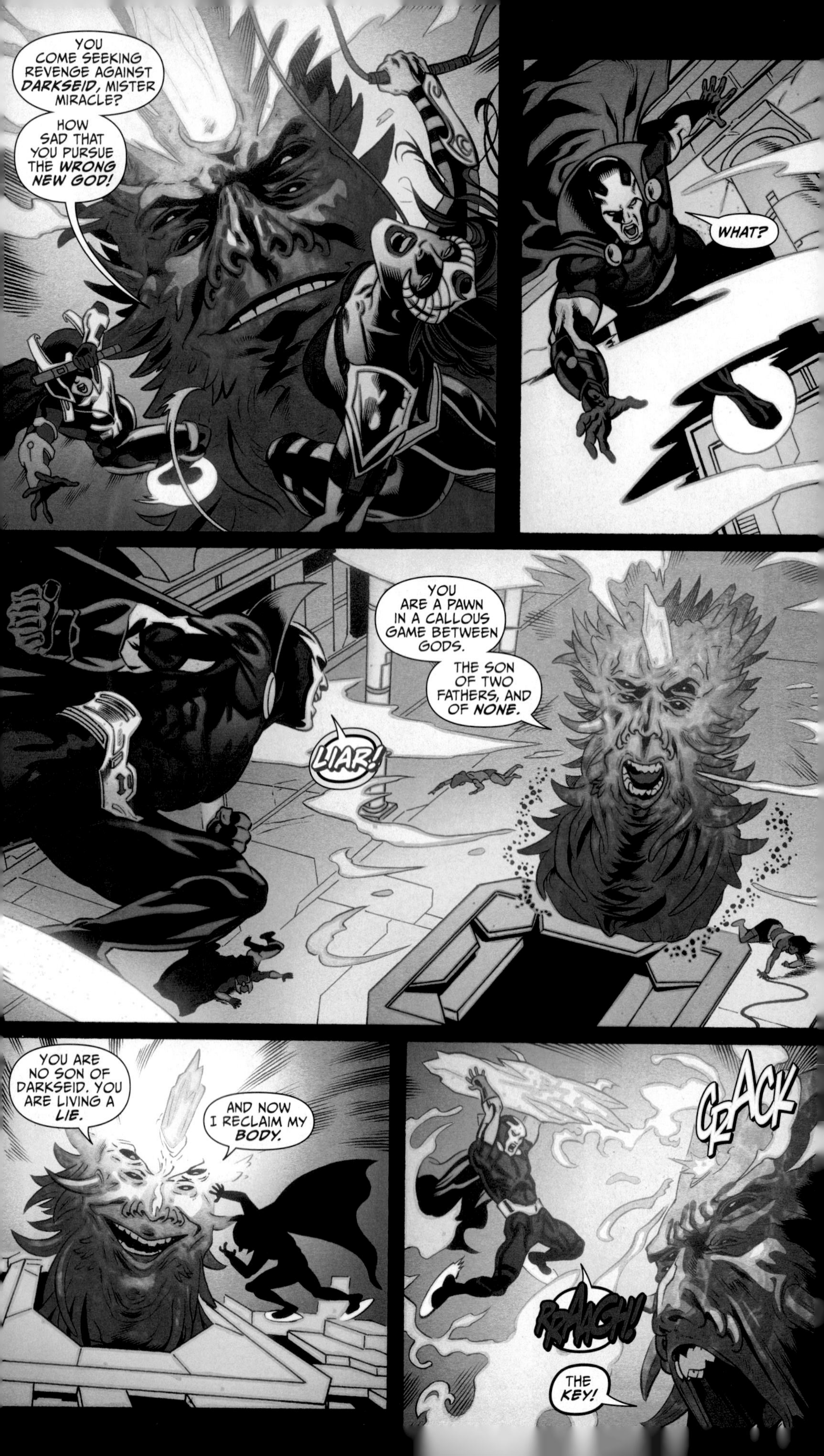
YOU COME SEEKING REVENGE AGAINST DARKSEID, MISTER MIRACLE?
HOW SAD THAT YOU PURSUE THE WRONG NEW GOD!
WHAT?
YOU ARE A PAWN IN A CALLOUS GAME BETWEEN GODS.
THE SON OF TWO FATHERS, AND OF NONE.
LIAR!
YOU ARE NO SON OF DARKSEID. YOU ARE LIVING A LIE.
AND NOW I RECLAIM MY BODY.
CRACK
RRAAGH!
THE KEY!

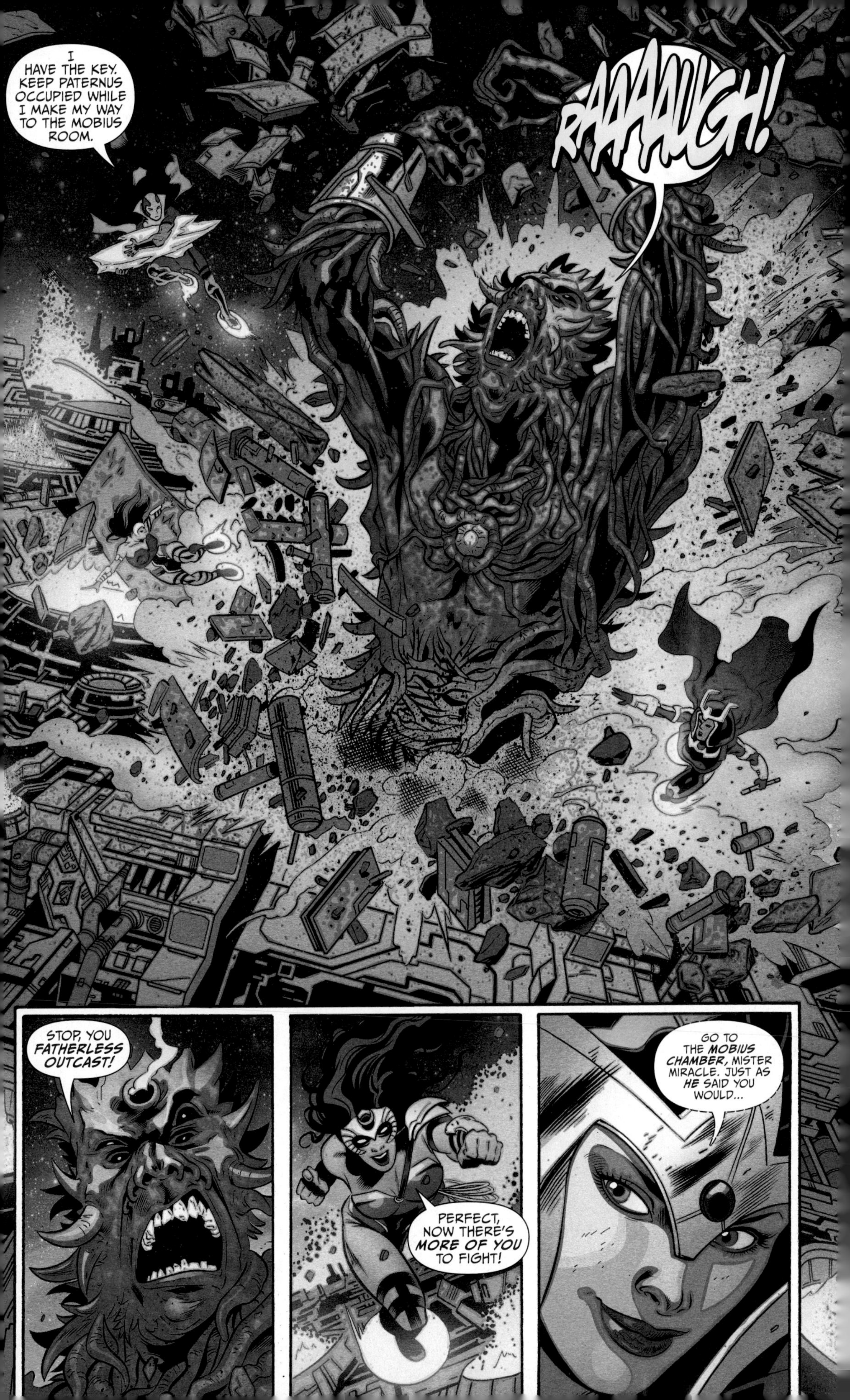
I HAVE THE KEY. KEEP PATERNUS OCCUPIED WHILE I MAKE MY WAY TO THE MOBIUS ROOM.
RAAAAUGH!
STOP, YOU FATHERLESS OUTCAST!
PERFECT, NOW THERE'S MORE OF YOU TO FIGHT!
GO TO THE MOBIUS CHAMBER, MISTER MIRACLE. JUST AS HE SAID YOU WOULD...

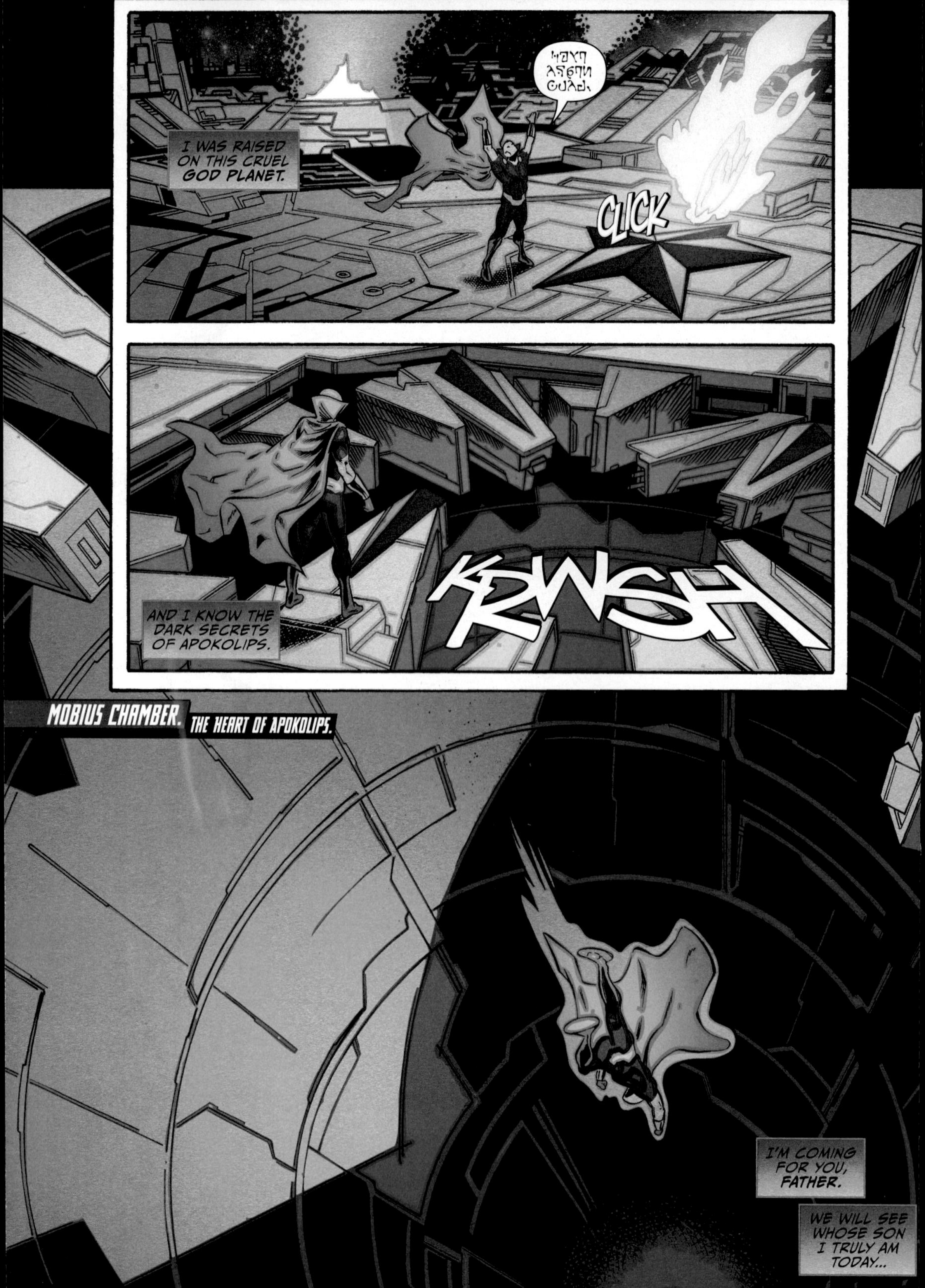
I WAS RAISED ON THIS CRUEL GOD PLANET.
CLICK
AND I KNOW THE DARK SECRETS OF APOKOLIPS.
KRWSH
MOBIUS CHAMBER. THE HEART OF APOKOLIPS.
I'M COMING FOR YOU, FATHER.
WE WILL SEE WHOSE SON I TRULY AM TODAY...

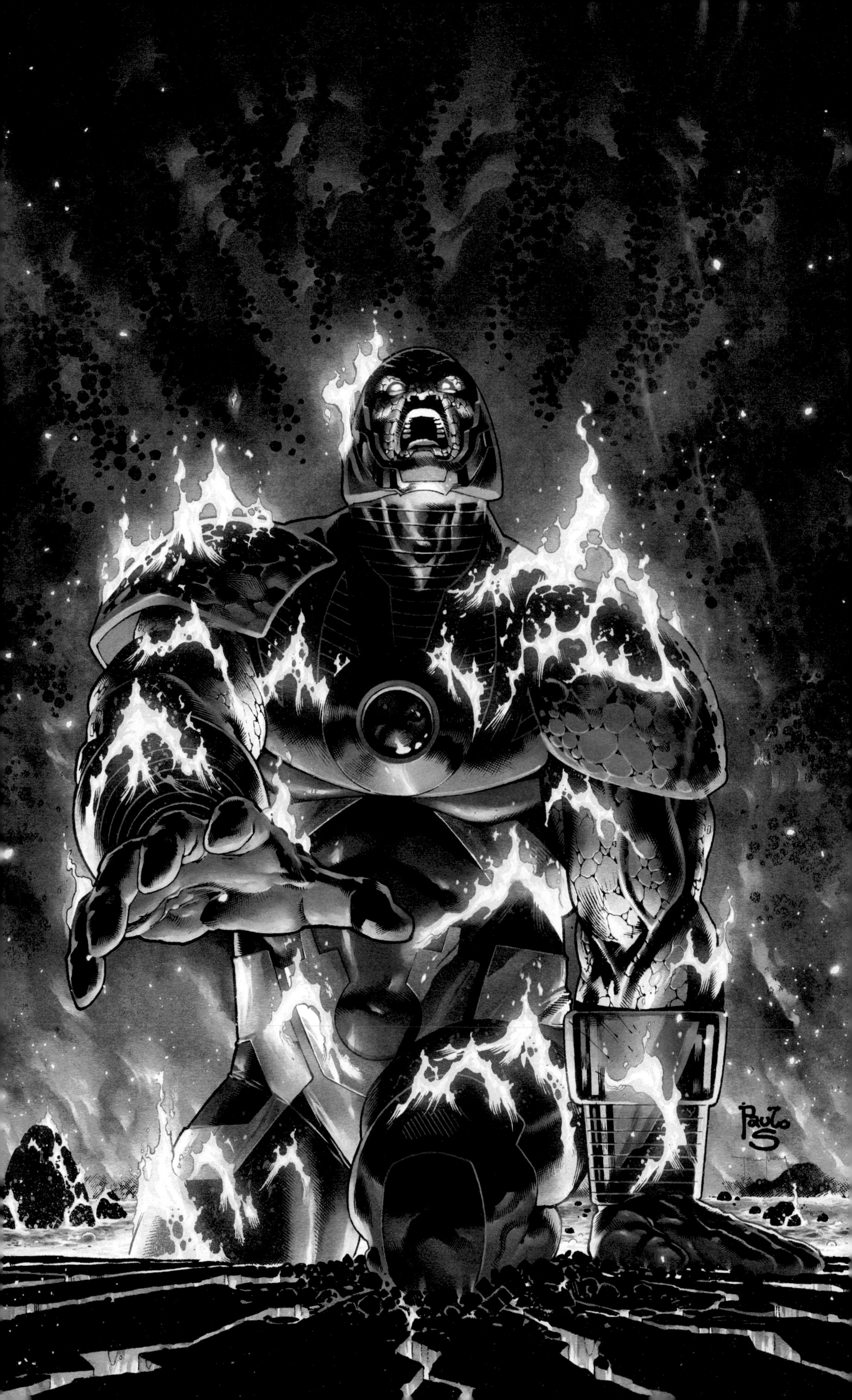

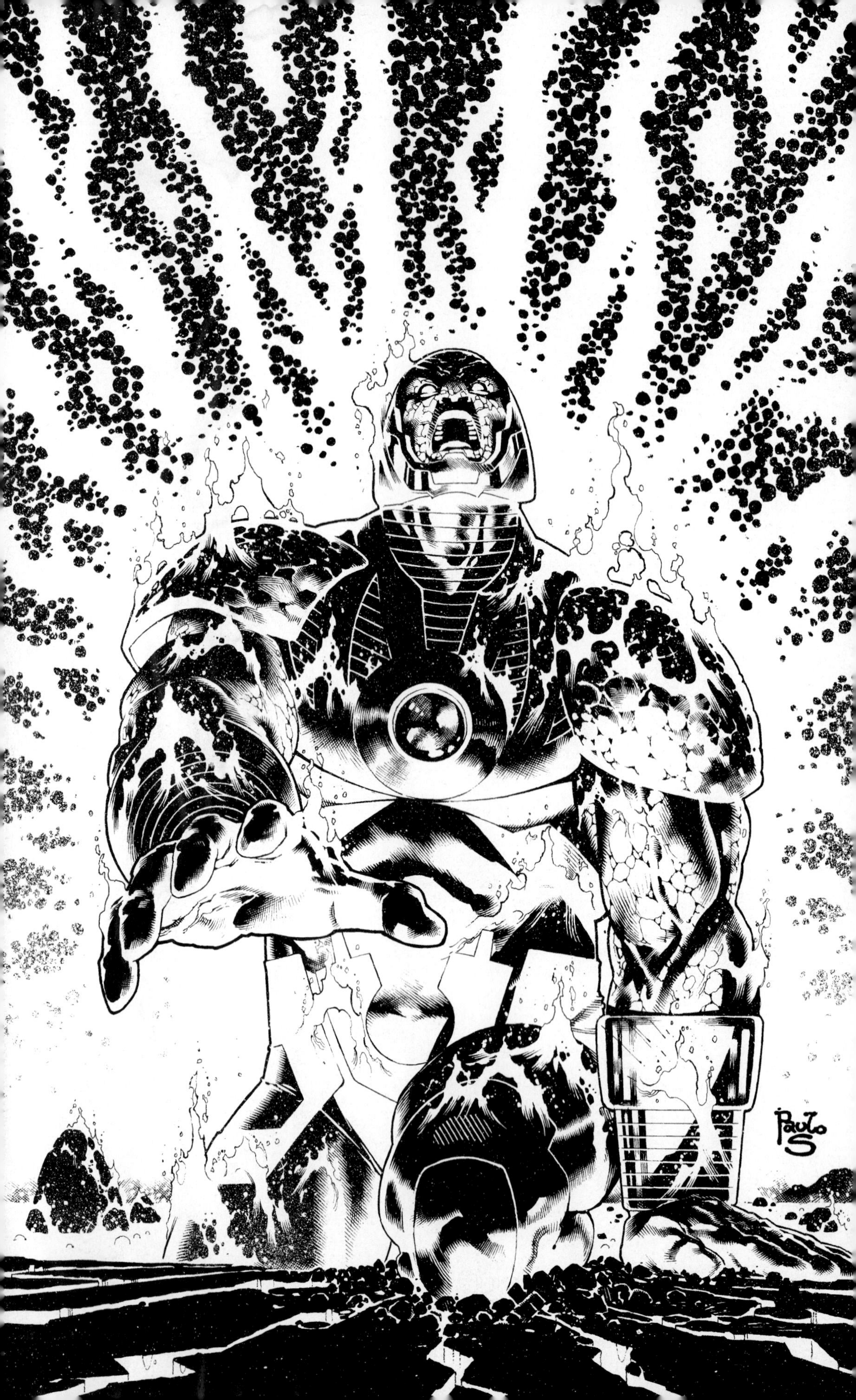
PAULO S

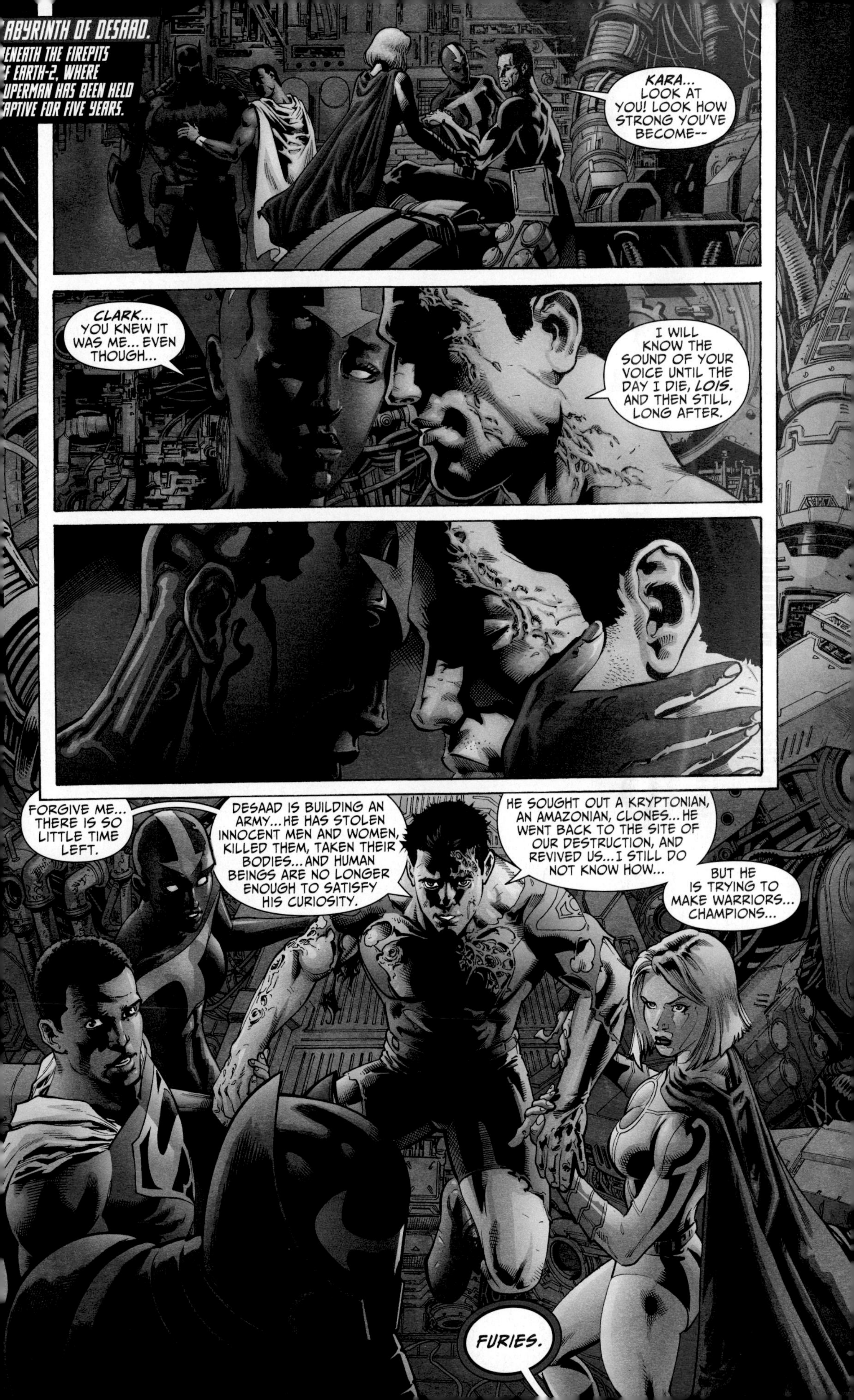
ABYRINTH OF DESAAD.
ENEATH THE FIREPITS 'F EARTH-2, WHERE UPERMAN HAS BEEN HELD APTIVE FOR FIVE YEARS.
KARA... LOOK AT YOU! LOOK HOW STRONG YOU'VE BECOME--
CLARK... YOU KNEW IT WAS ME... EVEN THOUGH...
I WILL KNOW THE SOUND OF YOUR VOICE UNTIL THE DAY I DIE, LOIS. AND THEN STILL, LONG AFTER.
FORGIVE ME... THERE IS SO LITTLE TIME LEFT.
DESAAD IS BUILDING AN ARMY... HE HAS STOLEN INNOCENT MEN AND WOMEN, KILLED THEM, TAKEN THEIR BODIES... AND HUMAN BEINGS ARE NO LONGER ENOUGH TO SATISFY HIS CURIOSITY.
HE SOUGHT OUT A KRYPTONIAN, AN AMAZONIAN, CLONES... HE WENT BACK TO THE SITE OF OUR DESTRUCTION, AND REVIVED US... I STILL DO NOT KNOW HOW...
BUT HE IS TRYING TO MAKE WARRIORS... CHAMPIONS...
FURIES.

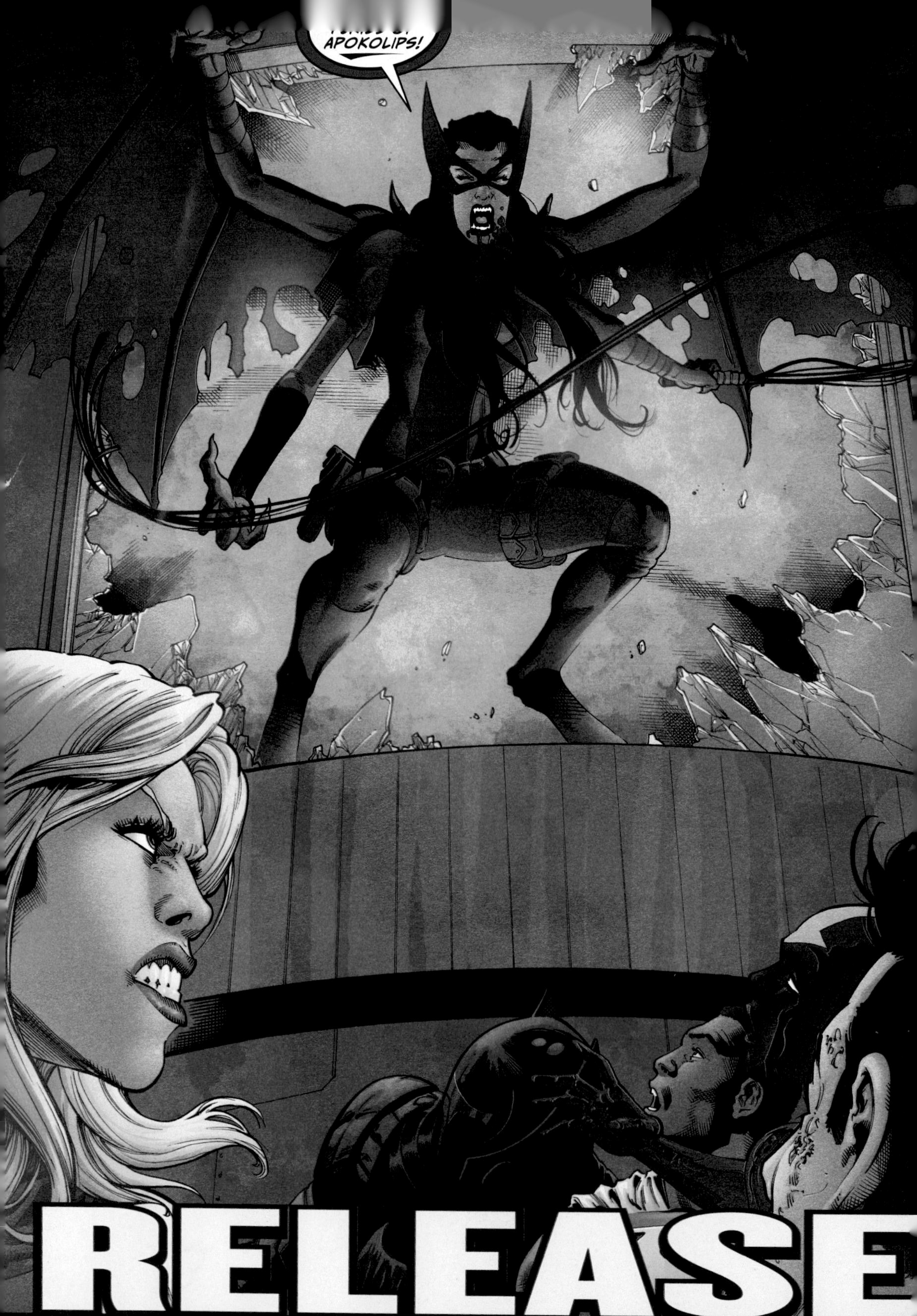
APOKOLIPS!

RELEASE

Story by DANIEL H. WILSON Written by DANIEL H. WILSON, MARGUERITE BENNETT and MIKE JOHNSON Breakdowns by SCOTT McDANI
Art by JACK HERBERT & VICENTE CIFUENTES, JORGE JIMENEZ, EDDY BARROWS & EBER FERREIRA, and JAN DUURSEMA & DREW GERAC
Colors by ALLEN PASSALAQUA Lettering by CARLOS M. MANGUAL Cover by PAULO SIQUEIRA AND HI-FI

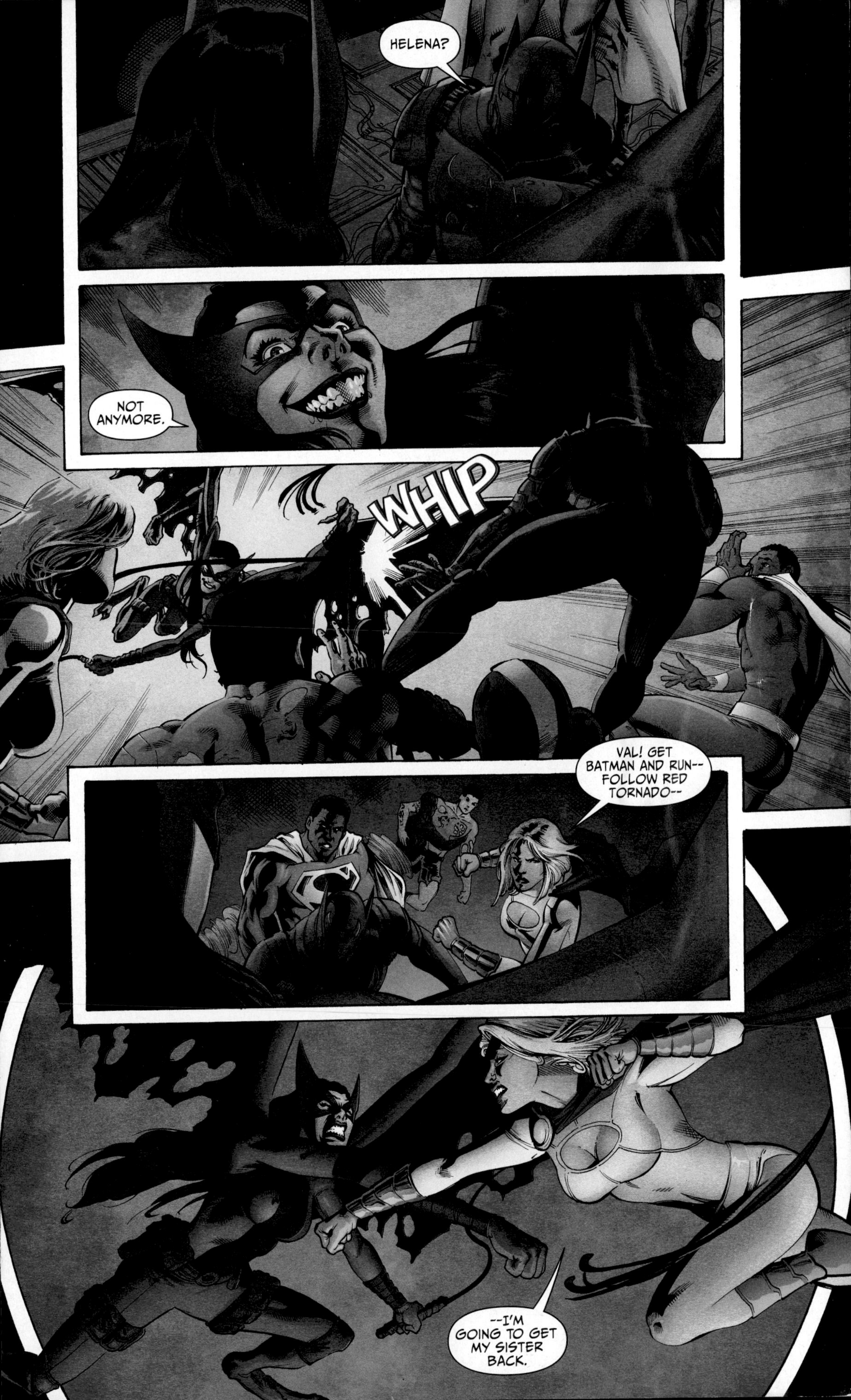

HELENA?
NOT ANYMORE.
WHIP
VAL! GET BATMAN AND RUN-- FOLLOW RED TORNADO--
--I'M GOING TO GET MY SISTER BACK.

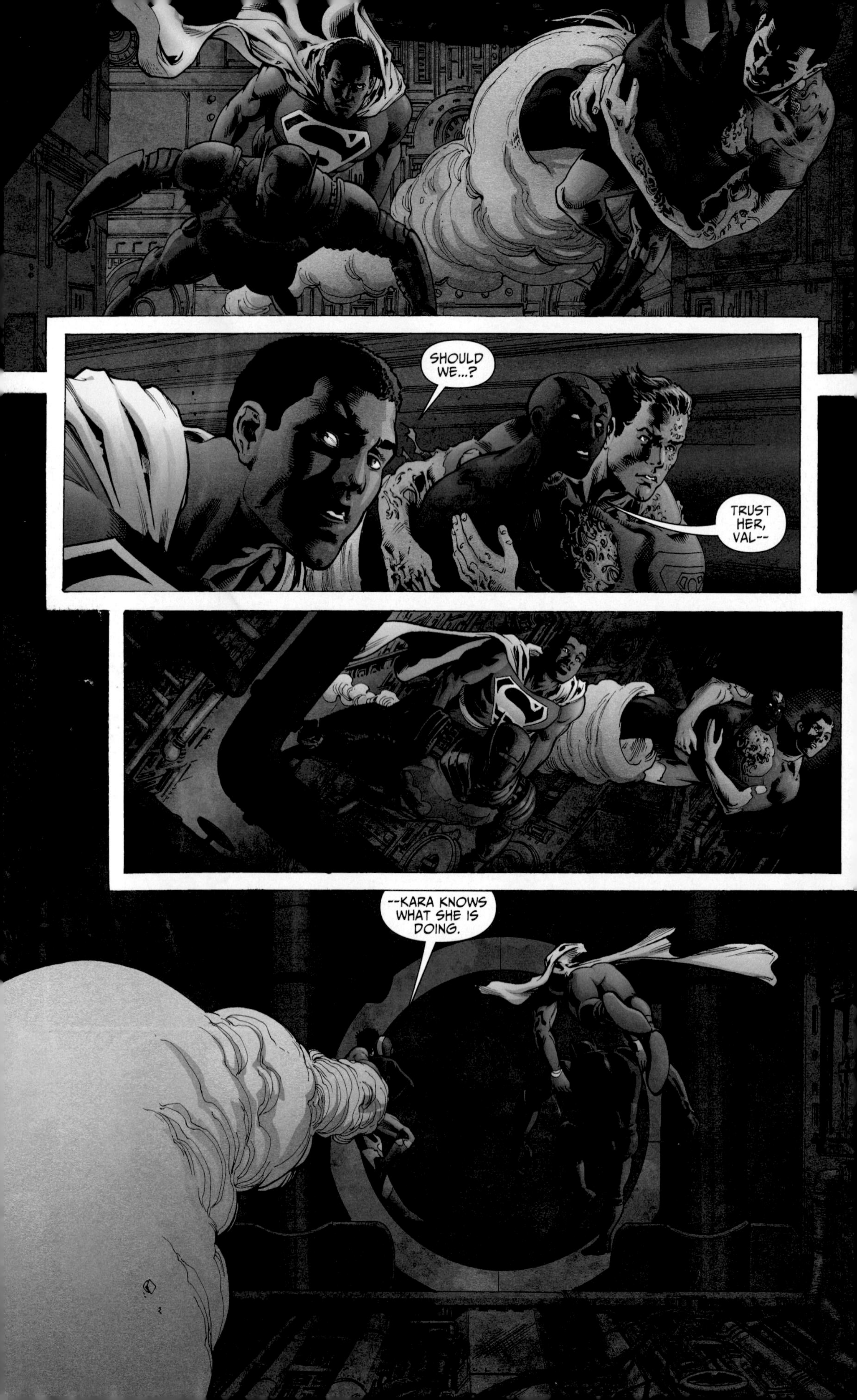
SHOULD WE...?
TRUST HER, VAL--
--KARA KNOWS WHAT SHE IS DOING.

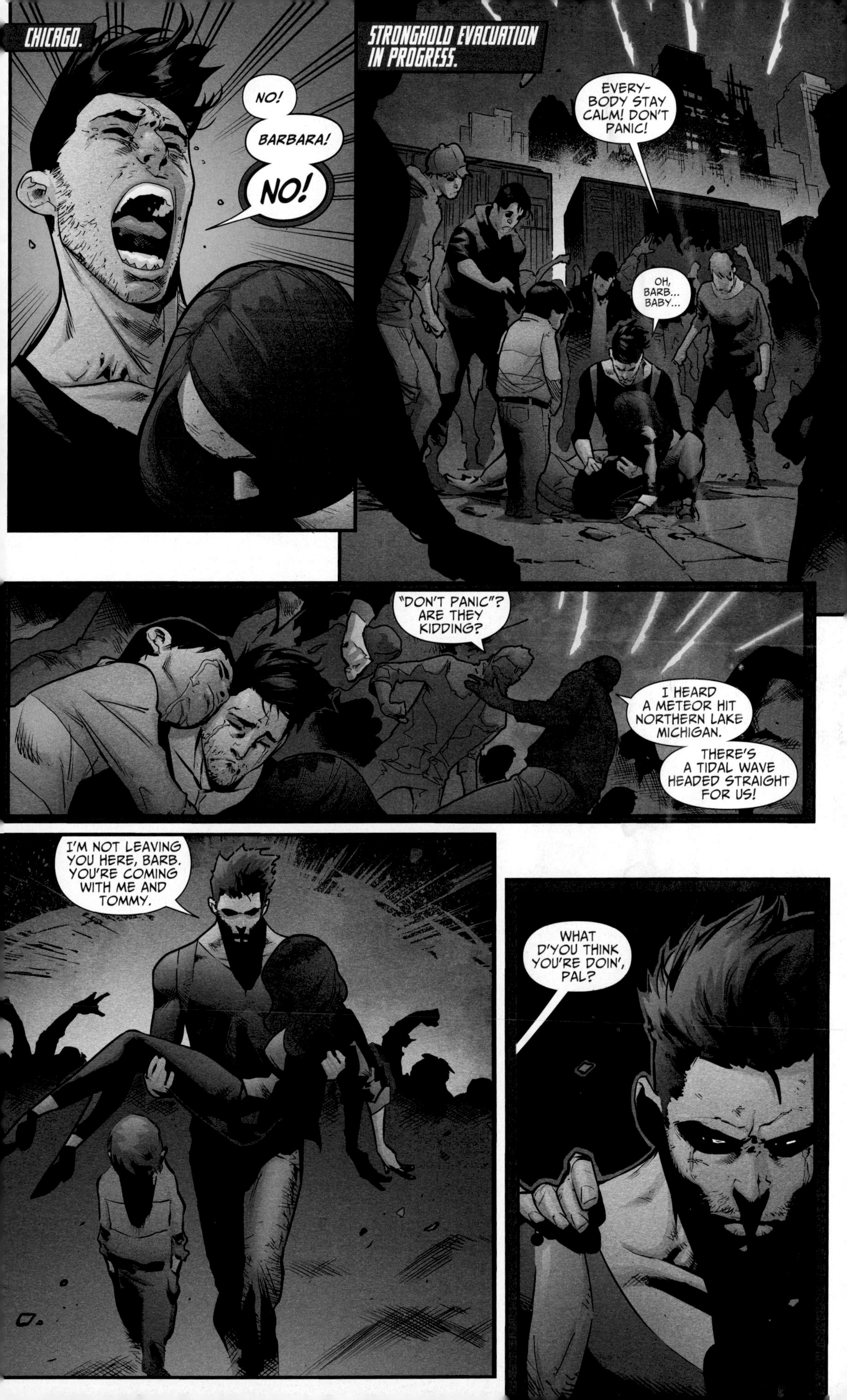
CHICAGO.
NO!
BARBARA!
NO!
STRONGHOLD EVACUATION IN PROGRESS.
EVERY-BODY STAY CALM! DON'T PANIC!
OH, BARB... BABY...
"DON'T PANIC"? ARE THEY KIDDING?
I HEARD A METEOR HIT NORTHERN LAKE MICHIGAN.
THERE'S A TIDAL WAVE HEADED STRAIGHT FOR US!
I'M NOT LEAVING YOU HERE, BARB. YOU'RE COMING WITH ME AND TOMMY.
WHAT D'YOU THINK YOU'RE DOIN', PAL?

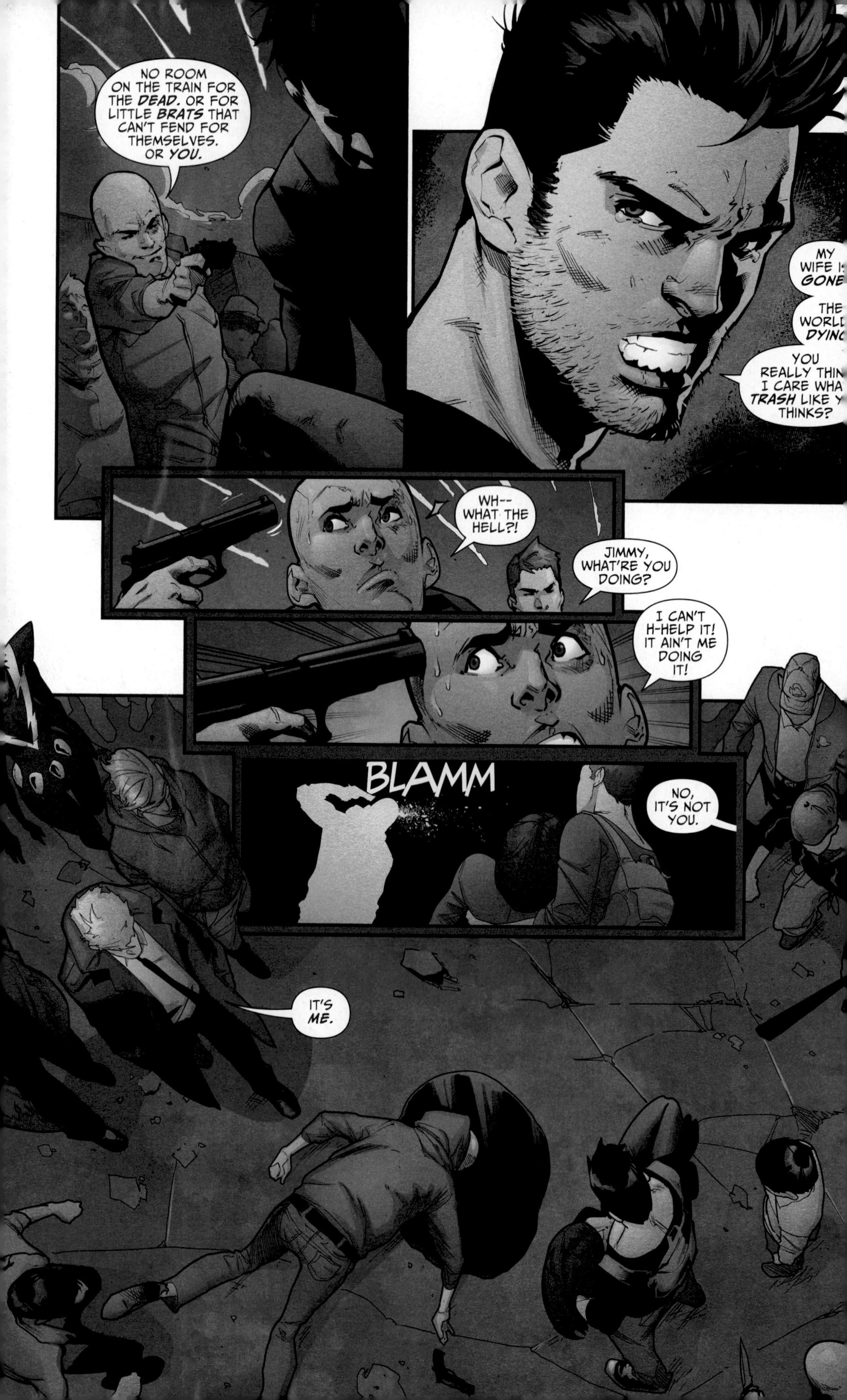
NO ROOM ON THE TRAIN FOR THE DEAD. OR FOR LITTLE BRATS THAT CAN'T FEND FOR THEMSELVES. OR YOU.
MY WIFE I GONE
THE WORLD DYING
YOU REALLY THIN I CARE WHA TRASH LIKE Y THINKS?
WH-- WHAT THE HELL?!
JIMMY, WHAT'RE YOU DOING?
I CAN'T H-HELP IT! IT AIN'T ME DOING IT!
BLAMM
NO, IT'S NOT YOU.
IT'S ME.

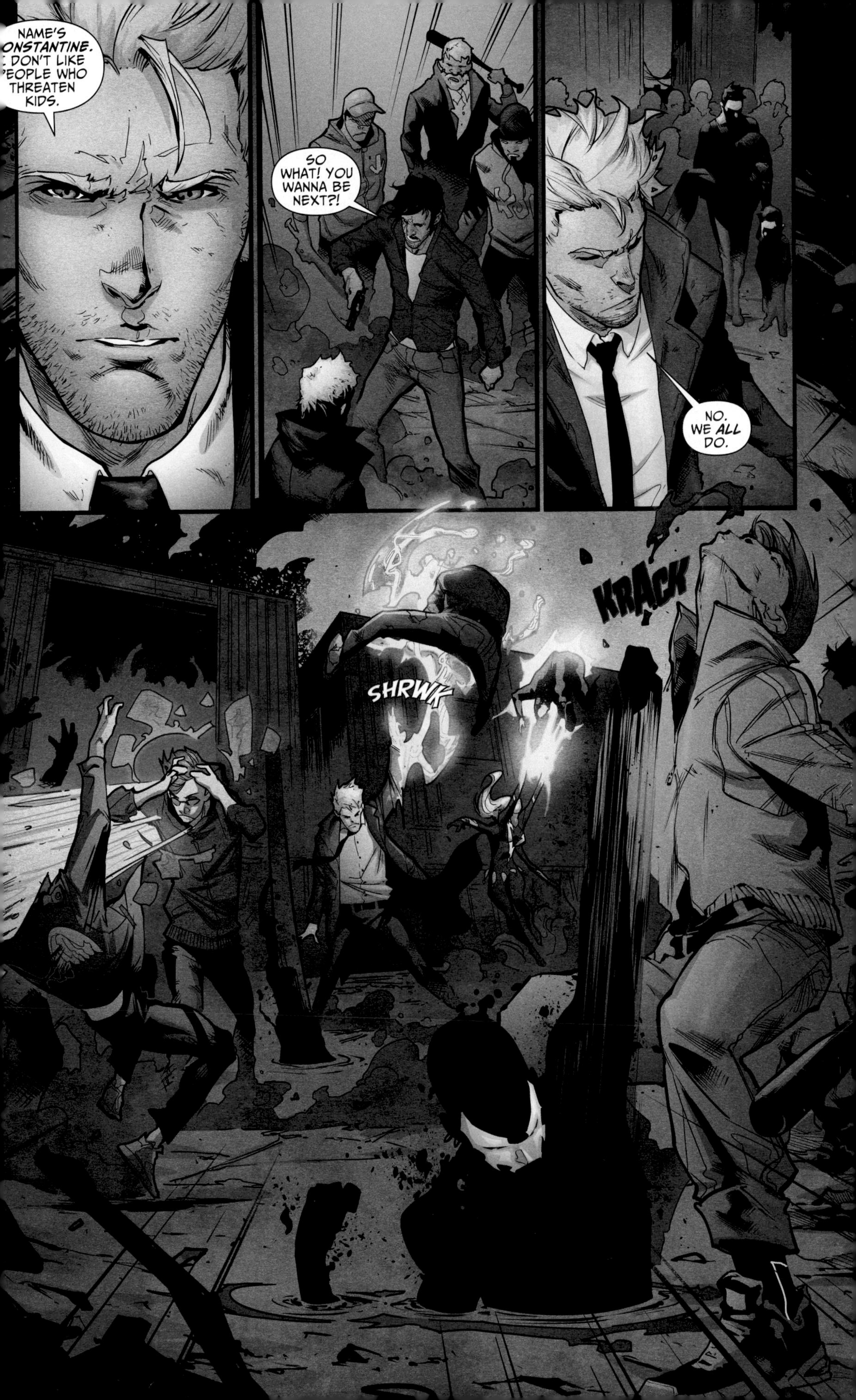
NAME'S CONSTANTINE. I DON'T LIKE PEOPLE WHO THREATEN KIDS.
SO WHAT! YOU WANNA BE NEXT?!
NO. WE ALL DO.
KRACK
SHRWK

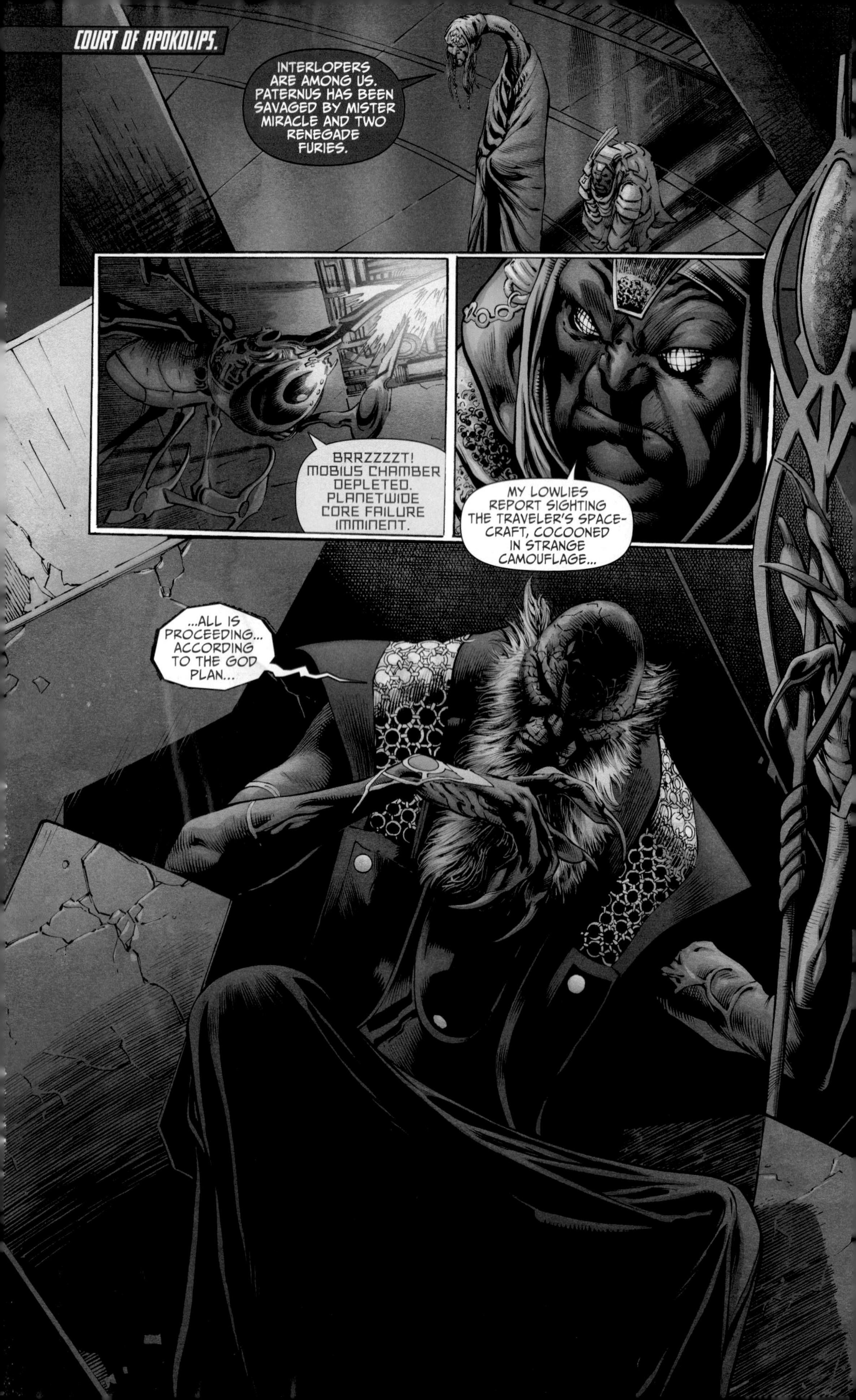
COURT OF APOKOLIPS.
INTERLOPERS ARE AMONG US. PATERNUS HAS BEEN SAVAGED BY MISTER MIRACLE AND TWO RENEGADE FURIES.
BRRZZZZT! MOBIUS CHAMBER DEPLETED. PLANETWIDE CORE FAILURE IMMINENT.
MY LOWLIES REPORT SIGHTING THE TRAVELER'S SPACE-CRAFT, COCOONED IN STRANGE CAMOUFLAGE...
...ALL IS PROCEEDING... ACCORDING TO THE GOD PLAN...

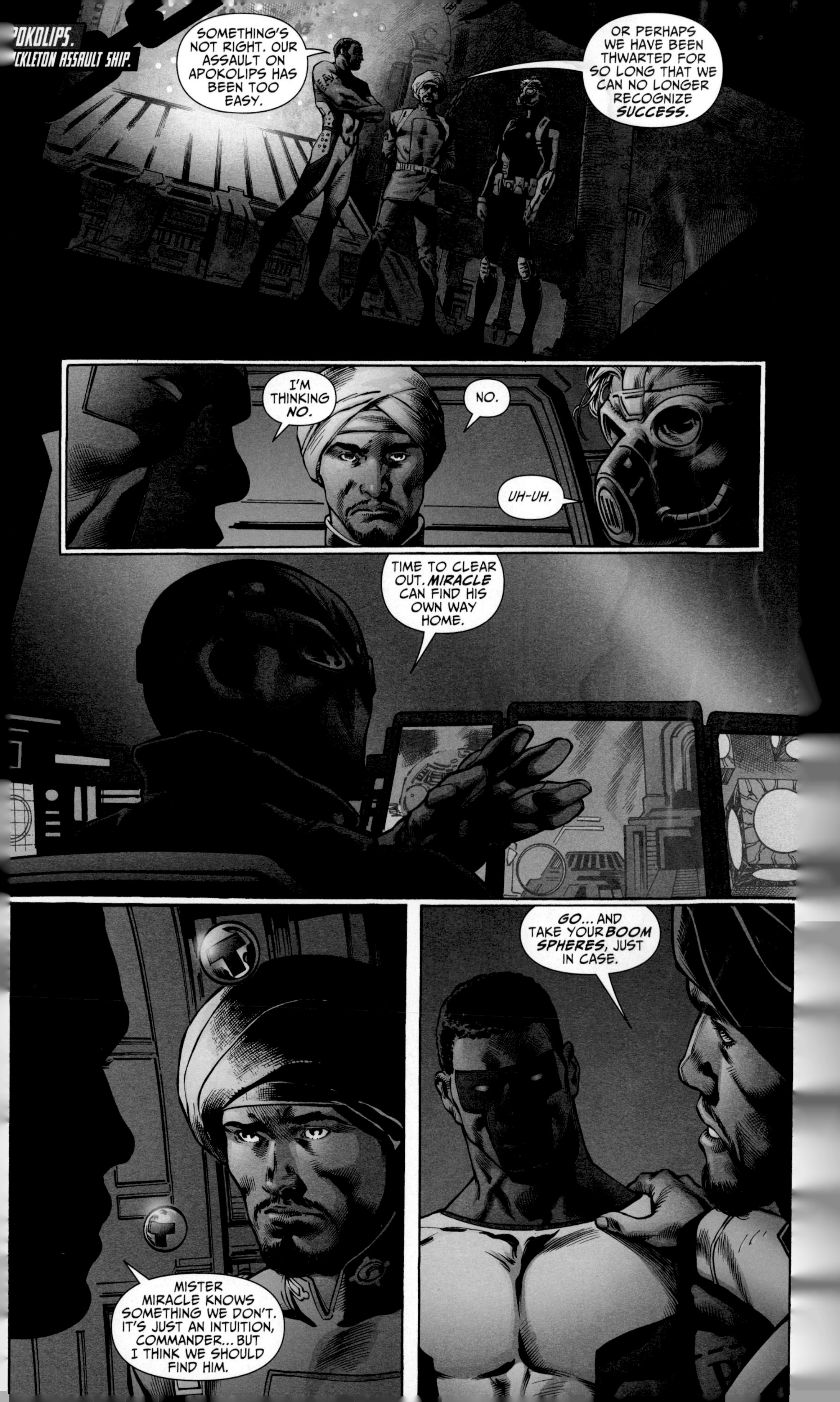
POKOLIPS.
CKLETON ASSAULT SHIP.
SOMETHING'S NOT RIGHT. OUR ASSAULT ON APOKOLIPS HAS BEEN TOO EASY.
OR PERHAPS WE HAVE BEEN THWARTED FOR SO LONG THAT WE CAN NO LONGER RECOGNIZE SUCCESS.
I'M THINKING NO.
NO.
UH-UH.
TIME TO CLEAR OUT. MIRACLE CAN FIND HIS OWN WAY HOME.
MISTER MIRACLE KNOWS SOMETHING WE DON'T. IT'S JUST AN INTUITION, COMMANDER... BUT I THINK WE SHOULD FIND HIM.
GO... AND TAKE YOUR BOOM SPHERES, JUST IN CASE.

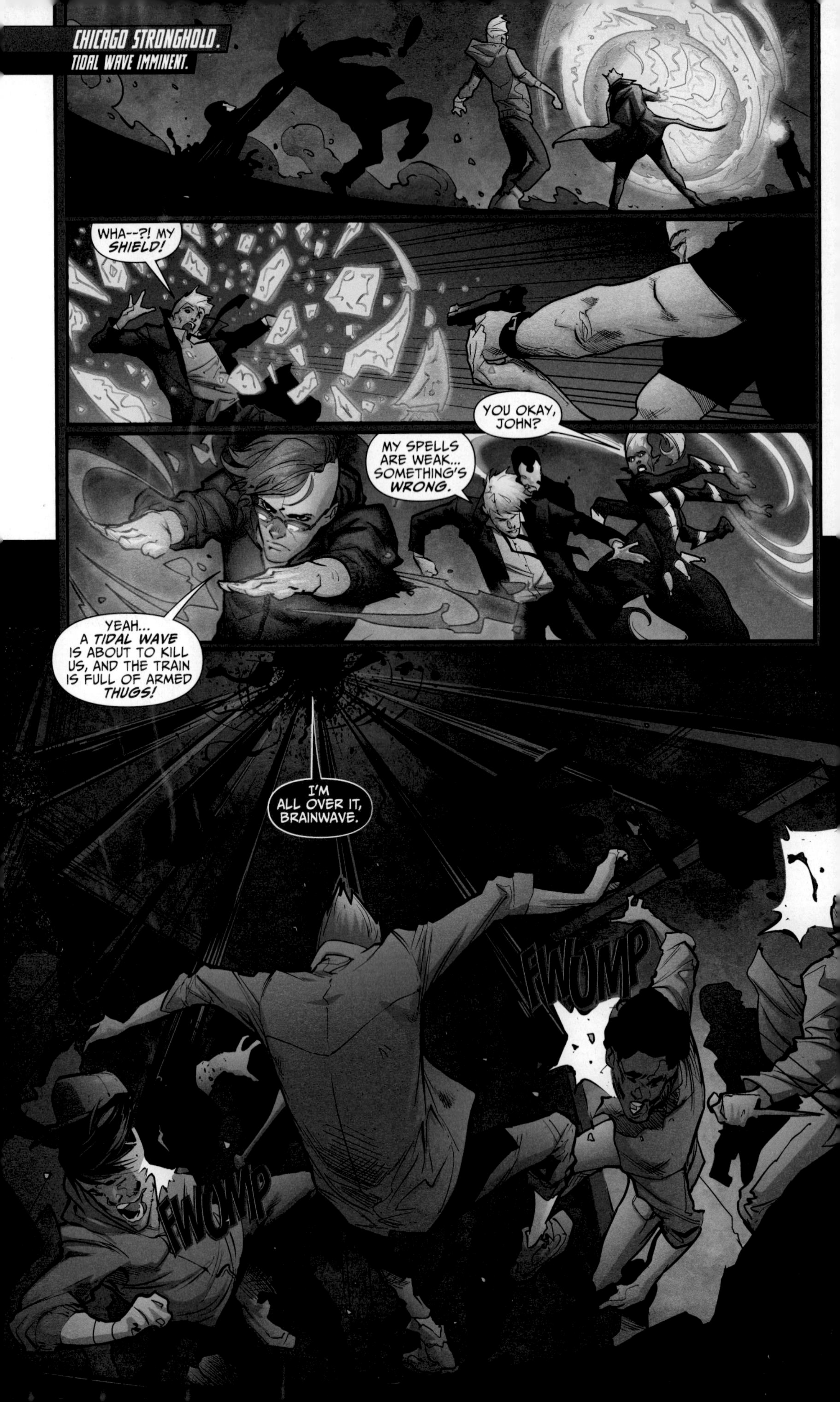

CHICAGO STRONGHOLD.
TIDAL WAVE IMMINENT.
WHA--?! MY SHIELD!
YOU OKAY, JOHN?
MY SPELLS ARE WEAK... SOMETHING'S WRONG.
YEAH... A TIDAL WAVE IS ABOUT TO KILL US, AND THE TRAIN IS FULL OF ARMED THUGS!
I'M ALL OVER IT, BRAINWAVE.
FWOMP
FWOMP

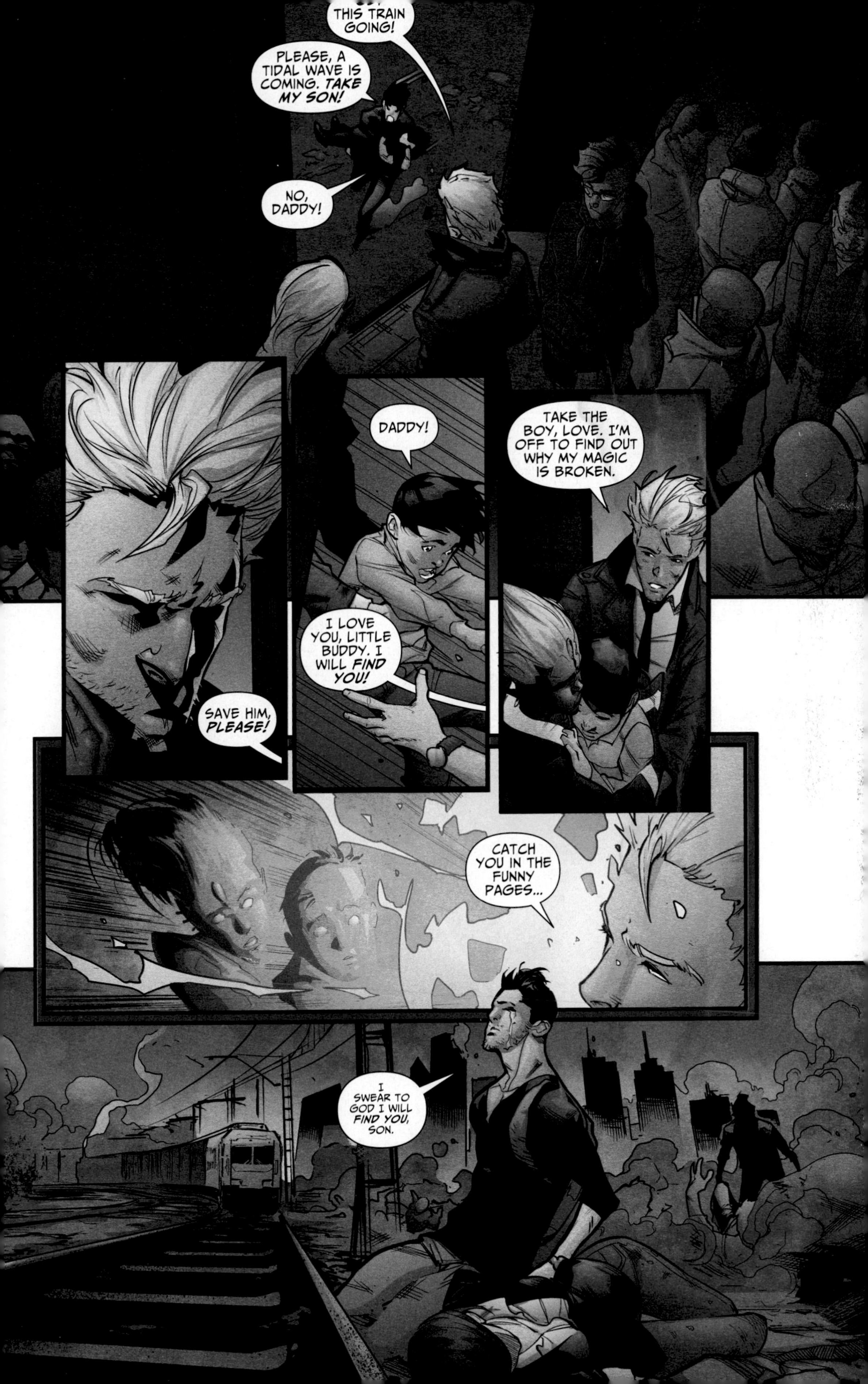
THIS TRAIN GOING!
PLEASE, A TIDAL WAVE IS COMING. TAKE MY SON!
NO, DADDY!
SAVE HIM, PLEASE!
DADDY!
I LOVE YOU, LITTLE BUDDY. I WILL FIND YOU!
TAKE THE BOY, LOVE. I'M OFF TO FIND OUT WHY MY MAGIC IS BROKEN.
CATCH YOU IN THE FUNNY PAGES...
I SWEAR TO GOD I WILL FIND YOU, SON.

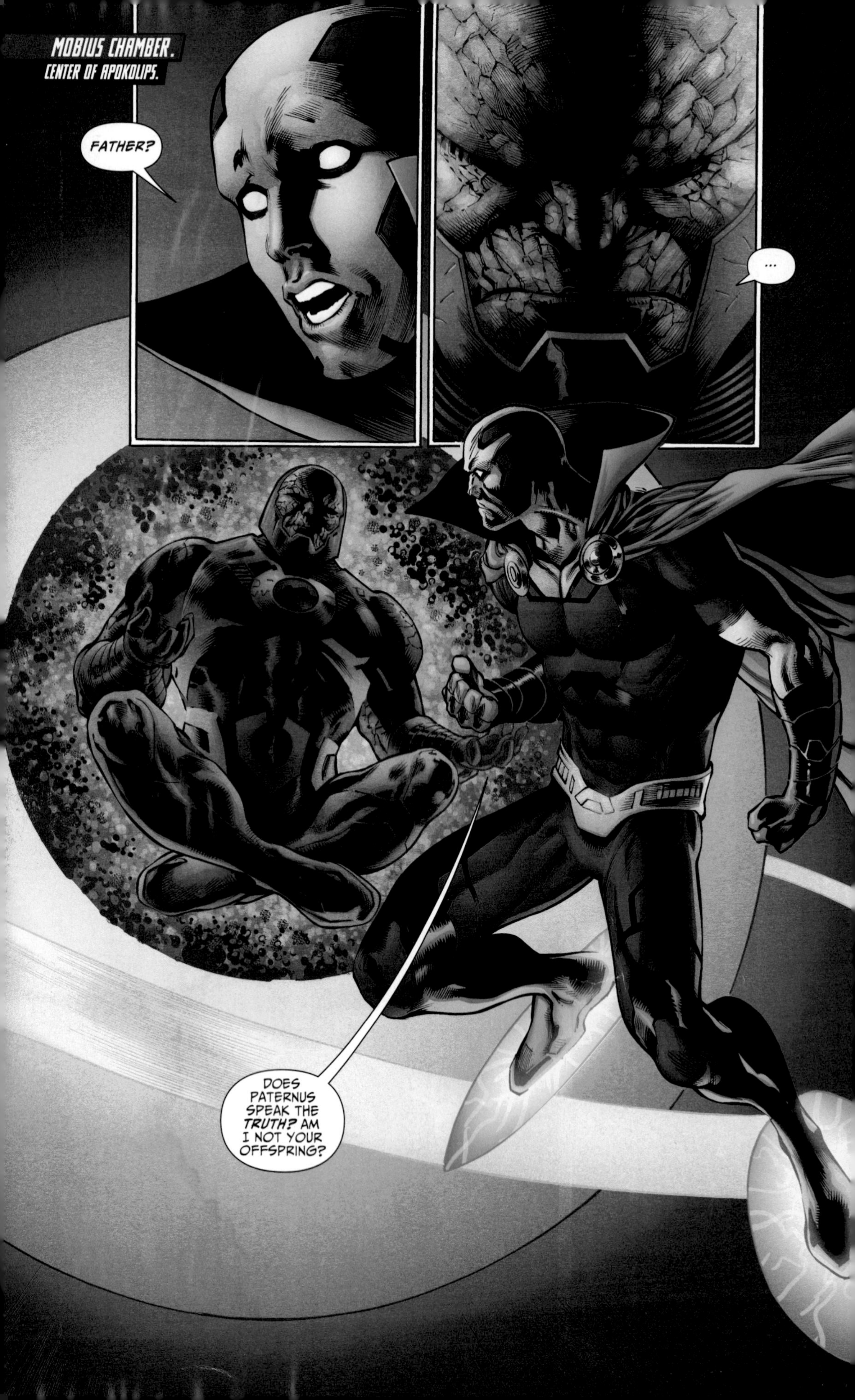
MOBIUS CHAMBER.
CENTER OF APOKOLIPS.
FATHER?
...
DOES PATERNUS SPEAK THE TRUTH? AM I NOT YOUR OFFSPRING?

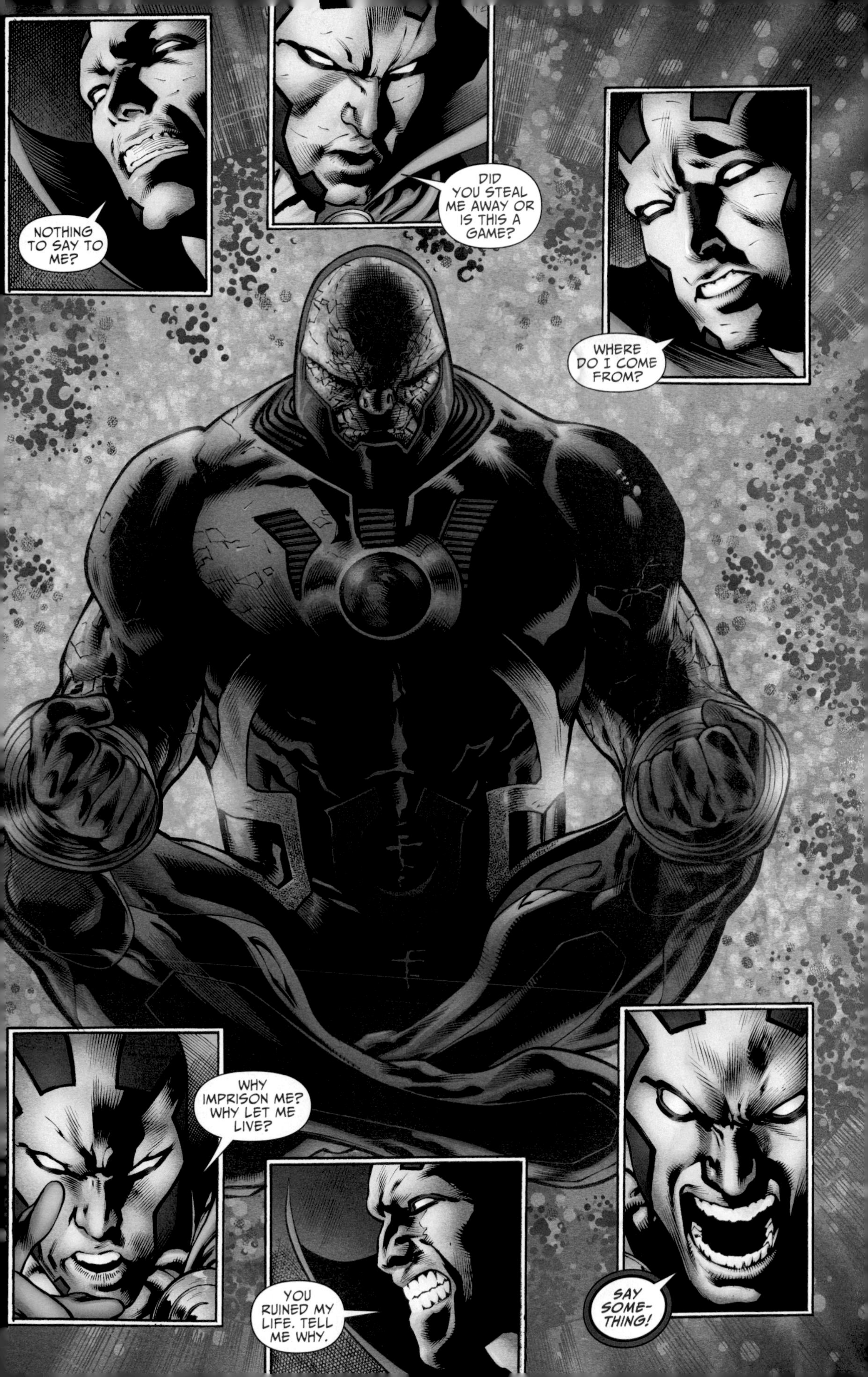
NOTHING TO SAY TO ME?
DID YOU STEAL ME AWAY OR IS THIS A GAME?
WHERE DO I COME FROM?
WHY IMPRISON ME? WHY LET ME LIVE?
YOU RUINED MY LIFE. TELL ME WHY.
SAY SOME-THING!

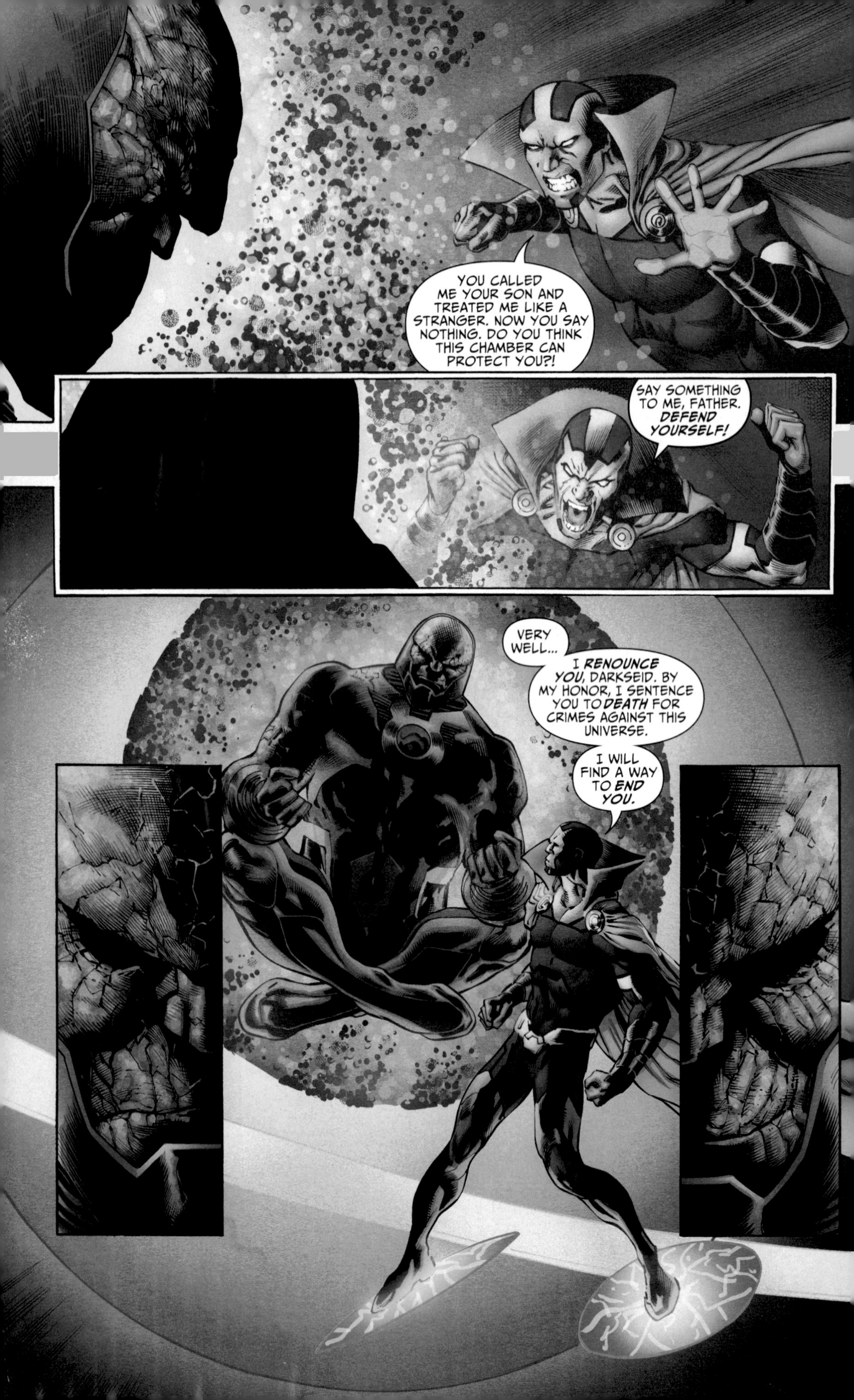
YOU CALLED ME YOUR SON AND TREATED ME LIKE A STRANGER. NOW YOU SAY NOTHING. DO YOU THINK THIS CHAMBER CAN PROTECT YOU?!
SAY SOMETHING TO ME, FATHER. DEFEND YOURSELF!
VERY WELL...
I RENOUNCE YOU, DARKSEID. BY MY HONOR, I SENTENCE YOU TO DEATH FOR CRIMES AGAINST THIS UNIVERSE.
I WILL FIND A WAY TO END YOU.

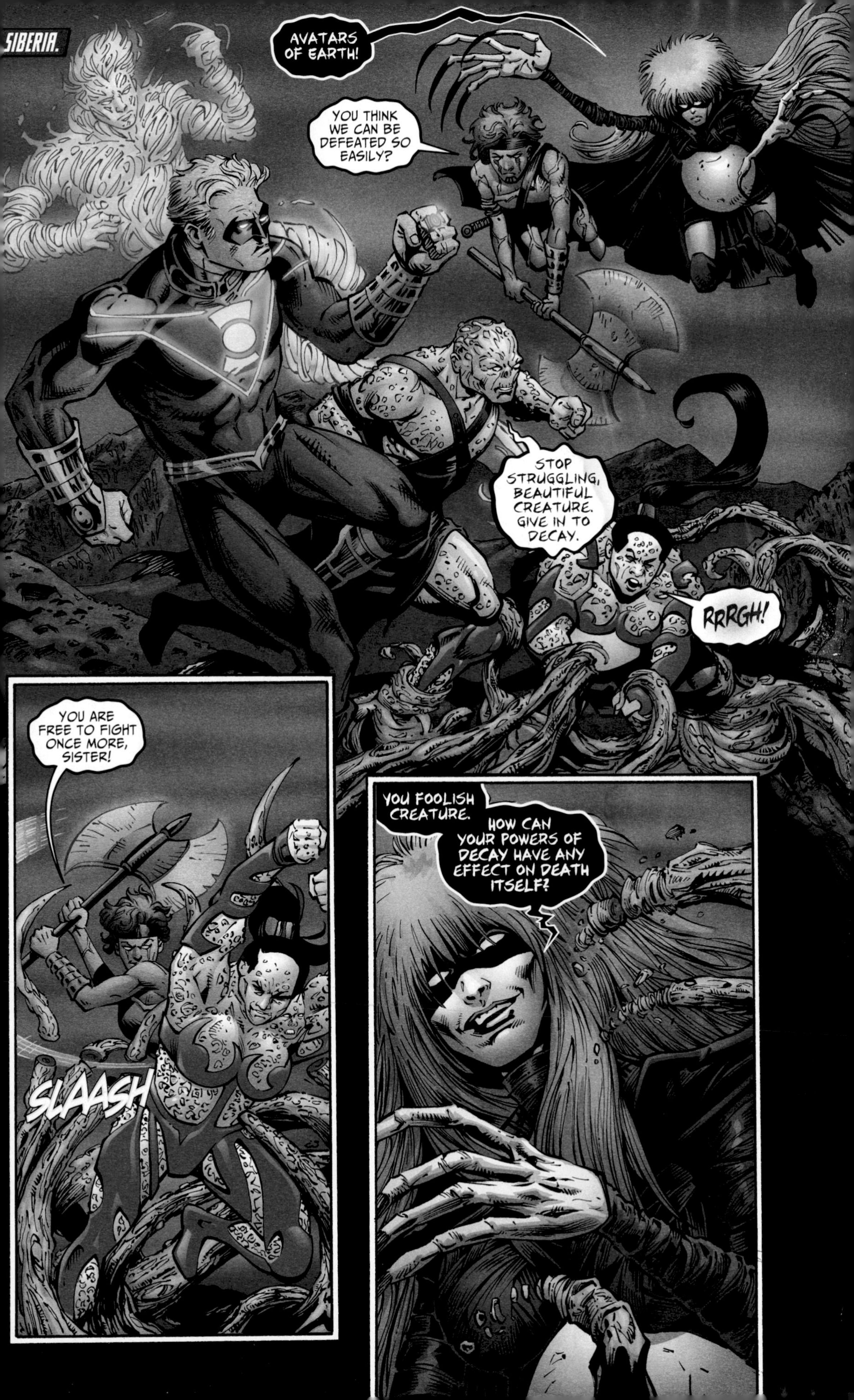
SIBERIA.
AVATARS OF EARTH!
YOU THINK WE CAN BE DEFEATED SO EASILY?
STOP STRUGGLING, BEAUTIFUL CREATURE. GIVE IN TO DECAY.
RRRGH!
YOU ARE FREE TO FIGHT ONCE MORE, SISTER!
SLAASH
YOU FOOLISH CREATURE.
HOW CAN YOUR POWERS OF DECAY HAVE ANY EFFECT ON DEATH ITSELF?

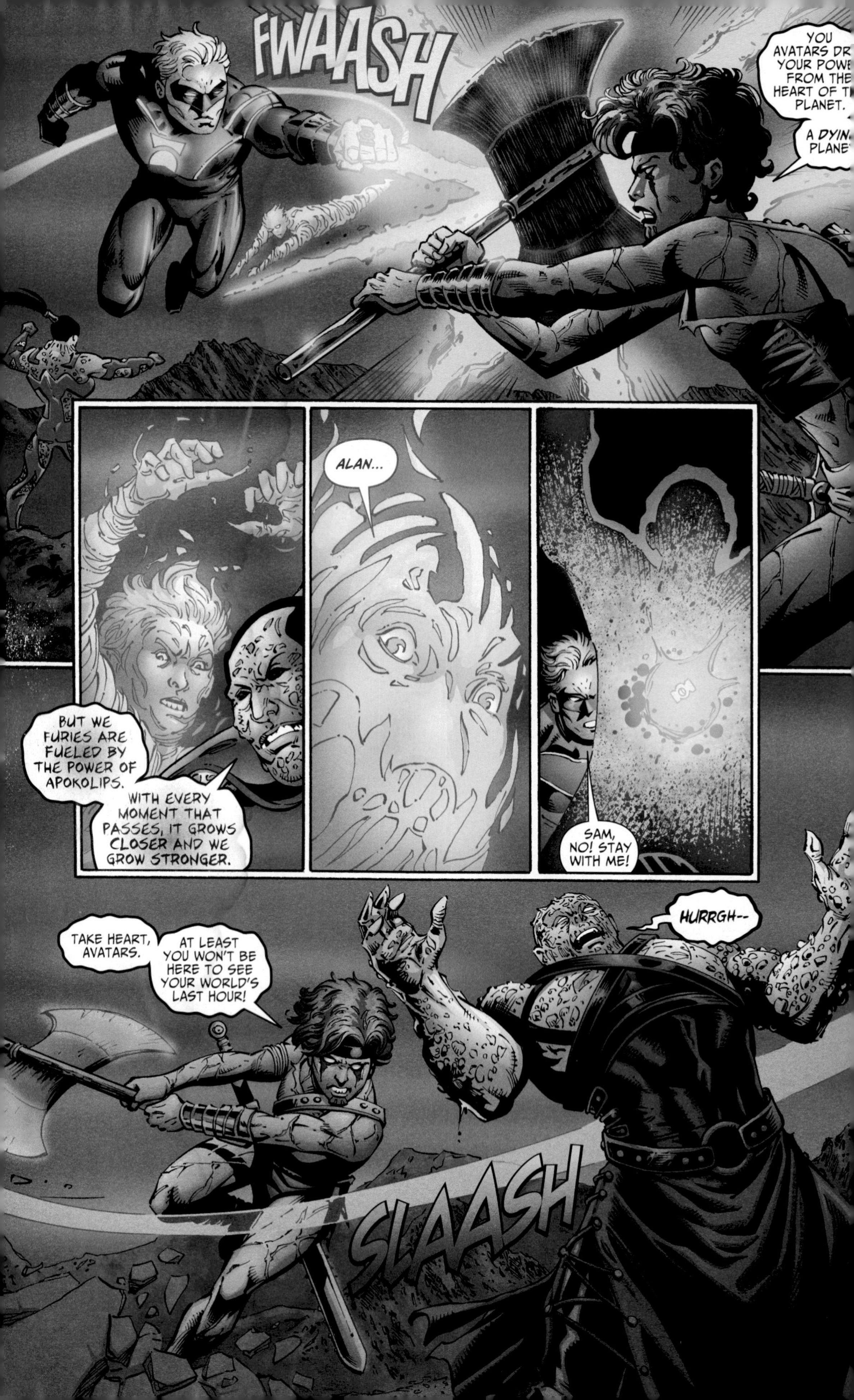
FWAASH
YOU AVATARS DR YOUR POWE FROM THE HEART OF T PLANET.
A DYIN PLANE
ALAN...
BUT WE FURIES ARE FUELED BY THE POWER OF APOKOLIPS.
WITH EVERY MOMENT THAT PASSES, IT GROWS CLOSER AND WE GROW STRONGER.
SAM, NO! STAY WITH ME!
TAKE HEART, AVATARS.
AT LEAST YOU WON'T BE HERE TO SEE YOUR WORLD'S LAST HOUR!
HURRGH--
SLAASH

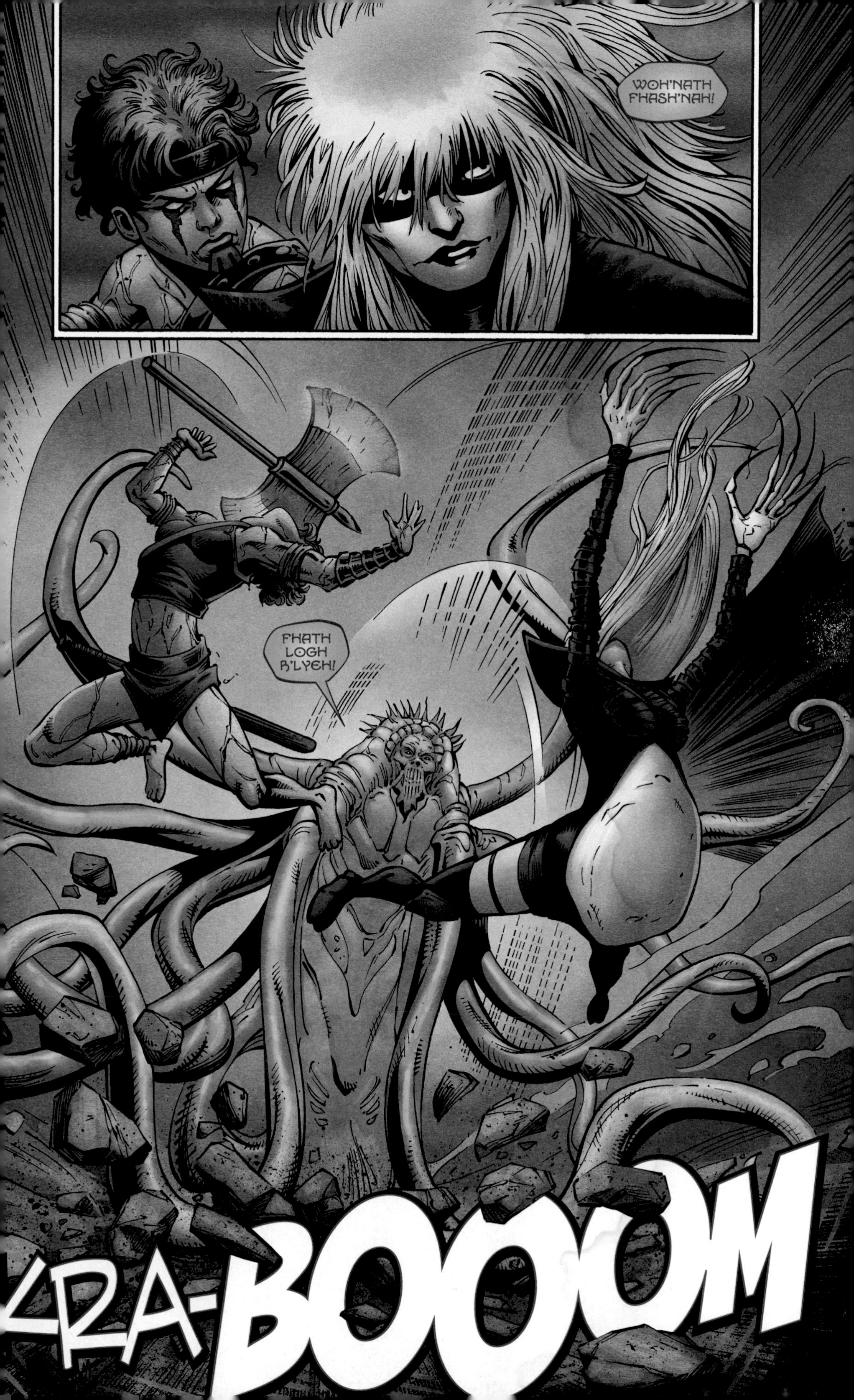
WOH'NATH FHASH'NAH!
FHATH LOGH R'LYEH!
KRA-BOOOOM

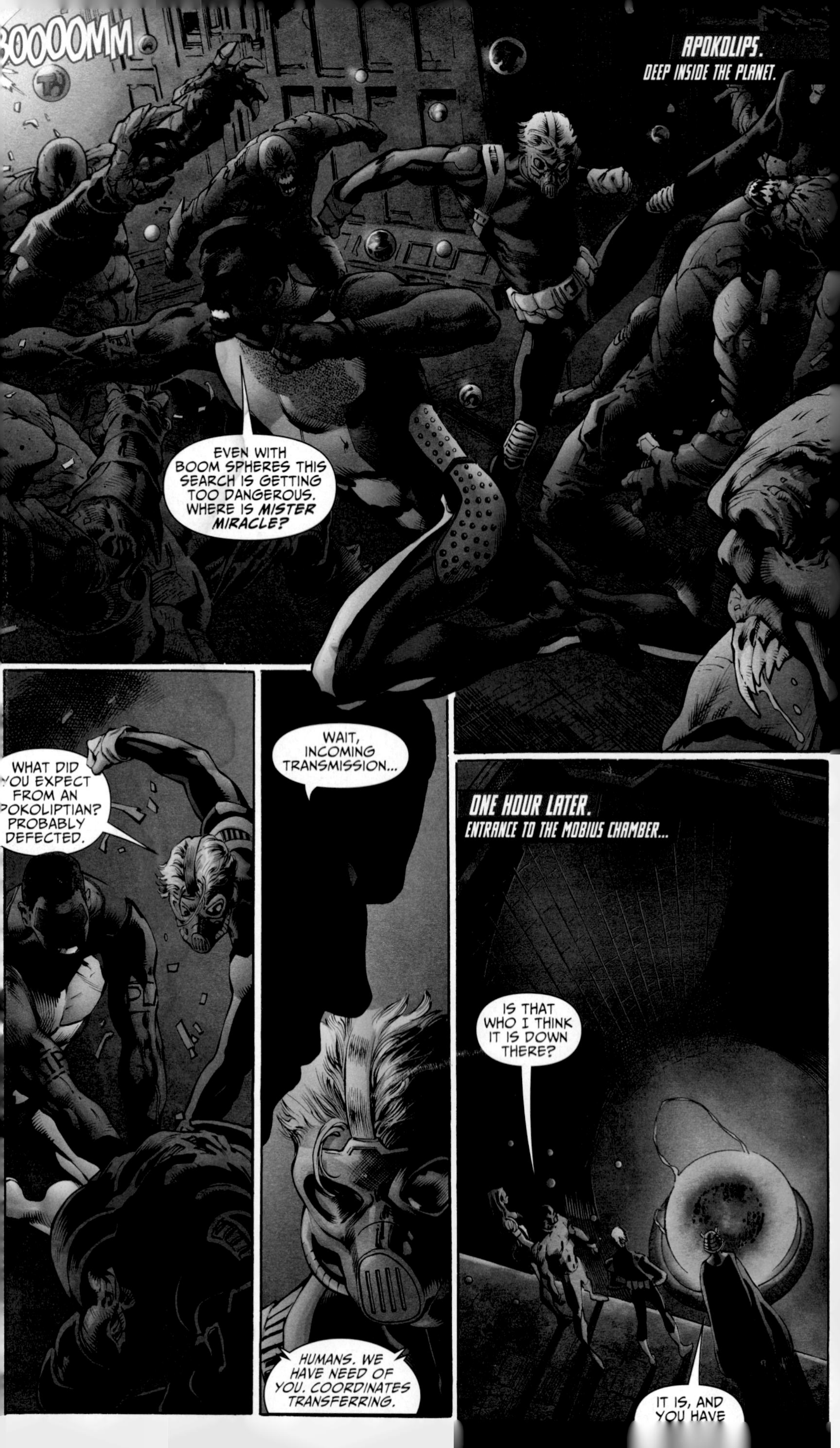
OOOOMM
APOKOLIPS.
DEEP INSIDE THE PLANET.
EVEN WITH BOOM SPHERES THIS SEARCH IS GETTING TOO DANGEROUS. WHERE IS *MISTER MIRACLE?*
WHAT DID OU EXPECT FROM AN POKOLIPTIAN? PROBABLY DEFECTED.
WAIT, INCOMING TRANSMISSION...
HUMANS. WE HAVE NEED OF YOU. COORDINATES TRANSFERRING.
ONE HOUR LATER.
ENTRANCE TO THE MOBIUS CHAMBER...
IS THAT WHO I THINK IT IS DOWN THERE?
IT IS, AND YOU HAVE

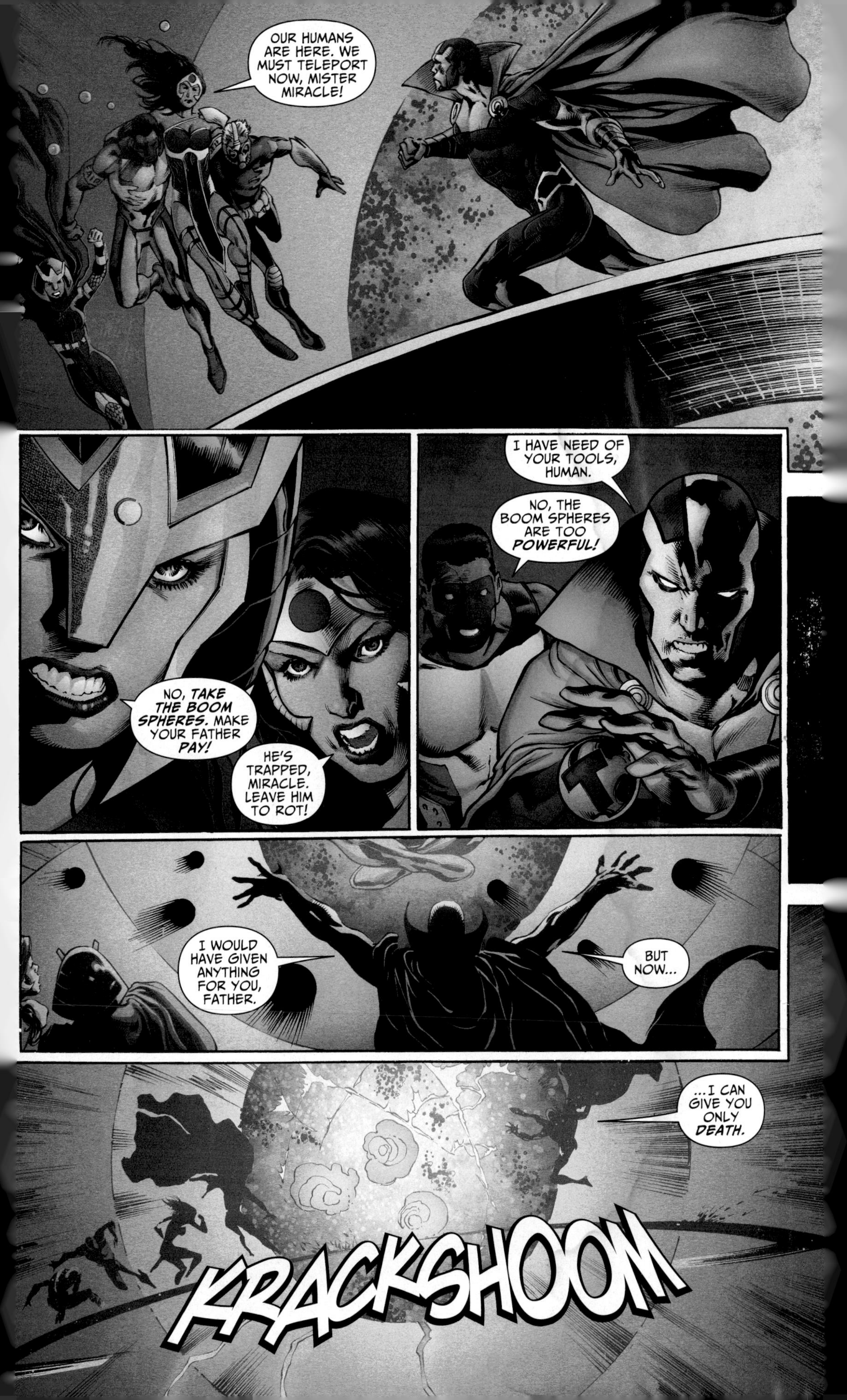
OUR HUMANS ARE HERE. WE MUST TELEPORT NOW, MISTER MIRACLE!
NO, *TAKE THE BOOM SPHERES*. MAKE YOUR FATHER *PAY!*
HE'S TRAPPED, MIRACLE. LEAVE HIM TO ROT!
I HAVE NEED OF YOUR TOOLS, HUMAN.
NO, THE BOOM SPHERES ARE TOO *POWERFUL!*
I WOULD HAVE GIVEN ANYTHING FOR YOU, FATHER.
BUT NOW...
...I CAN GIVE YOU ONLY *DEATH*.
KRACKSHOOM

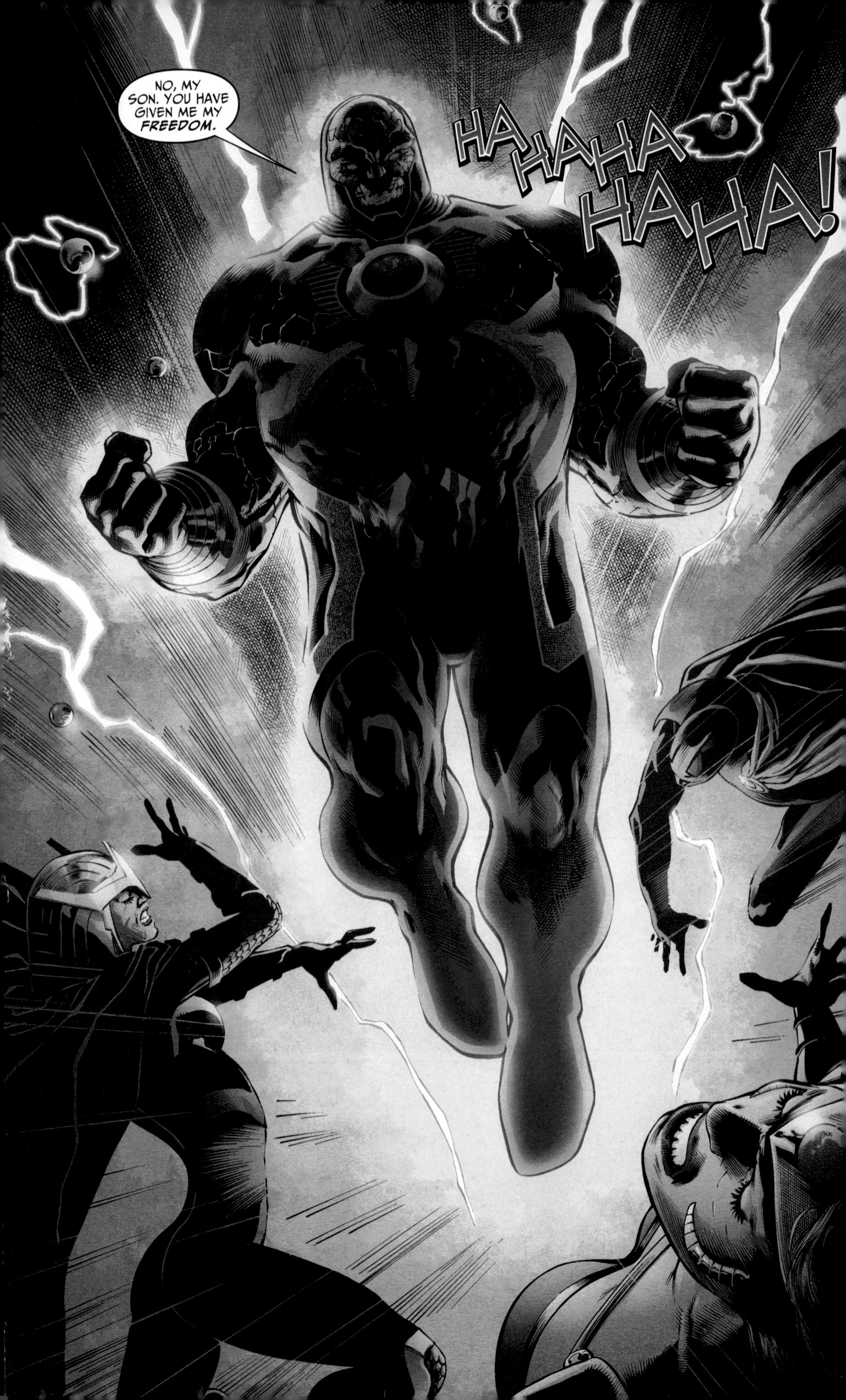
NO, MY SON. YOU HAVE GIVEN ME MY *FREEDOM.*
HAHAHAHA HAHA!

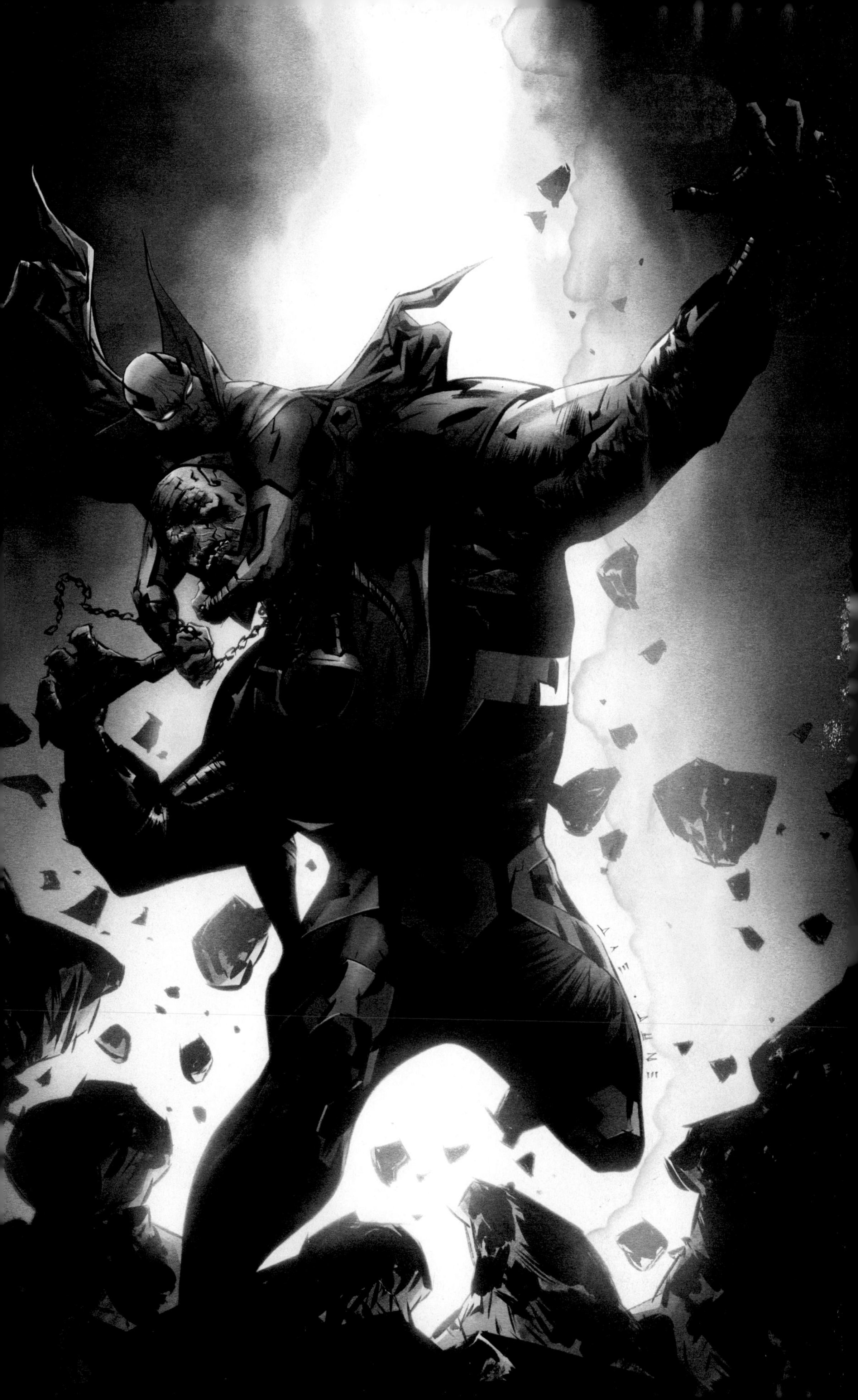

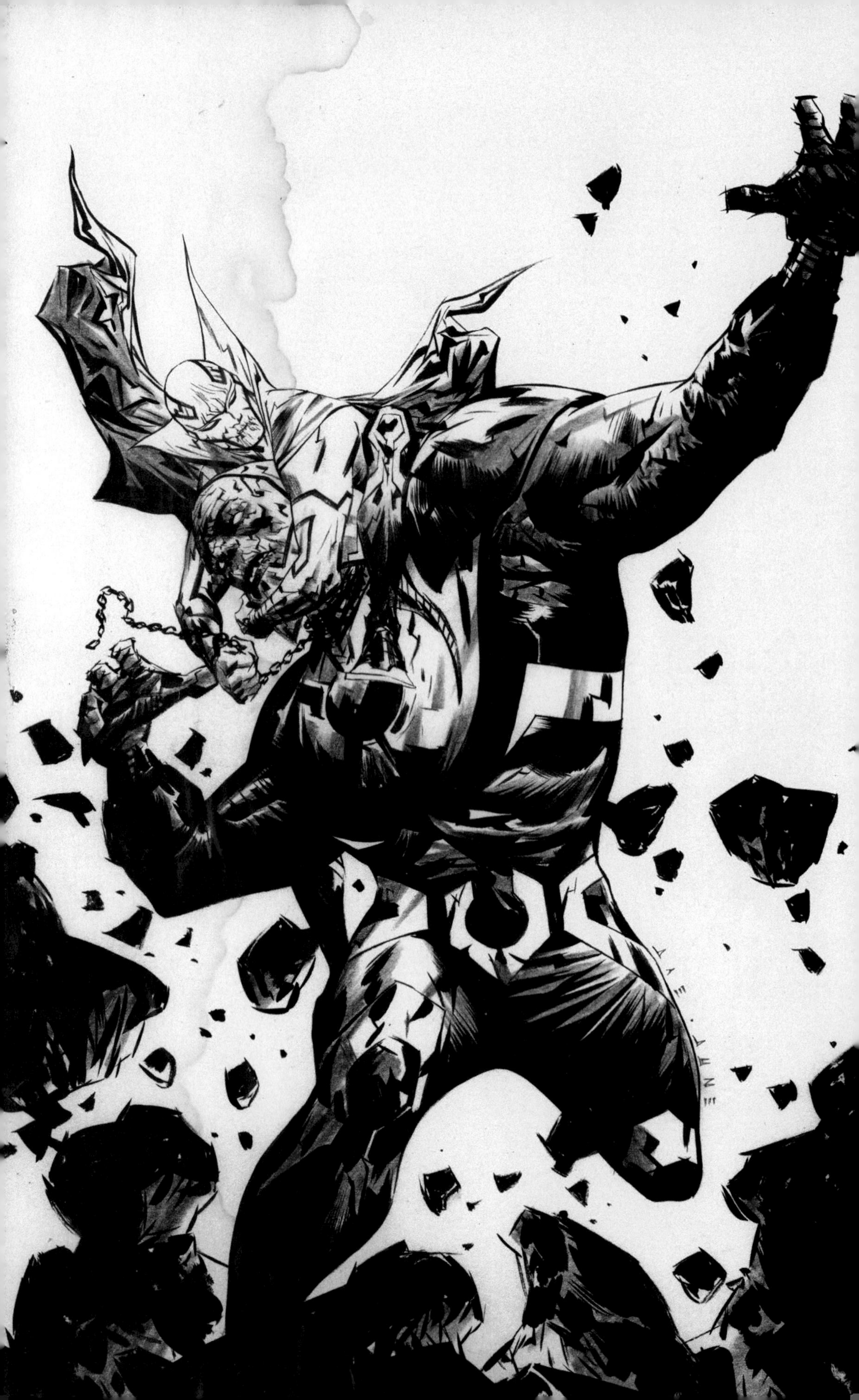

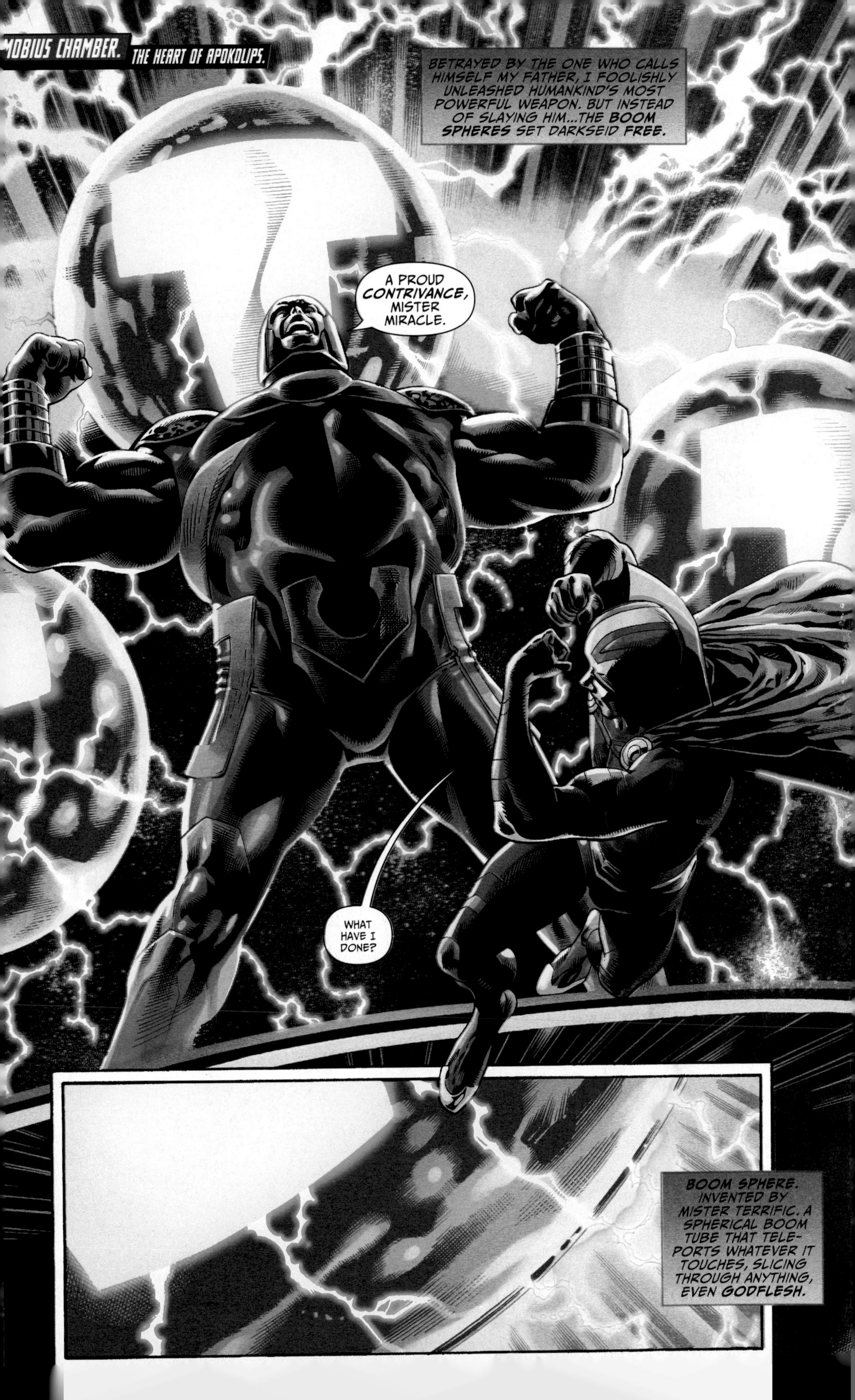
MOBIUS CHAMBER. THE HEART OF APOKOLIPS.
BETRAYED BY THE ONE WHO CALLS HIMSELF MY FATHER, I FOOLISHLY UNLEASHED HUMANKIND'S MOST POWERFUL WEAPON. BUT INSTEAD OF SLAYING HIM...THE BOOM SPHERES SET DARKSEID FREE.
A PROUD CONTRIVANCE, MISTER MIRACLE.
WHAT HAVE I DONE?
BOOM SPHERE. INVENTED BY MISTER TERRIFIC. A SPHERICAL BOOM TUBE THAT TELEPORTS WHATEVER IT TOUCHES, SLICING THROUGH ANYTHING, EVEN GODFLESH.

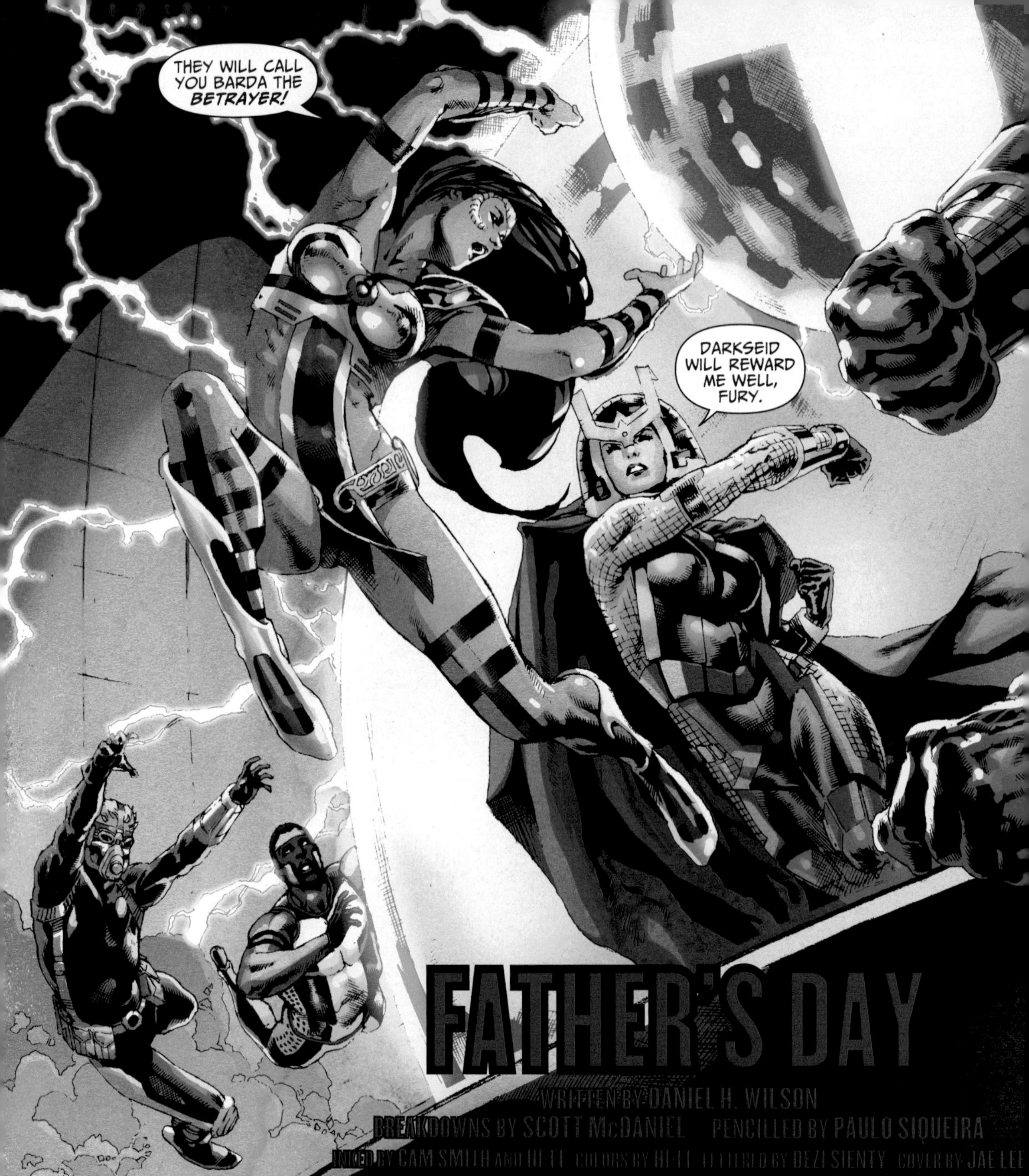
THEY WILL CALL YOU BARDA THE *BETRAYER!*
DARKSEID WILL REWARD ME WELL, FURY.
FATHER'S DAY
WRITTEN BY DANIEL H. WILSON
BREAKDOWNS BY SCOTT McDANIEL PENCILLED BY PAULO SIQUEIRA
INKED BY CAM SMITH AND HI-FI COLORS BY HI-FI LETTERED BY DEZI SIENTY COVER BY JAE LEE

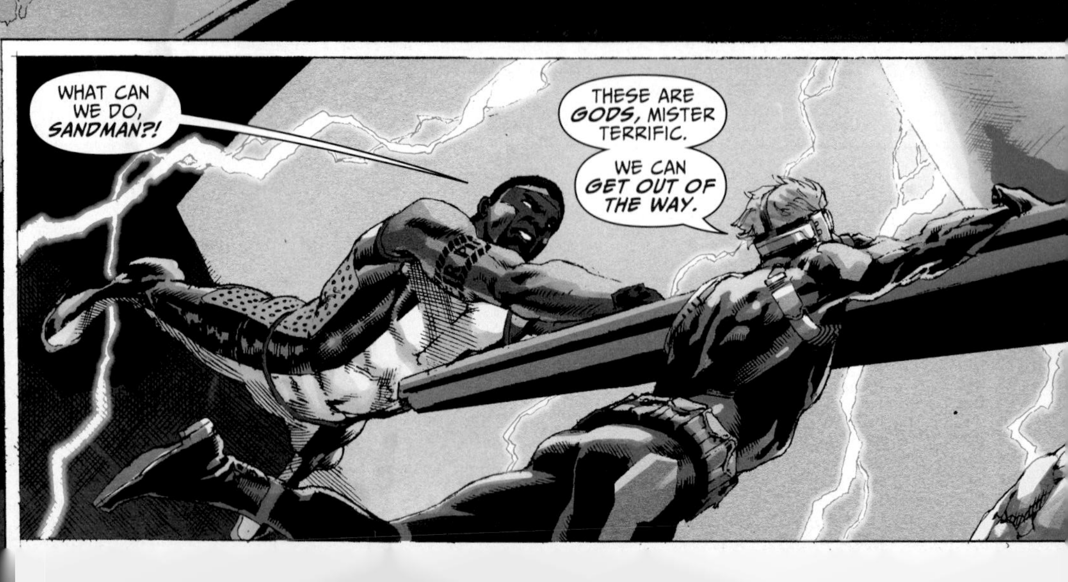
WHAT CAN WE DO, *SANDMAN?!*
THESE ARE *GODS,* MISTER TERRIFIC.
WE CAN *GET OUT OF THE WAY.*

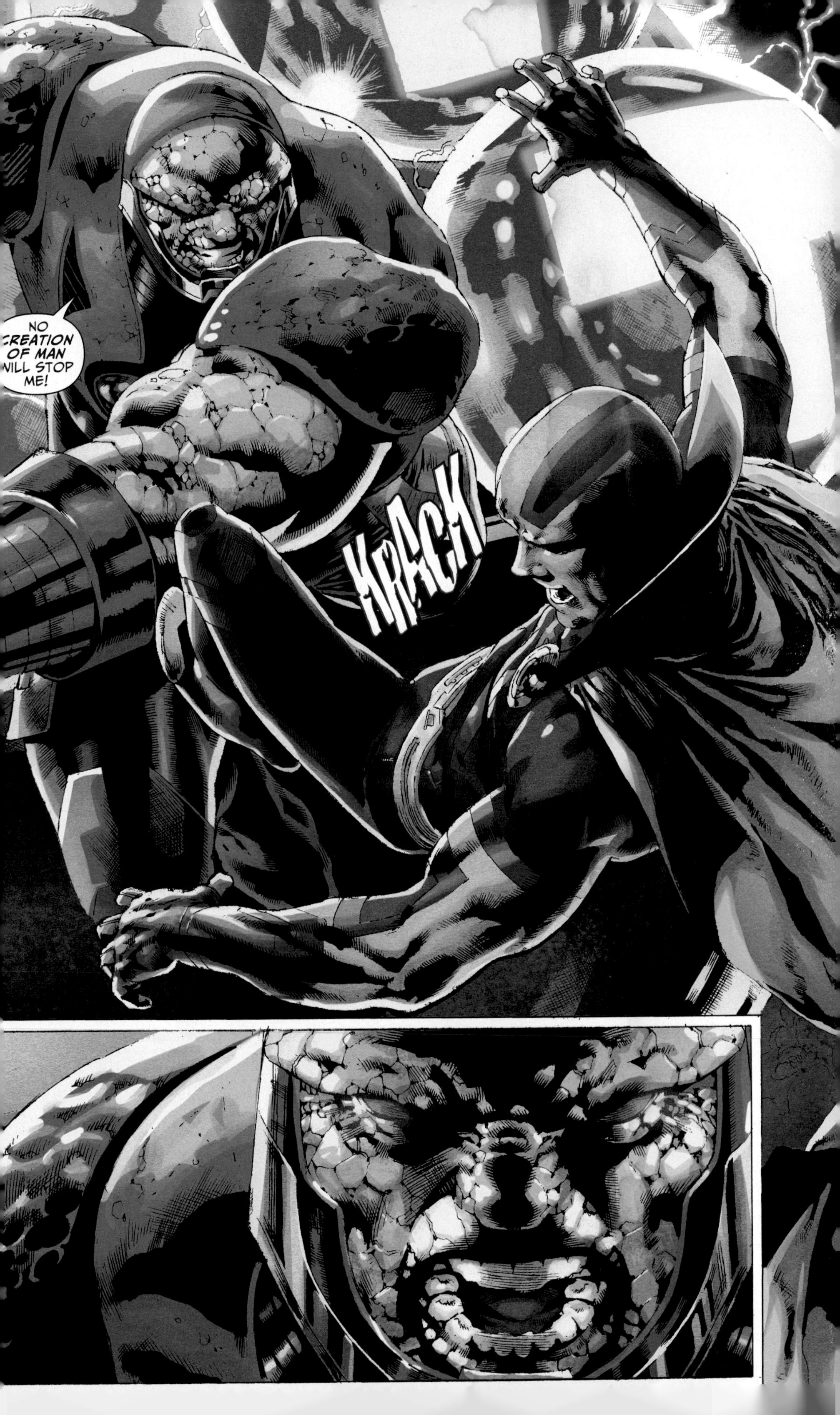

NO CREATION OF MAN WILL STOP ME!
KRACK

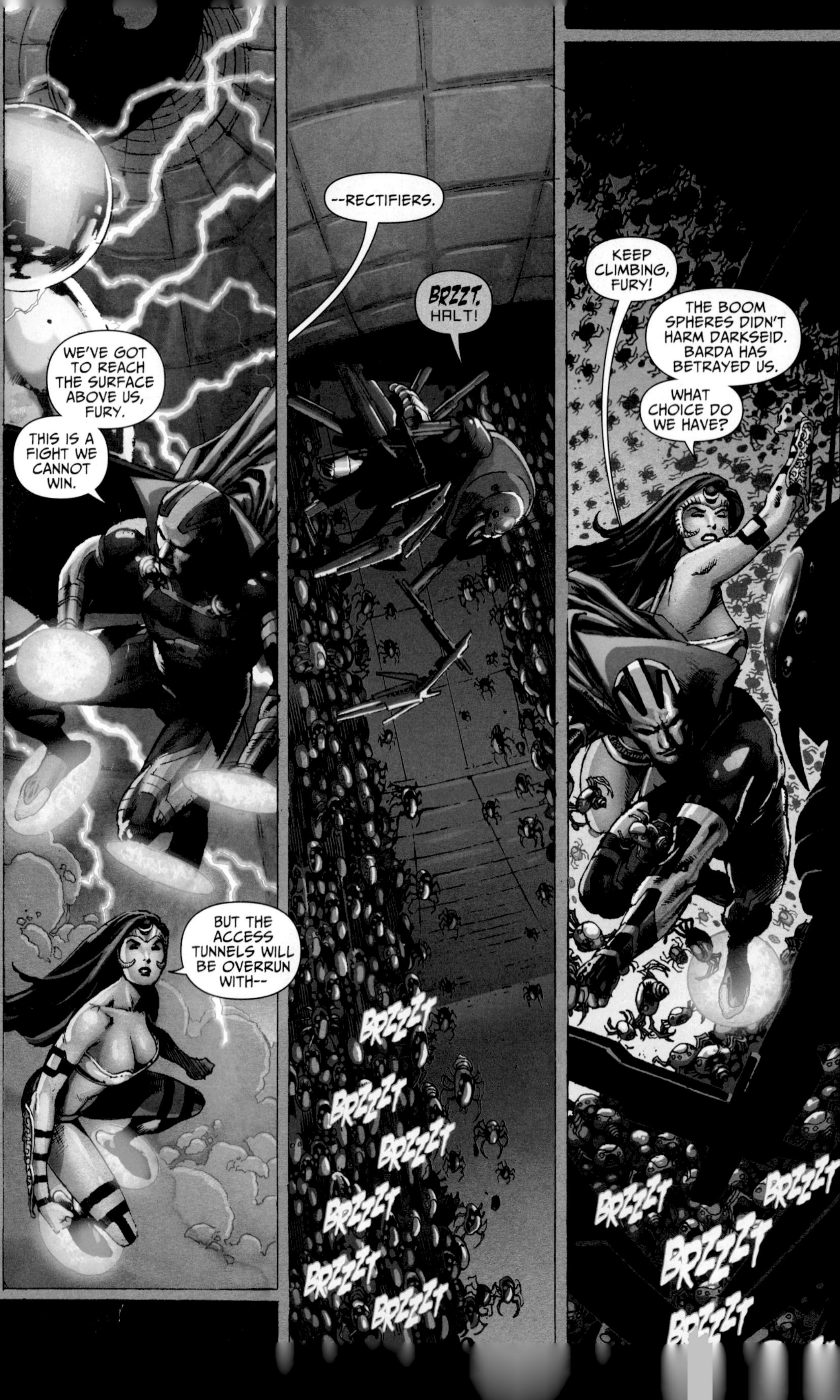

WE'VE GOT TO REACH THE SURFACE ABOVE US, FURY.
THIS IS A FIGHT WE CANNOT WIN.
BUT THE ACCESS TUNNELS WILL BE OVERRUN WITH--
--RECTIFIERS.
BRZZT. HALT!
BRZZZT
BRZZZT
BRZZZT
BRZZZT
BRZZZT
BRZZZT
KEEP CLIMBING, FURY!
THE BOOM SPHERES DIDN'T HARM DARKSEID. BARDA HAS BETRAYED US.
WHAT CHOICE DO WE HAVE?
BRZZZT
BRZZZT
BRZZZT
BRZZZT

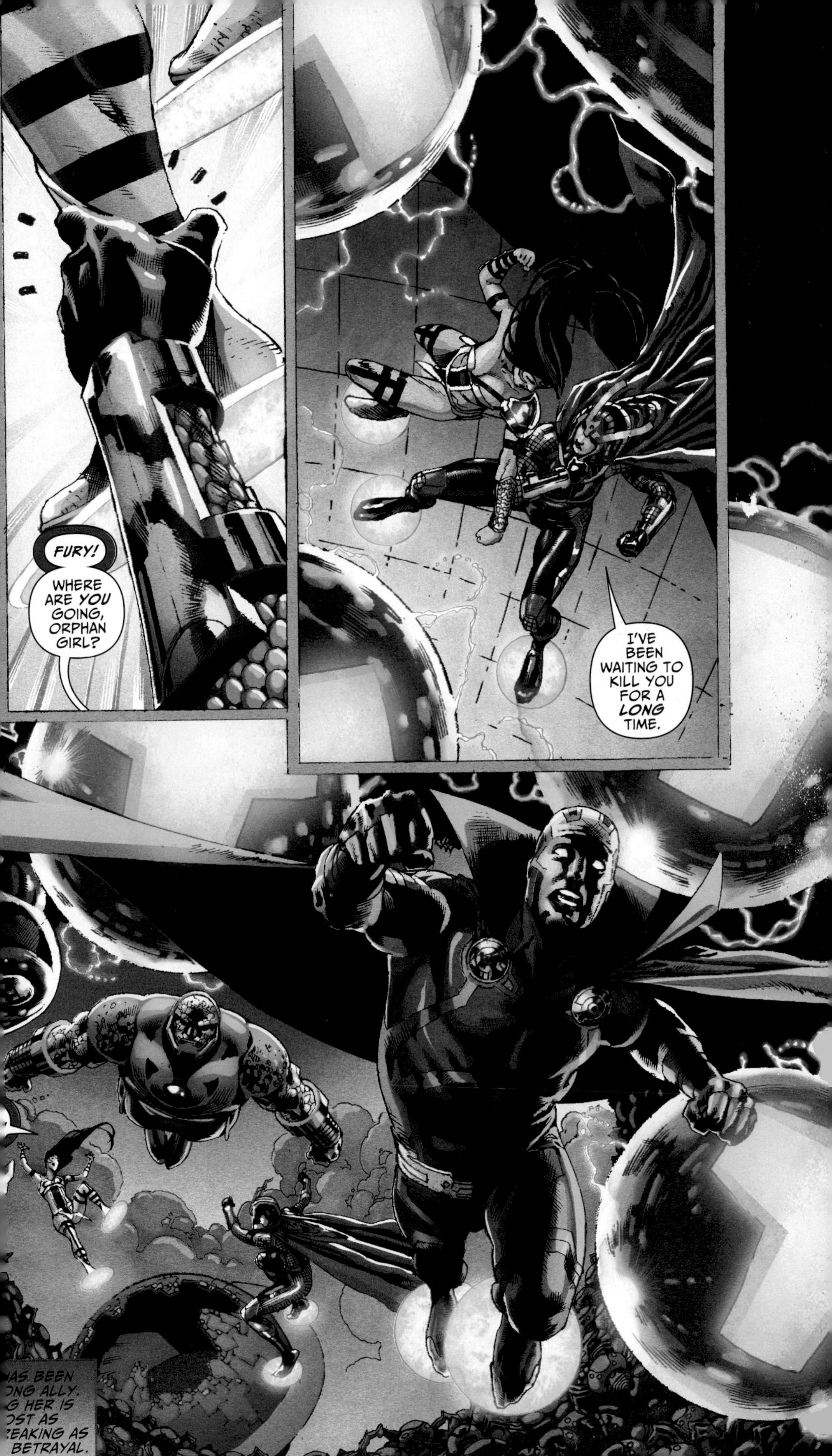
FURY!
WHERE ARE YOU GOING, ORPHAN GIRL?
I'VE BEEN WAITING TO KILL YOU FOR A LONG TIME.
BEEN
ALLY.
HER IS
AS
AS
BETRAYAL.

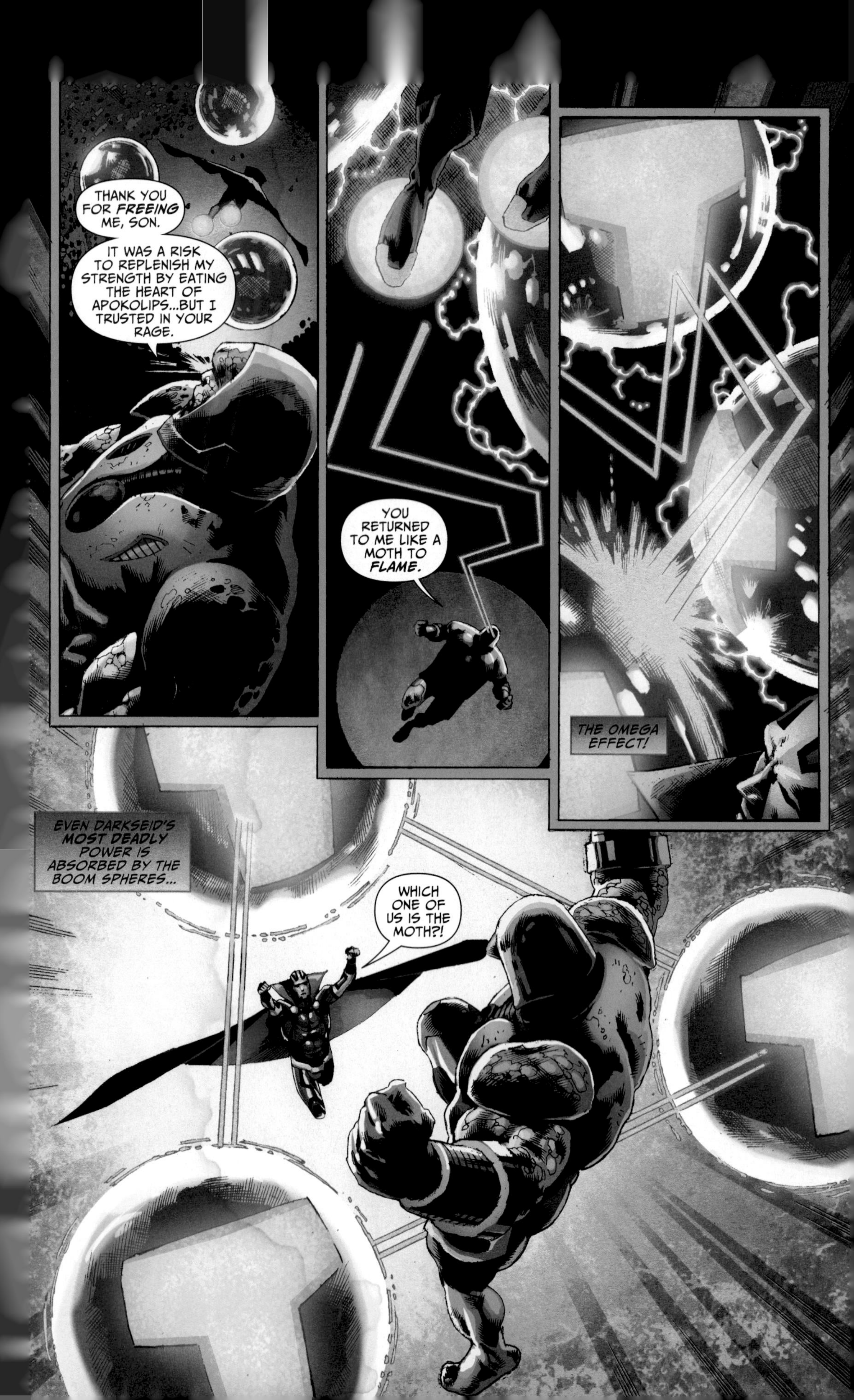
THANK YOU FOR FREEING ME, SON.
IT WAS A RISK TO REPLENISH MY STRENGTH BY EATING THE HEART OF APOKOLIPS...BUT I TRUSTED IN YOUR RAGE.
YOU RETURNED TO ME LIKE A MOTH TO FLAME.
THE OMEGA EFFECT!
EVEN DARKSEID'S MOST DEADLY POWER IS ABSORBED BY THE BOOM SPHERES...
WHICH ONE OF US IS THE MOTH?!

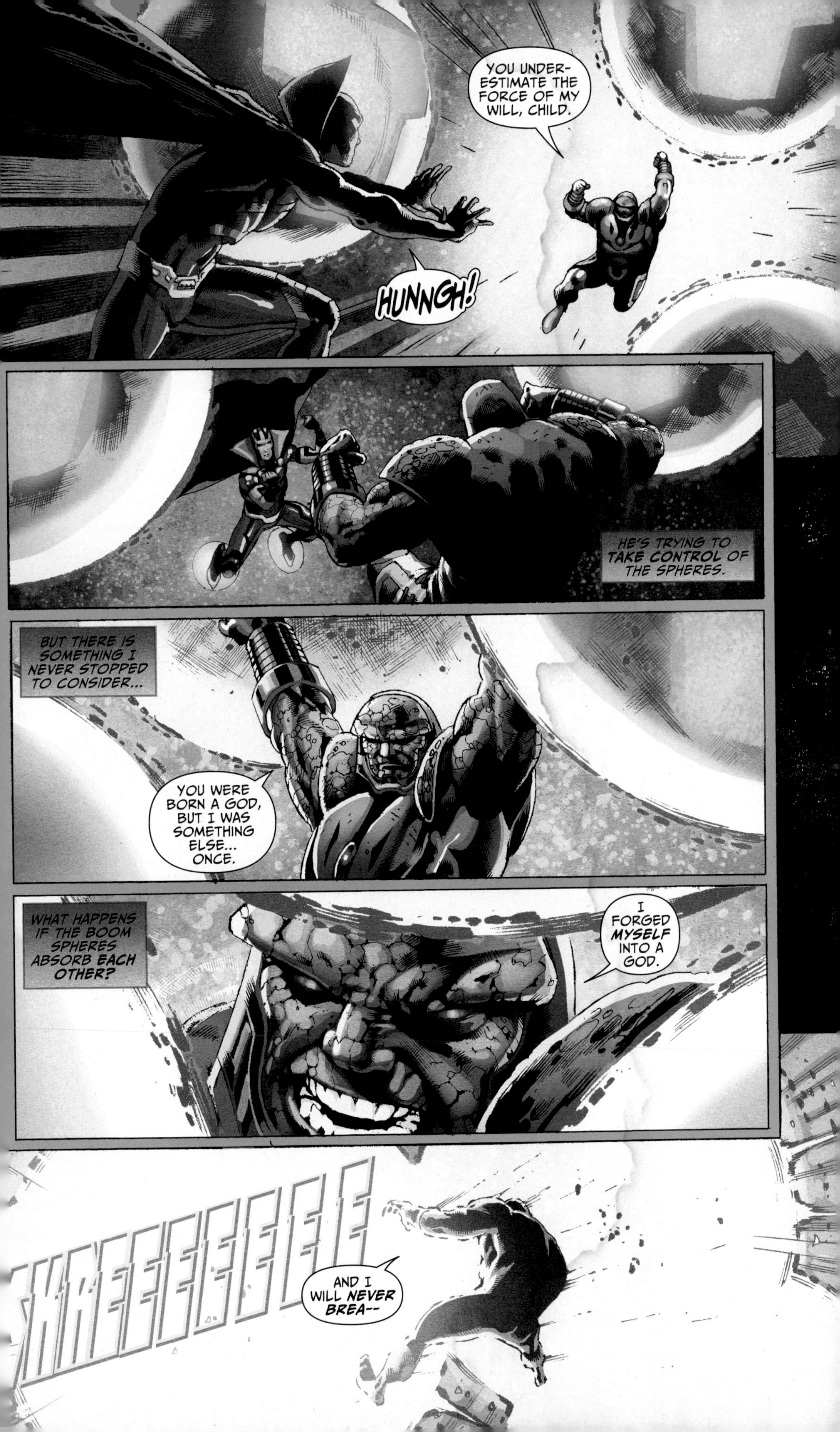
YOU UNDER-ESTIMATE THE FORCE OF MY WILL, CHILD.
HUNNGH!
HE'S TRYING TO TAKE CONTROL OF THE SPHERES.
BUT THERE IS SOMETHING I NEVER STOPPED TO CONSIDER...
YOU WERE BORN A GOD, BUT I WAS SOMETHING ELSE... ONCE.
WHAT HAPPENS IF THE BOOM SPHERES ABSORB EACH OTHER?
I FORGED MYSELF INTO A GOD.
SKREEEEEEEE
AND I WILL NEVER BREA--

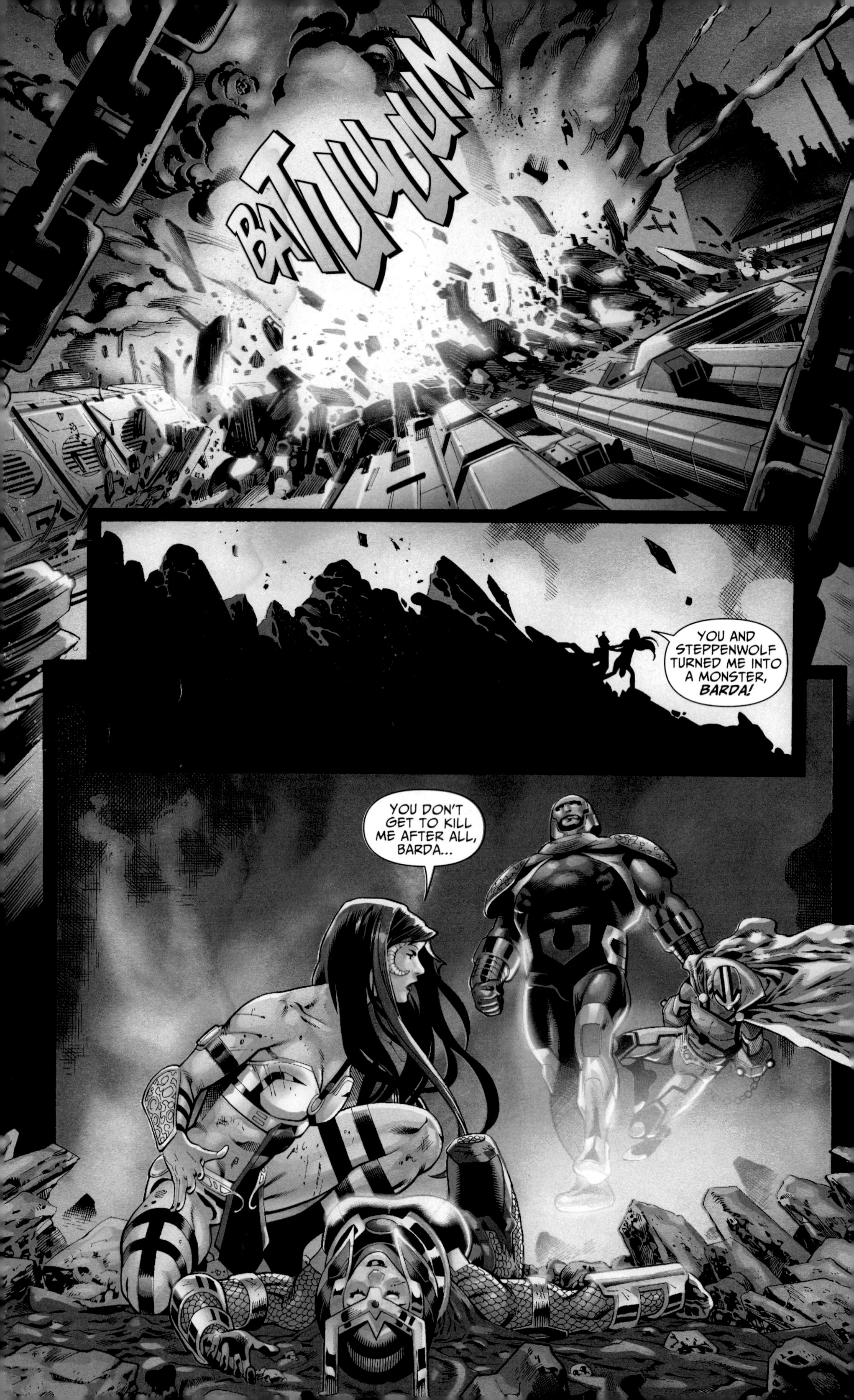
BATUMM
YOU AND STEPPENWOLF TURNED ME INTO A MONSTER, BARDA!
YOU DON'T GET TO KILL ME AFTER ALL, BARDA...

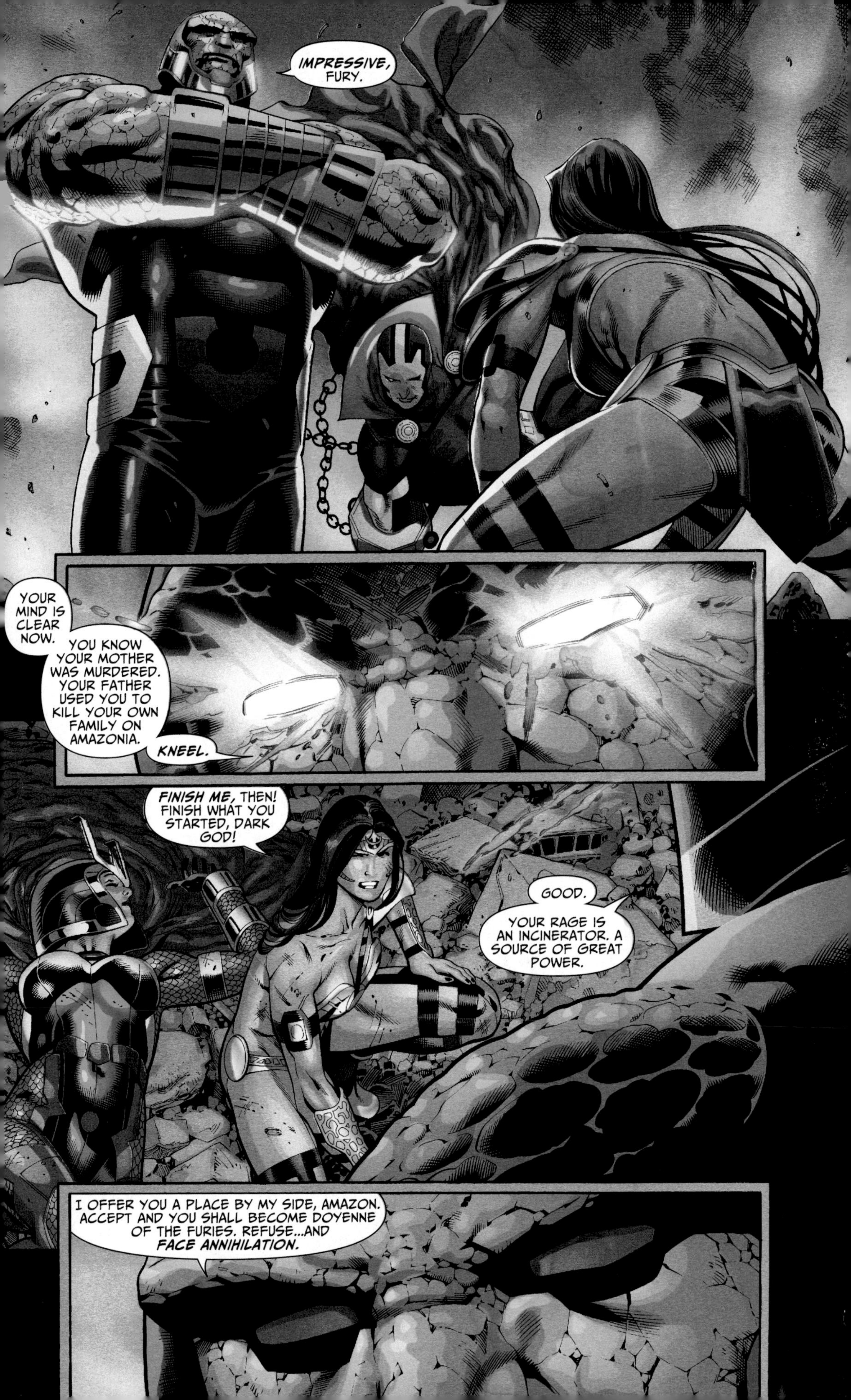
IMPRESSIVE, FURY.
YOUR MIND IS CLEAR NOW.
YOU KNOW YOUR MOTHER WAS MURDERED. YOUR FATHER USED YOU TO KILL YOUR OWN FAMILY ON AMAZONIA.
KNEEL.
FINISH ME, THEN! FINISH WHAT YOU STARTED, DARK GOD!
GOOD.
YOUR RAGE IS AN INCINERATOR. A SOURCE OF GREAT POWER.
I OFFER YOU A PLACE BY MY SIDE, AMAZON. ACCEPT AND YOU SHALL BECOME DOYENNE OF THE FURIES. REFUSE...AND FACE ANNIHILATION.

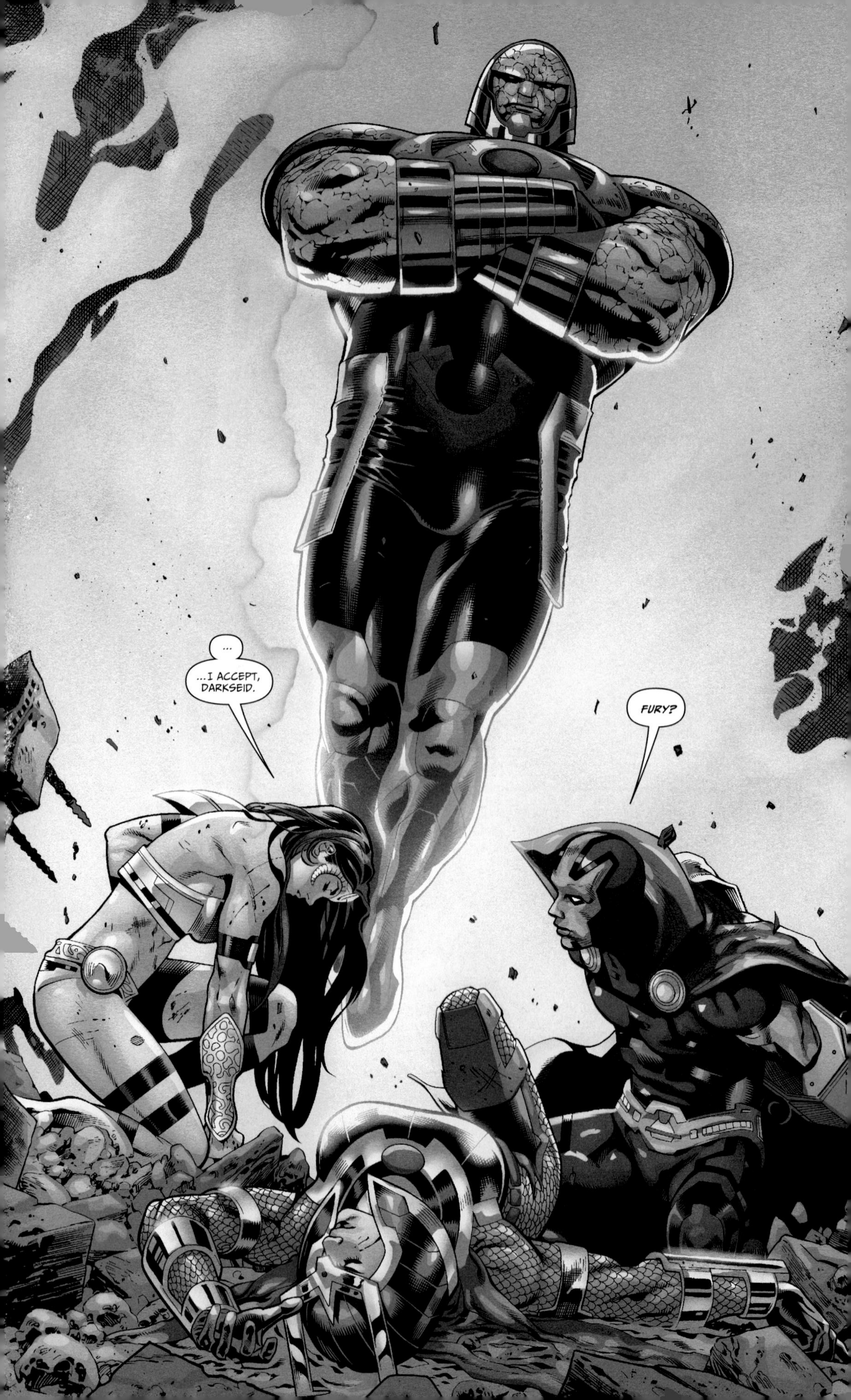
...
...I ACCEPT, DARKSEID.
FURY?

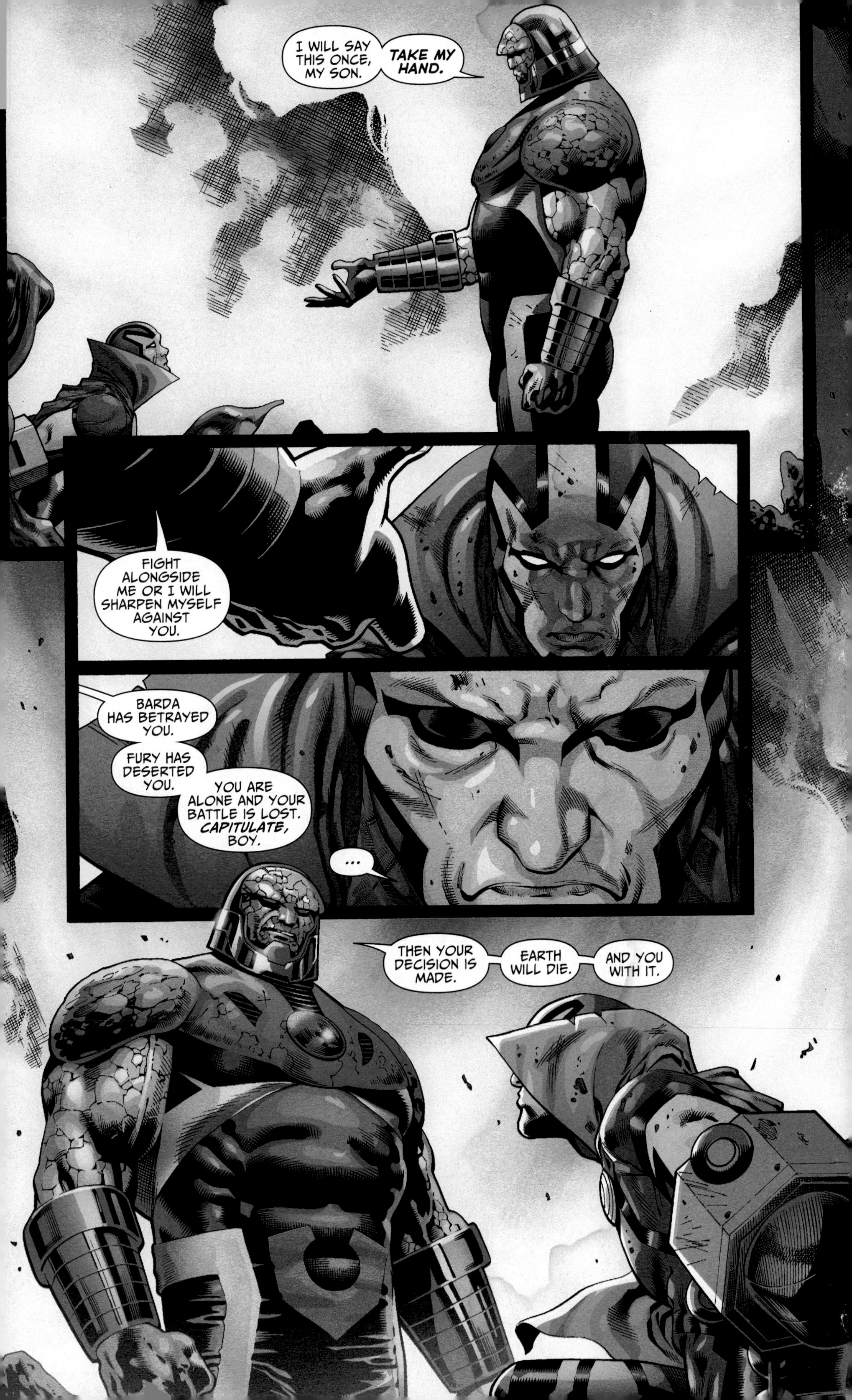
I WILL SAY THIS ONCE, MY SON.
TAKE MY HAND.
FIGHT ALONGSIDE ME OR I WILL SHARPEN MYSELF AGAINST YOU.
BARDA HAS BETRAYED YOU.
FURY HAS DESERTED YOU.
YOU ARE ALONE AND YOUR BATTLE IS LOST. CAPITULATE, BOY.
...
THEN YOUR DECISION IS MADE.
EARTH WILL DIE.
AND YOU WITH IT.

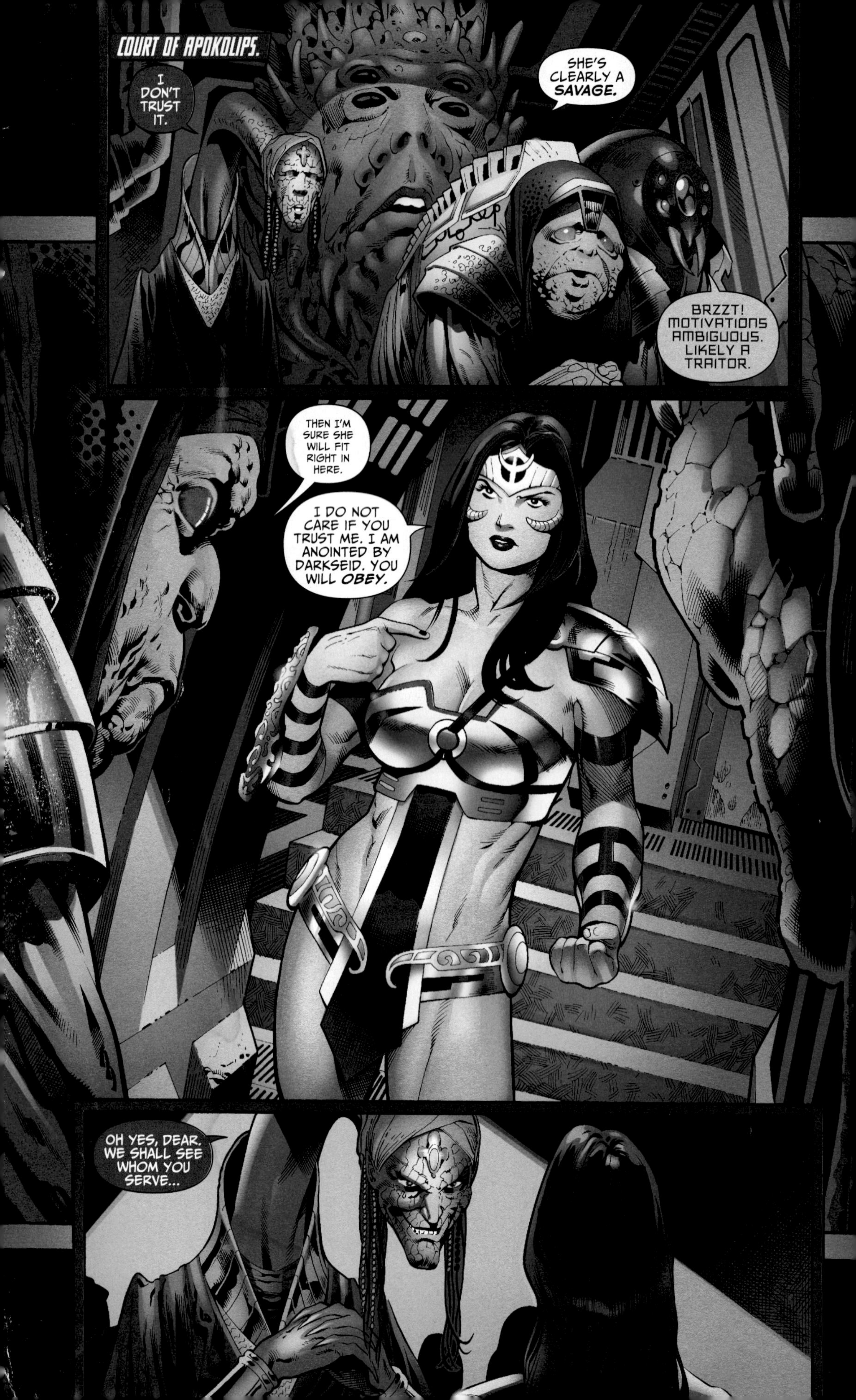
COURT OF APOKOLIPS.
I DON'T TRUST IT.
SHE'S CLEARLY A SAVAGE.
BRZZT! MOTIVATIONS AMBIGUOUS. LIKELY A TRAITOR.
THEN I'M SURE SHE WILL FIT RIGHT IN HERE.
I DO NOT CARE IF YOU TRUST ME. I AM ANOINTED BY DARKSEID. YOU WILL OBEY.
OH YES, DEAR. WE SHALL SEE WHOM YOU SERVE...

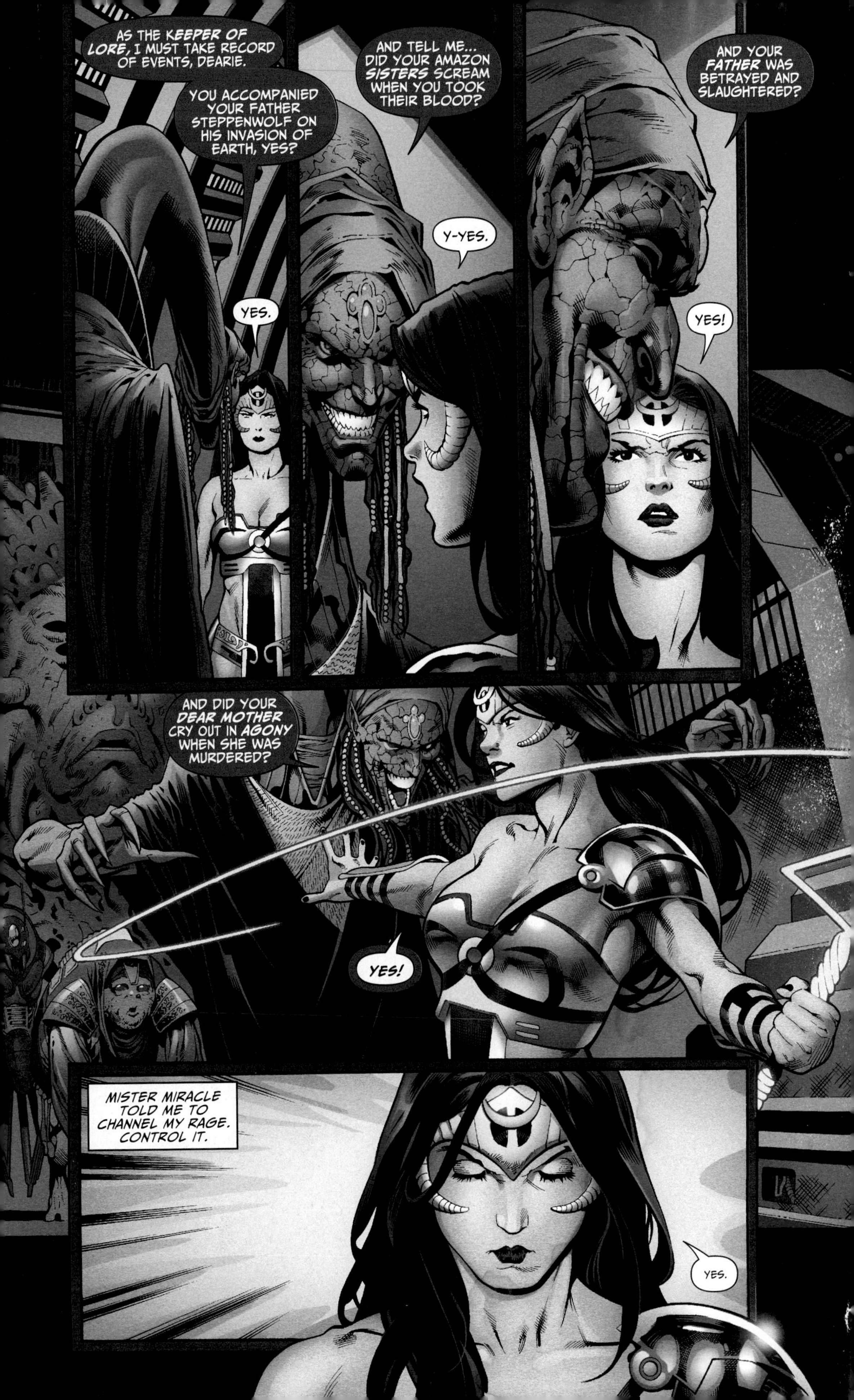

AS THE KEEPER OF LORE, I MUST TAKE RECORD OF EVENTS, DEARIE.
YOU ACCOMPANIED YOUR FATHER STEPPENWOLF ON HIS INVASION OF EARTH, YES?
YES.
AND TELL ME... DID YOUR AMAZON SISTERS SCREAM WHEN YOU TOOK THEIR BLOOD?
Y-YES.
AND YOUR FATHER WAS BETRAYED AND SLAUGHTERED?
YES!
AND DID YOUR DEAR MOTHER CRY OUT IN AGONY WHEN SHE WAS MURDERED?
YES!
MISTER MIRACLE TOLD ME TO CHANNEL MY RAGE. CONTROL IT.
YES.

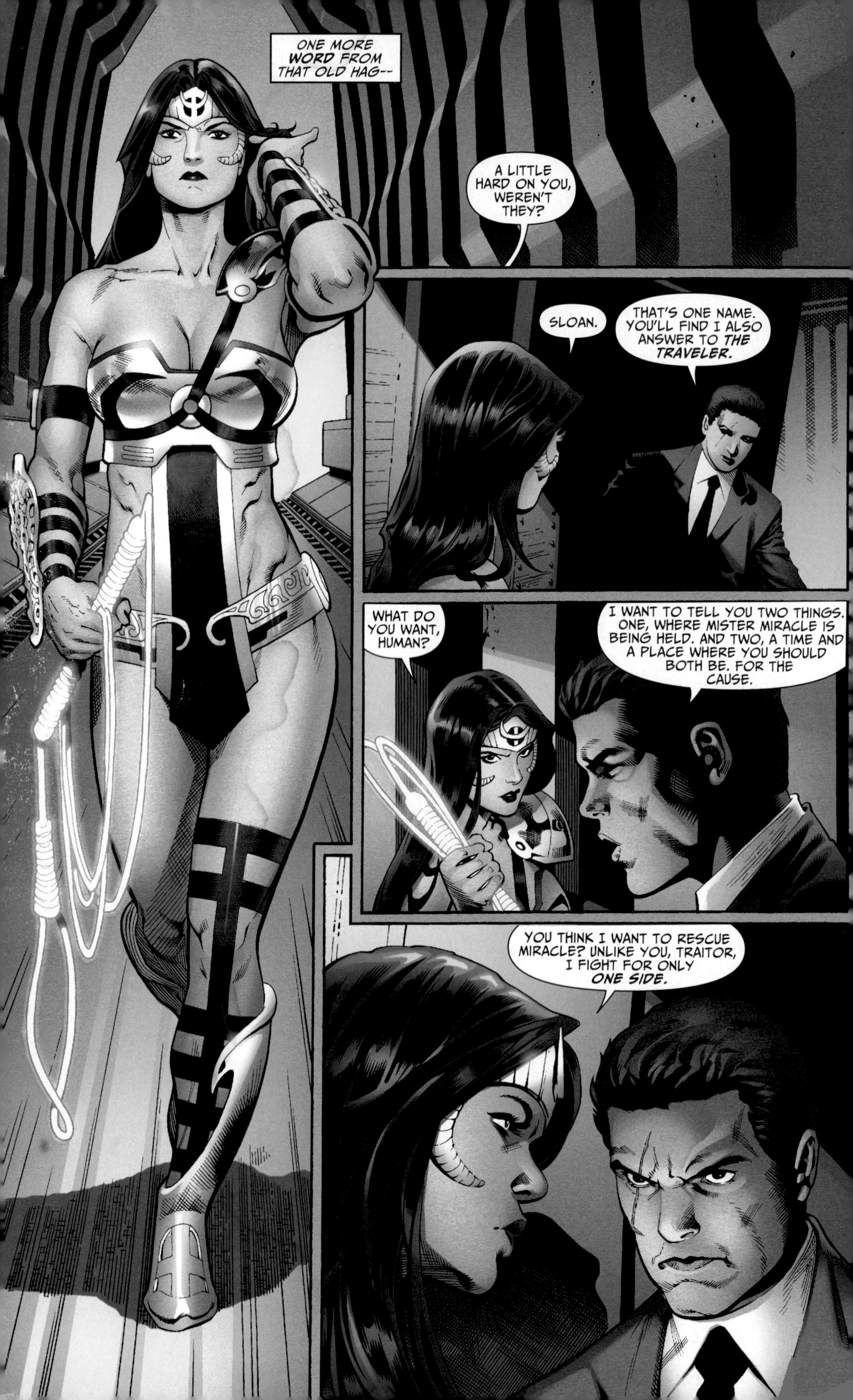
ONE MORE WORD FROM THAT OLD HAG--
A LITTLE HARD ON YOU, WEREN'T THEY?
SLOAN.
THAT'S ONE NAME. YOU'LL FIND I ALSO ANSWER TO THE TRAVELER.
WHAT DO YOU WANT, HUMAN?
I WANT TO TELL YOU TWO THINGS. ONE, WHERE MISTER MIRACLE IS BEING HELD. AND TWO, A TIME AND A PLACE WHERE YOU SHOULD BOTH BE. FOR THE CAUSE.
YOU THINK I WANT TO RESCUE MIRACLE? UNLIKE YOU, TRAITOR, I FIGHT FOR ONLY ONE SIDE.

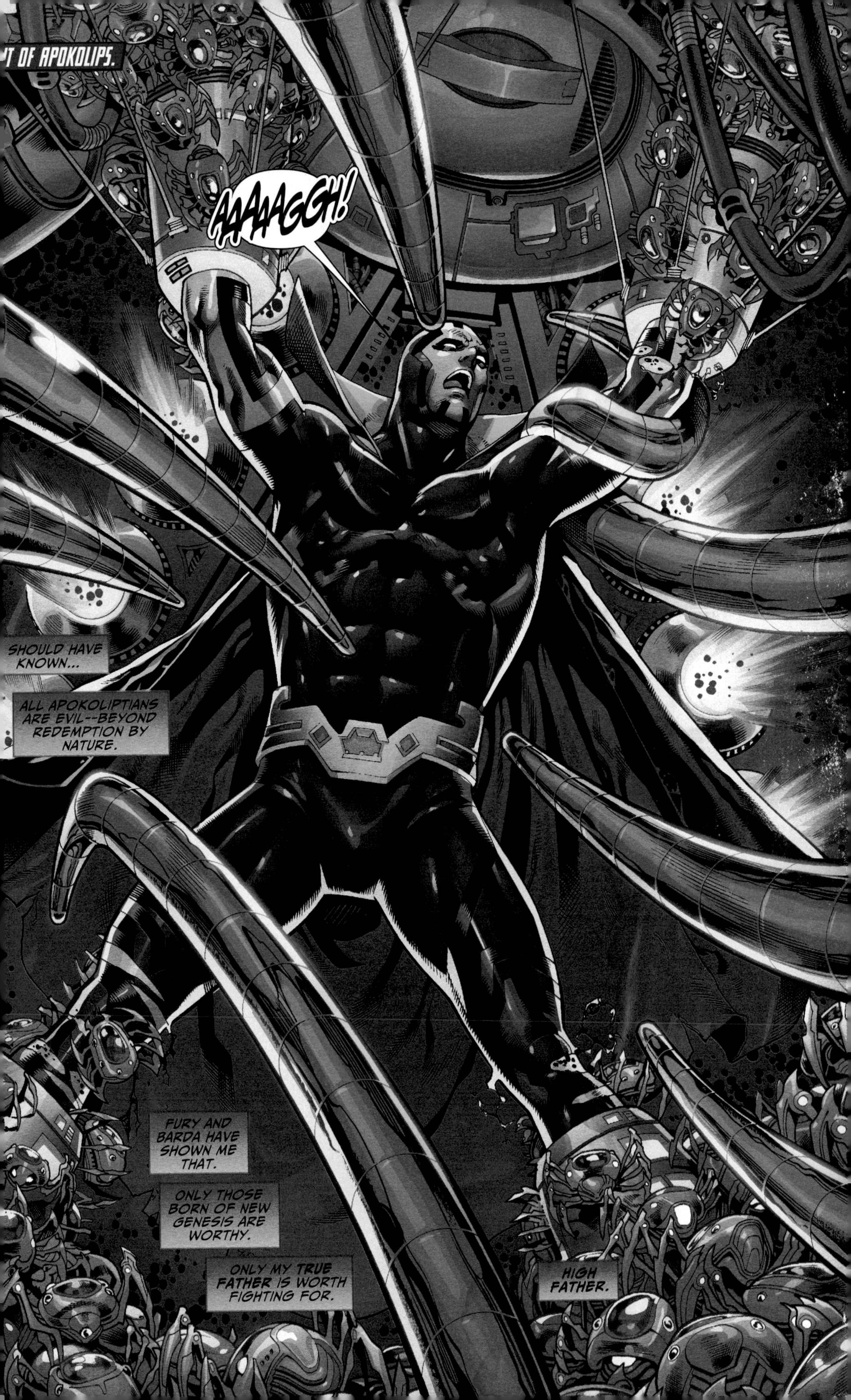
...T OF APOKOLIPS.
AAAAAGGH!
SHOULD HAVE KNOWN...
ALL APOKOLIPTIANS ARE EVIL--BEYOND REDEMPTION BY NATURE.
FURY AND BARDA HAVE SHOWN ME THAT.
ONLY THOSE BORN OF NEW GENESIS ARE WORTHY.
ONLY MY TRUE FATHER IS WORTH FIGHTING FOR.
HIGH FATHER.

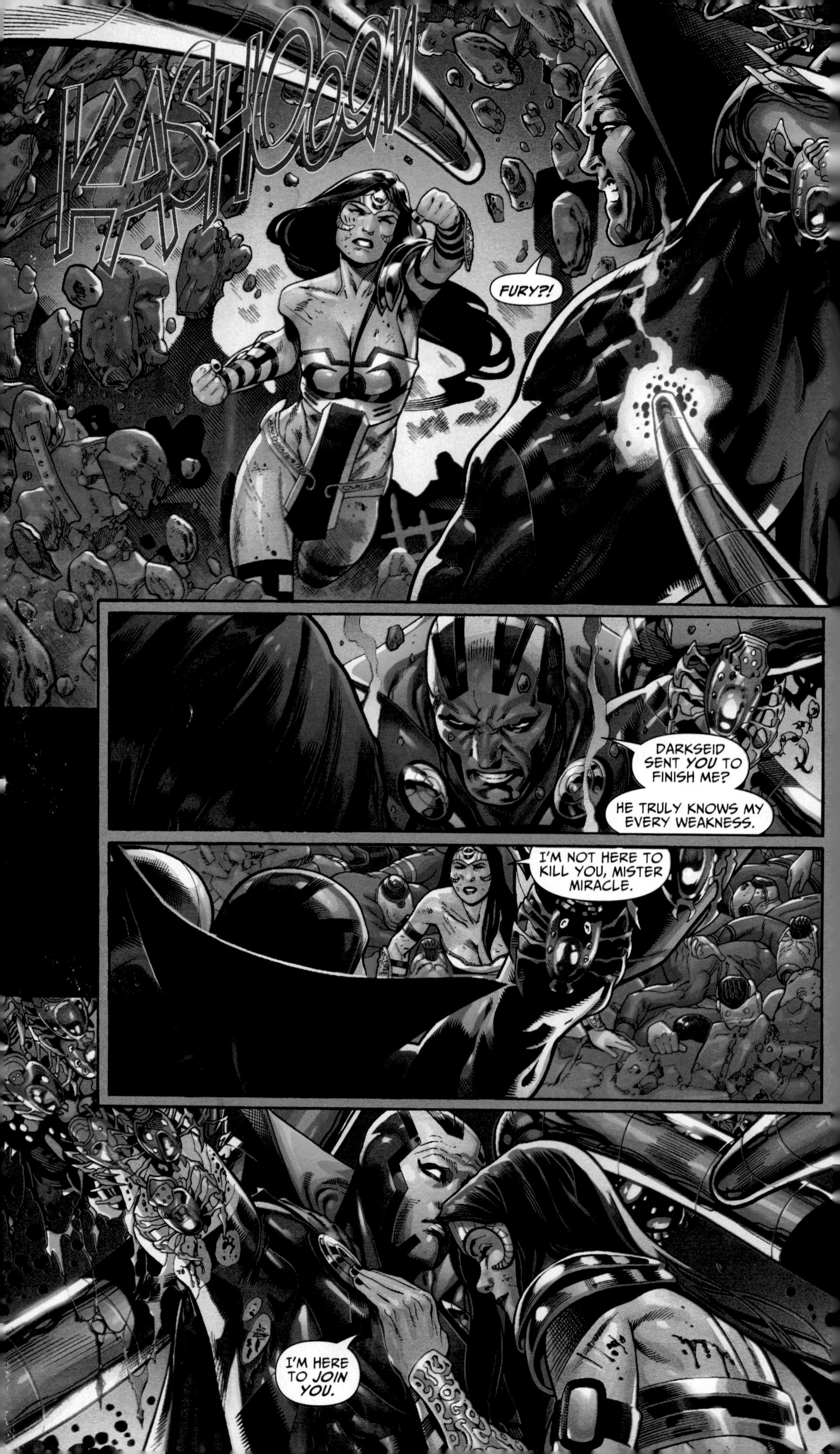
KASHOOOM
FURY?!
DARKSEID SENT YOU TO FINISH ME?
HE TRULY KNOWS MY EVERY WEAKNESS.
I'M NOT HERE TO KILL YOU, MISTER MIRACLE.
I'M HERE TO JOIN YOU.

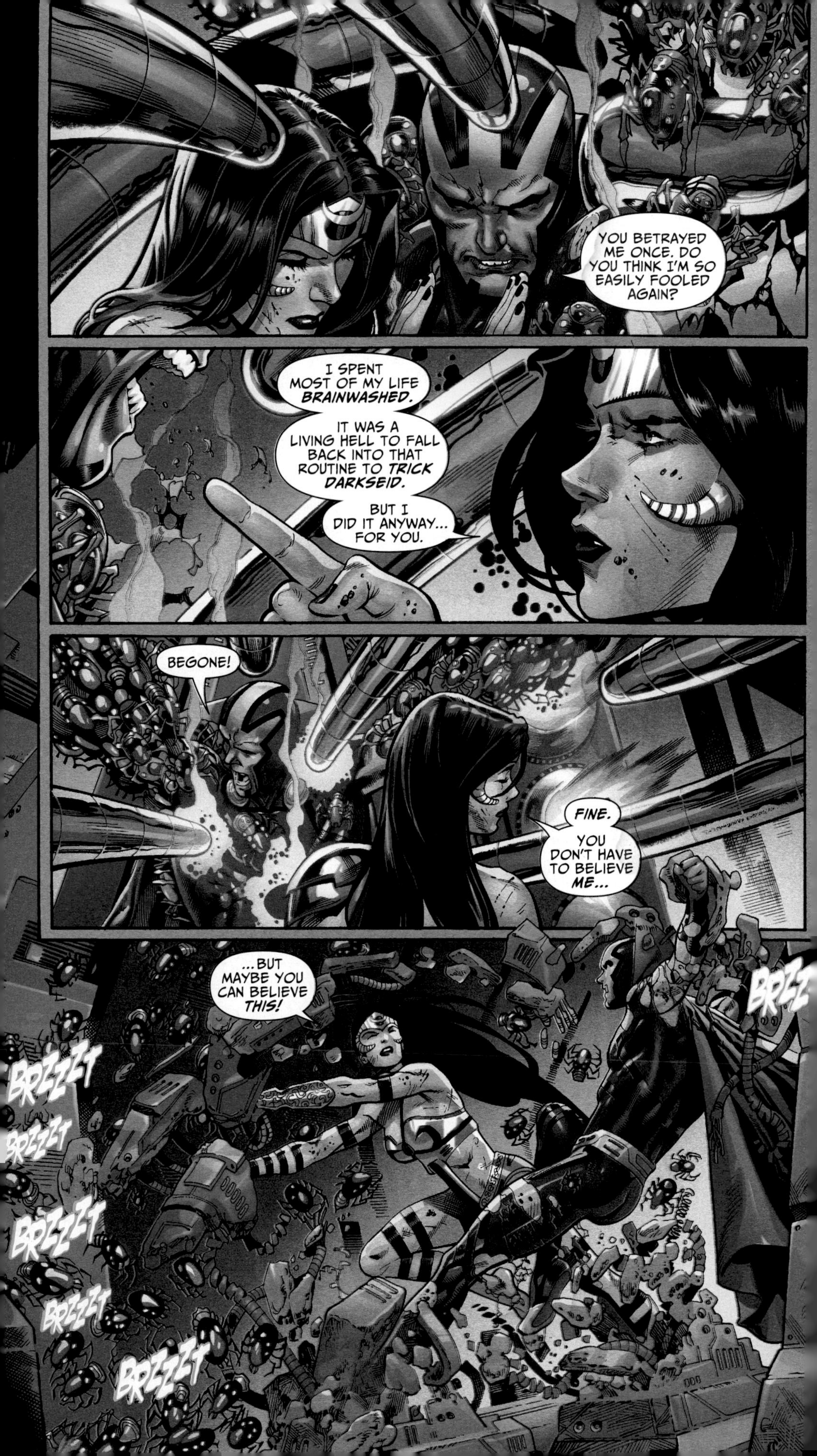
YOU BETRAYED ME ONCE. DO YOU THINK I'M SO EASILY FOOLED AGAIN?
I SPENT MOST OF MY LIFE BRAINWASHED.
IT WAS A LIVING HELL TO FALL BACK INTO THAT ROUTINE TO TRICK DARKSEID.
BUT I DID IT ANYWAY... FOR YOU.
BEGONE!
FINE.
YOU DON'T HAVE TO BELIEVE ME...
...BUT MAYBE YOU CAN BELIEVE THIS!
BRZZZT
BRZZZT
BRZZZT
BRZZZT
BRZZZT
BRZZ

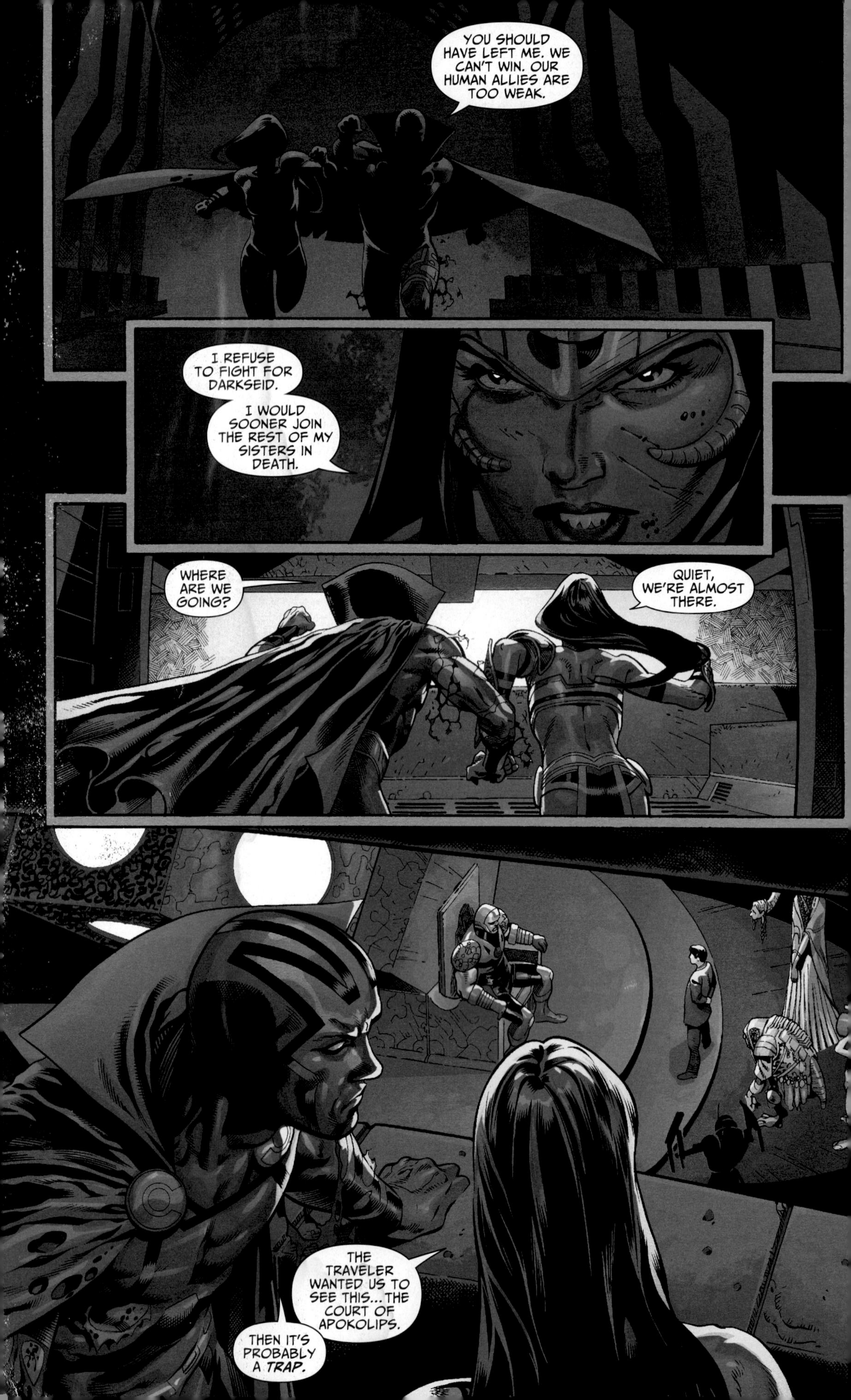
YOU SHOULD HAVE LEFT ME. WE CAN'T WIN. OUR HUMAN ALLIES ARE TOO WEAK.
I REFUSE TO FIGHT FOR DARKSEID.
I WOULD SOONER JOIN THE REST OF MY SISTERS IN DEATH.
WHERE ARE WE GOING?
QUIET, WE'RE ALMOST THERE.
THE TRAVELER WANTED US TO SEE THIS... THE COURT OF APOKOLIPS.
THEN IT'S PROBABLY A *TRAP*.

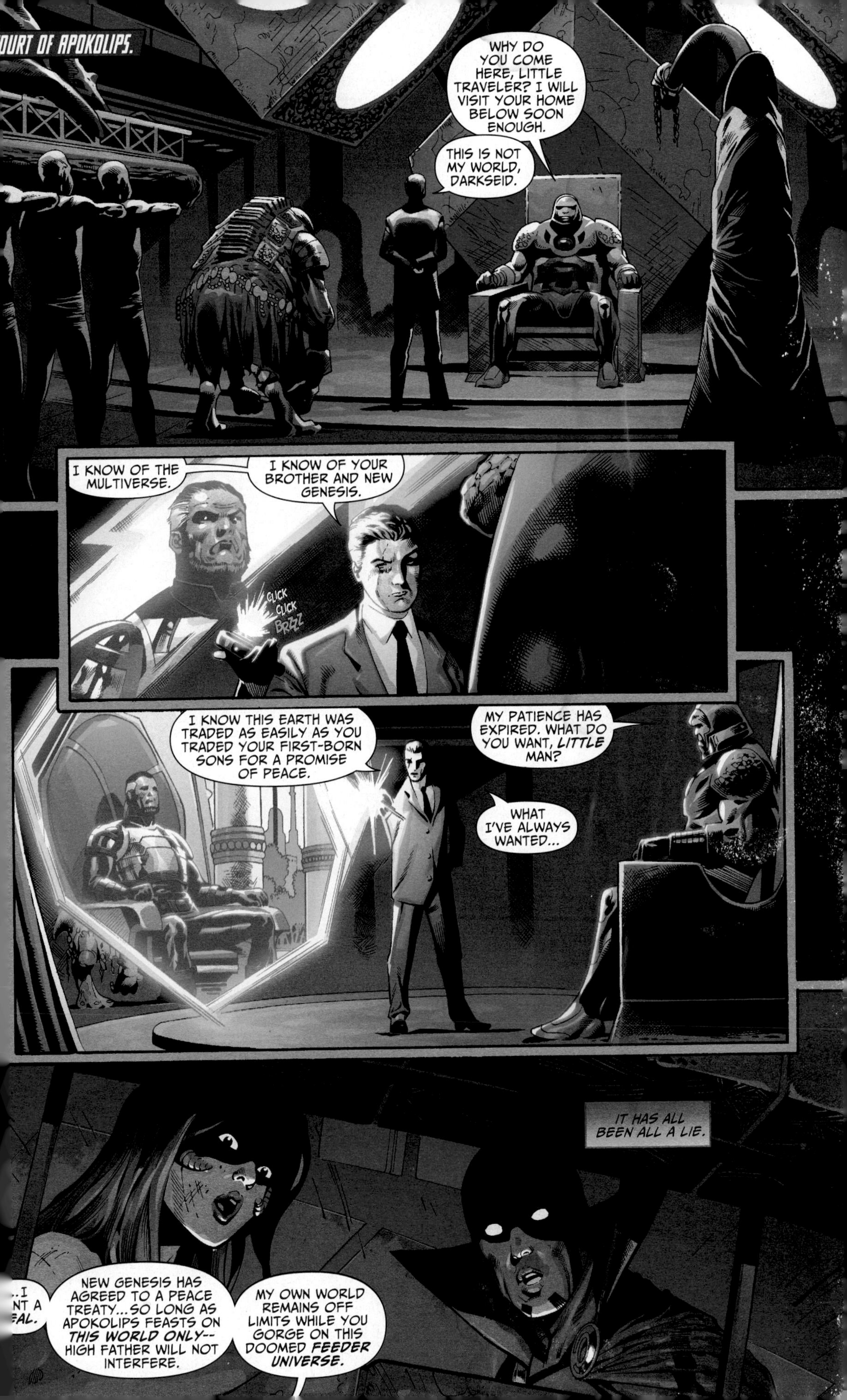
OURT OF APOKOLIPS.
WHY DO YOU COME HERE, LITTLE TRAVELER? I WILL VISIT YOUR HOME BELOW SOON ENOUGH.
THIS IS NOT MY WORLD, DARKSEID.
I KNOW OF THE MULTIVERSE.
I KNOW OF YOUR BROTHER AND NEW GENESIS.
CLICK CLICK BRZZZ
I KNOW THIS EARTH WAS TRADED AS EASILY AS YOU TRADED YOUR FIRST-BORN SONS FOR A PROMISE OF PEACE.
MY PATIENCE HAS EXPIRED. WHAT DO YOU WANT, *LITTLE* MAN?
WHAT I'VE ALWAYS WANTED...
IT HAS ALL BEEN ALL A LIE.
NEW GENESIS HAS AGREED TO A PEACE TREATY...SO LONG AS APOKOLIPS FEASTS ON *THIS WORLD ONLY*--HIGH FATHER WILL NOT INTERFERE.
MY OWN WORLD REMAINS OFF LIMITS WHILE YOU GORGE ON THIS DOOMED *FEEDER UNIVERSE*.

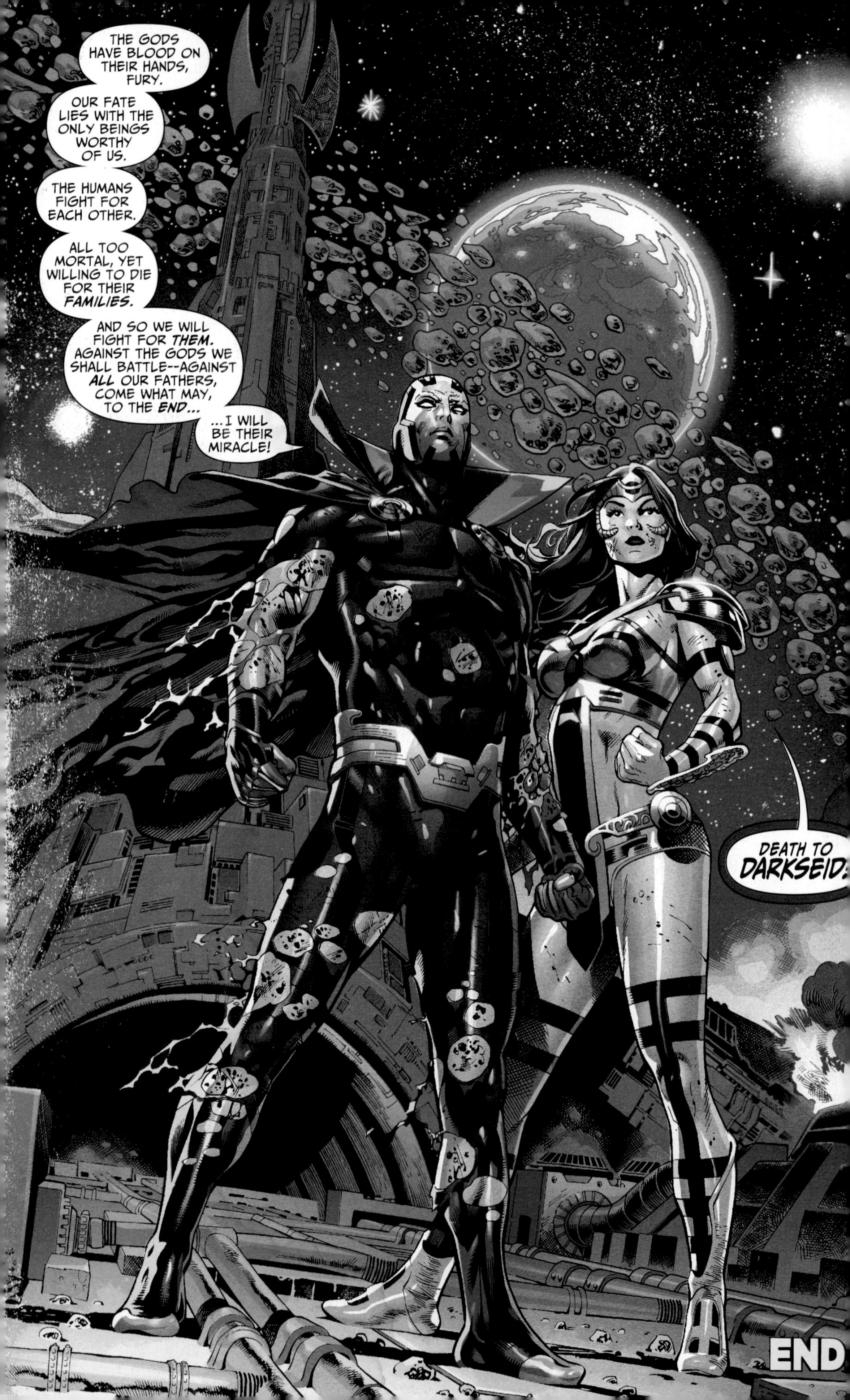
THE GODS HAVE BLOOD ON THEIR HANDS, FURY.
OUR FATE LIES WITH THE ONLY BEINGS WORTHY OF US.
THE HUMANS FIGHT FOR EACH OTHER.
ALL TOO MORTAL, YET WILLING TO DIE FOR THEIR FAMILIES.
AND SO WE WILL FIGHT FOR THEM. AGAINST THE GODS WE SHALL BATTLE--AGAINST ALL OUR FATHERS, COME WHAT MAY, TO THE END...
...I WILL BE THEIR MIRACLE!
DEATH TO DARKSEID!
END

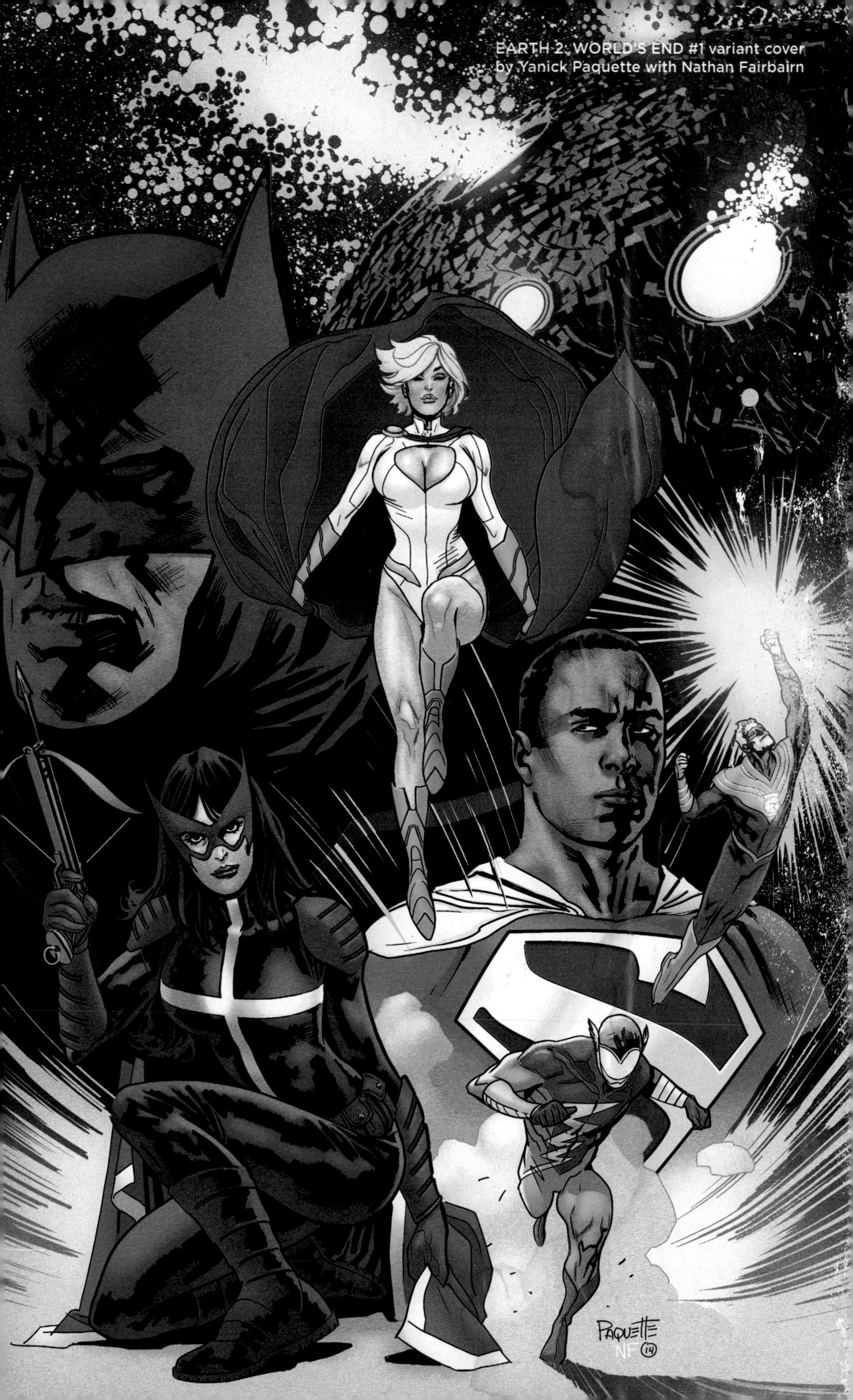
PAQUETTE
NF 14

EARTH 2: WORLD'S END #1 variant cover
by Yanick Paquette with Nathan Fairbairn

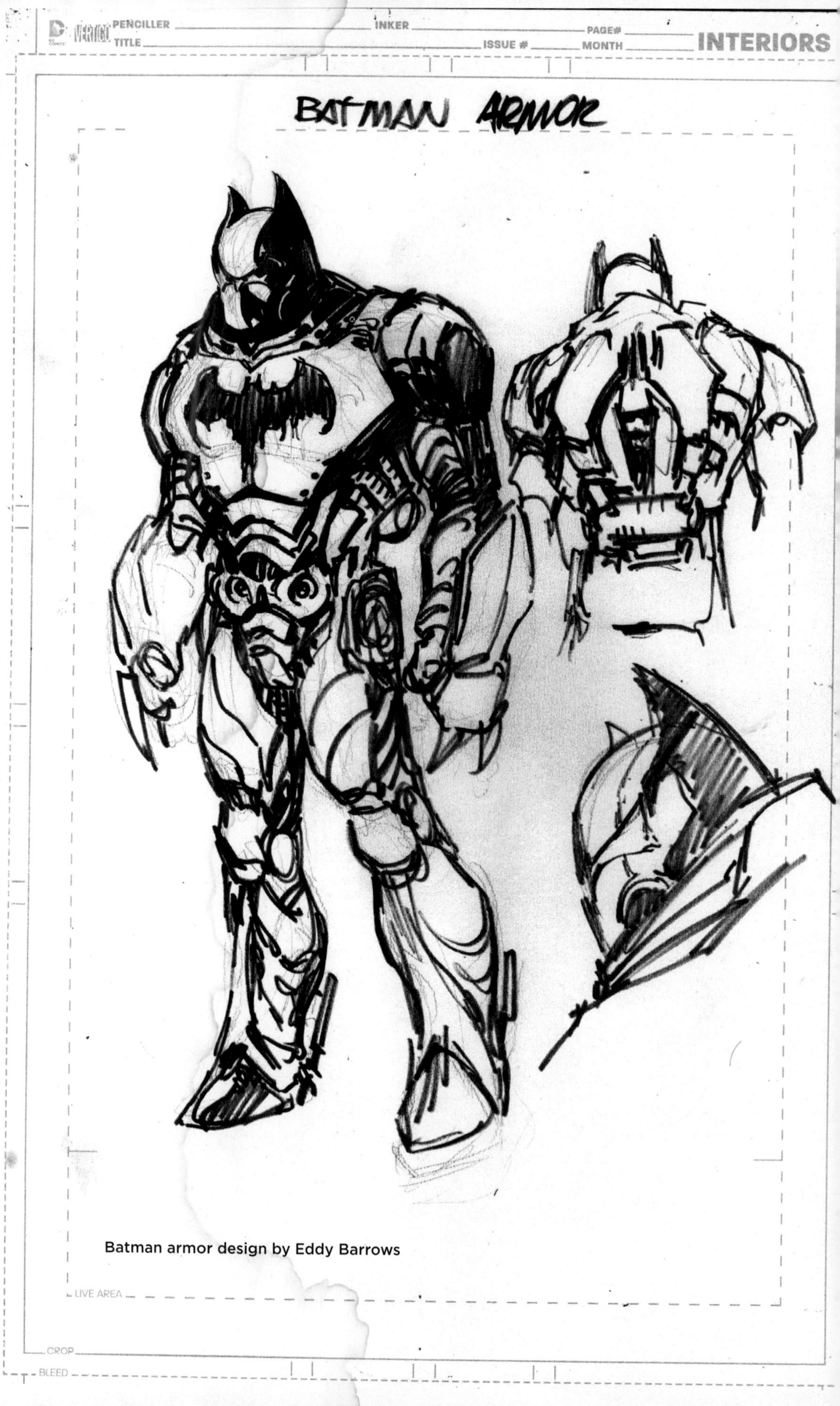
PENCILLER
INKER
PAGE#
TITLE
ISSUE #
MONTH
INTERIORS
BATMAN ARMOR
LIVE AREA
CROP
BLEED

Batman armor design by Eddy Barrows

Barda as Doyenne of the Furies design by Eduardo Pansica

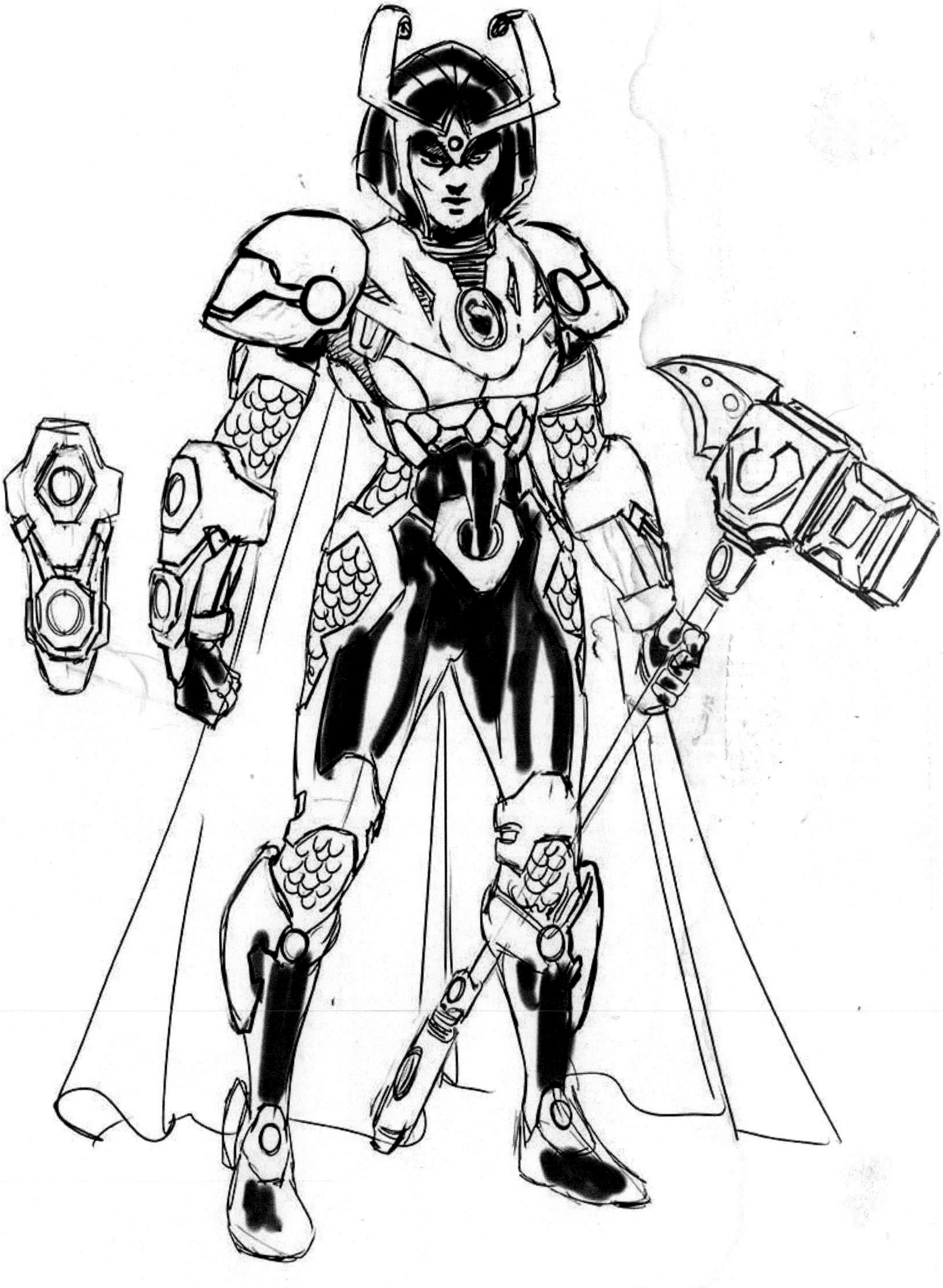

Famine Huntress designs by Phil Jimenez

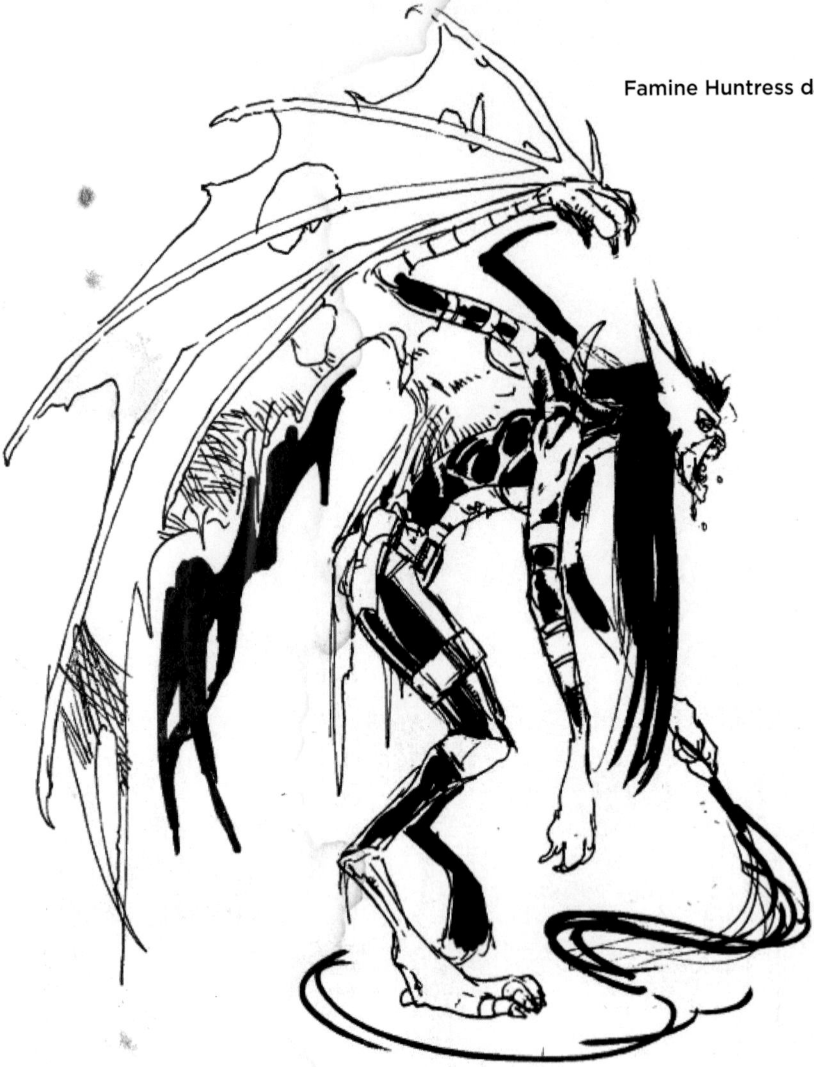

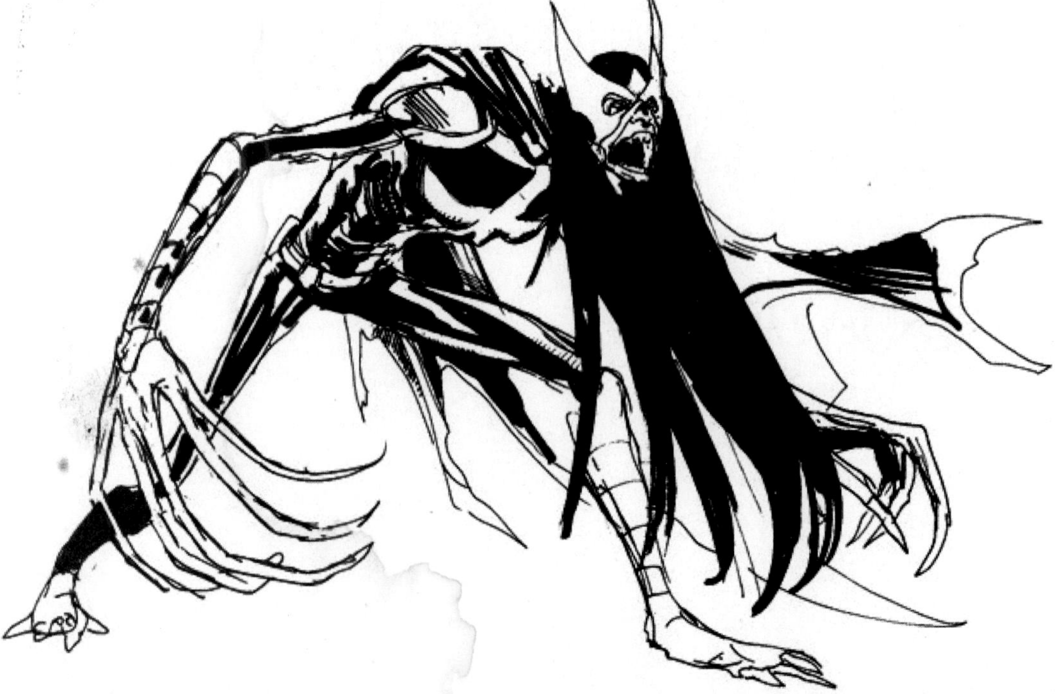

Arcanis designs by Phil Jimenez

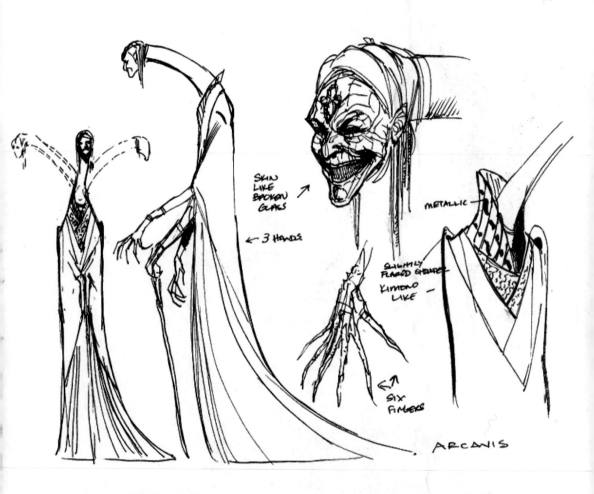

SKIN LIKE BROKEN GLASS
← 3 HANDS
METALLIC
SLIGHTLY FLARED SHOULDER
KIMONO LIKE
SIX FINGERS
ARCANIS